THE SCOTTISH SECRETARIES

David Torrance

BIRLINN

First published in 2006 by
Birlinn Limited
West Newington House
10 Newington Road
Edinburgh
EH9 1QS

www.birlinn.co.uk

ISBN 10: 1 84158 476 2
ISBN 13: 978 1 84158 476 8

British Library Cataloguing-in-Publication Data
A catalogue record for this book is available from the British Library

Typeset by Iolaire Typesetting, Newtonmore
Printed and bound by Antony Rowe, Chippenham

Contents

Foreword

James Naughtie

By the time a secretary of state for Scotland was celebrating the centenary of his office in the 1980s, the shadows were falling. Before long there would again be a parliament in Edinburgh and although the title would remain it would lose much of its lustre. Imagine one of the sturdy inhabitants of the past – a Tom Johnston or a Willie Ross – being asked to combine his duties with running the Department for Transport or Work and Pensions, with Scotland as the junior partner. Not only would he have refused, he would have found it difficult to believe that the thought could occur to anyone. He might have suspected a degree of insanity was at work.

Yet self-destruction became part of the job. To watch the last half dozen or so secretaries of state before the devolution referendum of 1997 was to understand how strange the position in Cabinet had become. From the moment the nationalist tide washed ashore with the first oil in the early seventies, and the worm of panic began to gnaw at government at Westminster, the role of secretary of state changed. Within a few years the pride with which its occupants had operated as half governor-general and licensed Cabinet troublemaker had become something more defensive. Under Labour and Conservative governments alike, they were preparing for a different kind of life. Those who wanted devolution shared with those who did not the knowledge that a certain part of Scottish government was about to be laid to rest.

It was always remarkable to try to explain to outsiders (mostly in England) how the phenomenon worked. George Younger, who served Margaret Thatcher with such patience and robust good humour for seven years as her first secretary of state, used to astonish even those Cabinet colleagues who had political memories by the way he could assemble cross-party coalitions. They would come charging over the border at regular intervals, accompanied by sundry churchmen, businessmen, trade unionists and Good Folk of every description, to assail Westminster in support of whatever it was that the Scottish Office had decided was in need of help. Sometimes, he won.

The freemasonry that stretched from St Andrew's House in Edinburgh and Dover House in London into every corner of Scottish life made it possible even for a Scottish secretary like Younger, with only around 20 MPs (out of 72) on his side, to stir up trouble in Cabinet of the sort that a mere minister of agriculture, fisheries and food – to take an obvious example – could only observe with impotent envy. Margaret Thatcher couldn't quite understand it, but had to accept it.

Younger, however, knew that he was likely to be one of the last. He had been a devolutionist in the seventies, after all, and never doubted that before too many years went by the Labour government's botched Scotland Bill and the messy referendum of 1979 would be superseded by a plan that worked, at least in so far as it established a Scottish parliament of some sort. The end game had begun.

His successor, Malcolm Rifkind, had his first great moment in the Commons as a result of that argument, from which everything else was to flow. He wound up the passionate debate on the Thatcher government's repeal of the Scotland Act a few weeks after the 1979 election, a mere parliamentary under-secretary at the Scottish Office speaking without a note to an overflowing chamber, riding the roars of derision from the opposition with elegant ease and relishing the moment with every gesture. A senior Scottish Office official watching from the gallery leaned over to me and said: 'There's our next secretary of state.' He was right.

The Scottish Office's sense of itself had been sharpened by devolution, perhaps because it was indeed the beginning of the end. Younger's predecessor, Bruce Millan, had the horrible task of leading a Scottish Labour group with a majority who were grumpily anti-devolution, even if lifelong habits forced some of them to keep it quiet, but he knew too that the Scottish Office was no longer simply an outpost of government in which a powerful secretary of state could exercise his peculiar freedoms: shuffling his allocated funds around from here to there, dispensing a surprising amount of patronage, and assembling 'national coalitions' when it suited him. It was in the middle of a constitutional revolution, one that was going to have a false start but which was not going to subside.

The Conservative secretaries of state in the eighties rather enjoyed that in a masochistic way, despite the nightmare of their disappearing troops. Both Ian Lang and Michael Forsyth had to labour in office with only 11 Scottish Tory MPs to support them, though Forsyth's political cunning and insight allowed him to perform in a way that surprised the officials who had served him as a junior minister and wrongly suspected that his ideological edge was too sharp for the big job. Like Rifkind and Lang before him, he understood the unique strengths of the office, even when they didn't produce victory.

Those were rollicking years. Those of us who heard it won't forget Nicky Fairbairn's speech from the back-benches, railing against his own government for some daft scheme invented, as he saw it, by time-serving Edinburgh bureaucrats. The secretary of state, he observed, had a very fine office in London – Dover House on Whitehall – where Lady Caroline Lamb had often entertained Lord Byron in her own special way. And, said Fairbairn, in full post-prandial flow, nothing so human or enjoyable had gone on in the Scottish Office since.

It had certainly changed, the last 20 years before devolution finding it locked in a constitutional argument of the sort that had only briefly troubled it in earlier times. But in that period Scottish politics was alive. It was one of the reasons for the preponderance of Scots in government when Tony Blair came to power, they had been blooded in the politics of devolution, when many English counterparts had fled from Labour's private battlefield. Before the Scottish Executive came into being, the Scottish Office was given more attention than ever before, its strengths, weaknesses, ambiguities, and its personality were revealed.

The story reached its climax with Donald Dewar, the secretary of state who became first minister. His Labour successors would have none of the old powers, and would tread an uncomfortable path. Dewar was an appropriate man to bring one chapter to a close: determinedly Scottish in style and speech, instinctively wedded to Scotland's institutions and with the serendipitous mind of the book-collecting polymath that fitted the role perfectly. As it came to an end – when he steered through the Bill that said simply in its first clause 'There shall be a Scottish Parliament' – he seemed the right kind of figure to sum up the secretary of state's role. For more than a hundred years they'd tried to balance loyalty to their governments with broader commitments to all Scots, and to find ways of turning to their advantage the unusual power conferred on them by their strange office.

There is no going back now to the old days of the Scottish Office, its headquarters hewn out of an Edinburgh rock and its traditions embedded in a Victorian notion of Westminster and its distant territories. But in its time it held a unique place in government, for better and for worse, and, like so many of its occupants for more than a century, it had character.

Acknowledgements

They were not men of major importance in their own party, and they were
doomed to political extinction when they left office. Indeed, so little mark
did most of them make that they were quite unknown to the general public,
just as they have been forgotten by historians.

H. J. Hanham, 1969

I finished writing this book during a remarkable period of political (and
therefore media) interest in the constitutional relationship between Scotland and England. Seven years after the creation of a Scottish parliament
and just a year before the 300th anniversary of the Act of Union,
everything from the Barnett formula to the voting rights of Scottish
MPs (the so-called West Lothian Question) came under prolonged
scrutiny. This, of course, was nothing more than a coincidence, but
provided an appropriate backdrop for a detailed look at the 114 years of
Scottish Office history which preceded devolution, and more specifically
the figures who commanded it.

I have wanted to write a biographical history of the Scottish Office
since I started working as a journalist in 2000. And far from discouraging
me, comments like that of H. J. Hanham above simply deepened my
interest. Why, I wanted to discover, were these men forgotten by
historians? Many, as I discovered, deserved to be, while others, as I
came to believe, ought to be much better known than they are. The
advent of devolution has seen a spate of books about the campaign for a
Scottish parliament, nationalism and the future of Scotland, but little on
the old Scottish Office. I did not study politics at university, nor have I any
formal training as an historian. On that basis, this book does not purport
to be an academic work of history, but rather an enthusiastic amateur's
biographical account of a government department now in its 121st year.

The last person to write a book on Scottish secretaries was George
Pottinger. An Edinburgh-born civil servant and amateur historian, he
probably dreamt up the idea for his tome – *Secretaries of State for Scotland
1926–76* – while serving a five-year prison sentence for his part in the
notorious Poulson Affair. I had no such solitude to produce this work,

although at times I contemplated some minor offence to give me the time I often found difficult to secure. I am therefore indebted to Pottinger's work, as I am to that of another civil servant, John Gibson, who produced a fine history of the Scottish Office to mark its centenary in 1985. I also owe a great deal to the research of Ian Levitt, who saved me hours of work at the Scottish Records Office in Edinburgh, and to academics like James Mitchell and Christopher Harvie, who have produced authoritative accounts of the political history of Scotland since 1885. Few aside from Pottinger, however, have dwelled upon the characters of the 40 secretaries for Scotland and secretaries of state, so for information on those I owe thanks to both archivists and surviving protagonists.

With regard to archive material, I am grateful for the assistance and courtesy shown to me by the staff of the National Library of Scotland in Edinburgh and the British Library in London. My thanks also go to other libraries whose archives I have consulted: the New Bodleian Library at Oxford University, the Churchill Archives Centre at Cambridge University, the House of Lords Record Office, the Mitchell Library in Glasgow, the National Library of Wales, the National Archives of Scotland (particular thanks to Tessa Spencer), St Andrews University Library, Edinburgh Central Library, the Carnegie Library in Dunfermline, the William Patrick Memorial Library in Kirkintilloch, Newcastle University Library, and last but by no means least, all the staff (especially Corie Chambers) at the superb House of Commons Library. Jane Gillies (the daughter of William Anstruther-Gray) was also a delightful host while I looked at her late father's papers at Kilmany in Fife.

Many former secretaries of state and ministers have been incredibly helpful. Back in 2002 I spoke to the late Lord Campbell of Croy, who died the week I began this project in earnest. More recently, I interviewed the surviving Scottish secretaries Bruce Millan, Sir Malcolm Rifkind, Lord Lang, Lord Forsyth, and (by email) Helen Liddell. Lord Forbes shared his memories of the Scottish Office in the 1950s with me by telephone and correspondence; Dr J. Dickson Mabon did likewise about the 1960s, while the late Lord Monro of Langholm, Sir Teddy Taylor (by letter), Lord Ewing, Hugh Brown and Lord Kirkhill (by letter) remembered the Scottish Office of the 1970s. For the Thatcher and Major years, the late Lord Gray of Contin, Lord Glenarthur, Lord Sanderson, Allan Stewart (by telephone), Lord James Douglas-Hamilton MSP, Michael Ancram MP, Lord Strathclyde, the Earl of Lindsay and Raymond Robertson all shared their recollections, while for the Blair years, Lord Sewel, Sam Galbraith, Lord Macdonald of Tradeston and Henry McLeish were all very co-operative.

Other politicians who spoke to me include Alex Neil, now an SNP MSP but formerly a Labour researcher in the early 1970s, Margo MacDonald MSP, Lord Maclennan of Rogart, Lord Thomson of Monifieth, Lord Baker, Jim Sillars, Winnie Ewing and Lord Donoughue, who kindly gave me a sneak preview of the second volume of his as yet unpublished diaries. Helen Liddell's special adviser, Nick Comfort, remembered the post-devolution Scotland Office, while Simon Turner, who worked closely with Michael Forsyth from 1990 to 1997, remembered those often fraught years. Relatives of Scottish Office incumbents also proved invaluable. The present Earl of Dalhousie kindly looked at my chapter on his ancestor, as did the present Lord Balfour of Burleigh on his. The latter's wife, the historian Janet Morgan, helpfully suggested amendments to the same chapter, while Mark Iain Tennant spoke to me about his grandfather, Harold John Tennant. Sir John Gilmour looked at my chapter on his father, and Joanna Davidson – George Younger's daughter – very kindly met me to discuss her late father, while John Thurso MP did the same to talk to me about his grandfather, Sir Archibald Sinclair.

But I owe the biggest debt of gratitude to the civil servants, both past and present, who shared their incredibly detailed memories of working with secretaries of state from the late 1950s until present. Sir William Kerr Fraser gave me an account of his career spanning 40 years, while Sir Norman Graham's anecdotes stretched back to the Second World War. Former private secretaries proved especially helpful. Archie Rennie spoke to me about his time with Jack Maclay and Michael Noble, and also suggested changes to my resulting chapters. The Rev. Norman Shanks, Kenneth MacKenzie, Godfrey Robson and Alan Fraser did likewise, but my biggest vote of thanks has to go to Peter Mackay, who served two Scottish secretaries as private secretary in the mid 1970s. He tirelessly supplied me with anecdotes, detailed recollections, correspondence and valuable advice on my manuscript over several years. Of those currently serving at the Scotland Office, Kenneth Robbie kindly gave me a tour of Dover House and helped in securing permission to use the many portraits which hang in the building for the book's cover. I would like to give special thanks to the Government Art Collection for allowing use of five of those images, to Trinity College Cambridge for the painting of Sir George Otto Trevelyan, to the Royal Bank of Scotland for the portrait of the 9th Marquis of Lothian and to the artist Anne H. Mackintosh, who kindly agreed to let the publisher reproduce her fine portrait of Donald Dewar.

Thanks also to Professor Chris Cunneen, who met with me on a visit to Sydney and helpfully suggested revisions to the chapters on the 1st Marquis of Linlithgow and Viscount Novar, and to the writer Colin Clifford, who supplied information and sources for my chapter on Harold John Tennant. My boss for much of the time taken to write the book,

David Mundell MP, also allowed me much flexibility in researching it while I worked for him in the Commons.

The former *Herald* editor, Harry Reid, deserves thanks (or perhaps the blame) for spurring me back into action on completing this project following an encounter in early 2005, and for putting me in touch with Hugh Andrew at Birlinn, who agreed to publish the book. On the production side, I could not have asked for a more enthusiastic and encouraging publisher than Hugh. All of his staff at Birlinn proved to be just as helpful, particularly Laura Esslemont, Jim Hutcheson, Sarah Ream, Kenny Redpath and Andrew Simmons. Aline Hill was also a diligent and sympathetic copy-editor. For help with the pictures, I must thank – among others – the National Portrait Gallery, the *Scotsman* picture library and the *Herald*'s photograph archive at the Mitchell Library in Glasgow.

Among family and friends, my parents, as ever, provided silent encouragement to my niche obsessions, as did my brother Michael, who helped enormously by researching and compiling the appendix on Scottish Office legislation. My good friends Dominic Heslop and Douglas Pattullo kindly read and suggested important amendments to some chapters, while another friend (and former colleague at Grampian TV), Andrew Kerr, enthusiastically read the whole manuscript and picked out inconsistencies and errors with a pedant's eye. Finally John Wilson, who was honest enough to say he could not tolerate anything past Chapter Ten, nevertheless endured hours of listening to me talk about dead Scottish politicians and provided moral and practical encouragement for which I will be forever grateful.

David Torrance
September 2006
www.scottishsecretaries.com

PROLOGUE

The fact cannot longer be concealed that Scotland is becoming
dissatisfied, impatient, even disaffected, in consequence of the treatment which her affairs have received and are receiving at the hands
of the Government which she did so much to put into power. There
have been mutterings of discontent in many quarters for some time,
but now the suppressed mutterings have given place to outspoken
and empathic remonstrances.

The Times, 24 May 1881

Quixotic expectations seem to dog Scottish constitutional reform, and
the campaign to give Scotland a minister of her own was no exception.
The aspirations of the Scots, as Lord Salisbury later remarked, were
'approaching the Arch-angelic', particularly those of a vocal group of
prominent Scottish politicians which included the 5th Earl of Rosebery.
Born in London in 1847, Rosebery did not allow his English origins to
distract from a growing indignation at the manner in which 'Scotch'
business was dealt with at Westminster, chiefly by the lord advocate. An
articulate orator, the petulant young peer expressed this discontent
whenever he found a platform beneath him. It was fuelled by the
perception that while Ireland was appeased with concessions like the
land legislation of 1881, Gladstone cared little for the country which had
produced not only his parents but a seat in the Commons (Midlothian).
Scotland's secretary of state had been abolished following the 1745
Jacobite uprising and Rosebery relentlessly pestered the prime minister
to revive the position with a seat in the Cabinet. Gladstone was unsympathetic and repeatedly fobbed him off, although in August 1881 the
prime minister made Rosebery an under-secretary at the Home Office,
with special responsibility for Scottish business. He repeatedly fell out with
the home secretary, Sir William Harcourt, and continued to agitate for
reform, threatening resignation if Gladstone did not concede. On 5 May
1883 the Cabinet finally discussed the Scottish question, if only to avoid
what would be the damaging loss of a rising star. 'The Scotch, instigated

by Rosebery,' recorded the Earl of Derby in his diary, 'are asking for a Secretary of State or a Minister on the same footing as the Irish Secretary: there is no work for him to do and in the judgment of most English persons the proposal is a mistake but it seems that a certain amount of Scotch feeling, real or fictitious, has been got up on the subject.'[1] The prime minister 'disliked the notion of a bill' but gave way. Nevertheless, a combination of boredom, petulance and an overreaction to a perceived slight from Harcourt caused Rosebery to quit just a month after the meeting. He later refused the post of minister for Scotland under the ill-fated Local Government Board (Scotland) Bill of 1883, on the contra-dictory grounds that he had lobbied for the ministry himself (and it would look bad), and more to the point, the post was not in the Cabinet.

A certain fickleness accompanied Rosebery's patriotism, and as he holidayed in Australia from September 1883 the continuing campaign fell to others. Hundreds of them gathered in Edinburgh's Free Church Assembly Hall under the auspices of the Convention of Royal Scottish Burghs on 16 January 1884. 'The doors of the Assembly Hall having been opened at twelve o'clock,' recounted the *Scotsman*, 'ticket-holders forthwith began to pour into the building, and were ushered to their places by assiduous stewards . . . So prompt were the arrivals that, long before the time gun announced the hour for commencing the proceedings, all the available seats in area and galleries were closely packed.'[2] Just after one o'clock, the Marquis of Lothian entered and was reluctantly induced to take the chair. To his right sat Arthur James Balfour, and to his left Lord Balfour of Burleigh. Sitting close by as an observer was the young Earl of Dalhousie. Remarkably, all four men were future holders of the position the meeting sought to create. Speaker after speaker lamented the handling of Scottish business at Westminster, and overwhelmingly supported the following resolution:

That in the opinion of this meeting more satisfactory arrangements for the administration of Scottish affairs are imperatively required; that the increasing wealth and population of Scotland make its proper administration most important to the empire, while its marked national characteristics and institu-tions, and separate legal and educational systems, render it impossible to govern Scotland solely through the Home Office and other existing depart-ments of State; and that, therefore, Government should create a separate and independent department for the conduct of distinctively Scottish affairs, responsible to Parliament and the country for its administration. That the department should be presided over by a Minister for Scotland of personal eminence and position in Parliament and the country; and it is suggested that this office be conjoined with that of the Lord Privy Seal.

'The meeting,' concluded *The Times*, 'which was very enthusiastic throughout, separated after giving three cheers for the Queen.'[3] Gladstone was still unconvinced, although conscious that his growing zeal for Irish home rule could not be reconciled with dogged resistance to a similar (if lesser) concession for Scotland. With his blessing, the Earl of Dalhousie introduced a Bill within months to create a 'Secretary for Scotland'. As he moved its Second Reading on 8 May, Dalhousie recalled the spirit of that January meeting:

> In the opinion of many whose judgments are much more worth having than mine, such a meeting has rarely, if ever, taken place in either Scotland or any other country of the world. There were representatives of every class, representatives of every section of the nation, representatives of every shade of opinion, political and religious. The discussion lasted for some three hours, and I think there were some 30 or 40 speeches; and, so far as I can recollect, there was not one single discordant note from beginning to end.[4]

'I am not in the least degree unfriendly to the object of this Bill,'[5] said Lord Salisbury, but others criticised what they called a 'second-class Secretary for Scotland'. Dalhousie unequivocally declared that the 'Secretaryship for Scotland will be a Secretaryship altogether inferior to that of a Secretary of State,'[6] but, sensing discontent, altered his tone 12 days later. 'I can see no possible reason why the Secretary for Scotland,' he said, 'if he is a strong and able man – as strong and as able as these other great Officers of State – should not also find his way into the Cabinet.'[7]

Peers gave the Secretary for Scotland Bill a unanimous Second Reading but it was withdrawn following a quarrel between the Upper and Lower House over the finer details of the Franchise Bill. It was reintroduced a year later by a mellower Lord Rosebery – still expected to be the new post's first holder – and even when the Liberal government fell in June the incoming Conservative administration promised to treat the Bill as non-political and graciously allowed Rosebery to see it through. 'A General Election is near,' remarked Sir Lyon Playfair, inducing 'both sides to throw a tub to the Scotch whale'. *The Times* was a little more generous: 'Not much positive legislation can be expected from the new Government; but the Secretary for Scotland Bill is a measure which they should be able to pass without difficulty, and the passing of which will gain them credit in Scotland, where their credit does not stand very high.'[8] At the revived Bill's Second Reading on 9 July, responsibility for education had by now been added to the new department's eclectic duties following a rare Cabinet vote. The Marquis of Lothian, speaking from the government benches, acknowledged that some believed the movement towards a separate administration for Scotland 'was practically a sham, and that a sham deserved no consideration'. But, he added, 'These things began in a whisper; but the whisper grew into a loud voice, which . . . those who were wise would stop to listen to before it developed into a sullen roar.'[9] The new prime minister, Lord Salisbury, also remained in favour:

> I have never concealed my opinion on the subject, that, on the whole – though I admit that a great deal may be said on the other side – that, on the whole, it is better to localize as far as possible, rather than centralize, a business of this kind; and that those vast administrative mechanisms which we are building up are not without their inconvenience, and even not without their danger; and I should be, therefore, prepared to see them divided into smaller Departments.[10]

Future Conservative prime ministers would not be quite so enthusiastic. As the Bill moved towards its Third Reading, *The Times* adopted a more cynical view. 'We have heard no very convincing arguments advanced to show that Scotland is likely to be better governed in the future under a single Secretary than it is at present under a variety of officials and departments,' said an editorial, continuing:

> One practical consideration is, however, we admit, conclusive. The Scotch people seem to have made up their minds in favour of the Bill, and the Scotch people, as Lord Salisbury said the other day, are of such a character that whatever form of Government is in power they generally get what they choose to have. The Scotch people want a Secretary for Scotland; the late Government were willing to listen to the demand, and the present Government are far too wise to resist it.[11]

And so, on 21 July, the Secretary for Scotland Bill was read for a third and final time and sent to the House of Commons. Within two weeks, the Lower House passed the Bill and it received Royal Assent on 14 August. Exactly five months earlier, Gilbert and Sullivan's new comic opera, *The Mikado*, had premiered at the Savoy Theatre in London. One character was called Pooh-Bah, a pompous official with the title of 'Lord High Everything Else'. Pooh-Bah's range of inconsistent duties were reminiscent of the fledgling secretary for Scotland's, and it was not long before political wits had come up with an inevitable nickname for the new occupant of Dover House.

6TH DUKE OF RICHMOND

17 AUGUST 1885 – 28 JANUARY 1886

The farmers' friend

The first Scottish secretary was impeccably aristocratic. With no less than four dukedoms – Richmond in England, Lennox in Scotland, Gordon in the United Kingdom and Aubigny in France – Charles Henry Gordon-Lennox was the most richly endowed nobleman on the peers' roll. History has not been kind to the 6th Duke of Richmond and Gordon, 'an amiable but ineffective nonentity'[1] being typical of his biographical write-ups. It would be charitable to shatter this myth, but the reality supplies plenty of evidence to support both traits.

The year 1885 perhaps represented the calm before the political storm: Gladstone was yet to finalise his scheme for Irish home rule, and when Lord Salisbury was reluctantly invited to form a caretaker ministry (until another election, based on the new franchise and constituencies, was possible)[2] Richmond became nothing more than a stop-gap Scottish secretary. 'I am astonished to find Richmond will take the Scotch Sec.-ship.,' wrote the lord president Viscount Cranbrook in his diary. 'He hardly knows what is before him.'[3]

The Duke of Richmond had spoken only occasionally as the first Secretary for Scotland Bill made its way through the Upper House in 1884. Richmond had opposed the transfer of the Scotch Education Department (SED) to the new minister, fearing it would end up in the hands of a man who knew nothing of his subject.[4] In fact, His Grace was suspicious of the Bill fullstop, especially when the Earl of Dalhousie claimed it was purely an experimental measure. 'It would be satisfactory to their Lordships to know how long they were to be occupied in experiments,' he said sarcastically, and 'how long they were to be kept in suspense, before they knew whether a Secretary for Scotland was to be one of the institutions of the country.'[5] Richmond suggested setting a time limit to assess the new minister's usefulness, allowing the office to be abolished if its holder did not prove up to the job.

From police to fisheries, wild bird protection to prisons, the new minister for Scotland was certainly spoilt for choice; Salisbury, however, was not. The Conservatives' few Scottish MPs, and even fewer peers, made the prime minister's job of filling the Scottish Office difficult. He first offered it to the 9th Marquis of Lothian, but, despite being an early supporter of the Bill, the marquis turned it down on health grounds. Only after three others had been approached did Salisbury write to Richmond, an old friend, on 7 August:

> What are your feelings about the Secretaryship for Scotland? The work is not very heavy – the dignity (measured by salary) is the same as your present office – but measured by the expectations of the people of Scotland it is approaching the Arch-angelic. We want a big man to float it – especially as there is so much sentiment about it. I think you seem pointed out by nature to be the man. Lothian's health would not be up to it – & Balfour of Burleigh or Dalrymple are too insignificant. The Scotch people would declare we were despising Scotland – & treating her as if she was a West Indian Colony. It really is a matter where the effulgence of two Dukedoms and the best salmon river in Scotland will go a long way.[6]

How could Richmond resist? He replied with humility, and a heavy dose of pragmatism:

> I am quite ready and willing to take the office of Secretary for Scotland if you would like me to do so and think that by doing so I can be useful to you. You know my opinion of the office, and that it is quite unnecessary, but the Country and Parliament think otherwise – and the office has been created, and someone must fill it. Under these circumstances I am quite ready to take it, and will do my best to make it a success (if this is possible!).[7]

Salisbury was relieved. His flattery had worked.

> I really am very grateful to you for your kindness in taking the Scotch Office. It makes it a success at once, for the whole object of the move is to redress the wounded dignities of the Scotch people – or a section of them – who think that enough is not made of Scotland: & your taking the office will make all the difference between the measure being a compliment to them, or a slight.[8]

Royal Assent was granted on 14 August and three days later the Duke of Richmond was appointed as Her Majesty's first secretary for Scotland, taking possession of the Great Seal of Scotland.

It was a strange end to a solid, if unremarkable, political career. A descendent of King Charles II, Charles Henry Gordon-Lennox was born at Richmond House in Whitehall on 27 February 1818. He was educated at Winchester and

Christ Church, Oxford, and entered parliament as the Earl of March in 1841, sitting for West Sussex until becoming 6th Duke of Richmond on his father's death in 1860. He briefly held office as president of the Poor Law Board in Lord Derby's second government but devoted much of his time to developing a reputation as an authority on agriculture in the House of Lords. He also had a parallel military career, acting as aide-de-camp for ten years to the Duke of Wellington, until the great soldier-statesman's death, and when General Peel resigned from Derby's third administration in March 1867 Richmond joined the 'leap in the dark' Cabinet as president of the Board of Trade. To everyone's surprise he then became Conservative leader in the House of Lords following Derby's death in 1869, proving to be a moderate leader of the opposition as he tried to water down Gladstonian reforms. Richmond continued as leader in the Lords when Disraeli formed his second government in 1874, also becoming lord president of the council, which gave him control of the education department. A future historian sneeringly described him as 'A man of little calibre with no particular interest in education, an aristocratic amateur of the old type, whose main concern seems to have been to get the business of the session over and depart to the Scottish moors with that other hammer of the grouse, Lord Cairns.'[9] Cairns proved a steady Cabinet ally, Richmond's rank supplementing the austere lord chancellor's considerable brainpower. Richmond also matched that intellect with ego, gaining ideas above his station. 'Letter from Salisbury,' wrote Derby in his diary, adding:

> who has got in his mind the notion that there is in some quarters a project for making the D of Richmond the next premier, when Disraeli's health compels him to resign, an event which Salisbury evidently considers as not far distant. He protests against this, says it must not be allowed, that the Duke is unfit for the post, that his appointment would justify the title of the 'stupid party' as applied to us.[10]

But when Disraeli became Lord Beaconsfield in 1876 Richmond stood down as leader[11] and instead applied himself to agricultural matters; the Prince of Wales even publicly dubbed him 'the farmers' friend' at a meeting of the Royal Agricultural Society in 1883. Richmond chaired a royal commission on the depressed state of British farming, which produced a number of recommendations including the creation of an agriculture ministry. But other than a brief return to the Board of Trade, his political career was over; over, that is, until Salisbury found himself with a new 'Scotch' department and no one to put in it.

The *Scotsman*, then a sycophantically Tory rag, was effusive about Scotland's new minister: 'By the appointment of the Duke of Richmond and Gordon, in brief, the new office has been stamped, at the earliest moment, with the hall-mark of Cabinet value . . . and invested with the highest dignity, with power behind that dignity to make the weight of Scottish wants felt in the councils of the Empire.'[12] An overzealous leader writer later hinted at the shape of things to come: 'The Scottish Secretary may before long be preparing Bills for discussion by a Scottish National Council. His appointment will make that easier because he will know what Scotland wants – while the English heads of the different departments would not.'[13] His 'dignity' was the princely sum of £2,000 a year (a figure which remained unchanged until 1914), which meant Richmond retained the same salary and Cabinet rank he had held at the Board of Trade.

Richmond was holidaying in the German spa town of Homburg when his appointment was finalised on 17 August, and he stayed there while the details of the new office were worked out. He instinctively turned to Sir Francis Sandford for help, an official he had worked with as head of the Education Department. Now retired, Sir Francis joined his old boss in Germany, where he was offered the post of permanent under-secretary at the Scottish Office.[14] He accepted, and the home secretary, Sir Richard Cross, also offered the services of W. C. Dunbar[15] – who had handled Scottish business at the Home Office – but otherwise the new secretary for Scotland was to have virtually no political or administrative support. Assistance did come from two law officers, whose existence pre-dated that of the Scottish secretary by centuries: the solicitor-general for Scotland and the lord advocate, the latter being an amiable and bumbling fellow known as Sir John 'Jumbo' Macdonald. Salisbury was impressed by Richmond's haste: 'I am very glad you are settling the matter so quickly – it will impress your vainglorious countrymen the more.'[16]

It could scarcely be claimed that the Duke of Richmond in any way controlled Scottish administration. He had a greater claim to being a rather remote co-ordinator, the real work being performed by a quagmire of county and burgh councils, the Crown Office and a series of ad-hoc Edinburgh-based boards (rather grand Victorian quangos), which controlled everything from fisheries to prisons. Yet Scottish affairs were, for the first time, directly accountable to a minister within parliament. 'I signed away Dover House for you to reside in,' wrote Salisbury flippantly. 'I believe I have as much right to sign away Westminster Abbey – but the Lord Advocate seemed to take it very easy . . . Anyhow it is better than twelve rooms over a Post Office. I wonder Plunkett [First Commissioner of Works] did not offer you the second pair back over a gin-shop.'[17]

A survivor of the days when Whitehall was at the heart of fashionable

London, Dover House had been offered to Gladstone as an alternative to Number 10 Downing Street, but the Grand Old Man declined. The grandeur of the building, he said, would oblige him to receive many visitors and Gladstone valued his privacy. Now lying vacant, Scottish Office legend has it that as the lord advocate chatted with Lord Salisbury in a railway compartment the prime minister asked whether a new home had yet been found for the new department. Sir John said no, but added that various suggestions had been made, including a house in Covent Garden, and others which seemed to him to be equally unsuitable. Salisbury said he wished the new office to be well housed; the lord advocate mentioned Dover House, and wasted no time in getting a note from Salisbury agreeing that it should be handed over for that very purpose. His haste was more than a little self-serving, Sir John being keen to desert his cramped quarters in the Home Office. Richmond, the Scotch Education Department (SED) and the lord advocate moved in to their new home at the end of September. The palatial classical dimensions were perhaps disproportionate for an office not yet considered in the first rank of government, especially given that only seven people, serving two ministers, occupied three floors. Perhaps the gin shop would have been a more economical option.

On 18 November 1885 the duke hosted a reception in the Faculty of Advocates' Library in Edinburgh after taking his oath as secretary for Scotland. Members of the legal fraternity hobnobbed with other dignitaries both local and national, and Richmond was clearly warming to the idea of his new position, reporting to Salisbury:

> My functions came off yesterday. I was sworn in as Keeper of the Great Seal . . . in the Court of Session. All the judges attended. After which I had a levee! of all the heads of Departments – Prisons Board, Fishery Board, Board of Supervision, &c., &c. The Provost and Town Council attended. In fact it was rather a grand affair and not much in my line . . . I am beginning to think the office is more thought of than I ever gave credit for. I received two deputations in my rooms, over the door of which Roseberry [sic] had painted Secretary of State for Scotland![18]

Although Richmond was never to speak in parliament as secretary for Scotland – a long summer recess soon giving way to a typically lengthy Victorian general election – he had still experienced an eventful few months. The home secretary wrote to the duke just a week after his appointment, alerting him to a situation of the 'utmost concern' in the Western Isles. Cattle, he said, had been forced off grazing ground and replaced with the 'beasts of crofters'.[19] But he also pointed out that as law and order were still Home Office responsibilities, the unrest was not solely a Scottish Office concern. Richmond, however, was responsible for local police and general administration on the island, so he could not be fully excluded from the action. The Scottish secretary wrote to the home secretary, Sir Richard Cross, on 2 September, saying that all one island landlord wanted was five extra policemen supported by a gunboat:

> I have a very strong opinion that the Gun Boat should not be there at all unless it is to be of some use . . . I quite understood when I wrote to you before, that a great deal still remains under the S. of State and in some cases for instance under the Police Acts the jurisdiction of the SofS and the Secy for Scotland are very much mixed up.[20]

More than two weeks later the situation was no better, and the tone of Richmond's letters became a little frantic. 'I can not imagine what induced the late Gov. to send a Gunboat and then do nothing with it,' he wrote. '[Joseph] Chamberlain seems to be going about trying to unite the people. I hear that he was at Inverness yesterday where he made a most violent speech trying to incite the Crofters.'[21] Richmond suggested that the chief officers of the fleet survey the affected island's coasts, while turning his mind to a legislative response. 'The more I look at the Crofter Bill question the more difficult I find it,' he wrote to the home secretary, adding that it would be difficult to sell politically to the crofters. 'I have not yet attempted to draft a Bill and shd much like to talk to you about it before I begin . . . I have great doubt if we ought to promise one in the Queens Speech. If we are all turned out we shall be pledged to a Crofter Bill. We can always promise to bring one in if we remain in office.'[22] Salisbury shared Richmond's instincts. 'I am very glad to hear you are resolved against any Irish Land Bill for the Crofters,' wrote the prime minister sagely. 'It would be a great pity to reduce the Highlands quite to the condition of Ireland.'[23] By early 1886 land league associations had started to spring up all over the Highlands and Islands, but the whole issue of crofters' unrest was soon to become a problem for another government.

The Highland conflict had also been mirrored by another dispute much closer to home. As soon as Richmond and Sir Henry Craik (head of the Scotch Education Department) began to appoint a small number of staff to the new department, the Treasury did its best to obstruct any progress. Sir Reginald Welby, the permanent under-secretary at the Treasury, offered no objections to Richmond's original proposals, but the financial secretary, Sir Henry Holland, took 'a very hostile view of the thing'.[24]

Richmond had proposed to pay Sandford £1,500 and Craik £1,200 a year, and to allow W. C. Dunbar to get £1,000, but the Treasury proposed cutting Sandford's salary to £1,200, with corresponding reductions to all other salaries. The Education Department also made trouble over SED staffing, while the Home Office continued to maintain that the Scottish Office had nothing to do. 'The [Scottish] office only exists within certain statutory powers,' said a typically territorial memo dated 14 October. 'The Secretary has no jurisdiction whatever beyond what is specially imposed on him by the Act. In every other respect, until experience has shown the necessity for alteration in the Law, and the Law has been altered accordingly, the Secretary of State [for Home Affairs] must still remain responsible.'[25] The dispute lasted throughout September and October, with the Treasury pushing each point to Cabinet level. And even when both Salisbury[26] and the Cabinet agreed that Sandford be paid £1,500 the Treasury refused to concede defeat, prompting Richmond, Sandford and Dunbar to threaten resignation at the end of October. 'I am very much disappointed and I may say disgusted at the conclusion they have arrived at,' wrote Richmond to Cross. 'I am much [angrier] because I thought the Cabinet had decided that my proposal was fair and right. Sandford and Dunbar both desire to go on, and I have written to Salisbury to say that under the circumstances I do not see how I can continue to hold the office. I think I have been badly and unfairly and improperly treated by the Treasury.'[27] The chancellor finally intervened to force his subordinates to give way, but not before one of them had scrawled across the corresponding file 'This is the worst Scotch job since the Caledonian Canal.'[28]

The general election of November/December 1885 saw the Conservatives outnumbered by the combined force of the Liberals and Charles Parnell's Irish Nationalists, so in the end Scotland's first secretary lasted only six months, resigning on 28 January 1886 along with the rest of Salisbury's ministry. Richmond took the opportunity to retire from public life, busying himself with dull but useful committee work while earning a reputation as an efficient chairman of private Bill committees. He reportedly ran a mile on being offered a return to the Scottish Office when Salisbury became prime minister again in July 1886, no doubt more interested in maintaining the hunt at his Sussex home of Goodwood, not to mention his famous party in race week. The Duchess of Richmond died in 1887 after many years of poor health, and her elder, unmarried, daughter Caroline became Richmond's companion, acting as hostess for him in his later years. The duke died at his Scottish residence, Gordon Castle, on 27 September 1903, having enjoyed a good summer there since

July; he was buried in the family vault in Chichester Cathedral (near Goodwood) on 3 October. He never showed any hint of pride at having been the first Scottish secretary, nor did he display any interest in the subsequent work of the Scottish Office. But as the first secretary for Scotland, the Duke of Richmond and Gordon – however uninterested – had prepared the groundwork for a department which, over the next century, was to play an ever greater role in the government of Scotland.

Sir George Otto Trevelyan, Baronet

12 February – 6 April 1886 & 18 August 1892 – 21 June 1895

A minor prophet

In the summer of 1867 George Otto Trevelyan travelled to Italy hoping to join Garibaldi's Redshirts for their attack on Rome, but as he made his way south by train he was overtaken by the Italian revolutionary's defeated troops retreating from the battle of Mentana. Disappointed, Trevelyan nevertheless always looked back on his adventure as 'the greatest romance of my life'. The first Liberal Scottish secretary was both an historian and an incurable romantic. Such flourishes littered Trevelyan's political career, often ending in resignation, but it was symptomatic of a vast hinterland. He moved easily between the worlds of learning, literature and public affairs, and if Trevelyan had never set foot in the House of Commons, he would still be remembered for his many volumes of history and biography.

After a brief Conservative interlude, Gladstone returned to government in February 1886, now convinced of the need for Irish home rule. Liberal sceptics were persuaded to join the Cabinet on the understanding that they were committed to no more than an inquiry into the feasibility of home rule, and on this basis Trevelyan became secretary for Scotland, although he had rather quixotically hoped to become chancellor. Like his predecessor, he was essentially English; while several acres of prime Scottish estate justified the Duke of Richmond's appointment, Trevelyan's Borders constituency justified his. Trevelyan was not really interested in the more obscure duties of his department, but it fell to him to make the parliamentary debut of the new ministry. Speaking in the debate on the Queen's Speech, Trevelyan defended the planned Crofters' Holdings (Scotland) Bill. The Crofters' Party had won five seats at the 1885 general election, and since then rent strikes and land raids had become commonplace. The Bill provided security of tenure to crofters in seven northern counties and established the first Crofters Commission, a land court which would mediate in disputes between landlords and their tenants. 'During the last six months, under a Conservative Government,' Trevelyan told MPs, 'no troops have been sent into that district; and I do not think it is very likely that, under a Liberal Government, any troops will be sent for such a purpose.'[1] He spoke too soon, as his successors – both Liberal and Conservative – would discover. The Bill came before Cabinet in February and although Trevelyan complained to Gladstone of not finding enough time for 'Scotch' business in the Commons, he moved the Second Reading on 25 February 1886. 'You have been very generous to Scotland in giving her legislative procedure,' Trevelyan wrote to Gladstone the following month, 'but in truth it is very necessary that the bill should pass promptly. The House is perfectly prepared to accept it now, if we can get time to consider it. Of course I am aware how very great an assumption that is.'[2] Gladstone replied whimsically the following day: 'I feel the force of what you say about the Crofters' Bill, & it seems a case to make hay while the sun shines.'[3] Trevelyan, however, had to hand the Bill over to his successor at the end of March as Cabinet divisions over Irish home rule reached breaking point.

Trevelyan had tried to resign after the Cabinet meeting of 13 March when Gladstone unveiled plans for an Irish legislature and a separate Bill to settle the land question. 'I am sorry to say that the experience of Saturday's Cabinet proved to me that I am not justified in continuing to be a member of the Government,' he wrote to the prime minister on 15 March. 'I shall be very much obliged if you will lay my Resignation before Her Majesty, and will yourself accept my warm thanks for the manner in which you have helped and supported me during the tenure of this office.'[4] The Grand Old Man was not impressed: 'I have seen many and many a resignation, but never one based upon the intentions, nay the immature intentions of the Prime Minister, and in a pure anticipation of what may happen . . . Bricks and rafters are prepared for a house, but are not themselves a house.'[5] Trevelyan was temporarily appeased but the foundations did not hold for long. On 26 March the Cabinet met once again, with Trevelyan not so much objecting to a restored Irish assembly, but unable to tolerate law and order being removed from direct British authority. Gladstone was in no mood for concessions and when Joseph Chamberlain posed four questions regarding the proposed powers and remit of the legislature, Gladstone answered yes to each. 'Then,' said Chamberlain, 'I resign.' And with that Chamberlain and Trevelyan stormed out of the Cabinet room. The prime minister made no effort to detain them. It was a turning point for the erstwhile Unitarian screw-manufacturer, but marked only a brief split with Gladstone for Trevelyan.

Gladstone did not hide his disgust. 'The Queen accepts your resignation and you are free to announce it as you please,' he wrote to Trevelyan. 'I witness the snapping of this tie with unfeighned [*sic*], and with unmixed regret. My heartiest good wishes wait upon your future career. I only grieve to think that I have lost all power to give effect to them.'[6] For Trevelyan the feeling was palpable. 'I cannot tell you what a relief it is being out,' he wrote to Sir Henry Campbell-Bannerman, 'because to be in a Government, with a great difference of view from one's colleagues, makes one critical, and rather unfair: whereas the effect of being out is to clear up all clouds, as far as personal considerations go, and make me even more friendly than before, which is saying not a little.'[7]

The first Irish Home Rule Bill was presented to parliament during April 1886 but was defeated at its Second Reading on 8 June when 93 Liberals, led by Chamberlain and Lord Hartington, voted with the Conservatives. Curiously, a greater proportion of Scottish Liberal members voted against the Bill than did their English counterparts; Trevelyan was one of them, marching defiantly into the Tory lobby. He stood as a Liberal Unionist in the resulting general election but was narrowly defeated, ending an association with the Border Burghs of nearly 20 years. There was also bad news for the Grand Old Man, now very much in a hurry, the election producing only 191 MPs under his banner against 316 for Salisbury's Conservatives. Trevelyan was deeply unhappy at being separated from old colleagues, and believed that Gladstone should have resigned rather than take his case to the country. Ironically, he converted to home rule within a year, having attended a round table conference contrived to appease former rebels. Trevelyan stood in a by-election for the Bridgeton Division of Glasgow in July 1887 and won, but his swift U-turn exposed him to the full acrimony of the Liberal Unionist press and some former colleagues. Chamberlain had a field day, depicting Trevelyan as a political weathercock.

Trevelyan's career to date had been inextricably bound up with that of Gladstone. He was first elected in 1865 to represent Tynemouth, but switched to the Border Burghs three years later. He was appointed civil lord of the admiralty in Gladstone's first government, a position he somehow retained until July 1870, when he resigned over the Education Bill's proposed allowances for denominational schools. Trevelyan had proved a hapless junior minister, managing to offend both the Queen and Gladstone by portraying the Duke of Cambridge (the Queen's cousin) as an obstacle to army reform. The prime minister was horrified and assured Her Majesty that Trevelyan had 'received a lesson for life'.

In 1882 the chief secretary in Ireland, Lord Frederick Cavendish, was assassinated in Dublin and Trevelyan replaced him. But he was not a success, the stress turning his hair and beard prematurely grey, and when Trevelyan returned to the mainland in 1884 he rejoined the government as chancellor of the Duchy of Lancaster. He came from a close-knit family, strongly evangelical in religion and intensely bookish. Trevelyan's bachelor uncle, Lord Macaulay (his mother's brother), had a considerable influence on his young nephew, later providing the subject matter for Trevelyan's first great work, *The Life and Letters of Lord Macaulay*, which was published in 1876. Trevelyan was educated at Harrow and Trinity College, Cambridge, and after graduating he went to India to work for his father, Sir Charles Trevelyan. On his return, he wrote *The Competition Wallah*, a humorous collection of fictional letters from an imaginary young Indian civil servant, who had won his post in the competitive examinations introduced under the influence of Sir Charles. By 1865 Trevelyan had decided upon a political career and quickly adopted strong radical views, particularly on questions of electoral and administrative reform.

Trevelyan returned to the Scottish Office in 1892, becoming the first recidivist Scottish secretary as Gladstone formed his fourth and final ministry. Once again Sir George, his father having died in 1886, was not Gladstone's first choice to fill the post. Although the prime minister considered Trevelyan to be a man of great talent and high character, he believed that 'by 1892 he had shown himself to be unfit for high places',[8] so a seat in the Cabinet was no more than a sop. But while Trevelyan had lacked the time to make his mark back in 1886, his second residency at Dover House proved to be a missed opportunity. Gladstone was by now dependent upon the Irish vote, and although Trevelyan was an able administrator and a loyal colleague he was not a compelling platform speaker (although strangely popular). His prepared speeches in the Commons benefited from a clear voice and a natural literary flourish, but that rare talent of instinctive debate was never his forte. He also had his critics, one polemicist sneering that with 'Home Rule in the ascendant, it was a sad blow to find the Scottish Office assigned to a Northumberland landlord with a Cornish name, whose performances as the Lot's wife of Liberal Unionism were rewarded by the fiat, "As you were in March 1886"'. Trevelyan's Scottish constituency, he added, was nothing more than a pied-a-terre for his political career.[9]

By the beginning of 1894 nothing substantial had materialised by way of specifically Scottish legislation. All Sir George had to boast of was a private Bill to give Glasgow 'an accession to dignity' by making it a county, and a Scottish Fisheries Bill which only got through the Commons due to the 'wonderful forbearance' of Scottish Unionist members. The Queen's Speech of 1893 had promised a Scottish Church Suspensory Bill but Trevelyan's pitch was muddled to say the least: 'A good thing cannot be done too soon, and a good thing cannot be begun too soon, and this is at any rate a beginning.' To others it was simply bemusing and unnecessary. A Registration Bill had also been promised, but again Trevelyan botched it so badly that he was openly accused of seeking to gerrymander, or 'Trevelyander' as one wag put it, constituencies in the Radical interest. Gladstone said the government would do everything in its power to get the Bill through but again it vanished without trace. MPs of both parties, not to mention the popular press, were scathing. Mr R. T. Reid lamented, 'He was a Scotsman. They had been there for a year. With the exception of one small uncontested bill, not a single thing had been done for Scotland. They might as well have forgotten that country existed.'[10]

On constitutional reform Trevelyan was on surer, and more productive territory. Lord Rosebery succeeded Gladstone as prime minister in 1894, and although his premiership was petulant and brief he was the first head of government with a direct interest in Scottish affairs. Luckily for Trevelyan, Rosebery was a fan of his uncle, having become hooked on Macaulay's *Essays* during a youthful illness. They also agreed on many things, not least Scottish disestablishment, for which a Bill also appeared that year, yet the reluctant prime minister considered his Scottish secretary to be the weakest man in his Cabinet, later admitting to the Queen that he would not himself have appointed him.[11] 'R. says he is lamentable as Secretary for Scotland,' wrote Sir Edward Hamilton in his diary, '& that an effort must be made to get him to exchange places with Bryce.'[12] Gladstone agreed, later telling an acquaintance that Trevelyan 'seemed to have lost his nerve and become useless, except for the power to make an occasional good speech'.[13]

Trevelyan's only lasting reform turned out to be the Scottish Grand Committee. A petition had been presented to Gladstone by Scottish MPs in December 1892 expressing discontent with the conduct of Scottish business, and in April 1894, just a month after Rosebery became prime minister, Trevelyan moved a resolution to create a standing committee (comprising all Scottish members together with 15 others) to solve the problem.[14] This had obvious practical and political benefits, but the debate surrounding it on 2 April threw up some enduring constitutional questions. 'Is it not in itself an abuse of very great magnitude that 70 busy men . . . should come to Parliament, and only every other year be able to do important business about the country which they represent?' asked

Sir George. 'The Scotch Grand Committee will not only be a sort of microcosm of the House in Committee of the whole House on Scotch business; it will be the House in Committee on Scotch business itself.' He quoted a Victorian incarnation of Tam Dalyell, who had warned 'It would be utterly unfair to English interests that, while the English were to have no voice in the framing of Scotch measures, Scotchmen and Irishmen should determine the form in which English measures were to be passed.' Trevelyan disputed that this would be so, but Arthur James Balfour, in the first of many anti-devolution speeches, took up the theme: 'I . . . am one of those who have always believed that these subordinate patriotisms, if I may use the expression, are a most useful element in our public life.'[15] But Balfour ridiculed the notion that any Bill could be deemed to relate exclusively to Scotland, warning that 'sham gifts' were a prelude to depriving Scotland of some of her most valuable political privileges.

Only the Second Reading of non-contentious Bills were to be considered by what quickly became known as the Scottish Grand Committee, with the final decision on the Third Reading and any amendments resting with the entire House. The new body also provided something new for the *Scotsman* to knock, and it met for the first time at the end of May 1894 with only Trevelyan and the solicitor-general present on the front-bench. The 15 'outsiders' did particularly well, according to a correspondent, but attendance occasionally dwindled to just 33 out of a possible 87 members.[16] Although its initial existence was short lived – Lord Salisbury scrapped it in 1895 – the Scottish Grand Committee was credited with producing good work on the Local Government (Scotland) Bill of 1894. Although Trevelyan was no fan of Scottish administration (he told Earl Spencer that 'these semi-independent, semi-representative Boards are the real difficulty of Scotch administration'[17]) this established a new Local Government Board for Scotland to replace the old Board of Supervision. It also completed earlier Conservative reforms by establishing directly elected parish councils which took control of poor relief from non-elected parochial boards, and it had a remarkably easy ride in parliament. The Bill was regarded as a minor triumph by government supporters who had half expected the Scottish secretary to make a mess of it. 'Now that the new Local Government Board is settled, (as far as I can judge, to the satisfaction of everybody,) they will take some work off my hands,' wrote Trevelyan to James Bryce. 'On the whole, we shall come all right out of it: but the local authorities require most careful handling.'[18]

On the wider question of Scottish administration it seems Trevelyan's conversion to Irish home rule now also applied to Scotland. 'The happy and successful experience of the Scotch Office has gone far towards solving the question of Home Rule,' he said in September 1892. 'It ha[s] proved that Scotland, and if Scotland other parts of the country too, would do very well with a separate Executive.'[19] And when the House later debated a Scottish home rule resolution, Trevelyan insisted that in 'this Parliament there is a Government which has, I maintain, done as much for Scotland as for the rest of the country'. He admitted, however, that all members regretted the lack of time for Scotch business. 'I have seized every opportunity I could find to give my vote in favour of a generous measure of self-government for Scotland, and I certainly shall not lose that opportunity to-night.'[20] Most of Trevelyan's Cabinet colleagues, however, abstained.[21]

Meanwhile, Gladstone had introduced his second Irish Home Rule Bill, sparking yet another political crisis. 'Time moves inexorably,' wrote Trevelyan to Sir James Donaldson at St Andrews University, 'and at last we appear to be approaching the threshold of the great event. Everybody is heartily tired of this House of Commons – except the Peers in the Cabinet who do not sit in it.'[22] The Government of Ireland Bill passed by a slim majority in the House of Commons on 1 September 1893.[23] 'You will see that we are still rolling up the stone of Sisyphus,' wrote Trevelyan, again to Sir James, 'an occupation which I fancy will last out this government.'[24] But the Bill floundered in the Lords, another popular target for Trevelyan, who told a meeting in York 'that it was humiliating and shameful to think that in our country alone of all the countries and colonies which spoke our tongue the representatives of the people were overridden and overruled by those who represented nobody but themselves'.[25]

'Sir George Trevelyan has sunk to the rank of a minor prophet,' declared the *Scotsman* on 16 January 1895, an appropriate insult for one so obsessed with the established church. Earlier in that parliament Scottish MPs had voted by 35 to 14 'in favour of religious equality' or Kirk disestablishment, an issue which occupied Trevelyan above all others. Rosebery had promised Bills for both Scottish and Welsh disestablishment the previous year, even attracting the support of Gladstone, but they came to nothing. It was said that Trevelyan removed a typical preamble about maintaining the Presbyterian Church of Scotland from the Queen's letter to one meeting of the General Assembly of the Church of Scotland. This caused great consternation among delegates and the lord high commissioner took prompt action. But before the Assembly began, the missing words 'were found in their place, and the Secretary for Scotland was put into his'.[26]

The other aspect of the Scottish Office which greatly excited Trevelyan was his wide powers of patronage. 'I have no feeling whatever about patronage except to get the thing rightly done,'[27] he said, but Trevelyan was indecisive and reckless when it came to appointing university chairs and members of commissions, often getting himself into trouble, not least with his monarch, who had very definite views on crown appointments. Relations with Queen Victoria had always been bumpy, and although he now considered her a 'very great lady' he had not in 1871 when he penned an anonymous pamphlet called 'What Does She Do With It?', an impertinent attack on the Queen's apparent hoarding of money. In 1894 Trevelyan appointed Professor Sorley from Cardiff University to a vacant chair at Aberdeen University, but Rosebery wrote to him outlining the Queen's complaints: 'She . . . says that your last nominee at Aberdeen has become crazy and will have to be removed.' Her Majesty also complained that Professor Sorley's 'experience is purely Welsh'. He was, protested Trevelyan, a 'Scotchman of Edinburgh' and of the highest intellect.[28] After prolonged correspondence with an irritated Rosebery, the Queen eventually approved Professor Sorley's nomination. 'In Glasgow academical appointments are regarded as their own right by a certain Tory and Unionist clique,' wrote Trevelyan to Lord Kimberley in September 1892, 'who work the press in the most improper manner whenever an appointment is in the wind.'[29] The suitability of his chosen deer forest commissioners in 1892 were also widely questioned, and in May 1895 he got wind of a 'scandalous production . . . showing that literally every legal appointment, properly so called, has been given to a liberal: which was right and normal, as they had been systematically passed over for so many years under the late government'. Trevelyan believed jealous Liberals were to blame rather than the Unionists, adding in a letter to Rosebery that 'of course no answer can be given as it would become public and create a scandal'.[30]

'I am deep in the Crofters Bill,' Trevelyan wrote on 5 April 1895, 'which, to the solid satisfaction of Scotch members, is to be introduced first of Scotch bills and as soon as possible.'[31] But his Bill to extend the Crofters' Act to all northern counties[32] disappeared when Rosebery was defeated at the general election. 'One likes being turned out better than being put in,'[33] he wrote to his sister Alice, clearly enjoying the freedom of opposition.

Trevelyan enjoyed another 31 years of busy life, none of them spoiled by even a fleeting return to party politics, having resigned his seat in 1897 aged only 59. He finished his six-volume history of the American War of Independence, but refused Asquith's offer of a peerage in 1908. He died at his Wallington estate in Northumberland on 17 August 1928 at the age of 90, six months after his wife. Trevelyan's family continued to produce politicians and historians with strong independent streaks,

Charles Trevelyan holding junior office in the Liberal government during 1908 and later becoming Labour's first education secretary, while his brother George Macaulay Trevelyan churned out many a standard historical text. Trevelyan had been well liked by most of his colleagues, but was too gentle and sensitive to exert a dominant influence on events, a streak of vanity leading him to overestimate his political abilities. He used to tell Earl Spencer that he could have been Liberal leader in view of his literary and political successes, but in reality Sir George Otto Trevelyan had been at best an intriguing and colourful, if not ultimately successful, secretary for Scotland.

13TH EARL OF DALHOUSIE

7 APRIL – 2 AUGUST 1886

The truest heart

The 13th Earl of Dalhousie's short life reads like one of Anthony Trollope's political novels: early political ambitions thwarted by his father, a brief spell in government which destroyed his health, and a tragically early death from a broken heart. Now almost completely forgotten, Sir John William Maule Ramsay was for a period considered one of the most promising young Liberal politicians of his day. John Morley thought him 'one of the truest hearts that ever was attracted to public life',[1] while Gladstone rated that 'admirable man'[2] so highly that efforts were made to track him down in South America, where he was travelling when the Grand Old Man formed his third ministry in February 1886.

The grandson of Fox Maule Ramsay, 11th Earl of Dalhousie and Lord Palmerston's war secretary during the Crimean War, Sir John was born on 29 January 1847 and entered the navy aged only 13, becoming a lieutenant just six years later. He was appointed flag-lieutenant to his father's ship, *Narcissus*, but instead joined the crew of the *Galatea*, then commanded by the Duke of Edinburgh. Dalhousie remained in the navy until 1879, rising to the rank of commander and spending three years as equerry to the duke before running the *Britannia* training ship of naval cadets. He flirted with academia in 1875, matriculating at Balliol College, Oxford, but spent only a few months as an undergraduate before returning to the navy. Dalhousie's career in the House of Commons did not last much longer. He stood at a Liverpool by-election in 1880 on a Liberal Gladstonian ticket, but was defeated, perhaps under the pernicious influence of his Conservative father. He stood again for Liverpool in the general election of that year and was elected, but was thwarted once again by his father, this time by his death, which elevated him to the House of Lords. Like his predecessor at the Scottish Office, Dalhousie had some experience of Ireland, having visited the colony in 1883 as a member of a royal commission charged with examining the state of the country. But, unlike Sir George Trevelyan, he returned convinced of the need for home rule. 'He has been over there for some weeks,' Lord Derby noted in his diary, 'talking in his frank sailor fashion to people of all sorts &, being receptive of new ideas . . . [he] is more than half inclined to doubt whether landlords have any right to exist.'[3]

Dalhousie had helped steer the Secretary for Scotland Bill through the Lords and his abilities were unquestionable, although let down by a naïve streak which was a source of amusement to some elder statesmen and an easy target for his Forfarshire tenants. Quite simply, he believed everything anybody told him and 'when you are dealing with politicians and Scotch tenants,' Lord Derby said, 'that won't do'.[4] It seems Dalhousie quickly occurred to Gladstone as a likely replacement for Trevelyan. 'J. Morley who knows D[alhousie] most intimately says he has no doubt of his capability,'[5] wrote the prime minister to Lord Spencer. But curiously, Dalhousie had written to Gladstone a few days earlier, saying:

> Please do not have any regret on my account, and be assured that my small support will be given to your Govt all the more heartily because I shall be free to say what I please. I have suffered somewhat for Home Rule already & the Irish question generally, so it will give me great pleasure to speak and vote for your Govt on those questions as an independent private member . . . I am extremely happy & content in my present position and hope & wish to retain it until your Irish legislation is well advanced. I would not exchange my freedom for any office in your gift, even if a seat in the Cabinet were attached to it.[6]

Whatever the agreement between Gladstone and his young protégé, Dalhousie was the obvious choice to succeed Trevelyan and he became Scottish secretary aged just 39, although without a place in the Cabinet. The *Scotsman* branded his exclusion a 'gross mistake' but predicted that he would make an excellent minister for Scotland.[7] Although Dalhousie lasted just four months, until the Liberal party split over home rule, he did manage to introduce and pass the first Scottish Office-sponsored Bill, which became the Crofters' Holdings (Scotland) Act of 1886. His predecessor had got as far as a Second Reading; Dalhousie's Bill was largely the same, and was confined to the crofting counties of Argyll, Inverness, Ross, Sutherland, Caithness, Orkney and Shetland, introducing fixed tenures and fair rents regulated by a Scottish Land Commission. Moving the Bill's Second Reading on 20 May, Dalhousie stressed the urgency of passing it to maintain law and order in the region. 'Of course it might be objected that this was very grandmotherly legislation,' he told peers, 'but a wise grandmother might do good.'[8] The Bill was largely based on the recommendations of the Napier Commission which had reported in 1884, and it included the appointment of three land commissioners, along similar lines to those appointed under the Irish Land Act. The Bill had a relatively easy passage through both chambers and on 20 July the new crofting commissioners were sworn in at the Court of Session in Edinburgh, meeting with Dalhousie in his Parliament Square offices afterwards. But the Act did not spell the end of Highland unrest: on 30 June the Scottish secretary was informed of lawless acts by crofters on the Duke of Argyll's land in Tiree. He was reluctant to call in military assistance but authorised a small civil force to be dispatched to the island. They only managed to serve five writs, so by the end of July Dalhousie arranged with the home secretary for the Admiralty to send 150 marines to support police on the island. On his last day at the Scottish Office, Dalhousie wrote to A. J. Balfour to brief him on the situation:

> Now I am very anxious that the expedition should not be overdone. The island is apparently quiet and an air of ridicule would be cast over the whole thing by having a much larger force on the spot than is necessary . . . These were and are my ideas on the subject and it is only fair to let you know them. I am sorry that you should find yourself confronted with a case of this kind immediately on taking office – but you are a man of wisdom and judgement and I am glad for my own sake that you are my successor.[9]

Ironically, land reform had not been among the arguments for the creation of a Scottish secretary, but it set the foundations of a relationship between central government and the Highlands which was to last for more than a hundred years. In legislative terms, the Crofters' Holdings Act was Dalhousie's main legacy, but his other (or rather his wife's) contribution to the fledgling Scottish Office was a 'brilliant' reception at Dover House on 26 May. The vestibule and staircase were decorated with flowers and effigies of men in armour, loaned from the Tower of London, and the supper room was hung with old tapestries from the earl's castle in Brechin. The full band of the Scots Guards played popular tunes while Lady Dalhousie greeted guests at the top of the grand staircase, including Grand Duke Michael of Russia, Mr and Mrs Gladstone, most of the leading Liberals of the day and a smattering of exotically named foreign representatives. The first official reception of the secretary for Scotland – illuminated with electric light – was declared a triumph and became known as the finest of Gladstone's home rule ministry. The *Scotsman* congratulated Dalhousie for making Dover House 'likely to prove a new and influential centre of London fashionable society'.[10]

'The new Scottish Department has now been in existence for nearly twelve months,' observed the *Scotsman* near the end of July, 'and for the greater part of that time it has been in tolerable working order. It may therefore interest the people of Scotland to consider whether it has turned out the complete sham and imposture which some superior critics in the West predicted, or whether it does not already give promise of becoming a vigorous and useful institution.'[11] Far from having nothing to do, Dalhousie had had a busy four months, both socially and politically, but the experience – however brief – proved stressful and his health never quite recovered.

In 1887 Lord and Lady Dalhousie embarked upon a tour of the United States. The countess's ill health forced them to stop at Le Havre in France in November as they worked their way home. She died there, and, unable to bear the shock, Dalhousie was seized by an apoplectic fit and also died the following day. *The Times* reported the death, 'in melancholy and pathetic circumstances', of the earl, aged just 40: 'A career, not only of promise but also of useful performance, is thus prematurely closed.'[12] The bard of Dundee, William McGonagall, commemorated their deaths with some typically bad verse:

> ALAS! Lord and Lady Dalhousie are dead, and buried at last,
> Which causes many people to feel a little downcast;
> And both lie side by side in one grave,
> But I hope God in His goodness their souls will save.[13]

ARTHUR JAMES BALFOUR

5 AUGUST 1886 – 11 MARCH 1887

Bob's your uncle

Philosopher, writer and intellectual, by the time Arthur James Balfour reached the Scottish Office he was clearly climbing the greasy pole faster than most. But many contemporaries believed Balfour was a lightweight, merely amusing himself with politics. 'Nothing matters very much,' Balfour is held to have said, appearing to justify such perceptions, 'and few things matter at all.'

Born on 25 July 1848 at Whittinghame House, East Lothian, Balfour was educated at Eton and Trinity College, Cambridge, before becoming the Conservative MP for Hertford, his political career no doubt aided by his uncle Lord Salisbury, whose private secretary he became in 1878. He also demonstrated intellectual capacity with the publication of his *Defence of Philosophic Doubt* in 1879. Following the 1880 general election he took a more active part in parliamentary affairs and was associated with Lord Randolph Churchill's 'Fourth Party', freely criticising prominent members of the 'old gang'. In June 1885 Salisbury made him president of the Local Government Board, a position for which he displayed little enthusiasm. Despite this, Balfour was disappointed to learn that his uncle planned to transfer him to the Scottish Office a year later. He wrote to his cousin Lord Cranborne demanding the 'unvarnished truth' behind the invitation. 'I feel no natural vocation for being a Great Man's Great Man . . . therefore there are obvious motives for not leaving these solitudes,' he wrote on 23 July, 'but of course they would not for a moment stand in the way of my coming up if I thought I could be the slightest use to Uncle R.'[1] A day or so later he was offered, and accepted, the secretaryship for Scotland. 'It was evidently necessary', replied Cranborne, 'you should have an office with which you would readily be put in the Cabinet where Papa, I know, considers you will be most useful to himself and the country.'

The general election of July 1886 had left the Tories with only 12 seats in Scotland, forcing the party to turn to Balfour, a Scottish member sitting for an English seat, to fill the Scottish Office. The new secretary for Scotland had never actually shown much enthusiasm for the work of administration; he was a typical philosopher, preferring to muse over concepts and ideas rather than put them into practice. But his seven months at Dover House would defy his critics and demonstrate his political potential.

'We are all too much accustomed to look at Highland questions from a romantic point of view,' Balfour told MPs in the debate on the Queen's Speech in September 1886, 'through a mist of romance.'[2] He was no admirer of the Crofters' Holdings Act passed by his predecessor, although he had voted for it. Balfour believed the problems of the Highlands did not stem from high rents but were caused by overpopulation, so he wanted to stop the lawlessness as a short-term fix and encourage emigration as a long-term solution. 'I do not think they [the crofters] are suffering from either bad Land Laws or bad landlords,' he told the House, 'and though I grant they have to contend with a barren soil, with inclement skies and stormy seas, yet neither soil, nor skies, nor seas are, in my opinion, the worst foes they have to contend with.'[3]

A military and naval force had been stationed for weeks on the Duke of Argyll's island of Tiree, but, while the Earl of Dalhousie had fretted and fussed about the continued presence of troops, Balfour got down to business, determined to crush the troublemakers. But the unrest spread and in September 1886 Balfour received reports of lawlessness in Skye. On visiting Inverness he was appalled to discover that not only were crofters refusing to pay rents, but landlords were also refusing to pay their rates. Balfour began to suspect that the Crofters Act had simply made things worse, as tenants had come to believe that the Crofters Commission would cancel outstanding debts. He composed an urgent memo to the Cabinet on 14 September:

> In Skye, at this moment, it may be said, that, broadly speaking, neither Rates nor Rents are paid by Crofters, excepting when it happens to suit them. No officer can serve a Writ without protection; and for purposes of protection, the Police are absolutely useless . . . All the authorities whom I have consulted are of opinion that the people will never for an instant attempt to resist the forces of the Crown; partly through some fear of the results, and partly because they recognise in them what they decline to recognise in the Police, i.e. that they are emissaries of the Central Authority.[4]

With Cabinet approval the Admiralty received an alarming message from the Scottish Office the following day: 'I am directed by the Secretary for

Scotland to request that you will inform the Lords Commissioners of the Admiralty that it is proposed to send a military force to Skye, to support the civil authorities in the administration of law in the island.'[5] Initially, the Admiralty complained it had neither the men nor the ships to carry them to Skye. Balfour protested to Lord Cranborne that he had asked for only a quarter of the force requested by, and granted to, Dalhousie: 'But the meek do not inherit the earth . . . All, however, is now going smoothly – ships, Marines, policemen and Sheriffs are all to rendezvous on Monday at Portree.' Two days later the HMS *Humber* began transporting police and marines from Portree to areas around the coast. 'So much for Skye,' wrote Balfour. 'The plot, as Shakespeare says, is a good plot; though I dare say the whole thing will come to grief over some unfortunate trifle.'[6]

The unlikely named local factotum, Sheriff Ivory ('He is known at Dover House as Pooh-Bah!' joked Balfour), got off to a bad start in executing Balfour's instructions. While defaulting tenants were served with writs, non-paying landlords were left untouched, throwing off balance what had been planned as a more even-handed operation. 'I confess that I am more angry than I care to say,' wrote Balfour. 'Mere stupidity I could have forgiven.'[7] The second phase kicked in two weeks later, this time to arrest those who had resisted the initial warrants. This sparked more trouble, with women in one township linking arms around a house targeted by police and marines. Fighting broke out and muck was thrown at the sheriff, but when the third and final phase took place two weeks after that, to remove poinded stock and goods, the operation went according to plan. Balfour had triumphed. 'The Skye business has so far gone exceedingly well,' he wrote to his uncle. 'A considerable number of crofters have paid up: - and the organization of the expedition seems to have worked as well as my most sanguine anticipations led me to expect.'[8] Salisbury replied on 22 October: 'Everything seems to be going on charmingly in Skye. By steady deliberate pressure, such as you have used, without either spirting or giving way, you will get them under surely enough.'[9]

Balfour was seen to have acted swiftly and the press was soon urging his inclusion in the Cabinet. In 1887 troops were also deployed to Lewis and Sutherland following further land raids, but Balfour was unrepentant and gave a spirited defence of his land policy to MPs on 16 February 1887: 'What would this House have said . . . if I had chosen the second course, instead of the first, and had come down here, and had to answer, not for the trifling accusations which have been brought in such detail against us, but, perhaps for the destruction of lives which, if I had taken a different course, might have been spared?' During this period Balfour had begun to develop gifts of oratory which soon made him one of the most effective public speakers of his generation. Impressive in terms of content rather than delivery, he seldom rose to the eloquence of Gladstone, but his speeches were logical and convincing, and engaged a wider audience. 'So long . . . as I hold the Office for which I am now responsible,' he continued, 'I shall not shrink if a similar case should arise for adopting similar means to put an end to it.' Balfour added:

> I look back with much pain to what has passed, but with no regret whatsoever. I deeply deplore the necessity that was put upon me; but I should have thought myself cowardly, and utterly unworthy of holding any office under the Crown, if I had shrunk from the responsibility, which I did not seek, but which was thrust upon me . . . Sir, we may have to face the displeasure of the democracy, but very much worse consequences will ensue to this country than the fall of this Government.[10]

So, fresh from his battle with Highland insurgents, Balfour was now convinced of the need to reform the Scottish Office and raise the status of the secretary for Scotland. The land disputes had highlighted a disparity between the powers of the Scottish secretary and the territorial Home Office, and on 21 August 1886 Balfour outlined his case to the Cabinet: 'The Secretary for Scotland has no more to do with restoring law and order in Skye and in Tyree [sic] than he has in restoring order in Belfast and Kerry,' he wrote. 'To have two Chief Secretaries for Scotland, one sitting at the Home Office, the other at Dover House, is as insane as it would be to have two Chief Secretaries for Ireland, with different offices and different staffs.'[11] Balfour also wrote directly to the home secretary, Henry Matthews, on 7 September: 'I do not wish to be troublesome, but the question of "Who is to govern Scotland" is really pressing. Little or nothing is being done in the Western Highlands and Islands to restore the beginnings of law and order: the Lord Advocate declines to move; I cannot move; and I apprehend that the Officials at the Home Office are not troubling their heads about the matter one way or another.'[12] His impression of the Home Office stance proved to be correct; Matthews responded the same day: 'It should not be forgotten in considering this question, that the proposed delegation of powers in respect of law and order to the Secretary for Scotland is apparently meant to include not merely the case of a few crofters resisting the service of writs in Tiree, but also the extreme case of a general insurrection in Scotland.'[13] The home secretary also protested that he was unable to divest himself of responsibilities conferred upon him by Common Law, but Balfour was quick to spot the weakness in that argument. 'All that I desire is that the holder of this Office should be placed in the same relation to law and order in

Scotland as the Chief Secretary to the Lord Lieutenant is in Ireland,' he argued. 'If the latter can exercise his functions without denigrating from the positions of Secretary of State, I am entirely unable to see why the former must do the same.'[14] Balfour also faced resistance from the lord advocate, who feared subordination by a more powerful secretary for Scotland, and in another memo, dated 6 September, he responded directly to hostile noises from his troublesome law officer. If, Balfour argued, the home secretary believed he could not delegate his powers over law and order in Scotland, how therefore did he expect to carry them out?

> Is the Home Secretary then going to carry out his business by the assistance solely of the Lord Advocate, who does not live in his Office, or does he expect to be aided by the Scotch Secretary, and the Scotch Secretary's staff? In the latter case, it would seem that the Scotch Secretary would be expected, for purposes of law and order, to take the place formerly occupied by Lord Rosebery as Under-Secretary. This, I conceive, would hardly be a convenient course, and is not one which the Cabinet would desire the Scotch Secretary to adopt.[15]

Luckily for Balfour the Cabinet agreed, but only after he had sent his sympathetic uncle a thinly veiled threat of resignation. 'I think you will find more difficulty than you anticipate in overcoming the red-tapeism of y. cabinet,' he wrote on 10 September, 'and if you fail it becomes rather an interesting question what I ought to do.'[16]

Soon after the Skye expedition came to an end, Salisbury wrote to his nephew with some surprising news: 'I informed the Cabinet to-day that, in view of the fact that much of our impending legislation had a Scotch side, and Scotland being in no way represented in the Cabinet, I thought it expedient that you should become a member of it. The announcement was very cordially received.'[17] Balfour was clearly taken aback and replied the same evening: 'The Scotch, moved not by liking for me but by national susceptibility, will highly approve – and (which is of more importance) it will make the administrative machine work more smoothly.'[18] As ever, Balfour feigned lack of interest in his elevation. 'I forgot to say what will probably interest you (though not me) – that I am in the cabinet,' he wrote to Lady Frances Balfour. 'I like it, but am provoked with myself for not liking it more.'[19]

Beyond power struggles and organising military raids, Balfour was far from busy. He did not find himself troubled with any major legislation, although he came close to amending the Crofters Act in early 1887. The Queen's Speech of that year promised university reform and the completion of an act to upgrade the powers of the Scottish secretary. Both of these, however, were to wait until Balfour had left Dover House to reach fruition. When the Kirkcaldy MP Sir George Campbell questioned whether Balfour could justify both his position and his salary, the Scottish secretary reminded him that not only was he responsible for the general administration of the country, he was vice president of the Scotch Education Department. 'These two Offices together may well prevent the duties of the Secretary for Scotland being those of a sinecurist,'[20] he quipped.

Already suspicious of Irish home rule, Balfour's thinking on the devolutionist instincts of some Scottish MPs also hardened. He exploded when Sir George tabled an amendment – 'Great Britain-Local Home Rule' – to a debate on the Queen's Speech, claiming a devolved assembly could deal with the 'special affairs' of Scotland. 'But what are the special affairs of Scotland?' snapped Balfour. 'That is precisely what I want to know. Are they only strictly speaking local affairs or are they larger affairs of policy?'[21] His anti-home rule fervour remained with him for another 30 years, as his successors were to discover. But by now Balfour was a young man in a hurry and when Randolph Churchill resigned over the Budget in late 1886, he was both restless and bored with the resulting crisis. 'I dare not go to London for fear of being seized on by the innumerable tribe of political bores who wander to and fro at such times seeking what minister they can devour,' he wrote to Lady Elcho in early January 1887. 'However here I dwell in safety far from this madding crowd: spending my mornings in playing Tennis (real) my afternoons in playing hockey on the ice, and squeezing my official work into the interstices as best I can. To say the truth I have been abominably idle.'[22]

Rumours began to circulate at the end of 1886 that Balfour was not to remain much longer at the Scottish Office. Congratulating him on his sagacity in dealing with the Skye agitation, Sheriff Ivory wrote to the secretary for Scotland on 30 December: 'I hope you are not going to leave us for a higher sphere of usefulness either in Ireland or elsewhere. But wherever you go I shall take the greatest interest in watching the career of a Scotsman in whom we may all be proud.'[23] In March 1887 Sir Michael Hicks Beach, the chief secretary of Ireland, was advised by his doctor that he would go blind if he did not resign, and Balfour was chosen to replace him. Irish Nationalists gloated: 'We have killed Forster, blinded Beach, and smashed up Trevelyan. What shall we do with this weakling?' This was an underestimation to say the least, but the appointment still took many by surprise. The phrase 'Bob's your uncle' was coined in reaction to what critics saw as Salisbury's nepotism, but the gamble paid off. Balfour surprised cynics with his ruthless enforcement of the Crimes Act, earning

him the nickname 'Bloody Balfour'. This, coupled with steady administration, did much to alter Balfour's reputation as a political lightweight.

The Scottish Office had been a brief but crucial stage in Balfour's
career. Without it, the Irish secretaryship would have eluded him, and
without that he may never have reached Downing Street. He later
became one of the great political survivors, returning to government
again and again, even when the prevailing mood of both colleagues and
voters seemed to be against him. And while the great issues of tariff reform
and a Jewish homeland were far removed from Scottish affairs, neither
would have been possible without a Highland skirmish and its handling by
the first substantial political occupant of Dover House: the only Scottish
secretary ever to become prime minister.

9TH Marquis of Lothian

11 March 1887 – 11 August 1892

The ambassador

In less than two years the Scottish Office had seen four incumbents; the 9th Marquis of Lothian was its fifth and in him the fledgling department at last found stability. Appropriately, he became Scottish secretary in Queen Victoria's jubilee year, for Schomberg Henry Kerr was a quintessentially Victorian figure.

Lothian came late to politics, having initially settled upon a diplomatic career. Descended from John Ker, 1st Duke of Roxburghe and a post-Union secretary of state for Scotland until he resigned in 1725, he was born on 2 December 1833. He left Oxford without a degree and travelled in the Far East for two years before being appointed attaché at Lisbon, also serving in that capacity in Tehran, Baghdad and Athens. In 1862 Lothian was appointed second secretary at Frankfurt, moving to Madrid in 1865, and finally to Vienna. He would no doubt have risen higher, and indeed, with his finely groomed beard and handsome features, he looked every inch the British ambassador.[1] But by 1884 Lothian was steeped not in international affairs, but in those of his native land.

A timid man with equal supplies of charm and candour, Lothian had succeeded his elder brother William, becoming 9th Marquis in 1870, and campaigned from the House of Lords for a dedicated Scottish minister throughout the early 1880s. 'What think you of the enclosed?' wrote Arthur James Balfour to Lord Salisbury (with whom Lothian had attended Eton) in submitting Lothian's name as his successor. 'I think there might be worse appointments.'[2] 'The new Scotch Secretary is known to be a clever diplomatist,' mused the *Dundee Courier* on his appointment, 'but as a politician he has yet to show his capabilities.'[3] These turned out to be formidable.

'A battle has to be fought for the completion of the efficiency of the Scottish Office,' said the *Scotsman*, welcoming Lothian's appointment but lamenting his exclusion from the top level of government, 'and it will have to be fought, in the first instance, in the Cabinet.'[4] Lothian considered the original Secretary for Scotland Act to be 'ill-drafted, and passed at the fag end of the session of 1885', but had the satisfaction of moving the amending Act proposed by Balfour soon after becoming Scottish secretary:

> I should have liked, if it were possible, to have added to this Bill a clause which would have provided that the Secretary for Scotland should be one of Her Majesty's Secretaries of State. I think that would have given satisfaction to the people of Scotland, who earnestly desire it, and it would also necessitate the Minister for Scotland being a Member of the Cabinet.[5]

This raise in status, however, would have to wait until 1926, but so comprehensive was the amending Act's transfer of powers – including those over law and order – that another Act was passed in 1889 to reassure the War Department that Lothian was not, in fact, responsible for forts, barracks and other military buildings in Scotland. 'The general lay business of Scotland has,' observed Lothian, 'in spite of every obstacle, flowed, by a gradual process, into this Department.'[6] Despite control of the Crofters Commission, Peterhead Harbour and postal services in the Western Hebrides all resting with the Home Office, the Scottish Office had come to be held responsible for all three. The Scottish secretary also set out to secure more staff to support his newly expanded office, but the Treasury dug in its heels, and actually tried to reduce both the status and pay of existing Scottish Office staff. In desperation, Lothian demanded a committee of inquiry, which ultimately recommended he be given most of what he had requested.[7] None of these efforts impressed Scottish Liberal MPs, however, who instigated a vote in December 1888 on whether the Scottish secretary should be a member of the House of Commons. Unsurprisingly, given the dearth of Tory MPs in Scotland, 37 Scottish members voted against the government and only 15 with it. Nevertheless, the Marquis of Lothian now had the tools, status and stability with which to govern Scotland.

Lord Lothian, like the Mikado, had a little list. He produced Scottish Bills at an alarming rate and remarkably, given he was a minister in the Lords without a Cabinet seat,[8] many of them passed into statute. Tackling pressing issues such as university governance and Scottish local government, neither of which fell under the Scottish Office remit (although the Scottish secretary exercised wide patronage in university appointments), Lothian proved himself to be a great reforming Scottish secretary.

A Universities Bill had been promised or presented to parliament each year since 1885, but all had floundered. The press was unanimous in saying that the question of reform had to be settled and a Bill finally appeared in 1888 which the *Scotsman* praised as 'thoroughly Liberal in its spirit'.[9] This brought an end to the traditional professor–student, master–pupil relationship in the four ancient Scottish universities, and created a more modern staffing structure of readers and lecturers – still in use today – while broadening the curriculum to allow for ordinary degrees and more honours subjects. It also introduced student governing bodies, commonly known as student representative councils, and gave more powers to the University Court. Some courses were also opened to women for the first time, and Lothian championed the student voice in university government, allowing them to nominate candidates for lord rector.[10] He also sought to address the complex issue of university finance. His predecessor had noted that the 'amount they respectively get seems to depend more on the casual powers of resistance of the Treasury than on any settled principle'.[11] But in doing so, Lothian encountered some hostility from the chancellor, George Goschen, who feared that money was simply being thrown at the institutions. Lothian argued it was 'essential this should be done by a fixed sum upon which they can safely depend', but Goschen wanted an annual vote in parliament to set fees, chiefly to stem the growing tide of local colleges in England. Lothian retorted that it was hardly reasonable to impose the same system upon the 'ancient, National, Universities of Scotland', and fought his corner tenaciously, concluding that the chancellor's proposed conditions 'might be as unacceptable to the Universities as to be fatal to the Bill, and this after so many years of waiting would create an amount of feeling in Scotland which would be exceedingly unfortunate'. The Scottish secretary was already becoming adept at wielding hostile Scottish opinion as a political bargaining chip. 'I fear that to quote your words,' he added, 'it might not be a case of cutting our coat according to out cloth, but of having no cloth at all to cut a coat of any kind from.'[12] Following some reluctant Treasury compromises, Lothian basically got his way. He displayed wit and charm in steering the Bill through parliament, and, despite initial unhappiness from the academic community, by 1889 there was a broad consensus which allowed the Universities Bill finally to pass. Moving its Second Reading, the secretary for Scotland stressed the difference of Scottish universities from those in England, boasting of the higher proportion of Scots attending university and paying cheaper fees than their English peers. 'Every year the number of students is increasing,' he said, and 'every year the demand for higher education and for new facilities [is] becoming stronger. At present the classes of some of the Professors are filled to overflowing.'[13]

Lothian also tackled what was then known as elementary education, promoting technical schools, and phasing out restrictions which had granted funding solely on the basis of academic results. A freer system of inspection and grants was established and provision was made to educate deaf, mute and blind children for the first time. Schooling remained fee-based but was boosted financially, helping children who wanted to go on to attend university, schools of law and medicine, and to join the civil service. Many school boards were bankrupt, particularly in the Highlands and Islands, so Lothian devised a scheme whereby the Scotch Education Department (SED) forged partnerships with certain school boards, enabling the SED not only to inspect, but to distribute grants to and take part in each school's general management.

Lord Salisbury, the prime minister, had committed himself to general reform of local government throughout the United Kingdom, and Lothian was charged with overseeing this in 'North Britain'. The resulting Local Government (Scotland) Bill virtually invented modern local authorities, replacing the outdated Commissioners of Supply with new county councils charged with improving public health provision in Scotland.[14] Furthermore, each county and small burgh council was to be directly elected on a triennial basis, bringing democracy to local government for the first time. Lothian moved the Second Reading of the Bill on 1 August 1889, telling peers that its passing would no doubt increase his own workload. 'A new system cannot be introduced without some friction, and some difficulty,' he said ominously. 'There may at first be some over zeal, which may be over zealous, some energy which may not be tempered with sufficient discretion, but on the whole the work will be satisfactorily done.' Members of the new Scottish parliament taking their places in May 1999 would have done well to take note of this prediction. Occasionally prone to oratorical flourish, Lothian concluded:

> Naturally, I myself do not think that my countrymen, the people of Scotland, are as Conservative as I should like to see them – not nearly so Conservative; but from one point of view, I do think the people of Scotland are strongly and thoroughly Conservative. They are so proud of their ancient history and institutions which affect themselves and everything connected with their daily life, that they would be reluctant to make any change which would tend to cut them off from the system of County Government which has gone before, and from their historic and local associations.[15]

Some Liberals, however, wanted to go much further, and on 9 April 1889 the Commons held its first ever debate on 'Home Rule for Scotland'. 'We do not want an elaborate Executive,' the Caithness MP Dr Clark told the House. 'I think the Scotch Secretary, supported by the Scotch people,

would be sufficient, and the Lord Advocate might be left to devote more
time to his practice at the Bar.'[16] Essentially Dr Clark – who was also
president of the Scottish Home Rule Association – wanted a federal
system with only the existing powers of the Scottish Office devolved to
Scotland. Gladstone later contributed to the debate in his capacity as an
MP for a Scottish seat (Midlothian). He held that 'Scotland and Ireland
are precisely equal in the face of England' when it came to making
demands upon the imperial parliament, but believed the practicalities
were very different. 'I freely admit, in the face of my kind, indulgent, and
generous constituency,' concluded Gladstone, 'that I do not think that this
question is ripe for our decision; and, until it is ripe for our decision, I
should forfeit any title I may have to the favorable attention and kindness
of the House and the confidence of my constituency were I to support the
proposal which is now brought before the House.'[17] Following a scathing
speech from Lothian's predecessor, A. J. Balfour, against the motion, it
was defeated by 200 votes to 79.

Lord Lothian was what would now be described as a paternalistic Tory of
the old school: involved with politics not because of personal ambition but
in the spirit of public service. The profound poverty affecting some parts
of the Western Highlands and Islands therefore concerned him deeply.
Within weeks of coming to office, Lothian had a taste of what Balfour had
been dealing with when crofters seized two of the Duke of Sutherland's
farms to steal peat. He wrote to the War Office saying he was 'anxious to
know at once whether some soldiers might be requisitioned from the
nearest station by the Sheriff. The affair may become serious if we lose
time. The Marines are distant, and Gun Boats are seemingly not
immediately available.'[18] The War Office was keen to help but protested
that the nearest troops were in Glasgow and gunboats were 'few and far
between . . . and deadly slow'. Later that year, news of a violent deer raid
on Lewis quickly spread, and there were soon both gunboats and marines
in Assynt and Sutherland, although by the beginning of the following year
the troubles in Stornoway had settled down. All was quiet during
Lothian's tenure until March 1891, when reports reached him of the
'unsettled state and condition of the people', again in Lewis.[19] The
Scottish secretary applied once more to the Admiralty for use of marines
and a gunboat, but in his handling of Highland unrest there was an
important difference in tone. While Balfour had almost relished suppres-
sing uprisings, Lothian was genuinely sympathetic to Highland concerns.
    The Scottish secretary quickly took up the idea of state-sponsored
emigration. Dalhousie had put a scheme involving New Zealand to the
Cabinet in 1886, but it was rejected. Balfour, meanwhile, had initiated

discussions with the Dominion of Canada which Lothian picked up, but he found pursuing such an ambitious scheme from outside the Cabinet difficult, not least in terms of communication. He became embroiled in more wrangling with Goschen about government funding for the scheme, the Treasury withholding funds until interest was guaranteed by landlords. Lothian wrote to Salisbury on 6 December 1887 saying his 'prognostications' on the land question had, alas, come true – in that violence had again flared up.[20] 'I confess I am somewhat in a difficulty to know how matters stand now,' he wrote to Lord Knutsford on 12 March 1888, adding:

> from what was said in the H. of C. by Arthur Balfour (himself a member of the sub-committee of the Cabinet) I understand that the Government undertook that some scheme of "Colonisation" should be started at once, and I have been hoping to hear on what lines some scheme could be organized & supported . . . The time is getting so very short, that unless something is done at once, I fear very much that we may drift away again with serious difficulties.[21]

The scheme finally got the go-ahead later that year, with Lothian authorising the transportation of 12 families from Harris and 18 from Lewis. Posters were displayed on the islands offering emigration to the Manitoba and North-western Territories of Canada during the spring of 1889 to a 'few selected families'. The Canadian government agreed to supply 160 acres of good land and advance £120 to each household, and on 26 December 1888, Lothian, Canada's High Commissioner in London and the lord provost of Glasgow were formally charged with overseeing the plan. The results were mixed, and although Lothian feared a negative report from the Select Committee on Colonisation in March 1891, it actually broadly supported his original scheme. Generally, the colonists appeared to have done well and had even been able to pay back their government advances much quicker than planned. The select committee even recommended that, if possible, colonisation should be extended to other colonies.

With a working emigration scheme now in place, Lothian turned to improving the infrastructure of the islands for their remaining inhabitants. On 26 July 1888 he minuted the Cabinet on the general situation in the Highlands, recommending that telegraph lines be extended, while proposing some sort of cut in local taxation. This became the nucleus of Lothian's plan for the region and in June 1889 he embarked upon on a tour of the Western Islands and Highlands to see for himself the conditions of the islanders.

'A Scotchman must be a very sturdy moralist,' said Dr Johnson during his own tour of the Western Isles a century earlier, 'who does not love Scotland more than truth.' The Scottish Office's very own sturdy moralist sailed from Oban on the Admiralty yacht *Enchantress*, accompanied by his permanent under-secretary, the former MP Robert Cochran-Patrick. This was the first such trip by any government representative to the islands and Lothian was received warmly wherever he went, telling islanders that what he saw on the trip would form the basis of any subsequent government policy. From Oban he called at Roshven and Mallaig on the mainland, sailed over to and around Skye, North Uist, Barra and Lewis, before concluding his trip at Ullapool two weeks later. It was a triumphant PR stunt, Lothian having sacrificed his Whitsun holiday to do the tour. *The Times* reported that he had 'delighted the Highlanders with his bland manner as much as he impressed them by his earnestness and tact'.[22] Although he talked freely with men 'of all classes' on the trip, the secretary for Scotland refused to be drawn on the land question, protesting that the remit of the visit was quite narrow and refusing to meet a deputation from the local land league. Later that year the Western Highlands and Islands Commission was established and Lothian managed to secure a massive Treasury grant for direct economic intervention in the formation of new roads, the improvement of harbours, the erecting of lighthouses, the extension of telegraph and postal systems and in aid of the construction of railways. He wrote to Goschen on 10 August 1889 asking for £150,000 to implement his plans, which 'while liberal, would not be [an] extravagant' sum of money:

> For so long as chronic destitution exists, so long must there be discontent, and a fruitful field for agitation. The only hope for a quiet and permanent solution of the difficult problem before us is to place at the disposal of the peoples of these far-off districts some means by which they may, by obtaining a market for their produce, receive some return for their labour, and thus have the hope and prospect of improving their position by their own exertions. At present, they have no such hope – as a rule their attitude is rather an attitude of despair – and under such a frame of mind good and earnest work is almost impossible.[23]

In June 1890 Lothian set sail on the *Enchantress* once more, this time for an official visit to Shetland. Although the island had not originally been included within the remit of the Western Highlands and Islands Commission, Lothian now ordered its addition. The commission reported in 1890, recommending total expenditure of more than £280,000, almost double what Lothian initially requested from the Treasury. On 3 August 1891 he moved the Second Reading of the Western Highlands and Islands (Scotland) Works Bill, a procedural measure designed to release cash already agreed by the Commons. 'Commission after commission has been appointed,' Lothian told the House of Lords, 'inquiry after inquiry has been made into the condition of the Western Highlands and Islands, with the uniform result of showing that owing to domestic misfortunes, such as the failure of harvests, and the failure of the fishing and other industries, the condition of that part of Scotland is very unfortunate.'[24] While Balfour had pursued a twin-track strategy of military coercion and emigration, Lothian continued with the latter but also showered the remaining islanders with cash. He recognised the Highlands and Islands as a distinctive part of a distinctive nation within the UK, and came closest of all the Scottish secretaries to understanding that region's particular needs and aspirations.

Rumours spread in early 1890 that Lothian was close to resignation because of ill health. In the event his doctor told him to take a complete rest although, as the *Scotsman* noted, 'there is nothing in the state of his health to cause him to contemplate resigning his office'.[25] A large injection of cash for the Western Islands and Islands proved to be Lothian's last hurrah as an energetic Scottish secretary, for his last two years in office were unusually quiet, although punctuated with occasional ill fortune. In April 1890 his Newbattle paper-mills closed following a dispute with its tenants over rent levels, and, worse still, in June 1892 Lothian's eldest son and heir, Walter William Schomberg Kerr, Earl of Ancram, died following a shooting accident in Australia. Ancram and a party had gone out for a day's duck-shooting when another of the party's horse began to buck violently. His gun was jerked and went off, striking Ancram in the back of the head. The Hon. Rupert Leigh called out 'Look out Ancram', but when they reached him he was dead.[26] Lothian was devastated and immediately left London to join his wife in Scotland. Mrs Gladstone wrote on 1 July expressing her husband's sympathy; Lothian replied, referring to the 'blow which has fallen' but adding that 'it is an unspeakable mercy that the boy was loving and good and so we can look back upon his short life with happiness in every way and think of him now with complete rest and peace'.[27]

   The Scottish secretary was already pessimistic about the government's chances in the forthcoming general election, but the death of his son no doubt overshadowed any political anxieties. Out of office, he spent the next eight years indulging his lifelong interests in botany and historical manuscripts. He owned the UK's largest private collection of orchids at his Midlothian home, Newbattle Abbey, and in the mid 1890s commissioned life-size watercolours of the finest specimens, which were published in 18 meticulously illustrated volumes, *The genus Masdevallia*, in 1896.

Lothian was also a competent amateur architect and designed the stables at his Jedburgh home Monteviot, where he also laid out the gardens. He died at his Grosvenor Square home in 1900 and was buried in the family chapel at Newbattle Abbey. Ninety years later his great-great-nephew Michael Ancram, later 13th Marquis of Lothian, arrived at Dover House as minister of state at the Scottish Office.

6TH Lord Balfour of Burleigh

29 June 1895 – 6 October 1903

The benevolent Despot

Lord Balfour of Burleigh was everything Sir George Otto Trevelyan was not: staunchly Unionist, conscientious and committed to the Church of Scotland. 'Between us,' he used to say, referring to the lord advocate Andrew Graham Murray, 'we know every man in Scotland.' The Presbyterian establishment was delighted at his appointment, having come close to despair during three years of his disestablishment-inclined predecessor.

Lord Balfour (no relation to A. J. Balfour) had a commanding but reassuring presence and much charm of manner; he was also a consummate public servant and the obvious choice for Lord Salisbury as his Scottish secretary. 'There was a good deal of the benevolent Despot about his character,' wrote his biographer Lady Frances Balfour (a niece of Lord Salisbury);[1] he disliked maladministration in any form but, like Harold Macmillan in the early 1960s, recognised that the old order was passing and, as a practical man, applied himself to developing a new one. 'Your help would've been better in another Cabinet post, than in this office without the Cabinet,' wrote Sir Henry Craik from the Scotch Education Department (SED). 'Now we have both advantages!'[2] The consensus on Lord Balfour's appointment to the Unionist coalition in 1895 was that Scotland had got the right man in the right place at the right time.

Born at the family seat of Kennet in Alloa on 13 January 1849, Alexander Hugh Bruce was educated at Loretto and Eton, and after leaving Oxford – where contemporaries included Cecil Rhodes and many prominent churchmen – he launched himself with peculiar zeal into public life.

Like the Marquis of Lothian, Lord Balfour was essentially an apolitical figure who worked well with Liberals, making him an ideal foot soldier on many a government commission. Disraeli kicked off a lifetime of appointments by making him a member of the Factory and Workshops Committee in 1874. 'He is a tactful fellow and the names of the Commissions over which he has presided are legion',[3] wrote *Vanity Fair*, and Lord Balfour's was indeed a formidable CV. He was chairman of the Royal Commission on Sunday Closing in Wales (1881–90), the Educational Endowments Commission (1882–89), the Metropolitan Water Supply Commission (1893–94), the Rating Commission (1896), the Royal Commission on Local Taxation (1899–1902), the Cable Communications Inter-departmental Committee (1902),[4] the Royal Commission on Food Supply in Time of War (1903), the Lords Select Committee on Overseas Life Insurance (1906), the Royal Commission on Closer Trade Relations Between Canada and the West Indies (1909), and the Committee on Commercial and Industrial Policy after the Great War (1916–17).

Politically, Lord Balfour was not as prolific, holding only two government positions: parliamentary secretary to the Board of Trade from 1889 to 1892 and secretary for Scotland for eight years from 1895. Even at the Scottish Office he was prevailed upon to act as an arbitrator – in November 1900 over a dispute about the running of the Flying Scotsman service between the Great Northern, North Eastern and the North British Railway Companies. His shrewdness, business ability, and sound knowledge of local government (he had presided over Clackmannanshire County Council since its inception in 1889) were valued, and his commission reports were authoritative documents, noted for their thorough accumulation of evidence rather than for any startling line of recommendation. Lord Balfour was the undisputed quango king of his day.

Although Lord Balfour was the fourth Scottish secretary with a seat in the Lords (the first Scottish representative peer of the nineteenth century to enter the Cabinet),[5] he was at the Scottish Office during an upturn in Unionist fortunes. The Liberals had dropped from 45 to 39 MPs at the 1895 general election, and from 39 to 34 five years later. By contrast, the Conservatives had gone from just ten Scottish seats in 1885 to 33 ten years later, with a little help from the breakaway Liberal Unionists.

Lord Balfour of Burleigh had two abiding interests as Scottish secretary: the Church of Scotland and Scottish education. He had been continuously elected a member of the General Assembly of the Church of Scotland since 1874, often mediated between Queen Victoria and the minister at Crathie on the Balmoral estate, and energetically defended the Kirk against sustained campaigns for disestablishment. Lord Balfour organised a fund for aged and infirm ministers, but drew a sharp distinction between the defence of the establishment and the accommodation of the Free Church. Lord Balfour was uncompromising on the former, becoming in 1882 convener of the Church Interests Committee of the General Assembly, which at the 1885 general election organised a highly effective petition against disestablishment. He combined this spirited campaign with movement towards union with the Free Church, something he supported both for itself and as a means of removing the chief cause of pressure for disestablishment. From the 1890s he was prominent in the talks which led eventually to the union of the Church of Scotland and the United Free Church, dying just days after a Bill passed through the Commons to that end. 'The last days of Lord Balfour of Burleigh were made happy by the certainty that his work was to be crowned with success',[6] said the *Scotsman*. In 1911 he published *An Historical Account of the Rise and Development of Presbyterianism in Scotland*. To Lord Balfour, Kirk and Crown were inextricably linked.

Ironically, although he had been an early supporter of the creation of a secretary for Scotland, Lord Balfour had opposed the transfer of the SED to the new department. Lord Lothian had flexed the Scottish Office's educational muscles during his five years at Dover House, and Lord Balfour also revelled in matters educational. In Sir Henry Craik, the gifted SED chief, the Scottish secretary found a kindred spirit. A son of the manse, Sir Henry was chosen as the SED's secretary on its transfer to the Scottish Office in 1885, remaining in that role for nearly 20 years. Occasionally irascible, his habit of always planning ahead earned him much respect, not only from his political masters but among his peers. He gained much credit for ending the discredited system of 'payment by results', under which schools were funded according to their academic records, and for the abolition of fees in elementary schools from 1890 onwards. The combined efforts of Sir Henry and Lord Balfour were impressive: in 1898 an improved payment scheme was introduced for elementary school teachers; the following year 'advanced departments' were created to give an additional two years of post-elementary schooling, while in 1901 the leaving age was fully established at 14 for the first time. The term 'primary', still in use more than a hundred years later, replaced that of elementary, clarifying each child's entitlement to a two-stage education. Post-compulsory education funding was brought under the SED in 1897 and defined in 1901 under various categories which allowed institutions like the Royal College of Science and Technology in Glasgow and Heriot Watt College in Edinburgh (both of which eventually became universities) to establish themselves. Lord Balfour's 1901 Education (Scotland) Bill made it the duty of 'every parent to provide efficient elementary education in reading, writing, and arithmetic for his children who are between five and fourteen years of age'. It also altered the number of exemptions allowed under the compulsory age of attendance, so, while the normal leaving age would remain 14, the Bill gave school boards the power to dispense with it in individual cases. 'There are, unfortunately, circumstances of poverty in which it is not fair to expect the boy or girl to remain at school until the age of fourteen,'[7] Lord Balfour told the Lords. The Scottish secretary was an educationalist, but also an unsentimental realist. He had more comprehensive plans which, due to lack of parliamentary time and his subsequent resignation, never came to fruition. In a Cabinet memo of 1899 Lord Balfour described a plan to consolidate education in Scotland, providing a system for administering the funding of higher and technical education and also establishing a consultative committee similar to a body being proposed for England, the Board of Education.[8] *The Times* reported that by April 1900 the Merchant Company of Edinburgh considered the Bill as 'of far more profound and far-reaching importance than any which has been introduced since the General Education Act of 1872'.[9] It singled out 11 burgh schools in Scotland's main towns and cities to be managed by the newly constituted school boards. In 1903 the Bill's passing finally looked to be inevitable but in September Lord Balfour quit the Cabinet over tariff reform, earning rare tributes (for a Scottish secretary) from Scotland's educational establishment. Sir Henry left the SED soon after, ending his days as a popular and productive MP for the Combined Scottish Universities.[10] He and Lord Balfour believed imperial service was the highest principle that any Scot could hope to attain, and the Scottish secretary's rectorial address to students at Edinburgh University gives some idea of his evangelical belief in King and Country. 'Will you not be enabled to rise to the vast burdens of Empire, to feel its grandeur, to rise to new enthusiasm for its great possibilities, and to new devotion to its service?' Lord Balfour asked rhetorically. 'Does not such a training make a backbone of national character, altogether independent of mood and temperament, or even of hereditary bias?' Yet Lord Balfour was fully conscious of Scotland's place within the Union and Empire, and acutely aware of the changes afoot as Britain prepared for a new century. He added:

We often hear the complaint that this is an age of little reverence or restraint, that our ideas are vague and unsettled, that we are recklessly enamoured of change, and that we are careless whither we are moving. I venture to suggest that much that we may deem irreverence is only the exuberance of newly asserted liberty; that it is the froth upon the surface, which leaves undisturbed the calm depths below. We know not what this new century so soon to open upon us has in store for our country, but may it not be that the spirit of restlessness and disquietude, of vague and impatient questioning, of rash and unthinking opposition to authority, may settle down into steadfastness of purpose. I would fain hope that this may be so; but whether it is to be so

or not must be mainly decided by the steadfast concentration of national
character. And if that national character is to preserve its identity and its
strength, it must rest upon trained and disciplined intellectual force.[11]

Lord Balfour's interest in Scotland's education also extended to its four
ancient seats of learning. In 1901 his friend, the philanthropist Andrew
Carnegie, founded the Carnegie Trust for the Universities of Scotland.
Carnegie attended a meeting of its trustees in Lord Balfour's Edinburgh
office in May 1902, together with Arthur James Balfour, John Morley and
James Bryce, all of whom were sympathetic to Carnegie's desire to scrap
university tuition fees in Scotland. 'It is of course obvious that if Mr
Carnegie has made up his mind to donate a million to paying Scottish
University fees,' wrote the Scottish secretary to Balfour, 'it is either useless
or superfluous for us to enquire how that will be accepted.'[12] Sir Henry
Craik analysed the proposals later that year and produced a memo packed
full of uncomfortable home truths. The 'lower middle class', he concluded, actually liked fees and would probably remove their children from
institutions which no longer charged them. 'The Secondary Schools are
not free; but, with Free Elementary and Free University Education, the
position of these Schools would become untenable,' he argued, also
dismissing Carnegie's offer of one or two million pounds as a counter-
productive drop in the ocean. 'A poor student must not only get his
Education free; it is of vastly greater importance that he should be helped
to live. If you merely pay fees and do not give *living* money you won't
increase the students by a single head, except for a few triflers who can live
in idleness, and who may think that if it costs nothing they may as well join
the University as not.' Sir Henry instead proposed beefing up fellowships
and existing bursaries, which would bypass legislative opposition, university negotiations and go straight to the neediest students.[13] The Scottish
secretary was clearly attracted to the idea but uncertain of its consequences. 'I cannot say that my mind is made up or that at present I am
doing more than searching for light on a difficult and important subject,'
he wrote to the Liberal leader, Sir Henry Campbell-Bannerman. 'As you
would see . . . I am apprehensive of the ultimate effect upon the great
Institutions concerned of the very generous proposal which was put before
us.'[14] University fees were not abolished, but 16 years later Lord Balfour
became chairman of the Carnegie Trust for the Universities of Scotland.
'For pair auld Scotland's sake,' lamented Carnegie to Lord Balfour on his
resignation, 'I am sorry you are no longer her Secretary.'[15]

Some of Lord Balfour's other reforms proved as enduring. His Public
Health (Scotland) Act gave county councils control over their own

medical inspectors and still form the basis of much local authority activity even today.[16] He also created a Scottish Congested Districts Board in 1897 – similar to that in Ireland – with powers to assist land settlement and other development activity. 'The Congested Districts Board is now only congested with officials and camp followers', quipped his biographer.[17]

Lord Balfour appears to have had no interest in constitutional reform, beyond some practical, if dull, procedural improvements. Trevelyan's Scottish Grand Committee was ditched in 1895, but in 1899 the Private Legislation Procedure (Scotland) Act allowed for the first time the meeting of commissions in Scotland to consider and initiate private legislation, freeing it from the London circuit. But while Lord Balfour was suspicious of Scottish home rule, his contemporaries' use of the catch-all term 'English' in place of 'Scottish' or 'British' irritated him. He often complained to Lord Salisbury about it, a frequent offender, and insisted that 'Scotland might be mentioned as an integral portion of the Empire'. Lord Balfour even prevented the removal of the Scottish crown to London for an exhibition, as he feared for the fragility of Scottish sensibilities. But Salisbury's terminology was considered and quite deliberate; he could not understand what all the fuss was about.[18]

Lord Balfour was at the Scottish Office for eight years – the longest serving of any incumbent – but by 1898 he was getting restless and felt his full potential was being ignored, first by Salisbury, and then by Arthur James Balfour, who took over from his uncle as prime minister in July 1902. He was mentioned as a replacement for Lord Elgin as governor-general of India in mid 1898, while by 1902 he was also rumoured as a possible successor to Lord Curzon as viceroy. Lord Balfour was certainly of gubernatorial calibre. In 1876 he married Lady Katherine Eliza, youngest daughter of the 5th Earl of Aberdeen, whose brother (the 1st Marquis of Aberdeen) was governor-general of Canada when his brother-in-law was longing to escape the Scottish Office. Lord Balfour was also offered the Irish Office in 1896 but declined,[19] and in 1900 Salisbury planned to demote Gerald Balfour, Arthur's younger brother and troubled chief secretary for Ireland, to the Scottish Office and move Lord Balfour, who 'does not make mistakes', to the Admiralty. Salisbury was fond of appointing Scots to government as he felt they always had a certain amount of prudence and common sense. 'In making appointments I can count on a Scotchman not falling below a certain level,' he said, 'they may not be very clever, but they are safe not to be stupid.'[20] But the Queen thought Lord Balfour 'too ponderous' for the Admiralty and so he remained, once again, at Dover House. The Scottish secretary's insecurity spilled over in a letter to Balfour on 12 November 1900, which expressed disappointment that recent Cabinet changes had brought him nothing new. Balfour replied on 18 November, 'I feel that the PM has as high an opinion of yr. merits as surely as have all your colleagues.' He suggested that the secretary for Scotland contact Salisbury direct with his concerns.[21] Lord Balfour would not be the first Scottish secretary to find it difficult to move on from the Scottish Office, but to the Earl of Crawford, who recorded a meeting with him in 1898, Lord Balfour was a model of his class.

> Lord Balfour of Burleigh illustrating the good government of Scotland and the satisfaction of the people with their parliamentary ministers, told me that on the opening day of the session his work at the Scots Office was concluded in twenty minutes. He received no letter and only two visits from M.P.s: one Radical and one Conservative, who in each case called in order to thank the Secretary for what he had done during the recess.[22]

In May 1903 Joseph Chamberlain launched his crusade for tariff reform in a speech at Birmingham, demanding that the government drop free trade in favour of a system of imperial preference, and therefore questioning an economic system unchallenged for 50 years. Its appeal was obvious: Britain was facing stiff competition from abroad and her traditional industries needed protection. By adopting a preferential tariff on imports from the colonies, the bonds of Empire would be strengthened. Chamberlain, who had led one Scottish secretary from a Liberal government in 1886, would force the resignation of another from a Unionist government 17 years later. Lord Balfour was a moderate free-trader and found himself caught between extreme tariff reformers, and the more uncompromising free-traders who found common ground with the Liberal opposition. The prime minister worked hard to unite the party with his compromise policy of selectively retaliating against unfair competition. This, he argued, would promote worldwide free trade to Britain's advantage while avoiding deliberate protection of domestic industries.

A contemporary cartoon depicted the 'slim' Balfour (A. J. Balfour) alongside the 'Burleigh' Balfour, but this implied a warmth which simply did not exist between the former and current Scottish secretaries. Balfour's Cabinet had never been harmonious, its political differences accentuated by cliques which the prime minister's political style simply encouraged. Despite Balfour's best efforts to prevent the dispute developing into open conflict, the summer of 1903 was grim. Lord Balfour's letters to the prime minister during this period become increasingly desperate. 'I suggest that we as a Cabinet must know where we are expected to stand before there is a campaign of oratory,' he wrote from the Scottish Office on 24 June 1903. 'Life is hard enough when we have to speak on platforms in reply to our opponents if we are also to argue with our friends & even amongst ourselves.'[23] Cabinet meetings became dominated by the fiscal question, and Sir Almeric Fitzroy remembered that Lord Balfour was 'very sore at the way the Prime Minister has allowed Chamberlain his head and complained bitterly of the insouciance with which he treated everything. For his own part, he did not care how soon he went.'[24] The prime minister eventually offered the Cabinet two options: Chamberlain's proposals for preferential tariffs (and food taxes), or his own policy of retaliation. Both were discussed by Cabinet on 13 August, the Chamberlains (Joseph and his son Austen) arguing for imperial preference and four ministers – the Duke of Devonshire, C. T. Ritchie, Lord Balfour and Lord George Hamilton – strongly defending free trade while disapproving of both memoranda. The majority favoured the prime minister's position although a final decision was deferred until another Cabinet meeting a month later.

During the intervening period, Balfour learned that Ritchie and Lord Balfour were pushing Devonshire to assume the leadership of the Unionists and retain free trade by forming a coalition with the Liberal Imperialists. In a memo to the Cabinet dated 19 August 1903, the Scottish secretary stated, 'I have come with whatever reluctance, with whatever sense of personal loss I may feel – and it is not small – to the conclusion that I cannot honestly make myself responsible for the policy now put forward.'[25] But even before the Cabinet of 'final decision' met on 14 September, the prime minister had resolved to rid himself of the free trade rebels. After a heated three-hour discussion on the two outstanding options, the majority voted for retaliation over imperial preference. But prior to that decision, Lord Balfour and Ritchie – who had circulated memoranda objecting to both proposals – were abruptly dismissed by Balfour. Sir Almeric Fitzroy later recalled that 'Ritchie and Balfour of Burleigh were practically drummed out' of Cabinet, while Devonshire wrote to the prime minister the following day, 'I never heard anything more summary and decisive than the dismissal of the two Ministers, and I should be very much surprised if every other member of the Cabinet did not share my impressions that it was their Minutes [memoranda] which made their resignations inevitable.'[26] Lord George Hamilton (secretary of state for India) and Devonshire, Conservative leader in the Lords, then resigned, although the latter was later persuaded to remain in Cabinet. To make matters worse, Lord Balfour had been summoned to Balmoral and it was from there, after a long audience with the King (who was furious at not being consulted by the prime minister) on 17 September, that he wrote a letter tendering his resignation to Balfour, but which he refrained from posting as he waited for word from the Duke of Devonshire. Lady Balfour, a glamorous redhead, wrote to her husband the following day: 'the news seemed like a dream. Even now I cannot believe in this sudden change of matters. My dear . . . was a man *ever* in such a difficult position as you? I know how beastly the crisis is for you.'[27] Devonshire soon became uncomfortable at the prospect of deserting his free-trade colleagues and ended up leading the free-trade opposition within the Unionists as originally planned by Lord Balfour et al. It was a political battle with no clear winners. Five ministers resigned within just a few days, fatally weakening the reputation of an already semi-discredited government.

'I will venture to say all Scotchmen appreciate the energy, the fairness, and the patriotic spirit with which you have discharged the functions of Secretary for Scotland,'[28] wrote James Bryce a few days after Lord Balfour's resignation was confirmed. Lord Balfour had become almost part of the furniture at Dover House and Scottish Office staff, who idolised him, were anxious about his successor, the lord advocate Andrew Graham Murray. 'I returned to the Office today,' wrote the civil servant James M. Dodds, 'a very unlucky day in its Kalendar [*sic*].'[29] In November, Lord Balfour made a valedictory speech in Glasgow defending free trade, which appears to have been well received. But despite the hopes of his friends, Lord Balfour never again held office, instead devoting himself to his first love – committees of inquiry and exhaustive reports. Politically, he was vindicated in 1906 when the Liberals – free-traders almost to a man – won a landslide victory. Lord Balfour had lost the political battle, but belatedly won the ideological war. He died on 6 July 1921 at his London residence, 47 Cadogan Square, aged 72.

Andrew Graham Murray

6 October 1903 – 2 February 1905

The miraculous Moses

Andrew Graham Murray reluctantly joined a Cabinet hastily recon-
structed along policy lines in October 1903. This also marked the
beginning of almost two years of stagnation at the Scottish Office, still
reeling from the loss of a popular and energetic Scottish secretary to
bitter political infighting. Having served as lord advocate since 1896,
and therefore as de facto secretary for Scotland in the House of
Commons, Murray provided much-needed continuity during this
traumatic period. He was also strictly on-message, telling his constituents at a meeting in Rothesay that free trade was all very well
in theory but, 'in practice it meant ruined villages, impoverished
families, people without work, and a future that looked dark indeed'.[1]
Murray joked with his audience that the handicap of being a lawyer in
parliament had not prevented him reaching Cabinet. He believed he
was following in the footsteps of Henry Dundas, later 1st Viscount
Melville, who had governed Scotland as lord advocate in the nineteenth
century.

Called to the Scottish Bar aged only 25, Murray's legal rise was as swift as
it was impressive, his instinctive legal ability and talent for cross-exam-
ination marking him out from the start. Born on 21 November 1849 in
Edinburgh, he was the only child of Thomas Graham Murray, writer to
the signet and crown agent for Scotland, and his wife Caroline Jane,
daughter of John Tod, also a writer to the signet. Tod was a founding
member of the leading Edinburgh solicitors' firm of Tod, Murray, and
Jamieson, in which Murray's father was a partner, and where he would
also work as a young legal graduate.

Privately educated in Tunbridge Wells and at Harrow, Murray secured
a scholarship to Trinity College, Cambridge, from which he graduated
with a second-class degree in classics in 1872. Much of his time as a student
was devoted to sporting activity, and together with a college friend he

created a pioneering eight-hole golf course on Midsummer Common. At Edinburgh University Murray studied law and was friendly with Robert Louis Stevenson, who was said to have consulted him when writing *Weir of Hermiston*. Tradition had it that Murray spent his year at the family firm studying Italian rather than law, and doubts were expressed about his ability to concentrate as he ostentatiously 'enjoyed himself in every lawful manner'.[2] 'He is so fond of sport that he studies each of its branches as though it were an exact science,' said *Vanity Fair*, 'for he is a Scotchman. He is a good shot, a keen golfer, and a precise billiard player.'[3] Murray also enjoyed dancing, even in old age staying out late and managing to begin work early the next morning. In his physical prime Murray was tall and athletic, with a muscular and energetic frame. He also devoted some of his plentiful energy to serious study of Scots Law, and although he was no orator he excelled in arguing a case with imperfect preparation, gifted as he was with both brevity and confidence.

In 1888 Murray was appointed an advocate-depute in the Crown Office, becoming solicitor-general for Scotland in 1891. Later that year he was elected to parliament as the Conservative member for Bute, the same seat Murray's uncle David Mure had represented some 30 years before. He represented the area for nearly 14 years but was not a natural constituency politician, displaying an absent-mindedness which often generated a bad impression. Out of office from 1892, Murray again became solicitor-general when the Conservatives returned to power in 1895, becoming lord advocate the following year. As such, he earned a reputation as an excellent and conciliatory administrator. He gained notoriety for driving a tandem bicycle up to Parliament House in Edinburgh and was said to have been one of the first MPs to cycle into Palace Yard in London. Murray was also a pioneer motorist, a talented architect (designing his Edinburgh home at 7 Rothesay Terrace), a keen amateur film-maker and enthusiastic traveller. This Scottish secretary had character.

Arthur James Balfour immediately decided upon Murray when Lord Balfour left the government in September 1903, but the lord advocate initially refused, pleading that he could not afford the resulting £3,000 drop in salary. He regarded his legal career as an insurance policy against the unpredictability of politics and feared the Scottish Office would wreck his chances of judicial advancement. Instead he suggested Balfour appoint a peer such as the Marquis of Linlithgow – who would succeed Murray little more than a year later – or even the Duke of Sutherland.[4] 'Of course the offer is a very tempting one,' he wrote to Balfour from Balmoral on 5 October, 'but I am too old – apart from gratification – to effect in the future senior cabinet office – whereas as I am I could fairly hope if there was an appropriate vacancy for high judicial office.'[5] But Murray quickly changed his mind on being assured by Balfour that he would retain any claims to a judicial appointment that would have been his as lord advocate. On 5 November he wrote to Sir Henry Craik at the Scotch Education Department (SED) saying he considered the appointment to be only temporary. 'I hear I am on safe ground and pray that we shall work together without difficulty', he wrote, adding that he would 'press for and I hope attain a high place for [an education] bill'. He felt confident that 'we shall survive the session', and assured Sir Henry that he would 'generally adhere to B of B's policy'.[6]

Murray dealt with only one Bill as secretary for Scotland, and that was the education legislation left over from Lord Balfour's tenure. He told the House that the Scottish people were 'anxious to march with the spirit of the time' and scrap school-board control of elementary education (as had happened in England two years before), placing it in the hands of new, directly elected education authorities. But Murray rejected calls to transfer the SED from London to Scotland – although an Edinburgh branch was opened that same year with a staff of seven – saying, 'I believe that so long as you have an Imperial Parliament in which you have the Minister for Scotland here, it is absolutely necessary that he should be in continual touch with his Education Department, and I am perfectly certain he could not be if that Department were in Scotland.' Ease of communication was a common argument, not just among Unionists, against administrative relocation. The secretary for Scotland concluded on another common refrain: 'It will be quite possible, with the resources which the Imperial Parliament with no stinting hand has placed at our disposal, to have what I hope will be the best educational system to be found in the United Kingdom.' The Liberal leader Sir Henry Campbell-Bannerman congratulated Murray on steering himself and the Bill 'between Scylla and Charybdis', but warned of 'little rocks and whirlpools with which he may find himself in difficulties'.[7] The *Scotsman* preferred a biblical anology: 'The Secretary for Scotland is the miraculous Moses whose rod has struck the dry rock and made the sweet waters gush over the waste howling wilderness.'[8] But even Moses could not rescue the Bill during its committee stage in June, where various amendments soon found Murray in difficulty. The opposition was bent on obstructing all of the ailing Unionist government's legislation, and two months later the Education (Scotland) Bill was ditched completely.

Outside parliament, Murray was involved in the negotiations which preceded the introduction of the Churches (Scotland) Bill (under his successor), bringing him into close official contact with King Edward VII, to whom he became a mentor on Scottish affairs for the remainder of his reign.

In early 1905 Lord Kinross, the lord president of the Court of Session, died and Murray was appointed in his place. The prime minister had kept his word. 'Mr Graham Murray always kept his eye on the opposite party,' reflected the *Scotsman*. 'To keen party loyalty he added acute perception of human nature, and his knowledge of character became part of his equipment as a successful Minister . . . A virile, tactful, successful, and popular statesman is at a stroke metamorphosed into a Judge, and active politics will know him no more.'[9] He was also raised to the peerage as Baron Dunedin, and his period at the Court of Session proved to be the summit of Murray's legal career. Comparisons between the English and Scottish legal systems became a theme in Dunedin's published writings. 'In England you have to find the remedy in order to discover the right,' he wrote in *The Times* on 20 April 1927, 'whereas in Scotland you have to find the right in order to discover the remedy.'[10] Murray was concerned above all with the rational administration of Scots Law; the Scottish Office had been no more than an enjoyable interlude. He retired as a judge in 1932 and died in an Edinburgh nursing home on 21 August 1942, aged 92.

1ˢᵀ Marquis of Linlithgow

2 February – 10 December 1905

The reluctant Scottish secretary

Never was there a more reluctant Scottish secretary than John Adrian Louis Hope, the 7ᵗʰ Earl of Hopetoun and later the 1ˢᵗ Marquis of Linlithgow. In 1905 he was in increasingly poor health and had retired from politics on returning from Australia as governor-general two years previously. But Arthur James Balfour's government was in terminal decline and he probably considered Linlithgow to be nothing more than a safe pair of hands to keep a dormant Scottish Office ticking along until the end of the year. Sir Almeric Fitzroy, the clerk to the Privy Council, recalled a rather shambolic handover of official seals in his memoirs years later. The outgoing Scottish secretary, Andrew Graham Murray, was running late, unprepared for an impatient king's punctuality. 'After an awkward pause he was seen with Hopetoun in close pursuit, scurrying down the corridor, and arrived breathless at the feet of His Majesty,' wrote Sir Almeric. 'Hopetoun looked ill and listless, and on my saying that presumably he did not expect a long term of office replied, "No; that is the one consideration that led me to accept the appointment." He retains all that gentle and engaging manner that made him so popular as Lord Chamberlain.'[1] It was an inauspicious start to a melancholy ten months at Dover House.

Born on 25 September 1860 at Hopetoun House in South Queensferry, the young earl was attracted to politics in his early twenties, becoming a junior Conservative whip in the House of Lords aged just 23. For a time he was seen as a possible rival to his friend and neighbour the 5ᵗʰ Earl of Rosebery, whose Dalmeny home was just along from the Hopetoun estate on the Forth estuary. But his was no match for the famous Rosebery oratory, speaking with 'a suggestion of hesitancy'[2] and relying instead on an emotional style sprinkled with some simple metaphors. 'He is an exceedingly cheerful, very amiable fellow,' profiled *Vanity Fair*, 'in whom there is no trace either of condescension or of self-consciousness.'[3]

In 1889 Hopetoun went to Melbourne as governor of Victoria, later speaking of his six years there as the happiest of his life. After Salisbury's victory in the 1895 general election he was made postmaster general, and then a reforming lord chamberlain. Hopetoun's popularity in Victoria made him a sensible choice to become the first governor-general of the new Australian Federation and he arrived in Sydney in December 1900. His first task was to appoint a prime minister, and since no federal elections had yet been held he followed protocol in appointing the premier of the senior colony, New South Wales. But Sir William Lyne had opposed federation and several prominent politicians refused to serve under him. He later withdrew, and Hopetoun sent instead for Edmund Barton, who had led the federalist movement. The fledgling governor-general was widely criticized for what became known as the 'Hopetoun blunder'. He entertained lavishly, spending heavily from his private income, and when the Australian parliament refused to vote him an annual allowance of £8,000 in addition to his salary of £10,000 Hopetoun asked the colonial secretary, Joseph Chamberlain, to recall him, and he relinquished his post on 17 July 1902. His career in Australia had come to a humiliating end and he was reduced to tears at farewell ceremonies in Melbourne, acutely aware that he had failed in an historic role.[4] As compensation, Hopetoun was created the 1st Marquis of Linlithgow on returning to the UK, and he soon withdrew from public life.

At the unveiling of Linlithgow's portrait in 1904, Lord Rosebery implored him not to indulge in any more Antipodean trips. 'We want to keep him among us,' he said, 'and though we shall all rejoice to see him hold high and eminent office once more under the Crown, we would rather see him holding it within the borders of the United Kingdom than at any external part of the Empire.'[5] His friends did not have to wait long as on 30 January 1905 Balfour wrote to Linlithgow from Downing Street: 'G. Murray (as you know) is leaving us. Will you consent & replace him? – of course with a seat in the Cabinet. All Scotland would welcome such an appointment, & it will give the utmost satisfaction to your old friends.'[6] It was an unusual request to say the least, especially considering the number of available Scottish Unionist MPs. Linlithgow's health had been failing since he caught typhoid fever en route to Australia, and even before that trip he had been generally frail (the effort of shaking hands at his first official engagement as governor of Victoria had caused him to faint). Lord Rosebery was clearly apprehensive, writing to his friend the day after Linlithgow accepted Balfour's offer, 'My dear Hopie, I am in two minds about the news announced this morning, I rather hoped that you had abandoned the stormy path of politics, but I [delight] in anything that pleases you and in anything that shows you are in good health and heart.'[7]

Questions had been raised about the amount of money paid to Linlithgow by the government in 1903 for property which was to become the Rosyth naval base, but the *Scotsman* considered him a Scottish secretary full of promise, and even welcomed the return of the Scottish Office to the House of Lords as Scotland would have two ministers (Linlithgow and the lord advocate) instead of just one in the Commons. 'I confess I feel anxious as to whether I am man enough for the very important job,' Linlithgow wrote to Sir Charles Dalrymple, 'but . . . a man can but do his best and that I certainly mean to do.'[8] But he found the strain unbearable and tried to resign after just five weeks in the job, begging Balfour's private secretary Jack Sandars to persuade the prime minister to let him go:

> This is not a very easy letter to write but I think the most honest & straightforward course to pursue *is* to write it. A month's experience of my new life has convinced me that I am not mentally or physically a fit and proper person to be a cabinet minister or to administer an important government department. Ten years ago . . . my abominable illness began to come upon me. I believe I might have done it [then] in a fairly satisfactory way but to day is not 10 years ago. Now . . . my memory has gone I have lost the power of coherent speech when I am on my legs. I cannot see at times when at work in my office . . . I want you to ask Mr Balfour to let me go; it will not be hard to find a better man to fill my place & . . . I hope Mr Balfour will believe that I accepted his offer a month ago with a strong sense of duty.[9]

Balfour, however, was unsympathetic and refused Linlithgow's request. Losing a Cabinet minister after only a month would have looked too bad for a government on its last legs.

'I think I am leaving your home in good order,'[10] wrote Andrew Graham Murray in a parting note to his successor, but in fact he bequeathed only the unenviable remains of his Education Bill, and the nucleus of a basis for Kirk reunion. Only the latter occupied much of Linlithgow's time in parliament, and he moved the Second Reading of the Churches (Scotland) Bill in July. This attempted to pick up the pieces from the 1900 union between the Free Church and the United Presbyterians under the United Free Church banner. A court ruling had decreed that the UFC had no right to the property of the old Free Church, now represented by a minority who had refused to join. A royal commission then recommended parliamentary interference, and Linlithgow told peers that he did not think 'it is a phase of the proceedings upon which any Scotsman can look back either with pleasure or satisfaction'. The Scottish secretary spoke with some historical authority. His ancestor Sir Thomas Hope was lord advocate during the reign of Charles I, and in 1606 his defence of six Kirk ministers charged with high treason for denying the King's authority in ecclesiastical matters brought him wide-spread acclaim. Linlithgow's aim was more modest, proposing to give the royal commission power to divide the total property between the Free and United Free Church as it saw fit. 'I belong to the Church of Scotland and am a well-wisher of the Church of Scotland,' he told the House of Lords, but 'those who know me in my own part of the world will tell you that I am not a bad friend to the Churches outside the Establishment.' His speech was lengthy, moderate in tone and not without eloquence. 'When the flame of the acute passions has burnt itself out,' he concluded, 'matters will settle themselves down, and all that has been best and most noble in this movement for the union of these two great Churches will be remembered, and all that is most regrettable will be forgotten.'[11] Otherwise, appearances by Linlithgow in the Upper House were rare and usually brief. 'It is not a difficult job in the Lords,' wrote a correspondent who had urged him to take the job earlier that year, and 'I do not think it will be a long term of office as I have a strong feeling that the Government will not last long. You would have . . . the satisfaction of having been a Cabinet Minister.'[12] Linlithgow's well-wisher was correct in so far as his first two points, but it is doubtful that he gleaned any satisfaction from regular meetings of an increasingly gloomy Cabinet. In August Linlithgow moved the Second Reading of the Fisheries (Scotland) Bill; it proved to be his final appearance in the Lords as well as his last as Scottish secretary.

Balfour eventually resigned as prime minister in December of 1905, losing his seat when the Conservatives were soundly defeated by the Liberals at the general election the following year. For Linlithgow it was a welcome escape from the burden, both emotional and physical, of government office. His health continued to decline and he died in France of pernicious anaemia on 29 February 1908. He was just 47 years old.

John Sinclair, 1st Lord Pentland

10 December 1905 – 13 February 1912

An angel with discordant wings

John Sinclair was a politician who attracted scorn and praise in almost equal measure. H. H. Asquith thought he had 'the brain of a rabbit, and the temper of a pig',[1] but to radical Scottish crofters he was something of a folk hero. It was these two extremes which made his seven years at the Scottish Office both so interesting and ultimately disappointing.

Born on 20 January 1860 to Captain George Sinclair, an officer in the Bengalese army, and his wife and cousin Agnes,[2] Sinclair had an impeccably middle-class upbringing. He was schooled at Edinburgh Academy and Wellington College before entering Sandhurst in 1878. He came fifth in his class and joined the 5th Royal Irish Lancers, serving in Ireland from 1881, where he often acted as an escort officer to the viceroy, Earl Spencer (to whom he 'owed the beginnings of his Liberal faith'). He also came into contact with the Irish chief secretary, Sir Henry Campbell-Bannerman, and a lifelong political and personal relationship was forged. Sinclair was devoted to him, becoming his parliamentary private secretary at the War Office, his Scottish whip, and from 1895 to 1905 (having lost his Dunbartonshire seat) his chief political assistant. Even after Sir Henry died in 1908 the association continued, with Sinclair acting as his literary executor and ambitious biographer.[3]

Sinclair left the army in 1887 to read law and economics at the recently founded Toynbee Hall, and in 1889 he was elected to represent East Finsbury as a Progressive on the first London County Council. Sinclair stood down three years later to make way for the candidature of Lord Rosebery, and to stand at the 1892 general election, in which he won Dunbartonshire for the Liberals. He was an instinctive political campaigner and re-entered parliament in 1897 at a by-election for Forfarshire, a constituency he retained until his elevation to the House of Lords in 1909. But on the formation of the Liberal government in 1905 the only appointment of Sir Henry Campbell-Bannerman's which attracted criticism was that of Sinclair, one contemporary commentator writing that his inclusion 'was the only thing . . . which looked like a job'.[4] The subsequent 1906 general election, however, produced the Liberals' greatest ever poll triumph, and with the government holding 60 out of 72 Scottish seats Sinclair had a massive mandate for reform north of the border. 'He had very definite ideas about Scottish administration,' wrote his wife after his death. 'He wanted Scotland to be governed according to Scottish ideas.'[5] The closeness of Sinclair's relationship with Sir Henry was often ridiculed, H. H. Asquith observing that at the Royal Court Sinclair was 'regarded as C.B.'s natural son',[6] but it gave him influence upon general party policy which previous Scottish secretaries could only have dreamed of.

The new secretary for Scotland began with some minor, but enduring, reforms. The National Galleries of Scotland Act of 1906 was the first Scottish Office foray into the arts world, providing additional funding and a board of trustees for the Edinburgh galleries and a new headquarters for the Royal Society of Edinburgh on George Street, as well as building a new school of art in the capital. Sinclair was also deeply interested in the care of historical monuments and in February 1908 the Royal Commission on the Ancient and Historical Monuments and Constructions of Scotland was established, originally to catalogue everything but later assuming a more permanent role.

Sinclair also finally brought Scottish education up to date after repeated attempts by Unionist Scottish secretaries since 1901. Sinclair got on well with the Glaswegian Sir John Struthers, who had succeeded Sir Henry Craik at the Scotch Education Department (SED) in 1904. His work with Sinclair was impressive: in 1906 school boards acquired the legal duty to provide for all handicapped children in cases where parents were unable to do so; the Education (Scotland) Act two years later made provision for medical supervision and school meals, adding a social welfare element to Scottish schools for the first time; an Education (Scotland) Fund was established to centralise educational finance, boosting teacher training and pay and substantially increasing the government grant to Scotland's four universities; and an obligation was also placed upon each local authority to provide the option of continuation classes for all children aged 14 to 17 who wished to attend.

One MP heckled Sinclair during the Second Reading of his Education (Scotland) Bill, asking why he would not transfer the SED from London to Edinburgh. 'I say transfer it tomorrow if you transfer with it the Parliament which controls it,' retorted Sinclair. 'A Scottish Education Department, with a Minister responsible to Parliament and under the control of Parliament, I can understand.'[7] Ironically, and despite this rhetoric, the secretary for Scotland moved some SED staff to Edinburgh in 1909 under pressure from Scottish colleagues who resented the lack of a strong base in Edinburgh. Sinclair also presided over the transfer of greater housing powers to the Local Government Board for Scotland following the Housing and Town Planning Act, and in November 1909 he installed his private secretary of the last three years, H. M. Conacher, in Edinburgh, to act as a liaison officer for the Scottish local authorities. His commitment to home rule for Ireland, however, did not extend to Scotland.[8] Sinclair did not believe the time was right, and besides, he was preserving his energy for a much bigger battle.

Both Arthur James Balfour and the Marquis of Lothian had planned to extend the original Crofters Act beyond the seven crofting counties to the whole of Scotland soon after it was passed in 1886,[9] but when Sinclair announced his intention to do something similar with his Small Landholders (Scotland) Bill in 1907, there was a colossal outcry – not just from Unionists but from the government benches too. Unlike Balfour, this Scottish secretary sympathised with the land raiders and sought to normalise their position by turning their moral claims into legal ones. Sinclair was alarmed by the declining rural population in his Forfarshire constituency, and he believed the exodus to the cities needed a radical solution. But it was the clause providing for the enlargement of existing holdings, whether by agreement or compulsory powers, which outraged the landed gentry – a significant proportion of both the Lords and the Commons. Two new bodies – one administrative (the Board of Agriculture for Scotland) and the other judicial (the Scottish Land Court) – were to be established, the former to handle the creation of new holdings, while the latter would intervene when necessary to take land by compulsion. Crucially, Sinclair had Sir Henry's backing. In his first speech as prime minister, Sir Henry said, 'We desire to give the farmer greater freedom and greater security; to secure a home and a career for the labourer. We wish to make the land less of a pleasure ground for the rich and more of a treasure home for the nation.'[10] The subsequent King's Speech promised a measure for amending and extending the Crofters Act, and over the next six months the new Bill was drafted as Sinclair dispatched deputations of farmers to examine small land holdings in Denmark, Canada and Australia. He finally introduced the Bill on 28 July 1906, squeezed in at the end of a Saturday afternoon session. When that first attempt ended in failure, Sinclair tried again in March 1907, and this time the Bill passed its Second Reading the following month with a majority of 239. Every aspect of the Bill was debated that summer, and it spent 23 days in a newly revived Scottish Grand Committee, not to mention nine days on the floor of the House. The Unionist leader, Arthur James Balfour, attacked what he called a 'wild and infantile experiment', and taunted Sinclair with the opposition of Chamber of Agriculture and the Highland and Agricultural Society of Scotland. The Scottish secretary put on a brave face, arguing that his reforms were 'not only in accordance with Scottish experience, but in accordance with Scottish opinion'.[11] The Upper House was just as hostile, with Lord Rosebery succumbing to his increasing conservatism with a scathing speech denouncing the principle of the Bill as 'essentially a vicious one'. Looking around the chamber he declared, somewhat melodramatically, 'If nobody else goes into the lobby [to vote against] . . . I will go alone.' He confessed to viewing the Bill's protagonist with nothing less than suspicion:

> The Secretary for Scotland, Captain Sinclair, has yet to win his spurs, and I have no doubt that he will win them . . . But I must say that he is a very young Minister . . . His record does not give us any encouragement for following him blindly in his agricultural experiments . . . I am willing to concede to the Secretary for Scotland every moral quality. He may be an angel for all I know; but an angel with discordant wings is not likely to fly very far . . . the danger of an old man in a hurry is as nothing to the danger of a young man in a hurry.[12]

Rosebery had a personal interest in the Bill through his estate at Dalmeny, as did most of his fellow peers. 'Ministers have chosen Scotland as their battle ground,' he wrote to a friend, 'the Scottish Land Bill as their standard, and the House of Lords as their object, not without an eye (far from friendly) to the humble individual who now addresses you.'[13]

Sinclair endured deeply personal attacks such as Rosebery's with admirable restraint, although by this point the House of Lords was increasingly flexing its constitutional muscles, having already blocked most of the government's radical programme. A. J. Balfour audaciously declared, 'The great Unionist party should still control, whether in power or opposition, the destinies of this great Empire.' The Liberal ministers Lords Elgin and Tweedmouth seemed to agree and opposed the Bill in Cabinet. It did not help that the English version of the Bill under Lord Ripon was more moderate, not least because there were no crofters in England. Sir Henry also remained upbeat, writing to a colleague that 'We think we are doing very well here . . . The Scotch Land Bill is a great stumbling block and rock of offence to the Tories, and even more to the Lib. Imps., who still rear their head now and then!'[14] But Sinclair withdrew the Bill on 22 August 1907 following a Lords vote to place it on hold. The secretary for Scotland wrote to Sir Henry on 12 December 1907, clearly at a loss:

I detest arguing and quarrelling – but I have no choice: and the matter is urgent . . . When I saw Elgin the other day, his only suggestion about it was – why not introduce it in the Lords, who always complain that they have nothing to do? Whereas on the other hand, we shall be very short of time in the Commons. No doubt we shall have to reckon with the usual desire of most people to get quit of Scottish business somehow.[15]

On 12 February 1908, in the last speech of his life, the prime minister outlined a new timetable for the land legislation and its 'twin brother' the Land Values (Scotland) Bill, which had also been thrown out by the Lords. It is the 'first time I believe in the history of this House that Bills have been a second time sent up to the House of Lords within the compass of a single Parliament,' he observed, believing it to be an issue of who controlled Scottish affairs: Scotland's Liberal MPs, or peers and a small section of the Commons. The Cabinet was uneasy at backing a Bill solely on the assurance of a young and inexperienced minister that public opinion was behind it. Its second Second Reading, however, passed with an increased majority of 244, and its third by 257 (only three Scottish Liberal MPs voted against). But once again its rejection in the Upper House was moved by the former Scottish secretary, Lord Balfour of Burleigh, and carried on 11 March by 153 votes to 33. Things got worse when Sir Reginald MacLeod of MacLeod, Sinclair's permanent under-secretary at the Scottish Office, resigned in disgust to contest the Inverness-shire constituency for the Conservatives (unsuccessfully), and in April the prime minister's health deteriorated badly, Sir Henry dying in Downing Street soon after. 'The sad news has come upon us all,' Sinclair had written to Sir Henry on 6 April 1908. 'I shudder to think of it. But I have no doubts, for you had none.'[16] Sinclair acted as a pall-bearer at his funeral and was also an executor of his will, a specific legacy giving Sinclair all the late prime minister's correspondence and papers 'to be dealt with solely by him at his absolute and unquestioned discretion'.[17] The Small Landholders (Scotland) Bill, meanwhile, was once again in political limbo.

Even beyond the land reform battleground Sinclair had been faring badly. There was growing unrest among the party faithful, and not only was the Scottish secretary at odds with Alexander Elibank, the Scottish Liberal whip, he also became locked in a petulant war of words with Thomas Shaw, the lord advocate. The MP for Hawick since 1892, Shaw was an ardent land reformer as well as an ambitious lawyer, but he upset the secretary for Scotland by arguing that his post was analogous to that of the lord chancellor in England, and claiming he had the right to appoint

judges. In turn, Sinclair accused Shaw of undermining the post of
secretary for Scotland and trying to restore 'Parliament House government'. Shaw wrote to Sinclair on 5 December 1906 saying that he wished
to be able to support him fully, both in the House and in the country, but
felt Sinclair's recent behaviour had made this difficult. Shaw had not been
consulted on the form and content of the recent National Galleries of
Scotland Bill, leading to an embarrassing incident under questioning in
the House. 'My only wish,' he wrote, 'is that, as has always been with Lord
Advocates of former times, the Lord Advocate should be consulted on
what he has to defend.'[18] The bad feeling was confounded when Lord
Kyllachy resigned as a Scottish judge and confusion arose as to who was
responsible for nominating his successor. Shaw claimed he could not
get hold of Sinclair and so interviewed a candidate called Guthrie, who
gladly accepted what he took to be a job offer. On 30 December Sinclair
telegraphed Shaw, snapping, 'Not so. Please prevent all publicity. Am
writing.'[19] The secretary for Scotland then wrote to the lord advocate,
declaring himself free of any responsibility for the appointment and saying
he was passing all correspondence to the prime minister for his judgement. 'Your action . . . leaves me no choice,' he wrote sadly, 'and I have
no doubt that in so doing I interpret your wishes. All the compliments of
the season.'[20] Sinclair wrote to Sir Henry the same day, enclosing the
correspondence to date. 'The man is v. pleased with himself in all that he
has done, & I dislike these squabbles so heartily, that I would willingly let
this whole thing go by the board. But there is more than childishness in it.
And the worm will turn.'[21] Indeed it did, after Shaw discovered that
Sinclair had consulted two of his predecessors, Lord Dunedin (formerly
Andrew Graham Murray) and Lord Balfour of Burleigh, who both
concurred rather vaguely with Sinclair's position. The lord advocate
was furious, and wrote at length to the Scottish secretary on 2 January
1907. He denied having appointed Guthrie, saying he had merely asked
him if he was interested, and added that the final decision lay with
Sinclair, 'But during these weeks, as I learn to my surprise from your
letter, you have been going afield and, both in communings and correspondence, have been submitting to others, not even members of the
Government or political associates, our relations with each other. I knew
nothing of this and it is speaking with much reserve about it to say that it is
an irregularity.' Shaw argued, not unreasonably, that Sinclair had yet to
make any mention of who he wanted as the new judge. 'So that, as I
began my letter, I end it,' he concluded. 'Your communication in its tone
and its claim has surprised me. Holding the views above expressed as to
my public duty, no other course is open to me than to perform it. I
accordingly request that you will at the proper time be pleased to carry my

selection into effect, by submitting to His Majesty the name of Mr. Guthrie as a Lord of Session.'[22] The secretary for Scotland turned, once again, to his patron in Downing Street:

> Now, as you will remember, one of the considerations in view in the creation of the office of Secretary for Scotland was to put some check upon the paramount influence of Parliament House in Scottish affairs; which was then considerable, and is now . . . In the meantime too, he has taken the matter into his own hands – against everybody's opinion. And this, if it is repeated, is bound to lead to trouble, & public criticism.[23]

Finally, Sir Henry reached a decision: 'The Lord Advoc. will recommend to. &. then S. for S. will submit his name.'[24] The Scottish Office in Whitehall had prevailed over Parliament House in Edinburgh, but the episode had hardly covered Sinclair in glory.

Meanwhile, ordinary party members were accusing the secretary for Scotland (now in the House of Lords as Lord Pentland) of ignoring both party, and public, opinion. At a particularly rowdy meeting of the Scottish Liberal Association in late 1909, Mr Allan McLardy of Glasgow moved a resolution claiming the Scottish Office was more autocratic than the House of Lords, and branding the Scottish secretary a 'mere tool in the hands of the permanent officials'. Worst of all, an old Liberal gripe about Sinclair's use of patronage resurfaced, the secretary for Scotland standing accused of having 'set aside Liberals against whose fitness nothing could be said, and appointed others less able, but less obnoxious to their Tory colleagues in the Scottish Office'. Another speaker, seconding McLardy's motion, said Sinclair had appointed a cousin of his wife (with a salary of £1,200 a year) to the chairmanship of the Prison Commissioners: 'The fact was, and they all knew it, that Lord Pentland was utterly incompetent . . . He had been like wax in the hands of the Tories, and he had flouted the opinions and wishes of his former supporters . . . They might blind themselves to the harm he was doing to Liberalism, but it existed.'[25] Only the Scottish whip, John Gulland, and Mr J. Wales Cameron, representing Edinburgh University, defended Pentland as a hardworking minister who had been sent to the Lords against his wishes. The motion was later withdrawn but, by July 1910, press reports said many Liberal members were openly calling upon Sinclair to resign.

The new prime minister, Herbert Henry Asquith, was also no fan of his secretary for Scotland, yet retained him at the Scottish Office on succeeding Sir Henry in April 1908. Not only did he compare Sinclair unfavourably with wild animals, but his chief whip, Jack Pease, recorded more prime ministerial thoughts in his diary on 21 December 1908: 'Never was a minister more painstaking obstinate & less brilliant was his criticism,' wrote Pease. 'He quoted the retiring Scotch Perm. Sec. to same effect Macleod & the latter's opinion of the Lord Advocate as being shifty & sharp.'[26] Sinclair was no doubt aware of this hostility and, fearing for his Land Bill, wrote to Asquith on 7 September 1908 claiming that the party remained united behind his proposals, being 'perfectly reasonable and willing to wait for what is clearly unattainable at present, for they see and know that the Lords stand in the way of what they desire'.[27] Sinclair's wife (and subsequently his biographer), Lady Marjorie Adeline,[28] would later claim her husband moved to the House of Lords reluctantly, but in fact the idea came from Sinclair himself. On 26 October 1908 he wrote to Asquith suggesting he be moved to the Upper House to keep an eye on 'Scotch Bills'. Asquith was not convinced, and told Pease that at the Royal Court Sinclair was 'regarded as C.B.'s natural son & to be promoted will really cause ridicule'.[29] Asquith had recently dropped the Land Values (Scotland) Bill, later incorporating it into the 1909 budget, but he still publicly backed the more contentious land legislation, though with less obvious enthusiasm than his predecessor.

By January 1909 the tension between Shaw and Sinclair had calmed down and Asquith finally resolved to move Sinclair to the Lords. 'Between ourselves,' he wrote to Lord Knollys seeking royal approval for Sinclair's peerage, 'I think it is in the interest of the Government & of public business: for Shaw is by a good deal a stronger man than his official chief, while Sinclair (who is painstaking) will at any rate be able to speak with first-hand knowledge in the Upper House.'[30] But Asquith's clever plan to get rid of Sinclair and leave Shaw in charge of Scottish business was scuppered by the death of Lord Robertson, a Scottish lord of appeal. Shaw held the same succession of offices as Robertson, and was keen to take his place. Still, elevating Sinclair was not without benefits: Hamilton of Dalzell had resigned as the Scottish Office spokesman in the Lords over the Small Landholders Bill, and Asquith rightly sensed that the Upper House would be crucial to the future success of several Bills, not least the 'People's Budget' of 1909. Sinclair's ancestors had lived by the Pentland Hills, so he took the title Lord Pentland of Lyth, Lyth being the original name of his family home in Caithness.

Lord Pentland now found himself a member of the very chamber he had once denounced as nothing more than 'a branch of the Tory Party . . . a mere registration office for Tory legislation'.[31] His reception there was predictably hostile. 'Lord Pentland has been described by a Parliamentary wit as resembling the riotous Firth from which he takes his title,' reported the *Scotsman* just months after he took his seat, 'in running ten knots an hour in one direction and then ten knots an hour in another.'[32]

In November 1909 the House of Lords rejected the Budget, even though constitutional precedent prevented the Upper House blocking a money Bill. When Lord Lansdowne suggested that peers should submit to the judgment of the country, Lord Balfour of Burleigh warned that this amounted to a referendum on the Budget, which risked destroying both the supremacy of the Commons and the prestige of the Lords.[33] But the Liberals sensed triumph and in January 1910 a general election was fought on the basis of reforming the House of Lords. The result in Scotland was mildly encouraging, with the Liberals actually gaining a seat from the Unionists. The result in England was very different, where the outcome meant increasing reliance on the Irish Nationalists. Asquith then introduced the Parliament Bill and, when an all-party constitutional conference failed, another election was held in December, at which the Liberals consolidated their position in Scotland. In 1911 the Parliament Bill finally became law, passing in the Lords by 131 votes to 114 after Asquith threatened to flood the Upper House with 500 new peers.[34] The National Insurance Bill now cleared both Houses of Parliament, and in November Pentland introduced his Land Bill for the last time. Lord Rosebery recycled some of his old arguments against it, but the appetite for continued obstruction had waned and some minor concessions ensured that the Bill finally became law on 14 December, peers grudgingly endorsing a Third Reading. When one opponent demanded to know if Pentland had consulted agricultural opinion in Scotland, the Scottish secretary replied that he had consulted the opinion of the House of Commons. Now, after all, that was all that mattered.

On 16 December 1911 Pentland was one of five peers who acted as the commission to prorogue parliament and give Royal Assent to both the National Insurance Act and the Small Landholders (Scotland) Act. Pentland was elated, and during a celebratory lunch his children chanted 'the Land Bill's through!'[35] as their father planned a celebratory party in Edinburgh for 1,500 people. The event, however, never took place as he was recalled from Edinburgh in January 1912 to be told by Asquith that he was now convinced the Scottish secretary ought to be in the Commons. Pentland was upset that his legislative baby was to be wrenched away from him just as it grew political teeth, and Lady Pentland later bitterly claimed that her husband's Bill had been the basis of the Liberals' Scottish success in the two general elections of 1910. 'In the party interest, therefore, it was impossible to get rid of the Secretary for Scotland before the Bill had been secured,' she wrote. 'So it was allowed to pass, in a form as weakened as possible, and immediately afterwards the blow was dealt.'[36] His sacking was so quietly contrived that it came to Pentland as a complete surprise; Asquith no doubt taking his reaction as further evidence of rabbit-like brains. The prime minister's daughter Margot snidely wrote in her diary, 'I am amused that the axe has at last fallen on Pentland – Father has offered him Madras – I'm afraid Marjorie will be very unhappy – & that the whole thing will have been a complete surprise & shock.'[37] Friends urged the outgoing Scottish secretary not to accept the Indian posting, and to seek more lucrative work in the City, but after some consideration he wrote to Asquith on 13 February 1912, 'In deference to your own strong wish, I accept Madras; and I can only hope that I may be happy enough to succeed in justifying in some measure your choice.'[38] Rather insincerely, Asquith replied, 'I am delighted that you see your way to go to Madras. Let me thank you once again, with all my heart, for the great services you have rendered to our party and the country during the last six years. They will always be remembered.'[39] The media reaction was balanced and largely sympathetic. 'Along with Lord Pentland, Lord Carrington leaves the Cabinet with the solace of a Marquisate,' said the *Scotsman*. 'There would appear to be some fatalistic connection between small holdings and disjuncture from the Cabinet; for the chief apostles of the policy in England and Scotland simultaneously withdraw from the Government circle.'[40] *The Times* generously noted that:

> There has been in the past something in the nature of a cabal against Lord Pentland among the rank and file on the Liberal side, to which, perhaps, these rumours were directly due. Lord Pentland was not a fighting politician, and his modesty, amiability, and lack of self-seeking qualities to which his friends bear witness were not calculated to impress his critics in debate, or help him to play a prominent part as a member of a Cabinet which includes so many fighting politicians . . . But, although as a Parliamentarian Lord Pentland did not achieve success, the Liberal Party owes not a little, from their point of view, to his political foresight, and it has not recently been the custom of Liberals to acknowledge the debt . . . This land policy has counted for much in the support given to Liberal Administrations in Scotland since . . . In the early days of the movement Lord Pentland did much spade-work in educating Liberal opinion in Scotland in this direction.[41]

One Scottish Office official wrote to his old chief, 'The announcement was a stab – I can't think of Dover House without you.'[42] Sinclair had been at the Scottish Office for almost seven years, acting as secretary for Scotland both in the Commons and in the Lords. The Freedom of Edinburgh was conferred upon him in 'happy recognition of the retiring

Minister's popularity in Scotland',[42] and four months later (and 50 degrees farther south) Sinclair crossed the Indian Ocean to take up his post as governor of Madras. In India he was remembered for his efforts to improve the health, social welfare and economic development of the region, and he remained in Madras until 1919.

Sinclair died of pneumonia at his home in London on 11 January 1925 and was buried at the Dean Cemetery in his native city four days later, 'Secretary for Scotland 1905–1912' proudly engraved on his headstone. From his colonial residence he must have watched with sadness as the 'Pentland Act', as it became known, failed to generate the anticipated flood of people from the cities to a new land of milk and honey in the Scottish countryside. After a year of operation nearly 4,000 requests had been made to create new holdings, mostly from the Western Isles, but the majority stalled due to lack of funding and cumbersome administration. By 1914, the new Board of Agriculture for Scotland had created only 500 new holdings and enlarged fewer than 300 existing ones.[43] A six-year constitutional battle had created little more than a damp squib, and in 1933 John Sinclair's radical experiment in land reform was officially abandoned.

THOMAS MCKINNON WOOD

13 FEBRUARY 1912 – 9 JULY 1916

Dry, uninspired, and uninspiring

Thomas McKinnon Wood was essentially a London politician, and H. H. Asquith's choice of him to replace Lord Pentland at the Scottish Office was both unexpected and uninspired.[1] And, although he scored some notable legislative triumphs during his four years as secretary for Scotland, Wood was bad-tempered, spectacularly rude to his colleagues and seemed ill-suited to the aggressive world of Scottish politics. 'McKinnon Wood should run in blinkers . . . when dealing with his opponents in politics,' wrote one critic to David Lloyd George, 'and I'm not sure they wouldn't come in hand when dealing with his friends.'[2]

Wood was born to Scottish parents in Stepney, London, on 26 January 1855. His father was a ship-owning merchant, and his second wife, Jessie, was the daughter of the Rev. Thomas McKinnon of Kincardineshire. He was educated at Mill Hill School and at University College, London, where he had a distinguished undergraduate career studying political economy and the philosophy of mind. Wood worked briefly on an eclectic mix of subjects for the ninth edition of the *Encyclopaedia Britannica* in Edinburgh, but returned to London in 1878 when his father became blind, joining the family firm as a partner. Like his predecessor, Wood's political career began with his election to London County Council, which he joined as a Progressive in 1892. He quickly rose through the party ranks, becoming group leader in 1897 and chairman of the council from 1898 to 1907. He presided over the Progressives' two most remarkable landslide victories in 1901 and 1904, but rather unimaginatively subscribed to standard urban radical views such as free trade and Irish home rule.

After three unsuccessful attempts to enter parliament he won the St Rollox Division of Glasgow in the Liberal landslide of 1906. Wood spoke mainly on London issues in the Commons, and two years later Asquith made him parliamentary secretary to the Board of Education, apparently to alleviate nonconformist misgivings over that year's Education Bill. In October 1908 he moved to the Foreign Office despite showing 'no obvious interest in foreign affairs',[3] where he served under Lord Grey, and two years later he became financial secretary to the Treasury having arrogantly convinced himself that he would 'have more power than three fourths of the Cabinet'.[4] 'McKinnon Wood did his work, though without any great distinction,' wrote the Irish Nationalist MP T. P. O'Connor. 'He was not a man who would do anything Parliamentary with distinction. His nature had no expansiveness; it was essentially dry, uninspired, and uninspiring . . . It did not seem possible that a career which had all the flow of a sluggish stream could ever be seriously interrupted.'[5] His four years at the Scottish Office proved that rather sarcastic point. With his big walrus moustache, the new secretary for Scotland was an able, yet slow-speaking, debater and an effective administrator. But there were bad omens: Wood collected his seals of office just days before a disastrous coal strike and the unpopularity of the National Insurance Act nearly lost him his seat at the by-election caused by his promotion. Wood hung on in St Rollox, but with a majority of only 469 votes.

Wood was a committed Congregationalist – his brother, brother-in-law and maternal grandfather all being men of the church – but not a teetotaller, so when he took up the cause of temperance reform it both puzzled and infuriated his opponents. The notion of 'local option' – granting local communities rights of veto over liquor licenses – was not new. The Peel Commission on Licensing Laws had recommended it in 1899, and a private members' bill for local option and general licensing reform had passed through the Scottish Grand Committee in 1909–10. The Bill became Wood's version of Sinclair's Small Landholders Bill, repeatedly being thrown out by the Lords and having very little impact when it finally became law.

The temperance lobby was noisy yet chaotic, but the Scottish secretary was convinced that public opinion was on his side and at the Temperance (Scotland) Bill's third Second Reading, on 1 April 1912, he told the House that just days before a petition signed by 2,000 ministers 'of all denominations' had been delivered to the prime minister. By this stage, Wood had been forced to compromise with a new clause providing that no local referendum could take place until 1917, and that no public house could actually be closed until May 1918. The Bill also stipulated that that no public house could open in Scotland before 10 a.m.: 'No one, I am sure the House agrees, desires to drink before that hour except the incorrigible toper.'[6] But the Bill was savaged in the Lords and critics accused Wood of steam-rollering his opponents. 'Mr. McKinnon Wood has turned the thumbscrew on all members of his own party,' wrote the *Scotsman*, 'who have had the audacity to express the heretical view that all wisdom does not reside either in him, or in his Bill.'[7] The secretary for Scotland came under attack in the Commons in February 1913, and for a while it looked as though the government would ditch the Bill on account of hostility from its own supporters. Wood refused conciliatory moves from both Lloyd George and Winston Churchill, and was heard to threaten resignation if the Bill was dropped; in the end Lloyd George 'faced the music and got a large majority'.[8] The *Scotsman* was typically scathing: 'He displayed all the attributes of a man who has ceased to think, and is contemptuous of every person's opinion but his own . . . he was intoxicated by his own ideas, and momentarily forgot that he was not the whole Cabinet.'[9] The irony of a temperance bill having so intemperate an advocate was not lost on the Liberal-baiting newspaper. To make matters worse, a Glasgow Corporation survey showed that the second city of the Empire, which included Wood's St Rollox constituency, was against any interference with existing licenses. 'An atmosphere of ineptitude pervades the Scottish Office,'[10] declared a leader writer, and by the time the Bill had its fourth Second Reading on 20 June 1913 Wood was running out of patience and threatened to use the new Parliament Act, which limited the power of the Lords to block Commons' legislation, to ensure its success. 'The idea that it was confined to constitutional questions never entered anyone's head,' stormed Wood during a fraught debate. 'But it is rather interesting to find to-day that when we are dealing with Scotch temperance it is all right that the Parliament Act should apply to Irish Home Rule on Welsh Disestablishment, but it is monstrous that it should apply to Scotch temperance . . . Then for what object do hon. Members think we passed that Act?' The secretary for Scotland was interrupted constantly, provoking his famously short temper. When an MP intervened to say that the Bill did not interest 20 per cent of Scots he heard Wood mutter 'Oh, rot!' to the member behind him; the prominent Unionist MP Sir George Younger even challenged Wood to fight him in Ayr on a temperance platform while claiming that Asquith had approved the Bill from the comfort of his bath. 'He was not in his bathroom,' sneered Wood. 'I mention that picturesque detail to show how fables grow, because a lot of fables have gone round about this scene. He was in an adjoining room.' The Scottish secretary concluded on a familiar refrain: 'It is perfectly well known that the majority of Scottish representatives are in favour of this Bill, and have been for a great many years, and in that they are supported by their constituents.'[11] This time the Lords reserved its sting for other battles and allowed the measure go through rather than see the Parliament Act invoked.

When Wood died in 1927 the United Kingdom Temperance Alliance wrote to his daughter with a glowing tribute: 'No one who was privileged to watch your Father's conduct of the fight in 1912 and 1913 could fail to be impressed with the courage, determination and prudence with which he piloted the Temperance (Scotland) Act across the stormy political seas into harbour. He has not lived to see the full harvest of his great effort, but even the first-fruits have brought much joy into many a Scottish home.'[12] But those first fruits were in reality – once the time limit was up – small, and Wood, like Lord Pentland with his treasured Small Landholdings Act, watched its implementation with ill-tempered dissatisfaction.

On the morning of 15 July 1914, as he stood talking to his butler on the steps of his home in Portland Place, a woman rushed at Wood with a dog whip, striking him across the chest. 'You Scotch pig,' she screamed, 'if you don't stop force feeding we shall smash you up, and you can't say you have not been thrashed by a woman.' A second woman also tried to strike the startled Scottish secretary but was stopped by the butler, who had already thrown the first assailant to the ground. 'You are a pig and a lot of hounds,' she shouted. 'Stop forcible feeding.'[13] Earlier that year Wood had also been covered in flour by a suffragette as he opened the new Boroughmuir Higher Grade School in Edinburgh. Although he person-ally supported votes for women, it was the government's Prisoners (Temporary Discharge for Ill Health) Act – the so-called 'Cat and Mouse Act' – which caused offence. This allowed hunger-striking female prisoners to be released in order to recover, only to be rearrested when they had.

On other issues of social reform, however, Wood proved to be sympathetic and far-sighted. The Mental Deficiency and Lunacy (Scot-land) Bill of 1913 sought to centralise government funding for Scotland's then crude mental health care facilities, while enlarging and renaming the Lunacy Board (to become the Board of Control) with an additional medical commissioner to relieve the burden currently placed upon Scotland's poorest parishes. In sharp contrast to his temperance crusade, the Scottish secretary won praise for the skill with which he steered this measure through the Commons. It coincided with an unprecedented period of expansion in Scottish Office control over health and social security: the National Insurance Act of 1911 had established a contributory system of insurance against illness and unemployment, and in Scotland was controlled by a distinct Scottish bureaucracy (the Scottish Insurance Commission) answerable to the Scottish secretary; the Education (Scot-land) Act, 1913, compelled education authorities to provide free medical attention for all schoolchildren; and, most significantly, the Highlands and

Islands Medical Service was also established that year. This latter service was given a free hand to spend its £42,000 annual grant as it saw fit. At first it created a comprehensive primary care service and then established an integrated hospital service. Wood, however, believed the funding of this would create unnecessary bureaucracy and suggested allowing the existing Local Government Board for Scotland to act as the central public health authority for Scotland. 'My main point is that it is undesirable and unnecessary to complicate local government in Scotland by setting up new hybrid authorities,' he argued in a Cabinet memo, 'that the type proposed is a very unsatisfactory one, and that it will involve an unnecessary expenditure of public money.'[14]

And just as he did not flinch from criticising government policy, he was brutally frank with his Liberal colleagues. Wood was often accused of giving evasive, apathetic answers when questioned in the House. Not only was his manner abrupt, said the *Scotsman*, 'but he seems to regard the question hour as an occasion for concealing information rather than imparting it'.[15] He was also moody, often taking refuge in silence. 'The firmness he displayed as Secretary for Scotland in dealing with malcontents of his own party was accompanied by a certain brusqueness which unnecessarily alienated some of his political friends,' judged the *Morning Post* after his death, 'while the cavalier way in which he sometimes treated opponents did not tend to smooth his political path.'[16] But Wood at least demonstrated some self-awareness, telling a meeting of the Scottish Liberal Club in Edinburgh that perhaps when they heard criticisms of the Scottish secretary they would bear in mind that however badly he might be playing, he was doing his best.[17]

Wood's period as Scottish secretary coincided with the home rule crisis of 1912–14. The trade-off for Irish support on the Parliament Bill was the third Irish Home Rule Bill, which almost sparked civil war in Ulster but was eventually passed by parliament – although never implemented due to the outbreak of war. This Bill also reignited demands for a similar measure in Scotland, a dormant cry since the 1890s. Asquith immediately regretted a resolution of 28 February 1912 which appeared to state that home rule should begin at home: 'That in the opinion of this House any measure providing for the delegation of Parliamentary powers to Ireland should be followed in this Parliament by the granting of similar powers of self-government to Scotland, as part of a general scheme of devolution.' Home rule all round had reared its awkward constitutional head once more, but Wood soon tried to ignore the resolution despite 226 Liberal MPs, including 15 ministers, having backed the motion. Asquith also qualified his position, telling a delegation of Scottish Liberal members, including the future

Scottish secretaries Ronald Munro Ferguson and Godfrey Collins, that 'sound statesmanship and sound business' made it impossible to apply a cast-iron rule on home rule, adding sympathetic noises but asserting that the Irish measure had priority.[18] 'When the Prime Minister desires an amusing hour,' sneered the *Scotsman*, 'he can find nothing more diverting than a solemn farce such as he lately enjoyed in an interview with a score or two of Scottish representatives, who presented themselves apparently for the sole purpose of making game of Scottish nationality . . . As a burlesque it is excellent, as a satire upon the native shrewdness of the national character it furnishes excessive entertainment to the Southerners.'[19] But a speech by Wood to a meeting of Young Scots[20] in April 1913 turned out to be 'rather a tepid affair'. He told them that a Bill would be reasonably easy to get through parliament and would help consolidate Radical majorities in Scotland. Again and again, Wood added, Scotland had sent overwhelming Liberal majorities to the imperial parliament only to find itself 'overborne by a Tory majority in England'.[21] Sir Henry Cowan, the Liberal MP for Aberdeen East, introduced a private members' bill the following month, but Wood did not rise to the occasion. 'Half an hour was left for the Secretary for Scotland,' said the *Scotsman*, 'but twenty minutes sufficed for his perfunctory defence of the Bill.'[22] Sir George Younger warned that a Scottish parliament would be left without adequate funds, and attacked the proposed retention of 72 Scottish members in the imperial parliament, claiming it would lead to an anti-Scottish feeling in England. The Unionist leader, Arthur James Balfour, also revived his anti-devolution rhetoric, arguing that even if it was desirable, this piecemeal method was not the way to set about it. Few Scottish MPs turned up to support Sir Henry's Bill and it was counted out. Another MP, Ian Macpherson, had more luck in 1914, when moving the Second Reading of his Government of Scotland Bill on 15 May:

> Except my right Hon. Friend the Prime Minister, there is no one in modern politics who is so comparable to Atlas as my right Hon. Friend the Secretary for Scotland. The whole of Scotland is upon his broad shoulders alone. He is a sort of political Pooh-bah. Land, law, lunacy, local government, agriculture, prisons, housing, roads, the Board of Agriculture, and a host of other things he has to administer, not in Scotland, not with the aid of a Scottish Board, but 400 miles away.[23]

Balfour again attacked what he called 'crazy methods' of devolution and mocked its insincere proponents. 'Do not recommend your administrative Bill by appealing to Scottish nationalism,' he said, 'and do not, when you are appealing to Scottish nationalism, talk about nothing but administration.' Wood was not exactly evangelical in response:

What does the whole course of this debate show? It shows, in the first place, that there is no passion in this matter, which is simply one of administrative and legislative convenience. Everybody admits that this Parliament is over-burdened, and that our work would be better done if we divided it. No one wants to interfere with the Imperial Union. It is a pure question of how best you can make laws for and administer the affairs of the different parts of the country, and after two years' experience at the Scottish Office I have no hesitation in saying that it would be a great improvement if we had Ministers in Edinburgh dealing with Scottish affairs on the spot, and if we had the right to deal on the spot with those matters of social necessity which are not even controversial, but the settlement of which is essential to the smooth working of the machine, in our own time and way.[24]

'The Scottish Secretary blundered on from one inconsequent and misdirected passage to another,'[25] observed the *Scotsman*, but when Macpherson twice tried to move that the question be put, it was talked out by Sir George Younger.[26]

This intoxicating mix of devolution and temperance, however, proved too much for Wood, and in May 1913 he was advised to take a complete rest by cancelling all his engagements until after the Whitsun recess. The outbreak of war in 1914 also instigated both the decline of the Liberals as a major party of government, and of the Scottish Office as a prolific legislator. Wood remained loyal to Asquith,[27] but he was one of ten ministers who considered quitting the government to form a 'Peace Party' on the declaration of war.[28]

In May 1915, the Shell Crisis[29] caused a Cabinet split and Asquith formed a new coalition government which included senior figures from the opposition. The resulting reshuffle caused Wood his share of un-certainty, and he wrote to Asquith on 20 May:

I see a suggestion in today's 'Times' and 'Morning Post', which I cannot credit, that the holder of the office of SforS is not to have a seat in the new Cabinet. I cannot believe that this suggestion will appeal to you, but I hear from a well-informed source that it is being seriously put forward. In the present situation I write impersonally – the question arises whoever may be your choice for the office. As a Scottish member of 9 years standing and as SforS for over 3 years I feel bound to express my views, in regard to which I have no doubt, that such a decision would be deeply resented in Scotland, and by the Scottish members as a degradation of the national position, nor do I think that any one can efficiently discharge the duties of a not very easy office in any inferior position – The 'Times' gives as a reason that the Scottish Office has nothing to do directly with the war, but this is mere ignorance as you know.[30]

The Scottish Liberal whip, John Gulland, sought to reassure the Scottish secretary in a letter two days later:

> I had a long talk today with the P.M . . . all endless difficulties about the Coalition, & very little is settled. It is a superhuman task to fit everyone into places. As to Scotland, I put again these propositions
>   1. That the Sec. for Scot. Must be in Cabinet. P.M. agrees
>   2. That he must be a Liberal. We have 55 Members, they 15. A Tory Sec. would be impossible + intolerable. P.M. agrees.
> These two positions are unassailable, + I can't imagine him going back on them. We discussed you fully, + and [*sic*] while he is not committing himself to names at present, I don't see who else he can appoint. The only thinkable person is Jack Tennant if he had to go from the War Office. Of course the P.M. did not suggest that + probably did not think of it. The Daily News mentions me, but of course that is stupid + ridiculous. I have to stay here – for my sins - + try to keep the Party together, which is not going to be the easiest kind of job.[31]

It was hardly a ringing endorsement from the prime minister, but Wood must have been relieved at the preservation of his Cabinet position.

In the summer reshuffle of 1916 Asquith considered sending Wood to the Irish Office, but 'in view of the very heavy responsibilities of the Treasury during the war the Prime Minister has invited Mr. McKinnon Wood to return to his former post of Financial Secretary'.[32] He remained in the Cabinet as chancellor of the Duchy of Lancaster but his ministerial career ended with the collapse of the first wartime coalition in December 1916.

Unsurprisingly, Wood did not have much time for Lloyd George, whom he blamed for his humiliation at St Rollox in the 'coupon election'[33] of 1918, where he gained just eight per cent of the vote and lost his deposit. 'Almost daily', wrote T. P. O'Connor, he 'could be seen at the Reform Club fighting the old battles over again and haunting the place where in the days of his glory he represented the prosperous, steady, and consistent members of the old Radical creed.'[34] Wood made one more attempt to return to parliament in 1922, but was defeated in his former London County Council constituency of Central Hackney. The remainder of his life was clouded by the death of his second daughter, Lorna, and by the long illness of his wife. She died in March 1927 and just two weeks later Thomas McKinnon Wood passed away at his home in South Kensington. Fittingly for an old Radical, he was buried in London's Highgate Cemetery, just yards from the imposing grave of Karl Marx.

Harold John Tennant

9 July – 10 December 1916

The little minister

'Mr. Tennant enters the Cabinet as Secretary for Scotland,' declared *The Times* in July 1916, 'though it is one of the mysteries of our system of government why the holder of this dull but blameless office should necessarily be a member of a War Cabinet. After being for two years the most questioned member of the Government, Mr. Tennant will now become the least questioned.'[1] Harold John Tennant, better known as Jack, had served at the War Office since the beginning of the First World War, and for most of that time as Lord Kitchener's man in the House of Commons. He was seen to have dealt with his duties in a pleasant and successful fashion, so his elevation to Cabinet was expected if not thought to be deserved. As his brother-in-law was the prime minister, Herbert Henry Asquith, this was the boldest example of Scottish Office nepotism since Lord Salisbury installed his nephew back in 1886.

Tennant's career began and ended with that of Asquith, whose over-bearing wife, Margot Tennant,[2] had dominated her younger brother since childhood. On his appointment as home secretary in 1892, Asquith made Tennant one of his three private secretaries, and on entering Downing Street in 1909, the new prime minister made his brother-in-law parliamentary secretary to the Board of Trade, before transferring him to the War Office in 1912. Tennant was devoted to Asquith, but the feeling was not reciprocated: the prime minister was torn between family ties and finding his wife's brother more than a little irritating.

Jack's father, Sir Charles Tennant, was one of wealthiest men in Victorian Britain and was known to his family as 'the Bart' (after his 1885 baronetcy). His three sons were introverted characters while Margot and her four sisters dominated the family home in Perthshire. Jack, who preferred memorising vast chunks of poetry to the kind of aggressive ebullience practiced by Margot, once described them as 'more like lions than sisters'. Sir Charles was an affectionate man and proud of his children, leaving Jack and his brother Frank £1 million each when he died in 1906. Margot was obsessed with her brothers' wealth but equally devoted to boosting Jack's political career.

It was while parliamentary private secretary to Asquith that Tennant first became aware of industrial suffering, and as chairman of the Dangerous Trades Committee he helped extend the provision of compensation payments and introduce minimum wages for certain 'sweated trades'. Another member of the committee was May Abraham, who had been England's first female factory inspector. She caught her chairman's eye and they married on 8 July 1896. (Tennant's first wife, Helen Gordon-Duff, had died of tuberculosis in 1982.) Tennant reacted petulantly on being excluded from Sir Henry Campbell-Bannerman's 1905 government, and for a while Asquith refused to do anything for Jack, whom he described as 'foolish and disloyal'. Tennant retaliated by becoming such a rebellious back-bencher that even his constituency association urged him to resign. 'I had done my very d-dest but my brothers are uninfluenceable,' lamented Margot. 'Jack has the best brains but poor darling he is not at all humble & is not big enough in a tight place.'[3]

'He is a serious, if not a very commanding personality,' judged *Vanity Fair*, 'and is capable of more than his appearance suggests. He thinks before he speaks, but thinks a great deal. And he laughs. He is not a big man.'[4] Dubbed 'the little Minister',[5] Tennant's appointment as secretary for Scotland sparked a by-election in the Berwickshire seat he had held since 1895. He told voters that 'To-day the nation has only one thought, how our men are doing over there – only one hope, to end the war successfully and as soon as possible.'[6] Tennant was successfully re-elected but the war meant domestic politics had been put on hold, so he dealt with nothing at the Scottish Office beyond routine wartime business and its implications for Scotland. His debut in parliament went well as he announced during a debate on Land Settlement a generous gift from the Duke of Sutherland of 12,000 acres to settle soldiers returning from the trenches.

'It never dawns on Eddy[7] that he owes everything to H.,' noted Margot in her diary, 'Jack also but in a lesser degree for tho' he would never have been in the Cabinet his industry, nature & enormous keenness & perpetual youth would always have got him in . . . if not so grossly self-centred & self-indulgent.'[8] In September, Tennant embarked on a general tour of the north of Scotland, visiting land settlement and afforestation schemes, but in December 1916 – with the war going badly and outmanoeuvred by David Lloyd George – Asquith resigned. This split the Liberals into two rival camps, led by a bitter Asquith and an exuberant Lloyd George, but with no compelling political or familial reason for retaining Tennant at the Scottish Office the new prime minister replaced him with the more substantial figure of Robert Munro, the lord advocate.

A hat trick of misfortune was completed when Tennant's eldest son Henry was killed in action the following year, and when Tennant's seat became Berwickshire and Haddingtonshire at the 1918 general election he was defeated by a coalition Liberal. He stood again in Central Glasgow in 1923, but quit politics after losing once more, retreating to his immense Whig mansion at Great Maytham in Kent. Tennant died shortly before his 70th birthday in November 1935. 'God bless them all wi' grace and gear', Robert Burns had written of the Tennants of the Glen, but Harold John Tennant – now the most obscure of 20th-century Scottish politicians – had little of either.

ROBERT MUNRO

10 DECEMBER 1916 – 24 OCTOBER 1922

The lord advocate

David Lloyd George's appointment of Robert Munro as his secretary for Scotland represented a return to the 'Parliament House Rule' so feared by his predecessor John Sinclair. The second (and last) lord advocate to be transferred to the Scottish Office, Munro was delighted with his promotion to the Cabinet. A vain and ambitious man, it also caused him some degree of anxiety. 'I hope you will not regard me as either ungrateful or unreasonable,' he wrote to Lloyd George just after his appointment, 'if I ask that my acceptance of the office of Secretary for Scotland should not, when . . . times are past, prejudice my claims to judicial preferment. Lord Dunedin [Andrew Graham Murray], under similar circumstances, I understand, made the same request.'[1] And like Dunedin Munro was assured (by the chancellor, Andrew Bonar Law) that this would indeed be the case. He arrived at the Scottish Office at an unenviable period in British politics, halfway through the First World War and following unrest both in Ireland and on Clydeside. Dismissed now as reactionary and weak,[2] Munro was in fact one of the most creative and talented Scottish secretaries since Lord Pentland – and equally as controversial.

Robert Munro was born on 28 May 1868 at Alness, Ross-shire, and grew up steeped in both the Scottish Highlands and the Kirk. 'Round it [his childhood] cluster the earliest, happiest, and most sacred of memories,' he later recalled. His mother, Margaret, was from Caithness, a daughter of the manse, and his Sutherland-born father, Alexander Rose Munro, was the local Free Church minister. Munro was fiercely proud of his Highland roots and in 1920 accepted the Freedom of Dingwall, saying that in 'all my plans and schemes for the future, the Highlands of Scotland will certainly not be forgotten. To them I am knit with bonds of birth and kinship which nothing can break. To them I owe anything that I am, and anything that I may have done. To them will be given my first thoughts in life and my last thoughts in death.'[3]

Munro was educated privately and then at Aberdeen Grammar School. He became active in student politics at Edinburgh University, being elected president both of the students' representative council and of the university's Liberal association. Munro graduated in 1889 and soon began his legal training, moving to London to become an official receiver in bankruptcy within the Board of Trade. He was called to the Scottish Bar on 3 November 1893, but as an advocate Munro's practice was successful without being extensive. In 1907 he was appointed as counsel to the Inland Revenue; in 1908, an advocate depute and in 1910, a king's counsel. Munro also continued his political activities, assisting the Liberals at by-elections, and he was himself unexpectedly elected for the Wick Burghs at the general election of January 1910, an event he later said caused him considerable personal and professional embarrassment. In October 1913 Munro became lord advocate, a position he enjoyed not only for its pomp and ceremony but because of its extensive influence over the Scottish legal fraternity. He was a colourful figure, with the familiar refined features of a music hall star. Contemporary photographs show a man who is both amused and amusing.

Munro turned out to be the longest-serving secretary for Scotland since Lord Pentland, holding the post for six years until his resignation in October 1922. Although he was a strong Liberal with reforming instincts, Munro was also inclined to be conservative when confronted with industrial unrest. Nowhere was this more prevalent than on Clydeside in the west of Scotland. Trouble had been growing there since 1915 when a shipping strike saw some shop stewards imprisoned. Thomas McKinnon Wood had tasked Lord Balfour of Burleigh with investigating the situation, and the former Scottish secretary concluded that a nation which had failed to give workmen decent housing could not expect good labour relations.[4] The situation was not helped by rapidly rising rents in areas producing munitions for the war. Wood had reported to the Cabinet on 17 November 1915 that 'the agitation is growing, and I think it is necessary that a prompt decision should be taken by the Government, otherwise there are signs that the demands for interference will become more clamant and will expand in scope and character.'[5] He concluded that working-class rentals should be limited to their pre-war level. During this whole period the Scottish Office proved itself remarkably feeble in tackling the situation and had arguably allowed the problem to get out of control. Both Wood's manner and Jack Tennant's lack of political clout had led to the Scottish Office being bypassed by the Ministry of Munitions, a department unhappy at being left to take all the flak. But, sitting in Dover House, Munro was not impressed by these displays of working-class solidarity and instead grew increasingly alarmed. In December 1915 he had supported (but doubted the effectiveness of) an attempt to prosecute the authors of a Clyde Workers' Committee leaflet opposing the Munitions Act. When Glasgow magistrates asked Munro (now secretary for Scotland) to ban a planned meeting of the Central Workers and Soldiers Committee for Glasgow in August 1917, he brought the request before the War Cabinet, which agreed to a ban on 8 August. The Scottish secretary also believed that the 40 hours' strike of January–February 1919, which aimed to reduce the working week, was the beginning of a revolutionary uprising and he urged the Cabinet to draft in 2,000 special constables to protect public utilities in Glasgow. On Friday 31 January 1919 around 60,000 demonstrators gathered in George Square to hear the lord provost's reply to their demands. While the strikers' deputation was in the City Chambers, the police mounted an apparently unprovoked attack on the demonstrators, felling unarmed men and women with their batons. The demonstrators quickly retaliated with their fists, iron railings and broken bottles, and forced the police into a retreat. During the ensuing riot, many protestors and policemen were injured and prominent strike leaders, including Emanuel Shinwell, William Gallacher and David Kirkwood, were arrested and charged with incitement to riot. The War Cabinet met on the afternoon of 'Bloody Friday' with a shaken Scottish secretary in attendance. The minute of that meeting famously recorded: 'The Secretary for Scotland said that, in his opinion, it was more clear than ever that it was a misnomer to call the situation in Glasgow a strike – it was a Bolshevist rising. It was, he thought, of limited dimensions in numbers, if not in effect.'[6]

It was, to say the least, an overreaction from the secretary for Scotland, although understandable in the context of wartime and following, as it did, the recent revolution in Russia. But, in the event, no further action was required from the Cabinet as 12,000 troops, six tanks and 100 motor lorries were already on their way to Glasgow. The second city of the Empire was soon alive with troops but the protest fizzled out, although the alleged uprising quickly became a potent political symbol for Scotland's growing labour movement.

The unrest did at least focus political minds in terms of housing policy, although this in itself created more political and logistical difficulties. Again, the roots lay with Munro's predecessor but one, McKinnon Wood. In response to growing unease about Scotland's appalling slum housing, Wood had appointed a Royal Commission on Housing in Scotland back in 1912; it reported in 1917 and its conclusion was groundbreaking: 'the state must at once take steps to make good the housing shortage and improve housing conditions, and this can only be done by or through the machinery of the public authorities'.[7] The coalition Cabinet largely accepted its findings and soon turned its attention to preparing 'homes fit for heroes'; the result was the 1919 Housing Act and a Scottish Board of Health to oversee its implementation in Scotland. This was in itself a political compromise, as Munro was keen to avoid possible subordination by a Scottish minister for health, to which a new health department in England would inevitably lead. Instead, the Scottish Office got a junior minister for the first time in the form of John William Pratt, who became parliamentary under-secretary for health (for Scotland) on 8 August 1919.[8]

The Housing Act had introduced government subsidies to local authorities for construction purposes, but the response was sluggish and in June 1920 plans to put 50,000 ex-servicemen to work in the building trade to revive house building ran into trade union trouble. Munro prepared a memo for the Cabinet on 9 June 1920, which said that 'Unless some very drastic measures are taken, the Government will be faced with a huge annual financial deficit. So far as Scotland is concerned, the deficit per house in future is likely to exceed £60 per annum unless costs are reduced.'[9] He also pointed to local authority hostility, the 'hopelessly deficient' supply of labour in Scotland, and a 50 per cent increase in building costs since the previous August. By July 1921 the Cabinet had decided to slash government spending due to the economic depression, and it resolved to withdraw its subsidy under the 1919 Housing Act. Munro was neither invited to the meeting (he was busy introducing the government's Railway Bill), nor was he immediately informed of the U-turn. He was furious and, at a subsequent meeting of ministers on housing policy on 13 July 1921, said his 'position was a difficult one because he would now be obliged to make a statement completely divergent from the policy which he had advocated only three or four weeks ago'. At that time, the Scottish secretary added, he had been in complete ignorance of the proposed change in housing policy and 'wished to make the strongest protest against his not having been summoned to the meeting of the Finance Committee of the Cabinet on which the housing policy of the country was revised, and he desired his protest to be placed on record'.[10]

In other areas, however, Munro found it possible to utilise his reforming instincts. Scotland's voluntary schools – mostly Roman Catholic institutions – had long been a source of concern for educationalists. Although government grants had previously been available, generally these schools were much worse off than those under state supervision. In 1917 Munro drafted a memo for the War Cabinet outlining proposals to deal with the problem:

There is no question that, because of the inadequate resources of the Managers, Roman Catholic children, who constitute upwards of $1/8^{th}$ of the school population in Scotland, are being deprived of the opportunities of education which are afforded by the public schools. There are only two possible remedies for this state of matters.

1) that state-aid to denominational schools should be provided in much fuller measure than to public schools . . . This solution, having regard to the state of public opinion in Scotland, is clearly out the question.

2) There remains the other solution, namely, that denominational schools providing elementary education should be compulsorily transferred to the local education authority and should be managed by them in all respects as public schools, but provision however being made for religious education according to the views of the former Managers, given by teachers who are acceptable to the representatives of these Managers, both as regards faith and character. This is the solution which I propose.[11]

For a son of the manse, and a Free Church one at that, it was a remarkably far-sighted proposal. It was endorsed by the Cabinet, and the subsequent Education (Scotland) Bill also proposed raising the school leaving age to 15, finally removing the anachronistic 'Scotch' from the Education Department, and creating 38 directly elected (by proportional representation) education authorities to replace school boards. In moving the Second Reading of the Bill Munro was on eloquent form: 'What is the main object of the Bill?' he asked rhetorically. 'It is, in a sentence, the better education of the whole people of Scotland, irrespective of social class, age, sex, or place of residence.' Getting into his stride, he waxed lyrical on his vision for modern Scottish education: 'Education shall become more and more a common possession, as befits a true democracy . . . we shall mobilise the intellectual resources of the nation as against those arduous times which are in front of us, when brains developed by education will be of more and more account.' Munro added that the provision for denominational schools was vital to the Bill:

Their separate schools are, generally speaking, inferior as regards building and equipment, their teachers are zealous but poorly paid, their provision of secondary schools is totally inadequate, and the educational outlook of the mass of their children is unduly narrowing . . . It is clearly not in the national interest that such a proportion of the population in Scotland should be left out of account in our endeavour to raise the general level of education for the mass of the people.

And the secretary for Scotland concluded on an evangelical note:

> My one aim, while I am responsible for education in Scotland, is to ensure, not
> only in the interests of Scotland, but of the world, that our country shall not lag
> behind in the educational race, but shall be in the van, which has always been
> in the past her appointed place. To that end let us strive. Let us have faith and
> vision in the matter. Let us repress all niggling and destructive criticism and
> unite in improving and strengthening the Bill in committee. If we do this, and
> place the Bill on the statute book, I am confident that future generations will
> remember with gratitude the Parliament which placed it there.[12]

By October 1918, the Bill had cleared the Commons and the Scottish Grand
Committee, but risked being held up in the Lords. Munro begged Lloyd
George to let it pass and, when it did, he wrote again on 15 November
imploring the prime minister to mention the Bill in a forthcoming speech
listing his government's achievements: 'It is unquestionably the greatest
educational measure affecting Scotland which has been passed for fifty
years. Indeed, it is not too much to say that it is one of the most important
Scottish measures which has been passed during that period.'[13]

   The Vatican had initially reserved its position on the Bill, but on being
assured it would not prevent the building of any new Catholic schools,
they accepted it in October. Sir John Struthers – head of the Scottish
Education Department since 1904 – then opened negotiations with
Catholic schools to come under state control. But while the Education
(Scotland) Act was impressive in tone, it was not without problems.
Its aims of raising the school leaving age to 15, and of developing
vocational and further education, were not realised in the years immediately following the war. Educational costs had also risen, as had
teachers' salaries, and Munro was held responsible. 'To-day in some
quarters I am being blamed for its passing,' he later told a meeting of the
Edinburgh Merchant Company, but 'If it had not been passed I would, I
think, also have been blamed – and with good cause. It was a necessary
measure in the reconstruction of a world bruised and battered by war.'[14]
Contemporary historians have also been unkind, pointing out that the
new education authorities only lasted for a decade, until they were
brought under direct local authority control in 1929. But that is a
minor quibble when compared with the Act's integration of Catholic
schools within the existing state system. That endures to this day, although
not without occasional rumblings of discontent from Munro's Liberal
successors.

   These reforms had upset the established Church of Scotland, which
viewed such sops to Rome as potentially dangerous to its religious

supremacy. As if to make amends, Munro also guided the Church of Scotland Bill through parliament in 1921. As a young advocate, the Scottish secretary had acted for the United Free Church in the property litigation arising from the church union of 1900. This Bill allowed the Kirk, without recourse to parliament, to adopt articles of a constitution, helping to clear the way for a merger with the United Free Church in 1929. 'You can never hope for complete unanimity amongst Scotsmen,' joked Munro at the Bill's Second Reading, 'for the Scot, as we know, has an independent mind – and certainly not amongst Scottish ecclesiastics, because, if I may say so with respect, they have exceptionally independent minds.'[15]

Also blessed (or burdened) with an independent mind was the liberal industrialist Lord Leverhulme. In November 1917 the Scottish secretary let it be known that he was considering a proposal from the Lewis Crofters Association for the government to purchase the island of Lewis as a 'colony for crofters, fishermen and cottars to settle on and cultivate after the war.' But the previous month Leverhulme had landed on the island with very different plans. He soon purchased Lewis and, in the summer of 1918, the Scottish Office began negotiations with him to break up some of the farms using powers under Lord Pentland's Small Landholders (Scotland) Act. Inevitably, Leverhulme was hostile to this idea, having already formulated his own scheme of industrial and transportation improvements to revolutionise the lives of the island's 30,000 inhabitants. The Board of Agriculture for Scotland argued that both schemes could operate concurrently, and Munro was anxious not to alienate Leverhulme, who, as the self-made 'Soap Man', was a powerful figure. But the Scottish secretary and Leverhulme soon reached stalemate. 'It does seem a pity', commented Munro, 'that the whole future of the islands for years to come should be jeopardised, and indeed wrecked, on account of a difference of policy regarding two small farms.'[16] In the meantime, soldiers had returned from the trenches to find themselves with a new landlord, and land raids broke out across the island. In August 1919 Leverhulme threatened to stop all his development work unless the raiding ceased and the Scottish Office changed its policy. Munro too came under pressure, with MPs demanding to know why the Scottish secretary was not using his powers to acquire land. 'It is true that I can take Lord Leverhulme's land under compulsory powers,' Munro told the Commons. 'But if I do that, the result will be that Lord Leverhulme's operations in the islands will not only be suspended, but permanently stopped. As at present advised, I do not feel disposed at the present moment to undertake that responsibility.'[17] Munro was convinced he had all-party support for breaking up the farms, but also realised that Leverhulme too had strong backing. 'I felt that basically Stornoway was for Leverhulme,' he later told the writer Nigel Nicolson. 'But that the country people were uncommitted.'[18] Munro let it be known that should Leverhulme have any of the land raiders imprisoned, as was his right, he would release them the same day, as was his right as Scottish secretary. Leverhulme's hands were tied and the raiders felt vindicated, taking over land at will with no fear of the consequences. He responded by ordering the suspension of all improvement works on the island, cleverly giving the impression that it was Munro's refusal to properly condemn the raiders which had forced his hand. *The Times* commented on 22 November 1920 that the Scottish Office 'must be rather a sleepy retreat' to have allowed things to reach breaking point. Munro at last gave way on 22 January 1921, writing to Leverhulme suggesting a compromise:

> I have come to the conclusion that it is in the interests of the community as a whole that the assurances which you seek should be given. Accordingly . . . I am prepared on behalf of the Government, to undertake that the compulsory powers of taking your land for small-holdings, shall not, while your schemes go on, be put in operation . . . Should your development schemes for any reason not proceed, the hands of the Government will of course be free.[19]

This amounted to a compromise on both sides, with Leverhulme agreeing to surrender six farms for use as smallholdings, and Munro pledging not to divide farms near Stornoway while also promising that the issue would not be raised again for ten years. The works were due to resume in April 1921, but in the meantime Leverhulme's company Lever Brothers had run into financial difficulty and he suspended some of the work begun in the interim. Munro sensed his opportunity and wrote to Leverhulme a few days later saying he considered their previous agreement to have been breached: 'In my view the latter contingency has, through no fault of yours, now arisen, and I am bound to reconsider the situation – freed from the undertaking above mentioned. In the circumstances as they are now, I feel that I would not be justified in refraining any longer from putting into operation a generous measure of land settlement.'[20] The letter deeply hurt Leverhulme, who felt, as land raids continued, that it was in fact Munro who had breached the agreement. But by October 1921 he gave way, worn down by events and diminishing local support. 'The whole affair became a dialectical tussle', concluded the incident's historian Nigel Nicolson, 'between Leverhulme, Munro, and, in its final phase, Lord Novar, in which the islanders themselves ceased to play much part.'[21] Lord Pentland's beloved land legislation had again proved controversial, only this time in practice rather than in theory.

Despite these power struggles Munro remained acutely aware of his junior political status, having only joined the Cabinet in 1919 (he was excluded from the previous War Cabinet). And although the creation of a Scottish Board of Health was widely welcomed, the press still lamented the Scottish Office's lack of prestige. Scottish supply (budget) debates, noted the *Scotsman*, were only held on 'inconvenient, odd days where there was no other business'.[22] After the 1918 'khaki' general election, Munro faced even more pressure from parliament, local authorities and the press, portions of each believing Scottish administration was fundamentally defective.

The secretary for Scotland, who always had half an eye on self-aggrandisement, wrote to Lloyd George at the end of December arguing that he be elevated to a secretary of state. The news, he said, 'would be very well received north of the Tweed, and would be generally interpreted as conveying some recognition of the great part played by Scotland in the War'.[23] In July 1919 a Bill was introduced to increase the number of secretaries of state, including one for Scotland, but it quickly stalled after running into opposition from Liberal MPs appalled at such extravagance during a period of financial restraints.[24] Munro then tried another approach, suggesting a fundamental restructuring of the Scottish departments with three divisions each headed up by an assistant secretary. He believed this would highlight the Scottish secretary's ministerial importance as the guardian of Scottish interests, but while the Treasury acknowledged that some reorganisation was desirable, it made clear that it was not considered a priority.

Munro felt more of his powers slip away as a new Ministry of Transport assumed control of Scotland's ferries, roads and trains, while electricity was also moved under Whitehall supervision. Yet he enjoyed his new Cabinet status, however limited, memorably telling an audience that it forced him 'to think of Upper Silesia as well as, let us say, Auchtermuchty'.[25] But even when the Cabinet met in Inverness Town Hall (the only recorded meeting of the Cabinet outside London) in September 1921 to discuss the Irish question, there was no sense that Munro was among colleagues on home turf; he was merely a junior member of the government summoned like any other by the prime minister.[26] Inevitably demands for Scottish home rule once again resurfaced, this time given added momentum by the Government of Ireland Act in 1920, which created not only an Irish Free State but a largely autonomous Northern Ireland parliament. If Ulster could have home rule, argued some, why not

Scotland? Once again, a private member's bill (Sir Henry Cowan's) reached a Second Reading in parliament, and Munro appeared to be sympathetic:

> I was in favour of this principle long before I entered this House . . . and my experience as a Minister has strengthened my belief in the principle still further . . . I see no solution of the difficulty except on the lines of the establishment of a Scottish Legislature and a Scottish Executive. That is my own personal view, but I know it is shared by the Prime Minister, who, when receiving deputations from Scotland, on more than one occasion in my presence, has avowed himself as a definite supporter of the principle which we are discussing to-day.

Too often, Munro added, Scotland had 'to be content with the crumbs which fall from the rich man's table'. But, he concluded, 'I blame no one; I blame the system.' Although the motion was granted a free vote, Munro predictably argued that such a radical constitutional change could not be left to a mere private members' bill. What's more, he argued, it made no provision for disputes between the two institutions. 'What is to become of the Secretary for Scotland?' he asked. 'Is that office to continue? Is he to remain in the United Kingdom Parliament as a member, and to sit in the Cabinet of the United Kingdom?' The Scottish secretary concluded by referring to a motion which had established a Speaker's Conference on Devolution the previous year. 'I am informed that that Conference is now upon the eve of reporting,' he told MPs. 'It seems to me that it would be barely respectful or indeed decent to proceed with this Bill to its subsequent stages without awaiting and considering the report of Mr Speaker's Conference when it is ready for issue and for consideration.'[27] It reported just a few weeks later on 27 April 1920,[28] proposing two devolutionary schemes – one from Speaker (James William) Lowther,[29] and another from Murray Macdonald, a member of the conference – both of which had 13 firm supporters and five more uncertain proponents.

The first, in the name of the Speaker, proposed an experimental system of subordinate 'Grand Councils' for Scotland, Wales and England consisting of two chambers, the 'Council of the Commons' and the 'Council of Peers'. The Speaker suggested reserving the spring and summer months for ordinary sessions of parliament and autumn for the new assemblies, while the UK parliament remained free to override any Grand Council Bill. Macdonald's scheme instead proposed similarly subordinate, but permanent, parliaments for each nation. *The Times* was broadly supportive, saying both plans had much to recommend them although the Speaker's was 'less likely to lead to large expenditure on new legislative buildings', while warning that 'electors called upon to choose a single member to represent them at Westminster and in the local legislature would be likely to be guided by local rather than central and national interests'. But, the editorial concluded, 'For the present, as we have already implied, there seems to be a good reason for supporting the Speaker's scheme, if only on the grounds that in so radical a departure from the constitutional practice of the kingdom it is well to look before we leap.'[30] But no official reaction from Munro was ever recorded and his promised debate never took place in the Commons, where neither scheme so much as received a mention. The Speaker's Conference on Devolution effectively neutralised devolution as a political issue for the next quarter of a century.

At a meeting of the Liberal Roxburgh and Selkirk Council in St Boswells in April 1922 delegates resolved not to support a coalition candidate (i.e. the incumbent) at the next general election, effectively deselecting Munro.[31] The secretary for Scotland hit back the following month, saying the St Boswell's resolution had not cost him a single hour's sleep. 'I was condemned unheard,' he said. 'The only effective policy of the Independent Liberal party to-day would seem to be one of excommunication. I ask, what have I or the Government of which, despite this resolution, I am proud to be a member done to merit this sentence of excommunication? The resolution does not enlighten me. It is silent on the subject.'[32]

Munro was nearing the end of an eventful six years at the Scottish Office, the last few of which were marked by personal tragedy. On 19 July 1920 his mother died in Edinburgh, and just over a month later his wife Edith also passed away at their home in London, having been seriously ill with heart trouble. Munro quickly recovered from the loss, and just a year later he became engaged to a French woman, Olga Marie Grumler, marrying her on 29 October. Against the backdrop of a bitter coal strike, his old financial and career anxieties had also returned to haunt him. Munro had rather shamefully used his mother's illness to lobby for a salary hike,[33] and the Scottish secretary also began to remind Lloyd George of previous assurances as to his claims to judicial advancement. 'So far as I know there is no precedent for the existing situation,' he wrote, giving the prime minister an unwelcome history lesson, 'except that which Dunedin[34] himself provided. He became S. for S. after being Lord Advocate, and, when the Lord President's position opened, he was appointed to it. Should my claims be overlooked . . . I shall be no better off when the next vacancy occurs.'[35] It seems Lloyd George ignored, or at the very most, appeased Munro, for on 25 March 1922 he wrote again to the prime minister: 'I have faith in the future of the coalition. I have faced many risks now. Delivering on you & your policy. I am prepared to face still more.'[36] But later that year he had again become impatient, a feeling no doubt fuelled by the impending collapse of the coalition. 'It seems to me that I have come to the parting of the ways,' wrote Munro, with a typical hint of melodrama. 'If I had a private fortune or a business – which I have not – I should prefer to remain in political life. But when I reflect on the financial condition, in which I should be if I lost office, I am really alarmed.'[37] The lord justice clerk, Lord Scott Dickson, had died the previous month and Lloyd George had been procrastinating over appointing his successor. Munro's claims were good, but the timing was not ideal from the prime minister's point of view, faced as he was with the likely withdrawal of the Conservatives from his increasingly fragile government. Nevertheless, Munro was installed as the new lord justice clerk and president of the second division of the Court of Session on 19 October 1922, with the judicial title of Lord Alness. Ill health forced him to retire in 1933, but his subsequent recovery allowed him to accept a barony in June 1934, again with the title of Lord Alness. Munro moved to London and began a new parliamentary career, this time aloof from party politics, and he introduced a reform of Scottish divorce law which became law in 1938. He also busied himself with the usual commission appointments which often accompany the life of a former Cabinet minister, but the advent of the Second World War finally concluded Alness's judicial career. He was appointed a lord-in-waiting in May 1940, so that he could take charge of government legislation in the House of Lords, a position he held until July 1945. In later life Munro made his home in Bournemouth, where he died in a nursing home on 6 October 1955.[38]

In many ways Robert Munro represented a rapidly disappearing political era. He was the last properly Liberal Scottish secretary, in that his party was still a significant force, both in Scotland and in the UK. Always prone to hyperbole, Munro had seen it as his fate to preside over the Scottish Office during a 'dark and critical time'. 'I trust, however, that the clouds are now beginning to pass away,' he said in an inaugural address to the Philosophical Institution of Edinburgh. 'Whether that be so or not, it will be the duty of the Scottish Office to carry on, and to see that in fair or in stormy weather the interests of Scotland are properly considered and conserved.'[39] He indulged in similar rhetoric on accepting the Freedom of Dingwall in early 1920, an honour he seems to have valued above all others. His speech on that occasion serves as a fitting, if a little egocentric, epitaph:

> It [the Scottish Office] is a great office, involving great responsibilities, and no one realises more than I do my inadequacy for the tasks which have devolved

upon me, and which confront me in the future. It has been my lot to serve as Lord Advocate and as Secretary for Scotland in war-time when problems more bewildering and responsibilities more crushing were laid upon Ministers than upon any of their predecessors. It has been a time to make, not to follow, precedents. I desire to acknowledge with gratitude the support and confidence which I have been fortunate to receive from the public and the Press of Scotland throughout these difficult years. Without these, I could not have carried on; with these, the burden though heavy, can be borne. And if I can confer any lasting benefit on my fellow countrymen, then I shall feel that my life has not been lived in vain.[40]

1st Viscount Novar

The governor-general

As the year 1922 drew to a close, British politics was in a perilous state. At a now famous meeting in the Carlton Club on 19 October 1922, Austen Chamberlain lost his plea for the Conservatives to remain in coalition with David Lloyd George's Liberals by 185 votes to 88, and Andrew Bonar Law, a Glaswegian by birth but Canadian by upbringing, became party leader. Law, alongside Stanley Baldwin, had led the revolt aided by the influential MP for the Ayr Burghs, Sir George Younger.[1] Only four other Scottish Unionists voted with Younger, while 17 backed Chamberlain, including the Scottish whip, Sir John Gilmour. Lloyd George resigned as prime minister the same day, and the age-old problem of finding a Scottish Unionist MP able enough to fill the Scottish Office began.

'Jack Gilmour came to see me,' recorded the Earl of Crawford, a Conservative minister, in his diary. 'He says George Younger is in a fright about Scotland, and furious that Jack supports Chamberlain. George offered Jack the Secretaryship for Scotland – twice! It was loyal of him to refuse it, for the offer must have been very tempting – however he did so . . . The Scottish members are independent of London, and a large majority of the Unionists are anxious to maintain the coalition understanding.'[2] The ultimate solution to the Scottish Office vacancy perhaps took that spirit just a little too far, as the suggestion of Viscount Novar began to be aired. Novar had recently returned from abroad, having served since before the war as governor-general of Australia. But there were drawbacks: not only was he a peer but he was also a lifelong Liberal. Two other names were also floated, that of Lord Linlithgow, son of the former Scottish secretary, and that of the leading Catholic peer Lord Lovat.[3] Sir George (who had himself refused the offer) had by now been charged with finding a suitable candidate, and sent the prime minister a memo summarising his recommendations on 21 October 1922:

> I find it is not thought wise to appoint Lovat. He is an able fellow and would, I think, fill the post very well, but it is believed that it would greatly inflame

Scottish feeling if a Catholic occupied the position. Novar would be an excellent man and a most typical Scotchman, if we could induce him to accept Office. He has been absolutely with us ever since he returned from Australia, and if we could secure him, it would be rather a score.[4]

Sir George added that Lord Clinton[5] was admirable, but perceived as more English than Scottish, while the Scottish Office might be regarded as too big a job for Linlithgow. 'I should put these three in the order of Novar first, Clinton second and Linlithgow third,' concluded Sir George. 'I am afraid it would be imprudent to touch Lovat, and we must not add to our difficulties in the North.' But Lovat would not have been the first Roman Catholic Scottish secretary: Salisbury, despite his High Anglican beliefs, had appointed the Marquis of Lothian in 1887. Finally, in November 1922, Bonar Law unveiled a smaller Cabinet of only 16, including five peers – many of them obscure. One of this number was Viscount Novar. 'There are too many peers in the cabinet,' wrote Crawford. 'Novar to the Scottish Office – a lifelong Liberal who though reticent on political matters during the last year or two has never declared himself a Conservative. A truly amazing appointment showing our poverty in Scotland. While he joins us . . . there are still practical proofs of coalition!'[6] Indeed, the handover from Robert Munro to Novar was all the more natural considering the two were distantly related.[7] 'The first feeling evoked by the announcement will be surprise, followed by satisfaction,' declared the *Scotsman*. 'Lord Novar was out of touch with domestic politics during the seven years he spent in Australia, and since his return home he has taken no concern with party affairs though it has been generally understood that he found himself out of sympathy with his former political associates.'[8]

Born in Kirkcaldy on 6 March 1860, Ronald Crauford Munro Ferguson was the eldest of three sons and one daughter of Colonel Robert Ferguson of Raith. Ronald was educated at home, and in 1875 he joined the 1st Fife Light Horse, later being gazetted to the Grenadier Guards after attending Sandhurst. He served in the Guards for five years until leaving to embark on a long-planned political career, although his initial efforts to become an MP did not bode well. Elected in 1884 at a by-election in Ross and Cromarty, Munro Ferguson was defeated just a year later by a Crofters candidate, and on moving to Dunbartonshire in 1886, he was again defeated following the Liberal split over Irish home rule. He had, however, become friendly with Lord Rosebery and on the latter's intervention was finally returned at a by-election for the Leith burghs a few weeks later (Gladstone having surrendered the seat which he had won as well as Midlothian). Munro Ferguson held the seat until 1914 and associated himself in parliament with figures like Richard Burdon Haldane, Sir Edward Grey and H. H. Asquith, a group which later became known as the Liberal Imperialists. The 'Lib Imps' looked upon Rosebery as their natural leader, and Munro Ferguson became particularly close to him, serving as his parliamentary private secretary during his two spells as foreign secretary in 1886, and from 1892–94. During Rosebery's subsequent, but brief, premiership, Munro Ferguson was a junior whip, with special responsibility for Scotland. But he found politics frustrating and proved inept at liaising with Rosebery's numerous Liberal opponents, and found himself without a job when the Liberals returned to office in 1905. Munro Ferguson's longed-for ministerial career now seemed out of reach, although he was granted a privy councillorship in 1910. His relations with Rosebery also grew strained, as his patron's political behaviour became increasingly erratic. Munro Ferguson feared his career was being stunted by this continuing association, and in 1912 rather coldly decided to stop speaking to his old friend. 'What a strange idea of friendship and a strange friend',[9] wrote Rosebery wistfully on learning of his former protégé's decision. Munro Ferguson instead set his sights on an imperial career. He had declined the governorship of South Australia in 1895 but later sought the same status in Bombay. This, too, seemed to elude Munro Ferguson, and instead he had to settle for being provost of Kirkcaldy from 1906–14.

Ironically, the First World War reversed his bad luck when Asquith – who did not think much of the ambitious MP – made him governor-general of Australia in February 1914. It was a risky appointment given Munro Ferguson's short temper, and indeed he was initially resented by some Australian socialists who felt they had been short-changed with a failed British politician. But he quickly proved himself one of the ablest governors to date. Grey-haired, tall, with a strong physique and an upright, military bearing, the new governor-general had a 'splendid presence'. Munro Ferguson was also a successful forester and, like Gladstone, would chop down a tree for exercise. His private secretary later described him as 'essentially kind', but 'choleric' and 'subject to outbursts of temper . . . often followed by quite touching displays of remorse'.[10] Like Lord Hopetoun, Munro Ferguson was not an impressive orator, but he spoke vigorously on public occasions of the need to fight for Empire. He arrived in Australia in May, and was at once faced with a request for dissolution of both houses of the federal Australian parliament. This he granted and Australia's role in the war, which broke out during the ensuing election campaign, proved to be Munro Ferguson's finest hour, offering a platform for his somewhat abrasive strengths as a leader. He was cautious in his dealings with two prime ministers, initially a fellow

Scot, Andrew Fisher, and later William Morris Hughes. He supported the latter's unsuccessful attempts to introduce conscription, though not his tactics, and a referendum failed to produce a resolution. Munro Ferguson was annoyed that he did not personally represent Australia at the Imperial War Conference in 1918 and wanted to resign, only being persuaded to remain in his post until 1920, partly to oversee the visit of the Prince of Wales. 'One thing I won't do,' he wrote to his friend William Anstruther-Gray, 'and that is to rejoin you in the H of C. I hated the place so much for some years before I left it that I will never look upon it again.'[11] His elevation to the peerage as Viscount Novar of Raith in December 1920 neatly avoided the need, and, having completed his swing from Liberal to Conservative,[12] the Unionists granted Novar the ministerial career he had always dreamed of, as he become secretary for Scotland under Bonar Law's short-lived premiership. He was the second Australian governor-general to move from the Dominion to Dover House, the Marquis of Linlithgow having followed a similar career path 17 years earlier.

Novar returned to parliament to find Scotland, and in particular Clyde-side, in a pretty shabby state. Initially, he supported Bonar Law's tight fiscal controls and was even optimistic, declaring that Scotland would soon enjoy a boom from private investment. But as more and more delegations trundled in and out of Dover House with tales of industrial woe, Novar soon changed his mind. In Thatcherite parlance, the new Scottish secretary went from being 'one of us', to requiring a towel remarkably quickly. A case in point was Scottish housing, which had still to recover from the U-turn over government subsidies in 1919. Novar 'reluctantly concurred' with legislation which set out to subsidise each new house by £6 over the next 20 years, but it ran into immediate difficulties with Scottish local authorities, who complained that building costs in Scotland were higher due to adverse market and atmospheric conditions. The secretary for Scotland did not accept this at first, but by 27 March 1923 he had 'reluctantly come to the conclusion that a higher rate of subsidy would be necessary in Scotland if full advantage of the Act was to be obtained'.[13]

The wider concern of Clydeside unrest also began to occupy Novar's mind, and he sent a rather alarmist memo to the Cabinet on 31 July 1923:

I am gravely concerned at the present conditions prevailing in Glasgow and the other great industrial centres of the Clyde . . . The not unnatural consequence is that there is at present existing in this area a spirit of hopelessness and sullen discontent which is very disquieting. This area as my colleagues know has always been one of the storm centres in the Kingdom, and unless some substantial contribution of work can be made to provide employment to a number of these men, I am very apprehensive as to what may happen in the coming winter.[14]

Novar's Cabinet colleagues were largely unsympathetic, and many refused to believe there was any potent political dimension to the unrest. The Scottish secretary's pleas for more investment in shipping were also rejected; it would disrupt the market, claimed some sceptical ministers, and besides, the shipyards did not want special treatment. The Cabinet, however, approved Novar's memo and charged J. W. Peck, chairman of the Scottish Board of Health, with investigating possible relief schemes. There was immediate hostility from numerous government departments, all wary of the likely recommendation (bigger subsidies). C. A. Montague Barlow, from the Ministry of Labour, wrote to Novar claiming that he was not unsympathetic but had decided against 'any special form of State subsidy'.[15] The Conservative minister, Sir Laming Worthington-Evans also wrote, warning that any such scheme would produce 'fictitious activity in the yards' and threaten the government's policy of deflation. 'I am anxious to flatten out the depression,' he told Novar, 'but if a direct subsidy is given as part of the cost of the ship I cannot see how we can refuse to give a similar subsidy to any manufacturer in nearly all the staple industries . . . We would be temporarily prosperous, living again on our capital. We should not have cured the evil of unemployment though we might have postponed its manifestation at the cost of increasing its virulence.'[16] Novar replied on 5 September 1923, agreeing with Evans but protesting that 'The fact is that the range of staple industries and minor industries here is much less varied than in England and our eggs are too much in the one basket, therefore the collapse in shipbuilding and engineering has produced a crisis more grave even than in the South.'[17] This was to become a common Scottish Office argument, even into the 1980s. Novar, perhaps through desperation, also began to name-drop to shore up his case. He wrote to Evans again later that month, saying that the King had spoken with him about unemployment, a subject on which he expressed 'deep anxiety'. 'I had another report from Glasgow,' continued Novar. 'Stress is laid on the need for exceptional treatment for "Black Spots" & for even more generous backing for imaginative undertakings.'[18]

In October 1923, Peck also began a 'discreet inquiry' into the possibility of a government grant to help Clydeside shipbuilders develop a new motorised liner service to Novar's old stomping ground of Australia. But the design and construction of the engines required were still at the experimental stage and Novar's claim that this justified a government subsidy sounded unconvincing. The Post Office and the Board of Trade both seemed tentatively keen on the idea, if only to speed up mail services. The idea was discussed at the Unemployment Committee of the Cabinet on 8 January 1924, but, predictably, it was rejected.

Throughout his career as a Liberal MP Novar had been a cautious backer of Irish home rule, and later an enthusiastic proponent of it for Scotland. In a debate on home rule in February 1912, Munro Ferguson had launched a scathing attack on the record of the Scottish Office.

> Its failure through twenty-five years is alone a strong reason in favour of Scottish national self-government . . . Bureaucracy has no enthusiasm. It destroys it. Great reforms are carried by a living administration, are secured for the country through the dogged, persistent zeal of the representative individual whose place is found mainly under a free system of representative Government. That free system we have not got.[19]

Novar would not be the first Scottish secretary to alter his thinking on devolution,[20] but he at least retained a desire to tidy up Scottish administration. The appointment of a junior Scottish Office minister for health[21] in 1919 had weakened the Edinburgh board system, something Novar hated even more than Robert Munro, describing it as 'a rabbit warren of Departments'. He complained that his political control of them was 'thin' and 'indirect' and instead wanted Scotland to be administered by a 'directorate', centralising the boards on a 'cheap, but convenient slum site'.[22] Novar got as far as getting leave to introduce a Reorganisation of Offices (Scotland) Bill on 30 July 1923, which would have scrapped the Scottish Board of Health and established a new department with its own director, but the issue fell with the Conservative government just months later. Meanwhile, the Scottish Grand Committee had been suspended owing to the weakness of the Unionists in Scotland, with even its 15 English MPs having failed to produce a Tory majority. As secretary for Scotland, Novar was never in a strong position, either politically or intellectually.

Early in 1923 the chancellor, Stanley Baldwin, sparked a political crisis by bouncing the Cabinet into accepting an American offer on Britain's war debt, without the prime minister's prior knowledge. Bonar Law said he would rather resign than support what he viewed as a fait accompli, but was supported by just two of his ministers, one of whom was his old friend Novar. The Scottish secretary was later left as Bonar Law's only backer when leading members of the Cabinet held an informal meeting without the prime minister. Novar later described the incident to Rosebery, with whom he was now back on friendly terms:

> I went straight to B.L. to see him before . . . a complete min of the Meeting, which of course he knew all about, arrived. He said "well something must be done. What do you think of it". I hadn't the knowledge to justify trying to offer advice. An hour later he told the Cabinet he gave in. Derby said "Thank God" & the rest were jubilant. Had not B.L. been dying probably Baldwin wd have had to resign, but it would have been hard to keep the Cabinet together & the Coalition might have found its feet again . . . If Baldwin was hoodwinked so was England & Winston now joins in his praise.[23]

Baldwin persuaded a humiliated Bonar Law to withdraw his resignation, but the prime minister was by then enduring the final stages of terminal cancer and he resigned on 20 May 1923, after just 209 days as premier. The King invited Baldwin to form the next Cabinet, and the new prime minister set about launching an ambitious scheme of tariff reform, dramatically switching from free trade to protection in a speech at the Conservative Party conference in Plymouth.

Despite his Scottish ancestry, Baldwin clearly did not think much of Novar and kept him out of the loop. 'Great anxiety about Scotland,' wrote the Earl of Crawford. 'Jack Gilmour told me last week that the party organisers at Edinburgh had never been consulted, and this evening George Younger said that Novar had never heard of a comprehensive scheme of tariff reform until he read the report of Baldwin's Plymouth speech.'[24] Despite a clear majority in the House, Baldwin felt bound by Bonar Law's pledge that there would be no new tariffs without a further election, and although this move healed the party's Carlton Club wounds, Novar was now completely at odds with his new chief. He wrote to Baldwin to warn him that a snap general election risked handing the government over to socialists. 'I should say that I cannot well see how our chief industries in Scotland, Engineering, Shipbuilding, Linen etc can be assisted by Protection,' he added, 'and I anticipate therefore that Protection will receive little support there . . . It might be worth considering whether the Australian plan of a referendum, which does not entail the defeat of a government, might be tried to decide this issue.'[25] Novar was correct on at least one point: although the Conservatives won 258 seats in the following poll, they had no clear majority and Baldwin resigned as prime minister in January 1924 following a vote of no confidence. Labour then formed its first minority government, although Baldwin returned to Downing Street ten months later, this time having decided not to take Novar with him. He wrote:

My dear Novar, It was with real regret that I was unable to avail myself of your services in the formation of the new Cabinet. You were so acceptable to Scotland and such a loyal colleague that my regret was intensified on personal grounds. But I have always felt it a weakness not to have the Scottish Secretary in the Commons and after the popular verdict in Scotland I regard it as more than ever essential. You will believe me when I say that Cabinet making is the most difficult, troublesome, and painful task to which man is called to put his hand.[26]

Novar clearly doubted Baldwin's sincerity, scrawling on Baldwin's letter (for Rosebery's attention) 'This is weak but his best line of argument. The reasons were quite different & originated possibly in Scotland – though I don't trust Mr B!' He responded formally, and more contritely, on 12 November:

I am touched by your kind letter. The Scotch Press of November 1st announced a probable change at the S.O. and I felt no cause, personally, for complaint. I only joined the Conservative Party in 1922 and I did so then because I thought the safety of the country was at stake and that everyone should back Mr. Bonar Law and you in your efforts to bring the Coalition to an end and to keep out the Socialists. Your reference to "loyalty" is welcome as showing that you understand my opposition to Protection and to the Dissolution of 1923 was actuated solely by my fear of its ill consequence to the country and party. I can well believe that your task in framing the Government was a difficult and painful one but you need not count me amongst the aggrieved. I recognise that my original nomination was due to the friendship of Mr. Bonar Law and not to party claims. It was an interesting episode and I have every confidence that my successor will carry out many of the reforms I had hoped to initiate, but which had to be deferred on account of our weakness, last year, on the Scotch Grand Committee. And, wishing you all success, Believe me.[27]

Novar had not exactly been a heavyweight figure even in a lightweight Cabinet, but he no doubt felt aggrieved at losing high office after little more than a year at the Scottish Office. His political career was now over, and without a colonial comeback in sight. In 1925 Novar chaired a committee on political honours and was a member of the Royal Commission on the Ancient and Historical Monuments of Scotland.

He died at Raith in Kirkcaldy on 30 March 1934, and was cremated in Edinburgh on 4 April. The Australian governor-general, Sir Isaac Isaacs, sent a message of sympathy on behalf of the Australian people; it was in that Dominion, after all, where the high point of Sir Ronald Munro Ferguson's otherwise unremarkable political career truly lay.

WILLIAM ADAMSON

22 JANUARY – 6 NOVEMBER 1924,
7 JUNE 1929 – 25 AUGUST 1931

Old Willie

The first Labour Scottish secretary could not have been more of a contrast to Viscount Novar. Known as 'Old Willie', William Adamson was a gruff, plainly spoken miner with a solid trade union pedigree but little political sophistication. He joined Ramsay MacDonald's fledgling government largely on the basis of his track record in the labour movement, and, in no small part, his friendship with the new prime minister. 'There are so many considerations which have nothing to do with merit,' wrote Beatrice Webb. 'The Labour Party has its "Dukes" – in its 18th century meaning of the term – the great trade unions have to be represented – viz Adamson!'[1] But he was not an impressive figure: unimaginative, cautious and possessed of ideas, one might say, above his station. 'Mr. Adamson certainly looked the part of Scottish secretary,' observed one contemporary biography, 'and he enjoyed letting his temporary subjects see him in his official capacity.'[2] One historian condemned him as 'dim and incompetent', while he also gained a reputation as the only boring speaker in the 1924 Cabinet. This, however, was a minority government, and the notion that any truly radical legislation could actually be passed did not cross MacDonald's mind. He instead concentrated on foreign affairs (the prime minister also became foreign secretary), aiming to correct the damage of the 1919 Treaty of Versailles.

The new government also embarked upon a massive public relations exercise, to prove to the nation that Labour was fit to govern. 'Without fuss, the firing of guns, the flying of flags, the Labour Govt. has come in,' wrote MacDonald in his diary. 'At noon there was a Privy Council at Buck. Pal; the seals were handed to us – and there we were Ministers of State. At 4 we held our first Cabinet. A wonderful country. Now for burdens & worries.'[3] Adamson had his share of both, not least a shortage of socialist-inclined Scots law officers. He nominated a fellow Labour MP, James Brown, as lord high commissioner to the General Assembly of the Church of Scotland, but enlisted the help of the Duke of Atholl as a

member of the 'auld aristocracy' to offer guidance.[4] Also recruited was
Lord Macmillan, neither an MP nor a socialist (he had once been a
Unionist candidate), who now became lord advocate. He later recalled his
first meeting with Adamson:

> On my first arrival I stepped through the communicating doors to make the
> acquaintance of Mr. Adamson, with whom I soon struck up the most pleasant
> relations. Almost his first remark to me was: 'You'll help us, won't you? You
> must remember I'm only a miner'; and then he added with a twinkle, 'You'll be
> surprised to find what a Tory I am'. I am bound to say that throughout our
> subsequent association I found him far from revolutionary. He was a real canny
> Scot and a very engaging personality, simple, straightforward, and friendly.[5]

Under Adamson, Lord Macmillan guided two small Bills through the
House – the Conveyancing (Scotland) Act and the Church of Scotland
(Property and Endowments) Bill – but otherwise the lack of a majority
meant the Scottish secretary's hands were tied. John Wheatley's landmark
Housing Act did get through, massively increasing house-building subsidies, but, although Wheatley was a Scot and his Act benefited Scotland,
its passing had nothing to do with Adamson. 'The Government has a lot
on hand,' Adamson told the House a few weeks after occupying his office
at Dover House. 'Its time will be taxed to the uttermost, but . . . We wish
to do everything possible to assist our people, either in the Highlands or
the Lowlands, and any step that it is possible for us to take we will take
gladly. We are here for one thing only, and that is to serve to the best of
our ability the people whom we represent.'[6]

In May 1924 Adamson appointed the Hospital Services (Scotland) Committee, under the chairmanship of Lord Mackenzie, to investigate Scotland's
myriad of health services,[7] and that same month a Scottish home rule Bill
introduced by the Gorbals MP George Buchanan (later an under-secretary
at the Scottish Office) reached its Second Reading in the Commons. This
time, the long-standing issue had a good chance: all Labour back-benchers
supported it (home rule was one of the Labour Party's founding pledges), as
did Adamson and the prime minister, who had been chairman of the London
branch of the Scottish Home Rule Association (SHRA). Many of Asquith's
Liberals, who were tacitly propping up the minority government, also
remained committed to home rule. But when it came to the crunch Adamson
offered a classic political fudge: 'The Government give the general principle
of this Bill their approval,' he said, adding:

> At the same time they recognise that it raises a large and vital issue which is of
> importance to this country as well as to Scotland, and what they suggest they are

prepared to do is to appoint a Committee to examine this whole question and report to the House . . . I hope the Bill will get a Second Reading, and in this way will express the feelings of the present Parliament on this important question.[8]

But when the call came that the question be put, the Speaker inexplicably withheld his assent. 'This is shameful', cried Buchanan amid rowdy scenes which did the public reputation of the Clydeside group of Labour MPs no favours. The House was adjourned without a vote; seemingly undeterred, Adamson later attended SHRA's annual rally to mark the anniversary of William Wallace's death. The secretary for Scotland whipped himself up into an evangelical fervour:

> Those of [us] who [are] looking forward in these times to a real, vitalising democracy [are] beginning to realise that the most pressing needs [are] the rousing, the invigoration, the educating, and the organisation of the people to a sense of their responsibility for the promotion of their own well-being. [I look] forward with confidence to the time when Scottish legislation [will] be enacted by Scotsmen in a Scottish Assembly.[9]

But the first Labour government did not last long enough to make this 'vitalising' democracy a reality. When a Liberal amendment to a Conservative censure motion against the government was passed,[10] the King granted MacDonald a dissolution of parliament. In the general election of October 1924 Labour fell from 191 to 151 seats, and the Conservatives returned to power.

William Adamson was born at Halbeath, near Dunfermline, on 2 April 1863, the son of James Armstrong Adamson, a coal miner, and Flora Cunningham. He attended a local school run by the wife of a mining engineer, but left at the age of 11 to work in the mines, where he remained for the next 27 years. Adamson first became active in the Fife and Kinross Miners' Association as a branch delegate, rising to become general-secretary in 1908. He was an active Baptist, a teetotaller, a Burns enthusiast and conciliatory when it came to industrial relations. Initially a Liberal, he was elected to Dunfermline Town Council on a Labour ticket in 1905, and became the first Scottish miners' union-sponsored MP in 1910. But Adamson was no revolutionary, strongly supporting Britain's involvement in the First World War, even though it claimed the life of his eldest son. He became the first chairman of the Parliamentary Labour Party in 1917, holding the post until 1921 when an illness which had seen him absent from parliament for long periods led him to resign. 'Adamson was a dour and phlegmatic Scottish miners' leader very much out of his depth in the Commons,' recalled his colleague Emmanuel Shinwell. 'His selection had been motivated by a desire to have a chairman who would create the minimum of trouble, so the movement got the results it deserved.'[11] Adamson's experience as (effectively) party leader was not a happy one, and he was derided for saying that to become the official opposition all he needed were two additional clerks, a typist and a messenger. He was fond of using words like 'statesmanship' in his platform speeches, often getting howled down as a result. The acerbic socialist intellectual Beatrice Webb recorded the following, typically detailed, impression of Adamson:

> He is a middle-aged Scottish miner, typical British proletarian in body and mind, with an instinctive suspicion of all intellectuals or enthusiasts: a thick, broad-shouldered and relatively short man, clumsy in movement, with straight sandy hair cropped close round a low forehead, big jaw and mouth, formless but slightly upward-tending nose, and lifeless blue eyes. In private conversation he is painfully slow in speech, every word seems to need deliberate effort. He is a total abstainer and is, I am told, domesticated and pious. He had neither wit, fervour nor intellect; he is most decidedly not a leader, not even, like [Arthur] Henderson, a manager of men. He has pushed his way up from miners' agent to miners' M.P., by industry and trustworthiness and the habit of keeping himself to himself, making no enemies and never giving himself away.[12]

Adamson was also that rare thing, a right-wing trade unionist, and therefore a determined opponent of a movement among some Fife miners who wanted a more accountable and democratic trade union. Adamson's critics emphasised his responsiveness to coal owners' demands and the lack of democracy within the union. The culmination was a split at the end of 1922 which saw the formation of a separate Reform Union under Philip Hodge of the Independent Labour Party. Hodge stood against Adamson in West Fife at the 1923 general election and managed to poll more than 34 per cent of the vote, evidence of the significant opposition among miners to Adamson's politics and union leadership. The two unions reunified in 1927 when fresh elections swept Adamson and his allies from the leading posts, but the situation then descended into chaos, the Fife county board suspending Adamson as secretary on charges of misrepresenting his members. Adamson responded by resigning and establishing a new union, the Fife, Clackmannan, and Kinross Miners' Union, which became the official Fife union within both the National Union of Scottish Mineworkers and the Miners' Federation of Great Britain. Adamson had triumphed, but not without sowing the seeds of bitter political trouble for his future.

At the May 1929 election Labour won 288 seats to the Conservatives' 260, with 59 Liberals under Lloyd George holding the balance of power.

Adamson was again returned in West Fife but the communist candidate, Willie Gallacher, dented his majority by polling more than 6,000 votes. This time, Ramsay MacDonald knew he had to concentrate on domestic matters, passing a revised Old Age Pensions Act and a more generous Unemployment Insurance Act, to improve wages and conditions in coalmining communities like those represented (or misrepresented) by Adamson in Fife. He returned to the Scottish Office, this time as secretary of state for Scotland, an elevation he no doubt relished. MacDonald actually proposed that Adamson move to the Lords as Scottish secretary, leaving his junior minister, the more capable Tom Johnston, to answer for the Scottish Office in the Commons. 'He [MacDonald] hoped we would both agree quickly,' recalled Johnston, 'for he was very busy, and time was precious, and he had other appointments.' He added:

> I said I was quite willing to work under Mr. Adamson and Willie then shook hands with me, and said he would go to the Lords!
> "Thank you both," said the P.M. "But not a word about this until you see it announced in the newspapers."
> "Can I no' tell my wife about the Lords?" asked Willie.
> "Oh you can tell your wife," replied the P.M.
> "And my son?"
> "Your what!" shouted the P.M. "I didn't know you had a son. That arrangement is off. I am against appointing peers who have heirs to inherit their titles."[13]

'And so suddenly was blotted out a noble lord,' added Johnston. Nevertheless, Adamson's under-secretary did effectively function as the de facto Scottish secretary with Adamson as a ceremonial head. Adamson allowed Johnston to do as he liked and although the Scottish secretary did become more involved than before in domestic legislation, he was happier attending freedom ceremonies and civic occasions than doing the legwork on parliamentary committees, which was left to Johnston. Civil servants also took their lead from the under-secretary, and as Adamson was terrified of the chancellor, Philip Snowden, Johnston was often dispatched as a 'commercial traveller' to the Treasury whenever more money was required.[14]

Adamson faced two immediately pressing issues on returning to Dover House, both of which had been bequeathed by the outgoing Conservative government. The Tories had phased out the Wheatley Act's housing subsidies, which Labour now restored, and had also passed, despite heavy opposition, the Local Government (Scotland) Act. MacDonald approved a slum clearance Bill, which saw Adamson successfully argue for 'special treatment' for Scotland, but an election pledge to repeal the local government reforms proved trickier. 'We opposed it', said Adamson during the Debate on the Address in July, 'and did our best, both inside and outside the House, to defeat it, but the state of parties in the House then was such that all our efforts, to secure the rejection of the Bill, or even its amendment in any material particular, were unavailing.' He outlined a number of options ranging from full repeal, to suspending the abolition of the education authorities until an inquiry could be held. 'We have reluctantly come to the conclusion that the last suggestion only is practicable.'[15] Ultimately, even this came to nothing, and Adamson disposed of the Bill to suspend the Act 'like an unwanted kitten'.[16] This damaged Adamson's prestige, and he was soon being attacked for including too many Labour supporters in the Royal Commission on Licensing in Scotland, and for his perceived inactivity following an East Anglian fishing disaster which killed several Scottish fishermen and destroyed 31,000 fishing nets.

Adamson also suffered physically when, in December 1929, he was hit by a car as he crossed Southampton Row to catch a bus to the North Temperance Hotel, his London home for nearly 25 years. He was pushed along the road in front of the car for about ten yards before it stopped. It took eight men to lift the car up so that Adamson could be removed; his clothes had been torn to shreds, although he was still clutching his umbrella and constituency briefcase. 'I purposefully withheld my identity – I was just a man to them,' recalled Adamson modestly. 'I remember when I was being set down on the pavement one of them saying with perfect candour, "Now you're all right, dad." It was then that I felt the most excruciating pains in my legs. I thought they were broken, and asked the folks to lift me on my feet in order that I might ascertain the extent of the damage . . . When they did so, I recall saying to myself, "Thank God, my legs are not broken, anyway." ' Adamson was taken by ambulance to the University College Hospital, where his left leg, left hand and head were bandaged. Gamely, he still made it to the House that afternoon, having been given notice of several questions. 'Some of my colleagues observed that all was not well with me,' remembered Adamson, 'but in reply to their inquiries I merely said that I had got a bump on my leg. I went down to the Scottish Office before going to the House of Commons. In the House I felt all right so long as I sat, but if I moved I experienced the most excruciating pain.'[17]

In March 1930 Tom Johnston was forced to publicly defend Adamson following a scathing attack from Miss Ellen Wilkinson MP in the official journal of the Independent Labour Party. She accused him of being unfit for the job and useless in the House. 'Who the devil cares whether or not some Liberals and Tories are displeased with him at question time?' retorted Johnston. 'But it's a matter of some [importance] that a man who is carrying one of the heaviest tasks in the Government should be so suddenly stabbed in the back – stabbed wantonly, and woundingly and patronisingly.'[18] But Wilkinson had a point when it came to the Scottish secretary's performance at the despatch box. A *Scotsman* sketch (under the heading 'Mr Adamson's Canniness') from April 1931 goes some way to capturing his peculiar, yet disarming, style. A common refrain of Adamson's was to assure a questioning MP that the 'matter is receiving my closest attention'. This caused much mirth, and on this occasion one member asked a supplementary question regarding a report on piers and harbours. Adamson hesitated; the House was silent. 'The Scottish Secretary pondered on the perilous adventure of an answer to a supplementary question,' reported the *Scotsman*. 'Slowly he gathered himself up from the Front Bench. There was tense silence. It was broken by the anxious cry of a Socialist colleague – "Be careful, Wullie," he exclaimed. Now the House rocked with laughter.' I am not one given to boasting, Adamson avowed, before proceeding to do exactly that, claiming he had done more than any other for the Scottish fishing industry. 'In this his parting shot the secretary for Scotland emerged from the question hour with the cheers and laughter of the whole House on his side,' continued the sketch. 'Mr Arthur Henderson, the acting Leader of the House, in the absence of the Prime Minister, beamed pleasure. Mr Adamson's caution is not to be shaken, but his "attention" is incurable.'[19]

Like many worldwide, MacDonald's second government had no effective response to the economic crisis which followed the Stock Market Crash of 1929. Unemployment in Scotland rose by around 200,000 in the first six months of the Labour government and during 1931 the economic situation deteriorated even further. MacDonald and his chancellor supported calls from economists for sharp spending cuts, but several ministers made it clear they would rather resign than sanction them. Adamson was one of them. 'I've never voted against the poor yet,' he told colleagues, 'and I can't now.'[20] On 24 August MacDonald submitted his resignation to the King but was persuaded to stay on as head of a National government including Conservatives and Liberals. Adamson joined the majority of the Cabinet in rejecting this idea and MacDonald, Snowden and two other ministers were expelled from the Labour Party. MacDonald pressed on, and called a general election in October. This proved disastrous for the Labour Party – not least because of the faked Zinoviev Letter, which implied Soviet collusion with the government and appeared in the *Daily Mail* four days before polling – and it returned just 46 members. Despite Adamson's principled stand he was humiliated in West Fife, losing to a Unionist when Gallacher split working-class support by polling nearly 7,000 votes.[21] His chances were even slimmer when he contested the seat again in November 1935. Several villages were now communist strong-holds and Adamson's pleas for his members to go back to work during a 12-week dispute at the Valleyfield colliery saw them instead side with the communist-controlled United Mineworkers of Scotland. By now in his early seventies and recently widowed, Adamson was defeated by just 593 votes and West Fife gained notoriety by returning Scotland's first com-munist MP, Willie Gallacher.

'He was the soul of loyalty and good comradeship,' said Johnston of Adamson in his memoirs, 'caution personified with a capital P; he carried on for years a relentless warfare with the communists in his county, and his motto in that warfare as I once told him was the Covenanters' banner at Tippermuir "Jesus and No Quarter".'[22] Devastated, Adamson died just months later in a nursing home near Dunfermline on 23 February 1936. 'Neither as a politician nor as a trade union leader can Mr. Adamson be said to have become widely known,' said *The Times* in its obituary, 'but he exercised much greater influence in the inner counsels of organised labour than in the working-class movement at large.'[23] Another contemporary commentator judged:

> Were he less long-suffering and had a trifle more of the devil in his composition, he would have been a really admirable Scottish Secretary, but in his patience and his subordination of self he was, surely, quite representative of the country of which he was the official head . . . Mr. Adamson has little of the revolu-tionary in his nature. But whoever in the Labour Party succeeds him in the fullness of time will, I should imagine, find that sound foundations have been laid by the first Labour Secretary of State for Scotland.[24]

SIR JOHN GILMOUR, BARONET

6 NOVEMBER 1924 – 7 JUNE 1929

The wax-work laird

The October 1924 general election resulted in a landslide victory for the Conservatives, who returned to government with a majority of 223. Sir John Gilmour, the 48-year-old second baronet of Montrave, therefore became the first substantial Conservative secretary for Scotland since Lord Balfour of Burleigh almost 30 years before. Sir John shared Lord Balfour's rather humourless dedication to public service, but soon proved a capable administrator and a robust leader of a Scottish Office emerging from two years of political instability. 'A ginger-headed soldier who will be most useful,' assessed the Conservative minister the Earl of Crawford; 'A stooping, sandy-haired figure with fleeting resemblances to Mr. Churchill', said a contemporary cigarette card of Sir John. 'Speaks in round tones and rounded sentences.'[1] It helped that the new Scottish secretary sat for what was said to be the safest Unionist seat in Scotland, the Pollok Division of Glasgow, a constituency he had won in 1918 and held until his death in 1940. As Scottish whip, Sir John had notably refused to accept the verdict of the Carlton Club meeting, which saw the Conservatives withdraw from the Liberal-led coalition, or indeed two offers of the Scottish Office in Andrew Bonar Law's government. Nevertheless, Baldwin offered him the Scottish Office once again. This time, he accepted.

Sir John Gilmour's career was, for minor Scottish landed gentry, typically solid. He served in no fewer than three great departments of state – the Scottish Office, the Ministry of Agriculture, and latterly the Home Office – but is nevertheless largely unknown today. He was the second, but eldest surviving, son of Sir John Gilmour, who was created a baronet in 1897 as a reward for his presidency of the Scottish Union of Conservative Associations. Educated at Glenalmond and the universities of Edinburgh and Cambridge, Gilmour later served with distinction in the second Boer War, twice earning a mention in dispatches and reaching the rank of major in the Fife and Forfar Company of the Imperial Yeomanry. From the army, he was elected to Fife County Council, and he also stood unsuccessfully against the future prime minister H. H. Asquith in his native seat of East Fife. Gilmour won the Liberal seat of East Renfrewshire in the first election of 1910, and quickly became popular among the Conservative ranks. Gilmour was made a whip in January 1913, but despite being exempt from military service, he willingly interrupted his political career to re-enlist at the start of the First World War. He was present at the Gallipoli landings, and also served in Egypt and Palestine, where he was wounded. Gilmour returned to the whips' office in 1919 with a Distinguished Service Order, and after succeeding to his father's baronetcy in July 1920, he formally joined the government in April 1921 as a junior lord of the Treasury.

Sir John was faced with a conflict of loyalty during the coalition crisis of 1922, and threatened to resign in May because he felt the whips' advice was so consistently ignored. He took part in the 'under-secretaries' revolt' that summer, but voted with Austen Chamberlain at the Carlton Club meeting in October, as he took the 'gravest exception to shutting out the possibility of working usefully with the coalition Liberals'. Sir John's sister Maud had married Sir George Younger, later 1st Viscount Younger of Leckie, and so although not in government for two years from 1922 he was still very much in the Unionist loop. Only when the rift was healed in 1924 and the former coalitionists rejoined the front-bench did Gilmour's career take off once again. 'Dined with Willie Bridgeman, Jack Gilmour, and Lord Peel,' noted the Earl of Crawford in his diary. 'If politics are indeed as dull as these three cabinet ministers, the peaceful outlook of these realms is indeed assured.'[2]

Sir John's first few years at the Scottish Office were dominated by agriculture and housing. The former he dealt with easily, for he had long been a practical and experienced farmer on his father's Fife estates, but the latter was an altogether more complex problem. In 1925, Sir John invited the prime minister, Stanley Baldwin, to Glasgow to see first-hand the slum conditions of the Gorbals and Cowcaddens. Despite a generous increase in the central government housing subsidy granted by the Housing Act of 1924, few local authorities had enthusiastically proposed schemes, and even those that did had failed to implement them vigorously. Acutely aware that the Tory mandate in Scotland was not as strong as that in England, especially in Glasgow, Sir John pushed for an additional house-building programme. He argued that British housing policy had barely 'touched the fringe' of the problems in Clydeside, and looked to a local industrialist for the answer, Lord Weir. He had boldly offered his services (and his cheap steel-framed houses) during a Lords

debate on the Housing Bill, his only caveat being that to ensure profit-
ability the majority of his workers would be paid at shipyard rates – lower
than normal construction pay levels. This infuriated the building unions,
who accused the Conservatives of trying to smash the organised labour
movement. When compliant local authorities were threatened with strike
action, Sir John initially supported the councils before suggesting the
government instead use its Office of Works to build the new homes. The
minister for health, Neville Chamberlain, pointed out that local authorities would still need to supply local services so that without them any
scheme 'was doomed to failure'. Gilmour, he said, should instead mobilise
public opinion behind Weir, and particularly housewives. Chamberlain
believed that owner-occupation 'increased self-respect' and would dam-
pen hostility towards Conservatives, but by the summer of 1925 the
secretary for Scotland had endured five heated Commons debates on
the subject, and he warned Baldwin that unrest was likely. Baldwin over-
ruled Chamberlain's objections and the Second Scottish National
Housing Company was established with the task of building 2,500 new
homes. 'I really went up to London yesterday to look after my colleagues
the Sec. for Scotland & the Minister for Labour who were proposing to
see the Ch. of Ex. & the PM about a new proposition to push Weir houses
in Scotland,' wrote Chamberlain to his sister. 'I thought they were both
vague & wild so I put down my own ideas on paper and the natural result
was that . . . it was unanimously adopted and I hope something may come
of it. There is no doubt that Scotland presents a far more favourable
battleground for the fight with the TU's than England.'

Chamberlain was fond of Sir John but was convinced that the task at
hand was beyond his abilities. 'I wish I had the conduct of Scottish affairs
instead of Gilmour,' he added. 'He is thoroughly honest, courageous and
well meaning but he strikes me as lacking in knowledge of how to deal
with his people.'[3] By November, the Cabinet had agreed to an additional
Scottish subsidy of £40 per house. And, if local authorities refused to work
with the private businessman Lord Weir, up to 1,000 homes would instead
be ordered direct from the Scottish Office. 'I regret to say that I have very
little confidence in the Scottish Office who will always make a bungle if
it is possible to do so or in Walter Elliott [sic Gilmour's under-secretary]
who is a clever windbag,' wrote Chamberlain on 15 November. 'But I
have told my people that this matter is too important to be allowed to go
wrong and that we must therefore hold the Scotsmen firmly by the hand
all through these difficult times.'[4] But still the wider dispute rumbled on.
'If houses could be built by talk,' wrote the *Scotsman*, 'the housing problem
in Scotland should have been solved long ago.'[5] The Scottish secretary
insisted that, in spite of Weir's involvement, the building trade would still

have 13,000 houses to construct, while the Labour leader, Ramsay MacDonald, argued that steel houses were 'dull, drab, and ugly'. As it was a government contract, argued MacDonald, there was an obligation to pay fair wages. 'We want houses,' he said, 'and there is no member of this House who will stand up and say that a matter of prejudice or taste or sentiment should stand in the way of building shelters for the people of Scotland.'[6] But denying working-class voters new housing over a labour dispute did not look good, and Labour's opposition soon softened as work on hundreds of homes in Edinburgh, Glasgow and Dundee continued regardless. In July 1927 some Weir Homes built in the Lochend area of Edinburgh received the royal seal of approval with a visit from the King and Queen. The following month Sir John issued a state-of-the-nation press release, boasting that while in 1924 only 4,000 houses had been built, that figure had increased to almost 13,000 in 1926, with an expected total of up to 17,000 in 1927.

Baldwin's visit to the Glasgow slums in 1925 had also convinced the prime minister that the time was now right to raise the status of the secretary for Scotland to that of a secretary of state. The Wilson Committee on the Remuneration of Ministers had proposed in 1920 that the Scottish secretary be 'raised to first class rank', and in 1921 Lord Birkenhead urged the Cabinet to do the same, declaring that 'the Secretary for Scotland represents not a Department but a country'.[7] By 1925 the Convention of Royal Scottish Burghs had also begun lobbying the prime minister, and helped along by mounting pressure from back-benchers, Baldwin finally promised to give the matter further consideration. It seems that Sir John remained aloof from such developments, although the former Scottish Office permanent under-secretary Reginald MacLeod of MacLeod told him, 'It is preposterous that this should be denied.'[8] On 17 December 1925 Baldwin announced that Gilmour was to become secretary of state for Scotland, news which the Scotsman greeted as 'extremely gratifying'.

The news came during an unhappy period for the Scottish secretary. The previous month, Sir John's butler had been sentenced to six months' hard labour for consuming a large portion of the wine cellar at Montrave and stealing items from his employer's London residence. And at the end of December, not only did Captain Harry Gilmour, Sir John's younger brother, die, but the shock proved too much for his mother and she too passed away. While Gilmour was en route to her funeral in Fife, a motor cycle and sidecar collided with his motor car, damaging both vehicles but injuring no one. It was also a bad year for the government as a whole. A disastrous coal stoppage had given way to the catastrophic General Strike of 1926, a crisis the government managed to weather despite the havoc it caused nationally. In June 1926, Baldwin was presented with the Freedom of Edinburgh and hailed as 'the man of the hour', fresh from the greatest triumph of his career. 'I think you could not get five more typical and better men in their several walks from Scotland than now occupy the five posts in the Government peculiarly connected with Scotland,' Baldwin told a crowd of 1,500 in the McEwan Hall, 'and I am glad it has fallen to me to introduce into Parliament that Bill which will convert my old friend Sir John Gilmour into a Secretary of State.'[9] But although the 1926 Secretaries of State Act elevated Sir John's status, it did not alter his bank balance. Baldwin was able to tell the Cabinet that the secretary for Scotland had 'waived the question of any increase in emoluments in the case of the present holder of the office'.[10] On Monday 26 July Sir John presented himself to His Majesty at 11 a.m. and took the oath of the secretary of state for Scotland. The *Scotsman* regarded him as successor to the Marquis of Tweeddale, who resigned as secretary of state in 1746, just before the office was abolished as payback for the '45 uprising. But this time, said the newspaper, 'There will be no Jacobite troubles or Malt Taxes to upset the new arrangement, and Sir John Gilmour will be able to secure for Scotland a consideration which was not obtained in the troubled days after the Union.'[11] The ebullient MP Walter Elliot, parliamentary secretary for health since November 1924, was also upgraded to a full under-secretary of state, and congratulated the government on giving the 'country a status unknown since the '45'.

Apparently re-energised by his newly elevated status, Sir John set to work on reorganising what was now considered to be one of His Majesty's principal departments of state. The result was the innocuous-sounding Reorganisation of Offices (Scotland) Bill, which was introduced to parliament in 1927. It sought to abolish the Scottish Board of Health, and also Lord Pentland's creation, the Board of Agriculture for Scotland, replacing them with corresponding departments of health and agriculture. 'I am satisfied that there is no advantage, under modern circumstances,' argued Sir John in a Cabinet memo on 4 March, 'in administering such services as health and agriculture through a Board rather than through a Civil Service Department on the ordinary lines, with a single Head directly responsible to the Secretary of State for Scotland.' He cited the 1913 Royal Commission on the Civil Service, which had been highly critical of the Scottish boards, in his support, but while his memo reads today as a reasonably modest set of administrative reforms, it caused uproar among Labour and Liberal MPs. They accused the Scottish secretary of engineering greater London control over the Edinburgh boards by installing

English civil servants as the new departmental chiefs. The former Labour secretary for Scotland, William Adamson, said it would remove 'the last vestige of independent Government and nationhood'.[12] The Bill was withdrawn without a vote but was reintroduced the following year with certain qualifications. This time, Sir John made it clear that the headquarters of the new departments would remain in Edinburgh, and by 1928 Sir John's desire for administrative reform had also found an architectural focus:

> we shall in course of time, when the clamant demands for economy shall have been overcome, centralise in Edinburgh under one roof all the Departments concerned with Scottish affairs. Then I can visualise the linking up of Parliament and Dover House with a central office in Edinburgh, where the Minister responsible to Parliament and the Scottish Members can be in close and easy touch with the heads of every one of his Departments.[13]

On 13 October 1927, the Scottish secretary had put in a second bid for what was known as the Calton Hill site, once home to Edinburgh's forbidding central prison. The Edinburgh outposts of the Scottish Office by now occupied no fewer than 18 buildings, only three of which were Crown property. And although he ceased to be secretary of state after the 1929 general election, Sir John would later chair a committee which produced plans for what eventually became the modern Scottish Office. The first secretary of state for Scotland would prove to be the dominant architect of Scottish government in the twentieth century.

Next the Scottish Office turned its attention to reforming local government. As in 1889, this was a UK-wide exercise, with Neville Chamberlain the driving force in England and Wales, and the Scottish secretary providing rearguard support north of the border. Since Lord Lothian created the original 33 county councils, supplemented by a network of parish councils established by Sir George Otto Trevelyan in 1894, Scotland had become congested with a panoply of autonomous bodies. By June 1928 there were no fewer than 869 parish councils, 201 town councils, 98 district councils, 37 education authorities, 33 county councils and 27 district boards of control. 'Many of them operate for areas of very small population and rateable value, and the multiplicity of authorities, in type and number, tends to overlapping and waste,' observed Sir John in a Cabinet memo. 'It is proposed to abolish Parish Councils, District Councils, education Authorities, and District Boards of Control. The functions of these bodies will devolve upon reconstituted County Councils, and upon Town Councils of Burghs with a population of 20,000 or over.' But as a former councillor himself, the Scottish secretary knew these reforms would not be popular and warned that 'Strenuous opposition to these proposals is to be expected from the Authorities to be abolished, and from the Councils of the smaller burghs . . .' But most importantly, he added, 'The results in the selected counties are also satisfactory from a ratepayer's point of view.'[14]

In June 1928 Sir John moved the Second Reading of the Local Government (Scotland) Bill. He said the status quo was cumbersome, expensive and confusing for the electorate. 'What I am submitting to the House is, that the new and freshly-constituted county councils will have the power of surveying the situation for themselves . . . altering the boundaries, and possibly linking parishes, or cutting from one parish and adding to another.'[15] As Sir John had predicted, the White Paper was not greeted enthusiastically, particularly by those bodies now under threat of extinction. But others praised its boldness, and the promise of increased revenue numbed criticism from financial quarters. Far from conserving Scottish institutions, the Reorganisation of Offices (Scotland) Act, and now the Local Government (Scotland) Bill, generated the distinct impression that the Scottish secretary considered nothing to be sacred. 'I am having at the moment a stormy time with Local authorities and some of your Highland Chieftans!' wrote Gilmour to Sir Ian Zachary Malcolm. 'Fortunately I know most of them and I am not kept awake at nights!'[16]

'A stranger listening to this Debate,' Sir John told the House, 'would suppose that the policy which the Government have laid before the Committee, and the proposals which they are making, were being thrust upon an unwilling Scotland.'[17] He constantly reassured MPs that his proposals offered no reflection upon the performance of the outgoing institutions, and insisted that the transfer of education was integral to his scheme. The novelist and Conservative MP, John Buchan, said education could no longer be left within a kind of walled garden in a suburb: 'We must bring it in sight of the market place, where the business of life is being conducted.'[18] But, as with his plans for reorganising the Scottish departments, Sir John was forced to compromise. He accepted at the committee stage that scrapping parish and district councils would leave too much of a gap and accepted an amendment from Sir Archibald Sinclair for their retention. Nevertheless, Labour and the Liberals formally opposed the Bill and the future Scottish secretary Tom Johnston likened Sir John to the Herod of the Scots, with the smaller councils being compared with the massacred innocents. Johnston also claimed that it attacked the democratic foundations of Scottish government,[19] but once the final committee stages had been handled by the lord advocate (Sir

John was ill and Elliot's mother had died), the Bill passed its Third Reading and received Royal Assent.

The year 1927 saw a mini economic boom in Britain. Unemployment was down and even the Clyde shipyards appeared to have full order books. Baldwin and his Scottish secretary could be forgiven for believing that the government's policy of protection was at last beginning to work. 'Nowadays,' Sir John told students at Edinburgh University on his election as lord rector, and 'in strange contrast to the period of buoyant optimism that followed the Armistice . . . a mood of pessimism as to our future has become rather fashionable.' Personally, he added, 'I cannot share these gloomy views. We have been through difficult times before, and I refuse to despair of the future now. But of one thing I am certain. If we are to ride the storm successfully, we must show not only courage, but initiative.'[20]

Conservatives in Scotland, having merged with the Scottish Liberal Unionists in 1912 to form the Scottish Unionist Association, also had reason to be optimistic. In four of the seven inter-war elections the Tories had returned the most MPs in Scotland – a degree of success unthinkable before the First World War (and after the Korean conflict). Scottish Unionism had at last carved out a distinctive political niche within the United Kingdom, but the Scottish Office was still criticised for being Anglo-centric in both political style and in practice. The loudest cries came from the newly formed National Party of Scotland (later the SNP), which claimed the Local Government (Scotland) Act typified the anglicisation of Scottish institutions. Sir John responded by reminding them that it was a Conservative government which had elevated his position to that of a secretary of state.

The Scottish secretary was also present at the Second Reading of the Rev. James Barr's Government of Scotland Bill in May 1927, but declined to speak. Barr's scheme was an odd mix of political devolution (he proposed a single chamber of 148 members) and the Kirk (the lord high commissioner – it was proposed – would represent the King in Scotland). His argument was more historical than political, and he compared Sir John with James VI writing from England centuries before: 'Here I sit and govern Scotland with my pen. I write and it is done; and by the Clerk of the Council I govern Scotland now, which others could not do by the sword.' The Bill's co-sponsor, Tom Johnston, implored the Scottish secretary to support the Bill. 'I submit that the time has come when this pooh-bah business,' he said, 'this conglomeration of sixteen offices in the person of one individual, is an insult to a proud nation.'[21] But the short debate ended without the question being put, and both Barr and Johnston later admitted the Bill had been a mistake. The Scottish secretary, meanwhile, was baffled by all this talk of Scottish self-government, which he depicted in speeches as a retrograde step. But on the other hand, he said Scots 'should never lose their love of country, and in its Imperial Parliament their knack of presenting things affecting their own problems from a Scottish point of view'.[22] He was, said Sir John, 'a keen Scotsman and a nationalist, but he hoped he had some sanity'.[23] As if to emphasise this point, Sir John went to great lengths to assemble a collection of portraits depicting his post-1707 predecessors as secretary of state to decorate his room in Dover House. To complete the set, he was himself presented in early 1929 with a full-length portrait by the leading portrait painter Sir James Guthrie, which still hangs in Dover House.

There was an air of complacency as the Unionists prepared for the 1929 general election, even though a string of recent by-election defeats had hinted at growing Labour strength in Scotland. The economy was worsening and Sir John's local government reforms were perceived to have been executed without consultation.[24] Although the Scottish secretary's own majority rose in Pollok, the Tories lost 16 seats in Scotland and the government was succeeded by a second minority Labour administration. 'Sir John Gilmour was not seen,' said the *Scotsman*, describing ministers as they took leave of Baldwin, 'but it is presumed that he took his usual route to the Prime Minister's house through the corridors of the Scottish Office and the Treasury.'[25]

Gilmour's style as Scottish secretary was unobtrusive and unflamboyant. He was often disarmingly reasonable and officials admired the way in which he tempered potentially explosive situations. The Conservative MP, William Bridgeman, later assessed his term of office thus:

> Sir J. Gilmour was a very industrious & successful Secretary for Scotland, and won respect from all sides by straightforwardness in speech and conduct. He never shirked a difficult job & always spoke plainly and expressed his opposition to any proposal in direct and unmistakeable language without giving offence. He has a quick temper, but controls it well, and was always loyal to those he was working with and ready to take his share of any unpopular course of policy which was found to be necessary.[26]

Baldwin had previously considered transferring Sir John to the India Office, but the civil servant Tom Jones urged against it, saying 'he had no imagination and could not rise to the quality of a speech demanded in the House when big issues are at stake'.[27] But on the formation of the cross-party National government in 1931 Gilmour continued his rise through the ranks, going to the Ministry of Agriculture and then to the Home

Office in September 1932. As home secretary, Sir John tackled corruption and low morale in the Metropolitan Police, a task no doubt aided by his experience at the Scottish Office. He also reformed gambling laws, but when Baldwin returned to the premiership in June 1935 Gilmour willingly retired from the Cabinet. His old friend Neville Chamberlain made him shipping minister in his short-lived wartime government, but his appointment was criticised on the basis of Sir John's obvious lack of expertise in such a critical field. Yet he was diligent, and overwork probably contributed to his premature death in London on 30 March 1940, aged only 63. 'The sudden death of Sir John Gilmour on Saturday morning represents the first casualty of the war in the ranks of the Government,' noted *The Times*. A bland but capable figure, Sir John had always been loyal to Baldwin and to his party, but lacked the aggressive edge which might have taken him further in politics. However, with his five years at the Scottish Office in the 1920s, and his enduring administrative reforms of the 1930s (of which more later), Sir John Gilmour's Scottish political legacy is significant, and 'It is difficult to suppose', as the *The Times* concluded, 'that he had an enemy in the world.'[28]

Sir Archibald Sinclair, Baronet

25 August 1931 – 28 September 1932

The Liberal crusader

Sir Archibald Sinclair became secretary of state for Scotland against a backdrop of bitter political divisions, not only within a traumatised Labour Party, but among a slowly disintegrating group of Liberal MPs. The Simonites, led by Sir John Simon, favoured outright opposition to Labour in alliance with the Conservatives; while the Samuelites – of which Sir Archibald was a member – led by Sir Herbert Samuel, were prepared to support the National government while fighting for free trade from within. Lloyd George was initially within the latter group, and after Ramsay MacDonald's 'great betrayal' in August 1931, the former Liberal prime minister awarded the spoils of coalition government from his sick bed. He gave Sinclair the Scottish Office – but without a seat in the Cabinet – and within months both he and the government were preparing for a general election. The National government won an overwhelming majority with 554 seats (470 of which were Conservative), but it left MacDonald as a prisoner of the Conservatives, still led by Stanley Baldwin.

In November, Sir Archibald was promoted to the Cabinet and his close friend Winston Churchill doled out career advice: 'You must carefully but ruthlessly detach yourself from the Samuelite group and establish solid Tory or Simonite connections,' he wrote. 'The Samuelites are wilderness headed and there they will [likely] find their friend L.G.'[1]

Sir Archibald was the first of several Liberals to occupy the Scottish Office throughout the next 14 years,[2] and he certainly cut a dashing figure. Endowed with striking good looks (not unlike a young Marlon Brando) and much charm of manner, he had long settled upon the standard City attire of striped trousers, winged-collar shirt and black bow tie. His 11 months in Dover House were dominated by events outside his department, so Sir Archibald emerged as a distinctly national – and not a Scottish – politician. 'I hope you are enjoying your office and taking great pains with your work,' wrote Churchill on 30 December 1931, 'and that you will always bear in mind the advice I gave you in the "ruthless letter" I wrote you some time ago, so that when the sheep are parted from the goats you may gamble safely with the righteous . . . The late Lord Salisbury said, quoting an American, there were two ways of governing a man, "bamboozle or bamboo". You seem to be trying both at once. I hope that you will be effective.'[3]

Archibald Henry Macdonald Sinclair was born on 22 October 1890, the only son of Clarence Granville Sinclair, a lieutenant in the Scots Guards, and his wife Mabel Sands, the daughter of a wealthy New York business-man and a noted beauty of her day. She died just days after her son's birth, but left him with her handsome genes. Archibald's father died five years later, so he was raised by a variety of relatives, spending a lot of time with his grandfather Sir Tollemache, and his uncle Archdeacon William Macdonald Sinclair, Canon of St Paul's. Another uncle, Lieutenant-General Owen Williams, gave Sinclair an entry into fashionable London society, for he was friendly with the then Prince of Wales. After Eton and Sandhurst, Sinclair entered the army in 1910 and two years later succeeded to his grandfather's baronetcy, and with it some hundred thousand acres in Caithness.

A contemporary portrait by Augustus John shows a glamorous young man with a hint of daredevilry in his eyes. This attracted the attention of H. H. Asquith's daughter Violet, and, for more platonic reasons, that of Winston Churchill, then a Liberal MP and soon a firm friend. Both Churchill and Sinclair had American mothers and felt deprived of parental affection, even sharing a slight speech impediment which later proved useful to both: Churchill's flattened vowels lent a dramatic aura to his wartime oratory, and Sinclair's slight stammer provided emphasis to his speeches in the House. They grew extremely close, and when in January 1916 Churchill (subdued by his handling of Gallipoli) took charge of the 6th Royal Scots Fusiliers on the Western Front, Sir Archibald served as his second-in-command for four months. 'He is most courageous conscientious and hard-working,' wrote Churchill to his wife, 'but he hates every hour of it [the war] with a profound loathing.'[4] Sir Archibald saw out the war as a major in the Guards Machine-Gun regiment and subsequently worked again for Churchill, first as his personal military secretary at the War Office, and then as his private secretary when he became colonial secretary in 1921. The following year Sinclair entered the House as the MP for Caithness and Sutherland, opting for the Lloyd George wing of the party and building a reputation as a talented opposition speaker. He also helped craft the Scottish version of the party's *Green Book* on agricultural reform (nicknamed the '*Tartan Book*'), as part of a comprehensive policy review instigated by Lloyd George. In 1930 Sir Archibald gained the thankless task of acting as Liberal chief whip, so by contrast the Scottish Office was to him a new and exciting challenge.

But the post of secretary of state for Scotland, even when in the Cabinet, in fact offered Sir Archibald limited scope for his talents, coming as it did at a moment of financial stringency and political instability. 'I talked with Archie Sinclair (new Secretary of State for Scotland) and the egregious Philip Kerr (Lothian) (Chancellor of the Duchy of Lancaster),' wrote the Conservative MP Sir Cuthbert Headlam in his diary, 'two flat-headed Liberals – both of them adopted the line that they were to be commiserated upon on being in the Government! and yet neither of them was really a bit depressed. Archie finds the position full of interest – but is evidently glad that L.G. is hors de combat.'[5]

Sir David Milne, later permanent under-secretary at the Scottish Office, remembered his political chief as a fine administrator with an agile and forensic mind. This, however, was only applied to such legislation as the Educational Endowments Bill and the Small Landholders and Agricultural Holdings (Scotland) Act of 1931, which gave greater powers of mediation to the Scottish Land Court. While Sinclair had been raised to accept the argument for Scottish home rule without question, he had now mellowed, believing the international situation presented a greater case for pooling sovereignty rather than splitting it up.[6]

Meanwhile, the National government's agricultural policy also caused acute problems for Sir Archibald in his largely rural constituency. A policy of cheap credit and low interest rates suited the south-east of England but did little for Scotland. The financial depression also prompted Sir Archibald into sporadic acts of generosity to his constituents which would nowadays lose an MP his seat. 'Meanwhile,' wrote Sir Archibald to Churchill, 'the National Government continues its majestic, toilsome but exciting progress. Like a charabanc without brakes, we go tearing around awkward corners but we cling patriotically to our seats & none of us has been flung out yet!'[7]

By now Lloyd George had quit the Samuelite Group and evicted his former colleagues from their Westminster headquarters on Abingdon Street. The party was also starved of cash and loyal party workers were sacked, further wrecking its already fragile morale. On 18 January 1932 the government proposed a ten per cent general tariff, prompting Sir Archibald to urge Samuel and his troops to cross the floor. Three days later there were chaotic scenes in the Cabinet as Sinclair, Samuel and the

Labour party minister, Philip Snowden, all announced their intention to resign. Lord Hailsham defused the situation by proposing that the Samuelites be allowed to differ with the policy publicly while remaining in the government; Sinclair and the others agreed to disagree. In a letter to Bob Boothby, Sir Archibald elaborated on what the prime minister had said: 'You may not only abstain, you may vote against protectionist proposals, you may not only vote against them but you may speak against them in debate; you may not only speak against them in the House of Commons – you may denounce them in the country.'[8] This shoddy compromise proved to be politically unsustainable, and zapped party morale even further. But things settled down enough for Sinclair to move the Second Reading of the Hire Purchase (Scotland) Bill, which prevented the oppressive use of imprisonment to enforce hire-purchase contracts, and work on the Scottish version of the Town and Country Planning Bill. 'He makes a bad impression on us in Cabinet,' wrote Neville Chamberlain in February, 'where he talks much too much and fails to carry conviction.'[9]

The political situation had again deteriorated when the National Liberal Federation met in April 1932. The Samuelite Liberal faction was now split into three parts – those supporting the National government; those who did not but backed the Samuelite ministers; and those who condemned both. Sir Archibald feebly tried to regain ground with a passionate attack on protectionism, which he compared with a dangerous drug, doing nothing for the economic disease but making the people feel better.

Sir Archibald's last Scottish Office policy consideration came in August 1932 when the Cabinet approved an English Education Bill. The Scottish secretary contemplated a radical change to the Goschen system of funding Scottish education, whereby eleven eightieths of the English grant was allocated to Scotland. He felt a needs-based grant was preferable, having told his under-secretary, Noel Skelton, the previous year that he wanted to take 'a careful look at Education administration – not because I have any reason to think it faulty, but because I don't believe that any of your immediate predecessors, or of mine, have ever devoted much attention to it'.[10] Sir Archibald endeavoured to do so, but events, as ever, disrupted his best intentions.

The Scottish secretary stuck doggedly to his 'national unity and trust our judgement' line, but by mid 1932 it was wearing a bit thin, and the Imperial Economic Conference which opened in Ottawa on 21 July 1932 proved to be the final straw. Baldwin excluded free traders from the British delegation and used the conference as an opportunity to introduce a system of imperial preference in international trade. Senior Samuelite Liberals met at Sir Archibald's Caithness home over the summer and eventually resolved to resign from the government. Churchill believed this was a mistake and telegrammed his friend on 22 September, saying 'On no account now',[11] but six days later the free trade ministers quit the government, therefore ending Sir Archibald's brief tenure at the Scottish Office. Many opposition friends urged him to reconsider. Walter Elliot, widely tipped to be his replacement, wrote to him soon after: 'I know the queer double feeling that comes over one on going out – so well – the physical relief at the lifting of the almost intolerable burden of work and the hankering that always remains for a hand on the tiller.'[12] The Samuelite ministers' resignations were also attacked for imperilling British unity. 'It would be an insult to condone with you upon leaving the administration. You should be warmly congratulated,' wrote the Conservative MP and publisher Brendan Bracken on 29 September. 'If it is good to be a secretary of state, it is something greater and better to have surrendered place and power for the sake of principle.'[13]

Sir Archibald told well-wishers that he found it a 'wrench' to leave what he called a very happy office. 'It seemed to us, however,' he added in one letter, 'that we had reached a point where the Government had ceased to be national or to pursue a national as distinct from a party policy, and we concluded that resignation was our only course.'[14] And Churchill, still unsure as to his friend's tactics, said he should have waited for the outcome of the forthcoming World Economic Conference. 'Well anyhow you will be Liberal leader in Scotland,' wrote Churchill, 'and there is nothing like having an official dunghill of one's own to crow from, however small and redolent it may be.'[15] It proved to be a fertile dunghill, when at the 1935 general election Samuel lost his seat and Sir Archibald replaced him as Liberal leader (albeit of only 21 MPs). He steered the party towards a moderate anti-appeasement line as storm clouds gathered in Europe, and refused office under Chamberlain once war broke out in September 1939. Sir Archibald accepted, however, when the call came from Churchill in May 1940 and he became a loyal yet unimpressive secretary of state for air.

The war years meant an unavoidable neglect of his constituency affairs, and at the 1945 Labour landslide Sir Archibald lost his seat, coming last in a remarkable result in which only 61 votes divided three candidates. He accepted a peerage in 1952, becoming 1st Viscount Thurso of Ulbster, although plans for him to re-enter politics as Liberal leader in the House of Lords were abandoned due to his ill health. Thurso spoke actively in the Upper House for three years but spent the last years of his life as an invalid, dying at his London home in Twickenham on 15 June 1970.

Churchill's wartime secretary, John Colville, wrote that 'Sinclair had an air of distinction. With his fine features, black hair, and swarthy complexion he resembled a Spanish grandee rather than the Highland chieftain that he was.'[16] This theatrical demeanour is shared by Sir Archibald's grandson, the 3rd Viscount John Thurso. He now sits as the Liberal Democrat MP for his grandfather's old seat in Caithness, Sutherland and Easter Ross. Thurso was the first hereditary peer to be elected to the Commons and, appropriately, was his party's Scottish affairs spokesman from 2001 until Sir Menzies Campbell took over as Liberal Democrat leader in March 2006.

Sir Godfrey Collins

28 September 1932 – 29 October 1936

Surely one of the dullest men on earth

'The Samuelites have gone for which the Lord be praised,' exclaimed the Conservative MP Sir Cuthbert Headlam, 'and Walter Elliot, Godfrey Collins (of all men!) and Gilmour are the changes – all Scots – and Gilmour gets the Home Office.'[1] The political establishment was more than a little scathing about the appointment of Sir Godfrey Collins as the new secretary of state for Scotland. 'Surely one of the dullest men on earth,' wrote Sir Cuthbert again the following month, adding 'He is a publisher by trade,'[2] as if that detail explained everything. But while the meek may not inherit the earth, the 57-year-old Liberal National Sir Godfrey Collins did find himself entrusted with the Scottish Office more than a decade after his resignation as Liberal chief whip, and what he had assumed would be the end of his ministerial career. The new Scottish secretary, it seems, shared his critics' surprise, later admitting to his 'utter amazement' at receiving the call from Ramsay MacDonald. He was not an instinctively partisan politician so the broad church of the National Government suited Sir Godfrey, who believed that the old party labels had died in 1914 along with the hopes of a whole generation. He did not, however, shine in the House, his physical lameness accounting for an obvious shyness, which also deprived him of the lighter touch so useful in politics. Sir Godfrey also arrived at Dover House just as the devolution issue began, once again, to gather ground. 'The debate on the Address continued and was duller than ever as it was devoted to the discussion of Scottish Home Rule!' wrote Sir Cuthbert, 'apparently this movement is becoming a serious one – what an age of absurdity we live in!'[3]

Sir Cuthbert was referring, indirectly, to a speech from Sir Robert Horne, a Scottish Unionist politician somewhat past his prime. He was, as Stanley Baldwin memorably remarked, 'that rare thing, a Scots cad', and epitomised modern Unionist thinking. Sir Robert was depressed at the quality of the new ministers, including Sir Godfrey, but saw an opportunity to influence future Scottish Office policy. He said:

> There is, in my view, far too much of the departmental work of Scotland done in Whitehall . . . there should be retained at Whitehall only that kind of Department which is necessary for the Parliamentary side of their proceedings. There should be concentrated in Edinburgh – I say boldly "in Edinburgh" – all the main work of the Departments which look after the business of Scotland . . .[4]

This was typical of the small 'n' nationalism being espoused by Scottish Unionists of the period. Sir Godfrey had already reached the same conclusion, and this twin-track political approach (administrative reform coupled with Scottish symbolism) dominated his four years at the Scottish Office. 'He is, indeed, a Cabinet in himself,' said Sir Robert of the Scottish secretary. 'He has got to do for Scotland what the whole Cabinet has to do for the rest of the country.'

Sir Godfrey responded later in the same debate, promising to continue his predecessor's policy of 'full-steam ahead within the means at his disposal'. 'Naturally,' he added, 'in times of distress, people turn to various remedies to improve their economic situation. Let me turn now to this demand. So far as the Government are concerned, Home Rule for Scotland is an academic question, and I have not asked my colleagues to consider it.' However, he continued:

> During my first official visit there it was apparent to me, as it had been to my predecessors, that the existing arrangement, whereby 10 different Departments are scattered in 22 different buildings throughout the city, is neither conducive to economy or efficiency . . . A centralised building in Edinburgh to which all sections of public life could come for the transaction of business with responsible heads would have real and obvious advantages, and I feel that sooner or later, such a building must be provided.[5]

Accordingly, Sir Godfrey revealed, he was now working with the first commissioner of works on such a scheme, but warned MPs that as 'financial considerations are paramount' he could not say for certain whether the Treasury would approve. This was to become the nucleus of St Andrew's House in Edinburgh, the architectural manifestation of consolidated Scottish administration. Sir Godfrey also announced plans to transfer further administrative work to Edinburgh in the interim, largely to deal with local authorities, and revealed that the chancellor (Neville Chamberlain) had agreed to prepare a balance sheet detailing the financial relations between Scotland and England.[6] He did not directly address Sir Robert's workload concerns, but gave his under-secretary, Noel Skelton ('who, I may say, has been very helpful to me'), additional responsibilities for education as well as housing and health.

The firm of Collins was, by the time of Sir Godfrey's appointment in 1932, an established Scottish publishing company. It was founded by a schoolmaster, William Collins, in Glasgow in 1819, and when it was renamed William Collins, Sons & Co. in 1868 it began to specialise in religious and educational books. When Sir Godfrey took charge in 1917 the firm began publishing fiction, including all but the first six of Agatha Christie's now famous crime novels.[7] He later joked that he would never admit whether the publication of his first classic or his elevation to Cabinet had given him the most pleasure.

Godfrey Pattison Collins was born on 26 June 1875 in Glasgow, the second of three children of Alexander Glen Collins, and his wife Cornelia, daughter of Godfrey Pattison, a Glasgow merchant. Following preparatory school, aged just 13, Godfrey joined HMS *Britannia*, but retired from the navy in 1893 in order to join the expanding family firm. Collins went to London to train as a compositor, and from there went to Germany to investigate the latest printing technology. He discovered state-of-the-art rotary printing presses in Leipzig, which he swiftly had installed in Glasgow. The Collins firm now churned out cheap books, beginning with the Collins Illustrated Pocket Classics, followed by the Nation's Library and the even cheaper Sevenpennies editions.

By now successful, both professionally and financially, Collins decided to follow in the family tradition of public service, standing in – and winning – a seat for the Liberals in Greenock at the first general election of 1910. An enthusiastic proponent of the New Liberalism championed by David Lloyd George, he soon became parliamentary private secretary to the war secretary and a member of the War Office supplies committee. Collins' administrative talents came to the fore when he served in Mesopotamia (now Iraq) during the First World War, where he reorganised the chaotic systems of supply and accounting, saving the army millions of pounds. He returned to the House of Commons after the war and established himself as an expert on financial matters, receiving a knighthood in 1919; he became a junior lord of the Treasury in Lloyd George's coalition government soon after. However, Sir Godfrey soon became disillusioned with the increasingly divided Liberal Party, and when the government (in his eyes) failed to stabilise either the economy or the international situation, he resigned in February 1920. He joined H. H. Asquith's Liberals and four years later became the faction's chief whip, but was removed when Lloyd George became party leader once again in 1926.

Outside parliament, Sir Godfrey was an enthusiastic stalker, a talented tennis player and an experienced yachtsman (representing Britain in the British–American six-metre cup in 1931). He also remained active in publishing, commissioning 'new' authors such as H. G. Wells and Walter de la Mare.

In 1931 Sir Godfrey decided to tie his colours to the National government's mast and managed to retain his Greenock seat with an increased majority. This, combined with his previous resignation and known dislike for German reparations (which he thought damaged an important trading partner), meant that when Sir Godfrey joined the Cabinet as Scottish secretary in 1932, he did so with a considerable amount of respect for his political judgement. He was, however, also thought boring and unimpressive in debate. 'He had a very sharp ear for Parliamentary opinion and a very sharp nose for Parliamentary trouble,' recalled his former private secretary Sir Charles Cunningham. 'But he was, although a man of ideas, essentially an inarticulate man.'[8]

But Sir Godfrey did, fortunately, have a knack for seeing things through. Therefore, when he promised in his maiden speech as Scottish secretary to develop a scheme for transferring Scottish administration to Edinburgh, he worked towards doing exactly that. Just over a year later, Sir Godfrey announced to the House that:

> I have made arrangements that a branch of the Scottish Office should be established in Edinburgh at as early a date as possible for the transaction of such business as can be conveniently carried on there, including in particular work connected with local authority administration in its various aspects. I have also in view a further transfer, at the earliest practicable date, of officers of the Scottish Education Department.[9]

The Clydeside MP James Maxton sarcastically asked if the Scottish secretary intended to deprive the House of the benefit of his presence. 'On no account,' replied Collins, and in January 1935 the new Whitehall outpost opened at 28 Drumsheugh Gardens in Edinburgh, with a staff of 20 under the guidance of Sir David Milne (later permanent under-secretary at the Scottish Office). The National Galleries of Scotland loaned some of its treasures to decorate the new office, Sir Godfrey wryly noting on his first visit that these amounted to a large canvass depicting the rape of the sabines and a 'slightly randy looking bust of Nero' outside the door to his room.[10]

'In a few years the new Government Building [will] arise on the Calton Hill site in Edinburgh – the loveliest capital in Europe,' he told civil servants at its official opening. 'Scottish administration [will] then have a home worthy of its responsibilities and the status of the capital of Scotland as the centre of public administration [will] be adequately symbolised.'[11] The Royal Fine Art Commission of Scotland had approved the Calton Hill site in July 1933, and a year later the architect Thomas Tait's plans for the new government buildings – as yet un-named – were given the go ahead. By the end of 1935 Scottish Office officials were also busy preparing the case for a Committee of Enquiry into Scottish Administration. Sir Godfrey was enthusiastic, and, as the whole exercise effectively built upon Sir John Gilmour's vision and administrative reforms of the 1920s, he chose the former Scottish secretary as its chairman. Sadly, Sir Godfrey's premature death a few months later meant he neither lived to see the completion of St Andrew's House on Calton Hill, nor had the satisfaction of announcing the inquiry's formation to the House.

Alongside Sir Godfrey's successful pursuit of administrative consolidation came an equally dedicated assault upon three of Scotland's greatest ills: health, housing and industrial depression. The picture when Collins joined the government in 1932 was bleak. Four hundred thousand Scots – more than 26 per cent of the insured workforce – were out of work; 20 new factories had opening in 1932 but 29 had closed; and in the industrial west the situation was even worse. In October 1934 the Cabinet agreed to review proposals for the so-called depressed areas. It identified four regions, including part of Lanarkshire, which were to receive additional funding. Sir Godfrey had reservations about the special areas being supervised by a single UK Commissioner, and pushed for a separate Scottish co-ordinator. The government eventually agreed to his request and awarded the new Scottish commissioner[12] a budget based on twice the Goschen formula (which calculated Scottish public expenditure), a significant achievement for the Scottish secretary. Sir Godfrey's already substantial ministerial brief now included economic development, and he also saw that a Scottish Economic Committee was established, under the chairmanship of the industrialist Sir James Lithgow, to consider methods of improving economic conditions in Scotland.

Another battlefront was the still woeful state of Scottish housing. Nineteen-thirty-two had seen a housing boom in England, but little change in Scotland beyond Edinburgh and a few other towns. In November, the health minister Sir Hilton Young proposed withdrawing the housing subsidy in England and Wales, while Sir Godfrey argued that in Scotland it should remain. Again, the Cabinet agreed, and retained a Scottish subsidy of £3 for the next two years. 'In spite of all our efforts since 1919,' observed Sir Godfrey in a Cabinet memo, 'the housing shortage in Scotland is still acute . . . It is obvious, therefore, that, if [the] subsidy were wholly withdrawn, private enterprise would have to fill a much wider gap in Scotland than in England.'[13]

By 1934 government policy was moving towards state-assisted slum clearance and the relief of overcrowding. The Scottish secretary secured a separate Scottish Housing Bill and was granted a £6 15s subsidy per house for the next 40 years – significantly higher than the £3 per house that was agreed for England and Wales. His moving of the Second Reading of the Housing (Scotland) Bill in February 1935 was, Sir Godfrey admitted later, the only speech of his on which he looked back with pride. 'We intend to destroy 60,000 slum houses and rehouse the occupants in healthy homes,' he told MPs. 'By destroying the slums and abolishing overcrowding we are performing an act of social justice which will ensure health and happiness to many who are alive to-day and to generations yet unborn.'[14] The Scottish secretary was also concerned about aesthetics and appointed a committee of 'well-known Scottish architects' to advise on the look of any new housing. 'Drab and mean surroundings do not encourage a bright and healthy outlook,' he advised. 'If we make the homes of our people more attractive, shall we not help encourage an appreciation of beauty?'[15] But Sir Godfrey's admirable vision proved to be overambitious. Although by 1936 one fifth of Scots lived in houses built with state aid, even a local authority building rate of 20,000 homes a year was not enough.

Forever linked with housing conditions was public health, and in June 1933 the Scottish secretary established the Cathcart Committee on Scottish Health Services to advise on possible legislation. This did not, as Sir Godfrey expected, recommend state co-ordination of Scotland's disparate medical services. Instead, it proposed an extension of the National Health Insurance scheme to cover the dependants of insured workers, using surplus funds to finance what became the 1936 Maternity Services (Scotland) Bill: an attempt to tackle Scotland's disproportionately high infant mortality rate.[16]

Sir Godfrey had a rather Victorian belief in the virtues of hard work, but on education he had some remarkably modern ideas. Speaking in Edinburgh on 5 April 1933, he called for schools and industry to move closer together, and for the removal of what he called 'lumber' from lessons, such as 'Obscure tributaries of rivers; lists of dates of the early English and Scottish Kings; pedantic insistence on grammar; [and] impossible questions of arithmetic the children would never have to solve.' 'Away with all this lumber,' he said, 'dull, useless, and not educative, and then concentrate on the essentials.'[17] Sir Godfrey's interest in education sprang, in part, from his previous experience of publishing school textbooks. On learning that children often spent a large part of their summer holidays waiting for exam results, he reduced the time taken to publish them. Moreover, in his Education (Scotland) Bill of 1936, he sought to raise the school leaving age to 15 (starting from 1939), and to scrap the granting of exemptions between the age of 12 and 14 for children who had obtained 'beneficial employment'. Secondary education was divided into junior and senior schools, while the Scottish secretary also intended 'to promote the intellectual and physical well-being of our children so that they may be enabled to undertake with resource, intelligence and courage the responsibilities of life and citizenship.'[18] Again, however, Sir Godfrey's public-spirited reforms were not ultimately successful; the outbreak of the Second World War prevented the leaving age from rising until 1947.

Sir Godfrey produced a prolific number of Bills during his four years at the Scottish Office, an impressive feat given the constraints of the period. He legislated to introduce a minimum wage for land workers and created several hundred smallholdings for pig and poultry farming; the Herring Industry (Scotland) Bill of 1935 set up the Herring Industry Board, while the Illegal Trawling (Scotland) Bill was much welcomed by inshore fishermen. Two officials, Sir David Milne and Sir Charles Cunningham, admired the Scottish secretary's political style. His deliberations were crisp, often laconic, and he disliked being surrounded by paperwork, usually returning whatever correspondence was sent to him with an additional note from himself.[19]

Like his successor Tom Johnston, Sir Godfrey also proved adept at promoting Scotland's commercial potential. In April 1934 he opened an exhibition at the Imperial Institute in South Kensington entitled 'Scotland Calling'. Organised by the Scottish Travel Association, this included everything from a model of Robert Burns' cottage to performances by the London Gaelic Choir, all aimed at promoting Scotland as a holiday destination. Sir Godfrey boasted of a land of cheap golf, state-of-the-art roads, scenic beauty and even a monster.[20] On the latter attraction the Scottish secretary proved himself perhaps a little too dedicated. In response to a letter from Sir Murdoch MacDonald in December 1933, Sir Godfrey contacted the chief constable of Inverness-shire, who assured him that five constables were stationed around Loch Ness, none of whom had seen so much as a fin flap. 'The Chief Constable has,' responded Sir Godfrey, 'however, offered to cause warning to be given to as many of the residents and visitors as possible for the purpose of preventing any attack on the animal if sighted, and I have told him that I shall be glad if he would do so.'[21] Perhaps mischievously, the Scottish Unionist MP William Anstruther-Gray asked the Scottish secretary during question time if, in the interests of science, he would investigate the existence of the fabled creature. 'There appears to be no reason to suspect the presence of any baneful monster in Loch Ness,' replied Sir Godfrey, 'and as regards scientific interests, I think that, in present circumstances, further researches are properly a matter for the private enterprise of scientists, aided by the zeal of the Press and of photographers.' The Labour MP Neil Maclean chipped in – not unreasonably – and asked, 'Would not the Scottish Office find their time better occupied in trying to capture the monster of unemployment in Scotland?'[22]

Sir Godfrey's battle to retain his Greenock seat at the 1935 general election proved to be a rowdy affair. Finding that he could not be heard during a hustings in the town hall, he armed members of his family with a bell and instead addressed bemused voters at the open windows of their tenements. 'We shall miss Sir Godfrey Collins from the House,' declared a Sunday newspaper. 'There seems very little doubt that he will be defeated.' But Sir Godfrey polled the highest number of votes in the seat's history; an impressive result, especially considering that he had recently informed his astonished parliamentary private secretary (a young Alec Douglas-Home) that he had visited his constituency 'about five times in thirty years'.[23] Sir Godfrey, therefore, did not impress everyone. 'Collins did his best I am sure, but he had no health and can bring no energy to an office which lacks it,' wrote the former Unionist MP Sir John Stirling Maxwell to Sir John Gilmour in 1935. 'Now that the Housing Act is on the Statute Book it is a good opportunity to tackle new questions which want tackling . . . no one seems capable of more than messing about with a Deer Forest Bill which is ten years out of date'.[24]

Collins' health was, generally speaking, indifferent, and he was absent from his duties for weeks on end at several points during his four years at the Scottish Office. Poor health also dogged Noel Skelton, Sir Godfrey's under-secretary throughout this time. A lifelong bachelor, Skelton was a talented Unionist MP with a wide outlook and an enquiring mind. In four lively articles for the *Spectator* in 1923 – later republished as *Constructive Conservatism* – he contributed the phrase 'a property-owning democracy' to the political lexicon. However, despite his standing among younger Tory MPs, Skelton's ministerial career had an inexplicably slow start, and he only entered government in 1931 as a Tory counterbalance to the Samuelite Scottish secretary Sir Archibald Sinclair. He proved to be a stimulating, if un-remarkable, junior minister and was re-elected for the Combined Scottish Universities seat at the 1935 election. But just weeks later, Skelton died of cancer in an Edinburgh nursing home aged only 55. Sir Godfrey paid tribute the following day: 'We shall miss him more than I care to think: but the memory of his work and personality will long remain as an inspiration to the many friends who mourn him.'[25] And for Sir Godfrey, too, poor health meant that time was short. In August 1936 he embarked upon an official tour of the Western Isles before heading to the south of France on holiday.

The Scottish secretary had been feeling tired but was convinced that a few weeks of sunshine and sea-bathing would restore him. Nevertheless, his health deteriorated and he travelled to Switzerland in the hope that its bracing climate would help him recover. 'I see that Godfrey Collins is seriously ill,' wrote Chamberlain, 'we are rather a groggy Cabinet!'[26] Some old nasal trouble had returned and in September Sir Godfrey underwent a small operation. This appeared to work and he began to make a good recovery, but a few weeks later he suffered a relapse and died of septicaemia in a Zurich nursing home on 13 October 1936. 'By the untimely death of Sir Godfrey Collins,' said the *Scotsman*, 'the public life of Scotland has been impoverished by the loss of a distinguished and devoted servant of the State, whose record of humane and sympathetic administration has left a permanent mark upon the Scottish Departments over which he was so proud to preside.' The obituary continued:

> If the times had been more propitious, he would have accomplished more for the Scotland which he loved; but although he had many disappointments, he achieved enough to show that in him the Scottish Office had an administrator of initiative and insight, who worked with single-minded purpose for the improvement of the social and industrial conditions in his native country, and left it better equipped than he found it to face its present and future problems.[27]

'It is probable that his four years as Scottish secretary were the happiest of his life,'[28] wrote another old friend, while in the House. Stanley Baldwin (once again prime minister following MacDonald's resignation) led the tributes to Sir Godfrey:

> It is no secret to many of us that he had more than his share of private sorrow . . . I never said good-bye to him, when we were separating for a holiday, without some such words passing as passed only last July between us. He said: "I want to tell you how much I enjoy my work, how I love working for Scotland, and with what pleasure I work with all of you."[29]

Sir Godfrey's funeral took place three days after his death at the Glasgow Necropolis. The coffin – draped in purple and gold – arrived by train from London in the morning, and the Rev. Neville Davidson led a simple service which included Sir Godfrey's favourite hymns, 'There is a green hill far away' and 'Abide with me'. Sixty-four years later Scotland would bid farewell to another of its political leaders at Glasgow Cathedral. Donald Dewar was of course first minister by the time he died in the year 2000, so Sir Godfrey Collins holds the tragic honour of being the only Scottish secretary to die in office.

WALTER ELLIOT

29 OCTOBER 1936 – 16 MAY 1938

Hamlet without the gloom

Shortly after midnight on 11 May 1941, Colonel Walter Elliot, the Conservative MP for the Kelvingrove Division of Glasgow and former Scottish secretary, could be seen laying into the main doors of the 900-year-old Westminster Hall with a double-headed axe. The Luftwaffe had showered London with bombs and this historic part of the old Westminster Palace was at risk from fire, but its doors were locked. The flames needed to be tackled from within, and Elliot had advised that fire services be switched from the doomed House of Commons chamber to the hall. Colonel Elliot was a romantic figure with an acute sense of heritage.[1] As one contemporary historian has observed, if Elliot did not exactly look the part of a Renaissance man he had many of the necessary attributes: learned, erudite, creative and amusing, he oozed character and was easily the most intriguing Scottish secretary since the late nineteenth century. Elliot was also the first secretary of state to be entirely educated in Scotland, and was overtly Scottish in outlook, even describing himself on one occasion as 'an unrepentant Scottish nationalist'.[2]

'Unpunctual, unpartisan, indecisive, a real political Hamlet without the gloom,' judged his friend and biographer Sir Colin Coote; he 'could argue so brilliantly on both sides that a conflict in his mind too often ended in a draw.'[3] Elliot was, as a result, often an indecisive minister and not everyone's cup of tea, so when he succeeded the late Sir Godfrey Collins as Scottish secretary in late 1936, it took many by surprise. 'Elliot had grown stale in Agriculture and I have no doubt he is very glad to be rid of it although he didn't much fancy Scotland,' wrote Neville Chamberlain. 'But I think he will do it well and appeal to the Scots while I should have been nervous about him in one of the English offices.'[4] The *Scotsman* had tipped John Colville as Collins' successor, but observed that:

> Mr Elliot will not be altogether sorry to leave the Department of Agriculture, where he has had many worries and anxieties. At the same time he is not

stepping from a difficult job to an easy one. Agriculture problems will follow him to the Scottish Office, and, in addition, he will have multifarious duties of a worrying nature. The Scottish Office has not been a bed of roses for many years, and it is not likely to provide a rest cure for its new occupant.[5]

The new Scottish secretary was actually an Elliot twice over. Born Walter Elliot Elliot in Lanark on 19 September 1888, he was the eldest son of William Elliott, a self-made man and livestock auctioneer, and his wife Elizabeth. In 1892 she died following childbirth and so all the Elliot children were largely raised by their maternal grandmother in Glasgow, where Walter was influenced by the rather eccentric interests of his uncle, Dr Shiels, who later went bust trying to turn base metals into gold. Elliot progressed from Lanark High School to the Glasgow Academy and in 1905 he matriculated at Glasgow University to study medicine. He joined a group of 'half-baked men of letters' which included the playwright James Bridie, and the future socialist politicians James Maxton and Tom Johnston. A star debater, Elliot refused to be bound by conventional party labels, fuelling later rumours that he had initially flirted with socialism. In the rectorial election of 1908 he simultaneously supported the Conservative candidate Lord Curzon, helped the Liberal Club in nominating David Lloyd George, and, according to Bridie, ended up voting for Keir Hardie. Elliot became president of the union in 1911, following a year as editor of the university magazine, and after graduating he worked at Glasgow Royal Infirmary. In the First World War he served as a medical officer with the Royal Scots Greys on the Western Front, and he was awarded the Military Cross for his part in the action at Wancourt in April 1917.

Elliot refused to enter the family business (Lawrie and Symington auctioneers) and was recovering from a leg wound when he was asked to stand for the Lanark Division of Lanarkshire as a coalition candidate in October 1918. 'Yes,' he reputedly replied, 'for which side?' He opted for the Unionists and sat for Lanark until losing the seat in December 1923. In 1919 Elliot began a ten-year association with the Scottish Office, first as parliamentary private secretary (PPS) to its first parliamentary under-secretary for health, John William Pratt, and latterly as the health minister when Pratt lost his seat. Elliot was an unconventional MP, forming a dining club called the Alternative Government Group (mostly comprising PPSs), while also becoming a member of the New Coalition Group under Oscar Guest, which promoted the idea of a new centrist party. He was also unusual in policy terms, pushing for full devolution to the Irish Free State in 1920, and making sympathetic noises over the miners' strike of 1921. He seems to have worked well with both Pratt and the Liberal Scottish Secretary Robert Munro, but his impression of Viscount Novar –

who replaced Munro in 1922 – fluctuated between frustration and affection, feelings not helped by the Scottish secretary's presence in the House of Lords, which effectively left Elliot to handle departmental work in the Commons.

'There is only one leader for a Conservative Party,' Elliot wrote to a friend in April 1923, 'Winston Churchill . . . I really shouldn't think Baldwin is much good – a capable business man – can't talk – never will be able to talk . . . As for Bonar, well, here's a Premier sitting all through the stormiest scene for ten years and not able to move his larynx to utter a syllable. That alone would demand his resignation if it went on 5 weeks more.'[6] But even if Elliot did not consider Baldwin 'much good', the future prime minister rated Elliot highly and when the minority Labour government fell in late 1924 (Elliot having returned to parliament in a by-election),[7] he returned him to the Scottish Office, this time with Sir John Gilmour as Scottish secretary. Elliot was disappointed to say the least. ' "I want you to carry on",' wrote Elliot, quoting Baldwin. 'And I said "All right." So that was that. He mumbled the usual insincerity about "seeing if I could do something better for you later" but he obviously didn't mean it. Well there's that. I don't think I could have refused. I did not want to but I don't think I could have – it would have looked horrid.'[8] Baldwin had toyed with the idea of making Elliot minister for labour, but thought better of it. 'Well, I had him in mind,' he wrote to the Whitehall mandarin Tom Jones, 'but my courage failed me.'[9] Sir John and Elliot had voted to sustain the coalition government at the Carlton Club meeting in late 1922 so got on well, and Elliot's five years as under-secretary for health proved to be both prolific and creative.

At around this time Elliot forged close friendships with the coalition Liberal MP Sir Colin Coote, later his biographer, and Blanche 'Baffy' Dugdale, a niece and biographer of the former Scottish secretary (and prime minister) Arthur James Balfour. She introduced him to Zionism and their flirtatious correspondence from the period provides an invaluable insight into Elliot's thoughts and experiences. As an under-secretary, he sat on the research committee of the Empire Marketing Board, and as a leading authority on nutrition,[10] Elliot used the board to pilot a scheme for providing free milk to schoolchildren in 1927. He also expanded and modernised Scotland's hospitals, badgered local authorities and building unions to accept Weir's steel housing scheme, and worked with Sir John on his plans for reforming local government and Scottish Office admin-istration. 'They are a pretty contrast,' noted the *Saturday Review*. 'Sir John Gilmour, rather stiff of movement and precise of utterance, but ever courteous withal; Major Elliot loose-limbed, voluble and pungent; the wax-work Laird and the animated Gogmagog.'[11] Elliot would not be the first under-secretary to outshine his superior, but they made a good team, Sir John commenting that his junior was 'a tower of strength to any office'.[12]

In 1927 Elliot was appointed a British delegate to the League of Nations conference in Geneva, consolidating an interest in foreign affairs which was to last for the rest of his career. Elliot was a colourful figure and the press loved his playful sarcasm and elegant irony. 'You cannot possibly feel in awe of a man who is so ready to laugh at himself,' wrote the *Aberdeen Press & Journal* in February 1928, 'so unostentatiously learned, and so deeply interested in the lives and opinions of other people'.[13] English newspapers were similarly enthused. 'He is a brilliant young man,' gushed the *Yorkshire Evening Post* in May 1928. 'If one could imagine Parliament where a competition was being held as to which member could talk longest on the greatest variety of subjects without boring the House, then certainly Major Elliot would be well in the running for the prize.'[14]

Elliot engineered Baldwin's campaign to become rector of Glasgow University in March 1928, in many ways a wise career move despite his private views of the prime minister. The year before, Baldwin had contributed a flattering introduction to Elliot's book *Toryism in the Twentieth Century*, a thoughtful plea that in the current scientific and political climate Conservatives should not only be instinctive reformers, but they could be more successful than dogmatic radicals. Elliot had been dreaming of promotion to become financial secretary to the Treasury since 1925, an ambition fuelled by constant press speculation to the same effect. Instead, in May 1928, Baldwin charged Elliot with assisting Arthur Samuel, the financial secretary to the Treasury, and the chancellor, Winston Churchill, on that year's Budget. Churchill was impressed, writing to Baldwin that among government under-secretaries 'Walter Elliot is by far the best'.[15] Like his academic and political contemporary Tom Johnston (who served as William Adamson's junior in 1929–31), Elliot's lengthy ministerial apprenticeship was valuable preparation for the top job he would hold some years later.

'The Scot was the dominant figure,' wrote the socialist intellectual Beatrice Webb of Elliot following one of her famous mutton suppers, 'a big loosely made man trained as an MD . . . with good manners and personal charm, an ugly but pleasing face, homely but well-bred manner.'[16] Elliot continued to thrive, at least socially, out of government following the 1929 election. He had a wide range of friends from across the political spectrum, and was even a welcome guest at the *New Statesman*. And at the Lord North Street home of his future wife, Katherine Tennant,[17] Elliot also mixed with young Tories like Alec Dunglass (later Alec Douglas-Home), Noel Skelton and Harold

Macmillan. But his judgement did, on occasion, fail him. He commended Oswald Mosley's radical plans for economic recovery, which resulted in a rebuke from Baldwin but not exclusion from the National government in 1932. 'Elliot's entry into the Cabinet was assured,' wrote the Conservative MP Sir Cuthbert Headlam. 'He is a clever man and has taken his chances, but I don't look upon him as a leader. He is too loquacious – however, he may get over this.'[18] Elliot became a successful minister for agriculture, combining modest protectionist policies with imaginative marketing schemes to reverse the recent slump in British farming. His best-known scheme, the Milk Marketing Board, began in 1933 and continued his Scottish Office policy of providing low-priced milk to schools.

So when Sir Godfrey Collins died in October 1936 the last thing Elliot wanted was a sideways move to another department, and especially not to the Scottish Office.[19] Officials liked him, as did the media, but he annoyed some colleagues with his rapid-fire style of speaking, and he failed to make much of an impact at Cabinet meetings. The move also meant Elliot's treasured marketing schemes were left in the lurch, although he quickly adjusted to his new brief, even maintaining his irreverent correspondence with the infatuated Baffy Dugdale. '[o]ff to Edinburgh to be sworn in on Friday by the Court of Session (I had forgotten about that),' he wrote on 3 November. 'Shall be racing against time for a week or two. If I get time I shall have grand plans for Coronating the King and Governing Scotland, but time may be denied me.'[20]

Elliot became Scottish secretary just as the abdication crisis was nearing its dramatic conclusion, but the old ebullience about King and Country was still there. 'Is democracy rising to the height of the events of the day, the great and terrible events which we see all around us?' he asked MPs during the debate on the Address:

> We have a young King opening his first Parliament, we have a House of Commons fresh from the polls, with its mandate still unexhausted, we have the whole world looking to us to see whether this country can rise to the level demanded by the events of the day . . . whether our country is great enough to seize the opportunity of prosperity which the machines have held out for us.[21]

Elliot's approach to the Scottish Office largely followed this theme. The department gave him an excellent opportunity to continue his moderately interventionist policies, and he quickly set to work on developing housing policy and the depressed areas. He had helped craft the original 'Special Areas' policy and now used it as a framework to extend the state house-building scheme begun by his old boss Sir John Gilmour. He wrote

to Neville Chamberlain suggesting that the Steel Housing Company be
used to build between 2,000 and 4,000 houses per annum in areas where
labour and housing shortages were the most acute. The chancellor ruled
out the use of steel due to rearmament measures, but he sympathised
with the Scottish position and instead proposed that a special housing
association should operate a limited programme within the Scottish
Special Area. Elliot was especially interested in Glasgow, which was
not only his home town but the location of his largely working-class
constituency; he told one official that 'it was a quarter of the problem for
population, but two thirds of it in sentiment'.[22] Elliot pushed for a
Government Housing Board to build in areas of greatest need, but
instead got the Scottish (Special Areas) Housing Association. On housing,
recalled his under-secretary Colonel James Scrymgeour-Wedderburn,
Elliot's 'mind was always on fire to get things done', [23] and the new
association went some way to satisfying that desire. Financed directly by
the Treasury, it proved useful in supplementing housing stock let down
by underwhelming take-up from local authorities, and by 1938 it had
built a total of 26,000 new homes.

On the wider economy, Elliot believed, 'The Scottish picture was not
one dotted with a number of black spots, but was generally grey
throughout.'[24] Chamberlain wanted to scrap the Special Areas Act in
1937 but instead agreed to a new one which included financing industrial
estates. The Scottish manifestation of this new thinking was the Hillington
Industrial Estate, four miles west of Glasgow. Elliot formally opened it on
26 November 1937 with some typically colourful rhetoric. 'Scotland is on
the march again,' he said, adding:

> Twice – once in the eighteenth century with the revolution in agriculture and
> once in the nineteenth century with the industrial revolution – the nation of
> Scotland has seized its dwelling place and transformed it with a furious energy
> to which there are few parallels in Europe . . . Hillington is the sign that the
> second industrial revolution, the mastery of the machine, can bring both health
> and wealth.[25]

Sadly, while industrial estates were a novel and enduring idea, Hillington
failed to fulfill those dreams. Elliot later asked for additional state aid from
the chancellor Sir John Simon, but the Treasury remained suspicious of
giving Scotland special treatment, not least for fear of consequent claims
from other regions of the country. 'Walter Elliot was a delight to work with',
recalled the civil servant Sir Charles Cunningham. 'He had one of the most
acute and lively minds I think I've come across . . . [and] he teemed with
ideas on every possible subject, he had a wide experience of life, a pretty

shrewd political mind.'[26] As Scottish secretary, Elliot was widely considered to be a possible party leader, if not a future prime minister.

One of Elliot's first tasks at the Scottish Office was to announce the long-expected inquiry into Scottish government under the chairmanship of Sir John Gilmour. 'Before a new building is completed,' he told the House, 'I think it desirable that a review of the present Scottish administrative arrangements should be undertaken.'[27] The Gilmour Committee contained cross-party elements – Tom Johnston for Labour and Sir Robert Hamilton for the Liberals – and it reported a year later in October 1937:

> The duties of the other great offices of state are in general defined functionally. The duties of the Secretary of State are, on the other hand, defined on a geographical basis . . . He is popularly regarded as 'Scotland's Minister' and our evidence shows that there is an increasing tendency to appeal to him on all matters which have a Scottish aspect, even if on a strict view they are outside the province of his duties as statutorily defined . . . there is a wide and undefined area in which he is expected to be the mouthpiece of Scottish opinion in the Cabinet and elsewhere.[28]

This was the apex of modern Unionist thinking, that effective administrative devolution would also be an effective neutraliser of home rule aspirations, an analysis Elliot more or less agreed with. The Scottish Office was to become centred upon one man, the Scottish secretary, and the board system was finally to be abolished – completing a decade-old ambition of Sir John's. The committee settled upon four new departments: Agriculture, Health, Education, and the Scottish Home Department, which included prisons and fisheries. Each was to be headed by an assistant secretary based in Edinburgh and co-ordinated by a non-departmental permanent under-secretary mainly based in London. Elliot gave his reaction to the Scottish Unionist Association's Political School of Study a few days later:

> I do not deny that there will be difficulties and anomalies. There are always anomalies in any system of government, but the fact remains that in perfect peace without Parliamentary fury or agitation, without the necessity for great popular demonstrations up and down the country, the principle that we should now decant a great deal of Scottish administration from London and concentrate it in Edinburgh has been accepted, and will be put into effect as soon as arrangements can be made.[29]

Crafting a Bill to implement Sir John's proposals actually fell to Elliot's successor, John Colville, but the Scottish secretary did compose a Cabinet memo on where Scotland now stood. 'I have my memorandum on the Scottish Totalitarian State nearly ready for the Cabinet,'[30] he joked to Baffy on 19 November, and submitted it soon after. While he concurred with the Gilmour Report, he warned that its proposals 'will not in themselves dispose of the problems upon whose solution a general improvement in Scottish social and economic conditions depends. It is the consciousness of their existence which is reflected, not in the small and unimportant Nationalist Party, but in the dissatisfaction and unease amongst moderate and reason-able people of every rank.'[31] Disaffection, he added, which had been expressed in every recent book written about Scotland. 'I am revolving in my mind the continuality of the Kingdom of Scotland', he mused again to Baffy near the end of 1937. 'Neville will yet find it dangerous to intern me there. I will break up the United Kingdom.'[32]

Elliot was, like many Unionist MPs, a Scottish cultural nationalist without ever becoming a political one. Speaking in the same debate which Sir Robert Horne used to set out his vision for Scotland in 1932, Elliot said the idea of a national parliament for Scotland was 'utterly fantastic and absolutely anachronistic', but added that 'We have to get Devolution undoubtedly.' 'We all know that the original self-determinationist was the man who went down to Hades,' he quipped, 'but could not get into Hell and was given matches and sulphur and told to go and self-determine himself somewhere else.'[33]

On 19 March 1937, Elliot and Lady Elgin cut the first sod at Bellahouston Park in Glasgow for what was become the Empire Exhibition of 1938. This was much more in Elliot's line: an expression of Scotland's achieve-ments within a UK context. He also showed his commitment to Sco-tland's heritage by introducing a Bill to improve the upkeep of historical records, the Public Records (Scotland) Act, which allowed for the return of documents 'borrowed' by England centuries before. The Scottish secretary also established the Films of Scotland Committee in the run up to the £11 million Empire Exhibition. Elliot admired the pioneering documentary maker John Grierson, especially his films *Drifters* and *Night Mail*, and Grierson found in Elliot a man who understood well the power of film. With the Scottish secretary's encouragement, Grierson advised on the production of a series of seven films which were to reflect 'modern Scotland' and form the centrepiece of the exhibition's film programme. Elliot was himself a gifted broadcaster, bemusing his Kelvingrove con-stituents with a pre-recorded new year's message which was shown in two local cinemas.[34] He also gave regular radio talks on everything from the local authority block grant to the 'wonders of Scotland'. Elliot had an endearing style, but it failed to impress his nationalist critics, who were

unmoved by his cultural activities. 'If Mr Elliot wants to be a great figure
in Scottish history,' said the SNP's honorary secretary, John MacCormick, after one broadcast, 'or a great power in British politics if he prefers
the phrase – then my advice to him is that to-morrow he should hand in
his resignation as Secretary of State for Scotland to the Prime Minister
and say "I cannot go on, for this is an impossible task." 'If Mr Elliot had
the courage and vision to do that,' added MacCormick, 'he would rank in
history as one of the greatest men that Scotland ever produced.'[35]

Elliot's incumbency coincided with a dramatic period in international
affairs, beginning with the Spanish Civil War in 1936, taking in the
German invasion of the Rhineland, the Austrian Anschluss, and culmi-
nating in 1938's Munich debacle. Elliot had always travelled widely,
making regular trips to Europe, Africa and South America while at the
Scottish Office in the 1920s. In 1927, he was a member of the British
delegation (led by Sir Austen Chamberlain) to the League of Nations
conference in Geneva, a duty he repeated ten years later, cancelling a trip
to Canada to join Sir Anthony Eden. 'Here we are much moved by the
Japs,' he wrote to his wife Katherine from the Assembly, 'but find London
is not at all. I mean Whitehall. Anthony [Eden] has gone on leave to
Yorkshire, nobody is running the Office (I mean no Minister) and Alec
Cadogan is also on leave.'[36] Elliot clearly saw this as an opportunity to
further his own ambitions, writing again to Katherine on 2 October: 'The
Foreign Office and I are now on close terms.'[37] But in reality the Scottish
secretary was deeply unhappy with the course of European politics, and
especially the government's reaction to it. 'A strong and prosperous nation
will be formidable to its enemies whatever its armaments may be,' he told
the House in October 1937, 'and a weak and divided nation will inevitably
be ridden over roughshod whatever it may have in tortoise-like armour or
machine guns. Unless we have a prosperous nation at home, we shall be
unable to take any line at all in affairs abroad.'[38]

Elliot had come close to resigning in 1936 when Germany invaded the
Rhineland, and again with Eden over Italy the following year. But having
failed to do so, he believed his duty was to remain with Chamberlain.
'Well well. First as to News Here,' Elliot wrote to Baffy in January 1938.
'That is quite simple. There isn't any. Foreign Affairs are as you see them
– but the Cabinet doesn't meet & Neville quite sincerely goes shooting at
Chequers.'[39] Publicly, Elliot remained loyal, but from February 1938 he
spoke privately of the need for a 'Government of National Safety'. His
letters to Baffy reveal his growing anxiety. 'All I can say is,' he wrote on 21
February, 'I think it would be dishonest [to resign]. Perhaps I should
discard reason and go upon instinct. I cannot do that unless I have some

overwhelming instinct which will take charge. But no such instinct is apparent.' The following month he wrote again: 'Without question we are merely asking people to be slaughtered. And till you & I have done affectual repentance we must take what comes. I know it's unpleasant. I know it will be worse.'[40] By April 1938 it was rumoured that five Cabinet ministers – Elliot, Leslie Hore-Belisha, William Morrison, Oliver Stanley and William Ormsby-Gore – were prepared to resign and join a new National government, with Churchill as prime minister and Eden as foreign secretary.

In May 1938 Elliot was moved from the Scottish Office to become minister for health after a Cabinet reshuffle. He was undoubtedly pleased to escape Dover House, having suspected that Chamberlain intended to isolate him there, but the change did not save him from more agonising produced by the Munich crisis. Although Elliot did not believe it represented, as Chamberlain claimed, 'peace in our time', he publicly condoned the policy and was savaged by Duff Cooper, Churchill, and Sir Archibald Sinclair at a meeting of the Other Club in September 1938. Bob Boothby thought that 'Munich broke the spring' in Elliot's step, but Chamberlain appears to have rated Elliot, even describing him and his wife as 'excellent company' in his diary. It probably helped that he soon proved a success as minister for health, making a major contribution to the country's war preparations by arranging evacuation schemes and establishing the Emergency Medical Service. But Elliot's dithering over Munich proved fatal to his future career. He was ignored in Churchill's wartime coalition government and never again held office. Winston did offer Elliot the governorship of Burma in October 1940, which he refused, although he performed well as a member of Tom Johnston's council of former Scottish secretaries for the duration of the war. Elliot also chaired the Public Accounts Committee, aided the War Office with his skills as a propagandist, and continued to write prolifically.

Elliot fell trying to board a train in January 1943 and was seriously injured, but had recovered by the spring of 1945, when he led a parliamentary delegation to Russia (which included a meeting with Stalin). However, in the Labour landslide of the same year, Elliot lost his Kelvingrove seat. He returned to the Commons in a by-election for the Combined Scottish Universities seat[41] a year later and became opposition NHS spokesman. 'Yesterday's man of tomorrow,' was Michael Foot's rather unkind assessment of Elliot in 1948, 'with the best future behind him.'[42] When his Universities seat was abolished at the general election of February 1950, Elliot succeeded in recapturing Kelvingrove, and when Churchill formed his second government in 1951, Brendan Bracken tried to convince the prime minister to make Elliot minister for education. Churchill instead offered Elliot either pensions or the junior position of postmaster general, both outside the Cabinet. 'He talks too much,' explained Churchill; Elliot declined and instead devoted himself to foreign affairs and his love of travel. On 8 January 1958, he suffered a heart attack while walking in the grounds of his Borders home, Harwood House, and died at the age of 69. His equally ebullient wife Katherine stood for Kelvingrove at the resulting by-election, but was narrowly defeated. Soon after, Harold Macmillan made her one of the first life peeresses, and Katherine became not only the first peeress to speak in the Lords, but also the first to steer a private bill through the House (on the request of Margaret Thatcher). Katherine had been the perfect political match for Walter, who was perhaps the first truly modern secretary of state for Scotland.

DAVID JOHN COLVILLE

16 MAY 1938 – 14 MAY 1940

A dull public clerk

Thomas Johnston is well known as Scotland's wartime secretary of state. In fact, there were three; the story of the first, David John Colville, is also that of St Andrew's House – the then new Scottish Office headquarters in Edinburgh. 'Since I took up this appointment with the Ministry I have seen three Secretaries of State,' wrote Sir William Darling when he worked at St Andrew's House. 'They have no common characteristic that I can discover.'[1]

The 44-year-old Colville attended his first Cabinet meeting on 18 May 1938, where he found discussion dominated by the European situation. On 30 August he told Cabinet colleagues that he believed 'the question of going to war on behalf of Czechoslovakia, or indeed the imminence of war at the present time, had not really found its way into the mind of the public'.[2] Colville did not make much of an impact in Cabinet meetings, or at the Scottish Office. 'He had the great strength of being extraordinarily good with people, and everybody liked him,' recalled Sir Charles Cunningham diplomatically. 'He didn't always find it easy to make up his mind because he was so anxious to come to the right conclusion . . . but he was a very easy Minister to work for, a very attractive Minister.'[3] Another senior official, Sir Ronald Johnson, remembered that Cunningham found the new Scottish secretary 'dull', but to Sir Ronald 'his lower intellectual pressure made him more approachable and he chatted about normal things, about the Scottish countryside'.[4] The Rev. James Barr likened him to a dull public clerk,[5] but he was popular with officials and his capacity for juggling the logistics of high office was formidable. Although generally decisive, Colville would often announce 'a pause for reflection' just before reaching a final decision. Haste was not one of his traits, and he was a solid, if unenthusiastic, supporter of Chamberlain. 'The Government refuse to accept the doctrine that war is inevitable,' Colville told the House in November 1938. 'Other evils have been stamped out. The evils of disease can be coped with, and we believe that the evils of war can be coped with too . . . I emphasise that the Prime

Minister's policy of appeasement, quite apart from its political value, which involves life and death to many people, also means employment to many of our people.'[6] But beneath the appeasement rhetoric, the Cabinet also realised that the country had to be prepared for any eventuality. In September 1938 a programme of emergency hospital accommodation was approved, and Colville formed a successful partnership with his predecessor Walter Elliot, now minister for health. They created a network of medical facilities in Killearn, Law and Peel – all far from likely bombing targets – to deal with potential civilian casualties from air-raids. This formed the basis of Scotland's post-war National Health Service, and while new facilities in England came under local authority control, Colville ensured that responsibility in Scotland was invested in the secretary of state. He also worked with another fellow Scot, Sir John Anderson, in organising the UK's evacuation scheme, which saw 3.5 million people, mainly women and children, moved from cities to country districts in the first weeks of the war. Colville's dedication in executing these war preparations impressed his staff, but his other activities were more typical of the Scottish Office in peacetime. He reorganised the Herring Industry Board and supplied aid to Scotland's herring fishermen, while in March 1939 Colville found time to abolish 'irregular' marriages, thus ending the romantic tradition of English couples eloping to Gretna Green to get hitched. But all non-emergency legislation was soon put on hold, including proposals for a Highland development commissioner, which had recently been recommended by the Hilleary Report.

Colville had a laconic, laid-back side to his personality. One morning he received a call from Sir John Gilmour, whose Montrave home had been offered as an emergency hospital. Sir John complained that the Department of Health had not properly converted it for use. 'Hell's bells man,' he exclaimed, 'war may be upon us any day and there aren't any lavatories.' Colville listened to him with gentlemanly calm and said after a pause: 'By the way Jack, are you going to the garden party on Thursday?'[7] War, and undoubtedly also the garden party, did come, and despite his pro-appeasement instincts, Colville was fully aware of its significance. 'This is a struggle of democracy against dictatorship,' he told constituents in North Midlothian, adding:

All history shows that democracy has an inherent strength, sooner or later, freedom triumphs, else we should never have emerged from barbarism. But sooner or later is not good enough. There have been dark ages in Europe before; and free nations have gone down for a time before the barbarians. We are not going to risk any such reverse. This war must be won, as decisively and as quickly as our wills and energies can achieve.[8]

David John Colville represented the third generation of a pioneering steel-making family. His paternal grandfather's firm, David Colville and Sons, had been a giant in the Scottish steel industry, producing iron bars for the Tay Bridge, and also material for the ill-fated *Titanic*. David was born at Motherwell House in Lanarkshire on 13 February 1894, the only son and younger child of John Colville, an industrialist and the Liberal MP for North-East Lanarkshire (1895–1901). Born into prosperity unknown to his grandfather, Colville attended Charterhouse School and Trinity College, Cambridge, where he only managed a third. Already an officer in the Territorial Force of the Cameronians (Scottish Rifles) when war broke out, he was wounded three times during his time on the Western Front. Following the armistice, Colville served as a dedicated member of Lanarkshire County Council, and also on the board of the family firm. He initially followed his father by standing in the 1922 general election as a Lloyd George Liberal, coming fourth in Motherwell, and, after switching to the Unionists, he narrowly lost Midlothian and Peeblesshire North at a by-election in January 1929, but took it at the general election five months later. In parliament, Colville spoke mainly on economic matters and he strongly supported protective tariffs. He claimed the best way to beat unemployment was to 'safeguard' British iron and steel, hardly surprising given that by 1931 Colvilles Ltd had a virtual monopoly of steel making in Scotland.

Colville was for two months parliamentary private secretary to Noel Skelton, then under-secretary at the Scottish Office, before moving to the Overseas Trade Department as parliamentary secretary. Following Skelton's death in November 1935, Colville moved back to the Scottish Office as under-secretary. Always on top of his brief, Colville's tone was businesslike but courteous, his narrow eyes and military moustache giving him a determined air. His hinterland comprised the predictable pursuits of shooting and fishing, and the less predictable hobby of touring the Western Isles on his yacht, *Iolanthe*.

Colville was widely expected to succeed Sir Godfrey Collins as Scottish secretary after his sudden death in October 1936, but instead he was promoted to become financial secretary to the Treasury, working alongside Sir John Simon and the chancellor, Neville Chamberlain. 'Colville is a good plodding chap,' wrote Chamberlain at the time, 'but I don't think he would have been very successful with those unpleasant Clydesiders nor would he have been much of an addition to the Cabinet. But he will have a new chance to show what he is made of as Financial Secretary.'[9] Colville ably defended the National Defence Contribution, a new tax on the growth of profits, and also imposed a tariff on imported beef. In 1937

Chamberlain succeeded Stanley Baldwin as prime minister, and the following year he moved Colville to the Scottish Office.

On 3 September 1939, air-raid sirens sounded in London for the first time. Meanwhile, in Edinburgh, officials were preparing to begin work in the gleaming new Art Deco edifice of St Andrew's House, the architectural culmination of a decade-long consolidation of Scottish government. Its construction was a saga of delays and rising costs not unlike that of the new Scottish parliament building at Holyrood (which can be seen from St Andrew's House on Regent Terrace) more than 60 years later. Another parallel with that troubled project was the controversy over the St Andrew's house design.[10] Sir Godfrey Collins had favoured an open competition, but the Scottish Office wanted an architect selected on the basis of past experience. In December 1933 Sir Godfrey accepted the proposal of architect Thomas Tait, and contracted the practice of Sir John Burnet, Tait and Lorne. Tait designed everything himself, down to the smallest details, but he had only four and a half months to plan the actual building. His original cost prediction was just under half a million pounds, but he later reduced the floor space and therefore this figure. However, before the ink was even dry on planning approval for the scheme, the floor area had to increase by 6,000 square feet to accommodate extra staff, and costs began to rise as the design constantly changed. In late 1936 Sir Godfrey died, and his successor Walter Elliot watched as the foundation stone was laid by the Duke of Gloucester on 28 April 1937. Again there were complications. When Sir John Gilmour's reorganisation added the prisons department to a newly restructured Scottish Office, not to mention additional staff for the departments of health and agriculture, even more floor space was required.

The location of the secretary of state's office had shifted back and forth between the fourth and fifth floors, finally settling on the latter, and Colville could not resist interfering during a site visit. He discovered that a parapet obstructed the view from his desk, and asked that it be altered at great additional expense so that the secretary of state could have both an upward and downward view from his office window. Colville also disliked the turreted Governor's House, a hangover from the old Calton Gaol on whose original foundations the new building now stood. Colville ordered its demolition, but, fearing another scandal, the first commissioner of works persuaded him to change his mind. There was also the question of a name for the new building. A radio programme proposed everything from the New Tolbooth, to the unlikely sounding Thistleneuk, but St Andrew's House was Colville's personal choice. 'It is hoped that the new Government building on the Calton Hill, Edinburgh, will be ready for occupation

early in September,' Colville told MPs in early 1939. 'I am glad to be able
to announce that His Majesty the King, accompanied by Her Majesty
the Queen, has graciously agreed to open the building formally on the
afternoon of Thursday, 12th October. With the King's approval, the new
building will be known as St. Andrew's House.'[11] The outbreak of war
meant the royal opening was cancelled, the calling up of removal men for
service also causing headaches when it came to transferring furniture to
the new building. A gold key specially produced for the King was never
used, although His Majesty, accompanied by Colville and the architect
Thomas Tait, eventually visited the building on 26 February 1940. St
Andrew's House certainly had presence, when viewed either from Calton
Hill or from Edinburgh's Old Town. Tait had developed his distinctive
Art Deco style, and even reproduced some features from his *Daily Telegraph*
building on Fleet Street. Interior rooms featured discreet lighting and
wood panelling, the most ornate adorning the Scottish secretary's office
on the top floor, where the wood was said to have come from a walnut
tree planted by Mary, Queen of Scots.[12]

Colville was also busy with the Reorganisation of Offices (Scotland) Bill,
the legislative product of the Gilmour Committee's recommendations.
'The cry at one time is for more central control in order to secure
standards of administration; at another time the cry is against a central
bureaucracy,' said Colville in mid 1938, identifying the central paradox of
the debate. 'The essential thing, and one of the most important functions
of the Secretary of State, is to see that the pendulum never swings too far
either way.'[13] So this Reorganisation Bill was another classic Unionist
compromise, apparently satisfying both sides of the argument. The new
Scottish Office was undeniably a central bureaucracy, but it was also a
potent symbol of Scottish nationhood, based in Edinburgh, not London.
This time, the government had learned the lessons of Gilmour's 1928 Bill
and purposefully sought cross-party support for its reforms. Crucially, the
Bill allowed for future internal reorganisations without the need for
legislation, and was timed to become law just before the completion of
St Andrew's House.
    Aiding Colville was the new permanent under-secretary at the Scottish
Office, Sir Horace Hamilton. The Kent-born civil servant was persuaded
to take the job in anticipation of the Gilmour proposals being accepted by
the government, and he helped reorganise the Scottish departments along
more traditional Whitehall lines. Sir Horace was rather aloof, and he
offended many by choosing not to move to Edinburgh on taking up the
post, but his Whitehall contacts were impeccable, and by the time he
stood down in 1946 Scottish Office clout had increased significantly.

Colville secured Cabinet backing to proceed with legislation on 28 July 1938, and on 9 November it approved the blandly named Reorganisation of Offices (Scotland) Bill. Moving its Second Reading on 13 December, Colville described the Bill 'as the most comprehensive reform of Government in Scotland since 1885'. But somehow it sounded anticlimactic as the Scottish secretary continued his lucid, yet mundane explanation of the Bill's main features. 'As far as possible, the day-to-day administration of all the Departments will be carried out in Edinburgh,' he told MPs, adding:

> I do not for a moment wish to shift the burden from Parliament, but the importance that the machine itself should be human and should be in close touch with public opinion in Scotland is immense . . . I do not claim that it is a Bill which deals with policy in the broad sense but I claim that in the efficient running of our Scottish administration this Bill will be a great landmark.[14]

Opposition MPs were not exactly enthralled. The former Scottish secretary, Sir Archibald Sinclair, lamented the abolition of the Fisheries Board, while Tom Johnston, a future Scottish secretary (who had sat on the Gilmour Committee) complained that the Bill's terms of reference were too restrictive, adding that 'what we desire is less bureaucracy and more democracy'.[15] Another future Scottish secretary, Joseph Westwood, wound up for the opposition by dismissing the Bill as a farthing-a-head revolutionary measure. But thereafter the Bill had an easy ride, with no debate at the Report Stage or Third Reading, and it received Royal Assent in May 1939 just as the finishing touches were being made to St Andrew's House. Within months the Scottish Office would have a new administrative structure, and a new home, at one of the most dramatic turning points in European history.

On 10 May 1940 Neville Chamberlain tendered his resignation as prime minister and recommended Winston Churchill as his successor. As Churchill formed his coalition Cabinet it became clear that there was no place for Colville (often confused with Sir John 'Jock' Colville, Churchill's wartime private secretary). He accepted his exclusion with humility, and immediately became a full-time colonel on the staff of the Lowland District, where he was responsible for raising the Home Guard.

From 1941 he played a full part in Tom Johnston's council of ex-Scottish secretaries, warning that industrial concentration threatened Scotland's postwar economy. And in November 1942 Colville replaced Sir John Dill as governor designate of the Bombay province in India. Colville's backing for Churchill in a censure debate of July 1942 had been unenthusiastic, and many saw this move as the prime minister exiling another pro-appeasement relic. But Sir John, as he became in February 1943, came into his own during his four years as governor, his sense of history and capacity for sensitive administration finding a perfect outlet. He arrived in Bombay in March 1943 to find the situation still tense following the suppression of the anti-British 'Quit India' campaign. With Congress Party leaders imprisoned in the province, Colville now governed without a Cabinet, or legislature, under Section 93 of the Government of India Act (1935). Despite these adverse circumstances, Colville managed to secure the trust of the Congress Party, and he handled successive crises, such as the accidental Bombay docks explosion in 1944 and the Royal Indian Mutiny of 1946, with shrewd skill and tact. As the only former secretary of state to hold a governorship in India since Crown rule began in 1858, Colville deputised several times for two viceroys, Lords Wavell and Mountbatten, while they were in London. He offered to resign when plans to end imperial rule were announced in 1947, but instead Sir John continued as governor for another five months after Indian independence, retiring on 6 January 1948. He was raised to the peerage as Baron Clydesmuir two months later and spoke frequently in the House of Lords on Scottish, industrial and army matters. He was suggested as the new minister of state at the Scottish Office in 1951, but was passed over in favour of Lord Home and died at his Braidwood home four years later on 31 October 1954. Historians have largely ignored Colville, perhaps because his modest technocratic style does not lend itself to interesting reading, his contributions to both Scottish administrative reform and imperial transition being more efficient than memorable.

ERNEST BROWN

14 MAY 1940 – 8 FEBRUARY 1941

The preacher

Ernest Brown was an unlikely secretary of state for Scotland. A gifted public speaker and strict teetotaller, he reputedly had the loudest, most penetrating voice in parliament. On seeing Brown in a House of Commons phone booth, Stanley Baldwin was said to have remarked, 'I didn't think he needed a phone to communicate with his constituents.' He was not only loud, but English, and the SNP attacked his appointment on that basis, conveniently ignoring that he had represented Leith in parliament for 14 years. Brown, however, was not the first English Scottish secretary: the Duke of Richmond was essentially an Englishman with a Scottish title and estates, while Sir George Otto Trevelyan was a Northumbrian with, like Brown, a Scottish pied-à-terre in the House of Commons. Brown was nonplussed. 'My duty is quite plain,' he said a week after his appointment. 'I have been charged by the Prime Minister with an honourable and onerous post in war-time. It is my duty to do my utmost for Scotland and all the interests of Scotland.'[1] Sir Thomas Moore MP ironically welcomed Brown as the representative of an alien minority.

Alfred Ernest Brown was born in Torquay on 27 August 1881, the eldest son of William Henry Brown, a fisherman, and his wife Anna Badcock. His father was a prominent Baptist who involved his son from an early age with his religious activities, Ernest quickly becoming a natural preacher not only in church but for the local Liberal Party. After attending a local school Brown trained as a clerk, embarking on an unremarkable career which was interrupted by the First World War. He joined the Sportsmen's Battalion in 1914, and two years later was commissioned in the Somerset Light Infantry, picking up a trio of medals – the Military Medal, Military Cross and later the Italian Silver Star – for valour as an officer. Following various attempts to enter parliament, Brown won Rugby in November 1923, but lost it the following year, and gained the Leith Burghs three years later.[2] He opposed propping up Labour during its 1929 minority government, and joined Sir John Simon in 1931 as a Liberal National (as opposed to Sir Archibald Sinclair, who became a Samuelite Liberal National). From then until he entered the Scottish Office, Brown held several posts, including that of minister for labour in 1935. There, he introduced the Unemployment Insurance (Agriculture) Act of 1936, which covered nearly all workers in agriculture, horticulture and forestry. War preparations added the Ministry of National Service to his duties in 1939, and the following year he replaced David John Colville as Scottish secretary.

Brown took up the reins at Dover House in the same week that Germany invaded the Netherlands, Belgium and Luxembourg. His nine months as Scottish secretary were therefore dominated by the war, and are largely unmemorable as a result. Sir John Gilmour's reforms, and Colville's subsequent legislation, had by then transformed the Scottish Office into the formidable northern wing of an increasingly well-prepared wartime government. The department also had a temporary new home at Fielden House on Little College Street in Westminster, Dover House having been vacated following bomb damage to a neighbouring building.[3]

On 16 May 1940 the Liberal MP Leslie Burgin wrote to Brown to offer his congratulations: 'I was lunching at No 11 Downing Street to-day with [Sir John] Simon,' he said, 'and we both agreed that as you are the senior member of the House of Commons of our Liberal National Group who holds Government office the natural and proper course would be to elect you Chairman of the Parliamentary Party.'[4] Brown, therefore, became not only Scottish secretary but also a party leader, albeit of a very small band of MPs. He took this additional duty seriously, attempting to engineer a reunion between the Simonite and Samuelite Liberals, the latter group now led by Sir Archibald Sinclair, but although negotiations were lengthy they were ultimately unsuccessful.

Brown had the unenviable task of making his Commons debut as Scottish secretary just after Churchill's classic 'finest hour' oration, but he was a competent Commons performer and dealt chiefly with agricultural issues. He commissioned a special study of hill sheep-farming in Scotland, and secured a special subsidy for breeding ewes. Such humdrum issues were an important feature of wartime politics, given that millions of mouths had to be fed with domestic produce. Brown even gave a wireless talk urging Scottish farmers to wage war on weeds, rats and rabbits. Such matters must have seemed like small-fry to Brown, no matter how loudly he espoused them, as he was also infamously egotistical. Alastair Dunnett, a future *Scotsman* editor who worked with both Brown and his

successor Tom Johnston at the Scottish Office, left this vivid portrait of his
old boss:

> He was the absolute in egocentricity, believing that he was universally well-
> known and indeed popular. It was a study to walk with him through his
> constituency of Leith, when he would pause every now and again to wave
> enthusiastically to some woman working at the kitchen sink, three storeys
> above, and she would stare down at him in ignorance of who this forward
> stranger might be. He was even more dangerous to accompany on the streets of
> London. He would sally, with one or two of us as his entourage, out from the
> front door of Dover House, the Scottish Office in Whitehall, and walk smartly
> across the road heedless of the rushing traffic. Buses and taxis would squeal to a
> halt with drivers screaming personal curses at him. 'They all know me,' he
> would say contentedly, continuing on his way.[5]

Consequently, Brown was not universally popular as an MP or minister.
'Ernest Brown to me is an example of a good politician,' declared Sir
William Darling, Edinburgh's wartime lord provost. 'I assert this boldly,
because I would not expect to find everyone in agreement.'[6] He was also
not an original political thinker, annoying officials by consuming their
briefs and then proclaiming them as if they were his own work. Pre-
sumably the Land Drainage (Scotland) Bill, which was presented to
parliament during Brown's last week as Scottish secretary, came about
in this way. 'In his customary black suit and come-to-Jesus collar,' recalled
the civil servant George Pottinger, 'Brown was essentially a performer, an
impresario.'[7] Throughout his life, and even as Scottish secretary, Brown
was much in demand as an evangelical lay preacher.

In February 1941 Brown left the Scottish Office and was succeeded by the
ostentatiously Scottish, and more substantial figure of Thomas Johnston.
'Ernest Brown was only on the job for a little while,' wrote Sir William
Darling, 'but he was, for an Englishman, surprisingly acceptable.'[8] He
moved to the Ministry of Health, where he faced criticisms, and even a
motion of no confidence, over his handling of evacuation procedures and
the lack of accommodation for workers during a period of severe housing
shortages.

In 1943, Brown was demoted to become chancellor of the Duchy of
Lancaster, and during Churchill's caretaker government in 1945 he served
as minister of aircraft production. Thereafter out of government, the still
ebullient Brown devoted himself to maintaining an extensive library in his
'improbable flat' (it was very small) on Shaftsbury Avenue, and to his
religious activities. He became president of the Baptist Union of Great

Britain and Ireland in 1948, and was a delegate to the Amsterdam assembly of the World Council of Churches the same year. As a member of the council's central committee, Brown visited India in 1952–53, and also toured Australia as a guest of the federal government, addressing religious meetings throughout the country. In his later years he suffered a stroke, and he died at St Pancras Hospital in London on 16 February 1962.

Thomas Johnston

8 February 1941 – 25 May 1945

The moderate extremist

On the afternoon of 27 October 1941 St Andrew's House played host to a remarkable gathering of former Scottish secretaries, all brought together to discuss Scotland's post-war reconstruction. The oldest, Lord Alness (previously Robert Munro), was now in charge of government legislation in the House of Lords. He sat alongside the loud and egotistical Ernest Brown, until recently Scottish secretary and now minister of health, and two distinguished figures in military dress: the ebullient Walter Elliot and the somewhat blander David John Colville. Both now had the rank of colonel having been excluded from the wartime coalition, a slight Elliot found harder to accept than the stoic Colville. The only absentee was Sir Archibald Sinclair, who was busy in London in his new capacity as secretary of state for air. Chairing the meeting was the 60-year-old Labour MP Thomas Johnston, a tall, dark and gallicly handsome polymath with raven hair and captivating eyes. He had been Scottish secretary for nearly nine months, reluctantly recruited to the wartime government by Winston Churchill. As one of the original Clydeside MPs, Johnston had once been seen as a dangerous revolutionary, but by 1941 he had completed a remarkable political journey from leftwing firebrand to pragmatic centrist.

Although not quite an establishment figure, Johnston was certainly palatable to it and an immensely attractive figure. Moderate Conservatives saw him as a man with whom they could do business; Liberals approved of his centrist approach; nationalists saw him as instinctively one of their own; and mainstream Labour figures considered him an articulate proponent of the New Jerusalem. In fact, Johnston had the support of almost everyone from the prime minister down to the man in the street.

The Council of State (or the Advisory Council of ex-Secretaries of State on Post War Problems, to give it its fuller, more cumbersome title) represented a long-cherished dream of Johnston's: a gathering of politicians from all parties to consider Scotland's problems free from partisan point-scoring. 'I am confident that the appointment of this Council,'

Johnston told MPs two weeks before it met for the first time, 'constituted as it is on the basis of national unity, will commend itself to public opinion in Scotland as a guarantee of the Government's intention to see that Scottish problems of reconstruction are competently and authoritatively surveyed and reported upon.' The Scottish secretary's former Clydeside comrades were not impressed, and resented his journey to the political centre ground. 'Could not the right hon. Gentleman get any more die-hard Tories to put on this organisation?' spat the Independent Labour Party (ILP) MP for Glasgow Shettleston, John McGovern. 'Does he think these people have the mind for any progress for the ordinary people of Scotland.'[1] Another critic, the Labour MP Emrys Hughes, wrote in *Forward*, 'Who would have dreamt that Tom Johnston of Forward, who had so scornfully derided the Lloyd George coalition in the First World War, would become Secretary of State for Scotland in a coalition Government headed by Winston Churchill?'[2] The Clydesiders feared Johnston would become a prisoner of the Liberals and Tories. Of that they should have had no fear, for Tom Johnston was also very much his own man. Like Lord Lothian in 1887, this Scottish secretary had a little list, although it was more comprehensive than even the Mikado could have imagined. Luckily for Johnston, he also proved to be in the right place at the right time. The Second World War had created exactly the climate which favoured his ecumenical approach. One of Johnston's new Tory friends, the wartime lord provost of Edinburgh, Sir William Darling, assessed him within months of his arrival at Fielden House:

> Gone, apparently, is the ardent propagandist of a political theory. He has no theories now – he asks if this is desirable, practical, worthwhile, and if so – on with it. Don't inquire – don't stop – don't write about it – don't harangue – don't ask if it is Christian or Marxian – on with it. This turbulent intensity commends itself to me. He knows he has his chance, his opportunity, his hour, and he wants to give it all to Scotland.[3]

Just as a sense of destiny had brought Churchill to power at a crucial moment in British history, Johnston too had been preparing for most of his political life for this juncture in Scotland's.

Thomas Johnston – always Tom in conversation but Thomas in corre-spondence – was born on 2 November 1881, in Kirkintilloch, Dunbarton-shire. He was the eldest of four children of David Johnston, a licensed victualler, and his wife, Mary Blackwood Alexander. Johnston's was a lower middle-class childhood. Both his parents were conservative Pres-byterians who schooled their son at Lairdslaw Public School, and later at

Lenzie Academy, where Thomas received a classical education which infused him with a love of history. Johnston was a bright, articulate child, and on leaving school he became a clerk in an iron-founding business, and then in an insurance office. By now interested in Labour politics and journalism Johnston began to apply himself to both with vigour. He stood unsuccessfully in a local election for the ILP in 1903, but he was soon distracted by an old printing press he had inherited from a relative.

Johnston launched the weekly newspaper, *Forward*, in 1906, and it soon acquired a reputation as the leading socialist newspaper in Scotland. *Forward* was polemical, original and crusading, and he edited the paper with flair and humour. But Johnston was no typical party apparatchik, commissioning mavericks like George Bernard Shaw and H. G. Wells to write articles, while also promoting a homespun moralistic tone. Johnston was a teetotaller, so *Forward* was devoid of advertisements for alcohol, and avoided romanticising what its editor saw as the more unattractive characteristics of working-class life. Johnston also dressed accordingly, wearing a Homburg hat and floppy bow tie as his standard attire. He later combined his editorial duties with studies as a mature student at Glasgow University, where contemporaries included Walter Elliot, his future ILP comrade James Maxton, and the playwright James Bridie. Like Elliot, Johnston voted for Keir Hardie (who had a profound influence) in a lively rectorial contest, but left university in 1909 without completing his degree. The same year, Johnston wrote his first book, *Our Scots Noble Families*, a savage assault on Scotland's landed gentry which sold more than 120,000 copies.[4] In 1920, the more substantial *History of the Working Classes in Scotland* was published, a combination of his polemical writing talents and love of Scottish history.

From 1913 Johnston was a member of Kirkintilloch Town Council, which provided a valuable platform for some imaginative experiments in town hall socialism. It also became a 'dry town' – much to Johnston's pride – under Thomas McKinnon Wood's Temperance (Scotland) Act. On his initiative, Kirkintilloch gained Scotland's first municipal-sponsored cinema, fire insurance, bank and even jam manufacturer. In sharp contrast to his later patriotic support for the war against Nazism, Johnston was deeply opposed to the First World War. And, although he was careful to abide by government regulations for wartime journalism, *Forward*'s coverage of the hostile reception received by the minister of munitions, David Lloyd George, during a speech to Clydeside workers in 1916, led to a pivotal test of press freedom. In a decidedly illiberal act, Lloyd George ordered that *Forward* be suppressed, and it ceased publication for five weeks. Johnston eventually met with the Welsh Wizard, who oozed charm and assured him that he was the last person to stop a newspaper saying what it thought. 'You were,' responded Johnston cleverly, earning Lloyd George's respect and ensuring that *Forward* hit the presses once more. For years afterwards, a portrait of Lloyd George was an ironic fixture in the newspaper's offices.

Having stood unsuccessfully for the ILP in West Stirlingshire at the general election of 1918, Johnston won the same seat four years later and became one of 29 Labour MPs in Scotland. A savage verbal attack on H. H. Asquith prevented Johnston joining the first minority Labour government, and when that administration fell in late 1924 he lost his seat in the subsequent election. Returning to parliament at a Dundee by-election a few months later, Johnston was seen as a key figure within the Red Clydeside group. But in reality he was increasingly semi-detached and preferred a softer approach to dealing with the opposition than did the more revolutionary-inclined Maxton and John Wheatley.[5]

In the 1929 election Johnston returned to his old seat of West Stirlingshire and became under-secretary to the gruff miner William Adamson as Scottish secretary. Like Elliot under Sir John Gilmour, Johnston quickly outshone his political superior and impressed colleagues with his work on a number of Bills, including the Housing (Scotland) Act of 1930. He also handled the evacuation of St Kilda with sensitivity, and built upon Elliot's milk schemes by giving 10,000 school children a daily bottle of Grade 'A' milk to demonstrate the benefits of produce from tubercle-free cattle.

Again like Elliot, Johnston acquired duties outside the Scottish Office, relishing his work on the Empire Marketing Board and becoming a member of the shambolic Thomas Committee on unemployment, a toothless body (headed by the lord privy seal James Henry Thomas and including the young Labour MP, and future fascist, Oswald Mosley) established by the prime minister Ramsay MacDonald to contemplate solutions to the mass unemployment caused by the depression. It met only twice in six months, but Johnston took his work on it seriously, proposing a Scottish Development Board to make Scotland 'a health centre and tourist resort', with a budget of £50,000. But, although he was sympathetic, MacDonald left Johnston to plead on his own with a Treasury suspicious of expensive job-creation schemes.[6] A Scottish National Development Council was eventually set up in May 1930, but it was just another talking shop. A few months earlier, the Cabinet had rejected the 'Mosley memorandum', which proposed, among other radical suggestions, public ownership of banking. Mosley then resigned, and although Johnston was supportive he despaired of his colleague's overtly partisan tone. Instead, he urged MacDonald to work with Liberals and Conservatives, and envisaged his old nemesis Lloyd George running a 'Council of State for Agriculture'. Increasingly cynical about party politics, Johnston held a weekly meeting of Scottish MPs at Dover House, and struck up a rapport with moderate Unionist MPs like Elliot, Bob Boothby and the writer John Buchan.[7]

Johnston was promoted to the Cabinet as lord privy seal in March 1931, but he joined Adamson in opposing MacDonald's proposed cuts to unemployment benefit and once again lost his seat in the resulting general election.[8] His stock within the Labour Party was high, but, rather than pressing his claims to the leadership, the experience of 1931 had consolidated Johnston's belief that certain issues, chiefly unemployment, had to be extracted from party politics. However, although he regained West Stirlingshire in 1935, Johnston announced (in 1937) his intention to stand down at the next general election. The prospect of war in Europe postponed an election, and therefore Johnston's planned retirement, and, although he was initially opposed to any increase in defence expenditure, he soon found himself in sympathy with Winston Churchill's calls for Nazi aggression to be taken seriously. In May 1939 Johnston became regional commissioner for Scotland and energetically prepared for civil defence against an enemy attack. Within two years he had become a zealous advocate of government by consent.

Churchill had tried several times to persuade Johnston to join his government, but without success. Johnston was happy in his role as regional commissioner and, besides, he hated London, often telling his daughter that it was the loneliest place in the world.[9] Nevertheless, he arrived at Downing Street in February 1941, having been summoned by Churchill.[10] Johnston later recalled the meeting in his memoirs:

> "What ails you about joining the National Government?"
> "Well for one thing I want to get out of partisan politics and write books!"
> "Write books? What kind of books?"
> "History books."
> "History!" (a disdainful snort). "Good heavens, man, come in here and help me make history!"[11]

That argument appears to have won Johnston over, and he agreed to replace Ernest Brown at the Scottish Office. However, he declined to take a salary, and extracted an assurance from Churchill that the Cabinet would look kindly upon any resolution produced by a committee of surviving Scottish secretaries. Given that the wartime coalition was based on the same principle, Churchill gave his assent. 'The PM told me he was delighted with "the lay-out",' wrote Churchill's private secretary Colville a few days later, 'which includes the Editor of *Forward* (Tom Johnston) and the premier Duke (Under Sec. For Agriculture) and thus shows the breadth of the Administration.'[12] The Labour MP Joseph Westwood continued as under-secretary (he had been appointed in May 1940), and political balance was attained with the addition of a second under-secretary for the first time, initially Colonel James Scrymgeour-Wedderburn, and later the Rutherglen MP Allan Chapman – both Conservative MPs. Johnston also recruited Arthur Woodburn as his parliamentary private secretary, and a young civil servant called Douglas Haddow became his private secretary (he learned much from Johnston's assertive approach to Scottish administration and became permanent under-secretary in 1965).[13]

The original intention was for Johnston to continue as regional commissioner as well as being secretary of state, but when it became clear that this was impractical, his former deputy, Lord Rosebery, took command of Scotland's civil defence. But, far from planning a long Cabinet career, Johnston saw his appointment as nothing more than short term. 'I have agreed to accept temporarily the post of Secretary of State for Scotland,' he wrote to Mr Dunlop at *Forward*, and therefore he had 'to resign once again (for what I trust will be but another brief break) from the Chairmanship and the Directorship of the Company.'[14] Johnston made almost an immediate impression as Scottish secretary. 'Your old chief appeared at the Cabinet for the first time, as far as I have been in attendance, on Thursday,' wrote the press baron Lord Beaverbrook to Lord Rosebery on 1 March. 'With his Scottish accent and his brief and vigorous explanations, he made the most immense impression on me.'[15]

Johnston entered the Scottish Office with a good reputation as an excellent front-bencher and an able administrator. His speeches in the House could not match Churchill's eloquence, but the new secretary of state could quickly detect the weakness in an opponent's argument and ruthlessly destroy it. Otherwise, Johnston was a modest man who disliked social occasions, although he was skilful in his dealings with the Scottish press, his experience as a journalist giving him a good nose for a story. But, while dour in speech, he had an explosive laugh and enjoyed telling anecdotes while mimicking his contemporaries.[16]

'The Cabinet met at the House and I had a conversation with the dynamic and excellent Tom Johnston, S. of S. for Scotland,' wrote Colville in his diary, 'who told me of the incredible tactlessness shown by many employers in Lanarkshire. He said the morale of the workers on Clydeside was much better since they had been bombed and he could not help wishing Lanarkshire would be bombed too.'[17] To Johnston, the Second World War represented an opportunity to cure Scotland of her political ills. He had a noble vision of society, infused with citizenship and pragmatic goals, and was determined that after the war Scotland would not revert to the kind of economic depression it had known before the conflict. Johnston and the Scottish Office gelled perfectly; to Sir William Darling he was the man of the hour. 'The propagandist idealist applies his ideas to his task,' he wrote. 'It is not easy. He has his discouragements but he has united Scottish public opinion most successfully. He impresses me as a man who has got everything he wants for himself. He isn't after anything except Scotland, and for its welfare, betterment, progress he would give all.'[18] Johnston also had the perfect administrative tool at his disposal: a reorganised Scottish Office, which until now had lacked dynamic leadership. But the new Scottish secretary felt that the 1939 Reorganisation of Offices (Scotland) Act had not completely solved the problems of Scottish governance; he wanted to channel often disparate Scottish opinion through one voice, effectively making the Scottish Office a large lobbying mechanism. His Council of State was the most obvious manifestation of this, but Johnston also experimented with some other procedural reforms. He revived weekly meetings of Scottish MPs at Fielden House, gatherings which had previously taken place at Dover House when Johnston was an under-secretary. Johnston had long wanted to hold regular conferences of all Scottish MPs at St Andrew's House in Edinburgh, but was 'strongly advised' soon after becoming Scottish secretary that wartime travelling restrictions made this almost impossible. MPs continually pressed the secretary of state on the idea during Scottish Questions, but he protested that statutory meetings in Edinburgh would require legislation due to the 'grave perils and anxieties of the war emergency'.[19] Eventually, these problems were overcome, and on 30 October 1941 27 MPs turned up at St Andrew's House, many of whom had never before set foot in the imposing building. Each was introduced to the departmental heads and given a pep talk by Johnston:

> Nearly two and a half centuries ago the Scots Parliament was adjourned, not abandoned or abolished – Chancellor Seafield with some picturesque levity declaring it was the end of 'an auld sang'. But whatever our respective views might be upon whether the old Scots song will be sung again and by a new choir, I am sure that every member of Parliament in Scotland desires to serve his constituencies to the best of his ability, to get any bona-fide grievances observed and obeyed.[20]

Tied up with Johnston's plan was the steady accumulation of more powers for the Scottish Office, while resisting the centralising instincts of White-hall. This inevitably led to tension between Edinburgh and London, not least with Johnston's fellow Scot Lord Reith, who wanted to establish a UK-wide Central Planning Authority to co-ordinate Britain's postwar reconstruction. Using the same argument as Sir Godfrey Collins (with whom Johnston shared many characteristics) nearly a decade earlier, Johnston warned that such an approach would antagonise both Scottish local authorities and popular opinion. 'In the first place I take it that you agreed that Scottish public opinion would be exceedingly restive if Town Planning powers were taken away from the office of the Secretary of State for Scotland and entrusted to a UK Planning Minister,' Johnston wrote to Reith on 24 September 1941, 'There would be a howl in the House of Commons from Conservatives, Liberal and Labour members alike and there would be a pretty strong Press against this proposal.'[21] Reith rejected this argument, and replied in November claiming that it looked 'as if the Scottish Office were unfriendly and suspicious of an ignorant flatfooted Sassenach'. Johnston responded in diplomatic terms: 'As for . . . being a flatfooted Sassenach and the Scottish Office being unfriendly to you – really and truly there is no justification for it. You are Scots and not Sassenach, and I am sure there is no feeling in the Scottish Office but goodwill and a desire to co-operate in every way.'[22] Johnston eventually won his corner, although Reith does not seem to have harboured any grudges. 'Lunched with T. Johnston, secretary of state for Scotland,' he wrote on 25 March 1943. 'He is very decent. He is very bothered by [Ernest] Bevin and other English ministers who do things affecting Scotland without consulting him.'[23] So perhaps the Council of State was a specific reaction to Reith's centralising instinct, in which case it proved successful. It met 16 times in less than four years, and at its first gathering Johnston reiterated what he had told parliament about considering Scotland's post-war problems before establishing committees to investigate them. On that basis, the Council of State was more an instigator than an investigative body, but what a prolific ideas machine it was. Johnston's wish list included hydro-electricity, the herring industry, hill sheep-farming, gas grids, regionalisation of water supplies and the unification of hospital services; Walter Elliot suggested housing, health services and food production, while Colville emphasised industrial development. Lord Alness, removed from front-line politics for nearly 20 years, made no suggestions.

Although the Council of State was more a political novelty than a constitutional revolution, its backing was strategically useful for Johnston in the Cabinet. With Churchill's prior backing, the Scottish secretary would repeatedly stress how difficult it would be to backtrack on anything already agreed (and usually publicly announced) by the Council. In other words, he presented certain schemes as faits accomplis. 'Prime Minister,'

Johnston is said to have declared at one Cabinet meeting, 'if this disnae go through I'm gaun tae tell the 51st Division when they come hame tae bring their bloody bayonets with them.'[24] Johnston saw politics as a means to an end: the resolution of Scotland's problems in education, housing, health and industry. Within months of the Council of State meeting for the first time, the nation was well on course to tackle all four.

Johnston's four years as secretary of state found the Scottish Office in full 'nanny state' mode, controlling where Scots worked, what they bought, and even what they ate. 'The redoubtable Secretary of State is telling his countrymen that they must learn to cook, like – and live on – their native products,' wrote Sir William Darling. 'He is at them – the challengers – horse, foot and artillery and doubtless has tanks and dive bombers in his strategic reserve. He will have his difficulties. He is aware of that but he is catching them young. Prizes for the best plate of porridge, prizes for the best grilled herring – these will go a long way, but how far only time can tell.'[25] A large part of Johnston's style simply comprised creative public relations. Nationwide competitions to find the best herring and potato dishes were imaginative examples of this, the most unusual being a 'porridge party' at Fielden House to test dried tinned milk as a substitute ingredient for making the traditional breakfast fare. Johnston, and his under-secretary Allan Chapman, watched with Ministry of Food officials as 'test' cooks prepared the porridge using reconstituted milk. The Scottish secretary declared the finished product to be excellent. 'It is likely that the Secretary of State will take an early opportunity of advising his countrymen accordingly,'[26] noted an ironic report in the *Scotsman*.

Johnston's already excellent journalistic instincts were ably aided by a young press officer called Alastair Dunnett, who later successfully edited Scotland's national newspaper. He helped with initiatives like the Scots Ancestry Research Council, which Johnston joked would help find any American a Scottish granny or two.[27] 'Unless we get things going in Scotland now and develop our own resources,' he would tell officials during late-night discussions, 'you chaps will inherit a poors' house.'[28]

The first committee of inquiry backed by the Council of State, chaired by the lord justice clerk, Lord Cooper of Culross, was tasked with looking into establishing a North of Scotland Hydro-Electric Board. Cooper had a well-equipped legal mind, and had been a popular lord advocate under the last four Scottish secretaries. He reported in late 1942, giving his full backing to Johnston's cherished dream of reviving the Scottish Highlands. The Scottish secretary had visited Canada's Niagara hydro project in 1927, and he had also been impressed by the Tennessee Valley Authority's commitment to social development. A Bill swiftly appeared in January 1943, the seventh such scheme to come before parliament (all the others had failed), and on 24 February Johnston moved the Second Reading of the Hydro-Electric Development (Scotland) Bill. 'There are people, of course, who regard any large-scale industry in the Highlands as anathema – something approaching desecration of the Garden of Eden,' he told MPs, adding:

> But, occasionally, I could fain wish that some of the people who clamour for the preservation of amenities would remember that there are amenities other than landscape ones. For the people who live in the grandeur and the majesty of the Highlands, we could wish – some of us – that the definition of the word was widened and made more comprehensive. To some people, I gather, amenity means the provision of bathrooms in hotels marked by four stars in the automobile guide books, with a few poverty-stricken natives living in squalor amid picturesque reservations . . . I should like before I go from this place to offer some of the amenities of life to the peasant, his wife, and his family. The amenities and comforts of civilisation have largely passed by the class from which Robert Burns sprang.[29]

It was typically emotive – and romantic – oratory from Johnston. 'I am trying to show how this is the voice of Scotland for once,' he said, and, for the first time since 1832 a major Scottish Bill passed without a division. It was a triumph for the Scottish secretary, and a testament to his authority within the Cabinet. The first hydro project began with a damn at Loch Soy in 1945, the water flowing down to a lost glen lying below the western ridge of Loch Lomond. On the day the first sod was cut, Mrs Johnston (Margaret Freeland, who had married Johnston in 1914) climbed aboard a huge bulldozer and sliced up an immense carpet of turf. But while the board succeeded in generating and supplying electricity, its duty to stimulate the social and economic welfare of the Highlands failed to transpire.

On health Johnston scored another notable triumph. In October 1941 he opened the new Ayrshire Central Hospital and stated that 'the aim of the Government, in their plans for the post-war medical service, [is] to ensure that appropriate treatment is available to every person in need of it'.[30] A week later, Johnston met with the Scottish branch of the British Hospitals Association (BHA) at St Andrew's House, and afterwards he fleshed out his vision for Scotland's three groups of hospitals (local authority, voluntary and emergency): 'When account is taken of the hospital accommodation provided in Scotland to meet wartime needs, it is obvious that there is now sufficient accommodation to form the foundation of a hospital system capable of providing for the needs of every person who requires hospital treatment.'[31] This was essentially the nucleus of what later became the National Health Service, applied at first to the Clyde Valley. By the end of 1942 3,210 patients had been referred from voluntary hospital waiting lists to emergency hospitals, and when the scheme was rolled out nationwide the Scottish secretary could boast that he had wiped out a waiting list of 34,000 patients from voluntary hospitals by the end of the war. And when the groundbreaking Beveridge Report appeared in early 1943, the Scottish Office soon turned its finest minds to the issue of Scotland's post-war health service. Johnston was enthusiastic from the outset. 'It is obvious to everyone that voluntary hospitals, the great backbone of the existing hospital services in Britain, must be set into the mosaic of the new State Medical Service,'[32] he told reporters following negotiations with the BHA in Glasgow. The Cabinet had been considering the issue since early 1943, and it charged Johnston and Ernest Brown, the minister of health and Johnston's predecessor as secretary of state, with drafting a White Paper. Johnston worked hard at establishing a rapport with the Scottish medical profession and was anxious to reach a consensus on how the NHS would be run. He predicted problems with bringing GPs under local authority control, as was originally planned, suggesting instead that they would co-operate more constructively with a centrally administered authority. But Brown objected to the Scottish Office scheme, and Johnston was told to go away and think again. However, when the Conservative MP Henry Willink took over as health minister, he and Johnson completed a White Paper in January 1944. It recommended free medical treatment for all, and state control over distribution of public-sector doctors. Willink had argued for the retention of private provision, while Johnston had insisted against patient charges in hospitals. But, although the two ministers generally worked well together, the Ministry of Health was hostile to Johnston's request to allow fair-rent tribunals for furnished apartments in Scotland. 'In the old days that would have killed the proposal for legislation stone dead,' Johnston later recalled, adding:

Scotland, although perhaps with a growl, would have yielded; the big brother's decision would have been regarded as final. But not so during the war. Now we were fortified by a Scottish Council of State, and I went forward to the Cabinet for legislation, backed by the members of the Council, and despite England's refusal to come in, we got our legislation, and relieved thousands of poor folk from onerous and unjust burdens. Years afterwards England and Wales elected to follow our lead.[33]

The long plight of Scotland's industrial infrastructure was another of Johnston's long-standing concerns. He had argued since the mid 1920s that issues such as unemployment and manufacturing 'ought not to be . . . the shuttlecock of party politics', and once again the war finally made that dream a reality. The result was the Scottish Council on Industry, which had its roots in the inter-war activities of the industrialists Sir James Lithgow, Lord Elgin and Sir Steven Bilsland, and was inaugurated by Johnston in February 1942. He initially struggled to find a chairman, as the banks would not play ball with a Labour man, and the trade unions would not work with a Tory. Johnston, however, eventually settled upon Sir William Darling. 'I will be frank with you,' the Scottish secretary told him. 'You are not the first choice of any of the parties, but the second choice of them all!'[34] He also established two short-lived regional planning authorities covering the east and west of Scotland, and in a supply (budget) debate on Scottish Industry a few months later, Johnston recalled the lamentable record of industrial Scotland:

> That was the situation when I personally arrived on the scene at the Scottish Office. The stage then, I found, was set for a repetition, and indeed an intensification, of the disasters following the last war. I knew that it was pretty nearly useless for one man in a Government to try and reverse these processes. I had seen my predecessors, men in other parties with far greater influence and with deep concern for their country's welfare, trying and failing.

Johnston added:

> The worst disaster that could befall us, would be that the war should end with Scotland relying to an undue and disproportionate extent upon armament industries . . . We are planning for the future, so that we may leave to our children a heritage of economic security and well-being which our generation in Scotland has not known.

He reasoned that by mobilising industrial forces behind the Council of State, a united voice would ensure that Scotland received her fair share of government orders.[35] By the close of 1942, the Scottish industrial picture was already more vibrant: unemployment was down, factory storage space had been given over to production, and Johnston made sure that even the smallest detail did not escape his attention. He prevented pottery manufacturers going to England, textile industries moving to Northern Ireland, and even acquired a share of printing orders for Post Office directories covering Scottish regions. More significantly, the Ministry of Aircraft Production was cajoled into locating greater numbers of new projects north of the border. The press congratulated Johnston on reversing what it called the 'drift south', while the Scottish secretary repeatedly made clear that it was all due to the cessation of partisan politics.

In other areas, however, Johnston proved less effective. He constituted the Scottish Housing Advisory Committee in May 1942, using Walter Elliot's expertise to solve another particularly Scottish (at least in its severity) problem. His Housing (Scotland) Bill was introduced in September 1944, widening the secretary of state's existing remit beyond slum clearance and overcrowding, and allowing Elliot's creation, the Scottish Special Housing Association, to undertake a massively enlarged building programme. For the first time both local authority and private house building was actively encouraged, and although Johnston's target of 30,000 houses was ambitious the SSHA went some way to achieving it. The Scottish secretary also introduced a separate Town and Country Planning (Scotland) Bill – a product of Lord Reith's Central Planning Authority – to rebuild blitzed areas on the west coast.[36]

On Forestry, Johnston was only moderately successful. There was to be a single UK-wide Forestry Commission, but with a separate Scottish committee, of which Johnston became chairman after the war. And with the Ministry of Agriculture Johnston scored one victory and endured one failure: he assumed control of Crown lands in Scotland, but lost a bid to establish a uniform milk price across the British Isles.

It is an irony of Johnston's four energetic years as Scottish secretary that although he was a life-long home ruler, the cumulative effect of his achievements was to erode many well-rehearsed arguments in favour of a separate Scottish parliament. A nationalist intervention in the Dunbartonshire by-election of March 1932 had prevented Johnston making an early return to parliament, so his opinion of nationalists had cooled, even if his home rule instincts remained. Johnston seconded both Labour's home rule Bills of the 1920s, and in 1936 he declared that 'Scotland must have a legislative Assembly of its own, to deal with its own special grievances and own special needs', while in 1937 he became president of the newly formed London Scots Self-Government Committee. Johnston was also critical of the Gilmour Committee reforms (despite being a member), stressing the lack of democratic control voters would have over even a reorganised Scottish Office.

John MacCormick, then leader of what became the cross-party Scottish Convention,[37] and a vehement critic of previous Conservative Scottish secretaries, was therefore buoyed by Johnston's arrival at the Scottish

Office. Other nationalists were not quite as enthusiastic. In November 1942 the Duke of Montrose wrote to the *Scotsman* dismissing Johnston's advisory councils as being of little use without a Scottish legislative assembly to back them up. Roland Muirhead, previously one of *Forward's* wealthiest backers and now a prominent nationalist, agreed, and he wrote to Johnston to tell him so. 'I respect your opinion,' replied Johnston diplomatically, 'but I intend to make an effort to keep our country meanwhile "on the map" and to do my utmost – and within the limits imposed by the circumstances in which we find ourselves – to persuade Scots and English alike that it is desirable we should be allowed to work out our own problems in our own way.' Muirhead was also angry at Johnston's failure to intervene over the imprisonment of the anti-conscription nationalists Arthur Donaldson and the writer Douglas Young. 'I cannot at my own hand wipe out the provisions of an Act of Parliament dealing with national service,' wrote Johnston indignantly, 'and I am not an Appeal Court for revision of judicial decisions arrived at in the High Court at Edinburgh. I am sure you will appreciate that.'[38]

In 1943, Lord Reith recorded a meeting with Johnston in his diary: 'He thinks there is a great danger of Scottish Nationalism coming up, and a sort of Sinn Fein movement as he called it. The Lord Justice Clerk (Lord Cooper) had said in a letter that if he left off being a judge and went back to politics, he would be a nationalist.'[39] The writer Naomi Mitchison epitomised the paradoxical view nationalists took of Johnston, both attracted and disappointed by a figure they could not quite bring themselves to dislike. Mitchison, née Haldane,[40] was a beautiful Edinburgh-born feminist who even saw Johnston as an inspirational figure, immortalising him in her poem 'The Cleansing of the Knife'.

> And it seemed he might be the man
> Who could shake us surely awake and make us
> Lead ourselves, thirl ourselves to a service
> known and agreed
> And sing a new song.[41]

Mitchison's husband, Dick, was later a Labour MP, and both were ardent home rulers as well as members of the Scottish Convention. Naomi joined a delegation which visited Johnston on 10 November 1944 to push for home rule, and she later recorded the meeting in her specially commissioned wartime diary:

> T.J. very friendly and anxious to talk off the record, but won't do anything political during the coalition. Emphasised all the economic things he had done,

and the machinery for progress which he had produced, the Grand Council etc. The difficulty is it may all be swept away by his successor and he doesn't seem to want to stand again which is an awful pity. He told us a good deal about himself and I found it fascinating though it wasn't really what we wanted . . .[42]

Johnston told the deputation that an Edinburgh-based assembly might improve matters, but he maintained that there had to be a Scottish secretary in the Cabinet to ensure that Scottish problems attracted sufficient UK-wide attention. Johnston had recently been continuing his march towards more cohesive Scottish governance, submitting a memo to the Ministerial Machinery of Government Committee in December 1943, which argued for a wider transfer of functions: 'Today Scotland expects that the central administration of her domestic matters will be based on Edinburgh rather than on Whitehall unless there are overriding reasons to the contrary.' This statement, of course, had far-reaching implications and other government departments were wary. The committee reported on 24 December 1943, concluding that greater channelling of powers was desirable but 'if he [the Scottish secretary] is directly responsible in all matters which affect Scotland's welfare, Scotland is likely on balance to lose rather than gain. Moreover, the burden on the Secretary of State personally, already prodigious, would be well-nigh intolerable; his staff would be loaded with a bewildering variety of work . . .'[43] The Whitehall view of Johnston was that of a 'Little Scotlander'. He was certainly a cultural nationalist, much like the future Scottish secretary Donald Dewar, and even Walter Elliot, with whom Johnston had helped establish the nationalistic Saltire Society in the 1930s.

Scottish nationalism also provided a useful stick with which to beat sceptical Cabinet colleagues, much as another Labour Scottish secretary – Willie Ross – would do 20 years later. This tactic, however, received a nasty shock in April 1945, when the SNP, breaking a wartime truce by actually contesting a by-election, won its first ever seat in Motherwell. The victorious MP, Dr Robert McIntyre, refused to take sponsors or the oath of allegiance on arriving at Westminster. 'He was therefore told to go away and think it over,' the Conservative MP Harold Nicolson noted disdainfully in his diary, 'which he did, shrugging vain shoulders. Next day he thought better of it and accepted sponsorship; but even then, as he reached the box, he said, "I do this under protest", which was not liked at all. He is going to be a sad nuisance and pose as a martyr.'[44]

Johnston's last year and a half as Scottish secretary did not quite match the frenetic activity of his early years in office. The sniping from the

Clydesiders continued unabated, and the Council of State had dwindled, both in numbers present and in the frequency of its meetings. Colville was now in India, Elliot in Africa on a government mission, and Sir Archibald was too busy at the Air Ministry. Only Lord Alness and Ernest Brown turned up to its last ever gathering in 1945. At Scottish Questions on 25 January 1944, one MP complained that the council was not truly representative, as only one Tory was a member despite the party holding the majority of seats in Scotland. William Gallacher also objected to it having no communist member, while Bob Boothby enquired, 'What particular merit is there in an ex-Secretary of State for Scotland?'[45] But even in decline the council's record was formidable. 'Into that experiment of the Council of State had gone four years of effort,' reflected Johnston in his memoirs, 'and in it I had sunk many of my own energies and hopes. As we parted at our last meeting we knew our experiment had worked; we were now no longer representatives of an old nation in decay, but of a young virile people lit up with the assurance that whatever men dare in unison they can do.'[46]

Towards the end of Johnston's term of office he turned his attention to Scottish education. This area of policy had been lacking in any direction for some time, and was perhaps the biggest disappointment of his four years as Scottish secretary. Like Sir Godfrey Collins, Johnston was convinced that schoolchildren should be imbued with a notion of citizenship, and in April 1942 he issued a circular to all Scottish schools. 'Much of the civilization we have known is crashing about our ears,' Johnston told the press, 'and the troubles and difficulties that must confront the next generation will tax to the uttermost all its resources in good-will, mutual aid, and common purpose. It is therefore vital that there should be generally inculcated in the schools of Scotland a high standard of public spirit and citizenship, and that everyone concerned with education should do his or her utmost to assist.'[47] But there were complaints that the circular made no reference either to religion or temperance, and Johnston later conceded that his efforts in this field were a 'bad flop'. In 1942, he had established another council – or 'Parliament' – on education, with Naomi Mitchison among its members. Johnston gave it five points to consider, including citizenship, but his plan for a radical revision of Scottish education was overambitious, and when an Education (Scotland) Bill finally appeared in 1944 it was essentially nothing more than a Scottish version of Rab Butler's landmark Act for England and Wales. It raised the school leaving age and consolidated comprehensive education as a compulsory stage in a child's education, but Johnston decided against scrapping local authorities' right to charge fees in a limited number of primary and secondary schools. It was a political compromise, avoiding any fundamental changes to make sure the Bill actually passed.[48] Johnston was out of office by the time it reached its Third Reading, but Churchill ensured it got a clear run, provided it passed through the Scottish Grand Committee without any major trouble. It did, and required only two hours of debate before clearing its final stages in mid 1945.

Victory in Europe marked the end of the coalition government, and therefore Tom Johnston's period at the Scottish Office. He was pessimistic about what peace would bring, warning that 'We shall be split into groups and ideologies all scrambling for mastery.' Johnston had only ever intended to stay at the Scottish Office until the war was over, and he kept his word. He had toyed with staying on as Scottish secretary from the House of Lords, but even for Johnston it would have been one compromise too many.[49] 'It really is awful losing T.J.,' wrote Mitchison in her diary on 24 May 1945, and four days later the Scottish secretary surrendered his seals of office. The Scottish media was unanimous in its praise. 'He took over at a moment when the national fortunes were approaching the lowest ebb,' observed the *Glasgow Herald*. 'He departs just as the magnitude of Scottish domestic problems is beginning to be generally understood. It is due largely to his energy, intelligence and patience that these problems are not more numerous or more urgent.'[50] And the consistently supportive *Scotsman* was even more effusive:

> He accomplished much in his four years of office, not only in legislation but also in stimulating a Scottish spirit of enterprise and of determination to overcome the difficulties, social, industrial, and economic, with which Scotland is confronted. He laid the foundations and prepared the plans on which her future wellbeing must largely depend . . . It is to be hoped that the aim of securing progress by basing Scottish schemes on common agreement instead of on merely Party considerations will be kept steadily in view. If that is done, Mr Johnston's pioneering work will prove to be of permanent value and good to Scotland.[51]

Both Churchill, and his successor as prime minister, Clement Attlee, reputedly considered sending Johnston to India as its last viceroy, while both offered him a seat in the House of Lords so he could continue to speak for Scotland. But Johnston insisted upon leaving the House of Commons as his party geared up for its first general election in ten years. At a thanksgiving rally in Edinburgh's Usher Hall before the July poll, Johnston said unity of purpose had saved the country from the brink of destruction:

> It was this corporate all-in national effort, each for all, that enabled us to match the hour, and to withstand – at one period entirely alone in the world – the

organised fury of the fascist and Nazi powers of darkness . . . If only we could recapture part of that enthusiasm, elan and common purpose, recapture it for the much-needed reconstruction and betterment of our world – if only we could lift great social crusades like better housing and health from the arena of partisan strife, what magnificent achievements might yet be ours.[52]

Yet, ironically, Johnston's dream of a continuing political consensus was shattered when the Labour Party won an overwhelming majority at the subsequent election. An over-all majority of 146 seats meant that Attlee could build the New Jerusalem without seeking help from either the Liberals or Conservatives. 'I only hope they are able now to keep their heads,' Johnston wrote to his old PPS, Arthur Woodburn, on 31 July, 'and that they are given a fair chance to deliver the goods.'[53]

Johnston intended to devote himself to writing and research, but was instead distracted by a host of public appointments. Aptly, he succeeded Lord Airlee as chairman of the North of Scotland Hydro-Electric Board in April 1946, skilfully fielding criticism of the scheme and cleverly avoiding its absorption into a centralised authority when the Labour government nationalised electricity in 1947. From 1945 Johnston also acted as chairman of the Scottish National Forestry Commission, and represented Scottish interests on the council which devised the Festival of Britain in 1951. He remained a high-profile Scottish spokesman for the Labour Party, but his devolving instincts jarred with the centralising bent of the Labour government. Johnston revived his support for home rule, and even signed MacCormick's pro-home rule Scottish Covenant. By 1949 he was regularly stating that economic control for Scotland should come first, followed by political autonomy, which Johnston now claimed was not only desirable, but inevitable.[54]

Having refused a peerage in 1945, Johnston accepted Churchill's offer of the Companion of Honour in 1953, a year after publishing a surprisingly frivolous volume of memoirs. *Memories* effectively conveys Johnston's sense of humour but barely touches upon his political legacy, which was already perceived as significant even a decade after he had left office. Johnston's reputation half a century on is still substantial, though, as one historian has noted, he is often more revered than researched. Others have argued that his success was an accident of wartime, raising the question of what might have transpired had Scotland suffered more heavily from bombing raids. Even then, Johnston's restructuring of the health service and his formidable administrative abilities would still have ensured a more successful clear-up exercise than most. The context of wartime, however, undeniably played a large part in his success. What if Johnston had been Scottish secretary in 1929 instead of Adamson? His efforts would no doubt have been lost amid bitter domestic politics and an international depression. Timing, and some degree of luck, had been crucial.

Following a period of ill health, Johnston died at his home in Milngavie on 5 September 1965, aged 83. 'There was a time when he seemed a possible leader of the Labour Party and destined for the highest office,' said *The Times* in its obituary. 'But Johnston himself was almost too disinterested a Socialist, possibly too modest a person also, to aspire to the heights of political responsibility.'[55] His funeral was attended by both Arthur Woodburn – a successor of Johnston's who tried to build upon his old chief's legacy – and Willie Ross, the then incumbent, who perhaps came closest to replicating his success. 'He saw a place,' concluded another biographer of Johnston, 'a better place for Scotland within the existing system.' He did indeed, and, with style and dedication, Thomas Johnston has earned his place in Scottish Office history as perhaps its greatest ever minister.

6TH EARL OF ROSEBERY

25 MAY – 3 AUGUST 1945

Harry the Horse

The choice of the 6th Earl of Rosebery, a man more interested in horse-racing than politics, to replace Tom Johnston as Scottish secretary in Churchill's caretaker government was considered by many to be an eccentric one. Rosebery and Churchill were close friends, as their respective fathers had been, so Churchill was no doubt aware that the 5th Earl had helped create the Scottish Office back in 1885. Rosebery's appointment, therefore, was based upon an improbable mixture of historical indulgence and old family ties.[1] He was the first peer to inhabit the Scottish Office since Viscount Novar (another old friend of Rosebery's father) in 1924, and was himself a Liberal National in the mould of Ernest Brown, his predecessor but one.

'It is a happy choice and a pleasant surprise,' said the *Scotsman*. 'It will be no easy task to succeed such a resourceful and energetic Secretary of State as Mr Thomas Johnston, and he can hardly count upon the all-Party support which his predecessor deservedly gained.'[2] Indeed Rosebery could not, as Labour and the SNP soon had a field day. The recently elected SNP MP, Dr Robert McIntyre, said that, by reason of his wealth, background, and education, Rosebery had no right to be considered a representative of Scotland, while the future Labour Scottish secretary Hector McNeil said his appointment would anger many people and distress all. 'It is more than 40 years since Scotland had its Cabinet Minister remote from the House of Commons and in the House of Lords,' he argued, obviously unaware of Novar's brief tenure. 'There can be only two explanations of this action – either Mr Churchill felt that he had to pay off a political debt to the Liberals by making office for them, or, compelled as he is by law to have a certain number of Ministers in the House of Lords, he decided that the Secretary for Scotland was a convenient device.'[3] Meanwhile, Rosebery showed no signs of taking either these criticisms or his new position very seriously. A few days after his appointment, Rosebery resigned his membership of the Racecourse

Betting Control Board. Not, as one might expect, due to his new Cabinet position, but because he had just become a steward of his beloved Jockey Club.

Albert Edward Harry Mayer Archibald Primrose was born on 8 January 1882, the eldest son of the 5th Earl of Rosebery, and his wife Hannah Rothschild. One of his godfathers was the Prince of Wales, later King Edward VII, and Lord Dalmeny – his courtesy title as heir to the earldom – was educated at Eton College, from where he passed top of his class into Sandhurst before being commissioned in the Grenadier Guards.

Dalmeny had a difficult relationship with his father, whose favourite child was his younger son Neil. He regularly attacked both for their academic idleness and turf-centric social lives, and Dalmeny reluctantly resigned his commission in 1906 to fight Midlothian for the Liberals at his father's insistence. The Liberal landslide made him the country's youngest MP, and, in a generous attempt to end an old feud with his father, the new prime minister, Sir Henry Campbell-Bannerman, asked Dalmeny to second the motion on the Royal Address, a task the 5th Earl had performed 33 years earlier in the House of Lords. 'If you accept Campbell-Bannerman's invitation,' the 5th Earl told his son, 'you are no son of mine.' It was, Dalmeny later recalled, 'very embarrassing'.[4] Disillusioned, he left parliament at the next general election, although his brother Neil (also an MP, sitting for Wisbech) later achieved ministerial office in Lloyd George's wartime government.

While an MP, Dalmeny had also made a name for himself as a talented cricketer. He had distinguished himself in the Eton versus Harrow match at Lord's in 1900, and went on to play for Buckinghamshire in 1901, and twice for Middlesex in 1902. In 1905 became captain of Surrey, the youngest the county had ever had. But, having given up both cricket and the Commons, Dalmeny formed a successful partnership with General Allenby as his aide-de-camp, and latterly as his assistant military secretary in Palestine. Earning himself a mention in dispatches, Dalmeny was awarded the Military Cross in 1916 and admitted to the French Légion d'Honneur in 1917, also being given a Distinguished Service Order the following year. His brother Neil was killed in the last shot of the battle with the Turks at Gaza, a blow from which his father never recovered. The 5th Earl suffered a severe stroke in 1919, and Dalmeny effectively became head of the family, entering the Lords as the 2nd Earl of Midlothian (a title conferred upon his father in 1911 but never used), before succeeding to the main earldom on his father's death in 1929.

The 6th Earl's first marriage had produced a son and heir, Archibald Ronald, but he died suddenly at the age of 21 after contracting blood poisoning from a dental operation while he was at Oxford University. Rosebery was devastated, but distracted himself with the management of his great estates at Mentmore and Dalmeny, while also establishing himself as a successful racehorse breeder and owner. His most famous horse was Blue Peter, which won an impressive run of the Two Thousand Guineas, the Blue Riband at Epsom, the Eclipse stakes, and the Derby in 1939. Another of his horses, Ocean Swell (sired by Blue Peter) later won the Derby in 1944, and the Ascot gold cup.

Like his father, Rosebery was imbued with a deep love for his native land and was no doubt proud when he became regional commissioner for Scotland in 1941. 'I have had some conversation with Mr Harry Hopkins (the US Ambassador),' wrote the press baron and politician Max Beaverbrook to Rosebery in early 1941. 'He tells me that he was greatly impressed by Mr Tom Johnston. He also said that Tom Johnston looks on you as entirely essential to his administration.'[5] Sir William Darling, the wartime lord provost of Edinburgh, also considered Rosebery a success as regional commissioner. 'He is a man of the world without being a worldly man,' he wrote. 'He is shrewd, comprehending, understanding, and all without any affectation or pose. In fact, poise is his suit . . . Rosebery understands dumb animals. He knows how to train them – even to win races.'[6]

Rosebery later dined out on the story of his appointment as Scottish secretary:

> I was motoring home from Perth, where I had my last meeting as regional commissioner for Scotland, and coming through a village I was stopped by a policeman who said "you are wanted in the police station". I naturally thought I'd committed some motoring offence although I couldn't tell what it was. When I got there he said "we've been waiting; you're wanted on the telephone". The telephone rang and I answered it and the well-known voice of Winston Churchill said "Harry, I want you to be Secretary of State for Scotland, is that all right?" So I said yes. "Good, I'll see you tomorrow."[7]

So, having succeeded Tom Johnston as regional commissioner for Scotland, Rosebery now replaced him as secretary of state.[8] 'The Scottish Office was started by someone of the same name as myself,' he told the Glasgow Press Club on 13 June. 'My father dragged it out of a garret in the Home Office when he was Under Secretary there. He said it was necessary that Scotland should have an Office of its own. The Minister did not agree with him, but my father fought for it and won it, and I don't think that Minister, Sir William Harcourt, ever forgave him.' Indeed, when Rosebery was born, in 1882, his father was busy pestering Gladstone to take Scottish business more seriously.

The 6th Earl also rejected yet more criticism of his appointment: 'One thing I am quite sure about is this. In politics everybody can, and should, have his own convictions, but when it comes to things that are of necessity to Scotland, I do sincerely hope that they will not consider party politics, but back me up in the cry of "Scotland First".'[9] In reality, however, the consensual climate enjoyed by Tom Johnston had now been relegated to wartime nostalgia. The caretaker government of which Rosebery was a member worked against the backdrop of an election campaign in which Labour rightly sensed there was everything to play for.

From the House of Lords, Rosebery mainly tied up the remaining stages of Bills introduced by his predecessor. The Forestry Bill transferred responsibility for woodlands to the minister of agriculture and the secretary of state for Scotland, while the Town and Country Planning (Scotland) Bill (which he called 'formidable, even menacing' in its dimensions) tackled the redevelopment of blitzed areas. Rosebery also dealt with Johnston's Education (Scotland) Bill, which finally raised the school leaving age to 15 (something Sir Godfrey Collins' Bill of 1936 had also aimed to do), and established a system of junior colleges for the part-time instruction of children up to the age of 18.

Rosebery was a competent performer at the despatch box, but could be irritable with officials, angrily brushing away notes passed to him during question time, snapping 'why should I be fed by you fellows in front of all those Lords?'[10] His character was much like that of his wartime chief, General Allenby. Both could be difficult to get along with; each was outspoken and did not suffer fools gladly, but both were also gifted with acute common sense. Rosebery certainly did not endear himself to his two under-secretaries, the Conservative MP Tom Galbraith, and the member for Rutherglen, Allan Chapman. 'I don't think he had anything much to do,' recalled Galbraith, later Lord Strathclyde, in an interview 35 years later. 'You see, we were only there for a few weeks, and I don't know what he did. He certainly came into the Office, but he never spoke to any of us, or asked us any questions or anything.' When asked why Rosebery was made Scottish secretary, he replied:

Well I don't know and he didn't know himself, I don't think. He was horrified when he was stopped on the road in the south of Scotland one day on his way from Dalmeny . . . I don't think you could really call him clever. He was a very well versed chap and so he knew what he wanted to do and all that kind of thing, though we didn't actually come in touch with him. And then there was the Election, you see, and we were all out.[11]

Polling for the general election had taken place on 5 July, but the collection of forces' votes pushed the formal declaration back by another three weeks. Rosebery played a full part in electioneering, and he knew Churchill wanted him to stay on at the Scottish Office ('I'm too old,' he protested), although his political instincts told him the Conservatives would not win. During the campaign, and even after domestic polling had ceased, the opposition attacks continued. 'The Secretary for Scotland has duties which closely affect the daily lives and liberties of the Scottish people,' said the Labour MP Herbert Morrison on a campaigning visit to Edinburgh. 'It is well established that the Secretary for Scotland should be drawn from the House of Commons, because it is desirable that he should be in daily touch with the elected representatives of the people. Perhaps Mr Churchill came to the conclusion that there was not a single Scottish Tory MP fit for the job.'[12] Rosebery hit back by saying he objected to Englishmen with 'periodical' Scottish interests, also accusing Sir Archibald Sinclair's Liberals of operating a covert pact with Labour.[13] Churchill's broadcast on 4 June, as reported in *The Times* the next day, boasted that the government still had a 'Rosebery and a Lloyd George' (the former prime minister's son Gwilym, minister of fuel and power since 1942) to 'carry forward the flags of their fathers'. Sir Archibald, meanwhile, claimed that Rosebery's father would have been a follower of his were he still alive. 'Sir Archibald never met my father,' sneered Rosebery, 'and it is quite obvious that he has also never read his speeches.' He added:

> When I spoke at the annual meeting of the Liberal National Party I said that the Prime Minister had put forward a programme which I asserted with confidence every Liberal Prime Minister in my lifetime would have gladly accepted as a Liberal platform on which to fight an election . . . I can assert with absolute confidence that if my father had been in politics at the present time he would have been the leader of the National Liberals, and would have lashed the Sinclairites with a scorn of which he was a past-master.[14]

Rosebery, meanwhile, was having better luck on his beloved turf. On 7 July his colt Ocean Swell won the Ascot Gold Cup by a length and a half, watched by the King, Princess Elizabeth, and a record crowd of 50,000. And the day after the sheer scale of Labour's landslide victory became apparent, another of Rosebery's horses, Blue Smoke, won the Herne's Oak Stakes at Windsor, again by a length and a half.

As the early election results came in, the Scottish secretary turned to his official, Craig Mitchell, and declared, 'we're out', even before it was obvious that this was indeed the case. And, as he left Dover House for the last time, he looked at his private secretary and said: 'Well, I didn't make a bad job of this, did I? I didn't have time.'[15]

Although he continued to lead the Liberal Nationals in the House of Lords, Rosebery's brief ministerial career was now over. Attlee's government asked him to chair an inquiry into the export and slaughter of horses in 1949, and he continued to comment on Scottish politics, opposing the creation of a Scottish parliament but supporting an inquiry into Scottish affairs. 'No far-seeing Scotsman wants to build an Iron Curtain on the Cheviots,' remarked Rosebery. 'What Scotland really needs is the speedy build-up of a proper system of regionalisation. Scotland does not need the power to make her own exclusive laws; she does need the power to administer her own affairs.'[16] Otherwise, his activities were largely apolitical. Rosebery chaired the Royal Fine Art Commission for Scotland from 1952, and he kept up his sporting connections, becoming president of the Surrey County Cricket Club from 1947, and of the MCC for a year in 1953. From 1955 until 1965 he was chairman of the Scottish Tourist Board, and he also worked with his wife Eva to help establish the Edinburgh International Festival.

Even in old age, Rosebery remained energetic and fascinated by current affairs, forming close bonds with people he encountered from all walks of life. And there was one final – albeit eccentric – connection with the Scottish Office. In the early 1960s he requested a meeting with the Conservative Scottish secretary Michael Noble, nominally regarding Musselburgh Race Course, but actually concerning a gold teapot owned by Noble and coveted by Rosebery. Noble's father had won the teapot at an auction in which Rosebery also bid, and he still hankered after its ornamental beauty. Noble was used to fending off his now elderly predecessor and arranged for his private secretary to interrupt the meeting just as the discussion moved from horses to teapots.[17] The 6th Earl of Rosebery died at his Buckinghamshire home, Mentmore Towers, on 30 May 1974, aged 92.

Joseph Westwood

3 August 1945 – 7 October 1947

Little Joe

Joseph Westwood had a hard act to follow. He became Scottish secretary in the first non-coalition government since 1931, but, having been one of Tom Johnston's under-secretaries during the heady days of the war, Westwood was inevitably compared with his old chief. Unfortunately for Scotland's new minister, a combination of political events beyond his control and bad health meant that Westwood simply could not measure up, in more ways than one. Little more than five feet tall, the new secretary of state was dubbed 'Little Joe' or 'Wee Joe' by the press, who gave him a rough ride from the start. In a Cabinet dominated by Labour heavyweights like Aneurin Bevan, Sir Stafford Cripps and Ernest Bevin, Westwood simply could not compete. Commentators rightly suspected that, like his friend William Adamson, this Labour minister had not been appointed on merit, but purely because someone was needed to fill the post. The *Scotsman* said Westwood was an 'almost inevitable choice', adding that, although 'Modest in demeanor, he is nevertheless a man of determination, and he is not likely to be daunted by the tasks which lie ahead of him in the years of construction. But he will not be an extremist, and even his opponents will recognise his sincerity and good intentions.'[1]

Perhaps intimidated by the eloquence around him, Westwood quickly gained a reputation for only speaking on narrowly defined Scottish issues when he attended Cabinet. But, given that Clement Attlee's government was preoccupied with a massive programme of nationalisation, a territorial minister such as Westwood was always going to find it difficult to fight his corner. In fact, all three of Labour's postwar Scottish secretaries would find there was little they could do to prevent Whitehall clawing back the responsibilities Tom Johnston had fought so hard to transfer to Edinburgh.

Westwood's bad luck also extended to his health. Just six weeks after being appointed Scottish secretary, he was struck down by illness and entered an Edinburgh nursing home to undergo a small operation. Two weeks later Westwood had more serious surgery and spent the next few months recovering. By early December, he was well enough to do 'light work' at St Andrew's House, but all his engagements were cancelled until the New Year. Westwood did not attend another Cabinet meeting until January. Meanwhile, Attlee and his new government had been putting the finishing touches to the New Jerusalem, without the Scottish secretary. Westwood never quite recovered, either physically or politically.

Joseph Westwood was actually English by birth and parentage; born on 11 February 1884 at Wollescote in Worcestershire, he was the son of Solomon Westwood, a miner, and his wife Harriet. His father moved to Fife in 1887 to work in the fast-expanding coalfields there, and Westwood attended Buckhaven Higher Grade School, leaving aged 13. After a year as a draper's assistant, he followed his father into the mines, working at the Wemyss collieries from the late 1890s until halfway through the First World War. 'I would do absolutely anything in the world to stop mining,' Westwood later told Alastair Dunnett, 'to stop a man having to go underground to dig coal with a pick as a face. My father was killed in the mines and my grandfather was killed in the mines, and I had an uncle whose bits were brought home in a sack.'[2]

Westwood married Frances Scarlett in 1906, their partnership producing an impressive total of three sons and five daughters. The Wemyss colliery was notable for its paternalistic approach, providing good housing, welfare halls, and railway and tram systems. Westwood, therefore, was not part of the 'little Moscow' strand in the Fife mining unions which caused William Adamson, as secretary for Scotland, so much trouble between the wars. Indeed, he left the coalface in 1916 to become industrial organiser of the Fife Miners' Union under the future secretary for Scotland, with whom he quickly became friendly. They were a strange contrast: Westwood was short, slight and sallow; Adamson was tall, burly and ruddy-faced. A councillor and justice of the peace in Kirkcaldy, Westwood was also a key progressive on the Fife Education Authority, which left him with a lifelong dedication to both local government and education.

Westwood failed to enter parliament in a 1921 by-election but won the mining constituency of Peebles and South Midlothian the following year. In June 1929 he became Adamson's parliamentary private secretary at the Scottish Office, and on 25 March 1931 Westwood succeeded Tom Johnston as under-secretary. Like Johnston, he lost his seat at the disastrous (for Labour) general election just months later, and had a good, although unsuccessful, showing in the East Fife by-election in 1933. Five candidates stood, including the writer Eric Linklater, who later fictionalised the contest in his novel *Magnus Merriman*. Westwood re-entered the Commons along with Johnston in 1935, this time representing Stirling and Falkirk Burghs. Westwood had a strong debating voice and was credited with a sharp mind. 'He loves the thrill of debate,' noted a 1931 biography, 'and when his blood responds to the thrill his eyes sparkle, his body quivers, and every muscle rejoices in mobility.'[3] The future home secretary, James Chuter Ede, described Westwood in his diary as an unexceptional yet loyal rank-and-file MP with whom the Labour leadership liked to keep in touch. Westwood returned to the Scottish Office as a Labour member of the wartime coalition on 17 May 1940, first under Ernest Brown, and then under his successor, Tom Johnston, taking control of health and education. He piloted the Education (Scotland) Bill through the Commons just as Johnston was preparing to retire, and Labour was gearing up for an election which would turn the electoral map red.

The new Labour prime minister was perhaps the least sensitive to Scottish sentiment since David Lloyd George. Ironically, Winston Churchill – now leader of the opposition – better understood the quirks and aspirations of the northern kingdom having served for 12 years as an MP in Dundee. Attlee had tried to persuade Johnston to stay on, fully aware of how 'wedded' he was to Scotland, but the wartime Scottish secretary was set on retirement and the job fell instead to Westwood. Attlee wanted the Gorbals MP George Buchanan to become minister of National Insurance and was surprised when he instead requested to take the more junior position of under-secretary at the Scottish Office. With his broad physique and booming voice, Buchanan wanted to tackle Scotland's appalling housing problems which had now been made even worse by the war. Another under-secretary was Tom Fraser, who handled the development brief, lobbying for Whitehall's 'economic' ministries to relocate industry to Scotland. The Redistribution of Industries Act of 1945 and the Town and Country Planning Act of 1947 were passed with this in mind, while the Clyde Valley Plan of 1946 was a bold attempt to wean Scotland off its traditional reliance on heavy industries and towards consumer production.

'Scotland's future', said Westwood after receiving the Freedom of Kirkcaldy in 1946, 'must never again depend, as in the inter-war years, on heavy industries alone. Light industries must be attracted . . . If planning is pushed forward in this way, it will certainly lead to the building of the Forth Road Bridge.'[4] That did not happen for another two decades, although Westwood realised what had to be done. But while many light engineering and consumer goods plants were established in

Scotland, they supplied just 2.7 per cent of Scotland's jobs by 1947. At his annual 'State of the Nation' address in Edinburgh's City Chambers, the Scottish secretary announced the merger of Johnston's Scottish Council on Industry with the Scottish Development Council. 'Get on with the fusion,' said Westwood, 'there must be no delay, and then we can make a great national appeal for the funds necessary to make the new advisory body a real effective instrument in working for Scotland's economic and industrial development.'[5]

Westwood, egged on by Buchanan, also staked his reputation at the Scottish Office on housing, setting a target of constructing 20,000 permanent houses a year at his first press conference. 'That is my target,' he said, 'but I want to exceed it.' Not for the first time, however, reality interfered with such ambitions. Although the Housing (Financial Provisions) (Scotland) Bill of 1946 doubled the housing subsidy for local authorities, manual labour was still in short supply and nearly all the materials required – timber, steel, slates and electrical goods – were scarce. The realities of post-war economics even defeated the pugnacious Buchanan, who was frustrated by civil service bureaucracy. 'We musnae be laskadainical' [sic],[6] he told one head of department, but no amount of hard work could get things moving. In 1947 Westwood appointed a committee to examine the rising costs of house building, but he soon had to admit there was little hope of reaching his target.

The Town and Country Planning (Scotland) Bill of 1947 also aimed to shake up the existing planning system, and allow Treasury grants to aid local authorities in clearing bomb-damaged land. Within three years of the Bill's passing, each local authority was to submit a 'development plan' for the whole of their district. As a former councillor himself, Westwood was committed to local government and saw this Bill as a way of enhancing its role in post-war reconstruction. Meanwhile, large-scale state planning was beginning to emerge as the new political orthodoxy. Patrick Abercrombie's ground-breaking Clyde Valley Plan included proposals for New Towns to house a projected seven per cent of Scotland's population, a goal for which Westwood was particularly enthusiastic. The Scottish secretary suggested a total of six settlements to cope with Glasgow's overspill and the needs of new coalfields in Fife and the Lothians. The chancellor, Hugh Dalton, complained in Cabinet that this would give Scotland a disproportionate share of the action, so Tom Fraser worked hard at ensuring East Kilbride was the first to be designated, while arguing that another in the Lochgelly-Cowdenbeath area was also essential. Adapting an old Liberal idea, Westwood also announced the formation of a Highland Advisory Panel (which included Naomi Mitchison among its members) in 1946. It met for the first time on

24 January 1947, under the chairmanship of the Western Isles MP, Malcolm Macmillan. 'I want action, and early action,'[7] Westwood told the gathering in Inverness, but the panel's lack of any executive authority, or sizeable budget, meant all it could do, as its name implied, was advise.

In September 1945 the minister of health, Aneurin Bevan, announced his plans to nationalise the UK's hospital service and make medical treatment free at the point of delivery. Westwood had an easier time than Bevan in securing the backing of the medical profession in Scotland, partly because Johnston had laid the groundwork, but also because the Scottish secretary based his scheme on Scotland's four university medical schools and their associated hospitals. Attlee considered this more traditional framework of specialist/teacher/consultant to be better than Bevan's, and personally congratulated Westwood.[8] Moving the Second Reading of the National Health Service (Scotland) Bill on 10 December 1946, the Scottish secretary reminded the House that a form of state-subsidised national health service had been operating in the Highlands and Islands since 1913.[9] 'In framing the proposals in this Bill,' he told MPs, 'I have only one objective in mind, to provide Scotland with a Health Service that will, in years to come, be a source of strength to her own people and the admiration of all others.'[10]

Westwood also took pride in the Education (Scotland) Act of 1946, which allowed parents found breaking child employment laws to be fined. Both these Acts, however, were essentially kilted versions of UK legislation, which was probably a blessing as officials were often dismayed to see the Scottish secretary at a loss, both in debate and at private meetings. Sensing Westwood's weakness, some English departments knew they could tackle this Scottish secretary more easily than the assertive Johnston. The Scottish Office civil servant George Pottinger remembered one meeting where Westwood had to choose either a new school or hospital building for a vacant piece of land. After both sides had made their case there was an uncomfortable pause. An education official tried to fill the gap by reminding Westwood that he felt strongly that more schools should be built. Westwood assented, but, when a junior official from the Scottish Department of Health said 'you will remember, Secretary of State, that you feel equally strongly that we need another hospital', the meeting broke up in confusion.[11] In public, however, Westwood put on a brave face. 'I claim that I will set up a good record,' he told the House in June 1946, 'and I will leave it to the people of Scotland to determine whether or not I have been successful when I leave office.'[12]

Many observers believed that Labour's nationalisation of electricity by the Scottish MP and minister Manny Shinwell would sound the death knell of

Johnston's cherished North of Scotland Hydro-Electric Board, even though the former Scottish secretary was now its chairman. 'The Highlands must be led into a better future,' said the chancellor Hugh Dalton following a visit to the Board, 'not by the invisible private hand of Adam Smith, but by the visible public hand of the Labour Party.'[13] And, although Westwood initially had a fight on his hands, Johnston's shrewd political manoeuvring resulted in Shinwell agreeing to a separate Scottish electricity board within the nationalised scheme.

A 1947 Bill also re-devolved control over fire services to Scottish local authorities, but in other areas the Scottish Office failed to stem Whitehall's centralising instincts. Westwood lost powers over transport, and he even appeared to give up the fight, timidly declining when the Ministry of Town and Country Planning offered to establish a Scottish Committee of the Central Land Board. Instead, the Scottish secretary rather disingenuously attempted to argue that far from Whitehall snatching control away from Edinburgh, the new nationalised industries actually gave Scotland greater autonomy than before over coal, electricity, transport and tourism. 'In each claim . . . Scotland as a nation either has a better grip – or will have under legislation – than she has ever had,' he said, boasting that he had established a Scottish Advisory Council on Civil Aviation. But the *Scotsman*'s verdict was typical of the press at that time:

> It is a little inconsistent for a Socialist to say that the future of Scotland depends finally not on Government action, be it local or national, but on the response of Scotsmen and Scotswomen to the demands of our time. The trouble is that the Government, because of their nationalisation policy, cannot allow adequate devolution in Scottish affairs, nor, in spite of Mr Westwood's claim to the contrary, have they done so.[14]

Although Westwood was a political unionist 'by personal conviction',[15] he was also sympathetic to demands for home rule, and he politely received a delegation from John MacCormick's Scottish Convention in February 1946. Westwood had been pressing for a bigger ministerial team since his appointment in 1945 but had come up against a hostile civil service which feared it would spark calls for more devolution. 'What I have in mind,' Westwood said in a memo to the Cabinet Office, 'is an arrangement whereby, at the instance of the Secretary of State, a new Minister could be given formal authority and responsibility for the discharge in his name of specified statutory responsibilities of the Secretary of State.'[16] He envisaged a Scottish 'Minister of State', an idea which would eventually be taken up by the Conservatives and implemented in 1951, but in the post-war climate, the Cabinet Office was 'not enamoured' either by the likely expense, or its political benefits.

Westwood also supported calls from some Labour MPs for a general inquiry into Scottish administration. In June 1947, John Taylor, the secretary of the Scottish Council of the Labour Party, wrote to the lord president of the council, Herbert Morrison, asking for such an investigation. Morrison passed his letter on to Westwood, who replied, 'My own feeling – and that of party officials with whom I have discussed the matter – is that an enquiry by an independent committee is the only way to deal with the criticisms which are levelled at the Government to the effect that Scotland's affairs are subject to too much central control from Whitehall.'[17] But Morrison, a fourth-generation Scot (not to mention Peter Mandelson's grandfather), was hostile, telling Westwood that ordering an inquiry without knowing the likely outcome could prove dangerous. 'We have not really done enough to combat the sense of injury and grievance against the present machinery of government which is widespread in Scotland,' he wrote. 'There is a big public relations job here which ought to be tackled before it is too late.'[18] Attlee, however, was more open-minded, minuting on 23 June that 'While, I think, our Scots friends are apt to be unduly alarmed at Scottish Nationalism, I think it might be wise to have some kind of inquiry.'[19] Getting wind of this, Morrison then moved his opposition into the media, telling journalists that there was 'no real demand for home rule', although the government welcomed 'the case for lesser claims if they were more specific'. 'Post-war conditions', he added, 'make the time inopportune to bring devolution into prominence and perhaps sharp controversy.'[20] Faced with the twin pressures of Scottish Labour back-benchers, who did want an inquiry, and Cabinet colleagues, who did not, Westwood chopped and changed his own position, leading Morrison to conclude that he had lost control of events. Eventually, the Scottish secretary dropped his call for a second minister while awaiting a decision on an inquiry. 'I am doing all I can myself so far as the work of the Scottish Office is concerned,' he wrote to Morrison. 'But important parts of the field are covered by Great Britain Ministers, and it is essential that they, too, should do their utmost to see that the needs of the Scottish position are kept fully in view.'[21]

In August 1947 the Government ran into balance of payment difficulties, mainly over its trade with the USA, and the Cabinet decided to prioritise public spending. Attlee's response was a ministerial reshuffle in early October, which saw Westwood sacked along with six other Cabinet ministers. When the outgoing Scottish secretary asked Attlee for an explanation, he received one of the prime minister's famously abrupt explanations: 'Cos you don't measure up to the job. That's why,' said Attlee. 'Thanks for coming. Secretary will show you out.'[22]

The Scottish press was almost unanimous in declaring that Westwood had failed to stand up for Scottish issues in Cabinet, and the *Scotsman* judged that his was one of the weakest ministerial teams ever to preside over the Scottish Office. Meanwhile, Westwood had made his way to St Andrew's House to clear his desk and ordered two sausage-and-mash canteen lunches to be sent to his office as a last supper for him and George Buchanan. Westwood was hugely popular with ordinary Scottish Office staff, at least. 'Mrs Westwood thinks this is a grand opportunity to give me a bit of a rest,' he told the *Daily Herald*, 'for I have worked hard during these years.'[23]

Like Tony Blair, Westwood was preoccupied by his political legacy. He tried to preserve his name in Fife's first New Town, but the new Scottish secretary, Arthur Woodburn, preferred Glenrothes when it came to be christened in 1947. And when Woodburn unveiled plans to reform Scottish business at Westminster, Westwood made his last speech in the Commons, on 28 April 1948:

> I welcome these proposals as being a step in the right direction, but I am convinced that no one person can effectively carry out all the work involved. If I had remained longer in office, I would have had proposals ready for increasing the number of senior Ministers for Scotland. We ought to have a Minister of Health and Education, and two senior Ministers instead of one. I should be out of Order if I went into this subject any further, so I will conclude by saying again that one man cannot be made Pooh-Bah of Scotland and effectively carry through its administration.[24]

Just three months later Westwood and his wife were killed in a car accident at Strathmiglo in Fife. Paying tribute in the House, Walter Elliot quoted Edmund Burke: 'What shadows we are and what shadows we pursue,' he said, adding, 'There are some things which are not shadows: Work, courage, sympathy, sincerity. By those sentiments, men can add to the great influence and renown of these Houses of Parliament. It was in those virtues that the late Joseph Westwood made himself eminent in the service of Parliament and in the service of his country.' Woodburn also remembered his old colleague: 'All of us, in our own ways, will carry on the torch of progress, which he has been compelled to drop.'[25] Westwood and his wife were buried in Dysart cemetery in Kirkcaldy in July 1948, following a funeral service conducted by the general secretary of the Scottish Salvation Army.

Arthur Woodburn

7 October 1947 – 28 February 1950

Big Arthur

On arriving at St Andrew's House as secretary of state for Scotland, Arthur Woodburn must have had a double dose of déjà vu. Not only had he been Tom Johnston's parliamentary private secretary during the war years, but more than three decades earlier Woodburn had been imprisoned in the old Calton Gaol which once stood on the site. Along with his future Clydeside comrade James Maxton, Woodburn spent two years in the prison for speaking out against conscription. After being court-martialled for publicly declaring his intention not to fight, he was at one point incarcerated in the Tower of London, and spent long periods in solitary confinement. But Calton Gaol was the worst, Woodburn later describing it as 'the poorhouse of all prisons' with the 'cold chill of a grim fortress'.[1] His first 30 days in captivity were spent on bare boards, but he used the time to study shorthand and politics. The secretary for Scotland at that time, Robert Munro, kept a close watch over Maxton (who was considered the more dangerous) and would no doubt have been appalled to learn that his fellow inmate would someday replace him as Scottish secretary. Woodburn rarely spoke of this period but retained a sense of humour, buying some old paving stones when Calton Gaol was torn down and making them into a garden path at his Edinburgh home. One of Woodburn's first duties as Scottish secretary was to officiate at a Remembrance Service, attracting some hostility from ex-servicemen because of his wartime pacifism, but otherwise Joseph Westwood's successor arrived at St Andrew's House with a considerable degree of goodwill, and officials and the press were no doubt hopeful that this minister would carry more political clout. 'Mr Woodburn has an attractive personality which, during the war years, made him popular in Press circles,' judged the *Scotsman*. 'He is an inveterate Commons man, steeped in the traditions of the House, and with a very proper respect for its usages and customs.'[2]

The Scottish media was still misty-eyed about Tom Johnston's years as Scottish secretary, so Woodburn tried hard to hit a 'Johnstonian' note in his first few days by calling for the co-operation of all classes and shades of political opinion. On arriving at St Andrew's House, he assured waiting journalists that he knew the Scottish Office well, but proceeded to make for the room he had inhabited as Johnston's PPS.[3] He received several letters of congratulation: 'Two things it would seem are necessary for a Secretary of State for Scotland,' wrote Sir William Darling, 'ability and good luck. You have the former in rich abundance – may I as a political adversary wish for you the second? It is all you need!' The home secretary, James Chuter Ede, also wrote, saying he hoped to work with Woodburn in promoting as much legislation as possible without clogging up parliamentary time, and to 'remove comparisons between the parts of the UK which only hinder effective progress'.[4] Unfortunately for Woodburn, his luck would soon run out, while comparisons between Scotland and the rest of the UK would dominate his incumbency. 'Big Arthur' had replaced 'Wee Joe', but, like Westwood, Labour's new Scottish secretary would be overshadowed by his wartime predecessor, and frustrated by political events beyond his control.

Arthur Woodburn was born in Edinburgh on 25 October 1890, the youngest of seven sons and one daughter of Matthew Woodburn, a brass founder, and his wife Janet. After attending the city's Bruntsfield Primary and Boroughmuir Secondary, Arthur left school at 14, taking a number of jobs including work in his father's brass foundry. He also gained some early media experience through working for the Free Church on its lengthy lawsuit over property with the United Free Church (of which Woodburn was a member). He later moved to Miller's London Road foundry in Edinburgh, eventually spending more than 25 years in engineering and foundry administration, where he specialised in costing and foreign contracts. He had a natural aptitude for languages, speaking German, French, Italian and Spanish, a skill he honed through evening classes at Heriot-Watt College. Woodburn spent a total of 12 years at the college after leaving school, and took classes in economics under the tuition of William Graham, later president of the Board of Trade in the minority Labour government of 1929.

Woodburn joined the Independent Labour Party (ILP) in 1916, the same year he was incarcerated in Calton Gaol. On his release in 1919 he returned to work at the London Road foundry and married Barbara Halliday, who was later one of the first female members of Edinburgh Town Council. Woodburn also became active in the Scottish Labour College movement, lecturing on history, economics and finance for its Edinburgh branch. In 1937, he became president of the National Council of Labour Colleges, and never quite lost the lecturing style of speech he acquired there. Having travelled widely in Europe and Russia, Woodburn was initially an enthusiastic Stalinist, and wrote *An Outline of Finance* in 1931, a short tract which apparently proved influential within the Australian Labor Party. Woodburn also outlined his financial theories to the Macmillan Committee on banking in 1930. When asked his status by Lord Macmillan, Woodburn replied 'Scottish secretary' [of the Labour Party]. 'I congratulate you on your elevation,' responded Macmillan. 'I trust your salary has been raised correspondingly.'[5]

Woodburn had been appointed as full-time secretary to the Scottish Council of the Labour Party soon after returning from Russia in 1932. 'A delightful fellow,' wrote the Labour MP and future foreign secretary Patrick Gordon Walker on meeting him. 'He only just missed [James] Middleton's job as Secretary of the Labour Party . . . He is a humorous man, not ostentatious, prepared to do quiet steady work for the movement.'[6] Woodburn lost out on the position by 13 votes to 11, but he continued to work hard on expanding the Scottish Council's membership and control. His early attempts to enter parliament also brought disappointment, contesting South Edinburgh in 1929, and the Leith Burghs in 1931, both without success. Labour had only seven seats in Scotland following the 1931 general election and so Woodburn's position was a difficult one. It became even more so when the ILP split from Labour, taking away four of those seven, not to mention many of its grass-roots members and much of the party's property. Woodburn more or less had to set up a new party organisation from scratch and soon became a relentless disciplinarian. But his bluff manner hid tremendous ability, and looking somewhat older than his years gave Woodburn significant presence at party events.

In October 1939 Woodburn finally entered the Commons at a by-election in East Stirling and Clackmannanshire. He had by now abandoned his pacifism, and enthusiastically served Tom Johnston (who shared Woodburn's dislike of cigarettes and alcohol) as his PPS from 1941 until the end of the war. Between then and 1947, he was joint parliamentary secretary to the Ministry of Supply and Aircraft Production, impressing colleagues with his diligence and ability. So when Woodburn replaced Westwood at the Scottish Office in October 1947 he was seen as a rising star.

Woodburn entered Fielden House just as the King declared a state of emergency during a bitter London docks strike. He was determined to learn the lessons of his predecessor's unhappy experience in charge of Scottish affairs and immediately set to work on reforming his department's business at Westminister. Woodburn had more extensive contact with the Labour grass-roots than Westwood and was acutely aware of the perception that nationalisation meant centralisation. In November 1947 he submitted a memo to the Cabinet on 'Scottish Demands for Home Rule or Devolution'. Dismissing the Scottish National Party (SNP) as 'small, picturesque and articulate', Woodburn concluded that the majority of Scots believed 'that Scottish affairs should have more time devoted to them and should be dealt with by the Scots themselves within the British Constitution and the unity of the two countries'.[7] But the Scottish secretary, by his own admission, did not want to play 'St George slaying the English dragon', and he was convinced that Scots would not be prepared to make a large economic sacrifice for the satisfaction of 'governing themselves'.[8] Woodburn's solution was threefold: at Westminster, reorganise Scottish business; in Edinburgh, convene a Scottish Production Council to stimulate industry; and, over-arching both, establish an inquiry into Scottish government. Again, the deputy prime minister, Herbert Morrison, emerged as the chief opponent of any such concessions to nationalism. He wrote to Woodburn on 13 November, 'If you enlarge the scope of the Scottish Grand Committee in the way you propose and at the same time seem to open the door to further wide and unspecified concessions to be achieved after the fact-finding committee has completed its work, you may set afoot an agitation for concessions on a lavish scale which you will not be able to control.'[9] Ironically, although Morrison had actually recommended Woodburn to Attlee as a man who could sell Labour's policies to Scotland, the Scottish secretary felt unable to counter his patron's hyperbole. By 6 December Woodburn compromised with five suggested reforms in another Cabinet memo:

(1) that on agreed occasions Scottish Bills should be referred to the Scottish Grand Committee for debate before the Second Reading is taken formally in the House of Commons;
(2) that up to four days should be allocated in the Scottish Grand Committee, in addition to the normal Supply days in the House of Commons, for discussion of Scottish Estimates;
(3) that a Scottish Economic Conference should be established under the Chairmanship of the Secretary of State;
(4) that an annual review of Scottish economic affairs should be made and presented to Parliament;
(5) that special attention should be given to the arrangements for decentralization on executive responsibility in Scotland.[10]

Woodburn's desired inquiry had been dropped completely, as had Westwood's idea of an additional minister of state, while the Production Council had become a tamer Economic Conference.[11] 'I take the view that it would be ultimately highly dangerous to the relationship of Scotland if the Government were to adopt a purely negative attitude,' Woodburn concluded, but it 'is unlikely that any enquiry, however wide its scope, would satisfy the varying and far-reaching demands which have been made.' The Cabinet approved all five points on 11 December, and Woodburn moved swiftly to produce a White Paper on Scottish Affairs. 'We want to be ourselves, and will be ourselves,' he told reporters in early December. 'We have our own culture, education and laws, and our own contribution to make. We want to make that contribution as Scotsmen, and we will make it as Scotsmen. The problem to be solved was how to remain ourselves and also part of a corporate community.'[12] Woodburn's solution to that problem appeared on 29 January 1948, just as Labour learned of its defeat by a Conservative in the Glasgow Camlachie by-election. (The Indian nationalist, Ghandi, died the same day, a symbolic link some newspapers made much of.) Reaction was swift and critical. Sir William Darling said that 'After a great deal of labour the mountain has brought forth a mouse'; while Lord Rosebery branded the proposals 'inadequate'. 'We do not want Home Rule for Scotland . . . What we do want is greater power to manage our own affairs,' he said paradoxically. The *Scotsman* judged the White Paper to be an 'anti-climax', although *The Times* was more positive, praising its 'sober and practical sentiment'. 'I don't think I can say anything pertinent about Mr Woodburn's White Paper,' commented the playwright James Bridie, 'except that it gives me a pain in the neck.'[13] Only the Scottish Unionists appeared to support the White Paper, while Woodburn was even attacked by his host, Edinburgh's lord provost, at his State of the Nation speech the day after the White Paper was launched. The Scottish secretary defended his plan in hyperbolic terms: 'These proposals, to those who understand the working of Parliament, are almost a constitutional revolution, and I may say, from what I have seen, that the Welsh have evidently recognised the importance of them, even if some Scots have not yet seen what they mean.'[14] Indeed, Woodburn had actually been warned 'to avoid any statement that might encourage Welsh demand'.[15]

The Scottish secretary presented his White Paper to parliament on 28 April, having by now toned down his rhetoric. 'I make no claim that these proposals are in any way a revolution,' he told MPs, 'or that they create some new Parliament, or anything of that kind. They are for the simple and clear purpose of giving Scotland more time to discuss its affairs, and more control over its affairs.'[16] Some MPs accepted it as a first step, but the Ayr MP, Sir Thomas Moore, condemned the White Paper as 'nonsensical and a sop to Scottish Nationalists', while the Labour MP David Kirkwood said sarcastically, 'I can see in this the hand of the Artful

Dodger – and he is a not a Tory.'[17] Kirkwood perhaps meant the proposals for the Scottish Grand Committee. On the surface, these looked good, but in reality only non-controversial Bills would reach the committee before a Second Reading, with parliament reserving the power to prevent a transfer if it desired to. However, Woodburn's White Paper itself required no fresh legislation, and the Commons' standing orders were altered accordingly on 28 April, although only after frantic negotiations with wary clerks of the House. The newly reconstituted Scottish Grand Committee – dubbed the 'Little Parliament' by some – sat for the first time on 22 June to discuss education. Despite Standing Order 100 allowing for meetings outside London, Woodburn resisted calls for the committee to meet in Edinburgh – a discussion which took up a fifth of its maiden session. Shortly after becoming Scottish secretary, Woodburn had summarised the political situation to his officials:

> The Labour Party [in Scotland] now puts socialist unity before its feelings, but it can be said without exaggeration that Scots of all Parties are apprehensive of tendencies to absorb independent Scottish institutions in UK bodies and view with suspicion and resentment any reluctance to allow Scottish affairs to be dealt with in Scotland. This feeling is growing and it will thrive in any policy of apparent negation and in my view the urgent and desirable thing to do is to give it a positive lead into legitimate developments.[18]

Woodburn believed his 'legitimate developments' had closed down the issue of Scottish governance and he resolved to treat any further calls for home rule with ill-disguised contempt.

The Scottish secretary's thinking on devolution was, at best, muddled and inconsistent. Standing for parliament in 1929, Woodburn had favoured home rule, and even wrote to Churchill in 1940 to suggest the establishment of a Grand Scottish Consultative Council, something the then prime minister politely rejected. Woodburn's position was mirrored by that of the Labour Party, which after 1931 had also cooled on demands for home rule. But by the mid 1940s, Woodburn's stance hardened just as Tom Johnston's softened. In 1945 and 1947 the Scottish Council of the Labour Party passed resolutions backing an inquiry into devolution, and the 1948 conference decided that Woodburn's White Paper was to be given a trial. But compared with the ever-expanding Scottish Convention movement, Labour Party resolutions were the least of Woodburn's concerns.

Dreamt up by the SNP's former honorary secretary John MacCormick as a cross-party lobbying group for a Scottish parliament, the Scottish secretary viewed the Scottish Convention as nothing more than a clandestine Tory plot. MacCormick had initially supported Labour while at Glasgow University, but he later negotiated the merger between the Scottish Party and the National Party of Scotland, to form the SNP in 1934. When the SNP elected the anti-conscriptionist Douglas Young as its chairman in 1942, MacCormick and his followers left in disgust to set up the Scottish Convention. That established a Scottish National Assembly in 1947, which overwhelmingly endorsed home rule for Scotland.[19] The convention owed its success not only to genuine support among Scots for some degree of devolution but also to growing concerns that Labour's widespread programme of nationalisation was going to far. Even Churchill implied that Scotland would have to resort to home rule to escape the worse excesses of British state socialism.

MacCormick led a deputation from the convention to meet Woodburn on 9 January 1948 in St Andrew's House, just as the Scottish secretary was putting the finishing touches to his White Paper. As ever, MacCormick had done his best to present an cross-party front, bringing with him the Duke of Montrose (nominally a Liberal), and Professor Andrew Dewar Gibb (nominally a Conservative). MacCormick's prejudices about Woodburn simply hardened during the meeting. He was 'a typical party bureaucrat,' he recalled later, 'efficient, uninspired and totally incapable of looking at anything except through the narrow eyes of party bias'. The Scottish secretary praised the deputation for what he said was a reasonable and comprehensive scheme for devolution but added that he was yet to be convinced of widespread demand in Scotland. He also told them to wait for his White Paper. 'It consisted of three small pages,' wrote MacCormick dismissively, 'and proposed nothing more than a slight extension of the Parliamentary time given to the Scottish estimates and modest improvement in the procedure of the Scottish Grand Committee.' MacCormick stood at the Paisley by-election the following month, but the formal support of the Unionists and Liberals did not translate into votes, and, although he gained nearly 20,000 votes, Labour held on to the seat with a reduced majority. The prospect of a nationalist win in Paisley had loomed large in Woodburn's mind, but in the event it proved more damaging to MacCormick, the more left-leaning members of the convention resigning in disgust at him seeking Conservative endorsement. Never one to let electoral defeat numb his enthusiasm, MacCormick pressed ahead with both the Scottish Convention and the National Assembly, the latter producing the Scottish Covenant, a document deliberately evocative of its seventeenth-century precedent. 'We, the people of Scotland who subscribe this Engagement,' it read, 'declare our belief that reform in the constitution of our country is necessary to secure good government in accordance with our Scottish traditions and [pledge] to . . . do everything in our power to secure for Scotland a Parliament with adequate legislative authority in Scottish affairs.'[20] The first to sign it was the Duke of Montrose, whose ancestor signed the original covenant 300 years earlier. To Woodburn such gestures were simply further evidence of the 'colourful pageantry' he believed was typical of parochial nationalism. At the close of Labour's Scottish conference on 26 October 1947, the Scottish secretary warned that Scotland 'must be careful not to follow some of the Pied Pipers of Nationalism over the brink that leads to disaster'.[21] But after two years of relative plain sailing at the Scottish Office, it was Woodburn, and not the Pied Pipers of nationalism, who would find himself on the brink of political disaster.

The first of Woodburn's Scottish Economic Conferences (SEC) met on 23 April 1948 in Edinburgh, generating many column inches in the press if not much in way of political action. It included representatives from local government, industry and the trade unions; and it was said that only the doorman at the Caledonian Hotel was not invited, because he was too busy. Like all of Woodburn's initiatives, the SEC was well intentioned and deliberately Johnstonian in formation, as was another of his internal reforms:

> I invited all my fellow Scottish Ministers to join me in regular meetings to consider policy, to be informed about major decisions and to keep me advised as to what was happening in their departments . . . it was an instruction of mine that none of the Scottish Ministers was to seek kudos for what we were doing but to let our actions speak for themselves.[22]

By the late 1940s, however, such noble innovations were lost amid the noisy rebirth of party politics. The SEC's first meeting produced the suggestion of a 'Marshall Plan' for the Highlands, and Woodburn told the press that it was the first time since the Act of Union that all strands of Scottish economic life had been pulled together. He also fended off criticism about the meeting being in private, saying it was a conference with influential representatives, and not a debate. But, even though Woodburn tried to shore up the SEC's credibility by persuading Cabinet colleagues like Sir Stafford Cripps[23] to address it, it met only seven times between 1948 and 1950, and never made any real impact.

In 1948, the Scottish economy took a turn for the worse as Scotland's share of new factory building slumped from 14 per cent to under half that figure. Woodburn did his best to carry on his predecessor's work with the New Towns, designating Glenrothes in 1948 and working hard, although without success, to revive the idea of another in Renfrewshire.

Housing remained a policy battlefield and the former fruit-seller John James Robertson – known as 'J.J.' – took over as the responsible under-secretary from George Buchanan, who was promoted to become pensions minister in 1947.[24] While building materials were now more widely available, Woodburn granted few private contracts, preferring to let local authorities compete for public sector deals. 'I refused to be part of the political nonsense,' wrote Woodburn in his unpublished memoirs, 'that the number of houses built could be either credited to or blamed on the Government of the day.'[25] This was just as well, because although a lot of houses were constructed few became ready for occupation during Wood-burn's tenure.

The fledgling National Health Service in Scotland, however, proved more of a success. 'On July 5 we commence in this country what we believe to be the greatest health service in the world,'[26] declared Wood-burn at a press conference. But there were teething troubles: although seven in ten Scottish doctors had signed up to the new nationalised service a month before its launch date, most chemists refused. The Scottish secretary met a deputation, and negotiations went on long into the night. Having reached an agreement, Woodburn discovered that all the Scottish Office typists had gone home. 'I solved the dilemma,' he later recalled, 'by getting an old typewriter out of my cupboard which I had used as a PPS [parliamentary private secretary] for my correspondence and myself typed out the agreement we had come to about their starting the scheme.'[27] The Scotsman's diarist poked fun at Woodburn's secretarial skills: 'Judging from the specimen of his typescript which is reproduced in a newspaper the Secretary of State has a pretty feeble touch on the key-board. His line wobbles and he uses "X" to cross out mistakes.'[28] As planned, the Scottish NHS came into being on 5 July 1948, with a Scottish Health Services Council and various other advisory committees to guide the secretary of state for Scotland. On 29 December 1948 Woodburn wrote a glowing memo on how well the NHS was performing in Scotland, saying it had begun work with 'remarkable smoothness', while joking, 'One would not expect Scots to be slow in taking advantage of the free services provided.'[29] But costs rose quickly, and by early 1949 the Treasury was alarmed at the prospect of having to spend another £50 million on the health budget for 1949–50. Charges for some services were touted as a solution, but Woodburn, and the scheme's main architect, Nye Bevan, emerged as vehement opponents of any such compromise.

Woodburn was seen to be performing well as Scottish secretary. Government expenditure on housing and health were high, while revenue from hydro-electricity and Scotland's coalfields had reached record levels. In his State of the Nation speech on 1 February 1949 Woodburn boasted that both his administrative reforms – the Scottish Economic Conference and the reconstituted Scottish Grand Council – had been a success. 'We are living to-day in a new Scotland,' he said. 'In my view Scotland was reborn during the war. The defeatism which developed amidst the depression and misery of the inter-war period was dissipated by the great task of winning the war. Hard work and a great purpose revived the Scottish heart.'[30] Woodburn still prided himself on building upon Tom Johnston's legacy.

The Scottish Covenant movement resurfaced in 1949 with a more broad-based campaign than in 1947. Anxious about the number of signatures the covenant was attracting, Scottish Labour MPs began pressing Woodburn once again for an inquiry into Scottish administration. Meanwhile, the Scottish Plebiscite Society had conducted a mini referendum in Kirrie-muir which produced a large majority in favour of home rule. The Scottish secretary's stance simply hardened, telling his critics that the imminent general election would provide a real opportunity for voters to express their views. But the political pressure was building, and, when the government devalued sterling in September, wide-ranging cuts in public spending just added to Woodburn's worries.

The Scottish Council of the Labour Party gathered in Aberdeen on 23 October to consider various resolutions, including one calling for an inquiry. After a blistering speech from a popular female MP, Peggy Herbison, against the motion, it was rejected by a large majority of delegates. In sharp contrast to Labour's intransigence, the third Scottish National Assembly met a week later in the Church of Scotland's assembly hall on the Mound, and its 600 delegates overwhelmingly endorsed a motion to establish a Scottish parliament with full legislative powers. Woodburn was now faced with pressure from his own back-benchers (who were at odds with party officials), the Scottish Convention, and an increasingly excitable press. 'The present tone of the newspapers', minuted an official to the Scottish secretary on 8 November, 'is due to a combination of the proprietors' willingness to embarrass the Government and the journalists' pleasure in being allowed to write what they believe!'[31] That same day, Woodburn came under attack at Scottish Questions for refusing to make a statement on how the planned expenditure cuts would affect Scotland. But if anything, Woodburn grew even more complacent, writing to Hector McNeil (soon to replace him at the Scottish Office) on 14 November, following some nationalist successes in McNeil's Greenock constituency. 'When it became clear that there was no possibility of splitting our party,' he wrote, 'and that we had been consolidated on a clear position, they [the Scottish Convention] realised that any divisions accomplished by Scottish home rule agitation would be among the other parties . . . To revert to home rule, it is important to realise that the industrial and commercial side of Scotland have shown no interest in it.'[32]

The situation came to a head just two days later, during an adjourn-ment debate on Scottish nationalism obtained by the Tory MP for Dumfries, Niall Macpherson. The day's Commons business had con-cluded early, leaving around six hours for the debate, which quickly moved beyond home rule to cover the whole business of Scottish administration. Woodburn had prepared a short ten-minute response, but, given the time available, ended up giving vent to his private fears about possible nationalist activities. Crucially, and somewhat recklessly, he referred to various oratorical flourishes made by John MacCormick:

> I saw another speech of his recently in which on three occasions he mentioned the word "bomb". Now, in these emotional movements that is very dangerous talk, and we have already had experience of bombs being in existence in this movement on two separate occasions in Scotland. For a leader of a responsible movement to indulge in this type of talk is extremely dangerous indeed, even though he phrases it in language which does not make himself the primary instigator. We shall be wise, therefore, to take note of the irresponsible elements who control this movement, and not to allow perfectly reasonable and creditable sentiments, such as the hon. Gentleman has put forward tonight, to be misused for the ultimate purpose of some of those people concerned.[33]

MPs immediately sensed the seriousness of Woodburn's remarks. Mac-pherson asked the chair if the secretary of state was straying from correct form. 'I confess that I was getting a bit nervous,' replied the Speaker, while John McGovern condemned Woodburn's speech as 'unworthy'. The Labour MP Emrys Hughes said he would not be surprised if when the Scottish secretary next arrived at Waverley Station the Duke of Montrose was not waiting for him with a claymore. 'We have listened to a speech of absolute blood-curdling irrelevancies,' he added. 'It was like something written by some script writer who had taken part in the writing of "Whisky Galore." '[34] Meanwhile, reporters began to telephone MacCor-mick for his reaction. 'I knew at once that the man who was accusing me,' recalled MacCormick, 'protected though he was by all the privilege of Parliament, was blundering to his own destruction.'[35] The Scottish Convention leader immediately wrote to Woodburn asking him to with-draw his statements in the House, while the next morning's Scottish newspapers were dominated by news of Woodburn's blunder. 'Haven't we in Scotland had just about enough of Arthur Woodburn?' asked the

Bulletin in its editorial.[36] On Saturday 19 November Woodburn summoned the press to St Andrew's House in a feeble attempt to contain the situation, but he simply made matters worse. 'The question [of home rule] . . . is a practical one,' he said in a statement, 'and, while sympathising with moderate thought on this matter, I ventured to strike a cautionary note about the danger of allowing the issue to be raised to a highly emotional plane.' Woodburn then laid out three files of press cuttings before bemused journalists, the first of which detailed the arrest of 17 people in Paris, following the discovery of an alleged plot by Jewish terrorist leaders to bomb London. The second contained quotes from MacCormick after Attlee refused to meet a deputation from the Scottish National Assembly: 'If some young enthusiast for Scottish Home Rule were to throw a bomb in the region of Downing Street the question of Scottish self-government would leap into the headlines and become a matter of national urgency.' The third cutting described the six months' imprisonment in Glasgow of two youths – members of the Young Scotland Movement – who had pleaded guilty to possessing explosives between December 1947 and April 1948. This was all interesting stuff, but hardly an explanation for what had been a serious accusation against the nationalists. One reporter pointed out that MacCormick had also said he was sure that Scotland would achieve home rule only through moderate means. Woodburn, however, refused to answer any more questions and promptly left the room. 'In view of the fact that some foolish Scottish nationalists had already thrown bombs in Glasgow,' Woodburn reasoned in his memoirs, 'it seemed to me the suggestion might have been followed by the more fanatical section as I had information that other preparations for violence were in vain. This suggestion of Bombs created great headlines and the press poured ridicule on my head though later my warnings were fully justified.'[37] One newspaper resorted to comic verse:

> They mock you, Arthur, laughing when you bleat
> Of tartaned types with bombs in Downing Street.
> They bid you have a care lest the display
> Of Scotland's saltire on St. Andrew's Day
> Be but a cover for some fiendish trick
> Of sending Southward haggises that tick.[38]

'I think it is right to let my colleagues know that the protagonists of Parliamentary devolution are at present very active in Scotland,' wrote Woodburn in a Cabinet memo on 12 December, 'but for the moment my view is that no further action by the Government is called for.'[39] Egged on by Herbert Morrison, the Scottish secretary stuck doggedly to the strategy of inaction agreed two years before. But, with a general election approaching, the Scottish Convention movement had been handed a ready-made campaign, and its supporters heckled Woodburn at rallies across the country. Meanwhile, the Conservatives had unveiled their own plans for Scottish affairs, chiefly a minister of state and a royal commission. The Scottish secretary protested that he had tackled the question of devolution as soon as he entered the Scottish Office, but, although Woodburn secured a good majority in East Stirling and Clackmannanshire, Attlee had already decided to sack him after just two and a half years in the job. Instead, Woodburn was offered a demotion to the Ministry of Fuel and Power, which he refused. 'I . . . took the view', reasoned Woodburn, 'that the change would be misinterpreted because of the campaign of the Scottish nationalists of which incidentally he [Attlee] was almost unaware.'[40] Privately, Woodburn was upset, believing he had been made the scapegoat for a position propagated by Morrison. The lord advocate, Lord Wheatley, and the rest of the Scottish Office team, also believed the Scottish secretary had been badly treated, with Attlee paying too much attention to Woodburn's critics. The MP James Hoy, until then Woodburn's PPS, even refused promotion as a mark of loyalty to his old chief. 'Mr Woodburn has never been happy there,' said the *Scotsman* of his time at the Scottish Office, 'and certainly few were happy to see him there.'[41] Woodburn maintained that it was his decision, and his alone, to leave the government. 'My roots are too deeply embedded in Scotland to be easily torn up now unless for a compelling reason, which to me at the moment does not exist,' he said. 'The new Secretary of State [Hector McNeil] has long been a friend of mine. He has done a good job at UNO and he will not do less for Scotland. It is with some pleasure that I hand over to him a Scotland full of energy, hope, and, believe, good-will.'[42]

Now on the back-benches, aged 60, Woodburn devoted himself to the House of Commons, and to helping younger Labour MPs make their mark. A warm, generous and avuncular figure, he deliberately avoided becoming bitter about his sacking, and instead enthusiastically supported both the remainder of Attlee's government, and Harold Wilson's from 1964. Woodburn served on the Select Committee on Procedure from 1956 to 1968, and was also active in the British Inter-Parliamentary Union, where his linguistic skills served him well. He led the first Westminster delegation to the West German Bundestag, and became the first foreigner to address that assembly. Woodburn advocated a 'University of the Air' (later the Open University) as soon as Wilson became prime minister in 1964, and, after leaving the Commons in 1970, his enthusiasm for the Common Market led to his election the following year as joint president of the British Section of the Council of European

Municipalities. A keen golfer, gardener and motorist – even in old age – Woodburn died on 1 June 1978, aged 88, following an accident while driving to visit his ailing wife in hospital. The Scottish Office has been responsible for the premature end of many a political career, not least that of Arthur Woodburn.

HECTOR McNEIL

28 FEBRUARY 1950 – 30 OCTOBER 1951

Young Hector

When Hector McNeil, formerly minister of state at the Foreign Office, learned that his old private secretary Guy Burgess was to become second secretary at the British Embassy in Washington, he warned him to remember three things: 'Don't be too aggressively left-wing; Don't get involved in race relations; and above all, make sure that there aren't any homosexual incidents which might cause trouble.' 'I understand, Hector,' replied Burgess. 'What you mean is that I mustn't make a pass at Paul Robeson.'[1] Burgess, of course, became involved in something much more serious than flirting with American singers, and when the news broke that he had disappeared along with Donald Maclean (the son of a Scottish Liberal MP Sir Donald Maclean), his old Foreign Office chief was by then secretary of state for Scotland.

Friends had warned McNeil about Burgess, but he had defended the gifted civil servant as a useful man to have around, claiming he was not senior enough to be a risk. In fact, McNeil escaped any political damage from Burgess's defection to the Soviet Union. Indeed, he was the first Scottish secretary since the war to be taken seriously by colleagues and the press. 'Some may think that in taking over the Scottish Office he has jumped from the frying-pan into the fire,' assessed the *Scotsman*. 'It is true that the post of Secretary of State for Scotland offers almost unlimited opportunities for mistakes, and has proved the graveyard of more than one Ministerial reputation. But, if there are dangers, there are also opportunities, and for a young, ambitious, and able man like Mr McNeil the adventure will be worth while.'[2]

McNeil's years at the Foreign Office had been the high point of an impressive political career. Born at the Temperance Hotel in Gareloch-head on 10 March 1907, Hector McNeil was the second of seven children of Donald McNeil, a journeyman shipwright, and his wife Margaret. His family moved to Glasgow when he was still quite young, and McNeil attended Woodside School before matriculating at Glasgow University. Colleagues later joked that Hector had joined the wrong ministry, as he had originally intended to study for the church. But after graduating, having honed his formidable debating skills as president of the students' union, he opted instead for a career in journalism and politics. He joined the *Scottish Daily Express* (then Scotland's largest daily seller) as a freelancer and later a leader writer, becoming assistant to its editor in 1938. McNeil also forged a relationship with the newspaper's proprietor, Lord Beaver-brook, which was to last for the rest of his life.[3]

McNeil had been elected a Labour councillor on Glasgow Town Council in 1933. There, he was nicknamed 'Young Hector' to differentiate him from his namesake, another Hector McNeil (later Sir Hector), the city's lord provost. He stood against Walter Elliot in the Kelvingrove Division of Glasgow at the 1935 general election but was narrowly defeated (despite calling Elliot a 'self-avowed fascist'). Following another defeat at a by-election the following year, McNeil was finally elected in July 1941, when he was returned unopposed in Greenock. From 1942 until the end of the war he served as parliamentary private secretary to Philip Noel-Baker, then as parliamentary secretary to the Ministry of War Transport, and after the Labour landslide of 1945 he became an un-der-secretary at the Foreign Office under Ernest Bevin. McNeil's cautious yet extrovert nature gelled perfectly with Bevin's vigorous personality, and the foreign secretary pushed continually for his protégé's advancement until his death in 1951.

In 1946 McNeil was promoted to minister of state and became the government's main spokesman at the annual general assemblies of the United Nations (the conservative MP and diarist Harold Nicolson thought him 'Scotch and dour'[4] in this capacity). He was passionately committed to good Anglo–American relations, becoming a well-known figure in US political circles, and he was equally as strong in his criticism of the Soviet Union, famously 'hectoring' Stalin's UN representative, Andrey Vyshins-ky. McNeil loathed communism and resented any of his Labour collea-gues 'playing footsie' with them.[5] And as a former journalist, he proved an effective tool in the Western propaganda campaign at the height of the Cold War. McNeil also took part in the Paris Peace Conference of 1946, and he was involved in the negotiations that resulted in the Brussels treaty of 1948. He had impressed the Labour prime minister, Clement Attlee, especially when he deputised for an ill Bevin, and also caught the attention of Hugh Gaitskell, another young MP on the right of the party. 'We dined last Sunday with the McNeils and had a good political gossip,' recorded Gaitskell in his 1948 diary, adding:

Hector is a journalist and I think all this is very much the journalist's approach
. . . Hector himself is obviously extremely ambitious. He would have liked to be
Secretary of State for Scotland; alleges that he was unofficially approached but
Ernie [Bevin] would not agree. He has, perhaps for this reason, no opinion of
Arthur Woodburn. Hector is an attractive person and I like him. For the
moment I do not think his ambitions would be such as to make him hopelessly
untrustworthy as a friend.[6]

McNeil and Gaitskell later became firm friends, but the longer McNeil
served at the Foreign Office, the closer he came to succeeding Bevin as
foreign secretary. Bevin told Attlee that he considered McNeil to be his
natural successor, but the prime minister was reticent, instead proposing
that he replace Woodburn at the Scottish Office. McNeil later confessed
to his predecessor that he had not wanted to be Scottish secretary, but he
was a sensible choice. Unlike Westwood and Woodburn, McNeil had no
ties with Tom Johnston, and also lacked any troublesome home rule
baggage. The new Scottish secretary was tasked with taking on the pro-
home rule Scottish Convention and winning. As the movement's leader,
John MacCormick, later put it, McNeil had won his spurs with Vyshinsky
at the UN, and now he had been charged with pacifying his fellow
countrymen.

McNeil's opinion of the Scottish Covenant, a petition produced by the
Scottish Convention, was essentially the same as that of Woodburn
(scornful), but he immediately struck a more moderate tone. 'Mr. McNeil
has shown himself readier than Mr. Woodburn . . . to go into the whole
question of Scottish devolution,' noted *The Times*, which went on to
speculate that 'giving clear proofs that the possibility of greater administrative devolution is being fairly studied the Government could reinforce
the many Scotsmen who remain convinced that the hazardous enterprise
of a separate Parliament is not the right solution'.[7]
    Privately, McNeil did not think calls for Scottish home rule were either
timely or particularly appropriate, fearing Scotland's influence in UK and
world affairs would be marginalised as a result. But McNeil was determined not to repeat Woodburn's mistakes, and he told the Commons in
his maiden speech as Scottish secretary that:

There always will be a concern and a zeal among Scots people to protect these
Scottish characteristics, and they should be assisted. It must not be lightly
concluded that we will assist Scotland or Britain by pressing hurriedly towards
any measure of self-government. There has been a gradual transfer, and it is
unlikely that that transfer will be stopped at any one stage. I find myself in

complete sympathy with those who have pressed for more and more facts about this situation before we come to a conclusion . . . Anyone of sensitivity who hopes to be regarded as responsible will not push, or attempt to push, this movement aside off hand. I certainly will not.[8]

Having been a contemporary of MacCormick at both school and college, McNeil was well matched to his nationalist opponent, whom he regarded as nothing more than an agreeable romantic. By May 1950, the Scottish Covenant claimed more than a million signatures, but Attlee still resisted requests to meet with a deputation from the Scottish Convention, saying he could not negotiate with a body lacking any constitutional status. Instead, the prime minister instructed McNeil to hear their case. This the Scottish secretary did, reporting back to parliament on (appropriately enough) 4 July. 'I met on 17th June a deputation which submitted to me their case for the setting up of a Scottish Parliament for domestic affairs,' he told the House. 'I undertook to bring their submissions to the attention of my colleagues. This I have done.'[9] McNeil's tactic was one of benign neglect, supplemented with a minor concession to persistent demands for an inquiry into Scottish affairs. He actually wanted to establish a royal commission on devolution, but sensed the Cabinet would immediately reject that idea, so instead McNeil actively sought the chancellor's support for a fact-finding inquiry into the financial relations between Scotland and England. Sir Stafford Cripps was reluctant, arguing that obtaining such statistics would be logistically difficult and would not satisfy Scottish opinion. McNeil responded promptly, and firmly:

> The vast majority of Scottish people have always had a traditional respect for facts and if the enquiry displayed as I think no doubt it will display that the Scottish people were not being unfairly and perhaps even generously treated that would meet a great deal of the criticism. It is not the extremists in Scotland who worry and embarrass us, it is the impression among the population which the extremists have to some degree created precisely because there was a lack of information.[10]

McNeil believed that when the financial status of Scotland in relation to that of England was laid bare, voters would realise that further devolution would put Scotland at a disadvantage. Sir Stafford, however, held his ground. 'I hope . . . you will desist from any further effort to get figures', he wrote, 'which must be completely valueless and which will nevertheless waste much valuable time and energy that might otherwise be used to increase the Revenue collected.'[11] McNeil also maintained his position, responding, 'I have no doubt at all that to go on taking this line can do us nothing but harm in Scotland where it will be regarded by all moderate opinion as completely unreasonable.'[12] But both the Scottish secretary and the chancellor realised the need to compromise, and Sir Stafford suggested an inquiry into the 'practicability' of producing a return on Anglo–Scottish finance and trade. McNeil agreed, and on 25 May he announced to the House what was inevitably dubbed as 'an inquiry into an inquiry'. A former governor of the Bank of England, Lord Catto, was appointed to chair the committee of eight members, which included the former Scottish Office permanent under-secretary Sir Horace Hamilton. It produced the Catto Report in 1952 (by which time McNeil was out of office), which revealed the growing reliance of the Scottish economy on state subsidies, estimating that while Scotland received 12 per cent of government expenditure, it only contributed ten. McNeil also launched a new handbook on Scottish administration in July, designed to demonstrate just how many powers had already been transferred to the secretary of state. Both moves were creative attempts to combat growing nationalist sentiment, and by mid 1951 support for the Covenant had more or less fizzled out. McNeil's more gentle approach appeared to have worked, although luck had also played a part.

McNeil's Scottish Office team was the youngest and most dynamic Scotland had ever seen. Tom Fraser stayed on to oversee the development portfolio, while the ailing J. J. Robertson was replaced with the North Lanark MP Margaret Herbison, affectionately known as Peggy, the first female minister to set foot in St Andrew's House.[13] The daughter of a miner, Herbison quickly made her mark, leading a crusade to replace out-of-date Victorian buildings with new primary schools. But, above all, it was McNeil who energised officials, encouraging them to take a strong, positive line on his behalf. His approach to politics was essentially businesslike, and he tried hard to turn the Scottish Office into a modern political operation. However, he found the routine legislation of his new department dull compared with that of the Foreign Office, and he remained determined to keep a hand in world affairs, perhaps with half an eye on eventually succeeding Bevin as foreign secretary.

Unlike Woodburn, McNeil did not restrict himself to purely Scottish topics in Cabinet; and, like the Scottish first minister Jack McConnell half a century later, he rarely missed an opportunity to fly the Scottish flag overseas. In July 1950 he accompanied a group of Highland provosts on a trip to Saint-Valéry-en-Caux in Normandy for the unveiling of a memorial to the 51st Highland Division and the 2nd French Cavalry Division. The Scottish secretary also insisted on leading the British delegation to a meeting of UNESCO in Paris, a task usually undertaken by the education minister.

McNeil made use of his old UN contacts in an attempt to bring its general assembly to Edinburgh. It was well known that the UN was considering a temporary base in Europe while its permanent home in New York City was being built, so McNeil invited David Vaughan, a senior member of the UN staff, to visit Edinburgh in July 1950, offering to 'clear out of St Andrew's House' for the secretariat and secure the Usher Hall for the general assembly. 'If the question is one of interest, enthusiasm, energy and good-will,' remarked Vaughan, according to the *Scotsman* on 29 July, 'there should certainly be no doubt as to where the next session is going to be held.' But although he was impressed by McNeil's offer, the South Americans had the decisive vote on the conference committee and the Scottish secretary's bid failed. A proposed trip to Canada also floundered when an envious Commonwealth relations secretary refused to let McNeil miss a three-line whip, Patrick Gordon Walker's own visit to the Dominion having been less than successful.[14]

The Scottish secretary attracted attention with two eloquent speeches on foreign affairs, the first of which warned the General Assembly of the Church of Scotland not to expect a speedy end to the Cold War, while also sounding a more optimistic note:

> Sometimes our grandfathers found themselves in a calm sea where such wind as there was blew steadily and doubtless they thought themselves fortunate in being in such a position. I say we are more fortunate. We are having a part in redefining and reaffirming our outlook on life. We are having an opportunity to express our faith in our way of living.[15]

And, speaking at Stretford in Lancashire, McNeil supported rearmament among the Atlantic Powers, while denying that the search for a peaceful solution to the Korean crisis was a sign of weakness. This speech encompassed his twin beliefs in the special relationship between the US and the UK, and the threat posed by the Soviet Union:

> It would be ungenerous, irresponsible and inaccurate if we did not all recognise and acknowledge that the United States, with the other democratic peoples, has travelled far to find a possible solution palatable to Soviet Russia and to the Government of China. This spirit of conciliation should not be mistaken for weakness, because it is plain that in concert we are a most considerable force . . . No one could deny that up to this moment, with its controlled Press, its restriction on travel, its secret police, the Soviet Government had prohibited the battle of ideas, and, at the same time, by persistent aggressions, it has made the battle of the bombs more likely.[16]

But McNeil's attempts to raise the status of the Scottish Office failed to impress his fellow countrymen. When his State of the Nation speech at Edinburgh's city chambers failed to cover housing, as was expected, the Scottish secretary's old newspaper – the *Scottish Daily Express* – urged him to speak up for his country. Some Scottish MPs also complained that McNeil spent more time with his powerful American friends, like the US ambassador Averill Harriman, than in Scotland. Indeed, he did not even own or rent a home in his Greenock constituency, preferring to stay with friends in Glasgow.[17]

These friendships, however, served a purpose, and McNeil was always on the look out for an opportunity to attract foreign industry to Scotland. His most notable success in this field came from International Business Machines (IBM), which was looking for a UK base. McNeil invited one of his American friends, IBM's chairman Tom Watson, to look at the Caird Shipyard in his constituency. But when they reached the long-derelict yard Watson refused even to leave his car, saying he was only interested in new sites. They then moved on to a nearby torpedo factory which McNeil said the Ministry of Defence was willing to vacate, but again Watson would not budge. The Scottish secretary later admitted to officials that he was then at a loss, but continued to evangelise about Scotland's magnificent scenery and local sporting opportunities. It was a fine summer's day, and when the party reached Inverkip they turned inland and took a side road past the Spango Valley, which looked down over Greenock. Watson suddenly jumped out of the car and exclaimed, 'Here is the valley of opportunity; this is where we shall come.'[18] Although the site was actually in another constituency (the future Scottish secretary Jack Maclay's), IBM's UK headquarters was up and running within a year, and it remains there to this day.

Tom Fraser's dogged pursuit of regional policy also produced impressive results. After intense lobbying from Fraser, Harold Wilson – then a precociously young president of the Board of Trade – agreed to support the establishment of a subsidiary factory for Rolls-Royce at East Kilbride, therefore firmly securing the New Town's industrial base. McNeil was also acutely concerned with the future of Scotland's rural communities and took a keen interest in hill farming, visiting the Great Glen Cattle Ranch at Inverlochy, near Fort William. Its owner had transformed a few thousand acres of heather and scrub into land on which cattle could be reared and wintered. The fact that the herd had increased to more than a thousand caught McNeil's imagination, and he floated the idea of a Beef Board, a new nationalised industry to breed and market cattle. The Treasury and Ministry of Agriculture were initially keen, but they failed to appreciate the local circumstances of the Great Glen experiment, and the board failed to transpire. McNeil had more luck with another contact, the Duke of Westminster, whom he persuaded to develop his West Sutherland estate, undertaking extensive afforestation, introducing Galloway cattle onto the hills and improving the port of Kinlochbervie. And, just before Labour lost the 1951 election, the Scottish secretary established the Hill Lands (North of Scotland) Commission, with Lord Balfour of Burleigh[19] as chairman. But, while it was charged with exploring the possibilities of breeding and rearing greater numbers of cattle in the Highlands, its role was purely advisory.

McNeil had a reputation as a very direct person, who did not mess around with either civil servants, or the opposition. Although he was remarkably non-dogmatic politically, the Scottish secretary caused uproar in the House by launching a scathing attack on the Conservatives' housing policy.[20] McNeil hated red tape, and, in particular, petty disputes between officials. John Wheatley recalled one stand-off involving Parliament House and St Andrew's House over a legal bill and its presentation. Summoned to deliberate, the Scottish secretary delivered a blunt verdict: 'Does it matter a damn which way the Bill is presented? It's a legal Bill and you'll be doing all the work.' He then tossed a coin to resolve the issue, as officials watched in amazement.[21]

After nearly a year at the Scottish Office, McNeil was becoming frustrated. The Labour government now had a wafer-thin majority and there was growing talk of a coalition. 'Hector is still plodding up and down to Scotland every weekend,' wrote McNeil's wife Sheila to Lord Beaverbrook after a weekend at Chequers. 'I'm going to sue for divorce and cite British Railways. He spends two nights a week with them . . . The PM asked me how I liked Hector's new job. I said that from the domestic point of view it was hell, from the point of view of administrative experience of a varied kind for Hector it was wonderful. I wonder how long the PM expects one to spend "gaining experience"!'[22]

On Christmas Day 1950, a small group of nationalists stole the Stone of Scone – or Stone of Destiny as it became known – from Westminster Abbey. The 336-lb lump of yellow sandstone, believed to have been the coronation seal of Scottish kings for several centuries, had been taken to London in the 13th century by Edward I. The symbolism was obvious, but McNeil retained a dignified silence and refused to comment while investigations were ongoing. Instead, he sniffed around behind the scenes with the newspaper reporter Andrew Ewart, and a policeman called William Kerr, later chief constable of Dunbartonshire. The Scottish secretary, therefore, knew quite quickly who the culprits were, but said nothing, although he astounded John Rollo, a prominent nationalist thought to be involved, by telling him after a meeting of the Highland Panel: 'I know you. You are in the stone mason's business.' The stone was missing for several months, but on 11 April 1951 it was wrapped in a Saltire flag and left at Arbroath Abbey along with letters addressed to the King, and the moderator of the General Assembly of the Church of Scotland. The government came under pressure from the archbishop of Canterbury and dean of Westminster to have the four suspects brought to trial for theft, criminal damage and sacrilege. But McNeil and others immediately realised the political implications of such action, chiefly a boost to the declining Covenant movement. The attorney-general, Sir Hartley Shaw-cross (famed for his role in the Nuremberg war trials), agreed and persuaded Attlee that prosecuting the group would prove counterpro-ductive. 'I am satisfied that a prosecution would do no good except to the defendants, to whom it would give the opportunity of being regarded as martyrs if they were convicted, or heroes if they were acquitted,' he wrote on 18 April 1951. 'In Scotland a prosecution would produce a very adverse reaction.' All those involved – law student Ian Hamilton,[23] engineering students Gavin Vernon and Alan Stuart, and domestic science teacher Kay Matheson – confessed to removing the stone under police question-ing. The lord advocate, John Wheatley, shared Sir Hartley's concerns. 'The prevailing view in Scotland is that those who removed the Stone were foolish rather than criminal,' he wrote on 17 April, 'and that it would do no good, and might do considerable harm, to proceed against them.' He added that moderate Scottish opinion favoured the Stone being returned north of the border. But this approach also carried political risks, as it would look like 'a victory' for those who stole the Stone in the first place.[24] The Cabinet agreed with both analyses, and in his own Cabinet memo McNeil presented three options for action: return the Stone to Westminster Abbey; put it on show in various Commonwealth capitals as a display of British unity; or return it to Scotland. The Scottish secretary favoured its return and recommended St Margaret's Chapel in Edinburgh Castle as a new home; he suggested June 1951 – when the King would be in Edinburgh – as a suitable transfer date. 'The return of the Stone to Scotland would, I am sure, be regarded by moderate opinion in Scotland as a generous response,' said McNeil. The Cabinet approved this course of action when it met on 7 May, but they resolved to delay any move for a year, for fear of appearing to react to the theft too quickly. By then, however, Churchill had returned to Downing Street and the matter was quietly dropped.[25]

Despite McNeil's public reserve, the incident clearly took its toll on him. 'I'd like to get Hector away from Stones of Destiny and Hill Sheep Subsidies and have him to myself for just a little while . . . This job is

Above left. The 5th Earl of Rosebery. 'The Scotch, instigated by Rosebery,' wrote the Earl of Derby, 'are asking for a Secretary of State or a Minister on the same footing as the Irish Secretary: there is no work for him to do and in the judgment of most English persons the proposal is a mistake but it seems that a certain amount of Scotch feeling, real or fictitious, has been got up on the subject.'

Above right. The Duke of Richmond, the most richly endowed nobleman on the peers' roll and the first Scottish secretary. 'You know my opinion of the office,' he told Lord Salisbury, 'and that it is quite unnecessary.'

Left. Sir George Otto Trevelyan. Lord Rosebery thought him 'lamentable' and Gladstone judged him to be 'useless, except for the power to make an occasional good speech'. (© *Mary Evans Picture Library*)

Below. Lord Dalhousie as seen by *Punch*. John Morley thought him 'one of the truest hearts that ever was attracted to public life'. (*Reproduced by permission of Punch Ltd, www.punch.co.uk*)

Right. Arthur James Balfour, who proved that the Scottish Office could be used as a political launch pad; he later became prime minister and foreign secretary. (© *Mary Evans Picture Library*)

Below right. The 9th Marquis of Lothian. An energetic and colourful secretary for Scotland, he reformed local government, Scottish universities and showered the Western Isles with public funds.
(© *The Illustrated London News Picture Library*)

Three Scottish secretaries as featured in *Vanity Fair*. Clockwise from above, Lord Balfour of Burleigh was the longest-serving, while Andrew Graham Murray and Harold John Tennant had little chance to leave their mark.

Above. The reluctant Scottish secretary. The 1st
Marquis of Linlithgow was so ill that he tried to
resign just a month after his appointment.
(© *National Portrait Gallery*)

Above right. 'An angel with discordant wings.' John
Sinclair had many enemies, but successfully persisted
with his radical plan for Scottish land reform.
(© *National Portrait Gallery*)

Right. 'Dry, uninspired, and uninspiring.' Thomas
McKinnon Wood could be incredibly rude both to
colleagues and the opposition, but championed the
temperance movement and reformed mental health
services in Scotland.

Above left. An enigmatic Robert Munro. He achieved the impossible by integrating Scotland's Catholic schools into the public sector, a reform which endures to this day. (© *National Portrait Gallery*)

Above right. Viscount Novar, a former Liberal MP who joined a Conservative government as secretary for Scotland. He was happiest as governor-general of Australia but found governing Scotland much more difficult. (© *National Portrait Gallery*)

Left. A proud-looking Willie Adamson, Labour's first Scottish secretary. His stock refrain that a matter was receiving his 'due consideration' provoked affectionate ridicule in the House. (© *National Portrait Gallery*)

Below. 'A stooping, sandy-haired figure with fleeting resemblances to Mr. Churchill.' Sir John Gilmour modernised the Scottish Office both in and out of government. (© *National Portrait Gallery*)

Right. Marlon Brando meets the Scottish Office. Sir Archibald Sinclair certainly cut a dash, but the depression and unstable domestic politics prevented him becoming a more successful secretary of state. (© *National Portrait Gallery*)

Below right. The public-spirited publisher, Sir Godfrey Collins. He was passionately committed to 'social justice' but died in office aged just 51. (Courtesy of *The Herald* & *Evening Times* picture archive)

Top and above. Two secretaries of state as seen by the cartoonist David Low. Walter Elliot was 'Hamlet without the gloom' while Labour's Hector McNeil was charged with quelling a growing home rule movement.

Left. One MP likened David John Colville to a 'dull public clerk', but he helped prepare Scotland, and the Scottish Office, for the Second World War. (© *National Portrait Gallery*)

Below. The Chaplinesque Ernest Brown hands over to his more austere successor Tom Johnston in 1941. The Second World War would transform the Scottish secretary into a powerful lobbyist within the Cabinet (*Courtesy of* The Herald & Evening Times *picture archive*)

Above. The Scottish Council on Post-War Problems. Lord Alness (formerly Robert Munro), Ernest Brown, Colonel Walter Elliot and Colonel John Colville join Tom Johnston for its first meeting in 1941. It was the culmination of Johnston's consensual approach to politics.

Left. The 6th Earl of Rosebery at the races. 'Harry the horse' boasted that his father had dragged the Scottish Office 'out of a garret in the Home Office'. (*Courtesy of The Herald & Evening Times picture archive*)

Above. 'Wee Joe' Westwood dwarfed by the Scottish Office, in more ways than one. A decent man who found Tom Johnston a hard act to follow. (*Courtesy of The Herald & Evening Times picture archive*)

Left. The avuncular Arthur Woodburn leaves 10 Downing Street after his appointment as Scottish secretary. Despite initial good will he was soon vilified by the SNP and even his own party. (*Courtesy of The Herald & Evening Times picture archive*)

Above. A very aristocratic Scottish Office team. James Stuart, a descendent of King James V of Scotland, and the 14th Earl of Home prepare to kill Scottish nationalism with kindness.
(© *The Scotsman Publications Ltd*)

Right. Jack Maclay outside St. Andrew's House. He was perhaps too gentlemanly to be Scottish secretary but worked hard to prepare Scotland for the post-industrial age. (© *The Scotsman Publications Ltd*)

Above. Michael Noble with his Central Scotland Plan. He was unfortunate to become Scottish secretary just as Macmillan's – and later Sir Alec Douglas-Home's – government began its occasionally traumatic decline. (*Courtesy of The Herald & Evening Times picture archive*)

Right. An evangelical Willie Ross in full flow. He was a reluctant convert to devolution in the mid-1970s but still believed a strong Scottish secretary was preferable to a devolved Scottish Assembly. (*Courtesy of The Herald & Evening Times picture archive*)

Left. Gordon Campbell with Edward Heath. The prime minister's dynamic free-market style often clashed with Campbell's more genteel approach. (Courtesy of The Herald & Evening Times picture archive)

Below. Bruce Millan with the then general secretary of the Scottish Labour Party – and future Scottish secretary – Helen Liddell. Her brash nat-bashing contrasted sharply with Millan's blander technocratic manner. (© The Scotsman Publications Ltd)

Above. Scottish Office centenary celebrations in 1985. Bruce Millan, Lord Ross of Marnock, George Younger, Lord Campbell of Croy and Viscount Muirshiel with a seventeenth-century predecessor watching over them. (© *The Scotsman Publications Ltd*)

Below. Malcolm Rifkind and Michael Forsyth sharing a joke in 1990, despite ideological differences which often spilled over into open political warfare. (© *The Scotsman Publications Ltd*)

Left. Ian Lang at the Great Debate in Edinburgh's Usher Hall. His defence of the Union proved surprisingly successful at the 1992 general election, but it was to be a final reprieve. (© *The Scotsman Publications Ltd*)

Below. Time's up for Westminster rule; the academic Donald Dewar with the pugilistic John Reid. The pair almost came to blows at the Labour party conference: the transition from Scottish Office to Scottish parliament was not harmonious either. (© *The Scotsman Publications Ltd*)

Alistair Darling and Douglas
Alexander. Two part-time, post-
devolution Scottish secretaries
who shared a cautious approach
to the renamed Scotland Office.
(© David Partner)

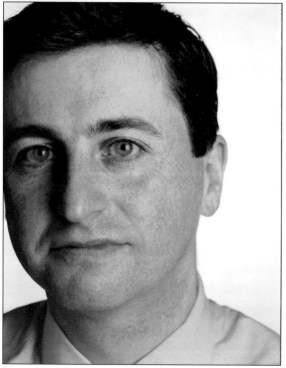

getting me down,' wrote Sheila McNeil to Beaverbrook on 1 June. 'The Monarch tore off a strip at poor Hector at the Gov. Reception to the Danish King about a speech that Lord Macdonald had made in the Lords about the Stone. It was really rather unfair and he had no right to do it in public.'[26] In a sublime piece of political irony it would fall to a staunchly Unionist Scottish secretary, Michael Forsyth, to finally return the Stone of Destiny to Scotland 45 years later.

On 14 April 1951 McNeil's mentor Ernest Bevin died after a long illness. He had been due to attend the England v. Scotland football match at Wembley, but on Bevin's insistence his wife went to the game without him, accompanied by McNeil and his wife. His health had been failing for some time, and in March he had been moved from the Foreign Office to become lord privy seal. The Scottish secretary, having served as Bevin's deputy before moving to the Scottish Office, must have thought he had a sporting chance of succeeding him. McNeil, however, was by no means universally popular among his colleagues. the former chancellor Hugh Dalton said he 'was a Scots gawk, who talked too much in Cabinet'.[27] Nevertheless, McNeil's name did make it to a shortlist of three – Shawcross and the deputy prime minister Herbert Morrison being the others – but the Scottish secretary was considered too inexperienced, and even his friend Gaitskell ranked him second to Morrison, who eventually moved to the Foreign Office.

Bevin's death, however, presented McNeil with another opportunity to move on from Scotland. 'Life in the Cabinet these days, as you will have gathered, is far from dull,' wrote Sheila McNeil to Beaverbrook on 20 April. 'I only wish the PM had the guts to sack him – and I don't mean Hector [she meant the increasingly troublesome Nye Bevan]. Now is the time if ever there was. He might just do it too – from exasperation if from nothing else. It would be interesting to see if Harold [Wilson, president of the Board of Trade] had the guts to follow him.'[28] Bevan was furious at NHS charges on spectacles and dentures recently proposed by Gaitskell, now the chancellor, to meet a massive shortfall in the health budget. Bevan threatened resignation, and Attlee typically failed to control the situation. After Gaitskell's Budget was unveiled to the House, Bevan attacked the decision publicly; he then sulked for two weeks before finally resigning in late April along with two junior colleagues, Harold Wilson and John Freeman. 'Give my love to Hector,' Beaverbrook wrote to McNeil's wife, 'and tell him he will shine out now brighter than ever if Attlee has the sense to give him the Board of Trade'.[29] But the prime minister had other plans, and McNeil once again remained at the Scottish Office. Many believed Bevan's threats to quit the government were a bluff, but, having pledged to resign with Gaitskell if the charges were dropped, McNeil and the health minister, Hilary Marquand, lobbied Attlee to sack Bevan on the basis of Collective Cabinet Responsibility. The Scottish secretary did not share his predecessor Arthur Woodburn's ideological approach to the NHS, and he was doubtful that there was any hope of recouping money through administrative reforms (as Wood-burn had tried to do). Therefore, he told the Cabinet, 'It means that we must admit publicly, with all its political consequences, that we are deserting the conception of a universal free service.'[30] McNeil also favoured dental charges, and backed Gaitskell's Budget to the hilt, telling the Commons:

> I therefore suggest that we have acted judiciously and wisely, that the charges have to be made, and that this is the place where the charges can be made without threat to the principle of the Act, and with comparatively little hardship to anyone affected. The need for dentures or spectacles is not a frequently recurring need, and it is not a need that normally descends suddenly upon anyone.[31]

His distrust of Bevan went back to the previous year, when McNeil had promoted a creative scheme to treat Scottish tuberculosis patients in Swiss sanatoria. It had emerged in July 1950 that many of these institutions were now lying empty due to the decline of TB on the Continent. McNeil, therefore, asked the UK Ministry of Health to fund the journeys, but Bevan, who had lower waiting lists for the same condition, was unenthu-siastic. The minister for economic affairs, Hugh Gaitskell, was more helpful but urged McNeil to find the cash from within his own budget. 'I quite see your difficulty,' responded McNeil in a private note, 'but I hope you will see mine and understand my slight feeling of resentment and my very definite feeling of frustration.'[32] The Scottish secretary eventually won the argument and the first Scottish patients flew to Switzerland on 15 June 1951. More than a thousand TB sufferers were eventually treated and the Ministry of Health soon followed suit, but Labour lost the general election in October and the Conservatives ended the scheme a month later.

Now in opposition, McNeil increasingly dedicated himself to his business interests, having felt the loss of four fifths of his salary quite severely.[33] He toyed with going back into journalism but eventually became managing director of the British company which produced the *Encyclopaedia Britannica*, making frequent trips to the United States on business. This attracted criticism from some Labour colleagues as it meant long periods away from parliament, but McNeil's decision was understandable. Sheila McNeil explained it to Beaverbrook in a letter on 11 January 1952:

> It was a hard struggle for him not to go back to the Express which he was longing to do. I'm afraid I was the one who dissuaded him. Maybe I was wrong but I asked him if he wanted to go on in politics and hope for the Colonial Office or the Foreign Office in the next Labour Gov. or remain a back bencher and go back to journalism and make some money. He said he wanted to stick in politics meantime so I'm afraid I went all out to dissuade him from joining the Express.[34]

McNeil's new role brought him an extra £2,000 a year, and he retained a high profile interest in foreign affairs from the Labour benches. Hostile to German rearmament in 1952, he remained a staunch defender of NATO while vehemently opposing the pacifist arguments of the Labour left. But McNeil played only a minor role in opposition, preferring to hedge his bets on the political rise of Gaitskell, who had grown in status since 1951, along with a group of 'Gaitskellite' MPs which included Dick Stokes and Alf Robens.

McNeil was crossing the Atlantic on the *Queen Mary* when he suffered a cerebral aneurism in October 1955. He was taken to the Columbia Presbyterian Medical Centre in New York City but died a few days later, aged only 48. It was a fitting resting place, as at one point in the late 1940s McNeil had arguably been better known in the United States than at home. Arthur Woodburn paid tribute in a BBC broadcast the day after his death. 'He burned with indignation against wrong and injustice and was immediate in his response to distress,' he said. 'He had a quick mind and loved an argument. There seemed no limit to his energies but alas they had been stretched to breaking point.'[35] Tragically, McNeil was just two months from a likely return to the Labour front-bench. In December Gaitskell emphatically beat Nye Bevan and Herbert Morrison to succeed Attlee as Labour leader, and he would almost certainly have given McNeil a prominent position shadowing foreign or Commonwealth affairs. 'He was an exceedingly unpushing man,' the future Labour foreign secretary George Brown later wrote of McNeil, 'and although he was an admirable Secretary of State for Scotland, his abilities would certainly have brought him back into a wider field. Had he lived in the Gaitskell period he would have been a very important member of the leadership team and would have had great influence on the Party.'[36]

In 1963 – just a year before the general election which would return Labour to power – Gaitskell also died, aged just 56. McNeil had a strong idea of where the UK stood in the postwar world, and he was the first

Scottish secretary to bring a truly international outlook to his department. But, although creative, he seemed less certain on domestic policy, even in his beloved Scotland. McNeil was also the first postwar secretary of state to free himself from Tom Johnston's legacy, but his full potential was cut short, first by the loss of the 1951 election, and then by his premature death four years later.

JAMES STUART

30 OCTOBER 1951 – 13 JANUARY 1957

The howitzer

Like his predecessor, James Stuart had no desire to end up at the Scottish Office, and he dreaded being asked to by Churchill. 'If he wants it,' wrote the future Conservative prime minister Harold Macmillan several weeks before the 1951 general election, 'James can be Secretary of State for Scotland, and will be a very good and popular minister. He said he cannot and will not do it. But I hope he will – for every reason, private and public.'[1]

The Conservatives' majority after the election was just 16, and Churchill formed his second – and only peacetime – government, aged 76. Stuart's result in Moray and Nairn was not declared until the following afternoon and he was then faced with a long drive south. The new prime minister could not understand what was taking Stuart so long, having given instructions to the police to intercept and redirect him to Chartwell, the Churchill family home, where he was forming his Cabinet. 'Among other minor problems,' wrote Macmillan in his diary, 'James Stuart, who is motoring south, has disappeared! But he is wanted, to be Secretary of State for Scotland. Nobody can say the Tories stand about waiting for office. It is a job to get hold of them!'[2] Word eventually reached Stuart from Harry Crookshank, an old friend who was soon to become leader of the House and lord privy seal. Crookshank confirmed Stuart's worst fears and so he prepared a short 'thanks, but no thanks' speech. 'I added that in office I would only let him down,' recalled Stuart. 'He [Churchill] took my arm and said, "No, you won't." I have often said that his powers of persuasion were remarkable. Anyway, before luncheon I found that I was a secretary of state and in the Cabinet.'[3]

To many Scottish Unionists Walter Elliot would have been the obvious choice to fill the Scottish Office. But Churchill thought he talked too much, and, having made Stuart the first Scottish Unionist Party chairman a year earlier, transferring him to St Andrew's House was trouble free. So Stuart became the first Conservative Scottish secretary since John Colville in 1938, a predecessor with whom he had much in common, even down to a tall, lean frame and a thin military moustache.

Stuart had fulfilled his political ambition by becoming chief whip during the war, so, perhaps by way of a recompense, Churchill gave his Scottish secretary a free reign when it came to choosing his ministerial team. This included the new position of minister of state for Scottish affairs (as Stuart later called it), and to fill it Stuart wanted the recently elevated Earl of Home. The prime minister was unimpressed, perhaps still resenting Home's role in the Munich debacle and the appeasement of Hitler (as Alec Dunglass he had been Chamberlain's parliamentary private secretary). But Churchill relented, and remarked drolly, 'Very well, Home Sweet Home it shall be.'

The Scottish Office at last had a second senior minister: a privy counsellor who would sit in the House of Lords, and attend Cabinet when necessary. This had been one of the suggestions produced by a Conservative policy committee appointed in the late 1940s, with Stuart as chairman and two former Scottish secretaries as members (Elliot and Colville). Their report, *Scottish Control of Scottish Affairs*, appeared in 1949 and suggested not only a minister of state, but an additional under-secretary and a royal commission into Scottish affairs. At the time, this trumped an increasingly divided Labour Party, elements of which wanted some, if not all, of what the Tories proposed. 'Union is not amalgamation,' said the report. 'Scotland is a nation . . . It is only since 1945, under the first socialist majority, that we have seen the policy of amalgamation superseding that of Union. This must inevitably result from the fulfilment of the socialist creed, which is basically one of amalgamation and centralisation. To this policy we are fundamentally opposed.'[4] The nationalist sentiment was perfectly deliberate, and built upon Unionist thinking which was already 15 years old: tackling nationalism through a combination of administrative reform and pseudo-nationalist political rhetoric. 'Go and quell those turbulent Scots,' Churchill told Home on appointing him minister of state, 'and don't come back till you've done it.'[5]

In a supply (budget) debate on Scottish affairs on 21 November 1951, Stuart laid claim to an extensive Conservative legacy in the history of Scottish governance, from the creation of the Scottish Office in 1885 to the elevation of its minister in 1926. The Scottish secretary then outlined the duties of his new deputy, who he said was to travel all over Scotland, maintain good relations with local authorities and other bodies like the consultative Highland Panel, take stock from each and, where possible, incorporate their views into legislation. 'It will, of course, be the duty of my noble Friend to deal with Scottish business in another place, as well as to be resident in Scotland to a great extent,' Stuart told MPs. 'That does not mean that I have no intention of visiting my native country. I shall go there whenever possible.'[6] That proved to be quite often, although Stuart delighted in affecting a laid-back existence. On their first day together at the Scottish Office, Stuart told Home, 'I think we ought to put a notice over our connecting doors.' 'All right,' said Home, 'what shall it be?' Stuart replied, 'We will not overwork.' Recounting the tale, Home said he 'was not deceived', while observing that 'he was apparently detached, work-shy, and bored with life. Nothing could have been more misleading; for his nonchalance was carefully cultivated to disarm.'[7]

The Conservatives had won the 1951 election with a promise to dismantle socialist controls and promote consumerism. Nowhere did this resonate more than in Scotland. 'The United Kingdom cannot be kept in a Whitehall straitjacket,' declared the manifesto. 'The Unionist policy for Scotland, including the practical steps proposed for effective Scottish control of Scottish affairs, will be vigorously pressed forward.'[8] However, 1951 was not a good time to inherit the reigns of power. Many wartime measures were still in force, restrictions the Conservatives had, in some cases, promised to lift. But beneath Stuart's uninterested exterior there lurked a shrewd political sense. The reluctant Scottish secretary was not only receptive to Scottish sentiment, but went out of his way to foster consensual dialogue with his Labour opponents, making it very hard for the opposition, led at first by Hector McNeil and later by the gentler Tom Fraser, to attack him. Liberals were another matter. 'I do not think I have ever suffered or enjoyed the friendship of a Liberal,'[9] recalled Stuart in his memoirs, having told colleagues: 'I never discuss politics with my con-stituents. They're all Liberals, really.'[10] Interestingly, Unionist strategy at this time also sought to incorporate the residual Liberalism which was still latent in some parts of Scotland. Two of Stuart's under-secretaries even styled themselves as Liberals: James Henderson-Stewart (the Liberal Unionist MP for East Fife), and Niall Macpherson (the National Liberal and Conservative MP for Dumfriesshire).

Churchill formed his second government just as Britain was entering a new Elizabethan Age of domestic optimism and imperial confidence. King George VI had died on 6 February 1952, and Stuart, who had once been the late monarch's equerry, signed Elizabeth's formal accession to the throne on behalf of Scotland. Following the ceremony, and still wearing full privy counsellor's uniform, Stuart was stopped by the former Labour MP and Scottish Office minister George Buchanan. 'I never thought ye were such a bloody fool, Jimmy,' he said, ignoring Stuart's greeting. 'I'm sorry Geordie,' replied Stuart, 'but what have I done wrong?' 'Och,' he said, 'to take on that job at the Scottish Office. Ye'll never make a bloody thing o' that.'[11] Queen Elizabeth II visited Edinburgh on 9 February for her proclamation at St Giles Cathedral, wearing day wear and, controversially, carrying a handbag. Stuart had assumed that as the Scottish peerage would be in full court dress then so would the royal party, and he attracted much criticism for the resulting contrast.

'The fact that I shall be resident in Scotland,' Home had told the House of Lords on 20 November 1951, 'in daily touch with industry and in daily contact with local authorities, will enable me or any other Minister of State to keep his finger on the pulse of the social and economic life of Scotland.' Whether the direct descendant of a Scottish king and the 14th Earl of Home were best equipped to keep their fingers on the pulse of anything, let alone 1950s Scotland, was debatable, although both were indisputably able. When Stuart finally conceded to Churchill's request that he become Scottish secretary, the prime minister declared, 'A Stuart shall rule again in Scotland.'[12]

King James V of Scotland produced one legitimate child, Mary, and several royal bastards, one of which was the Regent Moray (otherwise known as the Earl of Moray), James Stuart, the de facto ruler of Scotland. James Gray Stuart, the third son of the 17th Earl of Moray, used to joke that history might have brought him the crown; instead it brought him a typically aristocratic education at Eton, and almost Cambridge, although the outbreak of war instead saw Stuart join the 1st Battalion of the Royal Scots aged only 18. He was invalided home in 1915, but returned to the front with the 2nd Battalion in 1916, and by 1918 was a brigade major with a mention in dispatches, and a Military Cross and bar. On demobilisation Stuart spent a year studying law in Edinburgh, but found this uncongenial. Fittingly for a Moray, he was the first equerry in waiting to Prince Albert, later George VI, from 1919–21, a role which brought him into contact with Lady Elizabeth Bowes-Lyon, the future queen and queen mother. Stuart danced with Elizabeth during a ball at which she also caught the eye of 'Bertie', who asked his equerry to introduce him to her. They danced together but sparks did not fly. Elizabeth, it transpired, was keen on Stuart, a feeling which proved to be mutual. During their lengthy courtship the domineering Queen Mary got wind of the romance and plotted to have Stuart eased out of the scene. He eventually left for the Oklahoma oilfields in January 1922 after a few days at Glamis. 'That bitch Queen Mary, that cow, she ruined my life!' Stuart told Sir Anthony Nutting the year he became Scottish secretary. 'I was in love with the Queen Mother and she with me, but Queen Mary wanted her for the Duke of York.'[13]

Stuart did not return home until 1923, by which time Elizabeth was engaged to the smitten duke. Stuart soon found himself another partner in

the court circle. Lady Rachel Cavendish, fourth daughter of the 9th Duke
of Devonshire, had just returned from Canada where her father had been
governor-general. Her sister, Lady Dorothy, had already married a young
aide-de-camp called Harold Macmillan, and Stuart married Lady Rachel
in August 1923.[14] The same year, he was invited to stand in Moray and
Nairn for the Conservatives, and, against everyone's expectations, he
actually won the seat. 'This is bloody ridiculous,' commented Stuart,
bemused to find himself in parliament.

Initially, Stuart's political career was unremarkable, and only in 1935
did he rise to the dizzy heights of Scottish whip. He had been born for the
job, his gifts of persuasion and polite intimidation proving ideal, and he
was soon tipped to replace the late Noel Skelton as under-secretary at the
Scottish Office (the position actually went to John Colville). 'James is
doing well as a whip and I hope to see him Secretary of State for Scotland
before he has done,' wrote the Conservative MP Sir Cuthbert Headlam in
his diary, 'he is a wise and tactful person and has all the necessary
qualifications – birth, appearance, manner – so there is no reason why he
should not succeed. He speaks quite as well as Godfrey Collins whose
eloquence seems sufficient for the job.'[15]

In 1937 Stuart was promoted to become deputy chief Conservative
whip, rising to chief Conservative whip at the beginning of 1941, and joint
chief whip in Churchill's wartime coalition (working alongside his Labour
counterpart). The prime minister's staff judged that Churchill more
respected than liked Stuart in this role, but it did begin a particularly
close political relationship which was to serve Stuart well. He had a
difficult time keeping Conservative back-benchers in line during the
wartime truce, when party leadership and policy development grew
lax, and Stuart strongly disagreed with Churchill's election strategy in
1945. There was more tension in 1947 when Stuart was chosen as the party
grandee best placed to tell Winston that his time was up. He retired as
chief whip in 1948 following a minor operation, although it probably had
more to do with his being named as the co-respondent in a divorce case.
Thereafter, Stuart was a bit of an anachronistic cad, with immense charm
and a host of political tricks learned at the whips' office. Having gone to
the Scottish Office against his will, he affected a lack of interest, whether
on home turf or in the House. 'Speak up!' shouted an MP when Stuart
became incoherent during a long technical statement. 'Oh, all right,'
drawled the Scottish secretary amiably, 'but I didn't think anyone was
listening.'[16]

Labour MPs, however, were listening when Stuart announced that an
additional under-secretary – as well as a minister of state – was to be

added to his Scottish Office team under the Ministers of the Crown Bill. The opposition petulantly demanded to know what the new minister would do. Stuart said Commander Thomas Dunlop Galbraith would look after housing, health, police, fire and civil defence; William McNair Snadden (the MP for Kinross and West Perthshire and well known in farming circles) would oversee agriculture and forestry issues; while the as yet unnamed third under-secretary would take charge of education and Scottish Home Department responsibilities not already covered by Galbraith.

Commander Galbraith shone as the most capable of the junior Scottish Office team, having earned a reputation as a pragmatic and formidable debater on the Scottish Grand Committee in the late 1940s. At their 1950 party conference the Conservatives had committed themselves to building 300,000 houses per annum, although no specific Scottish total was mentioned. Stuart's brother-in-law, Harold Macmillan, had been made minister for housing, so Galbraith worked closely with him on an ambitious programme which eventually produced 38,000 houses in 1954 alone. The housing subsidy was one socialist control Stuart did not want to jettison; in fact, he doubled it, and for the first time in three decades housing construction and occupancy rose quickly. Most, however, were prefabs or wooden homes built with Norwegian timber. 'They were very quick to erect and that kind of thing,' Galbraith later boasted. 'And they were very, very good houses to live in. They had everything that was wanted.'[17] Everything, that is, except aesthetic quality. Galbraith also wanted to repeal the Rent Restriction Act, in place since the days of Thomas McKinnon Wood, as he believed it was reducing some Clydeside landlords to 'bankruptcy', and therefore damaging the rented housing supply. The Act was amended, and by the end of 1951 the Cabinet had also committed to continuing Labour's policy of building New Towns, another legacy of socialism which – like the NHS – the Conservatives had grown to love. Glasgow had serious overspill problems, and, despite opposition from Macmillan, Stuart persuaded the Cabinet to designate Cumbernauld as Scotland's third New Town. The planner Sir Patrick Abercrombie had first mentioned the town in his Clyde Valley Plan of 1946, and Stuart opened negotiations for it to accommodate up to 80,000 of Glasgow's surplus population. Stuart was particularly sensitive to the political impact of spending cuts, and when in 1956 Macmillan (now chancellor) pushed the Scottish secretary to reduce his housing subsidy, he refused to budge.

One Scottish Office official compared Stuart to a howitzer: the process of firing it exhausted teams of men, but, when it was, it obliterated everything in sight.[18] When the Scottish secretary wanted something, and particularly when he had Churchill's ear, he generally got it. One example was local government finance. On 30 January 1953 Stuart asked the Cabinet for permission to appoint a committee to consider 'the Scottish rating problem in all its aspects, including the practicability of abolishing owners' rates'.[19] The anomaly (which did not exist in England) whereby both the owner and occupier of a property paid rates was not only unfair but depressed Scotland's housing sector, and Stuart was determined to correct it. His friend Lord Sorn was charged with investigating the problem and reported in 1955.[20] Stuart called the subsequent Valuation and Rating (Scotland) Bill the most important reform of local government since Sir John Gilmour's in 1929. He emphasised that the current Scottish valuation system was based on legislation crafted in 1854, and elaborated on the Sorn Committee's recommendation that owners' rates should be abolished, and a comprehensive review of Scottish housing subsidies undertaken. 'We have here a matter which ought to be tackled,' Stuart told the House. 'We are doing our best to tackle it. If we fail, all I can say is that when I am dead the word "Sorn" will be found written on my heart.'[21] He did not fail, and he also turned his mind to local government finance in general, eventually scrapping the Goschen formula of allocating Treasury cash to Scottish local authorities.

Meanwhile, the Earl of Home was proving a success as minister of state, and his Highland remit produced two reforms designed to keep old Scottish Liberals happy. The Crofters (Scotland) Act harked back to Gladstonian reforms by establishing a Crofters Commission to develop Scottish crofting through the provision of grants and loans, while the Hydro-Electric Development (Scotland) Act built upon Tom Johnston's legacy by raising the board's borrowing limit to £200 million.

Reorganising Scotland's electricity supply had been another 1951 election pledge, and represented the first transfer of powers to the Scottish Office under Stuart's command. The Electricity Reorganisation (Scotland) Bill made the Scottish secretary responsible for all electricity matters in Scotland, and established a new board responsible to him, reversing an important shibboleth of Labour's centralisation. The North of Scotland Board had become responsible for the whole northern area in 1947, while the south of Scotland was divided into two regions. Stuart boasted that the Bill provided a 'measure of decentralisation', and that instead 'of remote control from England as at present, we shall have the management in Scotland in the hands of those who know the needs of the users or consumers in Scotland and are in close and constant touch with them'.[22] This was another common refrain of 1950s Unionism: satisfying consumer demand. The Butskellite spirit made this task easier, and Stuart worked hard at reformulating Scotland's industrial base to improve the standard of living, knowing this was an important factor in continuing Conservative success north of the border.

In April 1952, the Scottish Council's Cairncross Report had concluded that there was considerable scope for the government to take powers to build factories in any part of Scotland, and not just in designated development areas. Stuart was aware that public opinion remained concerned about the Scottish economy, and managed to secure additional steel contracts for the Clyde shipyards, while fighting attempts to move a British European Airways base from Renfrew to London. But he saved the big push for a fourth (steel) strip mill to be located in Scotland, heading up an enthusiastic lobbying operation which involved almost every minister at the Scottish Office. 'This is just what Scotland needs,' minuted Jack Nixon Browne, formerly Stuart's parliamentary private secretary and now an under-secretary, 'we must not lose it.'[23] They did not, and it eventually became Ravenscraig, a name which was to become totemic for the Conservatives 30 years later. The Scottish secretary also made sure that long-standing transport issues were addressed by authorising the electrification of Glasgow's railway network, and giving the go-ahead for the construction of the Forth Road Bridge, a project first touted during the war.

Stuart was a good operator who strove to keep a Scottish Office finger in every available Whitehall pie, regardless of whether it related to Scotland. He was proud of his connection with the Royal Scots, so he gelled with both Sir David Milne, his permanent under-secretary, and Sir P. J. Blair, who ran the Scottish Unionist Party organisation, both of whom had served in the same regiment. Sir David was an Edinburgh-born son of the manse who later wrote *The Scottish Office* in 1958, one of a series of books on Whitehall departments, and the first to examine the workings of St Andrew's House in any depth. Stuart also struck up a close friendship with Sir Charles Cunningham, who was head of the Scottish Home Department, and the trio – Stuart, Milne and Cunningham – were all of the view that the Scottish Office should not only become more visible, but also more powerful. Sir Charles regarded Stuart as the most influential minister he had ever worked with, and he approved of an arrangement which left the Scottish secretary free to concentrate on the bigger picture while officials got on with their work. Stuart did not like long policy meetings, and any he did have rarely lasted more than 20 minutes. 'And at the end when he had listened to what we all had to say,' recalled Galbraith, 'he used to say, "Well, gentlemen, I think we are agreed. We shall do so and so." And that was the end of it. You went off to your Department and did what had been agreed.'[24] MPs and officials found the secretary of state an incredibly easy minister to deal with. 'I once asked Mr Stuart – or rather he asked me – if I knew why people liked him,' Galbraith also recalled. 'And I said I couldn't understand why they did, but he said, "Well the reason is that they know I don't want anything. In fact there's nothing that they could give me." '[25] Stuart himself was a man of strong likes, and equally strong dislikes. Lord Home (as an MP) remembered following him out of the Commons chamber when one of his bêtes noires had just finished speaking. 'That man is a shit,' remarked Stuart. Unfortunately, the man concerned was close behind and demanded that Stuart apologise. 'Yes, I am sorry,' said Stuart. 'I should not have said it, I apologise. Have you anything better to suggest?'[26]

On health, the Scottish secretary found himself fighting a rearguard action. Shortly after the 1951 election, the Treasury tried to introduce additional health charges and scrap subsidised welfare food. Stuart argued that Scottish families would be worst hit, as those in need of welfare were more prevalent than in England, while also reasoning that any increase in revenue from health charges would soon be cancelled out by the need to increase benefits. But he did scrap Hector McNeil's initiative in which Scottish tuberculosis patients were treated in Swiss sanatoria, because, said Stuart, there were no longer any sufferers to treat. Galbraith flew to Switzerland to visit a Glaswegian lady from the slums, who told him, 'This is wonderful, I've never had a holiday in all my married years, and here I am enjoying a holiday at last.' The under-secretary for health concluded that this scenario 'was rather pathetic'.[27] However, in scrapping it, Stuart had miscalculated: by early 1956 Scotland was recording 18 new TB cases every day, and the Scottish secretary had to launch a mass X-ray survey in Glasgow in order to combat it.

Stuart also failed to resolve the anachronism of state-controlled liquor licensing in the Scottish New Towns, arguing that as a matter of principle the government should not be involved in the drinks trade. Two under-secretaries, Galbraith and Niall Macpherson, also fought to remove this relic of First World War restrictions, but the Home Office was opposed, and the Scottish Office had to settle for an amendment. Stuart's newly enlarged team of ministers worked well together, but Lord Home was the undisputed success. After nearly four years as minister-in-residence at St Andrew's House, Anthony Eden asked that Home be transferred to his department. 'Your old Home Sweet Home can't be too bad,' Churchill told Stuart. 'Anthony wants him at the Commonwealth Office.'

Initially, Stuart believed that Churchill would go on as prime minister until he died, but in April 1955 he finally retired, aged 80. Churchill had been confronted with a 'hanging jury' the previous December, comprising the seven most senior Cabinet ministers, which included the Scottish secretary. The ageing prime minister, who by then had suffered several strokes, reacted angrily to what Macmillan later described as a 'most painful affair'. But by the New Year Churchill accepted that resignation was now unavoidable, and Anthony Eden – who had played a waiting game akin to that of Gordon Brown 50 years later – took over as prime minister and immediately called a general election.

The 1955 contest found the Scottish Unionists riding high. Stuart, who remained at the Scottish Office after the poll, was rewarded with a unique result for a political party in Scotland: a majority of both seats and (albeit narrowly) the popular vote. A poor showing from the Liberals, who only fielded candidates in a handful of Scottish seats, helped, but the proportion of votes cast was better than that in England and Stuart had reason to take heart. A party which had often struggled to find Scottish MPs of a good enough calibre to fill the Scottish Office now had 36.

Perhaps a contributing factor was the report of the Royal Commission on Scottish Affairs, which had been published the previous year. An inquiry – long desired by a number of Labour MPs and ministers – was another of the Conservatives' 1951 election pledges, and when Hector McNeil's Catto Committee reported in June 1952, Stuart responded with a Cabinet memo suggesting a royal commission. The prime minister personally announced its formation in the House on 24 July, before handing over to the Scottish secretary. He later announced that the 3rd Earl of Balfour, a nephew of the former secretary for Scotland A. J. Balfour, was to be chairman, and Stuart, together with Sir David Milne, set about making the commission's remit as narrow as possible. Sir David revised its terms of reference 40 times, and its membership was tightly restricted to avoid discordant views. It was, essentially, a political fix, and the Cabinet Office even refused to allow the former Labour Scottish secretary Tom Johnston to become a member. Eventually, it was agreed that the commission would 'review with reference to the financial, economic, administrative and other considerations involved, the arrangements for exercising the functions of . . . Government in relation to Scotland'. Its remit, therefore, certainly did not include home rule. 'Legislative devolution is considered to be a matter for parliament,' the Scottish secretary told the House. 'The Royal Commission will deal with administrative devolution.'[28] But, added Stuart, Lord Balfour was free to take evidence on any aspect of Scottish affairs he wanted to. He did so in the grand surroundings of Edinburgh's Signet Library, hearing from three surviving secretaries of state, and even the 84-year-old Lord Alness, whose experience of the Scottish Office was now 30 years out of date. The commission also visited the Highlands and Islands and Northern Ireland, which then had the only functioning system of devolution within the

United Kingdom. Civil servants were invited to share their thoughts, and the Treasury's permanent under-secretary, Sir Edward Bridges, surprised everyone by insisting on giving evidence himself, mainly because he feared encroachment into his department's territory. In March 1954 the Cabinet was presented with a draft of the commission's report. This placed great emphasis on improving the standing of the British departments' Scottish officers. It also concluded that responsibility for roads should be transferred to the Scottish Office from the Ministry of Transport and Civil Aviation, along with the appointment of justices of the peace from the lord chancellor, and animal health from the Ministry of Agriculture and Fisheries. The Cabinet broadly approved, but when the final report was published in July 1954 it was not well received, its elaborately diplomatic language displaying all the signs of a whitewash. Balfour attributed any ill feeling among Scots to 'needless English thoughtlessness', but also to 'undue Scottish susceptibilities'. His report also laid down two important principles: that British ministers should consult fully with Scottish interests; and that the role of secretary of state for Scotland – that of 'Scotland's Minister' – should be seen as such and in no way limited. Stuart's tenure at the Scottish Office embodied them both, his gentle lobbying from behind the scenes making it difficult for colleagues ever to ignore the needs of his increasingly territorial department. The Scottish secretary, however, missed the Commons debate on the royal commission's findings, having been advised to rest after suffering from acute bronchial trouble. So just hours before MPs gathered in the Commons on 1 February 1955, Stuart was en route to the Mediterranean for a therapeutic holiday. Lord Home took control of the Scottish Office in his absence, and the three under-secretaries – Galbraith, Snadden and Henderson-Stewart – ably handled the debate.

Again, all of this was calculated to beat nationalism on its own terms. Stuart did not underestimate the resonance of home rule sentiment (indeed, his old constituency fell to the SNP in 1974), and he reasoned that if he demonstrated a slow but steady increase in his powers, his critics would quickly see the error of their ways. Stuart, however, had already compromised in a letter to the leading nationalist John MacCormick, which conceded that 'if the Scottish people were ultimately to decide in favour of a Scottish Parliament nothing could gainsay them'.[29] Of course, Stuart's tactics from then on were designed to prevent the issue even being raised. Such subtlety was lost on MacCormick, who launched a legal challenge to the new monarch styling herself Queen Elizabeth II, soon after she acceded to the throne.[30] The case was handled by Lord Cooper of Culross, who had chaired Tom Johnston's hydro committee during the war, and was now lord president of the Court of Session. The action fell on preliminary pleas, but Cooper criticised the English principle of sovereignty of parliament in relation to the Treaty of Union between Scotland and England. Some nationalists resorted to blowing up pillar boxes to vent their fury at such historical injustice, and even the Scottish secretary had a scare. Following his visit to Great Cumbrae Island in August 1954, someone discovered a lump of gelignite under Millport pier. It had been fitted with a fake fuse, and the police later concluded that it was a hoax designed to publicise the Scottish Republican Army.[31]

Stuart's tenure at the Scottish Office, unlike his predecessor's, was free of grand speeches about the Cold War, or indeed any other aspect of foreign affairs. But in April 1956, the Russian leaders Marshal Bulganin and Nikita Khrushchev visited Eden in London and agreed to spend a day in Edinburgh. 'B. and K. have gone to Scotland with James Stuart,' wrote Macmillan in his diary, 'a curious party.'[32] It was indeed; Stuart's idea of entertaining his guests involved consuming copious amounts of whisky and making inappropriate jokes about assassination attempts by his driver. It was a surreal situation: an old Etonian showing off the capital's finest roads and housing to the Soviet supremos, who refused to believe that what they saw was anything more than a carefully contrived showcase. Three years later, the US vice-president Richard Nixon would clash with Khrushchev during a visit to Moscow's version of the Ideal Homes Exhibition. Stuart's encounter was less argumentative, and an interesting 'and amusing' day ended with dinner at Edinburgh Castle – and more whisky.

For Anthony Eden, it was foreign affairs which signalled the end to his premiership, and also to Stuart's unwanted (although he had come to enjoy the job) spell at the Scottish Office. The Scottish secretary was actually absent when Eden told the Cabinet he was resigning, and Stuart's stand-in, Lord Strathclyde (Galbraith had been elevated to the peerage to replace Home as minister of state in 1955), 'was told to get Mr Stuart down as quickly as possible because his opinion would be required'.[33] Ironically, the Scottish secretary had actually backed Eden over the Suez debacle until he announced, under overwhelming international pressure, that British and French forces were to be withdrawn from Egypt. 'I did not object to our going IN,' Stuart recalled. 'What I did object to was our coming OUT.' He told Eden this in plain terms, arguing that troops could have reached the canal without any trouble, but Stuart accepted that Eden's decision was irreversible. 'It did, however, break my political heart,' he said, 'and I was glad when it became possible for me to quit the Government in the following year. I had lost interest and was tired.'[34] Stuart's relationship with Eden had always been ambivalent, Churchill's successor having never shown much interest in Scotland, and he saw the prime minister's ignominious climb-down as a good excuse to retire.

Stuart was now nearly 60, and he simply wanted a less arduous existence, so when Macmillan formed his first government he avoided any suggestion of nepotism by declining to stay on. His under-secretary William Snadden, who had never wanted to be a minister, also left the Scottish Office, and, although he was due for promotion, Henderson-Stewart got crowded out, so instead settled for a baronetcy. Scottish Office staff clubbed together to buy Stuart a gift, a rare display of affection from normally impassive civil servants. 'He was a very, very hard worker, though people didn't credit him with that,' remembered Lord Strathclyde. 'He would often work till 3am at the New Club in Edinburgh.' Stuart expected his ministers to be absolutely frank with him and, in turn, if he thought they were wrong about something, he would say so. 'And we were all very, very fond of him,' added Strathclyde. 'In fact, when we heard he was about to resign, all of us, independently, went and begged him not to. [It] didn't have any effect.'[35]

Stuart thought for a time that he might become leader of the House, a position free of departmental responsibility, but R. A. Butler insisted on combining it with his post of home secretary. Stuart admired Butler, and would probably have backed him as Eden's successor, but instead he used his remaining two years in the Commons to dispense advice to his brother-in-law, and mentor young MPs like Willie Whitelaw and Gordon Campbell, the future Scottish secretary who inherited Stuart's constituency at the 1959 general election. 'I would not dream of claiming any spectacular achievements for Scotland,'[36] said Stuart modestly in his amusing memoirs, *Within the Fringe*, which were largely ghost-written (by Stephen Watts) at the insistence of his publisher Alexander Frere. He had presided over the Scottish Office during a 'golden age', when the department was seen as a good and enjoyable place to work, a perception which had largely gone by the time Lord Balfour published his report into Scottish administration. Now elevated to the House of Lords as Viscount Stuart of Findhorn (the name of his local village), he skirted over his five years at the Scottish Office in just 14 pages of his book, reducing his experiences to a few choice anecdotes. Stuart's wartime experiences had left him with a confidence some mistook for arrogance, but he was wise enough not to aim for anything beyond the Scottish secretaryship. In retirement Stuart lived mainly at his home in Wiltshire, and he died at Salisbury Infirmary on 20 February 1971, aged 74.

JOHN MACLAY

13 JANUARY 1957 – 13 JULY 1962

A liberal Conservative

'If I had ever been offered the Scottish Office,' wrote the colourful Unionist MP Bob Boothby in the early 1960s, 'and at one moment, long ago, it was conceivable – I should have asked for an official residence in Edinburgh.' He continued:

> I should have driven round Scotland in an enormous black car, with the rampant lion flying proudly in the wind, and – if possible – outriders on motorcycles. I should have steamed round her coast every year in the fishery cruiser, rechristened a yacht for the purpose, with more flags. And all this not for the purpose of self-aggrandisement; but just to show that the Secretary of State for Scotland is, in his own right, a tremendous political figure whose presence at the British Cabinet table must be counted an honour to them.[1]

The ebullient Boothby must have considered John Maclay – James Stuart's successor at the Scottish Office – a rather bland secretary of state. Maclay did not go in for ostentation, preferring to continue his predecessor's approach of quiet persuasion, a style to which his pleasant and unobtrusive personality was perfectly suited.

He was not the first Maclay to sit in the Cabinet, his father, Joseph Paton Maclay, having been Lloyd George's shipping controller from 1916–21 (without being a member of either house of parliament). John Scott Maclay was 11 when his father joined the wartime coalition, and the youngest of seven children born and raised by Joseph and his wife in a middle-class part of industrial Glasgow. His father was a founding chairman of the shipping firm Maclay and McIntyre, and a friend of Andrew Bonar Law (destined to become Conservative prime minister), with whom he had been to Glasgow High School. Of John's four brothers, the two eldest, Ebenezer and William, were killed in action during the First World War, while the third, Joseph junior, was elected the Liberal MP for Paisley in 1931. John was educated at Winchester College and

Trinity College, Cambridge, and was in the crew that beat Oxford in the 1927 boat race. He joined the family shipping firm after graduating, and in the Second World War served briefly as a captain in the Royal Artillery. But Maclay was quickly seconded to the Ministry of War Transport and dispatched to Washington as deputy to Sir James Arthur Salter, then head of the British merchant shipping mission. Maclay had been elected unopposed as the National Liberal MP for the Montrose Burghs in July 1940, but was only in the Commons on four occasions until 1945, when he finally managed to make his maiden speech. He succeeded Sir James as mission head in 1944, and on returning from Washington he served briefly as parliamentary secretary to the Ministry of Production in Churchill's caretaker government of May–July 1945. Following the Labour landslide, Maclay contributed to Commons debates on shipping and trade, and, when his old Montrose seat was abolished in a 1950 reorganisation, he moved to West Renfrewshire as a National Liberal and Conservative MP.

In October 1951 Maclay became minister of transport and civil aviation (outside the Cabinet), but, following a crisis over increased fares for London transport, Maclay resigned after only seven months on grounds of ill health. In 1955 he served briefly (and 'rather surprisingly') as president of the assembly of the Western European Union. Maclay had occupied a room next door to the architect of European Unity, Jean Monnet, for about four months when he worked in Washington, and was a firm believer in some form of united Europe. In October 1956, he returned to the government as minister of state for the colonies, gaining wide acclaim for his work on the British response to the crises in Cyprus and Ghana. Maclay later said he would have preferred to have stayed longer at the Colonial Office, and, although he was flattered by Macmillan's offer of the Scottish Office, he was reluctant to leave.

Unlike his predecessor, Maclay was not really a Conservative at all. The National Liberals had been an independent group in parliament from 1945–50, but following the Woolton-Teviot Agreement their 17 MPs took the Conservative whip, and experimented with name changes (much as the Alliance did in the late 1980s) such as National Liberal Conservatives, and Liberal Unionists. In 1957 the former Scottish secretary Lord Rosebery stood down as president of the National Liberal Council, and, at a vote in Westminster's Caxton Hall, Maclay was elected his successor on 12 July. So, much like Ernest Brown in 1940, the Scottish secretary also found himself leading six Scottish National Liberal MPs, which included one of his under-secretaries, Niall Macpherson. Although a dwindling band (Maclay was the council's last president), this position proved useful in holding on to the last of Scotland's Liberal vote, and the Scottish secretary argued consistently that the Conservative government had implemented most of the National Liberals' desired policies.[2] Maclay, however, did not really consider himself a Conservative, often declaring disarmingly, 'I'll have to find out what the Tories think.' National Liberals believed that 'far too many decisions affecting Scotland are made by the central Government', as Maclay told the *People's Journal* just a few days after moving into Dover House (reoccupied by Stuart in 1955).[3]

Maclay knew that Stuart's retirement had thrown up a problem of succession, but did not expect to be the solution. 'I said to him, "Do tell me what goes on in this building, James",' recalled Maclay. 'All I got from him was, "You'll find out soon enough." We then talked about some other things; then, just as I was going out of the door he said, "Oh, I can tell you something about the job. If you've any friends in Scotland, prepare to lose them now!"'[4]

One of Maclay's first acts as secretary of state was to announce the approval of the Forth Road Bridge to the Commons. It was to cost more than £14 million (roughly £160 million today), £9 million of which would be advanced by the government and repaid through tolls. Maclay's five years at the Scottish Office saw the unveiling of many such infrastructure projects, and a marked change in the government's attitude to regional development. The affluence referred to in Macmillan's triumphant claim, 'you've never had it so good', had largely bypassed poorer parts of Scotland. From 1960, the Local Employment Act had allowed the government to offer grants to companies willing to establish themselves in so-called depressed areas. These were in the gift of the Board of Trade (which had an office in Glasgow), although such was Maclay's influence that 'the then President of the Board of Trade stopped [him] on going into Cabinet one morning and said to [him], "I do wish you'd tell me when you're going to take over my office in Scotland"!'

Maclay found in Macmillan the perfect prime minister ('He did not flap about things'), and also 'a very sympathetic Cabinet. They realised the Scottish problem was very often different in scale or in nature to the English one.' Maclay later said that his main aim as Scottish secretary was to have 'the economic base in Scotland altered and improved as quickly as humanly possible'. Here, Stuart had laid the groundwork, but it was Maclay who noted the paradox that, while neither labour nor industry was the domain of the Scottish Office, 'the whole infrastructure on which industrial development had to be based was the responsibility of the Secretary of State'.[5] Maclay sought to change this by continuing Stuart's campaign to secure a fourth UK steel strip mill for Scotland, for which Grangemouth was the preferred site. South Wales (which had the other three) was winning in the location stakes, but the Scottish secretary worked hard on a compromise whereby some of the mill would be sited in Scotland, if Colvilles (the firm run by the family of former Scottish secretary John Colville) agreed to run it. So Ravenscraig, as it became known, was essentially a political decision for which the Treasury was liable if it did not make a profit. Maclay argued that it would help broaden Scotland's industrial base, as well as rebalance steel production across the UK. Initially, the Cabinet feared that favouring the Grangemouth site over another in Wales would inflame Welsh nationalist sentiment, but by May 1958 Maclay had swung opinion behind Lanarkshire, a division of production that many economists found hard to justify.

The Scottish Office had less luck with two other companies. In the summer of 1957 Scottish Shale Oils Ltd told the government that it planned to close one of its mines at Niddry Castle in West Lothian, with the loss of several hundred jobs.[6] It was persuaded to delay its decision as the government devised a rescue package, while in November 1958 Scottish Aviation Ltd also ran into financial difficulties and announced redundancies of its own. The result of all this industrial activity, whether negative or positive, was that by the end of 1958 the Scottish Office, and not the Board of Trade, was, to a large extent, in control of economic development in Scotland. Scottish unemployment averaged double that in England, a statistic which gave the Scottish secretary a strong hand to play when it came to winning battles in Cabinet. The loss of five Scottish seats at the 1959 general election also shored up Maclay's position, as he could now point to imminent electoral disaster if the government failed to do more. Perhaps as a result, the industrial picture began to brighten the following year, when the British Motor Corporation announced plans to invest £9 million in a factory at Bathgate, with eventual employment for 5,600 workers. In October 1960 Rootes Cars announced its intention to build a plant at Linwood, near Paisley, employing another few thousand people. This impressive industrial trio of Ravenscraig-Bathgate-Linwood needed massive financial incentives from the government (from the Treasury and Board of Trade, not the Scottish Office), but still the Scottish economy struggled to adapt to the post-industrial age.

An economic boom during the Korean War was followed by a recession, spurred on by the Suez debacle, which hit Scotland especially hard. Studies showed that in 1958 Scotland was even more dependent upon heavy industry than she had been in the 1930s, while in the period 1958–59 unemployment doubled to reach 100,000. 'We managed to get a lot done,' reflected Maclay in 1980, 'but for the years I was there it was like a treadmill situation because you were hardly able to make any progress in absolute figures. Because as you got larger employment in the more modern industries, you were losing it on the traditional industries.' And he added mischievously, 'after about four years I did realise that (a) if it wasn't for the House of Commons, (b) if it wasn't for the press and (c) if it wasn't for the whole electorate, I'd really be able to get a great deal done for Scotland very quickly, but you would have had to shoot me every four years.'[7] Macmillan certainly did not want that to happen, at least not yet, and the prime minister did some lobbying of his own among Scottish business leaders, most notably Lord Polwarth from the Scottish Council (Development and Industry) (SCDI), and even George Middleton, then general secretary of the Scottish Trades Union Congress. The prime minister, however, hindered Maclay in other respects. His determination to reduce taxation in the run up to the 1959 election meant truncated public expenditure, while the Scottish secretary also had to tackle a reduction in housebuilding inherited from Stuart. He fought both, and secured more hospital building against heavy opposition.

The Housing and Town Development (Scotland) Bill, which had appeared just a month after Maclay joined the Cabinet, dealt with housing subsidies and worker overspill – a particular problem in Glasgow. A New Town at Cumbernauld had already been approved under Stuart to address this, but Maclay had the satisfaction of cutting its first sod. One negative aspect of the Bill was to encourage the building of high-rise tower blocks, with a special subsidy of £40 per flat, roughly £650 today, but little attention to aesthetics. Also inherited from Stuart was the Scottish Office permanent under-secretary Sir David Milne, who was replaced in 1959 by Sir William Murrie, both of whom were entirely on-side when it came to interventionist government. Maclay later remembered with satisfaction that as a result of his time in office 'Secretaries of State were now being judged by the performance of the Scottish economy', while traditional British departments such as the Board of Trade were regarded as marginal.

During a single week in July 1958 the Scottish secretary was required to introduce and discuss memoranda on the pay claim of doctors, forestry policy, compensation for the compulsory acquisition of land, a proposal to expand teacher training, the revision of Crown Land Act and the forthcoming 1961 census. So, despite Maclay's concentration on attracting new industries to Scotland, he still had to deal with a typically eclectic array of Scottish Office duties. The most substantial of these was the continuing reform of local government finance. Until 1957 most local services – the largest being education – were funded directly from central government through a series of ad hoc grants. Maclay announced the outcome of a Stuart-instigated review in February 1957, and, in December, the Local Government and Miscellaneous Financial Provisions (Scotland) Bill was introduced to parliament. This created a General Grant (nicknamed Major Grant by Lord Strathclyde) calculated on the basis of the total estimated expenditure from all Scottish local authorities. This was only the first stage, the next being another order which from 16 May 1959 allowed councils to decide for themselves how to spend the money allocated to them. Using language which would have made Thatcherite Conservatives flinch, Maclay often waxed lyrical about removing central controls from local government, and empowering Scottish authorities to spend their own money according to local needs.

Maclay's ministerial team was largely inherited from the previous regime. Lord Strathclyde remained as minister of state, but was replaced by Lord Forbes in October 1958,[8] who in turn was succeeded a year later by Lord Craigton. As Jack Nixon Browne, he had lost his Craigton constituency at the 1959 general election, but was kept on at the Scottish Office in the Upper House (much like Tom Galbraith had been in 1955).[9] Craigton was recognised as a smart political operator, as was another under-secretary, Niall Macpherson, who, despite a minor scandal in which it was implied he had forced the resignation of a local newspaper editor, went on to become minister of pensions in 1962.[10] Lord John Hope[11] joined the Scottish Office with Maclay in 1957, having moved from the Foreign Office, and served at Dover House for two years until he was replaced by another Thomas Galbraith, this time Lord Strathclyde's son (known as Tam).

Like Stuart, Maclay did not hold regular weekly meetings, instead summoning his team whenever a big issue arose. In January 1961, the Scottish secretary sanctioned the construction of another transport project, this time the Tay Road Bridge, again to be funded through tolls. There were also minor reforms to Scotland's licensing laws, fishing fleet, and mental welfare services, while Maclay also inaugurated Scotland's first commercial nuclear power station at Chapelcross, Dumfriesshire, in May 1959.

Maclay's concentration on industrial policy also marked the beginning of a shift towards state planning, which became the political orthodoxy throughout the 1960s and 1970s. As Scottish secretary, Maclay was involved with two planning exercises: the Fraser Plan to promote Highland tourism, and the Toothill Report, a more comprehensive survey of Scotland's whole economy. The former was presided over by Hugh, later Lord Fraser of Allander, who presented his report in the autumn of 1959, and the Highland Tourist Development Company was a direct result. It was floated as a regular commercial company providing loans for hoteliers who wished to expand, and Maclay enthusiastically used it to prove that tourism in the Highlands could be financially viable. Members of the

public were encouraged to buy shares, and the Scottish secretary encouraged Fraser to underwrite it as the Scottish banks were unwilling to
do so. Fraser said, 'we must produce something in bricks and mortar
without delay; otherwise we shall be lost in a cloud of Scotch mist'. He was
alluding to the Aviemore Tourist Centre, which finally opened after
Fraser's death. It was a private commercial undertaking, although
propped up by a government grant under the Local Employment Act.
Fraser took his inspiration from the French resort at Courchevel, where
the French government had tackled similar unemployment problems. But
more influential was the report of the committee chaired by John N.
Toothill, later Sir John, then managing director of Ferranti's Scottish
operation. Maclay was actually suspicious of such exercises, but when the
former minister Sir James Henderson-Stewart (who left the Scottish Office
in 1957) made a strong appeal for a Scottish five-year plan, the idea
emerged of asking the Scottish Council (Development and Industry) to
conduct an inquiry while the Scottish Office supplied resources and staff.[12]
Toothill reported in November 1961, recommending the co-ordination of
regional development bodies and a shift towards diversified industry based
around 'growth points' centred upon Scotland's New Towns. The report
– largely drafted by the committee's secretary, Dr Tom Burns (later a
professor of sociology at Edinburgh University), – also suggested 'a new
department which should bring together the present industrial and
planning functions of the Scottish departments'. The Scottish secretary
reacted swiftly to the recommendations, outlining a plan for another New
Town, this time at Livingston in West Lothian, while in April 1962 he
used, for the first time, the Scottish secretary's powers under the 1939
Reorganisation of Offices (Scotland) Act to reshape Scottish Office
departments without recourse to legislation. The health and home
departments came together as the Scottish Home and Health Department, while Maclay announced that the planning, housing, roads,
electricity and local government divisions at St Andrew's House were
to be consolidated to form a new Scottish Development Department. Sir
Douglas Haddow, later permanent under-secretary, became its head,
having pushed for a similar economic development department some
years previously. Maclay's vision of the Scottish Office as the lead
department for Scotland's economy was now a reality, both practically
and politically. No longer would it yap at the heels of Whitehall, but, as a
result, Maclay – and his successors – came to be judged, often harshly,
according to the performance of the Scottish economy.

Not everyone, however, was satisfied by Maclay's subtle style.[13] During
an otherwise routine debate on road estimates in the Scottish Grand

Committee, the Conservative MP for Caithness and Sutherland, Sir David Robertson, branded the Scottish secretary 'a Treasury lackey and a mouthpiece for officialdom'. He added, 'I can assure this committee that I will have the greatest difficulty in remaining in this party unless the problem of Highland roads is dealt with.'[14] Sir David later resigned the Conservative whip, citing neglect of his region, while the loss of Walter Elliot's Kelvingrove seat to Labour in 1958 also added to Maclay's worries.

By 1959 the Scottish Grand Committee had grown unwieldy, and it was felt that many measures were simply being rushed through. The consideration of Bills at committee stage was, therefore, transferred to a smaller Scottish Standing Committee consisting of at least 30 Scottish MPs, and up to 20 others to supply party balance. The Scottish Grand Committee, however, continued to take the Second Reading of Bills and the Scottish Estimates, while also gaining two days each session to debate any matter of general interest to Scotland. Such generic debates would give Conservative Scottish secretaries many headaches over the years, but for Maclay his time at the Scottish Office was already drawing to a close.

In April 1959 Maclay's wife, Betty, whom he had married in 1930, broke her leg after a fall at their Renfrewshire home. After three years of declining health, she became confined to a wheelchair and fell seriously ill in May 1962, leading her husband to cancel his parliamentary engagements to be near her. Maclay had decided that enough was enough earlier that year, telling Macmillan that he would like to retire at the next available opportunity.[15] 'I was very tired,' he later recalled. 'But it was really my family life that was the problem, because my wife had been out of action for many years, and she'd been much too much alone. She'd been frightfully good about it.'[16]

Unusually, the Scottish secretary decided to take the lead in announcing National Coal Board plans to close 20 pits over a four-year period, which meant the loss of 8,000 mining jobs in Scotland. Maclay announced the cuts on 11 July 1962, attracting immediate condemnation from both Labour MPs and the Scottish mining unions.

With the added stress of an ongoing dispute with teachers, it must have been almost a relief when, two days later, Macmillan sacked Maclay along with six other senior ministers (a third of the Cabinet), in what was dubbed the Night of the Long Knives. 'I knew that if there was going to be a major change I was bound to be in it,' recalled Maclay. 'I didn't know there was going to be a major change then, though. Nobody did. In retrospect, but I said it at the time, I do think it was a mistake to do such a sweeping thing in one fell swoop at that stage of the Parliament.'[17] Scottish Office colleagues resented the fact that Macmillan failed to make it clear that the Scottish secretary had already requested to retire, and instead it looked as if Maclay had been sacked for his handling of the coal board cuts. But he remained courteous, even in such unpleasant circumstances, and quietly returned to the back-benches. Macmillan, it seems, quickly realised that he had handled Maclay's departure badly, and he wrote to him on 15 July almost apologising for what had happened. 'The SofS Scotland is really a fantastic post,' he said, praising Maclay efforts in laying the foundations for Scotland's economic and social recovery. Ironically, he also paid tribute to Maclay's loyalty, concluding, 'It has been a good partnership.' Henry Brooke, who had just become home secretary following Macmillan's purge, also wrote to Maclay, calling his former department a 'truly horrible office', while Tam Galbraith said, 'This is all too sudden. I feel as though I had been thrown out naked on a winter's morning and dependent on the charity of one unknown to me. A most uncomfortable feeling.'[18]

Genuine sympathy greeted Maclay's departure from the Scottish Office, and, at a dinner party held in his honour by Scottish Unionist MPs at the House of Commons on 25 July, Macmillan once again paid him a warm tribute. He also made Maclay a Companion of Honour later in 1962. Two years later, Maclay went to the House of Lords as Viscount Muirshiel of Kilmacolm, the only one of Macmillan's evictees to receive a viscountcy. Maclay immersed himself in business interests, securing directorships of the National Provincial Bank, the Peninsular and Oriental Steamship Company, and the Clydesdale Bank. He also became a trustee of the National Galleries of Scotland, the founding chairman of the Scottish Civic Trust, and he was involved with finding a location for the Burrell Collection, a purpose-built museum which finally opened outside Glasgow in 1983. Maclay also contributed to Sir Alec Douglas-Home's investigations into Scottish devolution in the late 1960s, suggesting additional powers for new large regional councils. 'I am putting a wet towel round my head,' wrote Douglas-Home, thanking Maclay for his thoughts, 'and trying to see a way through.'[19] The former prime minister later settled for a directly elected consultative assembly, which probably suited Muirshiel, who had also written to Douglas-Home on 7 January 1969, saying, 'Legislative powers must result in direct conflict with Westminster.'[20] As Scottish secretary Maclay had sensed that the winds of change were blowing through industrial Scotland, but he perhaps had not sensed a similar shift in its constitutional fabric.

Viscount Muirshiel died of heart failure at his home, Knapps Wood, Kilmacolm, on 17 August 1992, having watched as all three of the heavy industries established in Scotland during his time at the Scottish Office closed down. The Linwood and Bathgate motor works were wound up in 1981, and, just two months before his death, aged 86, the Ravenscraig steelworks finally closed – after many expensive reprieves – on 24 June 1992.

MICHAEL NOBLE

13 JULY 1962 – 18 OCTOBER 1964

The tartan canary

Michael Antony Cristobal Noble was easily the most colourful of the three Conservative Scottish secretaries of the 1950s and early 60s, yet he has a reputation of being nothing more than a typically tweedy Tory grandee. Not many Conservative MPs, however, were born at Las Palmas in the Canary Islands, as Noble was, on 19 March 1913, the youngest son of Sir John Henry Brunel Noble,[1] 1st Baronet of Ardkinglas, and his wife Amie Grogan. He was educated at Eton and Magdalen College, Oxford, where his membership of a bridge team which took on Cambridge (and Noble's future Cabinet colleague Iain Macleod) in a famous varsity bridge league, perhaps explained his taking a third in *literae humaniores* in 1935. Following his graduation, Noble served in the Royal Air Force Volunteer Reserve, reaching the rank of squadron leader in 1943, and he was an Argyll county councillor for two years before winning a by-election in 1958. He later told an official that he could happily have stood as a nationalist, Liberal or Unionist, only opting for the latter because most of his friends were Conservatives.[2] Whatever the party, the Argyllshire constituency suited Noble perfectly, reflecting his farming interests, which included the presidency of the Black Face Sheep Breeders' Association, and the Highland Cattle Society.

Noble had briefly served as his predecessor Jack Maclay's parliamentary private secretary in 1959; he became Scottish Unionist whip in November 1960, and was a government whip and lord commissioner of the Treasury from the following year. Other than that, when he went to the Scottish Office following the July bloodbath, he had no ministerial experience. Lord John Hope, a former Scottish under-secretary and until then minister of works, had been tipped to succeed Maclay, but he was also sacked in Harold Macmillan's Night of the Long Knives. Noble had been an MP for just four years, and chairman of the Scottish Unionist Party for only three months when he joined the government, and he promptly gave up the latter position after less than a year.

Whether or not he knew of Bob Boothby's earlier vision of the secretary of state swanning around Scotland in a large black car with an official pennant, one of Noble's earliest acts was to order just that. It was done, despite some alleged difficulties of protocol, and in the process he discovered that Walter Elliot had attempted to do the same in 1936, but had given up in frustration at the same procedural difficulties encountered by Noble. He was unlucky to become Scottish secretary just as Macmillan's government, and a long period of Conservative rule, was coming – rather traumatically – to an end. And although Noble's comparative youth and enthusiasm was a deliberate attempt to revitalise the Cabinet, within months of the reshuffle he would lose one of his ministers in a messy spy scandal, another because of premature death, and one more through ill health. For Macmillan, and his successor Sir Alec Douglas-Home, things were not much better. Rising unemployment, Charles de Gaulle's European veto and the damaging resignation of John Profumo, all contributed to the perception that this was a regime on its last legs.

On 12 September 1962, the civil servant John Vassall, a cipher clerk at the British Embassy in Moscow, was arrested and charged with spying. He gave a full confession, and was sentenced to 18 years in prison the following month. Meanwhile, a whispering campaign had begun in Westminster which linked the young spy to Thomas 'Tam' Galbraith, who had worked with Vassall as a junior minister at the Admiralty in 1957. Galbraith (Lord Strathclyde's son) was now an under-secretary at the Scottish Office, and it soon emerged that letters had been exchanged between him and Vassall. The contents of these letters caused much speculation, some of which was sordid, and when it transpired that Vassall was also a homosexual the press moved in for the kill. The letters finally appeared in both *The Times* and the *Annual Gazette*, which decided that there was 'nothing more damaging than the former Civil Lord's interest in his office carpets, crockery, and paper clips. The most that could be said against Mr Galbraith was that he suffered a socially pressing and plausible junior a trifle too gladly.'[3] But, although an interim report from an inquiry set up by Macmillan cleared him of any wrong doing, Galbraith nevertheless offered to resign. 'I am glad that their report has made clear that any imputation against me is unfounded,' he wrote from the Scottish Office to the prime minister. 'But it is apparent to me that my long accustomed manner of dealing with officials and others who serve me has in the circumstances become an embarrassment to you and the Government. For this reason alone I feel that my only proper course is to tender my resignation.' Macmillan replied from Admiralty House (his temporary home while 10 Downing Street was being upgraded) the same night. 'I too am glad that my action in calling for an immediate interim report has cleared away the atmosphere of innuendo of which you have been the victim,' he wrote. 'In all the circumstances I think it right to accept your resignation, and I believe that your action will command universal respect.'[4] One journalist giving evidence at the so-called spy tribunal that followed told how he had heard from a police contact that Vassall had planned to join Galbraith on holiday in Italy, 'to do a Pontecorvo'.[5] The implication was that Galbraith, known to be politically pragmatic, also planned to defect, or at the very least help Vassall to do so.[6] The Radcliffe Tribunal (Lord Radcliffe had been appointed chair) eventually cleared Galbraith for a second time, and he returned to the government as parliamentary secretary to the Ministry of Transport in May 1963. But the whole affair had traumatised the British political establishment at the height of the Cold War, and provided an uncomfortable prelude to the following year's Profumo affair.

Galbraith's replacement was Lady Priscilla Tweedsmuir, daughter-in-law of the novelist John Buchan, and the first female Scottish Office minister since Peggy Herbison. 'At last the powers that be have done what they should have done as far back as 1951,' wrote Margaret Thatcher; congratulating her,[7] while the press dubbed her parliament's most 'glamorous granny'.[8] Lady Tweedsmuir took over responsibility for the Scottish Home and Health Department, which included education and criminal justice. Otherwise, Lord Craigton remained as minister of state from Maclay's team, as did the former journalist Richard Brooman-White, and William Gilmour Leburn, a Fife industrialist with a background in local government. Despite his inexperience, Noble enjoyed the loyalty of them all, as he did from Scottish Unionist MPs in general. He had just over two years at the Scottish Office, and like Maclay, his tenure was dominated by Scotland's economy.

Noble enthusiastically set about implementing the main principles of the Toothill Report as soon as he became Scottish secretary.[9] Indeed, his first appearance in the Commons came during a debate on that very report. 'I have tremendous faith in the people of Scotland,' Noble told MPs, 'the men and women whose work has shown that "Made in Scotland" can be a real selling point in world markets.' He continued with some florid rhetoric:

> If we in the Government can give them the technical colleges and the training facilities to equip them fully for the new industries, as well as the best of the old, we need fear no lack of craftsmanship. But we need to ask more still from them.

We need to provide the opportunities first, but then to inspire our younger generation with the feeling that there is still a great adventure for them. In this age, it is not necessary to cross the seas or even the English border. Their adventure lies at home – to rebuild a Scotland of which they and their children will be justly proud.[10]

The Toothill recommendations for modernising Scotland's economy, however, initially stalled. There was a meeting between Noble, the Scottish Council (Development and Industry), or SCDI, and Fred Errol, the president of the Board of Trade, in August 1962. Errol rejected the growth area concept out of hand, and refused to make the allocation of grants under the Local Employment Act more flexible. SCDI demanded to see the prime minister, who was more sympathetic, and in March 1963 Noble was able to unveil a one-off cash injection of £10 million for Scotland's electricity network, roads, and to help build a new reservoir. The Central Scotland Plan appeared in the autumn of 1962, and relied upon the Scottish Office's first professional economists; its publication had been delayed to allow the north-east of England to play catch-up with a similar plan, nominally headed up by Viscount Hailsham with his famous flat cap. The Scottish version was the first legislative manifestation of the Toothill Report, and designated all of Scotland's New Towns as 'growth areas', including a proposed new settlement in Irvine, with the promise of consistent funding for communications and housing. The fledgling Scottish Development Department (SDD) was to oversee the plan, and although Noble worked hard on the White Paper, the press response was less than enthusiastic. There were suspicions that the Scottish secretary lacked the political clout his predecessor had possessed, and, although he pressed the Scottish case with a good deal of support from Macmillan, he was less disposed than Maclay to be seen to take the lead in matters which primarily lay with another department. Often, therefore, both the SCDI and Scottish Trades Union Congress (STUC) would regularly bypass St Andrew's House to personally make their case in Whitehall.

Nevertheless, Noble did persuade the company Wiggins Teape to build a pulp mill in Fort William, and he also engineered the transfer of the Post Office Savings Bank to Glasgow following a last-minute Cabinet intervention, the first major government agency to leave London. And one of his most significant achievements was that, after initial reluctance from some Cabinet colleagues, Noble finally secured government approval for the concept of development growth areas in late 1963 (soon after he became a full member of the Cabinet's Economic Policy Committee). Edward Heath later wrote that Toothill, and Noble's reaction to it, 'brought about a complete change of attitude' in Scotland.[11] The Scottish secretary also established a Scottish Development Group, chaired by the SDD secretary, Sir Douglas Haddow. In another industry debate on 20 June 1963, Noble's hyperbole was undiminished. 'It needs boldness. It needs vision, radical change, and co-operation from everybody,' he evangelised, 'but I repeat that we are determined, and we are confident that the outcome will be the most prosperous Scottish economy that we have known since the beginning of the First World War.'[12] The Scottish secretary had visited the British Agricultural Exhibition in Moscow the previous month, stealing the show by sporting a kilt, although it did not produce any direct investment from the USSR. Noble later led a selling mission to the United States. Accompanied by the SCDI chairman, Lord Polwarth, he canvassed the views of all the leading US firms regarding their Scottish factories. 'Is he aware', asked Labour's future Scottish secretary Bruce Millan on Noble's return, 'that many of us feel that it is beneath the dignity of his office, and a humiliation to Scotland, that Scotland's Cabinet Minister should be trailing around the United States pleading with industrialists to come to Scotland as though we were some kind of under-developed area in Asia or Africa?'[13] The Scottish secretary, however, had the last laugh when IBM announced plans to expand, and Levis (the jeans manufacturers), whose chairman had met with Noble in the US, established factories in Lanarkshire and West Lothian. But he lost the argument over the formation of a Highland Development Board in 1963, mainly because the Board of Trade believed its existing Highland policy was perfectly adequate.[14] Noble, however, found the huge volume of paperwork generated by all this industrial activity tiresome, even to the point that it damaged his eyesight. After a few months staring at papers in Dover House, the Scottish secretary had to invest in his first pair of spectacles.[15]

In March 1963, the infamous Dr Beeching published his long-awaited findings, *The Reshaping of British Railways*, which immediately became known as the Beeching Report. It proposed drastic cuts to hundreds of railway stations and lines for economic reasons, many of which severely affected rural parts of Scotland. One initial proposal suggested scrapping the East Coast Main Line north of Newcastle, and leaving no lines at all north of Inverness. Noble did his best to convince MPs that nothing would be closed without his consent, but in reality the ultimate decision lay with the transport minister, Ernest Marples. The full extent of the cuts – most lines in the north and south of the country – only came into effect after the Conservatives had left office, although the eight minor lines which closed in the Highlands during Noble's incumbency undermined his claim to be committed to the north of Scotland's economy.

Also unhelpful in this respect was the failure of the Countryside and

Tourist Amenities (Scotland) Bill, which had been the main Scottish feature of the Queen's Speech for the 1963–64 session. Its main provision was a surtax on hotels to fund non-commercial tourist facilities, along the lines of various Continental models. A cross-party committee of MPs supported the idea after visiting the Highlands, and Noble won Cabinet backing despite Treasury suspicion, but the Bill bemused the Scottish Grand Committee (although it was approved), and a poll of hoteliers produced a result of 117 to 42 against. Noble protested that only 24 per cent of those asked had bothered to comment, but criticism from the Scottish Tourist Board, the National Trust and the British Hotels and Restaurants Association mounted, and the Scottish secretary was forced to abandon the Bill in February 1964. Also perceived as a threat to the Highlands was a recommendation from the Mackenzie Committee to merge the South of Scotland Electricity Board with the North of Scotland Hydro-Electric Board. Noble was swept along by a wave of Highland public opinion and blocked the proposal, a decision which baffled those who argued that following the completion of the network's construction phase, there was no justification for separate administration.

The Scottish secretary also had mixed results in other Scottish Office domains. The Education (Scotland) Bill of 1963 created an examinations board to oversee secondary school examinations, but Noble failed in an attempt to prevent a rise in the school leaving age to 16, arguing in vain that this would interfere with vocational training schemes the Scottish Education Department regarded as vital to the Scottish economy. Noble scored more of a success with his White Paper on *The Modernisation of Local Government in Scotland*,[16] which appeared in June 1963. Local authorities sticking doggedly to their boundaries had caused problems for the establishment of new industries at Bathgate and Linwood, and, for that and other reasons, it was felt that the 34-year-old structure was in dire need of reform. Noble proposed a two-tier system; the first comprising Scotland's four cities with extended boundaries and roughly 15 amalgamated counties; while the second would consist of expanded burgh councils with populations of around 40,000. Inevitably, and as former Scottish secretary Sir John Gilmour had correctly predicted in 1929, the smaller authorities were not enthusiastic about their proposed demise. The White Paper was meant to stimulate discussion and not necessarily produce legislation. It resulted in plenty of the former, but actual reform had to wait another ten years, and for another Conservative secretary of state, before it became a reality.

From March 1963, Noble had faced a Labour opposition increasingly well co-ordinated by the caustic Kilmarnock MP Willie Ross. He taunted the

Scottish secretary, who was not an impressive parliamentarian, with jibes that he was nothing more than a 'tartan canary' with no real interest in Scotland. Noble also had to endure indiscipline from within his own ranks, largely from rural Tory MPs who found themselves under pressure from a modest Liberal revival, led by the popular Orkney and Shetland MP Jo Grimond. The Scottish Unionist Party's organisation also left a lot to be desired. As chairman from 1962 to '63, Noble had appointed a public relations officer to give it a more professional edge, but it still lacked efficient planning and, more importantly, sufficient funds. Even the emergence of the Scottish peer Sir Alec Douglas-Home as Macmillan's successor did little to revive Conservative fortunes in Scotland. Noble was in the United States when the interregnum occurred, but admired Sir Alec and made it known that he favoured him as leader.[17] Macmillan had always been helpful to the Scottish Office, but not only was the new prime minister more ostentatiously Scottish himself, but he sat for a Scottish constituency, and had even served at St Andrew's House as a successful minister of state from 1951 to 1955. Ross quipped that Noble had left Scotland under one prime minister, and returned home under another, the implication being that the Scottish secretary was out of the loop. However, even Sir Alec's relative popularity during his year at Downing Street could not avert defeat at the general election of 1964, albeit by a narrow margin.

Adding to the air of decline at the Scottish Office was the sudden death while on holiday of one under-secretary, William Gilmour Leburn,[18] on 15 August 1963, and the resignation through ill health of another, the conspiratorial Richard Brooman-White, on 12 December (who died just weeks later). The former was replaced by the Edinburgh West MP (and a good friend of Noble's), Anthony Stodart, and the latter by Gordon Campbell, who would return to the Scottish Office in 1970 as secretary of state. Both, however, had barely a year to make their mark, and when Scotland went to the polls in October 1964 the youthful confidence of Harold Wilson easily outshone the aristocratic geniality of the (former) 14th Earl of Home. Noble was re-elected in Argyllshire with a reduced majority, but the Scottish Unionists lost six more MPs, and returned just 24 members with 41 per cent of the vote.

Although it is difficult to appreciate now, the existence of only 24 Scottish Conservative MPs after the 1964 election was seen as a disaster for the party, particularly the loss of Pollok in Glasgow, which pointed to the decline of a once-solid working-class Unionist vote. The result kick-started wide-ranging reforms, both administrative and political, which began to take effect when Noble was in the Shadow Cabinet as lead spokesman on Scotland. In 1965, the historic 'Unionist' portion of the party's name – which referred to union with Ireland, not England – was dropped, while the Scottish wing of the organisation lost much of its autonomy to Conservative Central Office in London.

In policy too, attitudes began to shift. Noble was sympathetic to the aims of the 'Thistle Group' of younger, less dogmatic Tory MPs, who eventually backed Sir Alec Douglas-Home's plans for a consultative Scottish Assembly in 1970. He wrote to his predecessor, Jack Maclay, on 23 June 1969 claiming that the 'nationalist bubble is lessening', while saying he favoured only 'a bit more' administrative devolution for Scotland. Noble also mooted an unusual plan to reduce income tax for long-domiciled Scots, and for companies with more than 75 per cent of their production based in Scotland.[19]

In 1970 Noble returned to the Cabinet as a short-lived president of the Board of Trade under Edward Heath.[20] The prime minister had been impressed with his centrist pursuit of regional policy at the Scottish Office, although a reorganisation of government departments meant that Noble was later downgraded to minister for trade within a restructured Department of Trade and Industry, from which he was embroiled in the Upper Clyde Shipbuilders dispute of 1971.

Noble stood down from the Commons following the February 1974 election, and was elevated to the Upper House as Lord Glenkinglas of Cairndow. Noble was a witty, chain-smoking raconteur, with excellent taste in wine and many smart friends in London. He loved the good life, and could bring the house down by singing specially adapted Scottish songs in his 'excellent sweet-toned true voice'.[21] But this lifestyle took its toll, and Noble developed emphysema caused by heavy smoking, not to mention other ailments brought about by drinking too much (he nicknamed himself Lord Clinking-glass). He died at home on his Argyllshire estate of a heart attack on 15 May 1984, aged 71. Noble's verdict on his two years as Scottish secretary was typically modest: 'One man can certainly do the job of the Secretary of State,' he said, 'but I think there's only half a dozen of those one men in the world, and I don't think I'm one of them.'[22]

WILLIAM ROSS

18 OCTOBER 1964 – 19 JUNE 1970,
5 MARCH 1974 – 8 APRIL 1976

Old Basso Profundo

The Wilson era in Britain was also that of William Ross in Scotland, yet the secretary of state for Scotland – who was to become the longest-serving minister since 1922 – did not inspire popular affection or make as lasting a mark in Scotland as his master did across the UK. The reasons for this are threefold: Ross had no time for the media manipulation so expertly deployed by Harold Wilson; his many achievements at the Scottish Office were overshadowed by his intransigence over devolution; and his reluctance to produce any memoir of his eight combined years as Scottish secretary. The end result is that Ross remains a seriously under-rated, or at the very least under-appreciated, secretary of state. He is also one of the most interesting, as his reign straddled some fundamental shifts in Scottish politics.

'How will the Scottish Office cope with the wrath of God?' quipped the former Scottish Office minister Peggy Herbison on hearing that Ross was to be Wilson's man in Scotland. Her reservations were not unreasonable, especially considering the new Scottish secretary's record of scathing attacks on the occupants – both political and administrative – of St Andrew's House. As in 1997, the arrival of a Labour government after such a long period of Conservative rule stimulated the civil service machine, not least at the Scottish Office, where officials used to being left alone by Michael Noble now had to face a stark contrast. One senior civil servant was even brave enough to challenge Ross about his previous criticisms. 'You can forget about all that,' he replied, but at first the Scottish secretary believed most of his team were probably card-carrying Conservatives, a suspicion that produced a tense and often hostile atmosphere.[1] Ross later mellowed and was relaxed and approachable in inverse proportion to the seniority of officials around him. His relations with junior ministers also varied a great deal. Some, Ross believed, were not particularly capable, and others he considered devious (a suspicion which also extended to Cabinet colleagues). There was, however, a sense of anticipation in the Scottish Office for the kind of administrative reforms only civil servants can get excited about. The new Department of Economic Affairs (commanded by the ebullient George Brown) and the government's National Plan heralded a bold new era of ambitious state planning, while the arrival of Sir Douglas Haddow as permanent under-secretary in 1965 saw the creation of a Regional Development Division reporting directly to his office. Sir Douglas's aim was to keep in close contact with the UK economic ministries, which chimed perfectly with Ross, who believed that until now power had limped 'lamely behind responsibility'.[2]

The post of Scottish secretary got its first pay rise in almost three decades, from £5,000 to £8,500, but also Cabinet competition in the form of a secretary of state for Wales, a territorial counterpart Ross argued strongly against.[3] The 1964 general election also produced the first decisive Labour majority in Scotland, with 43 seats to the Unionists' 24 and the Liberals' four. With a precarious overall majority of only four seats, Harold Wilson knew that Scotland was an important factor in the stability of his government. This gave Ross the kind of leverage which his Labour predecessors at the Scottish Office could only have dreamed of. His relationship with Wilson was therefore of key importance. Although never close, Wilson valued (at least initially) Ross's ultra-loyalism, and the Scottish secretary rated the prime minister's political judgment, not to mention his support in Cabinet. Yet they were a strange double act: Wilson the pipe-smoking populist promoting the white heat of technology, and Ross the austerely Presbyterian dominie who preferred Robert Burns to the Beatles. Through the years of sexual revolution, pop culture and the permissive society, Ross was an anachronism, yet he dominated the Scottish Labour Party for almost 14 years and was, above all, terribly, terribly Scottish.

William Ross was born in Ayr on 7 April 1911, the son of a locomotive driver and prominent member of Ayr Town Council, William Hendry Ross, and his wife Mary Smith Morrison. Ross – later known as Bill to close friends and colleagues – and his family were poor yet respectable, and steeped in trade unionism. Ross won a bursary to Ayr Academy, then the most famous school in the area, and later studied English at Glasgow University in 1929 with a Carnegie scholarship, graduating three years later. He became a primary school teacher, working in a number of inner-city Glasgow schools. The general strike of 1926, which saw Ross's father out of work, and the depression of the 1930s consolidated political convictions largely gleaned from his parents, and his political activities initially reflected the erratic nature of the inter-war Labour Party. He was active in the Independent Labour Party (ILP) Guild of Youth and later became a member of the Scottish Socialist Party, the loyalist remnant of the ILP which remained affiliated to Labour even after the 1932 split. Indeed, Ross only formally joined the Labour Party in 1936 when he was adopted as the candidate for the Ayr Burghs.

The Second World War, however, ended both Ross's teaching career and his political aspirations. He enlisted in the Highland Light Infantry, having already been identified as potential officer material, and guarded Rudolph Hess at the Maryhill barracks when he crashed in Scotland in 1941. Ross served at the north-west frontier of India and was later seconded to signals general headquarters in Delhi. In 1944 he became cipher officer to Lord Louis Mountbatten – then supreme commander in South-East Asia – and accompanied him on flights to Burma and Singapore for the signing of the peace treaty with the Japanese. For this, Major Ross received a military Member of the British Empire, and formed an association with the Queen's relative which would last until he was murdered by the Irish Republican Army in 1979. In India, Ross also met his future wife, a smart Wren officer called Elma Aitkenhead, the daughter of an Ayrshire publican.

Ross finally contested the Ayr Burghs at the 1945 general election, nine years after being adopted as its candidate, but the Labour landslide failed to sweep him into parliament and he was defeated by the Conservative Sir Thomas Moore. Moore's majority, however, had been heavily dented by Ross's vigorous campaign, and, when the Kilmarnock Division of Ayr became vacant a year later, Ross found himself with a safe Labour seat. The constituency had been held by Clarice McNab Shaw, perhaps Ross's strongest political influence. She was the widow of the legendary ILP scottish organiser Ben Shaw, and had won Kilmarnock in 1945 although ill health prevented her ever reaching the Commons. Ross often referred to her as the 'finest woman he had ever met', and Shaw cropped up in his conference speeches with regularity even 30 years later.

By the end of 1946 Clement Attlee's nationalising Labour government was in full swing, and Ross soon aligned himself with the right of the party, associating with figures like Hugh Gaitskell and Hector McNeil. The latter made Ross his parliamentary private secretary as Scottish secretary in 1951, giving him his first taste of a department he would later command.[4] But, despite his Gaitskellite bent, Ross appears to have supported Herbert Morrison in the 1955 Labour leadership contest, even inviting the Londoner to speak in Ayrshire. Gaitskell, however, won, and in early 1956 Ross was helping him with his speech to the Scottish Council of the Labour Party in North Berwick. The new Labour leader shared his predecessor's coolness towards Scottish home rule, but he promised delegates he would keep an open mind on the subject. Gaitskell was convinced that Scotland needed a Labour administration rather than a Scottish government. Ross agreed, but he remained on the back-benches throughout the rest of the 1950s and early 1960s. He used that period to hone what became a formidable debating style, firmly rooted in the Ayrshire Labour tradition and savagely deployed against his opponents on the Tory benches. Ross's maiden speech during a debate on the Town and Country Planning (Scotland) Bill gave a taste of what was to come: lashings of Burns; a gloomy survey of Scotland's many woes; and a strident attack on the Scottish National Party (SNP). But while Ross's rhetoric won plaudits from party colleagues, it also earned him a reputation as a mischievous and destructive back-bencher. He formed an effective double-act with the Edinburgh Labour MP George Willis, and together they utilised every delaying tactic known to parliament, especially in the Scottish Grand Committee, its cocooned nature allowing scope for even more mischief making. Ross's 'Morecambe and Wise' act with Willis not only annoyed the Conservatives, it even offended some in the Labour Party, prompting Attlee to warn the pair to tone down their negative antics.[5]

Throughout the 13 long years of Conservative government from 1951 to 1964, the former Scottish under-secretary Tom Fraser had been Labour's main spokesman on Scotland. He was a gentle soul who could not stomach Ross's more aggressive approach, and in 1962 Gaitskell made Ross shadow Scottish secretary in his place, following a period assisting Douglas Houghton on pensions, health and insurance from the back-benches. He blossomed in the role, stepping up his attacks on the Conservative Scottish secretary Michael Noble, whom he dubbed the 'tartan canary'.

When Gaitskell died in 1963 Ross shrewdly supported Harold Wilson for the leadership and cemented a political association which would prove essential to his future career. The domineering manner Ross acquired in the schoolroom, together with the military discipline instilled in him during the war, produced an imposing politician with formidable presence. It was said that he even scared Wilson, but above all Ross had a dedication to what he saw as Scotland's needs, a dedication which not only produced enormous benefits, but also a stubbornness which later loosened his grip on the Scottish Office during a crucial period of constitutional upheaval.

Ross was not by any account a creative politician. Neither ideology nor ideas were his forte, but he was an intensely practical Scottish secretary who would seize upon an initiative, make it his own, and see it through until the bitter end. Several examples of this emerge from his first six-year term as Scottish secretary. The Highlands and Islands Development Board (HIDB), though no longer in existence (at least under that name), was perhaps the most impressive. The notion of a Highland body to stimulate investment and promote tourism was not a new one: Sir Archibald Sinclair had floated the idea back in the 1920s, while Joseph Westwood's Highland Panel was a toothless precursor to what Ross had in mind. The Scottish Trades Union Congress (STUC) had also come out strongly in favour, so when Wilson formed his first government there was a broad consensus behind its creation. It was mentioned in the Queen's Speech of 1964 and, by March the following year, the Highlands and Islands Development (Scotland) Bill was presented to parliament by an emotive Scottish secretary:

> For 200 years the Highlander has been the man on Scotland's conscience . . . No part of Scotland has been given a shabbier deal by history from the '45 onwards. Too often there has been only one way out of his troubles for the person born in the Highlands – emigration. No country can claim happiness if one of its most splendid assets – in this case, its unsurpassed landscape – can only be enjoyed in the dreams of exiles.[6]

Ross harked back to the Napier Commission of 1884, which investigated the complaints of Highland crofters, and the subsequent reforms passed by his Liberal predecessors. But unlike the Crofters Commission, the HIDB had a huge budget and wide-ranging powers to acquire land and grant financial assistance to approved schemes. It covered 9 million acres, nearly 47 per cent of Scotland's land mass, and the shadow Scottish secretary Michael Noble, despite having considered a similar proposal himself two years earlier, condemned the Bill as 'undiluted Marxism'. Ross quipped that such objections came straight from Groucho, not Karl, Marx, and mischievously offered to amend the Bill so that Noble's Argyllshire constituency was excluded from the Board's remit. But, despite early teething troubles, the HIDB was a success and paved the way some ten years later for the Scottish Development Agency. By November 1971 it had dispersed grants totalling £9.5 million for more than 1,600 projects and could claim credit for the promotion of 5,000 new jobs. Wilson later called it 'one of our proudest achievements'. Ross's contribution was to secure Cabinet backing, while ensuring the Board had executive authority to spend money as it saw fit, a notable difference from the purely consultative Highland Panel.

The HIDB also tied in with the new political orthodoxy of regional, and national, economic planning. Ross would never acknowledge as much, but this approach had been pioneered by his three Conservative predecessors, although the Labour government took it to a much higher level. Five planning councils were established early in 1965, three for the English regions, and one each for Scotland and Wales. Each body comprised industrialists, trade unionists, financiers and members of local authorities, but, while the English councils each had ad hoc chairmen, Ross insisted upon chairing the Scottish Economic Planning Council (SEPC) himself. Delegates remember the Scottish secretary's schoolmasterly manner more inhibiting frank discussion than encouraging it, while Ross was fed advice by grandly titled Economic Consultants to the Secretary of State, who were selected from the senior economic professors at Scottish universities. The SEPC was serviced by the Regional Development Division, reporting direct to Sir Douglas Haddow (rather than being brigaded within one of the Scottish Office Departments), and also kept in close contact with the new Department of Economic Affairs in Whitehall. The result was the ambitious National Plan of September 1965, which set out the government's targets for the next five years; while another document published a few months later – in effect the Scottish Plan – designated the whole of Scotland, except for Edinburgh and Leith, as a development area. Command 2864, The Scottish Economy 1965–1970, also set out ambitious proposals to stem emigration and cut unemployment by rapidly developing Central Scotland and the Borders, while creating several New Towns; it was approved by the SEPC soon after.

Ross believed that 'you could make Scotland a proving ground for progressive legislation',[7] so another, more enduring, reform was the Social Work (Scotland) Bill. This sprang from his instinctive concern for the underprivileged, not least those in Glasgow and within his own constituency. The Bill drew together the disparate services provided by different local authority departments – education, welfare and the probation service – to form a single social work department for each Scottish council under its own director. It also set up controversial children's panels, but, again, the idea had not emanated from Ross: it had come from a committee chaired by Lord Kilbrandon. However, as with the HIDB, the Scottish secretary was responsible for pushing through a distinctly Scottish agenda with no direct correlation in England, and it is to his credit that the reforms endure to this day. The Bill even won warm praise from both the Conservatives and Dick Crossman, who, as the minister for social security, took a keen interest in the Bill's progress through parliament. An English Bill eventually appeared, but observers agreed the Scottish one was more comprehensive.

Supporting Ross with these reforms was his minister of state and friend

George Willis, who had aided the young Kilmarnock MP in his back-bench attacks on the Conservative governments of the 1950s. Willis was a former second-hand bookseller with special responsibility for the Highlands and the Scottish Home and Health Department. The Scottish secretary had less of a bond with his junior ministers, the ambitious and brash Judith Hart, who shared her predecessor Peggy Herbison's enthusiasm for school building, the ebullient Glaswegian medic Dick (Dickson) Mabon, and Lord (William) Hughes of Hawkhill, a former lord provost of Dundee who was widely respected. Ross was not an effective delegator and it was him rather than Hart who introduced a 1965 circular instructing Scottish local authorities to reorganise their secondary schools along comprehensive lines.

The Scottish secretary also successfully fought transport secretary Barbara Castle to create a separate Scottish Transport Group, arguing that as he already had responsibility for roads in Scotland then there was a case for him to assume more control over road passenger transport and ferries through a single transport agency. Castle, with whom Ross had battled during the Bevanite infighting of the 1950s, was not impressed, although the Scottish secretary later redeemed himself by supporting her over the Industrial Relations Bill (otherwise known as *In Place of Strife*), which was later killed off by what Ross saw as 'cold-blooded disloyalty' from James Callaghan.[8] There were also Bills to establish a General Teaching Council for Scotland and a Scottish Countryside Commission – both groundbreaking and eventually followed in England – but in other areas Ross was less successful. His plans to radically reform Scotland's feudal laws got off to a good start in 1969 with a jauntily titled consultation paper, *A Farewell to Feudalism*, but only the first step was implemented before an unexpected defeat in the 1970 general election. This also prevented any progress towards local government reform, as recommended by a royal commission, chaired by Lord Wheatley, in 1969.

Although by the end of the 1960s the Scottish secretary was still in place, his junior ministerial team had been transformed. In 1967 Willis was sacked as minister of state to make way for Dick Mabon, while Judith Hart moved to the Commonwealth Office after the election in 1966, despite harbouring ambitions to become the first female Scottish secretary. Bruce Millan, a Dundonian with a good head for figures, and Norman Buchan, a folk-singing schoolteacher from the Moray Firth, replaced them. Buchan was by far the most left-leaning of the team, a proclivity which later caused friction with both the Scottish Police Federation and Ross, while Millan was perhaps the only junior to earn Ross's respect and trust. Mabon, on the other hand, was not his cup of tea. A member of the fashionable political dining society, the Other Club, who loved the glitz of London,[9] Mabon was also a talented campaigner who used the media in a manner which was anathema to the more reserved secretary of state, often crying 'get me the editor of the *Greenock Telegraph*'. The Greenock MP was also at odds with Ross over the European Community, social reforms and devolution, and would later live up to his chief's worst suspicions by defecting to the Social Democratic Party (SDP) in the early 1980s.

The biggest row to hit the Scottish secretary during Wilson's first two governments came when the HIDB became embroiled in a bitter scandal which eventually claimed the scalps of two members, Frank Thomson and John Robertson. A prominent businessman in Easter Ross, Thomson and his fellow board member Robertson had a dream to create a major petrochemical complex at Invergordon. All was going well until March 1967, when a newspaper revealed that Thomson chaired a company called Invergordon Chemical Enterprises, which had entered an agreement with Occidental Petroleum to develop the complex. The whole affair then descended into a bitter farce as it also emerged that grants worth more than £38,000 had been awarded to companies with links to other HIDB members. Ross, who had invested a large amount of political credibility in the board, was deeply concerned, although he recognised that the sums involved were very small and had all been fully declared. He also confessed to *The Times* to having 'more than a feeling that someone is out to destroy the Board' when a series of unlikely tales of stolen documents, alleged phone tapping, character assassination, thinly veiled threats and secret meetings contributed to the impression that Ross's bold vision of a Highland revival was in tatters. Minutes of board meetings were leaked to the opposition, which scented blood and mounted a vigorous attack on the Scottish secretary. Matters came to a head on 21 March when Thomson was summoned to a crunch meeting with Ross to explain himself. Three days later, in a difficult Commons statement, the Scottish secretary gave full details of all the disputed grants, and announced the resignations of Thomson and Robertson.

Also in 1967, Tom Fraser resigned his Hamilton seat following problems with his constituency party. Ross felt sorry for Fraser and made him part-time chairman of the North of Scotland Hydro-Electric Board, while also adding him to the HIDB in an effort to stabilise the troubled authority. The result was a prolonged by-election campaign, the culmination of which was to shake Labour's dominant position in Scotland to its complacent core. Until then, Scottish home rule had been a non-issue since the decline of the Scottish Covenant campaign in the early 1950s. The SNP had no Commons representatives, few in local government, and a relatively low profile despite reasonable showings in several Scottish constituencies. Ross had no desire to change this, so when the media-friendly solicitor Winnie Ewing captured Hamilton in October 1967 the Scottish secretary's dislike for nationalists became pathological. As the veteran SNP wit Oliver Brown remarked, 'a shiver ran along the Scottish Labour benches looking for a spine to run up'.[10] It was felt acutely by Ross, who reacted by heaping caustic abuse on Ewing in particular, and the SNP – or 'Scottish Narks Party' as he called it – in general. It did not help that Ewing was one of Labour's own. She had grown up reading *Forward* and her family was steeped in the ILP; her second cousin was even the former Labour Scottish secretary Arthur Woodburn.

Other senior MPs, however, had a more thoughtful reaction. Dick Crossman, just the kind of socialist intellectual Ross disliked, floated the idea of a 'Scottish Stormont', while the staunch Unionist Teddy Taylor revived the idea that the Scottish Grand Committee should meet in Edinburgh as a kind of surrogate Scottish parliament. Ross blew hot and cold on the idea, but when Crossman took up Taylor's case he received a note from Ross's private secretary informing him that the secretary of state was of the opinion that 'half-baked nationalism is ridiculous and satisfies no one'.[11] Meanwhile, another socialist intellectual and leading academic authority on Cabinet government, the MP John P. Mackintosh, had formed a group of pro-devolution Scottish Labour MPs, including Donald Dewar and Robert Maclennan. Ross heaped scorn on what he saw as a fringe concern, but he also became aware that the rising threat of nationalism was a potent political weapon when it came to Cabinet negotiations. Just as Tom Johnston had done as Scottish secretary during the war, Ross used this weapon to extract more and more money from a reluctant Treasury. 'I urge my colleagues', Ross would plead, 'to think very carefully before doing anything that might make matters worse.' Ross also repeatedly warned Number 10 that 'the impression is gaining ground that we, as a Government, are discriminating against Scotland'. The results of this strategy, however, were mixed. The Scottish secretary lobbied successfully to secure a new prototype fast nuclear reactor for Dounreay, coming up against the minister of technology Frank Cousins, who favoured another site at Winfrith in Dorset. Wilson had promised to help forge the 'white heat of technology'; Ross was just trying to ensure that the far north of Scotland was bathed in its warm glow. But he failed to capture the Royal Mint for Cumbernauld after it was dispersed from Woolwich, and it went instead to Wales, as did the DVLA. This twin victory was a result of a canny Welsh secretary in the form of Cledwyn Hughes, by now an old hand at employing similar lobbying techniques to those used by his Scottish counterpart. Ross's influence also counted for nothing on the National Computer Centre, the British Steel Corporation and the Land Commission. But Crossman almost admired Ross's approach, writing in his diary, 'Willie is always grousing, he is always depressing and hopelessly narrow-minded and parochial, but if you are going to have in the Cabinet somebody for Scotland and for Wales, I suppose you can say that they have got to be like that by nature.'[12]

Crossman had written to Wilson a week after the Hamilton bombshell, urging the prime minister to at least consider some measure of devolution. The Cabinet secretary, Sir Burke Trend, instead advised the prime minister to consider a ministerial committee. Wilson agreed, and within days reports began to appear in newspapers to that effect. Ross had been kept out of the loop as his reaction to such a concession was all too predictable. The journalist Nora Beloff then produced a detailed account of the plan in the *Observer* on 18 February 1968, the Scottish secretary only receiving official notification that a committee had been set up under Crossman the following day. Ross hit the roof, and he wrote to Wilson complaining that he had just finished telling a group of back-benchers that there was nothing in the rumours. 'Miss Beloff is to be congratulated not only on the accuracy of her information, but the speed of delivery,' he wrote. 'My concern is my relations with Scottish Labour back-benchers. The most personally charitable conclusion they can reach, and not one that I relish, is that I was not consulted about the setting up of this committee, and was not aware of what was happening. I expect I will be hearing from them.'[13] Crossman's committee, however, proved ineffective.[14] Ross's opposition meant a Scottish parliament was out of the question, while the new Welsh secretary, George Thomas, said he would accept nothing less than an elected council for the principality. An exasperated Crossman wrote to Wilson on 25 June to report that he, Ross and Thomas could not come up with the 'warm-hearted' set of proposals the prime minister had requested. 'In my view a decision to move a major part of a major Whitehall office to Scotland, for example, would do more good than a lot of propaganda,' wrote Crossman. 'The one thing the Scots surely don't want is to be treated as exactly on a par with our English Northern region, just across the frontier.'[15] He added that the Scottish secretary had suggested 'bashing the nationalists' in the absence of an agreement; an unimaginative suggestion which remained Ross's only contribution to the constitutional debate for the next six years.

The Queen's Speech of October 1968 promised a royal commission to examine the issue. 'They take minutes but waste years' quipped Wilson, but he sanctioned it on the advice of the home secretary, Jim Callaghan, who saw it as a way out of the developing problems in Northern Ireland. Ross also grudgingly agreed, provided that England and Wales were included in its remit, and it was established under the chairmanship of Lord (Geoffrey) Crowther. The SNP had won 30 per cent of the vote in May's local government elections, which perhaps focussed the government's mind, and in April the following year a Select Committee on Scottish Affairs was also established to scrutinise the Scottish Office as part of a new structure of departmental select committees. It was now an increasingly high-spending department, and, with public expenditure per head in Scotland running at 20 per cent above the English average, the case for increased scrutiny was undeniable. But by the end of the 1960s Scotland was still losing jobs faster than new ones could be created, with a net loss of 35,000 between 1964 and 1968. Ross talked up some modest successes, including a fall in net emigration and a 19 per cent increase in industrial investment in the seven years from 1961. The Borders region, however, had been left untouched despite Labour's grand plans, and even the Scottish secretary could not prevent the closure of the Edinburgh–Hawick–Carlisle railway line as part of Dr Beeching's infrastructure cuts. Bad industrial relations, even under Labour, wildly optimistic planning and the bursting of many economic bubbles had produced a UK economy which was not exactly healthy; a downward trend that culminated with the devaluation of the pound in 1967.

Ross was a paradox: a cultural nationalist who hated nationalism; an austere Kirk member with a caustic wit; and a public abstainer who loved nothing more than a dram at the end of a long day.[16] Politically he was on the right of the party, but in such a non-dogmatic way that many colleagues found him impossible to pin down. Having witnessed the internal party divisions caused by the Bevanites in the 1950s, Ross valued loyalty above all else and expected everyone to support Wilson come what may; he therefore aimed to unite all elements within the Labour Party in Scotland. On social issues Ross was also difficult to classify. The 1960s were swinging, morals were loosening, and many assumed that Ross was largely aghast at the changes. As a committed Presbyterian he opposed just about every social reform which came before Cabinet, though often mellowed when a final decision went against his wishes. Even proposals to lower the voting age from 21 to 18 in January 1968 upset Ross, who feared it would bolster the SNP vote. His Kirk instincts also explained his stance when it came to the Northern Ireland issue, on which Ross always sided with the Protestant majority. Controversially, he ensured that the Sexual Offences Bill (which legalised homosexuality) did not apply to Scotland, but while Ross was privately opposed to David Steel's back-bench Bill to make abortion legal, he gave Bruce Millan a free hand on the Cabinet committee charged with making Steel's Bill acceptable to the government.

Many ministers from the 1960s also tell of how Ross refused to allow a drinks cabinet in any Dover House office, yet in the 1970s he cautiously embraced the 'Clayson' licensing reforms for Scotland, as he believed they would lead to more civilised imbibing.

In Cabinet, Ross could often be 'magnificent' when arguing against proposals like an increase in the price of school meals, but also annoyed colleagues with his constant gripes about their ignorance of all things Scottish. He would demolish arguments, both in the chamber and at the Cabinet table, with a daunting blend of irony, humour and rhetoric. When in 1968 Wilson admitted that his campaign to join the Common Market was nothing more than a 'minuet', Ross quipped, 'Let's make sure we aren't still dancing a minuet while everyone else is doing the twist.' Barbara Castle said it was the best 'crack I've heard him make in Cabinet'.[17] The Scottish secretary also clashed with the Oxbridge intellectuals he so distrusted, most memorably when Roy Jenkins launched a crusade to introduce permanent summertime, bringing the UK's clocks into line with the Continent. This would have meant that while in London midwinter sunrise was at 9.02 a.m., in Inverness it would occur almost an hour later, forcing young children to walk to school in the dark. 'The situation, therefore,' submitted Ross in a memo to the Cabinet Home Affairs Committee, 'is one where it's very easy to [suggest] that the interests of Scotland are being sacrificed to those of the South-East of England.' He particularly disliked Dick Crossman, criticising his dedication to socialism as purely intellectual. 'Dick possessed all the virtues of the intellectual except one,' wrote Ross privately. 'He never mastered the difference between truth & falsehood. He didn't think there was one. So he was eternally surprised that anyone should question his sincerity . . . or consistency. Truth was what he thought at any moment of time; it was personal, tactical and temporary.' He added:

As a minister he was inevitably indecisive, and by the time his officials had worked on his decision, Dick as often as not changed his mind. The archives of the Health Dept are weighed down by his favoured – then discarded schemes of reorganisation. Details bored him – they were for lesser mortals. Principles were the thing but he kept changing them. Of his work as a minister – in housing, health, pensions [or] Parliamentary procedure – nothing remains. Just his diaries – well paid and badly written. Where truth mingles with falsehood.[18]

In parliament Ross had few close friends, although he formed a close bond with Betty Harvie Anderson, the tweedy and witty Conservative MP for East Renfrewshire, even appointing her to the Wheatley Commission on Local Government. This caused trouble at one Labour conference, where Ross responded to criticisms by declaring that such appointments would end as soon as his own party started producing capable alternatives. He had a similarly low opinion of Commons colleagues, and John P. Mackintosh, the MP for Berwick and East Lothian, failed to satisfy Ross on three counts: class, morality and intellect.[19] 'He could be a terribly big man and a terribly small man,'[20] said Jim Sillars, who remembered him often castigating colleagues in a shockingly harsh fashion. As John Smith (Ross's parliamentary private secretary in 1974) later remembered, 'there were legions of people Ross did not like'.[21]

The Scottish secretary also shared Tom Johnston's disdain for London, and was so detached from it that he once was unable to give someone directions to Paddington, an area of which he had barely heard. Ross rarely left his office or the parliamentary complex and stayed at the same modest London hotel for decades, often eschewing it, in those days of frequent late-night sittings, for a simple camp bed at Westminster. A chain-smoker, he also disliked journalists – especially television reporters[22] – and would tick them off like naughty schoolboys while puffing on a cigarette during St Andrew's House press conferences. Ross was an orator rather than a speechwriter, and he preferred to come up with a few key ideas and phrases which he would then flesh out and deliver fluently. He was that rare kind of MP who could fill the Commons chamber rather than empty it on making a late-night speech. If there was a major policy decision to be made, Ross would often gather together all the relevant officials and hold up their pre-prepared brief as if it smelled. 'Who wrote this?' he would growl, a cigarette in one hand and foot tapping as a tense reflex, before criticising its drafting and gleefully pointing out any typing errors. This would set everyone on edge, but the Scottish secretary would then change tack and lead a 'perfectly sensible discussion' about the matter at hand.[23]

Although he did not suffer fools gladly, Ross had a very strongly developed sense of the dignity of his office and was highly deferential to certain establishment figures, particularly his old army chief Lord Mountbatten. The Scottish secretary was a Calvinist who occasionally enjoyed himself, although not in a conventional manner. He relaxed with *The Times* crossword (he rarely read a newspaper on the principle that they were mostly inaccurate and he would soon be told of anything important) and was a copious reader, albeit of light, if not escapist, novels, but he neglected the political social whirl which lay beyond the House of Commons tearoom. Public meetings, however, really fired him up and Ross thrived on the cut and thrust of town hall debates. He also had a creative edge which few knew of, including a talent for caricature (shared by Tom Johnston) which manifested itself during Wilson's typically rambling Cabinets in several 'most technically accomplished' doodles of Cabinet colleagues.[24]

Ross was an authority on Robert Burns, and much in demand at suppers in his constituency and across Scotland. He gave one civil servant a bound edition of the Bard's poems when he left his private office, the same official who had aided him in drafting Burns pastiches in response to similar, and highly critical, efforts sent to Ross during a bitter teachers' strike in 1974 (he was a natural target for take offs of 'Holy Willie's Prayer'). The Scottish secretary had almost complete contempt for the STUC ('the Scottish Trades Union Congrouse'), which he refused to accept was truly representative of the workers' movement, being instead full of communists and fellow travellers.

Although Ross was the undisputed leader of the Labour Party in Scotland, his power base was tenuous at best. His relations with back-bench Labour MPs were cordial yet detached, but more distant with party officials in Glasgow. The Scottish secretary also did not believe in building alliances in Cabinet, depriving him of heavyweight support when, on occasion, he most needed it. Ross's relationship with Wilson was therefore his most important political consideration. In many ways theirs was a strange alliance. Ross was strongly rooted in the working classes whereas Wilson displayed all the hallmarks of being exactly the kind of intellectual which roused the Scottish secretary's suspicion. But, like Ross, Wilson realised the importance of unity, and strove to achieve that at the expense of all else.

Labour had consolidated its position in Scotland at the 1966 general election, adding another three MPs to its 1964 tally. Nevertheless, there were persistent rumours that Ross was to be replaced, first by Judith Hart, and latterly by the Commonwealth secretary, George Thomson.[25] Wilson, however, retained Ross at the Scottish Office during two post-election reshuffles, and by 1970 he was one of only three Cabinet ministers (apart from Wilson) from the 1964 government to remain in the same department. But what of the public perception of Ross as Scottish secretary? This was largely favourable, hardly surprising given that he was a thoroughly Scottish figure. Voters who encountered him sensed that he was essentially one of their own: dour, critical and well-versed in the vernacular.

Labour's defeat at the 1970 general election was as unexpected as the Conservatives' victory. Ross remained on the front-bench as shadow Scottish secretary, thundering against 'the Government of Edward the Unready' and treating the new Scottish secretary, Gordon Campbell, to regular doses of caustic wit. The Royal Commission on the Constitution finally reported in October 1973 – now under the chairmanship of Lord Kilbrandon (Lord Crowther having died) – and recommended directly elected assemblies for Wales and Scotland, a related reduction in the number of Scottish MPs, and the scrapping of a dedicated Cabinet post of secretary of state for Scotland. The following month saw the so-called 'blonde bombshell' Margo MacDonald win the Govan by-election, supplying another nasty shock to a Labour Party which had hoped that nationalism was on the wane. MacDonald's experience of Ross was rather different to that of Winnie Ewing six years previously, and she remembers him gruffly explaining to her how to read through a Bill in the members' tea room. He also responded to her maiden speech in a typically witty fashion: 'We will not quarrel tonight with the things that the hon. Member for Glasgow, Govan said,' Ross told the House, 'hers was one of the best speeches that we have seen here for a long time – and I say "seen" quite rightly.'[26] Although MacDonald lost her seat just four months later at the first general election of 1974, a total of seven SNP MPs were returned to parliament after a campaign which had majored on 'It's Scotland's Oil' and 'Rich Scots or Poor British?'

Ross, meanwhile, returned to the Scottish Office resentful of the applause which had greeted his Tory predecessor,[27] but mellower than ten years earlier, even greeting his new private secretary as if he were a long-lost friend.[28] He had been initially reluctant to return to Dover House, and there was briefly some talk of Ross going instead to the Department of Agriculture, or becoming leader of the House.[29] The outcome of the February poll had finally convinced Wilson that something had to be done about devolution. The Queen's Speech committed ministers to discussing the Kilbrandon proposals and bringing forward legislation. Ross initially remained unreconstructed, joking to the STUC that Kilbrandon actually meant 'Kill-devolution', and telling the House that the SNP were 'conning the people of Scotland into tartan chaos'.[30] But the electoral success of the SNP had focussed other, more flexible, ministerial minds. 'It's not the seven SNP firsts I'm worried about,' said Michael Foot, 'it's the 13 seconds.' It also marked the beginning of the end for Ross's once influential association with the prime minister. Wilson did not even consult Ross (an echo of his reaction to the Hamilton by-election in 1967) when, in response to a question from Winnie Ewing, he announced in a written answer that proposals for devolution would soon be forthcoming.

In March 1974, the Scottish Council of the Labour Party (which included Ross) agreed that 'a measure of devolution could perhaps give the people a feeling of involvement in the process of decision making. We believe this might best be done by the setting up of an elected Scottish assembly'. This vague sentiment was endorsed by the Scottish Labour conference on 22 March, and on 22 June (a Saturday) the Executive Committee of the Scottish Council held an extraordinary meeting in Glasgow. The meeting clashed with Scotland taking on Yugoslavia in the final rounds of the World Cup, which meant that not only was Ross in Frankfurt watching the game, but many other office bearers had opted to stay away. Only 11 out of the executive's 29 members turned up, voting by six to five to condemn a Scottish Assembly as 'irrelevant to the real needs of the Scottish people'.[31] Apart from being acutely embarrassing for the prime minister, it also put Ross in a decidedly awkward position. Tam Dalyell has argued that even had the Scottish secretary been present the vote would still have gone against, but, whatever the case, an order soon left 10 Downing Street that the decision was to be reversed (an ironic commentary on devolution). In July, the National Executive Committee of the Labour Party formally endorsed devolution and in September a special conference at the Glasgow Co-Operative Hall in Dalintober Street called for a directly elected assembly. A consultation paper had appeared the same month, and by now even the Scottish secretary had become a convert, although he had no involvement in Labour's first dedicated Scottish manifesto, which was produced by the party researcher Alex Neil and Bruce Millan for the October 1974 election. By now back in Downing Street with an overall majority of only three and another four SNP MPs to contend with (making a total of 11), Wilson began to set the devolutionary wheels in motion. He set up a Constitution Unit within the Cabinet Office under the lord president, Ted Short, to work out the detail, while accepting Short's recommendation of the newly elected MP Harry Ewing as an additional Scottish Office under-secretary, with responsibility for devolution. As was usual with Wilson, Ross was not consulted about the composition of his team and viewed Ewing with suspicion, not least because he shared London digs with the increasingly troublesome MPs Alex Eadie and Jim Sillars. The Scottish secretary kept a close eye on what Ewing got up to with Short, and dedicated himself to excluding any economic powers from the remit of the Scottish Assembly.

The Scottish secretary continued to forecast doom and gloom as the proposals advanced, but his cynicism about devolution was at least well-intentioned. Like Hector McNeil, he feared that Scotland would lose its Cabinet clout (as Kilbrandon had recommended) and influence in defence and foreign affairs, becoming parochial and marginalised as a result. Ross also believed that a Scottish Assembly would fail to satisfy the domestic-policy concerns of Scots, and that big decisions on economic and industrial policy or the location of nuclear reactors could only effectively be made by a Cabinet of the UK. His analysis of the constitutional question was therefore practical rather than emotional. 'Do not let anyone under-estimate the complexities of the problems,' he told MPs during a debate on devolution in late 1974. 'Let them consider what has happened in the past. For example, let them consider the mistakes that were made when the secretary for Scotland was set up in 1885. Within a year absolute chaos was discovered. Certain matters had been overlooked and yet another Bill had to be introduced. We want to deal with the matter correctly and we wish to make our preparations now.'[32]

It was said that Ross often posed the rhetorical question 'Why does Scotland need an Assembly when it's got me?'[33] Again, there was some merit in what at first appeared to be a hubristic sentiment. Even as the debate on what form devolution should take raged on, more and more pro-Scottish decisions were taken. The headquarters of a new British National Oil Corporation were located in Glasgow, responsibility for regional selective assistance was passed to the Scottish Office from the Board of Trade, and the Department of Energy backed away from some of its more extreme proposals for 'streamlining' oil-related planning procedures and even recruited a Scottish MP to its ranks (John Smith), explicitly to ensure sensitivity to Scottish issues.

Wilson had accepted devolution purely on political grounds, as had Bernard Donoughue, the young academic (whom Ross considered wet behind the ears) who now headed up a new Downing Street Policy Unit. Donoughue's diary from the period provides a fascinating glimpse into the often shambolic discussions taking place behind the scenes. On 30 July 1974 he recorded a 'very depressing' Cabinet committee on devolution. 'Everyone now getting frightened at what we are doing – Ross, the Scottish secretary, rebuked them all.'[34] Even Wilson was getting cold feet, having failed to realise that Norman Crowther-Hunt[35] had been pressing for legislative (as distinct from administrative) devolution over the past four months. 'Now the PM is desperately trying to torpedo it by refusing to give them any money to do anything with,' wrote Donoughue.[36] And on 17 January 1975 Donoughue recorded an all-day devolution meeting at Chequers, observing that Tony Crosland, Reg Prentice and Eric Varley 'all felt they were on a slippery road towards the break-up of the UK'. He added:

> Ross then came in as Scottish Secretary to say there was no alternative. We were committed . . . Jenkins said he was a 'go-slower' because he 'didn't like the look of the destination'. He was 'afraid of the slippery slope to separatism'. Benn argued that the workers were against devolution because it would break up the UK trade union movement. Short preferred cabinet system, others opposed to either cabinet or committee like the GLC [Greater London

Council]. Short, Crowther-Hunt and Gerry Fowler all disagreed with one another. Everyone was 2:1 against the speed of proceeding . . . Short looking very irritable . . . Short said the committee had agreed his papers in principle; HW backed him trying to railroad it through but others, like Jenkins, made clear their opposition.[37]

What interested Barbara Castle (who was also keeping a diary during this period) about this meeting, was the 'extent to which Willie is now committed to making devolution work, on the sensible principle that, having been overruled in the first place, he wasn't going to get left out on a limb by the doubters now'.[38] But just months before a White Paper finally appeared, the wrangling continued. 'Every so often the meeting dissolved into grumblings of doubt about the whole exercise,' Donoughue wrote of another all-day Cabinet on devolution in September. 'But always Willie Ross stepped in to say it was too late.' He continued:

He had warned them years ago and they would not listen or support him. Now they must live with it. In fact Willie was being Calvinist, rubbing their faces in devolution, holding them wriggling on the hook because they had not listened to his Cassandra warnings earlier. It broke up at around 4 p.m., with Willie Ross booming on about the need to devolve agriculture to Scotland while ministers rushed desperately to the door and down the stairs.[39]

Labour's long-awaited proposals, *Our Changing Democracy: Devolution to Scotland and Wales*, finally appeared in November 1975. It committed the government to assemblies for Wales and Scotland (the latter with 142 members), but excluded the Scottish Development Agency from the new executive's remit. This compromise was too much for the pro-devolution Labour MPs Jim Sillars and John Robertson, who resigned their membership to launch the breakaway Scottish Labour Party.[40] Ross watched Sillars' departure with both disappointment – he had once spoken of his Ayrshire protégé as a future Scottish secretary – and also anger at his disloyalty. When MPs returned to parliament after the Christmas recess they were faced with a four-day debate on the government's proposals. Following an epic demonstration of just how split both Labour and the Conservatives were over the issue, Ross spoke on 19 January, praising Edward Heath's speech in favour of an assembly, and commending his successor's temerity in quoting Burns during her speech against. In particular, the Scottish secretary noted the expression on Tam Galbraith's face when Mrs Thatcher mentioned a legislative assembly:

> But Maggie stood right sair astonish'd,
> Till, by the heel and hand admonish'd,
> She ventur'd forward on the light;
> And, vow! Tam saw an unco sight![41]

Ross's Commons performances often reduced the Tory benches to fits of laughter, and this occasion was no exception. 'We want to retain the political integrity of this country, from which we have all benefited,' he continued. 'I suggest that there is only one thing to do tonight and that is to take note of the White Paper. There will be continuing discussions. There will be exchange of ideas. But we cannot and will not vote for anything which leads us towards separation.'[42] So at least some of Ross's old instincts remained undiminished, although delegates to Labour's Scottish Council began to hear strange words emerge from the Scottish secretary's mouth: 'It's devolution that we want,' he would thunder. 'Not separation.' Many found it difficult to believe that Ross desired either.[43]

So Ross's second throw of the Scottish Office dice found the Scottish secretary with declining authority, overseen by a prime minister who was a shadow of his former self. 'Ross is in some ways an impressive figure – stern and craggy and full of integrity, and trying to be master of the whole field of Scottish affairs,' wrote Donoughue after a meeting in late 1974. 'But he rambled on from subject to subject, and only after a quarter of an hour did he ask us who we were and where we came from.'[44] Always prone to paranoia, Wilson began to grow suspicious of his once staunch Cabinet ally. Harry Ewing had been appointed over Ross's head, as was Robert Hughes[45] and his excitable replacement Frank McElhone, who was added to the Scottish Office team to counter the impression that St Andrew's House was merely the political wing of the Church of Scotland. The Scottish secretary formally objected to McElhone's appointment but was over-ruled by the chief whip Bob Mellish, who was also a Catholic.

The debate over continuing UK membership of the European Community (EC) – which led to the first ever UK referendum in 1975 – also exposed Ross's increasing isolation. He was firmly against, a stance which alienated his natural supporters in Cabinet, who were all pro-marketeers. Ross believed the EC's record on regional development was woeful, while calculating that a negative position would outflank the nationalists. But Ross simply succeeded in annoying the prime minister. 'He [Wilson] then began to get angry,' recalled Donoughue, 'and said that none of the junior ministers who have joined in this [opposition to the EC] will get promotion. He added that Willie Ross and Barbara were "very vulnerable". He said he might promote Brian O'Malley in Castle's place and Bruce Millan instead of Ross at the Scottish Office.'[46]

There was, however, one final triumph for a Scottish secretary nearing the end of his career: the creation of a Scottish Development Agency in 1975. Actually the brainchild of Bruce Millan, Ross routed Treasury opposition and it was established with an enormous budget (£200 million) and wide-ranging powers. The threatened closure of the Chrysler's Linwood plant towards the end of 1975 also revived Ross's old campaigning instincts. He lobbied for substantial financial aid for the plant's workers, but Ross's friend, the industry secretary Eric Varley (who had replaced the unpopular Tony Benn), wanted Chrysler to go bust and threatened to resign if more cash was granted than he considered appropriate. The Scottish secretary responded with his own threat of resignation, creating a tense stand-off in the Cabinet. Wilson, however, wanted closure without losing either Ross or Varley, but deviously appeared to side with the Scottish Office. Ross argued that as Linwood was the only remaining part of the British motor industry located in Scotland, closure would be politically disastrous. He was also unwilling to face the resulting unemployment and was, essentially, pushing for the government to pay whatever it took to keep Chrysler at Linwood. Ross calculated that he would soon be sacked, so thought he 'might as well go out a hero of the Scottish Linwood workers'.[47]

When Wilson announced his surprise resignation in March 1976 speculation was rife that Ross would soon be joining him on the back-benches.[48] Harry Ewing remembers that he planned to pre-empt his inevitable demise by announcing his resignation at that year's conference in Troon. Ewing and Millan helped him write the speech on the evening before Ross was due to address delegates, but when the *Scottish Daily Express* ran a headline declaring 'Ross's Final Fling', he abandoned his plan because he did not want to prove the *Express* story correct. The Labour leadership election presented the Scottish secretary with a tough choice between two centre-right intellectuals (Jenkins and Crosland), Michael Foot and the untrustworthy Callaghan. Sunny Jim won, and therefore Ross's fate was sealed. Bernard, now Lord, Donoughue remembers chatting to the Scottish secretary as he waited outside Callaghan's office to be sacked, along with Barbara Castle, because the 64-year-old prime minister wanted to bring in younger blood.[49]

He was beaming away and was very funny. We had a chat while he waited and he told me he'd been reading of his sacking for years; every time there was a reshuffle the Scottish press would predict his sacking, but he actually believed this time it was true, he thought Jim was really going to sack him. He said

Wilson was really good at handling the Scots, he liked working under Wilson, [but] he didn't feel Jim would have been as good.

'I don't mind going,' added Ross firmly, 'as long as Mabon isn't succeeding me.'[50] According to Ewing, Ross threatened to go public and attack both Callaghan and Mabon if the latter was sent to the Scottish Office. Ewing also told Callaghan that he would not serve under Mabon. It seems the prime minister took these threats seriously, and instead appointed Ross's preferred successor and the clear front-runner, Bruce Millan.[51]

After a total of nearly eight years as Scottish secretary, 'Old Basso Profundo' (as Wilson once called Ross) was almost part of the furniture at St Andrew's, and now New St Andrew's, House (officially opened by the Queen in July 1975). So much so that as workmen fitted out the uncompromisingly modernist structure they scrawled 'Willie's Room' on the walls of the secretary of state's office, even though he was then in opposition. The *Scotsman*'s assessment of Ross was admirably evenhanded:

> If he had combined his attacks on that party's [the SNP] more fanatical aspects with an understanding of the reasonableness of the desire for a measure of self-government, and taken a positive instead of a negative approach to the subject before 1974, his long career as Secretary of State might have ended more happily, for himself as well as for Scotland. He will be missed, by his enemies as well as his friends, as the onerous, yet declining, job passes to Mr Millan.[52]

Even on the back-benches, and led by a man he distrusted, Ross remained terrifically loyal to the party he loved. He even told delegates to the 1977 Scottish conference that devolution had been Labour Party policy since 1945. As Hugo Young put it in the *Sunday Times*, Ross's speech 'rewrote autobiography with a passion that would make even a member of the politburo blush'.[53]

As Scottish secretary, he had been shocked by what he saw as the corrosive activities of diarists in the Cabinet. 'Chiels among you, taking notes,' he would curse (invoking Burns), while joking that Barbara Castle ended each meeting by slamming shut her diary. Arnold Kemp, the late editor of the *Glasgow Herald*, urged Ross to write his memoirs, or at the very least some reflective essays. He refused and produced only one account of his career in the *Scottish Government Yearbook*, which ended with this thought:

> It is a tough post for the expectations of Scots are still "approaching the Archangelic". Few men who have held it have taken any other ministerial

positions offered them. For the Scot it is the top job; any other job would be dull indeed after the hectic, crisis-ridden life as Scotland's Secretary of State. The post has changed beyond all recognition since 1885. The Secretary of State now has a new St. Andrew's House in Edinburgh. His Cabinet status is assured. But has his office a future? Devolution within the United Kingdom is the next logical step. But Scotland's voice will still be needed in the Cabinet of the U.K. government and further afield in Europe.[54]

Ross had very little to do with the devolution referendum in March 1979, but was angry at the wrecking tactics employed by some of his former colleagues. He now kept a low profile, although Callaghan did consider sending him to Africa to report back on the feasibility of a diplomatic conference, and for three years running (1978–80) Ross acted as lord high commissioner to the General Assembly of the Church of Scotland, an appointment he took very seriously.

He accepted a life peerage in 1979 and went to the Lords with his old friend Betty Harvie Anderson. Ross found the atmosphere congenial and never missed a day in the Upper Chamber, from which he railed against the Conservatives once more, particularly over the 'damnable' community charge. He watched with disapproval as some of his former ministers (like Dick Mabon) and Cabinet colleagues (such as Roy Jenkins) defected to the SDP, urging them to stay in the Labour Party to fight their corner, and he no doubt backed Neil Kinnock's stand against the Militant Tendency. Lord Ross's swansong came with the government's Poll Tax legislation in the late 1980s. He tabled hundreds of amendments and basically took the Bill apart, driving the Scottish Office minister Lord Glenarthur to distraction.

Apart from Burns, Ross's main leisure interest was watching football (he became honorary president of the Scottish Football Association in 1978), so it was fitting that his last public appearance was at the Scottish Cup final in May 1988. His years of chain-smoking had finally caught up with him and Ross died at home in Ayr of cancer on 10 June 1988. Ewing remembers that there was very little said at his funeral about his period as Scottish secretary; instead the eulogies focussed on Burns and the Boys' Brigade, of which Ross had been a staunch and lifelong supporter. But for a certain generation of Labour Party members in Scotland, their abiding memory of the longest-serving secretary of state is vivid: a striking figure with light-red hair, strong features, cleft chin and piercing eyes, taking to the podium on the last afternoon of the Scottish conference – be it in Perth, Dunoon or Largs – and railing against the evils of both Conservatism and nationalism; punctuated with quotations from Burns and delivered with a distinctive Ayrshire burr.

GORDON CAMPBELL

19 JUNE 1970 – 5 MARCH 1974

The forgotten Scottish secretary

In 1966 the Marquis of Bute gifted three Robert Adam-designed town-houses in Edinburgh's Charlotte Square to the government in lieu of taxes. Number 6 was quickly earmarked as the secretary of state's 'Number 10', or official residence, with a peppercorn rent of £1 a year.[1] Its first occupant was the Conservative Scottish secretary Gordon Campbell, whose background – like his Victorian predecessor the Marquis of Lothian – was diplomatic, and the Georgian surroundings of Bute House, as it came to be called, no doubt reminded him of the Continental embassies he had known as a young diplomat. He delighted in welcoming guests to his official residence, and journalists still remember an unfortunate remark made by Campbell's wife at one early press soiree: 'It really is very nice having it,' she said. 'It's like having a little embassy in Scotland.'

Officials believed the Foreign Office had left its mark on their new political chief, and, while this made Campbell an easy man to work with from a civil service point of view, it infuriated his elected colleagues. In fact, Campbell was not really a politician at all, and he would often cheerfully admit as much. Now almost completely forgotten (Edward Heath's memoirs do not mention him once), he was at the Scottish Office during a difficult period for both Scotland and the UK, yet he tackled many crises with care and patience, although without the political considerations which came instinctively to Willie Ross.

Gordon Thomas Calthrop Campbell was born on 8 June 1921 at Quetta in India, the son of Major-General James Campbell and his wife, the artist and novelist Violet. He was educated at Wellington, where he prepared for a history scholarship to Christchurch, Oxford. Hitler, however, had other plans and as Europe prepared for war Campbell passed his army exams, entered the Royal Military Academy at Woolwich and, when war broke out, took a concentrated course as a field gunner. He was retained at Woolwich as an instructor, aged just 18. A year later he was captain, and a major by the time he was 21. Campbell was soon in command of the 320 Field Battery in the 15th Scottish Division and became embroiled in some of the fiercest fighting of the war as the Germans retreated after D-Day. Earning the nickname 'Lucky' following two close shaves, he led his division in crossings of the Seine and the Rhine in assault boats.

In 1945, and just a day before Hitler committed suicide, Major Campbell found himself with one more river to cross, the mighty Elbe. Although half a mile wide and thickly wooded on the enemy bank, Major Campbell was in a confident mood as he led the crossing. Within minutes a bullet had smashed through him, severing his sciatic nerve and disabling him for life. 'Here's another bloody Gerry!' shouted one of his rescuers, failing to recognise Campbell beneath the blood and mud. 'That's not a bloody Gerry,' shouted another, having spotted his Military Cross and bar ribbon, 'it's Major Gordon Campbell!' He survived, unlike his brother Ian, a spitfire pilot who was shot after baling out over Italy. VE Day came just three days later, as Campbell was flown back to Britain where he spent more than a year in hospital.

Still on crutches, Campbell took the Foreign Office exam and began his diplomatic career with a desk job in London, dealing with Eastern Europe. He got to know the foreign secretary, Ernest Bevin, and pre-sumably also his deputy, Hector McNeil, and would often wake Bevin during the Berlin Blockade to pass on telegrams. During this period the so-called 'Campbell Solution' was also adopted over Trieste, marking the border between Italy and Yugoslavia. At the Foreign Office he formed a close friendship with Anthony Montague Browne, later Churchill's last private secretary, who remembered Campbell being 'in pain a good deal of the time and partially disabled'. He added, 'This did not stop him being both remarkably efficient and the most jolly and humorous of compa-nions. When he married the attractive and intelligent Nicola Madden, who worked in the Foreign Office, I was his best man and made a terrible botch of it.'[2] Madden counted the great 19th-century engineer and inventor Isambard Kingdom Brunel among her ancestors, as did the former Scottish secretary Michael Noble. The year of their marriage also took the couple to New York City as part of the UK delegation to the United Nations, just before the Korean War. Campbell still needed daily hospital care, a regime which continued in the United States.

After three years he returned to London, first as Foreign Office liaison officer with MI5, MI6 and Government Communications Headquarters, and then as private secretary to the legendary Cabinet secretary Norman Brook. Campbell used to help Churchill prepare for the twice-weekly Prime Minister's Questions in the Commons, impressing the ageing prime minister with his ideas for topical ripostes. He then went to Vienna at the time of the Hungarian uprising for what was to be his last posting before swapping the diplomatic service for active politics. The story goes that James Stuart once bemoaned the lack of suitable successors for his Moray and Nairn constituency after he quit as Scottish secretary in early 1957. Knowing that Campbell's appetite for politics had been whetted during his time at the Cabinet Office, Brook suggested his former private secretary. He was duly adopted, resigned from the Foreign Office and worked in the intellectual hotbed of the Conservative Research Department until the 1959 general election.

After a year on the back-benches, Campbell became a junior Scottish whip, and, having been passed over for promotion to the Scottish Office in 1962, he finally entered St Andrew's House the following year with responsibility for local government and housing.[3] In opposition from 1964, he joined Heath's front-bench (despite having voted for Reginald Maudling in the 1965 leadership contest) first as a shadow defence spokesman, and then replacing Michael Noble as shadow Scottish secretary in 1969.

The 1970 general election was the first at which the Conservatives were accused of having lost their Scottish mandate, with only 38 per cent of the vote and just 23 Scottish MPs. Campbell's relations with Heath were initially good, having come to know each other during the British negotiations to join the EC in 1961. The Scottish secretary, however, preferred the camaraderie of Cabinet colleagues who had been in 'Hitler's War' (Heath had not served in a combat unit). He also got on well with officials at the Scottish Office, particularly the permanent under-secretary, Sir Douglas Haddow, who found his reasonable and non-partisan approach a welcome contrast to the often difficult Willie Ross. When Campbell arrived at St Andrew's House for the first time as secretary of state, some staff had lined the art deco lobby and staircase to applaud him, the rash idea of an over-zealous Scottish Office press officer.[4] The Scottish secretary earned great respect for refusing to let his disability hinder his career; his left leg was permanently in a calliper and he often had to rely on two walking sticks to cover long distances. But although he remained outwardly uncomplaining, the Scottish secretary's lameness frustrated him, while his apolitical instincts made him equally as frustrating to his colleagues.

Campbell inherited many recommendations and Bills from the tail end of Ross's six years at the Scottish Office. Some, like land reform, he ignored; others, such as education, he reversed (restoring certain schools' rights to charge fees); and two – the major structural reforms of health and local government – he enthusiastically pursued. The Royal Commission on Local Government in Scotland, chaired by Lord Wheatley, had reported in 1969, but, as convention demanded, Campbell was not allowed to see his predecessor's planned response. The Scottish secretary broadly supported the general thrust of Wheatley, and by February 1971 he was ready to unveil his proposals, albeit with some concessions to local considerations. Wheatley had proposed a massive West of Scotland regional authority, covering 2.5 million people, and another covering the whole Highland area, as two of seven large regions. He had also recommended a second layer of 37 district councils, including the four cities, which would take up the more local functions. Campbell's White Paper differed in several important respects. Orkney, Shetland and the Western Isles were given separate status as 'island authorities', the Scottish Borders and Fife became regions in their own right after intensive lobbying, while some distinctive Conservative-voting areas on the fringes of Glasgow (such as Bearsden and East Renfrewshire) were kept out of the city's district authority. Wheatley's seven regions therefore became nine, and his 37 districts swelled to 53. On the face of it, the Scottish secretary had thoughtfully reshaped local government according to local desires, but grassroots Conservatives – and some Scottish Tory MPs – were furious, not least because of the new Strathclyde region, smaller than that planned by Wheatley but still guaranteed to consolidate socialist control in the west of Scotland. Campbell was unrepentant, and reasoned in his defence. He was aware that four local authorities – Renfrew, Lanark, Dumbarton and Glasgow itself – had been constantly at odds with each other, primarily over how to manage the dispersal of surplus population from Glasgow. Therefore, Campbell believed, the western region of Scotland needed a much larger authority to take planning and infrastructure decisions for the whole area, thereby avoiding inter-council conflict.

The first elections to the new two-tier councils were held in May 1974, several months after Campbell left the Scottish Office, and Conservative dismay grew as it became clear that the reorganisation had done nothing for the party's prospects in Scottish local government. Otherwise, Campbell's relationship with Scottish local authorities was often traumatic, and sometimes inexplicably remote. The Housing (Financial Provisions) Scotland Act of 1972 caused problems when some Labour-led councils refused to implement its new standard rate subsidy scheme, designed, among other things, to drive up council house rents from the low levels then prevalent in Labour-controlled councils. The Scottish secretary disliked confrontation and initially responded patiently, though eventually resorted to legal action. Default orders were issued until only the councils in Clydebank and Saltcoats persisted. But on local authority control of education, Campbell refused to adopt the then education secretary

Margaret Thatcher's approach of overruling councils which tried to abolish selective schools. He infuriated yet more natural Tory voters by declining to intervene when Glasgow Corporation announced plans to scrap the High School of Glasgow, and watched quietly as Edinburgh proceeded with making the rest of its schools comprehensive.

There was also a tremendous political row in 1972/73 over a proposed new runway at Edinburgh's Turnhouse Airport. It was then a relatively small airport with a single runway, and planes were frequently diverted (often to Glasgow) due to heavy cross-winds. The business lobby had long been pushing for an upgrade but the (largely Conservative) burghers of Cramond were up in arms about the planned route using airspace over their community. There was a public inquiry which produced a rather flawed report recommending against it, but the Conservative MP for West Edinburgh (which included Cramond), Tony Stodart, was appalled when Campbell decided to overturn the report, arguing that the national interest lay in having a second runway. Stodart, by then minister of state at the Ministry of Agriculture, Fisheries and Food, feared losing his seat and the Tory chief whip insisted that the issue come before Cabinet for a final decision.[5] Campbell stuck to his guns and got Cabinet backing. His private secretary remembers being with the Scottish secretary in a car at Cramond when angry residents beat his vehicle with their umbrellas; the perception grew that Campbell was a minister who was content to ignore his own party.

This feeling was also prevalent among the rest of the Scottish Office team. Lady Tweedsmuir, having lost her South Aberdeen seat to Donald Dewar in 1966, was sent to the Lords and returned to St Andrew's House in 1970 as a rather aloof minister of state responsible for agriculture and fisheries. Campbell's three under-secretaries – Alick Buchanan-Smith, who looked after law and order; George Younger, who dealt with industry and planning; and the folksy Teddy Taylor, who oversaw education and health – often wondered what she actually did. This trio were seen by commentators as promising young Conservatives, but two of them found the Scottish secretary both remote and frustrating. Taylor, who soon resigned over Heath's determination to join the EC, regarded Campbell as a helpful 'superior officer';[6] but Younger felt kept out of the loop over local government reform; while Buchanan-Smith and Hector Monro (who replaced Taylor) often resorted to the whips' office in order to find out what Campbell was going to do next. Instead, the permanent under-secretary, Sir Douglas Haddow, emerged as the most influential figure in the Scottish secretary's immediate circle.[7] Younger believed Campbell was in the pocket of the civil service machine, as initiatives of his would often be directly overruled by Sir Douglas. When the 1973 Hardman

Report[8] recommended the dispersal of the Ministry of Defence throughout the UK, Younger got wind of the fact that the defence secretary had minuted the prime minister with several reasons why Glasgow should be ruled out as a possible location. Campbell, however, refused to intervene as he had not officially seen the correspondence. Younger also became a conduit for the grievances of the Scottish Conservative Party. The Scottish secretary hated having to press the flesh at the annual party conference, so instead innumerable complaints reached the much more approachable member of parliament for Ayr. Officials remember that, at times, the Scottish Office relied upon Younger and Buchanan-Smith as its friendly face.

Some Cabinet colleagues, such as Mrs Thatcher, also held Campbell in very low regard. This was evident when in 1973 Campbell was due to wind up in a debate on museum charges, as it was a cross-border issue. He thought (like Heath, but, surprisingly, unlike Mrs Thatcher at that time) that there should be charges made, but when it looked as if the government would be defeated Thatcher decided to offer concessions, a U-turn which found its way into the *Evening Standard* on the day of the debate. No one had informed the Scottish secretary, and when his private secretary tracked the education secretary down in her office he asked what his minister was expected to say. 'Well,' said Thatcher dismissively, 'he'll just have to stand up and muddle his way through – same as he always does!'[9] Campbell did indeed muddle through, but he lacked presence in the House of Commons and dealt badly with the taunts of Ross and other Labour MPs. The late Hamish Gray, then the Scottish whip, remembered travelling with Campbell and finding him frustrated not by his standing in parliament or in the party, but by his disability. 'There were so many things he wanted to do but couldn't do,' Gray recalled. '[He] repeatedly said to me that one of the things that he felt most at the end of the war was not being able to play sport again.'[10] Gray felt that for Campbell, the Second World War had left an indelible mark.

The Kilbrandon Royal Commission on the Constitution finally reported at the end of October 1973, recommending a directly elected Scottish Assembly as well as major changes in Wales and Northern Ireland. The Conservatives, to varying degrees, had already reached the same conclusion. But as the report was published just as the government was limbering up for its ultimately unsuccessful battle with the miners, it received little media attention.

When Ross dug in his heels following the SNP's stunning win at Hamilton in 1967, moderate Tories had begun years of soul-searching over their response. An association of younger, centrist Conservatives –

including Malcolm Rifkind and Michael Ancram – came together the same year under the 'Thistle Group' banner. They began to examine the case for a Scottish Assembly, as did Sir William McEwan Younger for the party as a whole. Both reported favourably the following year, and, influenced by this, the Conservative leader Edward Heath made his Declaration of Perth – pledging to establish some kind of assembly – at the Scottish party conference in 1968. Heath then established a Scottish Constitutional Committee under Sir Alec Douglas-Home, which reported just months before the 1970 election. Home advocated an indirectly elected Scottish Convention with 125 members, and in May, conference delegates backed his proposals by a three to one majority. It therefore became a manifesto pledge, although with the caveat that local government reform would take precedence. The Queen's Speech following Heath's victory stated that the government would give the Scottish people a greater say over their own affairs, and from then until late 1973 the Scottish secretary was persistently pressed at Scottish Questions to say when proposals would be forthcoming. Campbell, not unreasonably given the manifesto pledge, stuck to the line about tackling local government reform first, while stating that 'Proposals on constitutional reform are intended during this Parliament and will precede any legislation on that subject.'[11] Even a threat from the veteran Scottish nationalist Wendy Wood to 'fast until death' did not spur Heath or his Scottish secretary into naming the day. 'I am extremely concerned about Miss Wood's health,' Campbell told MPs. 'I have managed to get messages through to her which I think have corrected her original misunderstanding. I hope that what I have said about a Green Paper coming forward at the appropriate time will meet her wishes.'[12] Following a televised appeal from Jim Sillars, Wood called off her hunger strike, but by the early 1970s the constitution of the UK was on the verge of great change.

In 1973, Northern Ireland's Stormont Assembly was suspended and direct rule imposed from Westminster. Control of the province's affairs was wrestled away from the home secretary, just as those of Scotland had been nearly 90 years before, and vested in a new Northern Ireland Office with the Scots-born Willie Whitelaw as its first secretary of state. The Cabinet now had a trio of territorial ministers, representing Scotland, Wales and the troubled six counties of Ulster. But even if Campbell had wanted to act sooner, the Conservative grassroots would have made things very difficult for him. At the 1973 Conservative Scottish conference in Perth, a proposal calling on the government to reaffirm its commitment to a semi-independent Scottish parliament was heavily defeated by a show of hands. An alliance of Young Conservative delegates and the South Aberdeen MP Iain Sproat (also Campbell's parliamentary private secretary) led an attempt to kill off any commitment to devolution. Campbell's speech after the result was rambling, and when Heath spoke the following Saturday he did not even mention his previous commitment to devolution, by now distracted by a miners' strike and a three-day week. The Scottish secretary argued that as the Local Government (Scotland) Act had only just come into effect when Kilbrandon reported there was no longer sufficient time for a consultation and legislation in that parliament. However, he said, a Bill would be forthcoming in the next. Ross pilloried what he called 'Grim Gordon's Fairy Tale', and sure enough a Conservative-created Scottish Assembly vanished into the ether when Heath failed to secure an overall majority in the February 1974 snap poll. Thirty years later Campbell still maintained that Heath's second government would have kept its word:

> If we had won in 1974 – [and] we only just lost it – if we'd won there's no doubt we'd have gone on with the next stage, which would have been very widely consulted, but we'd the idea of some form of assembly as recommended by the Home committee. That was what was in the plan but all that has been overwritten by what some people think good and what some people think bad.[13]

With drilling in the North Sea beginning in the early 1970s, cries of 'It's Scotland's Oil' – perhaps the SNP's most effective ever slogan – were ringing in Unionist ears and panicking some civil servants at the Treasury and Department of Trade and Industry (DTI).[14] While the Scottish secretary's Conservative predecessors had not hesitated in accepting some responsibility for Scotland's industrial base, Campbell's rigid sense of formal departmental boundaries led him to defer unequivocally over both industrial policy and oil exploration. He was also more hands-off than Ross when it came to regional planning. In December 1970 Campbell dropped the 'Planning' portion of the Scottish Economic Planning Council (although oddly he was to create a Scottish Economic Planning Department in the Scottish Office two years later) and made George Younger deputy chairman. He also secured a Scottish Industrial Development Office in Glasgow, which could dole out development grants without reference to Whitehall, but which was answerable to a minister at the DTI. Ross attacked the Scottish secretary's lack of influence, a perception which increased when an Offshore Oil Supplies Office cropped up in Glasgow, but again under the care of John Davies, the businessman-turned-trade and industry secretary.

The Whitehall view was that Campbell and the Scottish Office were needlessly stalling oil exploration projects through Scotland's overly bureaucratic planning process. One example of this was the proposal to construct a site for building oil-production platforms at Drumbeat on the Ross-shire coast. The site was owned by the National Trust for Scotland, which feared a detrimental impact on the ruggedly beautiful coastline and campaigned against the acquisition of land given 'inalienably' to the Trust. A public inquiry dragged on while Campbell came under increasing pressure from Heath and the DTI, including snide criticisms that his passion for ornithology clouded his judgement when it came to environmental considerations. Douglas Hurd,[15] then Heath's political adviser, would often lunch with executives from BP, and afterwards send the prime minister a note saying that oil would flow freely if only the Scots would get off their backs with all these planning laws. Heath would then minute Campbell asking why these laws were being allowed to hold up the balance of payments problem, and the Scottish secretary would respond defensively, saying, accurately, that many sites had already been approved without recourse to a public inquiry, the planning system in Scotland was no different in essence from that in England, and that he was doing his best.

In the middle of 1973 Heath drafted into government another businessman, this time Lord Polwarth, as an additional minister of state at the Scottish Office, to deal with North Sea oil development and chair the advisory Oil Development Council for Scotland. Polwarth was a former governor of the Bank of Scotland and a surprisingly effective speaker in the Lords, but, like Campbell, he did not have a political bone in his body. The formation of a Department of Energy under Lord Carrington shortly before the first election of 1974 just made matters worse, with several government departments now battling for control of oil development. Carrington produced a Bill which allowed the state to acquire land urgently needed for the construction of oil platforms (and bypass planning laws), but the Scottish secretary opposed it on a point of principle.

Campbell always regarded his greatest achievement as fast-tracking the construction of the A9 from the Central Belt to the Moray Firth, but even that was buried beneath the bitter industrial strife which gripped Scotland and the UK throughout the 1970s. His relationship with the Scottish Trades Union Congress was uneasy, although ironically not as bad as that of his predecessor in terms of access, and the Scottish secretary infuriated trade unionists by saying that the upward trend of unemployment in Scotland was 'worrying, though not unexpected'.[16] Matters came to a head in mid 1971 when the Upper Clyde Shipbuilders consortium ran into financial difficulties. It had faced liquidation in May 1969 with the immediate loss of thousands of jobs. Ross secured more than £3 million in aid, while Tony Benn merged the four private shipyards to become UCS. Campbell shared Heath's belief that 'lame-duck' industries should not be bailed out, although the dispute was actually handled by the DTI. There was an emergency debate on 2 August when John Davies sparked uproar by describing Benn as 'the evil genius of shipbuilding'. Campbell could barely be heard above the noise as he tried for 15 minutes to wind up the debate, adding to the furore by telling Benn that he had been acting like a demagogue.[17] Davies eventually announced a £35 million package of aid after Campbell lobbied quietly behind the scenes. He also had to contend with another crisis involving the collapse of Rolls Royce, which had factories in Scotland, although by then Heath's monetarist manifesto was beginning to unravel and he suddenly became sentimental about lame ducks. Prior to his U-turn, the prime minister had bombarded the Scottish secretary with memos urging him to break up the CalMac ferry monopoly and give the private sector a chance, including the shipbuilder Sir William Lithgow, a close contact of Heath who was the driving force behind the Western Ferries then operating to Islay. Campbell agreed there should be more competition, but feared the public service and electoral consequences of appearing to fragment CalMac. By the end of 1973 civil servants at the Scottish Office, as in Whitehall generally, were literally working by candlelight during the three-day week, and Heath's managerial (some might say bureaucratic) approach to government was beginning to run out of steam.

Shortly before Heath decided to call a snap election on the basis of 'Who Governs Britain?', he filled a gap at the Scottish Office (created by Younger's move to the Ministry of Defence) by bringing back the ebullient Teddy Taylor. Officials were used to his familiar refrain of 'I'll just have a wee release' (press, not toiletry) from his brief stint as education under-secretary until he resigned in 1971. Heath wanted him to shake things up in St Andrew's House, and also help run the Conservative's Scottish election campaign.[18] This was a slap in the face to Campbell, especially given that his Welsh counterpart had been deemed worthy of a similar role in the principality. But even Taylor's brash populism could not salvage the decaying urban Tory vote, and the three-week campaign did not go well. The nationalist commentator Douglas Young wrote that the Scottish secretary had 'made little impact on public opinion; he seems, indeed, to have little or no empathy with ordinary Scots folk'.[19] His profile also remained low, and Campbell's disdain for local politics had led him to neglect his constituency, although less in dealing with constituents' problems than in visible campaigning.[20] 'The trouble with the job is that everyone appreciates what you have done, but not until ten years afterwards,' Campbell told a *Times* journalist more than a week before polling day. 'The Secretary of State has a kind of Aunt Sally post,' he continued. 'He is in the headlines every day in Scotland, but seldom features south of the border.' The Scottish secretary also rejected the analysis that North Sea oil had lubricated Scottish nationalism, telling his interviewer that the SNP had reached its peak two years ago.[21] It was therefore ironical that on 29 February 1974 Campbell was defeated by the SNP candidate in Moray and Nairn with a 13 per cent swing, which was largely attributed to local concerns about the perceived adverse effect of the Common Fisheries Policy. His constituents had decided to 'Win with Winnie' rather than return the stiff and awkward Scottish secretary, who had refused to take part in any election fray he deemed inappropriate for a minister of the Crown. Campbell's lack of political judgement also surfaced when in his televised post-count speech he said that his defeat was a vote against the disabled.[22]

Campbell was devastated at being out of parliament, but travelled back to London and sat in his Dover House office, gazing out of the window while Heath conducted fruitless negotiations with the Liberals. When their leader, Jeremy Thorpe, rejected Heath's terms, Campbell was told to hand over his seals of office at Buckingham Palace. But his official driver failed to turn up and he had to drive himself to the palace in his own car. 'As I said on the telephone please do not have the Palace car on your conscience,' Campbell later wrote to his former private secretary Peter Mackay. 'I realise what must have happened and of course it would not have happened with Daphne [his usual driver]. The Police and others at the Palace thought that the mini was most appropriate for this final crisis.'[23]

Campbell was eventually given a peerage and moved to the more congenial surroundings of the House of Lords as Lord Campbell of Croy in 1974. The loss of his seat and ministerial salary had drastically reduced Campbell's income, so he became a diligent peer and Conservative front-bencher, speaking for the opposition on Scotland, industry, energy and EC affairs. And having failed to establish a commission to investigate discrimination against people with disabilities through a private member's bill in 1968, Lord Campbell tried again in 1982 when he steered his Disabled Persons Bill through the Upper House. For this, and his 1981 paper *Disablement in the UK, Problems and Perspectives*, he was awarded the first Nuffield Trust Queen Elizabeth the Queen Mother Fellowship. Its publication was a significant event at a time when disability discrimination issues were not yet in the political mainstream. Lord Campbell also became a patron of the National Schizophrenia Society, campaigning for better understanding of the condition, and was a creative practitioner in the art of asking parliamentary questions, covering everything from the extermination of Highland midges to security arrangements in pet shops. He was active in the Lords well into the new millennium but the constant travelling between his home in Nairnshire and the House of Lords took its toll on his health, and he died on 26 April 2005 in London, aged 83, almost exactly 60 years after he was shot crossing the River Elbe. John Biffen paid tribute to a 'man with an engaging lack of flamboyance',[24] while officials remembered a largely forgotten Scottish secretary. When asked in 2002 how he viewed his career, he said, 'Well I hoped I might have graduated to become a statesman at the end of my time, but I was a parliamentarian, and I don't think I was ever a politician, though I had to indulge in politics.'[25] Campbell was at least aware of his shortcomings in the political arena, but he deserves credit for refusing to bow to party pressure over key decisions when a lesser man would have buckled. He was out of kilter with the Selsdon Man[26] of the era, but was a good man who did his best during a difficult time in British politics, when the tide had begun to turn strongly against the Conservatives, and especially in Scotland.

BRUCE MILLAN

8 APRIL 1976 – 5 MAY 1979

The accountant

With the outgoing Labour secretary, Willie Ross, having won the battle over his successor, a disappointed Dick Mabon ended a long stretch on the back-benches and went to the Department of Energy as minister of state, while James Callaghan promoted Bruce Millan to become secretary of state for Scotland. He was well known at the Scottish Office having served as an under-secretary with Ross in the late 1960s, and, more recently, as minister of state since 1974. Many civil servants thought he behaved more like an auditor than a policy-maker, and the *Scotsman* hailed his appointment with the less than flattering headline, 'Bruce Millan: Dependable Heir Without Charisma'.

Millan came to the Scottish Office as Labour's precarious majority dwindled almost monthly and the party desperately tried to reach a compromise over the Scotland and Wales Bill, expected after the Easter recess. Importantly, he did not share his predecessor's antipathy towards Scottish home rule. 'Not that he is wildly enthusiastic about devolution,' noted the *Scotsman*. 'Bruce Millan is not wildly enthusiastic about any-thing. But he is efficient, with an ability quietly to master difficult detail, to grasp the essentials of a problem and reach a decision without fuss.'[1]

Bruce Millan was born on 5 October 1927 in Dundee, the son of David Millan, a shipyard worker. He was educated at the city's Harris Academy and trained as a chartered accountant, coming top of his class at college and working in Glasgow from 1950 until he entered parliament in 1959. Millan had unsuccessfully contested West Renfrewshire in 1951,[2] and the Craigton Division of Glasgow in 1955, but won the latter on his second attempt four years later. His election address in 1959 was typically cautious: 'I do not myself see any compelling reason for a separate Scottish Parliament, but I have by no means a closed mind on the matter.' Millan later opened his mind and came to support the case for an assembly, although he was not obviously pro-devolution until the late 1960s.[3]

Millan's first ministerial job was at the Ministry of Defence as under-secretary for the RAF, and after the 1966 general election he moved to the Scottish Office to take charge of education under Ross, with whom he was almost alone in getting along well. The Scottish Education Department provided a showcase for Millan's daunting ability with numbers; he once dazzled officials during negotiations with striking teachers by producing an array of statistics without reference to his briefing notes. He did not sparkle in the Commons but could argue a case in a manner which was difficult for the opposition to attack. After four years in opposition, Millan returned to the Scottish Office with Ross in 1974, this time as minister of state. He threatened to resign with the Scottish secretary over the Chrysler crisis in late 1975, but, when that dispute died down and as Ross's natural heir, he replaced him as Scottish secretary on 8 April, aged 48, giving Callaghan some of the younger blood he was said to desire in Cabinet.

While he was popular with colleagues, Millan lacked the instinctive leadership abilities which had served Ross well over the last 14 years. He was also not particularly close to Callaghan. Although Millan backed him in preference to Harold Wilson in 1963, he had voted for Denis Healey following Wilson's resignation in March 1976. On the other hand, the Rutherglen MP Gregor Mackenzie, now minister of state, was friendly with the new prime minister, having been his parliamentary private secretary at the Treasury and Home Office in the 1960s. Mackenzie and Millan were a very different combination to that of Millan and Ross, but they liked each other and worked well together. The more ebullient Mackenzie did the charming legwork while the Scottish secretary buried his head in the detail. Civil servants remember him working incredibly hard to understand his brief to a depth unheard of in other ministers, but Millan's shy and often solitary approach also meant he formed no natural power base within the Labour Party.

Officials accustomed to being consulted on almost everything by Ross suddenly found themselves reduced to nothing more than messengers, while the Scottish secretary also had a tendency to treat his under-secretaries like office boys, although allowing them greater autonomy than did Ross. Harry Ewing remained from Ross's team, as did Frank McElhone (whose – sometimes unrealistically – creative ideas on health and housing did not find an enthusiastic reception among officials), the Glasgow Provan MP Hugh Brown,[4] and the second minister of state, Lord Kirkhill.[5] But the Scottish secretary had great integrity and was tremendously loyal, always supporting his junior ministers, however wayward. Ewing, a great supporter of Millan, found that he delegated tasks better than his predecessor, and also allowed ministers to answer written questions in their own names, a courtesy Ross never sanctioned.[6]

He was unlucky to inherit the Scottish Office in the dying days of a Labour government under the command of a prime minister without an electoral mandate. The divisive issue of devolution dominated Millan's three years as Scottish secretary, often dwarfing other, more enduring, reforms that emanated from New St Andrew's House.

Labour's devolution plans were by now under the care of Michael Foot, the leader of the House and lord president of the council. He was the best Commons performer of his generation and well versed in the historical background to the home rule debate, but he was never really au fait with modern Scottish politics. A young advocate called John Smith, to whom Millan was close, did the legwork in both parliament and at the Cabinet Office Constitution Unit.[7] The Scotland and Wales Bill appeared in November 1976 and immediately ran into difficulties. It was attacked as costly and bureaucratic, bearing the marks of much Whitehall in-fighting among ministers and departments reluctant to see power devolved from Westminster, and it was greeted by a marked lack of enthusiasm among MPs, many of whom had moved from apathy to antipathy when it came to devolution. It helped Labour that the Bill's publication also threw the Conservative front-bench into disarray, later leading to several resignations, but it divided both main parties and attracted mischievous amendments from all sides of the House.

Unlike Labour's previous White Paper, the Scotland and Wales Bill retained the posts of Welsh and Scottish secretaries, and established two rival executives, one controlled by the Assembly's first secretary, and the other closely constrained by the secretary of state. The latter was to exercise a veto over Assembly legislation not deemed to be in the public interest, while control of the Scottish Development Agency and the Highlands and Islands Development Board would rest with the Scottish executive, but not come within the legislative remit of the Assembly. Callaghan had never viewed devolution with enthusiasm and found it difficult to make convincingly positive noises about the Bill. Bernard Donoughue, still at the Policy Unit even after the departure of Wilson, detected this and sent the prime minister a memo ('Scotland and Mr. Millan') urging him to be more positive about devolution. He also said Millan should inject some energy into the Scottish Office, which gave the impression of being an Anglicising influence, more focused on 'Tory Edinburgh than Labour Glasgow'.[8] Callaghan did give the Bill his blessing but, with a majority of only 11, even prime ministerial support could not guarantee the Bill's progress. Although the vote asking the House to note the White Paper was carried by 295 votes to 37 (the antis being a rag-bag of Tories, Ulster Unionists and one Labour MP), it had a rough reception and, despite the government conceding to a referendum at its Second Reading, an active group of Welsh and Scottish Labour back-benchers rejected the timetable motion by 312 votes to 283 on 22 February 1977. The debate languished, and the cumbersome and unpopular Scotland and Wales Bill effectively fell.

Beyond the lame duck of devolution, the eclectic world of the Scottish Office carried on more or less as normal. Millan, like Ross, had his share of crises, industrial disputes and tension with local authorities (never purely a Conservative problem in the Scottish context). He was criticised by a Scottish judge within weeks of becoming secretary of state for exercising the Royal Prerogative of Mercy to release Patrick Meehan, a Glaswegian accused of murder seven years earlier,[9] and in 1978 Millan led a parliamentary battle to sack Sheriff Peter Thompson,[10] who had infuriated the legal establishment by campaigning for a devolution referendum. A more positive development in the judicial arena was the Community Service by Offenders (Scotland) Act of 1978, a measure very much ahead of its time and still a live issue. On housing, the Scottish secretary asked each local authority to draw up a five-year plan beginning in 1978/79, while retiring teachers, marriage, and town and country planning all received legislative attention.

Millan remembers feeling 'hampered' by devolution and being unable to push aggressively on other measures because the two Scotland Bills took up so much parliamentary time, but perhaps his most enduring measure was a marked shift away from urban development (like New Towns) towards urban renewal. The Scottish Development Agency (SDA) had been Millan's brainchild, and he was determined to use it to regenerate decaying parts of Scotland's cities. The Glasgow East End Area Renewal project designated a large swathe of the city's eastern portion as a regeneration area, with funds reallocated from an abandoned New Town at Stonehouse. Plans were drawn up to clear derelict sites, renovate old tenements and promote industrial development, but Glasgow District Council was not keen, preferring to take the lead itself, while things became even more difficult when the Conservatives won control of the authority in 1977. Physically it was a success, with most of the demolition completed while Millan was still at the Scottish Office, but economically it was less so. Clydebank also received cash through the SDA and the Scottish secretary's meticulous attention, as did his native Dundee (e.g. at Discovery Point) and Leith in Edinburgh, perhaps the most successful (long-term) of them all. Urban renewal stalled briefly with the loss of the 1979 election, but soon reappeared in Glasgow, Edinburgh, Paisley and Dundee, and in Liverpool, under the theatrical auspices of Michael Heseltine.

Millan's ability to analyse figures proved useful during seemingly constant Treasury negotiations, as the Scottish Office fought to save the Clyde shipyards and subsidise Scottish coal prices for electricity generators to the tune of £35 million. 'With devolution a dead duck,' sneered *The Economist*, 'Labour fell back on its traditional way of keeping its grip on Scotland: buying votes by propping up its declining industries.'[11]

Millan struck up a special relationship with Joel Barnett, then chief secretary to the Treasury and, like the Scottish secretary, a former accountant. Barnett trusted him with figures and officials reckon Millan got things agreed with the Treasury much more quickly than other ministers as a result. The Millan-Barnett partnership also produced the so-called 'Barnett formula' in 1978, not actually a formula at all but rather the mundane result of annual spending talks, not to mention the men in grey suits (from the International Monetary Fund) demanding cuts in government expenditure. Millan cannot remember if he or Barnett suggested it, but, rather than make corresponding cuts in his department which reflected those in English ministries, they agreed to a proportion of spending increases or reductions which gave 85 per cent to England, ten per cent to Scotland and five to Wales. This was based on population rather than need, but it allowed the Scottish secretary to distribute savings or increases which accrued to the Scottish 'Block' according to Scotland's needs. The 'formula' was only supposed to last for one year (1978/79), but when George Younger replaced Millan he realised that it prevented traumatic annual negotiations and retained it.

Civil servants say there are two types of minister: those who like everything to be down on paper, and those who prefer talking about things. Millan was very much disposed to the former, preferring to work through his papers, often sent up to his Commons office using a dumbwaiter system.[12] Callaghan's Scottish secretary was shy and hard-working with an often difficult private life, and the last two years of his time at the Scottish Office were to be two of the most dramatic in Scottish politics.

'History repeats itself,' said Marx, 'first as tragedy, then as farce.' An apt description of Labour's two devolution Bills of the late 1970s. The history being repeated was that of Irish home rule, the Gladstonian dream which had so often ended in defeat during the 1880s and 1890s, only this time the political splits were not among Liberals, but the Conservatives and Labour. Even Michael Foot's eloquent pleas for his comrades not to repeat the mistakes of the past could not prevent the government's second Bill, this time affecting Scotland only (there was another for Wales), from running into almost immediate problems. The Scotland Bill appeared in late 1977, and on 14 November Millan moved its Second Reading with a competent, yet technocratic, speech:

> We cannot deal with these different characteristics and diversities of the Scottish situation by continuing to pile more and more powers on to the Secretary of State for Scotland. From that point of view, we have almost reached the end of the road. If we are not to pile yet more powers on the Secretary of State, the most sensible and satisfactory way in which we can meet the legitimate needs of the Scottish people is to set up an Assembly, as provided for in this Bill.[13]

Earlier that year, Callaghan had negotiated what became known as the Lib-Lab pact with the young Liberal leader David Steel, also a Scot. The deal came before Cabinet and Millan visibly surprised Callaghan by joining four other Cabinet ministers in voting against it. 'Bruce is a chartered accountant, quiet and steady,' wrote Tony Benn later, 'and, though his instincts are mainly cautious, he has something of a radical streak.'[14] Liberal support was crucial to the government, but even the pro-Assembly Steel and co. could not give the Scotland Bill an easy ride at its committee stage. Millan and John Smith were both very good on the detail of the Bill, and used to meet each morning in the office of Michael Foot, who was not. They would go over the previous day's events, then those presently before them, firming up the relevant 'line' and calculating likely levels of support. This was vital preparation, as on 28 January 1978 a group of Labour back-benchers conspired to pass an amendment which effectively killed devolution. The Cunningham amendment (named after George Cunningham, the expatriate Scottish Labour MP for Islington South and Finsbury) insisted that 40 per cent of the total electorate had to back an Assembly in the referendum, not merely a majority of those voting.[15] It passed with a majority of 26, which included a young Edinburgh MP called Robin Cook, who had long opposed devolution. And just minutes later, the former Liberal leader (and home ruler) Jo Grimond successfully moved an amendment which exempted majority no-voting parts of his Orkney and Shetland constituency from the devolved Assembly's remit.[16] Smith was confident that Cunningham's amendment would be defeated, but the abrasive and difficult Cunningham caught the mood of the House and spoke well without notes. Otherwise, an unholy alliance of Conservatives and unreconstructed Labour back-benchers (like Tam Dalyell), particularly those from the north of England, had basically set out to make sure that devolution would not happen. Millan was irritated, but believed turnout would be sufficiently good to meet the threshold.

There were also problems in Cabinet. Callaghan, who sat for a Welsh constituency, remained unenthusiastic, while Shirley Williams opposed anything which impinged upon her department (the now long-defunct Prices and Consumer Protection). But despite the defeats, four in all during the Committee Stage, the government pledged not to reverse them at the Third Reading.

The Scottish local government elections of May 1978 gave Labour reasons to be cheerful, gaining as many seats as the SNP lost. Labour also held on at three Scottish by-elections that year: George Robertson easily winning in Hamilton; Donald Dewar returning to parliament via Garscadden; and John Home Robertson succeeding the devolutionist academic John P. Mackintosh in Berwick and East Lothian. The contentious issue of abortion came up during the Garscadden campaign, as it had done at the previous year's Scottish party conference. Dewar was pro-choice, and there was controversy over whether the issue would fall under the Assembly's control. Labour's Scottish general secretary, Helen Liddell, became nervous – particularly when several Catholic priests began denouncing Labour from their pulpits – and contacted the governmental adviser Bernard Donoughue in London. He went to see Millan, who told him, 'There's no problem; it's not in the newspapers.'[17] But when Donoughue held up that day's *Glasgow Herald*, which carried the story on its front page, the Scottish secretary eventually changed his tune.

Millan believed that Labour's trio of by-election wins made an early October general election much more likely, but by the end of 1978 the so-called Winter of Discontent had started to grip the country. Millan argued against further spending cuts in Cabinet, saying they would only increase unemployment, and when the strikes began he found most of his time taken up with trade union meetings in London, as the minister responsible for the political aspect of industrial relations north of the border. Prices and incomes policy also weighed heavily on the Scottish secretary's time, as did a planned cull of some 4,000 grey seal pups to reduce population levels, the symbolism of which was hardly positive as Scots prepared for both a referendum and a general election. The first poll was on 1 March 1979, by which time Scotland's criminal justice system had also ground to a halt due to industrial action. Except for emergencies like murder charges, the High Court, Court of Session and all 49 Sheriff Courts were closed for several weeks over a pay dispute. Ross Harper, a moderate Tory and former president of the Glasgow Bar Association, telegraphed the prime minister to warn him, 'Justice is non-existent. We are approaching anarchy and law and order will break down in Scotland.'[18] On 20 March Millan moved the Second Reading of the Administration of Justice (Emergency Provisions) (Scotland) Bill. This suspended all legal time limits (like the 110–day rule) and allowed judges to do the work of their striking clerks. The Scottish secretary personally appealed to the strikers to call off their action, but all he got in response were accusations of trying to push through 'a strike breaker's charter'.[19]

Meanwhile, Millan also had to cope with the fallout from the referendum earlier that month. There had been a 63.8 per cent turnout, and although 51.6 per cent of those voting backed the Scotland Bill, 48.4 per cent voted no, and therefore the Cunningham threshold was not reached. The campaign had not gone well, with Labour having refused to join an umbrella 'yes' group (Liddell said it would amount to 'soiling our hands'), while the Tory-led 'no' campaign was seen to have had a good run. There were also problems with the electoral register, while the industrial climate had encouraged already apathetic voters to remain at home. Millan was a realist, and knew that a majority of only three per cent hardly amounted to a ringing endorsement of a bold new devolutionary age. The Scotland Act obliged him to bring forward an order-in-council to repeal the legislation, but he pledged publicly not to abandon the policy. In April the government lost a SNP-inspired vote of no confidence by just one vote, prompted by Callaghan's 'wait and see' statement on the future of the Scotland Act on 22 March.[20] The prime minister got his revenge by memorably comparing the nationalists with turkeys voting for an early Christmas.[21] Millan promised to double the SDA's budget during the ensuing election campaign, but, while Labour increased its number of Scottish seats to 44, it lost overall to the Conservatives led by Margaret Thatcher. Almost her first duty was to move the repeal of the Scotland Act just weeks after entering Downing Street. Sir William Kerr Fraser, who had become permanent under-secretary in April 1978, and Millan, now shadow Scottish secretary, watched in melancholy silence as an issue which had dominated parliament for the past five years was expunged from the statute books.

Callaghan continued as Labour leader for another year after his defeat, while Millan remained on the opposition front-bench until the 1983 general election. He had never been a Euro-enthusiast, but when Callaghan's successor Neil Kinnock suggested that Millan go to Europe as one of the UK's two commissioners he quickly agreed. Like Kinnock's own eventual conversion to Continental unity, this was an ironic move. Roy Jenkins recalls in his memoirs a meeting of the Parliamentary Labour Party on 3 November 1971. Jenkins had not yet declared his position as Edward Heath prepared to join the EC, and so 'an unflamboyant chartered accountant' decided to challenge the future commission president over his views. 'I thought him nice but pedestrian,' wrote Jenkins, 'which shows the danger of taking patronising views.'[22] Nevertheless, in 1988 Millan resigned his Glasgow Govan seat (which he had won five years previously) and set off for Brussels, sparking a by-election which returned the nationalist-convert Jim Sillars to parliament. With its paperwork, abundance of figures and backroom nature, Millan was in his element. He served a seven-year term and returned to Glasgow in 1995, but kept a curiously low political profile. Millan was uninvolved in the run up to the creation of the Scottish parliament in 1999, but won praise for his chairmanship of a committee which investigated mental health law in Scotland, producing a typically comprehensive and thoughtful report, *New Directions*, in January 2001.[23]

GEORGE YOUNGER

5 MAY 1979 – 11 JANUARY 1986

Gentleman George

While the similarities between George Younger's tenure as Scottish secretary and that of his great-great uncle, Sir John Gilmour, must surely be coincidental, they are nonetheless remarkable. Both tried to protect Scotland from spending cuts, both embarked on unpopular reforms of local government, and both tackled rating reform (although with different outcomes). The parallels did not begin at Dover House. Both men were heavily shaped by their army experiences, Sir John by the Second Boer War, and Younger by Korea, and they also had in common a famously charming manner which was calculated to ease their political paths. Younger, however, had considerably more personality than his rather bland relative, positively exuding bonhomie to everyone he encountered. But, despite his undisputed abilities and charm, he was bemused and a little shocked to find himself at the Scottish Office following the 1979 general election. Just a few years earlier he had not even spoken on Scotland from the front-bench, but the resignation of the shadow Scottish secretary Alick Buchanan-Smith over devolution, followed by the surprising defeat of his ebullient successor Teddy Taylor in Glasgow Cathcart,[1] meant that Younger was to be Mr Scotland.

'He's a classic old-time Tory paternalist,' remarked a colleague, 'with noblesse oblige to the poor.'[2] Younger was living proof that nice people could get on in modern politics. Unlike some contemporaries, his charm, friendliness and moderate language were all completely genuine. He came to the Scottish Office determined not to repeat the mistakes of his Conservative predecessor, Gordon Campbell, whom he had served under nine years earlier, and he immediately made it clear to his junior ministers that he would delegate with confidence, and support them in whatever decisions they made. Younger was close to heavyweights like Willie Whitelaw,[3] Geoffrey Howe, Jim Prior and Peter Walker, all of whom would support him in Cabinet, and he handled the prime minister cleverly, delivering just enough of what she expected, while subtly neglecting the policies he regarded as unpalatable. Younger also arrived at Dover House determined to reform the rates, as a revaluation loomed which he knew would impact most on Scotland's 21 Conservative seats.

Whether Younger was aware of his great-great uncle's record in office is doubtful, as he was only a boy when Sir John died, but he would certainly have passed Sir James Guthrie's splendid full-length portrait of Gilmour in Dover House. There was one more parallel: both were Conservative Scottish secretaries who managed to move on to other departments – Sir John to the Home Office and Younger to the Ministry of Defence. Gilmour was Scotland's first post-'45 secretary of state; his great-nephew was to become its longest continually serving secretary. When the Scottish Office celebrated its centenary, Younger's colleagues presented him with a silver-gilt miniature replica of a bed of nails. It was a fitting, and amusing, gift for that rare creature, a Conservative Scottish secretary who inspired both respect and affection in his native land.

Journalists often joked that George Kenneth Hotson Younger was a product of the 'beerage', a combined reference to the family viscountcy and brewery business. The first Viscount Younger of Leckie, previously the Ayr Burghs MP George Younger, had been an instrumental figure in the Carlton Club meeting of 1922, which saw the Conservatives withdraw from a Lloyd-George-led coalition government and a powerful chairman of the Scottish Unionists, for which the hereditary title was a reward. His great-grandson George was born in Stirling on 22 September 1931, just after Ramsay MacDonald formed his National government. He was educated at Cargilfield School in Edinburgh, and later Winchester (as was his equally well-mannered uncle, Kenneth Younger, who became a Labour MP and minister).[4] As a teenager Younger lost one finger on his left hand in a shooting accident, but at 19 he did his national service with the Argyll and Sutherland Highlanders and was posted to Korea in the early 1950s. He survived as a platoon leader, became a lieutenant, and served as an Argyll territorial until 1965. Before his posting to Korea Younger had also been studying modern history at New College, Oxford, and he joined the family firm after his graduation, becoming a director by his mid twenties. He enjoyed business life and soon became sales director in the wine and spirits division of Tennant Caledonian, the firm which acquired Younger's in 1960. In that role it was his responsibility to choose which scantily clad young lady appeared on cans of Sweetheart Stout, a process Younger probably neglected to mention at selection meetings.

As a schoolboy Younger had been 'thrilled' by Labour's 1945 landslide, but 'During the most formative years – between 14 and 20 – by the time I got to university, my views had changed. I identified with anything that was not socialism.'[5] Younger contested the safe Labour seat of North Lanarkshire in 1959, and in 1963 he was selected to fight the equally as safe Conservative seat of Kinross and West Perthshire. Then Harold Macmillan resigned, Sir Alec Douglas-Home became prime minister, and the hunt began for a seat to enable his return to the House of Commons. 'It was a lifetime's experience for me in a single week,' recalled Younger. 'Suddenly my telephone became red hot, all sorts of people ringing up and asking me if I was going to give Alec Douglas-Home the seat. Well, it was clear to me that it was the natural thing to do.'[6] Younger was offered the more marginal seat of Ayr (the same constituency his great-grandfather had held) as a reward for his loyalty, and he won it at the 1964 general election. The following year he was made Scottish whip by the then chief whip William Whitelaw, thereafter his mentor.

By 1968 Younger was spearheading a high-profile 'Save the Argylls' regimental campaign, and when Edward Heath unexpectedly won the 1970 election, he became a popular and effective under-secretary for industry and planning at the Scottish Office. He spent just over a month as minister of state at the Ministry of Defence in early 1974, and when the Conservatives lost the February election Younger became both chairman of the Scottish Conservative Party and deputy defence spokesman in the Commons. When Thatcher became party leader a year later, he was promoted to principal defence spokesman until being replaced by Sir Ian Gilmour just eight months later.[7]

By 1976 the Labour government was in turmoil over its plans for Scottish and Welsh devolution. The opposition was just as divided, and just as he had persuaded Heath to back devolution back in 1968, Younger remained pro-Assembly eight years later.[8] Thatcher was also initially keen to sustain her party's pro-devolution line, but things started to go wrong in May 1976 when the Scottish conference rejected the government's proposals. Delegates instead endorsed an alternative plan for a 'third chamber' of the UK parliament sitting in Edinburgh, with the final reading of any Bills taken at Westminster. Initially, the Conservatives planned to abstain at the Second Reading of the Scotland and Wales Bill to see what emerged before its Third. But when Thatcher and the Shadow Cabinet shifted towards imposing a three-line whip against, the shadow Scottish secretary Alick Buchanan-Smith felt his position had become untenable. Younger was one of seven Scottish front-benchers who told Thatcher they would resign en masse if she did not back down; she said their resignations would not be accepted and warned that their disloyalty would damage the party in Scotland.[9] On 8 December 1976 Buchanan-Smith finally quit along with his deputy Malcolm Rifkind, and his successor, Teddy Taylor, immediately condemned Labour's 'bureaucratic assembly'.[10] Younger had been offered the job but refused on the basis that his stance was basically the same as Buchanan-Smith's. So the mid 1970s found him at a low ebb, and when Thatcher removed Younger from the defence brief earlier in 1976 he considered leaving politics altogether. However, he later abandoned his support for devolution through political expediency and returned to the front-bench as a junior spokesman for Scotland in January 1977.[11]

Following the referendum of 1979, devolution began its demise as a mainstream political issue, and when Younger replaced Bruce Millan at the Scottish Office in May, he prepared to remove the Scotland Act from the statute books. 'Certainly we have definite views on the Scotland Act,' Thatcher told the Scottish Tory conference in her first speech as prime minister. 'We will ask Parliament to repeal it. But we have made it clear that we shall initiate all-party discussions aimed at bringing government closer to the people.'[12] Meanwhile, Younger suspended any use of the old Royal High School building in Edinburgh pending those all-party talks. It had been fully converted for use as the Assembly building, and Scottish Office civil servants had even cleared out of old St Andrew's House to make way for the new Assembly ministers. 'I ask the House to repeal the Scotland Act today,' the Scottish secretary told MPs on 20 June. 'In doing that I know, and every right hon. and hon. Gentleman in the House knows, that the Scotland Act has very few friends.'[13] Millan and Donald Dewar taunted him about his previous support for an Assembly, while Younger did his best to sound consensual.

The SNP refused to take part in the Inter-Party Group on the Government of Scotland, which concluded its talks in June 1981. The result was a select committee chaired by Labour back-bencher and future Scottish secretary Dewar, and on 15 February 1982 the Scottish Grand Committee met for the first time in Edinburgh, now shorn of its 15 English members, and therefore a Conservative majority. Younger used it to announce a package of measures to tackle youth unemployment, while the SNP's Donald Stewart derided the gathering (in the old Royal High School) as nothing more than a talking shop, a point echoed by three protestors who were led from the public gallery after interrupting a speech by Alex Fletcher. Later that year the Scottish secretary said in a speech that he now believed most people in Scotland were no longer interested in 'a Scottish Assembly as a practical proposition'.[14]

In retrospect, the early 1980s was an unenviable time to be Scottish secretary. Strikes still gripped Scotland and the rest of the UK, unemployment had climbed to 236,000 by 1980, and Margaret Thatcher was – by all accounts – set to lose the next election. Younger, on the other hand, was riding high, and his first four Bills could even be described as a radical programme of Scottish reforms. His Scottish Office team was more impressive than Millan's, although plucked from a much shallower pool of talent. Malcolm Rifkind (home affairs and environment) made his mark by summing up the debate on the repeal of the Scottish Act without using a note, Alexander Fletcher (that rare thing, a comprehensively schooled Tory) handled the then unusual combination of education and industry with aplomb, while the less able Russell Fairgreave (health and social work) and Lord Mansfield, the minister of state with Earl of Home-like responsibility for the Highlands and Islands, kept comparatively quiet. The most influential force at ministerial meetings, however, was the lord advocate James Mackay.

Younger realised the Scottish Office needed a strong identity and set about clarifying the junior ministerial titles and duties. So no longer did MPs have to introduce themselves with titles such as joint parliamentary under-secretary of state for Scotland with responsibility for education, becoming instead Scottish minister for education, health, etc. This clarity extended to Younger's first piece of legislation, the Tenants' Rights (Scotland) Bill, a title Rifkind insisted upon in face of civil service demands for 'Tenants etc'. It was, of course, that Skeltonian ideal of a property-owning democracy, this time by allowing tenants to buy their own council house, often at a massive discount.[15] Labour MPs dubbed it the 'Chancer's Charter' and Hugh Brown called it the 'bribe of the century',[16] but such a massive transfer of wealth was difficult for even the opposition to oppose and Rifkind cleverly threw the argument back at uncomfortable Scottish Labour MPs. The Criminal Justice (Scotland) Bill was the next big reform, its wider stop-and-search powers for police sparking fury in the civil liberties lobby despite strongly resembling a Millan Bill of the previous year.

Younger benefited from a Scottish Labour Party suffering low morale, and an SNP which had lost all but two of its MPs in what Callaghan memorably called 'an early Christmas'. Donald Dewar, despite right-wing Tory MP Iain Sproat's[17] best efforts, proved an effective chairman of the Scottish Affairs Select Committee, although the Conservatives' inbuilt seven–six majority reinforced complaints that Younger was paying lip service to devolution. The government's popularity sank even further in 1980, but two more Bills, Education and the innocuous-sounding Local Government (Miscellaneous Provisions) (Scotland) Bill, were just as radical and even more controversial. The former laid the basis for the assisted places scheme and allowed Scottish parents greater choice between local authority schools. The latter, meanwhile, allowed Younger to 'crusade' against high-spending Labour-controlled Scottish councils.

Again, it proved difficult for Labour to oppose either Bill effectively, even though the second reform became known at Westminster as the 'Lothian Regional Council (Abolition) Bill'. The most contentious clause allowed the Scottish secretary to cut a local authority's funding if it was deemed to be indulging in 'excessive and unreasonable' expenditure. Younger was himself accused of being 'excessive and unreasonable' when on 21 July 1981 he moved orders to cut the rate support grant to Lothian by £47 million, to Dundee District Council by £2 million and to his native Stirling by £1 million. Lothian was told to give £30 million back to its ratepayers or face the cut, but on 11 August 1981 the council defied the government and Younger made the unprecedented move. By the end of that month Lothian's grant had been almost halved with £1.4 million a week being clawed back by a confident Scottish Office.[18] Phyllis Herriot, the leader of the council's Labour group, announced she was quitting local government for personal reasons, and when Thatcher visited Scotland the following month she was jeered by more than a thousand protestors.

Meanwhile, the former Scottish Office minister Tony Stodart, now Lord Stodart of Leaston, had completed his review of Scottish local government.[19] The Local Government and Planning (Scotland) Bill followed at the end of 1981, implementing Stodart's recommendations in what Younger called a refining and tidying up exercise. Younger had won the battle, but with a smile on his face. Not only did Lothian have to back down, but the Conservatives (led by the pro-devolutionist Brian Meek) ousted Labour at the 1982 regional elections. Thatcher was delighted, asking conference delegates in 1984, 'Do the ratepayers of Lothian look on George as some ruthless tyrant because he has cut their rates by 25 per cent? Do the householders of Stirling quake at the name of Younger all because he took 6p in the pound off their bills for rates? On the contrary, they reckon he's a jolly good fellow, and so say all of us.'[20]

Justifying the Scottish secretary's crusade against high public sector spending were significant cuts in his own department. Thatcher had appointed a government consultant on efficiency, Sir Derek Rayner, and by the time he was finished reviewing the Scottish Office in 1982 it had shed 900 civil servants. Two years later a decree came from Downing Street that every departmental minister, accompanied by his permanent under-secretary, had to personally justify expenditure to the prime minister and her efficiency adviser. Younger was the third man in to the 'Star Chamber', having heard that Norman Tebbit (Department of Trade and Industry) and Leon Brittan (Home Office) had endured bruising encounters. He rehearsed his script with Sir William Kerr Fraser the night before and took a risk by including a postcard he had picked up on holiday among his projection slides. It depicted a kilted Scotsman climbing a hill with the caption 'Looking for lost coins among the heather'. Although not renowned for her sense of humour, the prime minister found it amusing and Younger departed with his spending plans intact.

By the end of his first term as Scottish secretary, Younger's team had more or less changed completely: Fletcher would move to the DTI in 1983, Fairgreave had been sacked in 1981, while Rifkind moved to the Foreign Office in 1982. The solicitor-general for Scotland, the colourful Sir Nicholas Fairbairn, had also resigned in spectacular circumstances. After foolishly speaking to the press about a Crown decision to abandon proceedings against three Glasgow youths accused of rape, Fairbairn was forced to admit to 'errors of judgement'. Details of an affair which ended with a woman trying to hang herself from a lamppost outside Fairbairn's London flat did not help, and in January 1982 Sir Nicholas finally quit.

The 'khaki' general election of 1983 was a triumph for Mrs Thatcher and a relief for Younger. The Conservatives won a landslide on the back of the Falklands campaign and, despite boundary changes, still had a total of 21 MPs in Scotland. The Scottish Office team was different but just as able. Michael Ancram – whose great-great-uncle the Marquis of Lothian had been secretary for Scotland in 1887 – became a minister, as did the impressive James Mackay (formerly a maths teacher in Oban and dubbed 'MacTebbit' by colleagues) and the mutton-chopped Allan Stewart. Peter Fraser had already replaced Fairbairn as solicitor-general and Hamish Gray, now Lord Gray of Contin, became minister of state in the Lords. He had just lost his Highland constituency (and his ministerial position at the Department of Energy) to the 23-year-old Charles Kennedy, a casualty of the recent closure of the Invergordon smelter at Easter Ross. The government had offered an £100 million grant to another buyer, but by mid 1982 Younger had been forced to concede that one could not be found. This was indicative of the other, more dominant, aspect of his six years as Scottish secretary – a constant battle against seemingly irreversible industrial decline. No sooner had North Sea Oil revenue begun to flow into the Treasury's coffers when closures began in its country of origin. In February 1981 PSA Peugeot Citroën announced it was closing its Chrysler car plant at Linwood with the loss of 4,800 jobs despite a government offer of £40 million in aid. Younger's acute political antennae knew that such losses were not only bad for unemployment, but unhelpful for the Scottish Conservatives. He also knew, however, that it was unsalvageable when he asked the owners what it would cost to keep the plant open and they replied, 'A guarantee from the Government to buy all the cars.' Younger also realised that the closure of Linwood was a matter of presentation, which Thatcher and other ministers so often got wrong. The Scottish secretary had to be in Brussels for fisheries talks and wanted the highly competent Alex Fletcher to make the Commons statement, and not the trade and industry secretary, Norman Tebbit, whom he considered unsympathetic. Private office ingenuity ensured that Fletcher's name appeared on the annunciator and therefore he made the statement. Tebbit was apoplectic and later burst into Younger's office demanding that he sack his private secretary. When the official asked the Scottish secretary what he had said in response, Younger replied, 'Absolutely', and they both laughed.[21] Delegates to May's party conference also voiced uneasiness about the destructive effect of spending cuts and damage to Scottish industry from the recession.

Linwood had come to Scotland under the watchful eye of Jack Maclay, who had also secured Ravenscraig for Lanarkshire. The steel stripmill first ran into trouble in December 1982, but both Younger and the industry secretary, Patrick Jenkin, argued that it should be kept open. The Scottish secretary believed the effect of closure would be economically, and politically, disastrous just before the election. Younger was also said to have threatened to resign should the strip mill be allowed to close. This, however, was never likely, as it simply was not his style. 'Mr Younger can be relied upon to do the decent thing,' observed *The Times*, 'and resigning over Ravenscraig would not be at all decent.'[22] While Scotland may have believed that the Scottish secretary would go, Westminster knew better. Younger authorised Ancram to tell a meeting of trade unionists in Motherwell that they would fight to save the plant, to everyone's great surprise. The prime minister was horrified, but when Younger and Ancram were summoned to see her they managed to convince Thatcher to abandon all her previous views and brought her round. Within weeks Younger had secured a three-year reprieve and Ravenscraig stayed open. He had acquired powers of Caledonian veto of which Willie Ross would have been proud.

Not all of Younger's fellow MPs, however, were impressed by these tactics: 'each SoS, instead of considering the National Interest – still less Government policy in the strategic sense – has to "fight his corner" ', complained the colourful Conservative back-bencher Alan Clark to his diary. 'So the three heavies (Jim Prior, Michael Heseltine and Peter Walker) get the support of ponces like Younger and Edwards (Nicholas, SoS for Wales) who need funds for their wanky little principalities.'[23] The Scottish secretary's principality certainly needed funds, and, like most of his predecessors, Younger was prepared to fight for them. He had also managed to fend off the closure of Ferranti's, but in February 1983 yet more job losses came when the Timex factory in Dundee announced redundancies. The Scottish secretary also managed to preserve spending in areas which suffered in England. Ancram remembers overseeing a massive road-building programme (like the A9) even while everything was being cut back south of the border. Thatcher, who initially did not 'understand' Scotland, appeared to tolerate this approach while simultaneously attacking 'subsidy junkies' in England. But although Younger's heart was in industrial development he had no real agenda beyond reacting sympathetically to proposed factory closures. Damage limitation had replaced radical domestic reform, and it was said that a once bold Scottish Office had lost its way by 1983. The new quango, Locate in Scotland, however, was a great success, and worked with the Scottish Development Agency (SDA) to secure £1,300 million of foreign investment and 30,000 jobs from 1981 to 1985. The SDA's survival was all the more remarkable considering Michael Heseltine's zeal for winding up its English counterparts, the Urban Development Corporations. New Towns, another Labour creation, also remained. By the end of 1984 English New Town Corporations had mostly been wound up and their powers transferred to local councils, but in Scotland Younger promised that none of Scotland's five would be wound up before 1990, and even then only once they had reached their target populations.

Younger had so far succeeded in managing Scotland in a Conservative, but not necessarily Thatcherite way. *The Times* called him the Scottish pro-consul of a monetarist government, and indeed the paternalistic Scottish secretary's relationship with the neo-Liberal Mrs Thatcher was an intriguing one. She distrusted party grandees but adored figures like Younger and Willie Whitelaw; the prime minister aggressively reformed the UK economy but gave Younger a free hand in Scotland; and while lame-duck industries in England were allowed to die, Thatcher backed the Scottish Office in keeping open Ravenscraig. Younger regarded the Iron Lady with bemused affection, even calling her 'Madame Tango' in private.[24] He was, however, uncomfortable with her jingoistic desire to exploit the Falklands conflict. 'It reminded me of the Nuremberg Rally,' he told a friend after witnessing an enthusiastic response to Thatcher's Scottish conference speech following the recapture of South Georgia. He also did not share the prime minister's rigidly ideological political outlook. Instead, the Scottish secretary was an old-fashioned pragmatist, prepared to examine policies on an impartial basis. But Younger differed from the likes of his predecessor Gordon Campbell in that he also had an acutely developed feel for politics: for what he could sell, and what would spark protest. If anything, he was a typically 'wet' Conservative like his mentor Whitelaw. He was thought to be socially liberal, but although he sanctioned a free vote on an amendment to the Criminal Justice (Scotland) Bill which legalised homosexuality in Scotland, he cautioned MPs not to back something which had yet to be fully debated.[25] Younger also consistently backed moves to restore the death penalty for murder, and pursued council house sales and local government spending cuts with good-natured zeal. He was also a marked contrast to his immediate predecessor in terms of personal style and working habits. While Millan shunned social functions for paperwork, Younger enjoyed a wide circle of friends in London and preferred officials to brief him verbally, dealing with paperwork in the back of his ministerial car. He was of the old school and believed that politics was a job like any other, making equal time for his children and his wife, Diana, always an important consideration in both his public and private life.

Unlike Millan, Younger would take officials into his confidence, relying on them for advice and even inviting some to family weddings. Consequently, they enjoyed working for him, although conscious that some issues were off-limits in terms of small talk.[26] His was an intuitive intelligence which did not need hard work; Younger was good at mastering his brief and reaching quick decisions, while enjoying the traditional trappings of his office. He was self-effacing and exuded reasonableness, never becoming difficult or losing his temper.[27] Younger was not a spellbinding orator in the House, but would genially poke fun at his opponents, even when under attack, making aggressive opposition barbs appear churlish. Unlike Willie Ross, Younger would happily rely on speeches prepared by officials, although he often added a little personal embellishment. His unruffled calm was as infuriating to his opponents as it was reassuring to his supporters, but above all, Thatcher's 'King of Scotland' was simply a nice person, although nice with a purpose. Tales of his handling of hostile delegations are legendary, not least those from the Convention of Scottish Local Authorities. Allan Stewart remembers a Labour councillor launching a vitriolic attack on Younger during one meeting, 'but George just looked at him and asked if he'd tried the chocolate biscuits'.[28] He was impossible to dislike, and although the Scottish secretary would rarely progress beyond a restatement of government policy, trade unionists would be happily out of the building before realising they had been fobbed off with tea and charm. The nationalist Paul Henderson Scott even left one meeting under the distinct impression that Younger favoured a federal solution to the constitutional question. But, although successful, this was the kind of subtle political act which could not be practised indefinitely. Delegations grew wise to the Scottish secretary's techniques and began to work round them. And by the end of 1984 even Mrs Thatcher had begun to grumble about her 'Highland hero', and the reluctance of the Scots to conform to her vision of a modern Britain.

For George Younger 1985 was a torrid year on several fronts. His desire to reform the rates caught up with him rather dramatically, and even his substantial powers of persuasion could not save the Gartcosh steel mill from closure. Back in 1894, Sir George Otto Trevelyan, then secretary for Scotland, referred to his fiefdom as a country 'where people have always been so much alive to the question of rating'.[29] A prescient observation, as on 24 January 1985 the Scottish secretary warned MPs that domestic rates would rise on average by 13 per cent following that year's quinquennial revaluation. Domestic and commercial ratepayers, not to mention Scottish Conservative members, were in uproar. Revaluation had been delayed in 1983 to hold off a crisis, and when it finally hit two years later it hit Tory voters hardest. The reaction which filtered back from Conservative constituencies took Younger off guard, but only when a shocked Whitelaw returned from a visit to Scotland and Sir James Goold, the Scottish party chairman, contacted Downing Street did the prime minister take notice.[30] Younger took an extra £38.5 million from his block grant to raise revaluation relief from five to eight pence in the pound, but it was not enough. At the Perth conference in May the Scottish secretary received an unusually hostile reception. 'The fact is, that for too many people, this year's rate demand has come as a thunderbolt,' said Thatcher in her speech. 'And I know how commercial ratepayers feel – I spent my early years living above the shop.' The prime minister announced another £50 million from Treasury coffers to ease the burden, and promised that once the rates were abolished 'The burden should fall, not heavily on the few, but fairly on the many.'[31] The chancellor, Nigel Lawson, was furious, but the prime minister now shared Younger's conviction that the rates had to go. 'This time we have got to deliver,' said the Scottish secretary before a summit meeting at Chequers. 'Nobody is prepared to put up with the system as it is, and I agree with them.' Back in March, the environment secretary Kenneth Baker had presented his proposals – for a community charge payable by all adults above a certain age – to a Sunday meeting of ministers at Chequers. 'All my political life I have been waiting for this,' said Younger.[32] And so the Poll Tax, as it became known, was born. Most other ministers, however, were not enthusiastic, and despite warnings from Michael Heseltine, Peter Walker and Tom King (all former environment secretaries with responsibility for local government), Younger resolved to go it alone, convinced that anything less than abolition would be disastrous for the Conservatives in Scotland. By November the Scottish secretary had won Cabinet backing to proceed.

Further dissent was sparked within the party by British Steel's decision to close the Gartcosh rolling mill – part of the Ravenscraig complex – in March 1986 with the loss of 700 jobs. Iain Lawson resigned as a Conservative candidate in protest, while the Cunninghame South constituency party also threatened to quit en masse if Gartcosh closed. And, closer to home, the Dumfries MP Sir Hector Monro joined Anna McCurley in making their views known to the government. Sir Hector was rewarded by being ousted as chairman of the Scottish Conservative back-bench committee by Bill Walker, the stridently right-wing MP for Tayside North, with support from English colleagues. Ravenscraig, however, was given another three-year reprieve, and Younger vainly tried to depict the closure of Gartcosh as to its advantage.

After six years the Scottish secretary's tightrope act was wearing thin, and his strategy of seeking Cabinet compromises for Scotland appeared to be subject to the law of diminishing returns. To make matters worse, an increasingly bitter teachers' strike continued, while in November Labour MPs demanded that Younger resign after he carelessly revealed Monopolies and Mergers Commission approval for an £100 million brewery takeover bid in a letter to a constituent. The Scottish secretary had been tipped to move to the Ministry of Defence in 1982; to Trade in 1983 after Cecil Parkinson resigned; to Northern Ireland in 1984 as a replacement for his friend Jim Prior; and, most recently, to Energy in 1985's autumn reshuffle, but still Younger remained at the Scottish Office. Now the longest-continually serving secretary of state for Scotland, he was desperate to leave Dover House.

At the Cabinet meeting on 11 January 1986, the issue of rating reform was one of the main items under discussion. Younger had put forward his case for abolition with typical forcefulness, but when the discussion turned to the so-called Westland Affair (concerning the relative merits of merging the ailing Westland helicopter manufacturer with European or American companies), the flamboyant defence secretary, Michael Heseltine, stormed out of Downing Street and out of the government. A stunned prime minister suspended the meeting, called the Scottish secretary into her study and asked him to take over at the Ministry of Defence, a job he had semi-openly coveted for two years. For Younger the timing could not have been better. At just before 6 p.m., he left the eighteenth-century splendour of Dover House and strolled across Whitehall to the more modern building which was to be his new departmental home. Younger found administrative chaos bequeathed to him by Heseltine, but he tried to curb the Ministry of Defences's expensive tastes and proved popular with both the armed Services and officials.[33]

Younger left the government in 1989 to become a director of the Royal Bank of Scotland, a role which finally made him financially secure, although he remained politically active by running both Mrs Thatcher's leadership campaigns. Younger became deputy chairman, then chairman of the bank, his acute business sense ably served by his political experience. In 1992 he was made a life peer, becoming Lord Younger of Prestwick, and on the death of his father in 1997 he swapped that for a hereditary peerage and became the 4th Viscount Younger of Leckie. That same year he lobbied Tony Blair against plans for a Scottish parliament, and was dismayed when it was finally established in May 1999, having by now shed completely his former pro-devolution sympathies. Younger spoke in the Scottish parliament's temporary chamber as lord high commissioner to the General Assembly of the Church of Scotland in 2002, but he was by then seriously ill with cancer. He died on 26 January 2003, aged 71. Tributes were warm and generous, and, curiously, hardly any Poll Tax stigma had attached itself to the instigator of rating reform in Scotland. When Mrs Thatcher unveiled his portrait at Dover House in 1988 she recalled always looking around the Cabinet table to find her Scottish pro-consul, who the prime minister believed spoke on behalf of the ordinary, reasonable man. George Younger was far from ordinary, but he exuded reasonableness during a period in Scotland's history which needed it most. And, like his great-great uncle Sir John Gilmour, Younger emerged from that time with his reputation intact.

Malcolm Rifkind

11 January 1986 – 28 November 1990

The Clark Kent of politics

The comedian Rikki Fulton used to say that Malcolm Rifkind was the secretary for Scotland in a state. He certainly was on the morning of 9 January 1986, when the prime minister's office phoned his Duddingston home to ask if he would consent to becoming Scottish secretary in place of George Younger. Rifkind was recovering from a bout of flu as Michael Heseltine dramatically stormed out of 10 Downing Street, soon to be replaced by George Younger at the Ministry of Defence. He enthusiastically agreed, and Mrs Thatcher completed her Cabinet meeting having executed perhaps the fastest ever reshuffle of senior ministers. 'It was not one of the things I woke up this morning expecting to happen,' Rifkind later told the press.

Rifkind was just 39, the youngest occupant of Dover House since the Earl of Dalhousie in 1887.[1] The prime minister had been suspicious of the Edinburgh advocate with an accent hand-carved in Morningside as he had resigned from the Conservative front-bench in 1976 over devolution and voted 'yes' in the referendum three years later. However, Rifkind had redeemed himself through his handling of council house sales under Younger in the early 1980s, and also by an impressive stint as minister of state at the Foreign Office, from which he now moved to the Scottish Office. He had often been spoken of as the natural successor to the long-suffering Younger, and Rifkind later said that Thatcher had indicated to him in as early as 1982 that, once he had gained wider experience of government, she would like to make him Scottish secretary.

Malcolm Leslie Rifkind was born on 21 June 1946 at 29 Morningside Road in Edinburgh, the eldest son of Elijah Rifkind, a credit draper, and his Mancunian wife, Ethel Cohen. His father's family were Lithuanian Jews who first came to Edinburgh in the late 1890s.[2] Rifkind grew up in a Marchmont flat, his father's small business making enough money to send him to the capital's George Watson's School. 'My schooldays were a period of very modest academic achievements and minimal sporting achievement,' he later recalled. 'As a result I was both happy and content.'[3] Rifkind was asked by his English master to take part in a school debate when he was just 13, and the experience gave him an enthusiasm for oratory which was to make him one of the most talented public speakers of his generation. He became president of debates while studying law at Edinburgh University (Robin Cook was secretary), and was also involved with the Conservative Association. As a student Rifkind toured India, and after graduating he lectured at the University of Rhodesia from 1967 to 1968, a job he later confessed to being 'unqualified' to do and in which he showed his strong liberal and anti-apartheid views.

Touring South Africa he met his wife Edith and returned to Edinburgh, where he was called to the Scottish Bar in 1970, and also joined the Edinburgh Corporation as a councillor. From there, his political rise was swift. Before leaving for Africa, Rifkind had been active in the Thistle Group (he came up with the nationalistic name), an energetic group of young Conservatives such as Michael Ancram and Peter Fraser, all of whom were politically centrist and inclined towards some kind of Scottish devolution. He contested Edinburgh Central at the 1970 general election but failed to be carried along by Edward Heath's surprise victory. Four years later Rifkind secured another seat in his native city, Edinburgh Pentlands, and went on to hold it for 23 years. Within a year of entering parliament Thatcher had appointed him as deputy to his Thistle Group colleague Alick Buchanan-Smith, who was made shadow Scottish secretary. But, despite the new Conservative leader's pro-devolution murmurings, the tide was already beginning to turn against figures like Buchanan-Smith and his 30-year-old deputy. They believed that as the party remained committed to an Assembly in principle, then it was wrong to vote against Labour's Scotland and Wales Bill at its Second Reading. Instead they urged abstention, and if Conservative amendments did not succeed in suitably altering the legislation then they would vote against at the Third Reading. However, Thatcher, and increasingly the Shadow Cabinet, did not agree with such tactics. 'So Alick decided to resign and I went to see Margaret to say that as his deputy I felt I should also go as well,' Rifkind later recalled, adding:

> She gave me the right to abstain if I wouldn't resign, a right she didn't give Alick. I thought that would compromise my position. I have never been an enthusiastic devolutionist; if the Scottish people had decided they didn't want it I would have been relieved. But I was also conscious that as a centre-right party we should want to decentralise power. I was never of the view that devolution, even with its faults, would lead to the break up of the UK. I never believed that the majority of Scots wanted independence.[4]

Three years later Rifkind voted 'yes' at the devolution referendum of 1 March 1979. '[But] there was no clear consensus in favour in Scotland,' he reflected, 'so I decided it shouldn't happen and I didn't depart from that view while we were in Government.'[5] Such a stance served him well, and he became one of Younger's under-secretaries when Thatcher won the general election two months later. Rifkind immediately made his mark as a minister, winding up the debate to repeal the Scotland Act without using notes. He also handled his responsibility for local government effectively and pushed through council house sales without resorting to a guillotine. In 1982 Rifkind moved to the Foreign Office as an under-secretary and was within a year minister of state, a rapid promotion which demonstrated that even the prime minister believed he was destined for the Cabinet.

When Rifkind arrived at Dover House in January 1986 civil servants noticed an immediate change in style from the gentlemanly Younger. Gone were lashings of charm for visiting delegations, Rifkind preferring to expose logical fallacies in their complaints, although he did earn respect as a good man to deal with. Quick, relaxed, friendly and ready to give credit when it was due, he and George Younger were easily the most effective of recent Scottish secretaries in getting the best out of Scottish Office civil servants. Also gone was a 'steady as she goes' approach to the party in Scotland; Rifkind set them a target of 30 per cent (of the votes) by the next general election. The new Scottish secretary, however, did inherit all of his predecessor's enthusiasm for the so-called Poll Tax, and he set about selling it to Scots with all the skill of an Edinburgh advocate. But the proposals, when they finally appeared just weeks after his appointment, proved to be a poisoned chalice. *Paying for Local Government* was immediately opposed by most Scottish local authorities and vociferously attacked by the Labour opposition. Rifkind responded by accusing his opponents of being 'wedded to a corrupt and out-of-date system'. The battle lines were set for what was to become the thorniest Scottish Office legislation since John Sinclair's Small Landholders Bill.

At first it was all relatively plain sailing. The White Paper was attacked but remained sellable on paper, and the Scottish secretary believed the proposals would be recognised for what they were: a stark improvement on the 'evil' of the rates. But although Younger had won Cabinet backing for a stand-alone Scottish Bill the previous November, certain ministers remained uneasy, and they grew more so as 1986 wore on. Michael Ancram, who remained as a minister at the Scottish Office despite Younger's departure, had been charged with handling the abolition of the rates the previous year. In September 1986 he asked the relevant Cabinet sub-committee for various exemptions within the community charge, such as non-working wives, those on benefits and students. Opposition came mainly from the chancellor, Nigel Lawson, who by now believed the whole plan was so doomed to failure that he planned to use the Scottish legislation to prove how flawed it was and therefore ensure it did not happen in England and Wales. But the still-prevalent political myth that Thatcher 'imposed' the Poll Tax upon Scotland first to 'suck it and see' is, as Rifkind has said, 'bollocks'. She, and a dubious Cabinet, reluctantly backed Younger's plea that five-yearly revaluations in Scotland were politically disastrous, and therefore the rates had to go before the 1987 election. Ironically, in rushing through the proposals in the course of 1986, the government believed it was doing Younger, and his successor, a favour.

The snappily titled Abolition of Domestic Rates etc. (Scotland) Bill (dubbed ADRES in St Andrew's House) finally appeared in late 1986 and received its Second Reading on 9 December. Rifkind hailed it as a 'radical and reforming measure which will abolish a discredited and unpopular local tax'.[6] The next stage was fraught. Last-minute concessions for OAPs and students made the once cohesive (if not popular) Bill seem complicated, while Labour's Dennis Canavan did his best to disrupt committee considerations. Following 100 hours of debate, and with only half its 34 clauses examined, the Bill was guillotined in early February. Sir Nicholas Fairbairn suggested as an epitaph, 'Delivered from death by boredom with a guillotine'.[7] Rifkind also surprised MPs by abandoning the planned three-year transitional period and instead announced a 'clean break' to take place in May 1989. The Bill then had a stormy time in the House of Lords, where the new minister of state Lord Glenarthur had to fend off savage attacks from Lord Ross of Marnock, previously a long-serving Labour Scottish secretary.[8] By the time it got back to the Commons for its Third Reading all hell had broken loose. The leader of the opposition, Neil Kinnock, said it should be fought all the way, and tempers frayed when another guillotine left just two hours for the House to cover 132 amendments. John Home Robertson, the Labour MP for Berwick and East Lothian, told Ancram to 'go to hell', even though he had finally succumbed to calling it the 'poll tax' (as had Thatcher), rather than the community charge he had been insisting upon until now. On 13 May – just four weeks before the 1987 general election – the Abolition of Domestic Rates etc. (Scotland) Bill completed its parliamentary stages. And, just days later, the prime minister told a delighted Scottish Conservative conference in Perth that the Queen had granted the Bill Royal Assent.

The electoral impact of the Poll Tax, together with tactical voting and a bitter teachers' strike, however, was devastating. The Conservatives lost 11 of their 21 Scottish seats, a result – beyond a partial reprieve in 1992 – the party would never recover from. 'The day after the general election was one of the most miserable in my political life,' Rifkind later recalled. 'We had won but in Scotland we had been humiliated . . . It was quite logical and not unreasonable for the SNP [as an independence party] to accuse us of governing Scotland with no mandate.'[9] This was the doomsday scenario many Tories had feared. The Scottish Office lost two of its ministers, John Mackay and Michael Ancram (whose relative the Marquis of Lothian had only become Scottish secretary due to similar problems with the Unionist mandate in 1887), and when both Allan Stewart and Buchanan-Smith refused to serve under Rifkind he had to resort to some creative tactics to fill his ministerial team.[10] The solicitor-general Peter Fraser, another casualty of the election, was simply kept on (by now it was unusual for law officers also to be MPs), while the Inverness-born English MP David Maclean became the Scottish whip. The under-secretary Ian Lang was also promoted to be minister of state, as was the ebullient Lord Sanderson of Bowden, while Michael Forsyth – who had retained Stirling by a narrow margin – took over health and education.[11] And Lord James Douglas-Hamilton (whose mother-in-law, Lady Tweedsmuir, had served at the Scottish Office in the 1960s and 1970s) was given prisons and the environment: in other words, responsibility for the community charge.

Labour, meanwhile, discovered that numerical strength (it had won 50 MPs in Scotland) was no guarantee of political success. Rifkind launched a spirited fight back, promising to review all existing policies and arguing that the Tory message simply had to be better sold. He drafted in Alex Pagett[12] to the Scottish party's Chester Street headquarters to oversee the 'Rifkind Revolution', while John Mackay applied his formidable intellect to the task of rebuilding the party in Scotland. Even as Labour's chaotic non-payment campaign got under way, the Scottish secretary continued to perform well, aided by the counterproductive antics of opposition MPs (Leith MP Ron Brown dropped the mace and refused to apologise; Canavan continued to disrupt committee meetings in protest at the presence of English MPs; while Tam Dalyell was twice suspended from the House and the SNP's Alex Salmond was thrown out for disrupting the chancellor's 1988 Budget statement). All the while Rifkind assured Cabinet colleagues that the introduction of the Poll Tax was actually going very well, but his efforts to give Thatcherism a human (and Scottish) face were often undermined by insensitive visiting ministers, and even the prime minister herself in two May 1988 speeches. The first, at the Scottish Conservative conference, promised a heavier dose of Thatcherism and pledged 'As long as I am leader of this Party we shall defend the Union and reject legislative devolution unequivocally.'[13] And at the second, the now famous 'Sermon on the Mound' to the General Assembly of the Church of Scotland, Thatcher attempted to marry her political thinking with scripture. 'But it is not the creation of wealth that is wrong but love of money for its own sake' was one such nugget of divine inspiration. An outraged clergyman described the speech as 'a disgraceful travesty of the gospel',[14] while the moderator, James Whyte, formally presented the prime minister with church reports on housing and poverty.

The Scottish secretary did not necessarily have a problem with either speech in terms of content, for he himself thought devolution had less support than Labour believed,[15] but, as ever, it was all a question of tone. This problem also extended to the Poll Tax. Thatcher insisted on presenting it as a charge *everyone* paid, as opposed to something the majority of taxpayers got some degree of rebate from. While Rifkind's relationship with the prime minister had actually been surprisingly good in his first year at the Scottish Office, it was now becoming decidedly ambivalent. 'Most of what Margaret was doing I thought was fantastic,' he later reflected, adding:

> I could have followed her to the ends of the earth. On a small minority of issues we clashed and in terms of Scottish matters if I had to sum up what the problem was, she just assumed that my job was to represent the Cabinet in Scotland; I saw it as the other way around and what she always found very difficult to understand was that in Scotland we were the minority party.[16]

But the fact that Rifkind had been trying to present himself as Thatcherite says a lot about his politics. In fact, he was almost as non-ideological as his predecessor George Younger. Some colleagues believed his formerly wet ways had by now dried out considerably, while others thought he simply had a lawyer's ability to espouse a policy in which he did not himself believe. Whatever the case, there had been a subtle shift in Rifkind's initial position as the Cabinet's man in Scotland, to that of 'a truculent tribal emissary' (as *The Economist* described Rifkind) for Scotland in the Cabinet. Crucially, the prime minister shared this impression:

> He was one of the Party's most brilliant and persuasive debaters. No one could doubt his intellect or grasp of ideas. Unfortunately he was as sensitive and highly strung as he was eloquent. His judgment was erratic and his behaviour unpredictable. Nor did he implement the radical Thatcherite approach he publicly espoused; for espouse it he did. After the 1987 election Malcolm made speeches up and down Scotland attacking dependency and extolling enterprise. But as political pressures mounted he changed his tune.[17]

These pressures included the Govan by-election in 1988, which appeared to show a revived SNP, and more moderate nationalist pressure in the form of the Campaign for a Scottish Assembly's 'Claim of Right' document, which after the by-election earned enthusiastic Labour support. And in England, the Local Government Finance Act began to take effect, provoking howls of outrage from Poll Tax payers and therefore an indignant knock-on reaction in Scotland. It was Disraeli who, as Lord Derby's chancellor, said, 'The Scotch shall have no favours from me until they return more Tory members to the House of Commons.'[18] By mid 1989 Mrs Thatcher had resolved to ensure the Scots earned those favours.

For a governing party with only ten Scottish MPs, the late 1980s was a remarkably busy period, and in some ways it recalled earlier Conservative (or Unionist) efforts to persuade Scotland that it was the true party of practical devolution. Rifkind sold electricity privatisation as a measure which would empower Scottish consumers used to English control,[19] and he won a battle with the Environment Department to merge the Scottish Countryside Commission with the Scottish operations of the UK Nature Conservancy Council to create Scottish Natural Heritage. Lord James Douglas-Hamilton also merged Walter Elliot's Scottish Special Housing Association with the Housing Corporation in Scotland to form Scottish Homes, an initiative warmly praised by the prime minister.

The development corporations of Scotland's five New Towns, however, were finally given notice that they were to be wound up – ending a planning consensus which was more than 40 years old. This was included in the Enterprise and New Towns (Scotland) Bill, the biggest aspect of which was a radical alteration to the 25-year-old Scottish Development Agency (SDA). While Younger had fought to protect it, the SDA was now to be combined with the Scottish operations of the Training Agency and renamed as the more Thatcherite-friendly Scottish Enterprise (SE). The Highlands and Islands Development Board (also established by Willie Ross, ten years before the SDA) was also revamped to become Highlands and Islands Enterprise (HIE), but the most important change was much more controversial. Instead of acting as arms-length agencies of central government, SE and HIE were to work in 'partnership' with the private sector, which would provide two thirds of each local enterprise company's board in order to develop local employment, business development and training initiatives. Bill Hughes, who was then chairman of the clothing company Grampian Holdings, and leader of the Confederation of British Industry in Scotland, had bypassed the Scottish secretary and presented Mrs Thatcher with his scheme to solve Scottish unemployment by reforming the SDA. Officials like Gavin McCrone had argued that changes of this scale would create a nightmare for accounting officers (by blurring responsibility for spending public money) and also demoralise staff. Indeed, the massive upheaval the change involved did result in a lot of key staff deserting what some feared might become a sinking ship. SE, however, was formally established in 1991, although subsequent events have tended to support those original fears.

The year 1988 ended on a tragic note: just before Christmas a passenger jet crashed in the small Dumfriesshire town of Lockerbie, killing everyone on board and dozens more on the ground. The local MP, former Scottish Office minister Sir Hector Monro, came close to tears when he made a short statement to the House. And within hours an ashen-faced Rifkind offered his Labour shadow, Donald Dewar, a space on the plane which was taking him to the disaster area. For a while at least, normal party politics were put on hold. However, within a few months the Scottish secretary would find himself locked in a battle, not with Labour or the SNP, but with his own party.

To Rifkind, 1990 was what 1985 had been to his predecessor: a torrid series of political disasters, internal party rebellions and fallings-out with the prime minister. And, like 1985, 1990 would be another Scottish secretary's last in office. One factor was an ideological tussle between the Scottish secretary and his junior minister for education, Michael Forsyth, which had its roots in the School Boards (Scotland) Bill of 1988. While Rifkind accepted the case for giving parents more say over how local authority schools were run, he drew the line at allowing individual state schools to 'opt out' of the public sector. Forsyth on the other hand, could not wait for what he believed would be an educational revolution, and, crucially, he had a hot line to Number 10. The prime minister sent Rifkind a personal minute on 22 January 1988 registering the strength of her views, particularly over the threatened closure by Strathclyde Regional Council of Paisley Grammar School. Forsyth had teamed up with Andrew Neil, an old Paisley boy who was also editor of the *Sunday Times*, to campaign for the school to be kept open, with the prime minister's blessing but not that of the Scottish secretary. Rifkind eventually took powers to overrule authorities like Strathclyde (unlike Gordon Campbell 30 years before) but continued to argue that there was insufficient parental demand for full-scale opting-out. But, as Thatcher says in her memoirs, 'I insisted and had my way.'[20] The incident marked the end of any residual fondness she had for her Scottish secretary, and, although she realised that sacking him would be politically impossible, the prime minister resolved to get things moving in Scotland by making her protégé, Forsyth, the Scottish party chairman. This was too much for Rifkind, who claimed

Forsyth could not be spared from his ministerial duties, suggesting instead the more moderate lawyer Ross Harper. Thatcher overruled him and in July 1989 Forsyth became chairman while remaining a minister, but shorn of his responsibility for education. 'Malcolm now also fell back with a vengeance', lamented Thatcher, 'on the old counter-productive tactic of proving his Scottish virility by posturing as Scotland's defender against Thatcherism.'[21] But in many ways, with Forsyth acting as the prime minister's eyes and ears in Chester Street, the Scottish secretary had little choice. The animosity between him and Forsyth was more a matter of style than substance. 'He thought the Thatcherite agenda could be implemented quickly in Scotland,' Rifkind later reflected. 'We didn't disagree as to end results, it was a question of pace and manner and tone.'[22]

The first major clash came in March 1990 with John Major's first Budget. He unveiled a hefty increase in community charge relief for England and Wales, but nothing for Scotland. To Scottish Poll Tax payers this looked like an unacceptable sop to southern protests while theirs continued to be ignored. The first concession had come the previous October. 'They have just announced an awful give-in on the community charge, spending £1,300 million quite unnecessarily,' bemoaned the Labour MP turned Thatcherite journalist Woodrow Wyatt to his diary. 'Norman Lamont told me that Malcolm Rifkind, secretary for Scotland, said, "Why do you want to do this? You will have to do the same for Scotland and we don't need it there at all. The poll tax is going very well there." '[23] But, however naive that belief was, Thatcher claimed that Rifkind had failed to voice any reservations about the Budget's additional relief measures when they had been discussed at Cabinet. When Donald Dewar intervened to articulate what everyone watching in Scotland was thinking (it was the first televised Budget), Rifkind realised the political ramifications were disastrous. Correspondence between him, Major and the prime minister negotiating Scottish relief was then heavily leaked, although Mrs Thatcher eventually sanctioned a special payment from within the existing Scottish Office block grant. The prime minister's press secretary Bernard Ingham told Lobby journalists that the Scottish secretary had been 'carpeted' by the prime minister, but, having already lost Lawson, Norman Fowler and Peter Walker (all of whom had a strange desire to spend more time with their respective families), even when Rifkind began declaring victory back in Scotland, Thatcher accepted that she could not afford to lose another Cabinet minister. But she was not amused, and when rioting broke out in London that April, the Thatcherite era entered its twilight months.

In May, the Scottish Conservative Party plunged into open warfare at its annual conference in Perth. The North Tayside MP, Bill Walker, had written to the prime minister criticising the Scottish secretary's handling of the Poll Tax issue, while leading a noisy band of right-wing Scottish Conservatives in an absurd attempt to oust Rifkind in a political coup. Rifkind brought down the house when he opened his keynote speech by looking at his watch and saying 'well it's 12 o'clock and I'm still here'. The party had just days to cool down before another crisis erupted, this time over the long-running sore of Ravenscraig. In 1987 Rifkind had convinced the British Steel Corporation (BSC) to keep it open for at least another two years. A year later BSC was privatised and it soon became obvious that the steel strip mill was not part of the company's long-term business plan. The Scottish secretary realised the plant was no longer essential to Scotland's economy, but felt its symbolic political value remained high. In a statement to the Commons on 16 May Rifkind said he 'deplored' BSC's decision and called for cross-party action to prevent it. The Lobby was soon being handed quotes from colleagues criticising the Scottish secretary's 'interventionist Labour-speak', but, while his approach isolated him in Cabinet, opposition MPs rallied round, as did some Scottish Conservative back-benchers who even signed a Labour-sponsored Early Day Motion condemning the closure. 'He was reverting to type', was Thatcher's assessment of Rifkind. Initially, however, the Scottish secretary was slow to accept that May's conference had been anything more than harmless troublemaking. Only when Walker led another revolt against the Law Reform (Miscellaneous Provisions) (Scotland) Bill did Rifkind sit up and take notice. Ironically, this legal reform was positively Thatcherite, ending the monopoly of Scottish solicitors to conveyance, but it was also the issue from which the Forsythite rebels chose to launch their last attack. Three Scottish Tory MPs, including the former solicitor-general Sir Nicholas Fairbairn, threatened to vote against the Bill in committee because they claimed it had not been given enough time. Sir Nicholas said he would not succumb to the 'thumbscrews of exhaustion' as it was rushed through. Rifkind offered some minor concessions and the Bill passed, but, finally the Scottish secretary added his voice to calls for Forsyth to be sacked for disloyalty.[24] By summer, heavyweights like Whitelaw and Younger had joined the chorus and in September Thatcher replaced him with the more palatable Lord Sanderson.

Forsyth's record during this year is mixed. He had proven himself an inspired campaigner, with a sustained attack on Labour's 'roof tax' proposals in the run up to the 1990 regional council elections, but he was not a natural chairman and soon ended up offending even some of his own supporters due to heavy-handed changes at Chester Street.[25] To save face, Rifkind suggested to Thatcher that, while he had to be removed, he had no objections to Forsyth being promoted to minister of state,[26] therefore swapping places with Lord Sanderson, who became chairman.[27] 'This combination of the Left and the traditional establishment of the Party to rebuff Thatcherism in Scotland,' she later wrote of the Forsyth affair, 'was a prelude to the formation of the same alliance to oust me as leader of the Conservative Party a few weeks later – although I did not know it at the time.'[28] The balance sheet of Thatcherism in Scotland was lopsided, as its protagonist later admitted, being economically positive but politically negative. Rifkind's verdict focussed on her style:

> She felt that the rest of Britain was embracing Thatcherism and Scotland wasn't. She was wrong. Scotland was, only they weren't prepared to vote for her. The council house sales policy was hugely popular in Scotland . . . the parents' charter whereby you could over-rule the local authority as to which school your child went to was hugely popular; privatization wasn't particularly unpopular, and the riots against the poll tax were in London. It wasn't that Thatcherism was rebuffed . . . the problem Margaret had was she was a woman; an English woman and a bossy English woman.[29]

When Thatcher's demise finally came at the end of November, the prime minister had already written Rifkind off as an ally. He told her bluntly that she should go, but promised not to campaign against her if she chose to continue. 'Silently,' said Thatcher, 'I thanked God for small mercies.'[30] The Scottish secretary had canvassed his team of ministers for their views, and, finding them all of the same mind (except, of course, Forsyth), knew that not only was the Thatcherite game up, but that it probably provided him with a chance to move on. Rifkind initially backed Douglas Hurd to succeed Thatcher, but eventually settled on John Major, who became leader and therefore prime minister on 28 November. Major moved Rifkind to the Department of Transport, then two years later to the Ministry of Defence, and finally back to the Foreign Office in 1995, always his main ambition since leaving that department as minister of state in 1986.

Like both his Conservative successors at the Scottish Office (Lang and Forsyth), Rifkind lost his seat in the 1997 Labour landslide. He was knighted in John Major's resignation honours and remained popular in Scotland, having mysteriously failed to become negatively associated with the Poll Tax (something Younger also escaped), but he failed to recapture Edinburgh Pentlands in 2001. Rifkind reluctantly moved south for the 2005 general election, succeeding Michael Portillo in the more comfortably Conservative seat of Kensington and Chelsea. Always a proud House of Commons man, he was glad to be back, and, after serving briefly as shadow work and pensions secretary, Rifkind launched a rather quixotic bid to succeed Michael Howard as Conservative leader. Perhaps ten years earlier his candidacy might have been taken seriously, but after eight years outside parliament it was instead greeted with bemused indifference from a new generation of Tory MPs. Rifkind had endured many crises during his five years at the Scottish Office, always with an admirably cheerful demeanour. He had moved on from Dover House to head three different government departments, more than any other Scottish secretary. But his bid for the top job was not to be.

IAN LANG

28 NOVEMBER 1990 – 6 JULY 1995

The iconoclast

'The royal barge is, as it were, sinking,' began a memorable sketch on the satirical television series *That Was The Week That Was*, with David Frost mimicking Richard Dimbleby. 'The sleek royal blue hull of the barge is sliding gracefully, almost regally, beneath the waters. Perhaps the lip readers amongst you will be able to make out what Prince Philip has just said to the captain of the barge. And now the Queen, smiling radiantly, is swimming for her life.' The script was written by Ian Lang, who three decades later would succeed Malcolm Rifkind as Scottish secretary. Originally, Lang, a talented mimic, performed the sketch himself, but later sold the rights to Peter Cook and David Frost. The lord chamberlain banned it from the duo's stage performances, and when they fell out over the rights to perform another Lang sketch its author decided not to pursue a career with his fellow Cambridge Footlights. It 'took the edge off my appetite', he later reflected. Instead Lang opted for the family firm and Conservative politics. Erring on the side of caution became a regular habit of Lang's, although this iconoclastic episode would also leave its mark.

Ian Bruce Lang was born on 27 June 1940 in Glasgow, the son of James Fulton Lang, an insurance broker, and Maude Margaret Lang, née Stewart. His parents later moved to Greenock, where Lang was raised, although his schooling at Lathallan in Kincardineshire and at Rugby meant he saw little of the town as a child. He won a place at Sidney Sussex College, Cambridge, in the late 1950s and soon fell in with budding comedians rather than the 'Cambridge mafia of politicians', many of whom would become future Cabinet colleagues. Lang's irreverent sense of humour gelled with that of John Cleese, Tim Brooke-Taylor and Graham Chapman, but he graduated a year before most of his contemporaries and therefore missed out on *Beyond the Fringe*'s triumphant debut at the Edinburgh International Festival, its London run and later its world tour. 'I would probably have been tempted to go with them,' recalled

Lang, 'but it wasn't yet clear you could make a reasonable living out of that.'[1] He had toyed with becoming an actor since his schooldays, but his father discouraged it. 'Very overcrowded and not at all secure. What about accountancy?'[2] Lang did not train in that field but did join the family insurance-broking business, where he worked from his graduation until 1979. He was by then a member of the Scottish Conservative and Unionist Party and remembers being impressed by Sir Alec Douglas-Home's poise and aristocratic charm. When the former prime minister was invited by Edward Heath to chair a party commission on Scottish devolution, Lang submitted evidence despite being instinctively against the Conservative leader's recent Declaration of Perth, which committed his party to Scottish devolution. However, he suggested regular meetings of a beefed-up Scottish Grand Committee in Edinburgh, with a regular question time and powers to initiate legislation.

Lang had contested Central Ayrshire in 1970 and Glasgow Pollock in February 1974, finally winning the rural seat of Galloway in 1979. At the second general election of 1974 he was appointed personal assistant to the Scottish Conservative chairman, and produced a thoughtful pamphlet on the party's future direction in May 1975. Co-authored with the computing executive Barry Henderson,[3] *The Scottish Conservatives – A Past and a Future*, pointed to the party's 'unparalleled devolutionary pedigree' and concluded: 'Conservatives have much to offer Scotland, if we can first carry conviction that we really do believe in one nation – socially, geographically, constitutionally – but, within that unity: diversity. Then we shall once again have earned the right to claim the trust of the people.'[4] It was innocuous stuff but was later exploited by the Labour shadow Scottish secretary George Robertson as proof that Lang had once been, like Malcolm Rifkind, a devolutionist. The reality was somewhat different, but it was fitting that his maiden speech came during the debate on the repeal of the Scotland Act. In 1981 Lang became an assistant government whip, a lord commander of the Treasury in 1983, and three years later moved to the Scottish Office as one of Rifkind's under-secretaries. When the disastrous 1987 election severely depleted the Scottish Conservative ranks, Lang was promoted to become minister of state with responsibility for industry at an unenviable time.

Like his Conservative predecessors George Younger and Rifkind, Lang's politics were ambiguously centrist. He often made unconvincing attempts at being partisan and even Thatcherite, but in truth he was more Rifkindite than Forsythite; naturally inclining towards consensus.[5] Lang's five years as Scottish secretary began and ended with John Major winning a leadership election. He voted first for Thatcher in November 1990, but switched to Major along with a majority of Conservative MPs on the second ballot. Lang had come to know Major in the closeted environment of the government whips' office, and, having been involved with the new prime minister's successful campaign, he received an unexpected call from Downing Street. 'He came straight to the point, offering me the Scottish Office,' remembered Lang. 'I replied, "If you can cope with all this, I suppose I can cope with Scotland."'[6] Major and Lang agreed that Michael Forsyth should remain as a minister of state, despite his divisive ideological battle with Malcolm Rifkind in 1990, while the prime minister personally asked Allan Stewart back, who had refused to serve under Rifkind in 1987. Officials remember the Scottish secretary being slightly intimidated at finding himself in a Cabinet with so many heavyweights, many of whom he remembered from the Cambridge Union. This feeling of intimidation deepened when he found himself charged with winding up a debate to abolish the Poll Tax. Not only that, Lang inherited the floatation of Scottish electricity from Rifkind, and also had a general election to look forward to.

Lang was conscientious, but found getting to grips with the eclectic range of Scottish Office responsibilities stressful. Civil servants sensed in him a perplexing contrast: on the one hand Lang was very much an establishment man with an acute sense of the dignity of office, but on the other he mimicked colleagues and poked fun at institutions he now found himself controlling. But the latter was very much a private face, and he often gave the impression of holding back in public. In his memoirs Lang confesses to eventually longing to work less than a 70-hour week, but for Major he was a figure perfectly suited for the job. 'Ian was steady, shrewd, highly intelligent and blessed with an ordered mind,' gushed Major in his autobiography. 'He was custom-made for the Cabinet, and in a less vulgar age he would have become prime minister.'[7] But the early 1990s was a vulgar political age, and Lang often found himself surrounded by vulgar people. 'I sensed that I might be in the job for some years and I preferred to play the long game,' judged Lang, 'seeking to persuade people by informed, courteous argument and to be judged by results.'[8] In electoral terms these were relatively impressive. Politically, however, his legacy amounted to some low-key constitutional reforms, and a major reorganisation of Scottish local government.

Initially it looked as if removing Margaret Thatcher had worked. Opinion poll ratings for both Major and the Conservative Party were good, but Lang – like Rifkind – had inherited a trio of poisoned chalices from his Scottish Office predecessor. Ravenscraig was in its death throes; the controversial community charge dragged on; and the question of the weak Tory mandate in Scotland remained unresolved. On the first, Lang could do little but manage industrial decline; on the Poll Tax he was at first strangely reluctant to let it die, but later assisted in its destruction; while on the constitution, the Scottish secretary had Woodburnian notions of how to proceed. Like Rifkind, Lang promised a wide-ranging policy review, while Allan Stewart returned to Dover House to handle the unenviable combination of Ravenscraig and the community charge. This time there was no saving the former, and when the Dalzell Plate Mill also closed in July 1991, the era of Scottish steel making disappeared with it. On the latter, Stewart and Lang were seemingly at odds. The Scottish secretary had never been enthusiastic about the Poll Tax, while Stewart, Forsyth and the researcher Douglas Mason (who had dreamt it up under the auspices of the Adam Smith Institute) were all committed to retaining it. There was a Hogmanay headache for Lang when Scottish local authorities published their community charge levels, provoking yet more squeals of anguish from those paying it. A portion of the increase was attributed to non-payment, leading the Scottish Office to suspect councils were simply trying to push the final nails into the Poll Tax coffin. But by February 1991 it became clear that Michael Heseltine's review was inclined towards a property-based charge, and Lang was soon committed to overseeing the Scottish end of the changeover.

On his first trip to Scotland as prime minister, John Major promised to 'listen' to Scots' concerns, but had ruled out a tax-raising Scottish assembly by the time of his second visit two months later. Nevertheless, Lang and his old friend were basically singing from the same constitutional hymn sheet. Tory devolvers remained within the Tory Reform Group, such as the Edinburgh councillor Brian Meek, while the future member of the European parliament Struan Stevenson also kept the devolutionary flag flying. Even Bill Walker, who had so destructively undermined the once pro-Assembly Rifkind, suggested an elected senate, but without tax-raising powers. Another internal party document proposed all-round Germanic devolution. 'Most Liberals think that the German Lander is a Berlin building society,' joked Lang dismissively. Instead, he continued the half-century old Unionist refrain that he was the true devolver of power to the Scottish people via initiatives like Major's Citizen's Charter, which aimed to improve public services. The Scottish secretary, however, privately realised that more had to be done. In the prime minister, Lang found someone who was immediately more sensitive to the Scottish dimension, unlike his uncomprehending predecessor. Following a Cabinet meeting the day before a November by-election in Kincardine and Deeside,[9] Major asked Lang, James Mackay, Rifkind and Douglas Hurd to stay behind and discuss the likely outcome of a general election expected in 1992. The prime minister judged that two out of three possible results – overall defeat or victory with no Scottish MPs – meant the party had to prepare a 'line'. The group was asked to form an ad hoc committee while Rifkind wasted no time by suggesting a referendum immediately after the poll.

Lang, meanwhile, began making enthusiastically pro-Union speeches, a daring break with the previous Scottish Office policy of not mentioning either the Union or devolution. He also initiated a series of Scottish Grand Committee debates on Labour's devolution plans. Strangely, Donald Dewar (still shadow Scottish secretary) failed to rise to the occasion and simply delivered a bland restatement of Scottish Constitutional Convention aims, a cross-party pro-devolution body the Scottish secretary believed to be nothing more than 'pretentious posturing'. The *Scotsman* editor Magnus Linklater, meanwhile, had been planning a much larger confrontation entitled the 'Great Debate', and finally convinced Lang to take part. More a novelty than a political event it was held at Edinburgh's Usher Hall and chaired by the broadcaster Kirsty Wark in the run up to the 1992 general election. The relatively new SNP leader Alex Salmond was deemed to be the outright winner, but Lang had held his own. A few days later, Major and senior colleagues endorsed the Scottish secretary's plan of attack – perhaps the first spirited defence of the Union in Scottish Office history – a strategy in which the prime minister was to play a high-profile part. By now Lang had ruled out a James Stuart-like royal commission after the general election, but believed a committee of inquiry into Scotland's constitutional relationship with England might be an option. He also published a Scottish Public Expenditure Paper, as had his predecessors Sir Godfrey Collins and Hector McNeil. The Scots-born chancellor, Norman Lamont, tried to stop it, fearing knock-on demands for higher expenditure elsewhere, but Lang persuaded Major to have him over-ruled. The anodyne phrase 'taking stock' also began to emerge, and it was enthusiastically taken up by the prime minister. In fact, Major became positively evangelical. 'The danger of Labour's devolution proposals is that they might feed any such grievance, not dispel them,' he said during a speech in Glasgow. 'Labour has chosen to ride on a tiger. That tiger, unless soon caged could consume the Union itself.' And even an election rally at that symbol of English football, Wembley Stadium, was not spared Major's rhetoric. 'If I could summon up all the authority of this office, I would put it into this single warning – the United Kingdom is in danger. Wake up, my fellow countrymen! Wake up now before it is too late!'[10] Oddly, this seemingly mutually exclusive approach of 'saving the Union' and promising to 'take stock' appeared to work. The Scottish secretary defiantly quoted Martin Luther – 'Here I stand' – and by polling day there was a late swing back to the Conservatives. Lang not only held his own Galloway and Upper Nithsdale seat, but added two to his pre-election tally of nine MPs, even chalking up a two per cent increase in the Scottish share of the vote. 'Congratulations,' said Alan Young (Lang's special adviser) ironically as they left the count. 'You've saved the Union.' 'Yes,' replied Lang, 'until next time.'[11]

Lang remained as Scottish secretary in a close partnership with Major, perhaps the warmest between a secretary of state and prime minister since the early days of Willie Ross and Harold Wilson.[12] Major retained his enthusiasm and continued to instigate symbolic gestures. A national thanksgiving service to mark the end of the Gulf War had been held at Glasgow Cathedral the previous year, and the prime minister also chose Edinburgh as the location for the 1992 European Summit. Meanwhile, Lang began to take stock. He consulted widely, meeting with leading Scotsmen and even seeking the advice of former Scottish Office minister and premier Lord Home, a valuable source of guidance even in his dotage. The result was a White Paper in the spring of 1993, an act highly reminiscent of Arthur Woodburn's similar exercise in 1948. The proposals were also remarkably similar: the Scottish Grand Committee was to debate more widely, taking the Second Reading of most Bills, questioning ministers and meeting at locations across Scotland. Ironically, most of this was already allowed under Woodburn's revised standing orders, but the similarities between the two White Papers ended with the second strand of Lang's plan. Training development responsibilities were to be 'devolved' to the Scottish Office from the Department of Employment, control of the Scottish Arts Council from the National Heritage Department, and some officials responsible for North Sea Oil were to be relocated from Whitehall to Aberdeen. *Scotland in the Union – A Partnership for Good* was drafted by Lang, Lord Fraser – who handled constitutional matters as minister of state – and Alan Young, who came up with the gently punning title. Eighteen months later the Scottish secretary boasted that every aspect of the White Paper had been implemented. 'But by then, in truth, it was really all too late,' Lang later concluded. 'It was a package which if implemented thirty or forty years earlier might have done the trick.'[13] The press reaction, as with Woodburn's 45 years earlier, was mixed but predominantly cynical. The SNP derided the White Paper, and Labour did its best to ignore it.

Taking stock fuelled a perception that Lang was nothing more than an overly cautious machine politician. Privately, he was warm and witty but had a puzzling deference for both Cabinet colleagues and institutions. Scottish Office officials were frustrated both at his unwillingness to engage in face-to-face battle with Cabinet colleagues (preferring to write letters from afar) and his reluctance to exude more of his natural charm when dealing with the public and public agencies. Lang was an adept, if unexciting, media performer, but the judgmental Scottish press viewed him with suspicion. One private secretary remembers the Scottish secretary agreeing to address a lunch with newspaper editors, most of whom did not expect much from their guest. But Lang dazzled them with effortless comic timing and fluent delivery. The Fourth Estate wondered where the real Ian Lang had been hiding.

Lang was a conscientious secretary of state who found the burdens of office grinding but enjoyable, perhaps lacking the confidence to believe that anything other than luck had brought him into the Cabinet. He was a committed family man who liked to get back to his Ayrshire home as often as possible, but among his ministerial team there was less of the warmth for which George Younger, and the good humour for which Rifkind were remembered. Lang admits in his memoirs that he was not a good delegator, preferring to work through all the official paperwork personally. Alan Young, therefore, emerged as the key figure in Lang's team. A talented special adviser inherited from Rifkind, Young's relationship with the Scottish secretary had grown closer during the 1992 general election campaign, and, although not politically ambitious, he remained at the Scottish Office until 1995.

Like Rifkind, Lang had his share of industrial battles. The Rosyth naval base was tipped for closure and he fought hard against the favoured Devonport site in the south-west of England. 'It was not an edifying experience,' recalled Lang, having found himself isolated in the Cabinet, with even his predecessor (now defence secretary) doing his best to remain neutral. But he won an important concession: Rosyth would not close – although its workforce was to halve from 6,000 – and it was to be guaranteed a high volume of surface ship refitting.[14] Responsibility for industry lay with the under-secretary Allan Stewart, who was heavily involved with the right-wing 'No Turning Back' group of MPs. A fellow member was Michael Forsyth, who surprised colleagues by remaining as minister of state (until 1992) despite the demise of his patron Margaret Thatcher. Forsyth had by now mellowed, although he continued to pursue vigorously what he regarded as a complacent educational and health establishment. Lord Strathclyde[15] had also been inherited from Rifkind, but was replaced as minister of state by Lord Fraser after the 1992 election. Also making a comeback following the poll was Sir Hector Monro, the popular MP for Dumfries, who had last been at the Scottish Office more than 20 years earlier. Compared with Rifkind's five-year tenure, however, Lang's was reasonably quiet in terms of legislation.

Scotland's water and sewage services were rationalised, and, while the Scottish secretary maintained that privatisation (along English lines) was never on the cards, a wave of noisy protests and an unofficial referendum in Strathclyde would have made such a change politically difficult.[16]

Lang dealt with the floatation of Scottish electricity suppliers, initiated by his predecessor, and also completed an outstanding commitment to establishing Scottish Natural Heritage, adding the Scottish Environmental Protection Agency in 1994. On education, Lang built upon the Howie Committee's inquiry into Scottish higher education, publishing proposals for Higher Still in March 1994. This mild reform was welcomed by the educational establishment, and the Scottish secretary also moved towards further devolving university finance, creating the Scottish Higher Education Funding Council and assuming responsibility from the Department of Education and Science. And on health, Lang authorised a new Royal Infirmary of Edinburgh building, the first private finance initiative for a teaching hospital in the UK, while in September 1991 he unveiled the Patient's Charter, which guaranteed treatment times and simplifying the complaints process.[17] Industrially, he built upon the success of Younger's Locate in Scotland by establishing Scotland Europa to guide Scottish businesses and public sector bodies through European Commission red tape, and also set up Scottish Trade International to do the same thing for exporters on a global scale.

But it was local government reform which was to provide Lang's major legislative legacy. It was the fourth such Scottish Office reorganisation,[18] and proved to be every bit as controversial as its predecessors. Lang believed that Gordon Campbell's 1973 attempt was 'cumbersome, illogical and wasteful',[19] particularly the socialist monolith that was Strathclyde Regional Council. When Lang stood up in the Commons to announce its abolition ('There is no possible justification for the size of Strathclyde. It varies from being two times to six times too big.'),[20] Scottish Labour MPs led a 'spontaneously premeditated' walkout to take their opposition direct to the prime minister, who happened to be in Japan. Instead the Scottish secretary proposed 32 unitary authorities to deal with all the functions previously controlled by what he characterised as a confusing overlap of regional and district councils. Beyond the loss of Strathclyde, Labour attacked the fact that ministers had decided the new council boundaries and not the Local Government Boundary Commission, with inevitable accusations of gerrymandering. But, ironically, it was the Conservatives who were to lose out electorally. At the first elections to the new authorities in April 1995, the governing party failed to take control of a single council in Scotland. This turned out to be an uncomfortable portent of things to come, while the following month's Perth by-election just added to Lang's woes with the SNP seizing Sir Nicholas Fairbairn's once impenetrably Tory stronghold.

Earlier that year Lang had also been faced with a ministerial resignation. Allan Stewart, who had until February been handling the Local
Government (Scotland) Bill, visited the site of the proposed M77 extension
in his Eastwood constituency with his son after a good lunch. The green
lobby was out in force, and when Stewart tried to get back to his car, he
was confronted by a group of protesters. 'There was a lot of pushing and
shoving going on but it calmed down and we left the scene,'[21] he later
recalled, neglecting to mention the presence of a pick axe and an air rifle.
Stewart resigned on 7 February when it became clear the story was not
going to go away. To make matters worse, the Crown Office later decided
to press charges. 'I denied the original charge because I was not guilty of
it. I did not brandish a pickaxe,' protested Stewart. 'I could not have
brandished the pickaxe even if I had wanted to as I suffer from arthritis
and would not have been able to lift it above shoulder height.'[22] Instead he
pleaded guilty to the reduced charge of 'presenting' the implement,
something Stewart accepted was true. George Kynoch, who had won
back Kincardine and Deeside at the 1992 election, replaced him, and
continued work on the changes to local government. But even before this
triumvirate of political disasters, Lang was already anxious for a change.
His relationship with Sir Russell Hillhouse, the permanent under-secretary who succeeded Sir William Kerr Fraser in 1988, was businesslike at
best, while Lang had been forced to fend off rumours that he was to
become UK party chairman in the reshuffle which followed the Labour
leader John Smith's death in May 1994.[23] Lang, however, was a realist
and knew that the shortage of Scottish Tory back-benchers meant he
would probably remain at the Scottish Office until at least the next
general election. 'I had found my five years at the Scottish Office testing
and exhilarating,' he wrote later. 'I do believe it was one of the best jobs in
government. But I was more than ready to move on.'[24]

On Thursday, 22 June 1995, Lang was summoned from his desk at Dover
House to Downing Street. John Major, he soon learned, was about to
resign as Conservative Party leader; his message – 'put up or shut up'. He
asked the Scottish secretary to handle the media aspect of his subsequent
campaign. Lang was in his element, and when Major won (albeit
narrowly) two weeks later, he was moved to the Department of Trade
and Industry.[25] He had been at the Scottish Office for an unbroken run of
nine years, the longest-serving minister in the department's history.[26]
Lang proved an able successor to Heseltine, displaying steadiness under
fire when it fell to him to present the outcome of the Scott Inquiry (into
illegal arms sales to Iraq) to a largely hostile opposition.
     Lang was one of seven Cabinet ministers to lose his seat in the May

1997 Labour landslide, but within a few months he returned to parliament, this time as a member of the House of Lords with the lyrical title of Lord Lang of Monkton of Merrick and the Rhinns of Kells. He remained opposed to devolution, even as it rapidly became a reality, and spoke against the Scotland Bill from the Upper House. Lang called the Scottish parliament the 'hobbled child of a troubled marriage'[27] in his memoirs, the gently amusing *Blue Remembered Years*, one of only three autobiographies produced by a secretary of state for Scotland.[28] Nevertheless, Lang remains better known for his two years as president of the Board of Trade. And, although he was occasionally spoken of as a possible successor to Major, of whom Lang was an eloquent defender, he still ranks as an able, yet lesser-known occupant of St Andrew's House.

Michael Forsyth

6 July 1995 – 5 May 1997

The Forsyth saga

George Robertson, Labour's shadow Scottish secretary from 1992 until 1997, used to joke that Michael Forsyth got out of bed at 5 a.m., had a bath, and then had an idea while bathing. This, he said, would be a White Paper by lunchtime and a Bill by early evening. Forsyth was an energetic politician who often gave the impression of being, like his predecessor John Sinclair, a young man in a hurry. And like another of his predecessors, Hector McNeil, it was Forsyth's misfortune to take control of the Scottish Office in the final years of a tired administration. He was also the first, and only, genuinely Thatcherite Scottish secretary. Although Margaret Thatcher had resigned nearly five years previously, this unashamedly populist and unmistakably right-wing figure finally gave St Andrew's House a sense of what Teddy Taylor might have been like had he become secretary of state in 1979. Forsyth had first encountered Mrs Thatcher in the mid 1970s through Keith Joseph and his Centre for Policy Studies,[1] and his outlook instinctively gelled with that of the future prime minister.

Michael Bruce Forsyth was born on 16 October 1954, to John T. Forsyth, a garage mechanic, and Mary Watson. He was educated at Arbroath High School before matriculating at St Andrews University in the early 1970s. Forsyth's choice of university was to become crucial to his political development, as it was there that he first encountered the radical right-wing arguments of St Andrews' graduates Madsen Pirie and Eamonn Butler, who would later establish the Adam Smith Institute. Forsyth became president of the university's Conservative association, and from 1976 he served one term as chairman of the notoriously forthright Federation of Conservative Students. He also debated, jousting with a young Alex Salmond, then a fledgling nationalist and later leader of the SNP when Forsyth was at the Scottish Office.[2] The Conservative crowd at St Andrews were liberal, market-minded, meritocratic and appalled by Edward Heath's series of U-turns over the free-market 1970 manifesto.

Devolution for Scotland was also a hot topic and, curiously, Forsyth actually supported it. In a 1975 pamphlet called 'The Scottish Conservative Party: A New Model for a New Dimension', 'Mike' Forsyth and a young Edinburgh solicitor called David McLetchie argued for a modernised Scottish party structure to reflect constitutional change largely undesired by party members. 'We understand this attitude yet regret it,' they wrote. 'We believe that any internal reform of the Party must now seek to prepare it for a future where a Scottish Assembly is a permanent feature of political life, and where under its aegis Scottish affairs will assume a still greater significance.' The pair also suggested that the post of Scottish secretary should be retained at Cabinet level:

> Our analysis sees the Assembly assuming an importance far greater than that formally allocated to it . . . If the Conservatives in Scotland fail to adapt to the new situation and to move away from the present unwieldy and inefficient structure then, in the opinion of the authors, they may look forward to further crippling defeats.[3]

'When I was young, before I grew up,' Forsyth later recalled, 'I found devolution superficially attractive. But later I came to realise that being pro-devolution was an easy sell; it's actually a hard sell to be against it.'[4] He soon opted for the hard sell, and when Thatcher U-turned on a Scottish Assembly in late 1976, Forsyth willingly acquiesced. By now, he had the ear of the Conservative leader[5] and moved to London on her suggestion, working in public relations and winning a seat on Westminster Council in 1979 (soon to be led by the notorious Dame Shirley Porter).[6] Forsyth quit local government to fight the marginal seat of Stirling, which he won against all the odds in 1983. He became a leading member of the No Turning Back group of MPs, thus named after a 1985 pamphlet of the same name which urged the government to press ahead with radical free-market reforms. The following year Forsyth was appointed parliamentary private secretary to the foreign secretary, and in 1987 he became minister for health and education at the Scottish Office.

In July 1989 Thatcher decided to shake up St Andrew's House and also made Forsyth Scottish party chairman, although he lost responsibility for education while retaining health. Rifkind was ambivalent, and when Forsyth secured Downing Street backing over the secretary of state's head to save Paisley Grammar School, the basis of a year-long feud was set. He overhauled the party's Chester Street headquarters, bringing in new Tory Turks and making it a more formidable campaigning operation. But Forsyth's style and reforms upset the old guard, and the new chairman's followers soon fought back. He believed that Scots overwhelmingly voted

Labour not due to some ideological predisposition, but because most of them lived and worked in the public sector. Forsyth also believed Labour had deprived Scots of his modest background from educational opportunity, and he set about establishing school boards and changing the law so that the Scottish secretary could intervene to stop local authorities closing certain schools. He also supported a voucher system for parents, and wanted schools to be able to opt out completely from the public sector. This was all too much for the more bourgeois Rifkind, and, after a series of messy coup attempts, Thatcher sacked Forsyth as chairman in September 1990. 'It had been a brave attempt to bring the Scottish Tory Party into the latter half of the twentieth century,' wrote Thatcher in her memoirs, 'and offer leadership and vision to people who had become all too used to losing or – even worse – winning on their opponents' terms.'[7]

Had Thatcher remained prime minister to fight a fourth general election, as she planned to do, Forsyth would probably have become Scottish secretary in 1992. Instead, he was promoted to minister of state after resigning as chairman, moving to the Department of Employment two years later, and to the Home Office in 1994. The experience of the latter softened many of Forsyth's harder edges, and together with the bruising experience of 1989–90, he had mellowed considerably by the time John Major challenged his party to 'put up or shut up' in June 1995. The month before, a taxi driver told the diarist and MP Alan Clark that he should have been prime minister. 'I went for a walk and my fantasy developed,' wrote Clark, 'even down to choosing the government, the first night in Scotland: "You've a PM and a Chancellor who are Scots – I doubt if you'd get better than that even with full independence." ' He even composed a Cabinet in faint pencil in his journal, writing 'Eric Forth, S of S Scotland'.[8] But when Major won his self-induced leadership election on 5 July, he replaced Ian Lang not with Forth, but with another outspoken right-wing populist.[9] It was the most controversial appointment of the reshuffle but ushered in an energetic two years which encapsulated the last colourful roar of Unionist Scotland.

Rarely had the appointment of a Scottish secretary elicited such a reaction from Scotland's cynical press: Forsyth was compared with Freddie Krueger, and he was even dubbed 'the Demon King' in one tabloid headline. He was just 40 years old and delighted to be in the Cabinet as secretary of state. 'Michael Forsyth now returns,' said the *Sunday Times*, 'rejuvenated and reformed, to govern Scotland for John Major and restore Unionist fortunes north of the border.'[10] The TV presenter-turned Chester MP Gyles Brandreth mused in his diary that just a few years earlier the party in Scotland would not have accepted him as Scottish secretary; 'he's a tough cookie,' he wrote, 'a sharp operator and who else was there?'[11] Forsyth still had his band of acolytes, but their tactics had changed. They saw Lang's five years at the Scottish Office as an uninspired throwback to patrician Tory politics, and considered his policy of 'taking stock' a wasted opportunity.

Unlike his three Conservative predecessors, Forsyth was a comprehensive boy made good. Most of his political instincts sprang from his Angus upbringing: his views on education were shaped by his experience of state education, and his attitudes to law and order by the reactions of 'ordinary' Scots, so when he finally voted for John Major following Mrs Thatcher's demise in 1990 it was because Major was an ordinary man from an ordinary background, just like him. Forsyth was determined to reverse the Scottish Office drift of the last three years by injecting some energy and populism into a political world obsessed with the constitutional question. This aim was well served by his speaking style; witty, engaging and occasionally electrifying, Forsyth oratory would soon become a popular conference fixture. Like Lang, he wanted to fight for the Union while being conscious of the fact that time was probably running out.

'We've got a teacher looking after education,' said the new Scottish secretary as he unveiled his team. 'We've got a lawyer looking after home affairs. We've got a businessman looking after industry. We've got a man who's a farmer, forester and environmentalist looking after these important areas as well.'[12] The teacher was Raymond Robertson, a unique gain for the Conservatives at the 1992 general election; James Douglas-Hamilton was the lawyer, now promoted to minister of state after renouncing his peerage to prevent a disastrous by-election in December 1994;[13] the businessman was George Kynoch, a former plant engineer for ICI; and the farmer was the Earl of Lindsay, dubbed the 'Robert Redford of Scottish politics', who was also given responsibility for the arts.

The four junior ministers found Forsyth both inspired and inspiring and as a result worked harder than ever before. The Scottish secretary demanded greater ministerial visibility in Scotland, dispatching an under-secretary to Stornoway or Dumfries whenever they had a spare 12 hours, and he also set about convincing Scotland that he was not the Forsyth of old. The reconstituted local authorities were given a generous financial settlement, trade union delegations were welcomed like old friends, and even journalists began to warm to a figure who had all but ignored them as Scottish party chairman. Civil servants, however, were distinctly unimpressed. Like Willie Ross, Forsyth would begin each meeting by attacking officials with his lip curled, just to show them who was boss.[14] Sir Russell Hillhouse, who had replaced Sir William Kerr Fraser as permanent under-secretary in 1988, was particularly appalled. He found

Forsyth difficult and resented his overtly political style of government. But the Scottish secretary was unconcerned; if Scotland was to be shaken out of its complacency, the revolution had to begin in St Andrew's House. Lord James was tasked with expanding the use of closed-circuit television and electronic tagging, while Raymond Robertson pursued the old Forsyth hobby-horse of nursery vouchers to promote parental choice, which the education secretary Gillian Shepherd was bounced into supporting. The prime minister, meanwhile, was initially suspicious of Forsyth, but soon warmed to the 'thinking-man's populist'. He wrote:

> Privately quite liberal, and by conviction something of a libertarian, he possessed a sharp-toothed feel for the saleable parts of his Thatcherite inheritance, particularly those saleable in Scotland. But he suffered from the fact that he always looked as if he was plotting, even when he was not . . . Michael was more attached to argument and creed than many of his blander contemporaries, and he was very ambitious. He had a way with words – he could rip into socialists with cruel skill – but he was no peacemaker, and a kind of anxiety, a vague sense of insecurity, always hung about him.[15]

Perhaps that air of vulnerability brought the pair closer together, but Forsyth was incredibly loyal to his prime minister – another indication of how much he had changed since 1990. There remained, however, old vestiges of the former firebrand. Smarting from a beef ban which kept prime cuts of Aberdeen Angus from Continental dinner tables, Forsyth refused to help mark Europe day on 9 May 1996 by not allowing the EU flag to fly from Scottish government buildings. And as the general election approached, the Scottish secretary's appetite for creative initiatives appeared to have no boundaries. He pledged cash to help Scotland's neglected towns spruce themselves up, while calling on his home town of Arbroath to reinstate an annual re-enactment of the signing of the Declaration of Arbroath. And, in the most unlikely move of all, Forsyth announced his intention to offer 250,000 acres of government-owned land to Highland crofters through the Transfer of Crofting Estates (Scotland) Bill, some of it for free, a move which harked back to the very origins of the Scottish Office and the Crofters Act.[16]

The Scottish secretary also had his share of political crises and tragedy to contend with. There was the BSE crisis, with its inevitable impact on Scotland's agricultural community, the e-coli outbreak, but worst of all, the Dunblane massacre in which 16 children and a teacher were killed on 14 March 1996. Like the Lockerbie disaster six years earlier, normal party politics came to a standstill. Forsyth immediately headed to the town, which was in his constituency, going out of his way to ensure that George

Robertson (who lived in Dunblane), his opposition shadow, was in the car with him as he arrived. Just hours after the shooting the Scottish secretary had the unenviable duty of making a short statement to the Commons. 'It was clear, simply expressed, softly spoken, exactly right,' wrote Gyles Brandreth. 'He was deeply impressive.'[17] There were immediate calls for an outright ban on the private ownership of handguns; a move Forsyth supported both politically and emotionally. But the Home Office was reluctant and although an inquiry conducted by the judge Lord Cullen was expected not to recommend a ban, the Scottish secretary pressed strongly for colleagues to back one regardless. The Cabinet was split, and although Major personally supported Forsyth's stance, the resulting handgun legislation did not satisfy Scottish Office expectations. But the Scottish secretary realised that resignation, or the threat of resignation, so close to an expected election was not an option, and he sold the new restrictions as best he could. It was a sobering experience for a Scottish secretary not yet a year in Cabinet. But Forsyth's style, humour, and creative intellect had impressed even his harshest critics. 'I used to think things were black and white,' he would concede to colleagues, 'and I now realise that most things are shades of grey.'[18] Newspaper editorials identified him as the one true success of Major's 1995 reshuffle, and as it became clear that the Conservatives would lose the next election, Forsyth was even spoken of as a possible leader.

The Scottish secretary privately believed that his predecessor's attempt at 'taking stock' of Scotland's place within the Union had been a wasted opportunity the revitalise the Conservatives' Scottish appeal, especially given the unexpected electoral reprieve of the 1992 general election. Forsyth, therefore, immediately began developing his own proposals for the government of Scotland when he replaced Lang at the Scottish Office. 'Taking Stock Mark II', as it inevitably became known, was to be unveiled at the annual Richard Stewart memorial lecture at Strathclyde University in November 1995.[19] Forsyth chose St Andrew's Night to play his political hand, the same day the Constitutional Convention was due to reveal its detailed proposals for a Scottish parliament. It was a tactical and media triumph; stealing some of the convention's thunder by unveiling his proposals in the House of Commons on Wednesday, and again at a lecture the following evening. Once again, the Scottish Grand Committee was to be beefed up, this time with powers to question ministers from other government departments with a remit in Scotland,[20] while local authorities were to be given more discretion over their budgets. The ghost of Arthur Woodburn once again appeared, as Forsyth announced his intention to revive his predecessor's long-defunct Scottish Economic Conference, to be chaired, once again, by the secretary of state. The Scottish Grand Committee was also to be given legs, becoming a 'parliament on wheels and meeting in every sizeable town across Scotland'. The proposals, however, actually fell short of the Scottish secretary's original plan:

> What people don't know regarding the idea I came up with about the Scottish Grand Committee going around Scotland . . . [is] the original proposal was that we should allow votes in the Scottish Grand Committee to count, which meant losing our majority in Scottish votes. We tried to find a way of moving it in that direction but at that time there was no real will in the party to concede the principle of votes in Scotland deciding Scottish issues.[21]

Instead, Forsyth implemented his truncated reforms and revived Lang's spirited defence of the Union. 'It is our birthright to be Scottish,' he told delegates to the May 1996 Scottish Conservative conference. 'It is our good fortune to be British. It is our duty to be Unionists. We will fight to win.'[22]

Forsyth also began to attack vigorously the now fully formed blueprint for a Scottish parliament, claiming it would cost £75 million to run in its first year, while destroying the United Kingdom and diminishing Scotland's influence at Westminster. 'It is a pygmy parliament,' he concluded, while in September 1996, he gathered his four Conservative predecessors as Scottish secretary in Perth to round off a summer campaign which asked Scots to sign a petition rejecting Labour's devolution plans. The proposals for the devolved parliament to have the power to vary the basic rate of income tax by up to three pence in the pound also came under particularly focussed attack. The phrase 'tartan tax' had originally been mooted by Ian Lang, but Forsyth made it his own. Labour began to get cold feet and annoyed the Liberal Democrats, not to mention some of its own Scottish front-benchers, by announcing that the tax-varying issue would now form the basis of a second question in the proposed referendum.[23] Forsyth, however, never believed that in doing any of this he was helping prevent imminent defeat at the next general election; far from it. To the Scottish secretary such tactics were political damage limitation, an effort to not only preach to, but to enthuse the converted. The same cautious logic applied to perhaps Forsyth's most famous 'tartan gesture', the return of the Stone of Destiny to Scotland. Alarm bells started ringing when he realised that 1996 was not only the 700th anniversary of the stone's original removal by Edward I, but the year in which official papers relating to its theft in 1950 were due to be released. Such a combination of factors, thought Forsyth, would be a gift to the SNP, so he resolved to beat them at their own game. The Scottish secretary told no one other than his special adviser (Gerald Warner) about the plan, but asked the prime minister to consult the Queen. Major was initially reluctant but Her Majesty took legal advice and said she would not oppose such a move. Forsyth later recalled an additional, more personal, factor:

> My daughter Katy had been to Westminster Abbey and she said: Dad, you know how you're secretary of state for Scotland? There's something you need to do; you need to get the Stone of Destiny back to Scotland. I gave her all the arguments against and she said: but it's ours; it was stolen; shouldn't it be brought back? That became the "Katy Question". I knew I'd have to face the nationalists and I didn't have an answer to that question.[24]

John Major made the surprise announcement to the Commons on 3 July 1996. 'I wish to inform the House that, on the advice of Her Majesty's Ministers, the Queen has agreed that the Stone should be returned to Scotland,' he said. 'The Stone will, of course, be taken to Westminster Abbey to play its traditional role in the coronation ceremonies of future sovereigns of the United Kingdom.'[25] As Forsyth recalled, 'there was a bit of mockery, but no one stood up and objected to it'. Outside parliament, the reaction was largely cynical. 'After 700 years it is to be yanked out of Westminster and carted off to Edinburgh,' wrote Gyles Brandreth in his diary, 'swirling [sic] bagpipes and wee Michael Forsyth in his tartan trews doubtless leading the parade.'[26] The writer Alan Bennett was even more scathing: 'The return of the largely unwanted Stone was intended to buoy up the hapless Mr Forsyth, though any favour the government might have hoped to curry north of the border has since been wiped out by the aftermath of Dunblane.'[27] The Stone arrived back on Scottish soil on 15 November, the first time the coronation stone of British monarchs had officially passed over the River Tweed since 1296. There was a solitary cry of 'Freedom!' from a member of the exuberant crowd as it was escorted by the Coldstream Guards onto Coldstream Bridge, where it was welcomed midway by Forsyth, before making its way to a special exhibition at Edinburgh Castle. Ironically, a staunchly Unionist secretary of state had finally carried out what a Labour Scottish secretary, Hector McNeil, had resolved to do almost 50 years earlier. A few months later Forsyth attacked the lack of knowledge about Scottish history among young Scots and set in motion changes to the curriculum, but by early 1997 it was clear that no amount of neo-nationalistic gestures would prevent Labour securing power, and therefore creating a devolved Scottish parliament.

Forsyth had formed a strong working relationship with the Welsh secretary, William Hague, in the Cabinet. The duo even rolled up their shirtsleeves and waxed lyrical about saving the Union during party conferences. But not everyone was as tuned into the Scottish secretary's devolutionary wavelength. The Health secretary Stephen Dorrell dropped a pre-election clanger by saying he could not envisage a Labour-created Scottish parliament being left 'unchanged' by a future Conservative government. Forsyth responded by warning that a parliament was 'not just for Christmas, it's for life'.[28] But, while the Scottish secretary was clearly losing the political argument, his status within the Scottish Conservative Party had been transformed in just under two years. No longer was Forsyth viewed as the divisive right-wing upstart of seven years earlier; rather, he was now the party's prodigal Thatcherite son, having returned to show members and activists just what could be done against all the odds. Nevertheless, the general election campaign of April 1997 was torrid for both Forsyth and his party. Sir Michael Hirst, the former Strathkelvin and Bearsden MP-turned-Scottish party chairman, resigned in March just before newspapers printed allegations about 'past indiscretions' in his private life, and in the Scottish secretary's marginal Stirling constituency even a visit from Mrs Thatcher failed to stem growing support for the Labour candidate.[29] But Forsyth was no fool and had long ago realised the game was up. His mischievous side had been busy setting up political landmines for his Labour successor, whom he always believed would be Donald Dewar rather than George Robertson. A toothless Convention of the Highlands and Islands (shades of Willie Ross) was established; a commitment given for a previously derided University of the Highlands and Islands; and the SNP-supporting actor Sean Connery was recommended for a knighthood, an honour Forsyth's successor would have to see through.

On 31 April 1997 the Scottish secretary held his last campaign press conference in Edinburgh. Forsyth had just delivered his final rousing endorsement of the Union when, hearing reporters' voices raised in the hall, he turned back and for another ten minutes argued his case with passion and precision. 'We're going to miss him,' lamented one formerly hostile reporter. *The Times* gave him the following credit:

Without him, the all-important constitutional issue in Scotland would have been a lacklustre affair, with Labour avoiding it wherever possible, and thorny questions left unresolved. He has explored the problems they have dodged, and if he does go he will at the very least have put them on the agenda, for others to raise again. He has pursued the anomalies of devolution, pointed out the risks, quantified the costs, and coined the most famous phrase of all, "the tartan tax".[30]

Forsyth had cleared his desk the day before polling, having admitted frankly to many officials that he did not expect to be back after the election, and when the results began flooding in this was confirmed; the Scottish secretary was one of seven Cabinet ministers to lose his seat. At a post-election press conference on 2 May he was delayed due to traffic and joked, 'I blame the Government', when he finally arrived.

Forsyth was the first incumbent secretary of state to lose his seat since Gordon Campbell in 1974, and like Campbell he was offered a similar move to the Upper House. He refused, and instead accepted a knighthood while he decided what to do. Only when Forsyth had ruled out standing for an English seat (like Rifkind in 2005) did he accept elevation as Lord Forsyth of Drumlean. He studied for and sat his City exams, carving out a successful second career as a director of Flemings until 1999, and then vice chairman of JP Morgan, Investment Banking Europe, of which he became deputy chairman in 2002.[31] He also began to heal old social wounds, cementing friendships with his old nemesis George Robertson and patching up differences with his predecessors Ian Lang and Sir Malcolm Rifkind. But still a hankering for the political limelight remained. Lord Forsyth resigned from JP Morgan in July 2005, agreed to chair a tax commission established by the shadow chancellor George Osborne and, when David Cameron was elected Conservative leader later that year he began to make unusually positive noises to journalists he had shunned since 1997. Michael Forsyth was a one-off while also undoubtedly being 'one of us'. He became Scottish secretary perhaps 16 years too late, but enlivened Scottish politics like no other Conservative secretary of state.

Donald Dewar

5 May 1997 – 17 May 1999

Father of the nation

Donald Dewar was the last fully fledged secretary of state for Scotland, and, as a man with a passion for both politics and history, he was probably well aware of the 112-year story he was about to bring to a close. Dewar was a political anachronism, more at home in the era of Salisbury or Gladstone (his hero) than in Tony Blair's New Britain, and driven by an unfaltering Gladstonian commitment to Scottish home rule. Dewar, therefore, cannot be subject to the usual assessments of Scottish Office performance, for this was a secretary of state whose raison d'être was the subversion of a UK government department by a directly elected Scottish parliament.

Donald Campbell Dewar was born on 21 August 1937 in Glasgow, the only child of Dr Alisdair Campbell Dewar – a consultant dermatologist – and his wife, Mary Howat, née Bennett. His father, 'A gentle liberal with nationalist overtones',[1] collected paintings by the Scottish Colourists and took his son to the first nights of James Bridie's plays, while his mother ran the Scottish Culture Society. Both Dewar's parents, however, fell ill soon after his birth – his father with tuberculosis and his mother with a brain tumour – and from the age of two Dewar was sent to a Perthshire preparatory school run by family friends, and then to Hawick. He returned to Glasgow aged nine, attending Moss Park Primary and then the Glasgow Academy. Dewar was a talented debater, and the *Glasgow Academy Chronicle* for 1956 presciently recorded, 'Dewar showed once again a developing talent for demagoguery that will, we understand, reach full fruition only when Scotland has a prime minister of her own.'[2] But Dewar was neither happy at school, nor did he excel academically, staying on an extra year to retake his higher leaving certificate. When he arrived at Glasgow University in 1957 to study history, however, he blossomed socially.

Dewar not only met his future wife at university, Alison McNair, but also a large circle of political friends – many of whom would eventually join him in parliament – including the future Labour leader John Smith, the future Liberal Democrat leader Menzies Campbell, and the Conservative lawyer Ross Harper. He took a second degree, in law, on finishing his first in 1961, but many assumed this was solely to further his political ambitions, by now fairly prominent. Dewar had joined the Labour Party along with Smith, with whom he won the *Scotsman* debating trophy in 1961, and both became enthusiastic followers of the Labour leader, Hugh Gaitskell. Dewar in many ways resembled the former Unionist Scottish secretary Walter Elliot, both in educational background and in their cross-party social circles. Elliot and Dewar were also both cultural nationalists, steeped in the art and history of their native land without ever becoming political separatists. But if Elliot was Hamlet without the gloom, as his biographer called him, then Dewar was Hamlet with the gloom, although perhaps without the subplot. He was straight as a die, the childishness of student politics being anathema to him, and on leaving university in 1964 Dewar became a solicitor.

Two years earlier he had been selected as the Labour candidate for Aberdeen South, a seat then held by the Scottish Office minister Lady Tweedsmuir. Dewar lost in 1964 but won it in 1966, much to everyone's – including his – surprise. Still in his late twenties, with an earnest air and black spectacles, Dewar still looked every inch the student politician. He was not a fan of Harold Wilson's ambiguous style, but served on the Public Accounts Committee and from 1967 to 1969 was parliamentary private secretary to Anthony Crosland, then president of the Board of Trade. The two did not get along. 'He was amazingly arrogant, an intellectual elitist,' remembered Dewar, 'if you couldn't keep up it was too bad. He also had this ludicrous Match of the Day side, Grimsby was the centre of his universe.'[3] Wilson's Scottish secretary, Willie Ross, would no doubt have agreed, but he was suspicious of Dewar because of his pro-devolution tendencies. This perhaps mitigated against him when, in April 1968, Roy Jenkins unsuccessfully proposed the Aberdeen South MP for junior ministerial office.

Dewar's commitment to devolution was unusual in that it was fully formed from an early age and remained virtually unchanged throughout his political career. In a book published just before the 1970 general election, *The Scottish Debate: Essays on Scottish Nationalism*, the member for Aberdeen South almost pleaded with his party to address the issue:

> If, as suggested, the structure of government in Scotland remains an issue, it is not one which should be allowed to go by default. This matter should not be reduced to a narrow exercise in political tactics when what is required is anxious debate about the case for change . . . The present Government had

been committed as no other to balanced industrial growth and the even spread of economic power. It would be in no way dishonourable or inconsistent for the Labour Party to think in terms of parallel political developments. I hope it is prepared to do so.[4]

But, sadly for Dewar, at that time political tactics were precisely the basis on which constitutional change was assessed, particularly by the Labour party.

The year 1970 marked a low point in Dewar's life, both politically and personally. He lost his seat at that year's general election, was incapacitated by a spinal condition which would later cause him to stoop and limp slightly, and he also lost his wife, who left him for Alexander (Derry) Irvine, another Scottish lawyer and the future lord chancellor. Dewar was devastated, not least because Irvine was almost the exact opposite of himself, and he never remarried. He returned to Glasgow and became a reporter to the East Lanarkshire Children's Panel, also accepting legal work from his old friend Ross Harper, becoming a partner in his firm, Ross Harper & Murphy, in 1975. Colleagues remember Dewar being a 'formidable advocate', while he also presented a political programme called 'Clyde Comment' on Jimmy Gordon's (another university acquaintance) Radio Clyde, all of which made him a more rounded human being by the time he returned to the Commons in 1978.

The Garscadden by-election was a fraught affair, and for a while Labour feared it might fall to the nationalists. But Dewar fought off a strong SNP challenge with his eloquent support for a Scottish Assembly, by then (rather cynically) party policy. He campaigned for a 'yes' vote in 1979 and despaired at the result, and, when Labour lost the subsequent general election, Dewar became involved in the centre-right's attempt to hold back the left, voting for Denis Healey and Roy Hattersley in their leadership and deputy leadership bids. They both lost, but Dewar continued to keep digs in Michael Foot's (who beat Healey) Hampstead attic, although he had less time for Tony Benn (who nearly beat Hattersley), whom he blamed for splitting the Labour Party. When Bruce Millan retired from the front-bench in 1983, Neil Kinnock made Dewar shadow Scottish secretary in his place,[5] a position he was to hold for a staggering nine years, shadowing three Conservative secretaries of state. He was an able shadow, deferential to his opponents but never lenient, although frustrated that with 50 MPs (following the 1987 election) he had twice the mandate Malcolm Rifkind ever would. When Labour lost the 1992 general election, Dewar began to believe that government would pass him by. Sensing that he needed a change, the new Labour leader – his old university friend John Smith – moved him to shadow social security, a post he retained until a year after Smith's premature death in 1994. 'It's all most unfortunate,' was Dewar's gloomy verdict on the ensuing leadership election. 'Most unfortunate.'[6] A natural supporter of Gordon Brown, he sensed that Tony Blair was the likely victor. Dewar was right (although Brown did not stand), and in 1995 Blair made him Labour chief whip, another position in which he thrived. The 'tartan tax' debacle and the decision to go for a two-question referendum in June 1996 (one on devolution itself and another on tax-raising powers) was seen to have damaged George Robertson, Blair's shadow Scottish secretary; so, as the historic general election of 1997 approached, those in the know were certain that Dewar, and not Robertson, would be on his way to Dover House.

The *Scotsman*, until 1997 a consistent supporter of Scottish devolution, accused the new Scottish secretary and his team of 'hitting the ground strolling'[7] just 12 days after polling day. It was a nice headline, but unfair. Within two weeks of Labour's landslide there appeared a short Bill to hold two statutory referenda on Welsh and Scottish devolution, the latter with two questions, and within weeks a White Paper – *Scotland's Parliament* – had been published, becoming an unexpected best-seller. In September, despite a truncated campaign owing to the death of Diana, Princess of Wales, both Scottish referendum questions were endorsed with decisive majorities. Dewar had led a cross-party double-yes campaign, including the SNP and Liberal Democrats, while the Conservatives' 'Think Twice' campaign floundered, not least because the party no longer had any Scottish MPs to sell the message. The Scottish secretary was relieved by the outcome and, aided by his advisers Murray (later Lord) Elder and Wendy Alexander (later a Scottish Executive minister), set to work on a weekend revision of the White Paper, which became the Scotland Bill. The blueprint drawn up by the Scottish Constitutional Convention in 1992 formed its basis, although Dewar's first draft was rejected by the prime minister for being 'too Braveheartish'.[8] Blair wanted to emphasise the Union, while the Scottish secretary wanted to highlight Scotland's newly enhanced place within it. Like Bruce Millan, Dewar had a great eye for detail, which turned out to be an invaluable asset during meetings of the Cabinet committee on devolution to Scotland and Wales. This was chaired by Derry Irvine, with whom Dewar tried hard to sustain a constructive working relationship under obviously difficult circumstances. Irvine was more cautious than Dewar, but realised the importance of getting most major aspects of the Bill agreed upon swiftly. 'He did find it [the Cabinet committee] stressful,' recalled Henry McLeish, Dewar's minister of state. 'When he came back from these committees he looked like he'd been through the mill.'[9] Jack Straw, in a viewpoint reminiscent of opponents to the last Scotland Bill, worried about what it all meant for northern constituencies like his in Blackburn, but otherwise the Cabinet – in contrast to 1976/77 – was on side. And, despite his pessimism, Dewar won almost every major committee battle, before returning to Dover House to tell everyone how disastrous it had been.

The Scottish secretary unveiled his long-awaited Scotland Bill in December 1997 to almost universal acclaim. 'In well under 300 days,' he said, 'we have set in train the biggest change in 300 years of Scottish history.'[10] Unlike its ill-fated 1970s counterpart, this Bill clearly set out the responsibilities of the devolved parliament, leaving everything else re-served to Westminister, which ranged from abortion (as in 1978) to the regulation of hypnotists. 'There shall be a Scottish Parliament,' said Dewar, quoting the Bill's opening gambit. 'I like that.' So did most other MPs, bar a demoralised Conservative rump, and the Scottish secretary moved the Bill's Second Reading on 12 January 1998. 'It is part of the most far-reaching programme of constitutional reform that the country has seen for well over a century,' he told the House. 'In years to come, people will look back on it as a decisive step in the fight to modernise our constitution. The intention, the objective, is a new covenant with the people.' Dewar continued:

> In 1999, a Scottish Parliament will sit in Edinburgh for the first time in almost 300 years. It is not the reincarnation of the nation state which, in 1707, entered a partnership which became the United Kingdom; it is unashamedly a settlement within the United Kingdom – unashamedly, because the majority of Scots are determined to maintain the bonds of friendship, trust and common interest built over time. It has been and always will be the views of the people of Scotland that will alone decide their future.[11]

And again, in stark contrast to the Scotland Bill of 1978, its parliamentary stages were spared wrecking amendments from unreconstructed Labour back-benchers (of which there were many), and instead received qualified goodwill from everyone but the Conservatives. One clause carried over from the Constitutional Convention was that providing for elections to the new parliament by proportional representation. Dewar called this 'the best example of charitable giving this century in politics',[12] but he knew that it would legitimise the new institution in the eyes of a Scottish electorate used to voting Labour, Liberal Democrat and SNP in over-whelming numbers but being rewarded with a Conservative government. The question of mandate that had dogged Unionist and Conservative Scottish secretaries for more than a century had finally been solved; but the fervently anti-home-rule Arthur James Balfour was probably turning in his grave.

Ministers remember finding Dewar at St Andrew's House on 2 May 1997 'as excited as a child with a new toy'.[13] Even for a man who did not often become elated, it was an understandable state of mind. Having first been elected to parliament in 1966 and having sat on the Labour front-bench since 1981, not many MPs had to wait 31 years to become a minister; especially not those with as acute a vision as Dewar. He had thrashed out the technicalities of devolution with John P. Mackintosh in the late 1960s; now as secretary of state for Scotland he was drafting legislation to make those details a reality. The prime minister's attitude towards devolution, however, was little different than that of Harold Wilson more than 20 years earlier. Tony Blair viewed it not with enthusiasm, but rather as a manifesto pledge which would help fend off the nationalists. Crucially, he also trusted Dewar to deliver it, and backed up by the chancellor, Gordon Brown (a devolution enthusiast second only to the Scottish secretary), deliver it he did. Like Wilson, Blair was bored by devolution, as was the only other Scot he trusted with constitutional affairs, Derry Irvine. The Scottish secretary suspected this ambivalent attitude but realised what was achievable; and he was not starstruck by the prime minister as showman. The Labour peer Giles Radice recorded a weekend visit from Dewar in August 1998:

> He is very tired, complains of his age . . . As for Blair, he is more critical than I expected, although one has to remember that Donald has a close relationship with Gordon Brown. 'Blair is not as good a PM as I thought he would be.' He says that Cabinet government is not really working and that even Cabinet Committees are not all that important: 'The Blair government is mostly government by bilateral meeting' – and he means the meetings between Blair and Brown . . . He is a bit worried by Blair's authoritarianism. He always wants, according to Donald, to discipline or get rid of people. He thinks that Tony is not really in favour of devolution.[14]

Dewar was a natural worrier, and never did he worry more than during the passage of the Scotland Bill. Rather than kill Scottish nationalism 'stone dead', as George Robertson had memorably predicted, by early 1998 the SNP was climbing in the opinion polls. Meanwhile, a deal to ship nuclear waste from Georgia to Dounreay was struck by the prime minister and President Clinton over Dewar's head; the Glasgow Govan MP Mohammed Sarwar was charged with electoral fraud; another Scottish Labour MP, Tommy Graham, was suspended from the Labour Party after he was implicated in the suicide of a fellow Labour MP, Gordon McMaster; it emerged that the Scottish secretary had vetoed Sean Connery's knighthood just as he was being recruited to the 'yes' campaign; and so it went on. By March 1998 one poll showed the SNP just a point behind Labour in voting intentions for the first Scottish parliamentary elections; two months later the SNP were five points ahead.

The prime minister, who had intervened only sparingly during the drafting of the Scotland Bill, began to interfere with what he saw as the 'Scottish problem'. Blair was fond of Dewar, calling him 'DD', but despaired of his reluctance to be transformed by Alastair Campbell et al. The Scottish secretary was not New Labour; in fact, he was not 'new' anything, but Dewar realised that Blair was actually part of the problem. The prime minister was heard to call Scottish journalists 'unreconstructed wankers' on one early trip to Scotland, while an inept comparison of the Scottish parliament with a parish council had not gone down well with the devolution chattering classes. Under pressure from Downing Street to improve the Scottish Office media operation, Dewar forced the resignation of Liz Drummond (a civil servant), head of the press office, and brought in David Whitton (a former Scottish TV journalist) as a special adviser to sharpen things up. Meanwhile, the party tried to sharpen up the Scottish secretary, removing the very scruffiness which made several Glaswegian lady friends want to mother him. 'They are supposed to re-create me, but actually they simply try to tidy me up,' Dewar joked to a reporter. 'And even that defies them.'[15] And when Alastair Campbell accused the Scottish Office of not changing anything in Scotland, it was subtly pointed out that a meagre pension increase and a cut in benefits for single mothers were more of a problem for Scots voters than the Scottish secretary's sartorial elegance.[16]

So there was a falling out between 'DD' and the prime minister, albeit temporary, and Dewar undoubtedly felt under pressure. In public, he spoke of an ambivalence about ministerial life. 'My job isn't the be-all and end-all of life,' he told the *Sunday Times*. 'Remember, I got sucked into politics. There are no pictures of me outside Downing Street practising.' He added:

> I find power very worrying – I dither and peer at papers anxiously. I also sometimes find it rather ridiculous. I've led a rather behind-the-counter life. I haven't been scrapping up at the top. I fear that in some ways I am seen as a safe pair of hands, which is like calling someone a good constituency MP: it's what you say when you can't think of anything else to say about them.[17]

But in private he went much further, and even on occasion contemplated resignation. He admitted to one close friend, the broadcaster Fiona

Ross,[18] that he lacked 'the killer instinct' of John Smith when it came to dealing with troublemakers, preferring to avoid confrontation. 'He was paralysed by indecision,' remembered Ross, 'totally convinced that everyone was against him – government colleagues at Westminster, activists in Scotland, the media and even his closest friends and advisers. Some were undoubtedly out to undermine him but the majority, like me, were trying to help.' After only a year in the job Dewar was exhausted. He toyed with not standing for the Scottish parliament at all and remaining at Westminster to take on another portfolio, possibly leader of the House or chief whip. But Ross recalled that his favoured option was to resign from the Cabinet and retire from politics altogether at the next general election. 'If I gave up this job,' Dewar told her, 'I would miss it but not much.'[19] Perhaps these were the melancholy thoughts of a weary Scottish secretary, but then Dewar's was a complicated personality.

His wit was legendary, but could occasionally become caustic and wounding; his abruptness was accepted by friends but seen as rude by mere acquaintances; and his usually sound political judgement could, on occasion, fail him. Dewar had many close friends, particularly those he had known since university, but he underestimated his capacity to inspire affection and would be bemused to discover a seemingly illogical act of generosity. 'Donald Dewar is off in the Cotswolds living like a hermit in a cottage,' wrote Paddy Ashdown in early 1997. 'He has taken a suitcase full of books with him. Apparently, this is his dream way to spend the New Year. What a strange man.'[20] Not since Ernest Brown had a Scottish secretary owned so many books, but while Brown's were neatly arranged at his flat on Shaftesbury Avenue, Dewar's lay mostly in boxes at his Glasgow home.

In July 1998, Helen Liddell was moved from the Treasury to the Scottish Office, declaring herself – Willie Ross-like – as the 'Hammer of the Nats' at her first press conference. Dewar had asked for her personally, with half an eye on her replacing him as secretary of state once the Scottish parliament was up and running. But Liddell's aggressive style proved more suited to the 1970s than the 1990s, and there were also other problems with the Scottish Office team. Malcolm Chisholm, the minister for health, had resigned in late 1997 over cuts in single parents' benefits, without consulting Dewar, while Brian Wilson – an anti-devolutionist in a pro-devolution government – ploughed a semi-detached furrow on Gaelic language policy and land reform. Wilson saw himself as the heir to Willie Ross's ambitious yet incomplete proposals to transform Scotland's feudal system of land tenure. Dewar established the Land Reform Policy Group under the chairmanship of John Sewel, another of his ministers in the Lords, although any legislative action was deferred until after the Scottish parliament had begun work in 1999. Henry McLeish, who would later succeed Dewar as first minister, was minister of state and seen as capable, if a little prone to 'phoning the *Daily Record*'. There was also Sam Galbraith who, like McLeish, would remain as a minister in the first Scottish Executive Cabinet, Calum MacDonald, and Gus Macdonald, who joined the Scottish Office in 1998 at the suggestion of Gordon Brown, who felt a team comprising mostly academics and lawyers needed more business experience.[21]

Dewar, like the last Labour Scottish secretary, Bruce Millan, was generally not good at delegating tasks, and although he led weekly ministerial meetings they tended to be rather perfunctory. Relations, however, between the secretary of state and Scottish Labour back-benchers were excellent, as were those with senior civil servants, who admired Dewar's intellect and strength of purpose.

On 19 September 1998 the Scottish secretary was formally selected as the first directly elected leader of the Labour Party in Scotland,[22] and thus began a year-long campaign for the first devolved elections. But there were yet more problems, mostly as a result of the authoritarianism Dewar had earlier identified as a hallmark of Blairism. A new centralised system of selecting candidates resulted in some high-profile exclusions, including the Falkirk West MP Dennis Canavan, who promptly declared his intention to stand as an independent.[23] The SNP leader Alex Salmond, however, also had his ups and downs, a low-point being his tactless condemnation of Blair's 'unpardonable folly' in bombing Kosovo, and by April 1999 Labour were once again out-polling the nationalists. At the last ever 45–minute Scottish Questions on Tuesday 27 April 1999, Sir Teddy Taylor asked the Scottish secretary how he planned to advise Westminster MPs of the devolved parliament's activities. Dewar replied that MPs could read about it in the parliament's official report. 'I am not sure that was the most exciting answer I have ever given,' he added, 'but I hope it may be my last.'[24]

On 5 May 1999 the first elections were held to the Scottish parliament, giving Labour the largest number of seats but, as predicted, no over-all control. Dewar was returned in Glasgow Anniesland, and became first minister of Scotland. Nearly two weeks after polling day, the Scottish Office was renamed the Scotland Office, and the post of Scottish secretary was reduced to nothing more than a shadow of its former self; it was no longer the 'Pooh-Bah' of old. But politics is full of ironies, and none more marked than the contrast between Dewar the Scottish secretary and Dewar the first minister. Having never doubted his motives for creating a Scottish parliament, he was uncertain what, in practice, devolution was for. Not only that, but within less than a year Dewar had become embroiled in disputes of both policy and personality. Several of his staff members quit following minor scandals, and, more seriously, the estimated cost of the new Scottish parliament building at Holyrood continued to rocket – a direct result of the choice of location being rushed through while he was still secretary of state. In another ironic twist, Dewar even found himself missing Westminster, the very institution the new parliament was trying hard not to emulate either procedurally or politically. He had never intended to serve more than one term as first minister, but in the end he barely managed more than a year.[25]

The strain of the last three years in government had taken its toll, and in May 2000 Dewar underwent major open-heart surgery to repair a damaged aortic valve. He returned to work three months later but on 10 October he suffered a massive brain haemorrhage after falling outside Bute House, and died a day later at Edinburgh's Western General Hospital, aged 63. Dewar was two years older than Sir Godfrey Collins, who as Scottish secretary had died in office more than 60 years earlier. Like Sir Godfrey, Dewar's funeral was held at Glasgow Cathedral, his ashes later being scattered at Lochgilphead in Argyllshire.

'It is a rare privilege in an old nation to open a new Parliament,' said Dewar as the Queen opened the new institution on 1 July 1999. 'Today is a celebration of the principles, the traditions, the democratic imperatives which have brought us to this point and will sustain us into the future.'[26] It was a fine speech, all the more so because it hid the anxiety of only a few months before. 'I'm an obvious choice for the job,' he had mused ironically to a reporter. 'Maybe I'm just seen as part of the machine, a significant loyalist. In the book of this political age there will be three references to me in the index.'[27]

JOHN REID

17 MAY 1999 – 25 JANUARY 2001

Labour's attack dog

The story of Scotland's first three post-devolution secretaries of state is also that of Westminster coming to terms with the fledgling Scottish parliament. John Reid was initially bemused and then hostile; Helen Liddell was less so, but still found herself in conflict with two first ministers; and Alistair Darling essentially knew his place. The first, Reid, arrived at the renamed Scotland Office on 17 May 1999, just as Donald Dewar and Jim Wallace, the leader of the Scottish Liberal Democrats, put the finishing touches to the first Scottish Executive partnership agreement. Reid was surprised, finding himself in the Cabinet as secretary of state, but without any of the associated power. 'I have been a long-standing supporter of devolution,' he apparently remarked, 'but I didn't realise that it had gone so far.'[1] And so began the legendary 'turf wars' of Scottish media lore, with officials on each side urging their minister to take a stand over some perceived intrusion. To paraphrase Dean Acheson, the Scottish secretary had lost an empire, but not yet found a role.

Perhaps the differences between Dewar and Reid stemmed from their markedly different backgrounds. While the first minister's socialism was forged in West End drawing rooms, Reid's had been shaped in the more traditional Labour heartland of Lanarkshire. Born on 8 May 1947 to Tommy Reid, a postman, and his wife, Mary, a cleaner, John grew up in Cardowan, a mining village to the east of Glasgow. He was educated at St Patrick's High School in Coatbridge, where a fellow pupil was the three-years younger Helen Reilly (later Liddell). A keen guitarist, Reid played with a local group called the Graduates, who came third in a 1965 Airdrie battle of the bands competition, and, after working in an insurance office and as a labourer, he enrolled at Stirling University as a mature student in the early 1970s. There, he studied for an MA in History and later for a PhD in economic history. This earned Reid a job as Scottish research officer for the Labour Party from 1979, and for two years from 1983 he was a political adviser to the Labour leader, Neil Kinnock.

Reid had been a member of the Communist Party of Great Britain,[2] in which capacity he supported the Soviet invasion of Afghanistan. A quarter of a century later Reid would back another assault on that Middle Eastern country, this time under the auspices of an alliance between the US President George W. Bush and the UK prime minister Tony Blair. This marked the conclusion of a remarkable political journey, but Reid's politics were Blairism spoken with the authentic sound of old Labour, and spoken well. He entered the Commons as MP for Motherwell North in 1987, becoming opposition spokesman on children in 1989, and then shadow defence secretary in the run up to the 1997 general election. When George Robertson went to the Ministry of Defence instead of the Scottish Office following the Labour landslide Reid joined him as minister of state, becoming minister of transport a year later. Looking every inch the political bruiser, he was a witty, skilled administrator and a perceptive watcher of both people and politics.

At the Department for Transport Reid had attended Cabinet without being of its rank, so when he became Scottish secretary in May 1999, it was his first top-level post. Naturally, therefore, Reid wanted to do something with it, and set about maintaining a UK presence for the Scotland Office, while keeping a watchful eye on the fledgling Edinburgh parliament. Initially, this looked feasible. The Kvaerner shipyards in Glasgow had run into difficulties just prior to the first Scottish parliamentary elections, and, together with Gus Macdonald, who remained at Dover House having been made an under-secretary in 1998, Reid put together a successful rescue package. He also had to face the House in a shorter, monthly Scottish Questions session, now a surreal affair in which the Scottish secretary found himself unable to answer most questions put to him unless they related to social security or the economy, and even then he was technically responding on behalf of another department. Other observers believed Reid took a more 'expansionist' view of his post, and this is what led to conflict with Dewar in Edinburgh. 'The Scotland Office was created as an empty shell,' remarked Brian Wilson three years after leaving the Scottish Office, 'because that is the way Donald Dewar wanted it to be.'[3] The empty shell had 85 civil servants divided between Edinburgh (as yet without official accommodation) and Dover House in London.

But if Reid had begun to grow restless in his truncated department, all that was to change in October 1999. The *Observer* newspaper secretly recorded Kevin Reid, Reid's lobbyist son, apparently boasting to a reporter posing as a potential client about having access to ministers.

The reaction to this story was the first test of the as yet untested relationship between the Scottish secretary and the first minister, and it proved to resemble a can of worms. Other Scottish Executive ministers were implicated, and as Dewar rushed to their defence Reid launched a bitter attack on the *Observer*, while maintaining that his son had done nothing wrong. He also denied that there was any problem between him and Dewar, telling a fringe meeting at Labour's annual conference in Bournemouth that while there were bound to be difficulties associated with devolution, 'Donald and I' were determined to sort them out. But beyond the fringe, the situation was far from amicable. Dewar had made positive noises about an official inquiry into the affair by the Scottish parliament's Standards Committee; Reid thought this gave the story unwarranted credence and was furious at the likely implications for his son. The resulting tension bubbled to the surface at the conference's Scots Night. Amazed delegates watched as two grown men stood toe-to-toe, jabbing fingers into one another's chests. Reid and Dewar apparently paused as Tony Blair approached, and then resumed their slanging match as the prime minister walked away.[4] The clash ensured that the story, dubbed the first scandal of the new parliament, refused to die down. Dewar was finally forced to make a statement to members of the Scottish parliament, which was swiftly followed by an announcement from Beattie Media that it had shut down its lobbying wing, meaning that Kevin Reid's job was under review.

The following weekend, a contrived photo call found the Scottish secretary and first minister signing concordats which set down the 'ground rules' for relations between the London and Edinburgh executives. But from then until Reid moved to the Northern Ireland Office in January 2001 – a department where there was no question of the continuing need for a secretary of state – relations between him and the first minister were relatively incident-free. Dewar died suddenly in October, but the Scottish secretary only had to endure his successor, Henry McLeish, for a few months. The new first minister later called Reid 'a patronising bastard', so it was perhaps timely that Peter Mandelson's resignation spared McLeish the trauma of dealing with him for long. To date, Reid has gone on to occupy another five Cabinet positions: minister without portfolio (as a newly created chairman of the Labour Party); leader of the House; health secretary;[5] defence secretary, a post, which, like George Younger, he had coveted from the beginning of his Cabinet career; and, from May 2006, home secretary.

Helen Liddell

25 January 2001 – 12 June 2003

Stalin's granny

' "At eleven fifty-five, the Prime Minister asked me to become Secretary of State for Scotland," declared Ann Clarke, the fictional heroine of Helen Liddell's 1990 political thriller, *Elite*. "He has also asked me to be Deputy Prime Minister. Should I take it?" A roar swept through the crowd . . ."[1] And so it continues, the Eva Peron of Scottish politics makes love in her dressing room, and then arrives triumphant at Bute House. Liddell, on the other hand, did not even want to be Scottish secretary, despite her literary efforts ten years before she replaced John Reid at the Scotland Office. Tony Blair, however, had other ideas and – sans lip-gloss – the 51-year-old MP for Airdrie and Shotts became the first female secretary of state for Scotland. Peggy Herbison had become the first lady minister at St Andrew's House in 1950, to be followed by Lady Tweedsmuir in 1962 and Judith Hart two years later, and although the last of that trio certainly wanted the top job, no other female MP had since come close to achieving it. When Anne McGuire joined the Scotland Office as an under-secretary it became the only all-female government department (Lynda Clark was advocate-general). Liddell had been Donald Dewar's preferred successor in 1999, having requested her as his deputy in July 1998, but instead Reid had replaced him.

Like Reid, Liddell had attended St Patrick's High School in Coatbridge, although three years and sexual segregation separated the two future ministers. Helen Lawrie Reilly was born on 6 December 1950 to Hugh Reilly, and his wife, Bridget. After leaving school, Liddell attended Strathclyde University, graduating to work for the Scottish Trades Union Congress as head of its economics department from 1971 and rising to assistant secretary four years later. After a year as economics correspondent for BBC Scotland, Liddell embarked upon a high-profile political career as general secretary of the Scottish Labour Party in 1977. She was an immediate success. Denis Healey considered Liddell a 'beautiful and attractive young woman', while less patronising colleagues admired her political judgement and administrative ability.[2] A big test of that was the devolution referendum campaign of 1979. Liddell was pro-Assembly, but declared 'we will not be soiling our hands by joining any umbrella "yes" group'.[3] She left Keir Hardie House in 1988 to become director of personnel and public affairs for Robert Maxwell's *Daily Record* and *Sunday Mail*, forming a relationship with the media mogul not unlike that of Hector McNeil's with Lord Beaverbrook.[4] When the Labour leader John Smith, a close friend of Liddell's, died in 1994, she was chosen to fight the resulting by-election in his Monklands East seat, a full 20 years after contesting her last election in Fife East. It was a torrid campaign, dominated by claims of sectarian corruption in the local council, but Liddell saw off a stiff challenge from the SNP and consolidated her reputation as the 'Hammer of the Nats'. She was a front-bench spokeswoman on Scotland from 1995 until the election, when Liddell joined Gordon Brown's team as economic secretary to the Treasury. In July 1998 she was transferred to the Scottish Office in order to give Dewar's team a more aggressive edge, and in 1999 Liddell spent a few months as transport minister before moving to the Department of Trade and Industry, where she handled energy and Europe. 'I was at my happiest in mainstream economic/industry jobs,' Liddell later reflected. 'I did not want to be Secretary of State.'[5]

Liddell's new Cabinet position meant she often found herself speaking at the same events as the prime minister. At one, much was made of the fact that a gender shift had taken place at the Scotland Office. 'Is that true? Are you the first female Secretary of State?' whispered Blair to Liddell in the wings. She confirmed that she was and he whispered again: 'Why didn't you tell me?' 'I just didn't think it was an issue,' remembered Liddell. 'I was in the job for two days before it dawned on us that I was the first woman Secretary of State. I try to bring a slightly different dimension to it. British politics is tough so I can't be a simpering shadow in the corner.'[6] The new Scottish secretary's relations with Henry McLeish, Dewar's successor as first minister, were good, as was apparent when the pair were recorded without their knowledge by Scot FM just after the 2001 general election. McLeish let off steam, attacking a number of colleagues including John Reid, whom the first minister described as 'a patronising bastard', while Liddell murmured assent.

   Meanwhile, the Scottish secretary was making a creative attempt to carve herself a role distinct from that of the hapless McLeish. 'Friends of Scotland' was supposed 'to reach out to the Scots around the world who are opinion-formers', but the practical benefits of an international roll call were unclear, and Liddell found both Executive and Scotland Office civil

servants hostile to Westminster initiatives. The *Scotsman* was also unimpressed, and, having recently stepped up its criticism of the Scottish
parliament, the newspaper detected another easy target sitting in the
Regency splendour of Dover House. 'What is the point of Helen Liddell?'
screamed one typically hostile headline, and when a leaked engagement
diary revealed that the Scottish secretary found time for French lessons in
her schedule the press coverage got even worse. Liddell, despite being
labelled 'Stalin's granny' by the *Scotsman*, arranged a meeting with its
editor-in-chief, Andrew Neil, in an attempt to clear the air. The Scottish
secretary also presented Neil with a dossier of 'alleged inaccuracies',
which proved to be a tactical mistake. 'Helen Liddell versus the Scotsman
group' was the subsequent two-page headline, as the newspaper gleefully
rebutted each 'inaccuracy' point by point.[7] Liddell protested that both she
and George Foulkes, her ebullient minister of state, had their hands full
with almost 20 Cabinet committees.

In Cabinet, Liddell spoke on a wide range of matters, particularly Iraq
and counter-terrorism. The aftermath of September 11th also produced at
least one practical success: the introduction of more direct flights from
Scotland to the United States after the Scottish secretary called an
Edinburgh summit for airline companies. Nick Comfort, who joined
the Scotland Office as Liddell's special adviser, remembers that Henry
McLeish actually 'needed and welcomed' the Scottish secretary's support,
while the relationship changed completely when the first minister resigned
following a badly handled, yet minor, error of judgement, and was
succeeded by Jack McConnell.[8] The controversial and expensive free
personal care policy had created tension between the Scottish Executive
and certain Whitehall departments, and Liddell found herself caught in
the crossfire. There was no similarly divisive issue with McConnell as first
minister, although the Scottish secretary had bad memories of his
previous role as general secretary of the Scottish Labour Party, particularly during the Monklands by-election. There was, however, a common
theme with both first ministers. 'Henry McLeish and Jack McConnell
seemed to perceive the secretary of state as a threat rather than a
colleague who could fight their corner,' recalled Liddell. 'As devolution
settles down there should be more self-confidence in the relationship.'[9]

By early 2003 newspaper reports began to suggest that the Scottish
secretary had told friends she was 'bored' with the job and wanted to
move on. A House of Lords committee had recently recommended that
Liddell's job be scrapped or merged with another department, a conclusion the prime minister had also apparently reached. On 12 June 2003 the
stand-alone post of Scottish secretary was abolished. 'The party is finally
over for Stalin's granny,' crowed the *Scotsman*. 'After two years, £18

million of taxpayers' money and several thousand air miles, the party is finally over for Helen Liddell.'[10]

Liddell clocked up a few more air miles that summer by flying to Australia in preparation for her new role as British high commissioner in Canberra. She had been Scottish secretary for longer than the Marquis of Linlithgow and Viscount Novar, both of whom had served as governor-general of the Australian Federation before embarking on unhappy and short spells at the Scottish Office. Liddell was making the same career move in reverse, from a declining Scottish department to a more agreeable diplomatic posting in another proud corner of the globe.

ALISTAIR DARLING

12 JUNE 2003 – 5 MAY 2006

A safe pair of hands

On the morning of 13 June 2003 Scottish newspaper front pages were dominated with the news that Helen Liddell was no longer secretary of state; the Scotland Office had been scrapped and Lord Falconer, the newly created constitutional affairs secretary, was now in charge of Scottish affairs in the Cabinet. It was not, however, one of Tony Blair's most successful reshuffles. The same newspapers labelled the resulting confusion a 'dog's breakfast', while SNP leader Alex Salmond complained that the last time a peer had been responsible for Scotland was Lord Rosebery in 1945. 'Unfortunately,' lamented the *Herald*, 'Scotland looks like paying for his [Blair's] botched reshuffle.'[1]

Emerging from the fallout was the Cabinet veteran Alistair Darling. Although he had been identified as the minister answerable for Scotland in the Commons, it was unclear whether he would carry the title of secretary of state for Scotland, or indeed if he would command a distinct department. It soon became clear that both would survive; the former receiving a legalistic reprieve, and the latter now forming part of the new Department for Constitutional Affairs (DCA). Lord Falconer would not, after all, speak for his homeland in Cabinet. Darling, who was already transport secretary, was typically cautious when asked to comment, calling the arrangement 'a logical solution that recognised the changes now that the Scottish Parliament was bedded in'.[2] Bedded in it may have, but the four-year-old legislature still had its peculiar troubles. On the same day that Darling found himself with additional duties for Scotland, the first minister, Jack McConnell, appointed the former Scottish Office minister Lord (Peter) Fraser to chair the Holyrood Inquiry. This would examine, among other issues, decisions made by the late Donald Dewar relating to the new Scottish parliament building. It was a fitting coincidence, as Darling was determined not to repeat the mistakes of his predecessors. Subsequently, his tenure as Scottish secretary was to be low key, but, importantly, deliberately low key.

Alistair was the great-nephew of Sir William Darling, the former Conservative Lord provost of Edinburgh and MP for Edinburgh South. This Tory background was oddly appropriate for his great-nephew, who, as one contemporary has observed, was a Conservative at university, a Marxist in local government, and a New Labour centrist in Blair's Cabinet.[3] But, above all, Darling was a safe pair of hands, a trait shaped by his impeccably middle-class upbringing. Born on 28 November 1953 in London, Darling was educated at Loretto School in Musselburgh, where his teachers included the future Conservative minister and MP for Salisbury, Robert Key, who taught him economics. University at Aberdeen followed, where he studied law and became a splendidly bearded president of the students' representative council.[4] Darling began work as a solicitor in 1978, becoming an advocate six years later. Meanwhile, he had also joined the Labour-led Lothian Regional Council in 1982, assuming the chair of its transport committee in 1986. Darling resigned from the council when he was elected to represent Edinburgh Central at the general election of 1987, beating the former Scottish Office minister Alex Fletcher. In the Commons his rise was swift: Neil Kinnock made him home affairs spokesman in 1988; he moved to treasury affairs in 1992; and in 1996 Tony Blair promoted him to the Shadow Cabinet as shadow chief secretary to the Treasury. With his close-cut grey hair, black beard and dark eyebrows, Darling looked quite sinister. He lost the beard, reputedly at the request of Labour spin-doctors, and swapped his shadow post for the same as a minister following the 1997 landslide election. He was promoted to social security secretary after the 2001 poll, a portfolio later rebranded as the Department for Work and Pensions. Darling's final move came in 2002, when he was chosen to replace Stephen Byers at the crisis-ridden Department for Transport. His brief was to take the department out of the headlines, which Darling did, for he retained the safe pair of hands which had served him well since entering local government 20 years before. The transport secretary was almost alone in not being prone to gaffes, personal (or political) scandal, or accusations of plotting.[5] Although closer to his fellow Scot, the chancellor Gordon Brown, than the prime minister, Darling never strayed from his public loyalty to Blair.

Despite the headlines, the handover from Liddell to Darling was surprisingly amicable. The outgoing Scottish secretary was pleased with her successor, and at the Trooping of the Colour (of which Dover House had a fine view) two days after the reshuffle, Darling welcomed guests as they arrived while Liddell received them inside the building. But this good will hid a degree of uncertainty: the Scotland Office's demise had been widely speculated upon and many civil servants feared for their jobs. Many were moved to other Whitehall departments or the Scottish Executive, while the Glasgow office at Meridian Court closed down. This downsizing reflected the declining role of the Scottish secretary. Liddell's Friends of Scotland initiative was transferred to the Executive, where it was quietly filed away, and Darling contented himself with handling the monthly Scottish Questions in the Commons, but little else. In fact, he even willingly surrendered some of his transport powers to the devolved administration: the Railway Bill of 2004 wound up the Strategic Rail Authority and distributed its power to the Scottish Executive, Welsh Assembly Government and Greater London Authority. On other transport issues, such as cross-border motorways and a long-awaited upgrade for Edinburgh's Waverley Station, Darling was in the unusual position of having to negotiate with himself. Anne McGuire, conqueror of Michael Forsyth in Stirling six years earlier, remained as an under-secretary, but now under a DCA umbrella instead of the Scotland Office. She was replaced by the Greenock MP David Cairns later in 2003,[6] while Lynda Clark – the under-worked advocate general for Scotland – remained as a UK law officer to oversee any inter-parliamentary disputes.[7] Darling's style as secretary of state was intentionally understated, although his rather bland manner hid a dry wit and a surprisingly frank analysis of contemporary politics. On assuming responsibility for Scottish affairs as well as transport, he reputedly joked to one reporter that 'two poisoned chalices are better than one'.

While the Scotland Office may once have been a poisoned chalice, by now it had lost most of its venom. As a result of the Scotland Act, the number of Scottish constituencies was reduced from 72 to 59 at the 2005 general election. Darling's own Edinburgh Central seat was abolished, and he moved to the Edinburgh South-west constituency (nominally vacated by Lynda Clark). The previous year he had established the Commission on Boundary Differences and Voting Systems under the chairmanship of Professor Sir John Arbuthnott, which was charged with examining the consequences of having four different electoral systems in Scotland (single transferable vote for local government, additional member system for Holyrood, first-past-the-post for Westminster and proportional representation for the European Parliament), as well as different boundaries for UK and Scottish parliamentary constituencies. Sir John reported on 19 January 2006, recommending various tidying-up measures for each level of Scottish government. Darling welcomed the report, but stated that any legislative response would have to wait until after the 2007 Holyrood elections.

With Darling, the relationship between Holyrood and Westminster finally became harmonious. There were no longer any turf wars, personality clashes or conflicting policy initiatives. He dealt coolly with Scottish Questions each month,[8] and many colleagues could be forgiven for not noticing one half of his dual portfolio. Darling left both transport and Scotland for the Department of Trade and Industry after Tony Blair's May 2006 reshuffle. A safe pair of hands had been rewarded with a long-awaited Cabinet promotion.

Douglas Alexander

5 May 2006 –

The young pretender

On hearing that he was to replace Alistair Darling as both secretary of state for transport and Scotland, Douglas Alexander celebrated by watching a Snow Patrol concert in Glasgow. It is difficult to think of another Scottish secretary who would have relaxed in such a way, but, at just 38, Alexander was the youngest ever occupant of Dover House, beating both Malcolm Rifkind and the Earl of Dalhousie by a year. In many ways he was a more youthful version of his predecessor: both were supporters of Gordon Brown, and, like Darling, this Scottish secretary did not make political mistakes. But while Alexander was very much a Westminster man, his sister Wendy was elected to the Scottish parliament in 1999 and latterly served as enterprise minister before resigning in 2002, so this Scottish secretary had a unique insight into not only the machinations of Whitehall, but the often uncertain workings of the devolved parliament.

Douglas Garven Alexander was born on 26 October 1967 in Glasgow, a son of the manse (like his future mentor Gordon Brown).[1] He was educated at Bishopton Primary and Park Mains High School in Erskine, Renfrewshire, from where he joined the Labour Party aged just 14 in 1982. The Alexander household was intensely political. 'Our house was where the UCS [Upper Clyde Shipbuilders] workers met,' he later recalled, 'where the first anti-apartheid meeting in Scotland was held, as well as the first Alcoholics Anonymous meeting in Glasgow. It was a home and a centre for community action.'[2] Like his sisters Wendy and Susan, Alexander proved to be a natural academic, winning a scholarship to attend the Lester B. Pearson College in Vancouver, where he gained the International Baccalaureate Diploma. He returned to Scotland to study politics and modern history at the University of Edinburgh, where he chaired what was then the largest student Labour association in the UK. He won another scholarship in 1988 to study at the University of

Pennsylvania, and while in the United States Alexander worked as a press aide to the Democrats' presidential candidate, Michael Dukakis, during the 1988 election campaign. Back in the UK, he began a long association with Gordon Brown while working as his speechwriter and researcher during the future chancellor's spell as shadow trade and industry secretary in 1990. Alexander also trained as a solicitor, qualifying soon after unsuccessfully fighting the 1995 Perth and Kinross by-election caused by the death of the colourful Conservative MP Sir Nicholas Fairbairn. He again contested the seat (now simply called Perth) at the 1997 general election, but was beaten once more by Roseanna Cunningham. Just months later the Labour MP Gordon McMaster committed suicide and Alexander was selected to contest the resulting by-election in Paisley South.

At first, the 30-year-old MP took a backroom role, co-ordinating both the Scottish Labour Party's campaign for the first elections to the Scottish parliament in 1999 (he coined the slogan 'Divorce is an expensive business') and the UK party's strategy for the 2001 general election. His reward was swift, becoming minister of state at the Department of Trade and Industry in June 2001 with special respon-sibility for e-commerce and competitiveness. In May 2002, Alexander moved to the Cabinet Office with a similar portfolio, and a year later was promoted to become chancellor of the Duchy of Lancaster. In both roles, he occupied a more political role than was the norm, overseeing the work of the government's influential Strategy Unit, the Central Office of Information, and the Civil Service, often reporting directly to an impressed prime minister. From September 2004 Alexander acted as minister of state for trade at both the DTI and the Foreign Office, and following the 2005 general election he remained at the Foreign Office as minister of state for Europe, becoming a privy councillor soon after. But even after a few years as a middle-ranking minister, Alexander retained the air of a backroom strategist, more content with scrutinising policy papers than indulging in the cut and thrust of frontline politics. His membership of Labour's National Executive Committee was symptomatic of this geeky tendency, although his commitment to ending poverty was indicative of a more authentically socialist motiva-tion.

Following a reshuffle in May 2006, Alexander finally joined the Cabinet as secretary of state for transport and Scotland, neatly inherit-ing Darling's twin portfolios and avoiding the need for the Scotland Office to be attached to another unsuspecting minister. He was slick, sharp and capably continued his predecessor's tactic of doing nothing in particular when it came to Scotland, while concentrating more on the

Department for Transport. Some commentators were bemused at the sight of Alexander fielding his first Scottish Questions. Simon Hoggart called him 'the impossibly young-looking fellow-my-lad who is now secretary of state for Scotland', in his *Guardian* sketch.[3] But while Darling had limited himself to fairly routine criticisms of the SNP, Alexander showed himself more willing to indulge in some of the old-fashioned nat-bashing favoured by Labour Scottish secretaries such as Willie Ross and Helen Liddell. At a Press Fund lunch in Glasgow soon after becoming Scottish secretary, he attacked the SNP for peddling the politics of 'grudge and grievance'. 'The essential difference between myself and the Nationalists is this,' added Alexander, 'they believe that what scars Scotland is the border with England. I believe that what scars Scotland is poverty, inequality and injustice.'[4]

Unlike the initially devolution-sceptical Darling, Alexander was utterly committed to constitutional reform and was somewhat dismayed at the resulting turf battles between Scottish Executive ministers and Whitehall. And, while his predecessor worked reasonably well with the Scottish first minister, Jack McConnell, Alexander took a cooler view of the increasingly nationalistic leader of the Labour Party in the Scottish parliament. In June the Scottish secretary announced that the consti-tuency and regional ballot papers for the 2007 Scottish parliamentary elections would be combined to make the voting process as straight-forward as possible.

Mid 2006 saw the first substantial backlash against devolution, with a series of rows over the voting rights of Scottish MPs, the Barnett formula and even the very basis of the Union between Scotland and England. Alexander responded with a strong attack on the Conservatives' plans to designate some Bills as England-only, so-called English Votes for English Laws. 'The government remains as committed now to devolution as it was in 1997,' concluded a Scotland Office paper, 'just as it remains committed to a single class of member in the UK Parliament.'[5] And in summer 2006 the Scottish secretary also launched the opening salvo in Labour's campaign against the new Conservative leader David Cameron, claiming that his apparent success was nothing more than 'lipstick on a pig',[6] while also intervening in the row over US planes carrying weapons for Israel landing to refuel at Prestwick Airport. Alexander reportedly told the foreign secretary, Margaret Beckett, that such activity would 'play very badly' in Scotland and RAF Mildenhall was used instead. The Scottish secretary did, after all, still speak for Scotland when it came to UK foreign policy.

As that rare beast, a zealous Brownite who also had the respect of Tony Blair, the fourth post-devolution Scottish secretary could afford to play the long game. Not only did Alexander's promotion to the Cabinet allow him to prepare to co-ordinate the Scottish Labour Party's campaign for the 2007 Holyrood elections, it also enabled the young pretender to prepare for the senior office which would inevitably befall him once Gordon Brown finally seized the top job – both in the Labour Party and in government.

EPILOGUE

We are fallible. We will make mistakes. But we will never lose sight
of what brought us here: the striving to do right by the people of
Scotland; to respect their priorities; to better their lot; and to
contribute to the commonweal.[1]

> Donald Dewar's speech at the opening
> of the Scottish parliament, 1 July 1999

One hundred and fifteen years after the Convention of Royal Scottish
Burghs came together in Edinburgh's Free Church Assembly Hall to
demand the creation of a minister for Scotland, another gathering took
place which effectively ended the dominant role of the Scottish secretary.
As 129 members of the new Scottish parliament took their oaths in what
was now the meeting place of the General Assembly of the Church of
Scotland, a similar mood of expectation perhaps emanated from the
chamber.

In a speech to constituents in 1943, the wartime Scottish secretary Tom
Johnston harked back to the original meeting in January 1884. 'That
remarkable gathering represented all shades of political opinion in Scotland,' he said, 'and the representatives had met to demand a new phase in
the administration of Scottish affairs. It was a supreme example of what
unity in Scotland could achieve.'[2] Half a century later, cross-party
representatives gathered on the Mound under the banner of Scottish
Constitutional Convention to demand another new phase in the administration of Scottish affairs, although something much more profound
than in 1884. No longer was Scotland to be governed exclusively from
Westminster, and no more was the Scottish secretary of state – for 114
years the dominant personality in Scottish politics – to call the political
shots. Home rule, or devolution as it became known, had finally come to
fruition. First debated in the House of Commons in 1889, and frequently
since, a Scottish parliament had been established following a referendum
which produced a decisive majority in favour. As with the creation of
a secretary for Scotland in the summer of 1885, the establishment of a

Scottish parliament had also been a specifically political reaction to a sustained and noisy political campaign.

Donald Dewar, secretary of state since Labour's victory in 1997, elegantly bridged the constitutional gap by becoming the first First Minister of Scotland following a vote by MSPs at the parliament's second meeting, on 13 May 1999.[3] 'This must be a Parliament of Scotland's people,' Dewar told MSPs. 'We must look beyond the walls of this place to the people of Scotland.'[4] Ever since that day – and despite its many problems – the Scottish parliament has become a fixture in Scottish public life. No longer do deputations march into Dover House to seek the Scottish secretary's backing in some bitter dispute, and no longer is Scottish legislation debated during late-night sittings at Westminster.

But even so it is difficult to ignore some of the more negative aspects of devolution, at least from the point of view of Scotland's political influence. The Scottish Office had always been the most effective lobbying tool in Whitehall, and the value of its chief lobbyist being present at Cabinet meetings was undeniable. Lack of legislative time for Scottish Bills at Westminster was one of the main justifications given for the devolution of power, but there is no evidence that important reforms failed to become law due to pressures on Commons business. What is more, it is arguably the case that quantity of legislation is not necessary better than quality.[5]

What devolution did address was the problem of mandate, which had dogged the Conservatives since 1885. Although this argument made no sense within the context of a unified British political state, it was a politically unsustainable position. However, the powers of the Scottish parliament as compared with those of the old Scottish Office are largely the same. The idea that a Scottish Assembly could have resisted the worst excesses of Thatcherism had it existed in the 1980s is simply a nonsense. With taxation, foreign affairs and social security all reserved issues, a devolved Scotland would still have been powerless in the face of Mrs Thatcher's monetarist reforms, the Falklands War and periodic mass unemployment. Nevertheless, the majority of domestic policy areas are now under the control of the Scottish Executive, a situation no politician would now suggest be reversed. What devolution did was to make the Scottish Office democratically accountable; and in that sense it has been undeniably successful.

Scottish influence has also diminished at Westminster in other respects. Although the Scottish Affairs Select Committee continues to meet almost weekly, it has to be rather imaginative when it comes to finding topics worthy of investigation. Sir George Otto Trevelyan's creation, the Scottish Grand Committee, met infrequently from 1999, and for the last time on 13 November 2003, although it could be revived at any time. The ministerial ranks of the Scotland Office have also been whittled away. Although John Reid and Helen Liddell sat in the Cabinet solely as Scottish secretary, when Alistair Darling took over in 2003 the portfolio was attached to the Department for Transport, an arrangement which continued when Douglas Alexander succeeded Darling in 2006. And while George Foulkes remained as minister of state at the Scotland Office post-devolution, the position was downgraded to an under-secretary in May 2002. And even then, as of May 2006, David Cairns found himself dividing his time between the Scotland Office and the Northern Ireland Office. Two part-time ministers running a department which does not really exist (technically the under-secretary comes under the Department for Constitutional Affairs, or DCA), and with no tangible responsibilities, hardly seems a permanent arrangement. Even the elegant residences have disappeared. Bute House, for 30 years home to the secretary of state when in Edinburgh, is now used by the first minister; the Art Deco splendour of St Andrew's House now houses Scottish Executive civil servants; and even Dover House is now officially a DCA building eyed jealously by other government departments.[6] All the Scottish secretary has to call home in the Scottish capital is a small office on Melville Crescent.

So what then for the future of the Scottish secretary as a Cabinet post? That it should be abolished is undeniable. Several former ministers, a former permanent under-secretary, and other key figures, have called for just that. 'The next junction for the Scotland Office will come when the devolution settlement for Northern Ireland is re-introduced,' says Helen Liddell, 'then the whole issue of territorial departments will have to be reviewed.'[7] And there lies encapsulated another irony of Scottish political history: the Scottish Office, an indirect product of the Irish question in the Victorian era, could well find itself abolished once the Irish question of the early 21st century is at last resolved. The notion of a Ministry for the Nations and Regions is not new. Indeed, it almost looked as if the prime minister meant to move in that direction with the formation of the DCA in 2003. And once – and if – the Stormont Assembly is successfully reinstated, a UK-wide ministry co-ordinating the work of the Scottish parliament, the National Assembly for Wales and the Greater London Assembly is both practical and desirable. But the stumbling block remains the Province, and unfortunately the politics of Ireland are not renowned for either haste or stability.

But whatever happens, the Scottish (and Scotland) Office has had a good innings. Forty Scottish secretaries have found themselves in control of a bewildering array of responsibilities, and all have acted as 'Pooh-Bah' to varying degrees, although devolution deprived the position of that

Gilbertian tag. As James Naughtie concludes in his introduction, the Scottish Office had character. In its incumbents too, character was often abundant, and as often lacking. Most left their mark, however small, on Scotland, and with this book I hope to have consolidated some already substantial reputations, while rescuing at least a few from historical obscurity.

APPENDIX

Scottish Office Legislation 1885–2004

1885
Secretary for Scotland Act 1885 (c. 61)
Sea Fisheries (Scotland) Amendment Act 1885 (c. 70)

1886
Sporting Lands Rating (Scotland) Act 1886 (c. 15)
Crofters' Holdings (Scotland) Act 1886 (c. 29)
Removal Terms (Scotland) Act 1886 (c. 50)
Poor Law Loans and Relief (Scotland) Act 1886 (c. 51)
Sea Fishing Boats (Scotland) Act 1886 (c. 53)
Returning Officers (Scotland) Act 1886 (c. 58)

1887
Trusts (Scotland) Act, 1867, Amendment Act 1887 (c. 18)
Crofters' Holdings (Scotland) Act 1887 (c. 24)
Criminal Procedure (Scotland) Act 1887 (c. 35)
Public Houses, Hours of Closing (Scotland) Act 1887 (c. 38)
Lunacy Districts (Scotland) Act 1887 (c. 39)
Sheriff of Lanarkshire Act 1887 (c. 41)
Public Libraries Consolidation (Scotland) Act 1887 (c. 42)
Valuation of Lands (Scotland) Amendment Act 1887 (c. 51)
Secretary for Scotland Act 1887 (c. 52)
Prison (Officers' Superannuation, Scotland) Act 1887 (c. 60)
Technical Schools (Scotland) Act 1887 (c. 64)
Conveyancing (Scotland) Acts (1874 and 1879) Amendment Act 1887 (c. 69)

1888
Roads and Bridges (Scotland) Act 1878, Amendment Act 1888 (c. 9)
Factory and Workshop Amendment (Scotland) Act 1888 (c. 22)
Bail (Scotland) Act 1888 (c. 36)

1889

Secretary for Scotland Act 1889 (c. 16)
Agricultural Holdings (Scotland) Act 1889 (c. 20)
Herring Fishery (Scotland) Act 1889 (c. 23)
Small Debt Amendment (Scotland) Act 1889 (c. 26)
Judicial Factors (Scotland) Act 1889 (c. 39)
Local Government (Scotland) Act 1889 (c. 50)
General Police and Improvement (Scotland) Act, 1862, Amendment Act 1889
    (c. 51)
Clerks of Session (Scotland) Regulation Act 1889 (c. 54)
Universities (Scotland) Act 1889 (c. 55)
Parliamentary Grant (Caithness and Sutherland) Act 1889 (c. 75)

1890

Herring Fishery (Scotland) Act 1889, Amendment Act 1890 (c. 10)
Municipal Elections (Scotland) Act 1890 (c. 11)
Electric Lighting (Scotland) Act 1890 (c. 13)
Public Health Amendment (Scotland) Act 1890 (c. 20)
Removal Terms (Scotland) Act, 1886, Amendment Act 1890 (c. 36)
Census (Scotland) Act 1890 (c. 38)
Factors (Scotland) Act 1890 (c. 40)
Education of Blind and Deaf Mute Children (Scotland) Act 1890 (c. 43)
Elections (Scotland) (Corrupt and Illegal Practices) Act 1890 (c. 55)
Police (Scotland) Act 1890 (c. 67)

1891

Registration of Certain Writs (Scotland) Act 1891 (c. 9)
Presumption of Life Limitation (Scotland) Act 1891 (c. 29)
Law Agents and Notaries Public (Scotland) Act 1891 (c. 30)
Roads and Streets in Police Burghs (Scotland) Act 1891 (c. 32)
Local Authorities Loans (Scotland) Act 1891 (c. 34)
Trusts (Scotland) Amendment Act 1891 (c. 44)
Returning Officers (Scotland) Act 1891 (c. 49)
Public Health (Scotland) Amendment Act 1891 (c. 52)
Western Highlands and Islands (Scotland) Works Act 1891 (c. 58)

1892

Roads and Bridges (Scotland) Amendment Act 1892 (c. 12)
Sheriff Courts (Scotland) Extracts Act 1892 (c. 17)
High Court of Justiciary (Scotland) Act 1892 (c. 21)
Housing of the Working Classes Act 1890 Amendment (Scotland) Act 1892
    (c. 22)
Education and Local Taxation Account (Scotland) Act 1892 (c. 51)
Allotments (Scotland) Act 1892 (c. 54)
Burgh Police (Scotland) Act 1892 (c. 55)
Technical Instruction Amendment (Scotland) Act 1892 (c. 63)

1893
Local Authorities Loans (Scotland) Act, 1891, Amendment Act 1893 (c. 8)
Day Industrial Schools (Scotland) Act 1893 (c. 12)
Reformatory Schools (Scotland) Act 1893 (c. 15)
Burgh Police (Scotland) Act 1893 (c. 25)
Improvement of Land (Scotland) Act 1893 (c. 34)
Sheriff Courts Consignations (Scotland) Act 1893 (c. 44)
Burghs Gas Supply (Scotland) Act 1893 (c. 52)

1894
County Councils Association (Scotland) Expenses Act 1894 (c. 5)
Arbitration (Scotland) Act 1894 (c. 13)
Fishery Board (Scotland) Extension of Powers Act 1894 (c. 14)
Burgh Police (Scotland) Act 1892, Amendment Act 1894 (c. 18)
Public Libraries (Scotland) Act 1984 (c. 20)
Valuation of Lands (Scotland) Acts, Amendment Act 1894 (c. 36)
Nautical Assessors (Scotland) Act 1894 (c. 40)
Heritable Securities (Scotland) Act 1894 (c. 44)
Local Government (Scotland) Act 1894 (c. 58)

1895
Local Government (Scotland) Act 1894, Amendment Act 1895 (c. 1)
Convention of Royal Burghs (Scotland) Act 1879, Amendment Act 1895 (c. 6)
Cruelty to Animals (Scotland) Act 1895 (c. 13)
Courts of Law Fees (Scotland) Act 1895 (c. 14)
Court of Session Consignations (Scotland) Act 1895 (c. 19)
Fatal Accidents Inquiry (Scotland) Act 1895 (c. 36)
Sea Fisheries Regulation (Scotland) Act 1895 (c. 42)

1896
Glasgow Parliamentary Divisions Act 1896 (c. 17)
Housing of the Working Classes Act, 1890, Amendment (Scotland) Act 1896 (c. 31)
Orkney and Zetland Small Piers and Harbours Act 1896 (c. 32)
Agricultural Rates, Congested Districts, and Burgh Land Tax Relief (Scotland)
    Act 1896 (c. 37)
Law Agents (Scotland) Act, Amendment Act 1896 (c. 49)

1897
Trusts (Scotland) Act 1897 (c. 8)
Railway Assessors (Scotland) Superannuation Act 1897 (c. 12)
Edinburgh University (Transfer of Patronage) Act 1897 (c. 13)
Market Gardeners Compensation (Scotland) Act 1897 (c. 22)
Municipal Elections (Scotland) Act 1897 (c. 34)
Public Health (Scotland) Act 1897 (c. 38)
Stipendiary Magistrates Jurisdiction (Scotland) Act 1897 (c. 48)
Parish Councils Casual Vacancies (Scotland) Act 1897 (c. 49)
Licensing Amendment (Scotland) Act 1897 (c. 50)
Congested Districts (Scotland) Act 1897 (c. 53)
Education (Scotland) Act 1897 (c. 62)

1898
Sheriff's Tenure of Office (Scotland) Act 1898 (c. 8)
Ex-officio Justices of the Peace (Scotland) Act 1898 (c. 20)
Poor Law (Scotland) Act 1898 (c. 21)
Rivers Pollution Prevention (Border Councils) Act 1898 (c. 34)
Vexatious Actions (Scotland) Act 1898 (c. 35)
Circuit Clerks (Scotland) Act 1898 (c. 40)
Trusts (Scotland) Act 1898 (c. 42)
Local Taxation Account (Scotland) Act 1898 (c. 56)

1899
Public Libraries (Scotland) Act 1899 (c. 5)
Fine or Imprisonment (Scotland and Ireland) Act 1899 (c. 11)
Private Legislation Procedure (Scotland) Act 1899 (c. 47)

1900
Ecclesiastical Assessments (Scotland) Act 1900 (c. 20)
Inebriates Amendment (Scotland) Act 1900 (c. 28)
Town Councils (Scotland) Act 1900 (c. 49)
Lunacy Board (Scotland) Salaries and Clerks Act 1900 (c. 54)
Executors (Scotland) Act 1900 (c. 55)

1901
Education (Scotland) Act 1901 (c. 9)
Burgh Sewerage, Drainage and Water Supply (Scotland) Act 1901 (c. 24)

1902
Immoral Traffic (Scotland) Act 1902 (c. 11)
Lands Valuation (Scotland) Amendment Act 1902 (c. 25)
Freshwater Fish (Scotland) Act 1902 (c. 29)
Electric Lighting (Scotland) Act 1902 (c. 35)

1903
Licensing (Scotland) Act 1903 (c. 25)
Burgh Police (Scotland) Act 1903 (c. 33)
Town Councils (Scotland) Act 1903 (c. 34)

1904
Wild Birds Protection (St Kilda) Act 1904 (c. 10)
Secretary for Scotland Act 1904 (c. 27)
Prisons (Scotland) Act 1904 (c. 35)

1905
Churches (Scotland) Act 1905 (c. 12)

1906
Education of Defective Children (Scotland) Act 1906 (c. 10)
Fatal Accidents and Sudden Deaths Inquiry (Scotland) Act 1906 (c. 35)
Statute Law Revision (Scotland) Act 1906 (c. 38)
National Galleries of Scotland Act 1906 (c. 50)

1907
Public Health (Scotland) Amendment Act 1907 (c. 30)
Whale Fisheries (Scotland) Act 1907 (c. 41)
Sea Fisheries (Scotland) Application of Penalties Act 1907 (c. 42)
Qualification of Women (County and Town Councils) (Scotland) Act 1907 (c. 48)
Vaccination (Scotland) Act 1907 (c. 49)
Sheriff Courts (Scotland) Act 1907 (c. 51)

1908
Tobacco Growing (Scotland) Act 1908 (c. 10)
Local Government (Scotland) Act 1908 (c. 62)
Education (Scotland) Act 1908 (c. 63)
Agricultural Holdings (Scotland) Act 1908 (c. 64)
Summary Jurisdiction (Scotland) Act 1908 (c. 65)

1909
Prisons (Scotland) Act 1909 (c. 27)
Summary Jurisdiction (Scotland) Act, 1908, Amendment Act 1909 (c. 28)
Wild Animals in Captivity Protection (Scotland) Act 1909 (c. 33)

1910
Police (Scotland) Act 1890, Amendment Act 1910 (c. 10)
Trusts (Scotland) Act 1910 (c. 22)
Agriculture Holdings (Scotland) Amendment Act 1910 (c. 30)
Jury Trials Amendment (Scotland) Act 1910 (c. 31)
Registration of Births, Deaths and Marriages (Scotland) Amendment Act 1910
  (c. 32)

1911
Intestate Husband's Estate (Scotland) Act 1911 (c. 10)
Public Health (Scotland) Act 1897, Amendment Act 1911 (c. 30)
Small Landholders (Scotland) Act 1911 (c. 49)
Burgh Police (Scotland) Amendment Act 1911 (c. 51)
House Letting and Rating (Scotland) Act 1911 (c. 53)

1912
Protection of Animals (Scotland) Act 1912 (c. 14)
Royal Scottish Museum (Extension) Act 1912 (c. 16)

1913
Clerks of Session (Scotland) Regulation Act 1913 (c. 23)
Sheriff Courts (Scotland) Act 1913 (c. 28)
Education (Scotland) Act 1913 (c. 12)
Education (Scotland) (Glasgow Electoral Districts) Act 1913 (c. 13)
Bankruptcy (Scotland) Act 1913 (c. 20)
Highlands and Islands (Medical Service) Grant Act 1913 (c. 26)
Temperance (Scotland) Act 1913 (c. 33)
Mental Deficiency and Lunacy (Scotland) Act 1913 (c. 38)

1914

Police (Weekly Rest-Day) (Scotland) Act 1914 (c. 8)
County, Towns and Parish Councils (Qualification) (Scotland) Act 1914 (c. 39)
Entail (Scotland) Act 1914 (c. 43)
Metropolitan Police (Employment in Scotland) Act 1914 (c. 44)
Milk and Dairies Small Landholders (Scotland) Act 1914 (c. 46)
Feudal Casualties (Scotland) Act 1914 (c. 48)
Special Constables (Scotland) Act 1914 (c. 53)
Education (Scotland) (War Service Superannuation) Act 1914 (c. 67)
Education (Scotland) (Provision of Meals) Act 1914 (c. 68)
Police (Scotland) (Limit of Age) Act 1914 (c. 69)
Local Government (Adjustments) (Scotland) Act 1914 (c. 74)
Sheriff Courts (Scotland) Amendment Act 1914 (c. 5)
Law Agents Apprenticeship (War Service) (Scotland) Act 1914 (c. 20)

1915

Special Constables (Scotland) Act 1915 (c. 47)
Housing (Rosyth Dockyard) Act 1915 (c. 49)
Scottish Universities (Emergency Powers) Act 1915 (c. 78)
Street Collections Regulation (Scotland) Act 1915 (c. 88)
Midwives (Scotland) Act 1915 (c. 91)

1916

Marriage (Scotland) Act 1916 (c. 7)
Court of Session (Extracts) Act 1916 (c. 49)

1917

Gaming Machines (Scotland) Act 1917 (c. 23)
Confirmation of Executors (War Service) (Scotland) Act 1917 (c. 27)

1918

Burgh Gas Supply (Scotland) Amendment Act 1918 (c. 45)
Education (Scotland) Act 1918 (c. 48)

1919

Intestate Husband's Estate (Scotland) Act 1919 (c. 9)
War Charities (Scotland) Act 1919 (c. 12)
Education (Scotland) (Superannuation) Act 1919 (c. 17)
Scottish Board of Health Act 1919 (c. 20)
Law Agents Apprenticeship (War Service) (Scotland) Act 1919 (c. 24)
Housing, Town Planning, etc. (Scotland) Act 1919 (c. 60)
Intestate Moveable Succession (Scotland) Act 1919 (c. 61)
Regimental Debts (Deposit of Wills) (Scotland) Act 1919 (c. 89)
Nurses Registration (Scotland) Act 1919 (c. 95)
Land Settlement (Scotland) Act 1919 (c. 97)

1920

House-Letting and Rating (Scotland) Act 1920 (c. 8)
Ejection (Suspensory Provisions) (Scotland) Act 1920 (c. 11)
Duplicands of Feu-duties (Scotland) Act 1920 (c. 34)
Merchant Shipping (Scottish Fishing Boats) Act 1920 (c. 39)
Public Libraries (Scotland) Act 1920 (c. 45)
Jurors (Enrolment of Women) (Scotland) Act 1920 (c. 53)
Married Women's Property (Scotland) Act 1920 (c. 64)
Registrar General (Scotland) Act 1920 (c. 69)
Housing (Scotland) Act 1920 (c. 71)

1921

Protection of Animals (Scotland) Act, 1912, Amendment Act 1921 (c. 22)
Church of Scotland Act 1921 (c. 29)
Housing (Scotland) Act 1921 (c. 33)
Criminal Procedure (Scotland) Act 1921 (c. 50)
Trusts (Scotland) Act 1921 (c. 58)
Poor Law Emergency Provisions (Scotland) Act 1921 (c. 64)

1922

Universities (Scotland) Act 1922 (c. 31)
Whale Fisheries (Scotland) (Amendment) Act 1922 (c. 34)
Education (Scotland) (Superannuation) Act 1922 (c. 48)
Allotments (Scotland) Act 1922 (c. 52)

1923

Agricultural Holdings (Scotland) Act 1923 (c. 10)
Town Councils (Scotland) Act 1923 (c. 41)

1924

Poor Law Emergency Provisions Continuance (Scotland) Act 1924 (c. 9)
Education (Scotland) (Superannuation) Act 1924 (c. 13)
Small Debt (Scotland) Act 1924 (c. 16)
Conveyancing (Scotland) Act 1924 (c. 27)
Local Authorities Loans (Scotland) Act 1924 (c. 36)

1925

Housing (Scotland) Act 1925 (c. 15)
Town Planning (Scotland) Act 1925 (c. 17)
Church of Scotland (Property and Endowments) Act 1925 (c. 33)
Poor Law Emergency Provisions Continuance (Scotland) Act 1925 (c. 35)
Education (Scotland) (Superannuation) Act 1925 (c. 55)
National Library of Scotland Act 1925 (c. 73)
Public Health (Scotland) Amendment Act 1925 (c. 75)
Circuit Courts and Criminal Procedure (Scotland) Act 1925 (c. 81)
Roads and Streets in Police Burghs (Scotland) Act 1925 (c. 82)
Education (Scotland) Act 1925 (c. 89)

1926
Allotments (Scotland) Act 1926 (c. 5)
Criminal Appeal (Scotland) Act 1926 (c. 15)
Execution of Diligence (Scotland) Act 1926 (c. 16)
Heather Burning (Scotland) Act 1926 (c. 30)
Rating (Scotland) Act 1926 (c. 47)
Burgh Registers (Scotland) Act 1926 (c. 50)
Prisons (Scotland) Act 1926 (c. 57)

1927
Poor Law Emergency Provisions (Scotland) Act 1927 (c. 3)
Midwives and Maternity Homes (Scotland) Act 1927 (c. 17)
Criminal Appeals (Scotland) Act 1927 (c. 26)
Sheriff Courts and Legal Officers (Scotland) Act 1927 (c. 35)

1928
Rating (Scotland) Amendment Act 1928 (c. 6)
Betting (Juvenile Messengers) (Scotland) Act 1928 (c. 27)
Education (Scotland) Act 1928 (c. 28)
Slaughter of Animals (Scotland) Act 1928 (c. 29)
Educational Endowments (Scotland) Act 1928 (c. 30)
Reorganisation of Offices (Scotland) Act 1928 (c. 34)
Western Highlands and Islands (Transport Services) Act 1928 (c. 6)

1929
Agricultural Credits (Scotland) Act 1929 (c. 13)
Local Government (Scotland) Act 1929 (c. 25)
Highlands and Islands (Medical Service) Additional Grant Act 1929 (c. 13)

1930
Land Drainage (Scotland) Act 1930 (c. 20)
Illegitimate Children (Scotland) Act 1930 (c. 33)
Education (Scotland) Act 1930 (c. 36)
Adoption of Children (Scotland) Act 1930 (c. 37)
Housing (Scotland) Act 1930 (c. 40)

1931
Acquisition of Land (Assessment of Compensation) (Scotland) Act 1931 (c. 11)
Probation of Offenders (Scotland) Act 1931 (c. 30)
Adoption of Children (Scotland) Act 1931 (c. 37)
Small Landholders and Agricultural Holdings (Scotland) Act 1931 (c. 44)
Educational Endowments (Scotland) Act 1931 (c. 5)

1932
Universities (Scotland) Act 1932 (c. 26)
Hire Purchase and Small Debt (Scotland) Act 1932 (c. 38)
Children and Young Persons (Scotland) Act 1932 (c. 47)
Town and Country Planning (Scotland) Act 1932 (c. 49)

1933
Housing (Financial Provisions) (Scotland) Act 1933 (c. 16)
False Oaths (Scotland) Act 1933 (c. 20)
Solicitors (Scotland) Act 1933 (c. 21)
Trout (Scotland) Act 1933 (c. 35)
Private Legislation Procedure (Scotland) Act 1933 (c. 37)
Administration of Justice (Scotland) Act 1933 (c. 41)
Church of Scotland (Property and Endowments) Amendment Act 1933 (c. 44)

1934
Illegal Trawling (Scotland) Act 1934 (c. 18)
Registration of Births, Deaths, and Marriages (Scotland) (Amendment) Act 1934
    (c. 19)
Assessor of Public Undertakings (Scotland) Act 1934 (c. 22)
Protection of Animals (Cruelty to Dogs) (Scotland) Act 1934 (c. 25)
Land Settlement (Scotland) Act 1934 (c. 35)
Poor Law (Scotland) Act 1934 (c. 52)

1935
Educational Endowments (Scotland) Act 1935 (c. 5)
Land Drainage (Scotland) Act 1935 (c. 19)
Criminal Lunatics (Scotland) Act 1935 (c. 32)
Public Health (Water and Sewerage) (Scotland) Act 1935 (c. 36)
Housing (Scotland) Act 1935 (c. 41)

1936
Education (Scotland) Act 1936 (c. 42)
Private Legislation Procedure (Scotland) Act 1936 (c. 52)
Weights and Measures, Sale of Coal (Scotland) Act 1936 (c. 54)

1937
Harbours, Piers and Ferries (Scotland) Act 1937 (c. 28)
Local Government (Financial Provisions) (Scotland) Act 1937 (c. 29)
Maternity Services (Scotland) Act 1937 (c. 30)
Sheep Stocks Valuation (Scotland) Act 1937 (c. 34)
Children and Young Persons (Scotland) Act 1937 (c. 37)
Public Records (Scotland) Act 1937 (c. 43)
Methylated Spirits (Sale by Retail) (Scotland) Act 1937 (c. 48)
Agricultural Wages (Regulation) (Scotland) Act 1937 (c. 53)
Local Government Superannuation (Scotland) Act 1937 (c. 69)

1938
Conveyancing Amendment (Scotland) Act 1938 (c. 24)
Scottish Land Court Act 1938 (c. 31)
Prevention and Treatment of Blindness (Scotland) Act 1938 (c. 32)
Housing (Agricultural Population) (Scotland) Act 1938 (c. 38)
Criminal Procedure (Scotland) Act 1938 (c. 48)
Divorce (Scotland) Act 1938 (c. 50)

1938—*contd*
Registration of Still-Births (Scotland) Act 1938 (c. 55)
Rating and Valuation (Air-Raid Works) (Scotland) Act 1938 (c. 66)
Nursing Homes Registration (Scotland) Act 1938 (c. 73)
Housing (Financial Provisions) (Scotland) Act 1938 (c. 3)

1939
Custody of Children (Scotland) Act 1939 (c. 4)
Reorganisation of Offices (Scotland) Act 1939 (c. 20)
Public Health (Coal Mine Refuse) Scotland Act 1939 (c. 23)
Local Government (Scotland) Act 1939 (c. 28)
Marriage (Scotland) Act 1939 (c. 34)
Administration of Justice (Emergency Provisions) Scotland Act 1939 (c. 79)
War Damage to Land (Scotland) Act 1939 (c. 80)
Education (Scotland) (War Service Superannuation) Act 1939 (c. 96)
Sheriff Courts (Scotland) Act 1939 (c. 98)
Education (Emergency) (Scotland) Act 1939 (c. 112)
Courts (Emergency Powers) (Scotland) Act 1939 (c. 113)

1940
Mental Deficiency (Scotland) Act 1940 (c. 8)
Agricultural Wages (Regulation) (Scotland) Act 1940 (c. 27)
Marriage (Scotland) (Emergency Provisions) Act 1940 (c. 30)
Confirmation of Executors (War Service) (Scotland) Act 1940 (c. 41)
Law Reform (Miscellaneous Provisions) (Scotland) Act 1940 (c. 42)
Scottish Fisheries Advisory Council Act 1940 (c. 1)

1941
Scottish Fisheries Advisory Council Act 1941 (c. 1)
Land Drainage (Scotland) Act 1941 (c. 13)
Rating (War Damage) (Scotland) Act 1941 (c. 25)
War Damage to Land (Scotland) Act 1941 (c. 40)
Local Government (Financial Provisions) (Scotland) Act 1941 (c. 45)

1942
Education (Scotland) Act 1942 (c. 5)
Marriage (Scotland) Act 1942 (c. 20)

1943
Housing (Agricultural Population) (Scotland) Act 1943 (c. 22)
Hydro-Electric Development (Scotland) Act 1943 (c. 32)
Nurses (Scotland) Act 1943 (c. 33)
Town and Country Planning (Interim Development) (Scotland) Act 1943 (c. 43)
Rent of Furnished Houses Control (Scotland) Act 1943 (c. 44)

1944
Courts (Emergency Powers) (Scotland) Act 1944 (c. 6)
Housing (Scotland) Act 1944 (c. 39)

1945
Liabilities (War-Time Adjustment) (Scotland) Act 1945 (c. 29)
Town and Country Planning (Scotland) Act 1945 (c. 33)
Hydro-Electric Undertakings (Valuation for Rating) (Scotland) Act 1945 (c. 34)
Education (Scotland) Act 1945 (c. 37)
Coatbridge and Springburn Elections (Validation) Act 1945 (c. 3)
Public Health (Scotland) Act 1945 (c. 15)

1946
Local Government (Financial Provisions) (Scotland) Act 1946 (c. 25)
Water (Scotland) Act 1946 (c. 42)
Housing (Financial Provisions) (Scotland) Act 1946 (c. 54)
Police (Scotland) Act 1946 (c. 71)
Education (Scotland) Act 1946 (c. 72)
Association of County Councils (Scotland) Act 1946 (c. 77)

1947
National Health Service (Scotland) Act 1947 (c. 27)
Education (Exemptions) (Scotland) Act 1947 (c. 36)
Acquisition of Land (Authorisation Procedure) (Scotland) Act 1947 (c. 42)
Local Government (Scotland) Act 1947 (c. 43)
Town and Country Planning (Scotland) Act 1947 (c. 53)

1948
Lord High Commissioner (Church of Scotland) Act 1948 (c. 30)
Agriculture (Scotland) Act 1948 (c. 45)
Public Registers and Records (Scotland) Act 1948 (c. 57)
Administration of Justice (Scotland) Act 1948 (c. 10)

1949
Education (Scotland) Act 1949 (c. 19)
Tenancy of Shops (Scotland) Act 1949 (c. 25)
Agricultural Wages (Scotland) Act 1949 (c. 30)
Water (Scotland) Act 1949 (c. 31)
Slaughter of Animals (Scotland) Act 1949 (c. 52)
Housing (Scotland) Act 1949 (c. 61)
Legal Aid and Solicitors (Scotland) Act 1949 (c. 63)
Agricultural Holdings (Scotland) Act 1949 (c. 75)
Criminal Justice (Scotland) Act 1949 (c. 94)
Nurses (Scotland) Act 1949 (c. 95)

1950
Public Registers and Records (Scotland) Act 1950 (c. 11)
Housing (Scotland) Act 1950 (c. 34)
Allotments (Scotland) Act 1950 (c. 38)

1951
Local Government (Scotland) Act 1951 (c. 15)
Alkali, etc, Works Regulations (Scotland) Act 1951 (c. 21)
Salmon and Freshwater Fisheries (Protection) (Scotland) Act 1951 (c. 26)

1951—*contd*
Midwives (Scotland) Act 1951 (c. 54)
Nurses (Scotland) Act 1951 (c. 55)
Rivers (Prevention of Pollution) (Scotland) Act 1951 (c. 66)

1952
Hydro-Electricity Development (Scotland) Act 1952 (c. 22)
Rating and Valuation (Scotland) Act 1952 (c. 47)
Prisons (Scotland) Act 1952 (c. 61)
Housing (Scotland) Act 1952 (c. 63)

1953
Harbours, Piers and Ferries (Scotland) Act 1953 (c. 11)
Leasehold Property Act and Long Leases (Scotland) Act Extension 1953
    (c. 12)
University of St Andrews Act 1953 (c. 40)
Hospital Endowments (Scotland) Act 1953 (c. 41)

1954
Local Government (Financial Provisions) (Scotland) Act 1954 (c. 13)
National Museum of Antiquities (Scotland) Act 1954 (c. 14)
Summary Jurisdiction (Scotland) Act 1954 (c. 48)
Long Leases (Scotland) Act 1954 (c. 49)
Housing (Repair and Rents) (Scotland) Act 1954 (c. 50)
Electricity Reorganisation (Scotland) Act 1954 (c. 60)
Town and Country Planning (Scotland) Act 1954 (c. 73)

1955
Crofters (Scotland) Act 1955 (c. 21)
Public Libraries (Scotland) Act 1955 (c. 27)

1956
Police (Scotland) Act 1956 (c. 26)
Food and Drugs (Scotland) Act 1956 (c. 30)
Local Government (Street Works) (Scotland) Act 1956 (c. 40)
Valuation and Rating (Scotland) Act 1956 (c. 60)
Marriage (Scotland) Act 1956 (c. 70)
Education (Scotland) Act 1956 (c. 75)

1957
Church of Scotland (Property and Endowments) Act 1957 (c. 30)
Housing and Town Development (Scotland) Act 1957 (c. 38)

1958
Land Drainage (Scotland) Act 1958 (c. 24)
Solicitors (Scotland) Act 1958 (c. 28)
Local Government (Omnibus Shelters and Queue Barriers) (Scotland) Act 1958
    (c. 50)

1958—*contd*
Interest on Damages (Scotland) Act 1958 (c. 61)
Local Government and Miscellaneous Financial Provisions (Scotland) Act 1958
    (c. 64)

1959
Intestate Husband's Estate (Scotland) Act 1959 (c. 21)
Building (Scotland) Act 1959 (c. 24)
Sea Fisheries (Compensation) (Scotland) Act 1959 (c. 27)
Deer (Scotland) Act 1959 (c. 40)
Licensing (Scotland) Act 1959 (c. 51)
National Galleries of Scotland Act 1959 (c. 61)
Town and Country Planning (Scotland) Act 1959 (c. 70)
Lord High Commissioner (Church of Scotland) Act 1959 (c. 8)

1960
Wages Arrestment Limitation (Amendment) (Scotland) Act 1960 (c. 21)
First Offenders (Scotland) Act 1960 (c. 23)
Occupier's Liability (Scotland) Act 1960 (c. 30)
Highlands and Islands Shipping Services (Scotland) Act 1960 (c. 31)
Mental Health (Scotland) Act 1960 (c. 61)

1961
Local Authorities (Expenditure on Special Purposes) (Scotland) Act 1961 (c. 32)
Flood Prevention (Scotland) Act 1961 (c. 41)
Sheriffs' Pensions (Scotland) Act 1961 (c. 42)
Companies (Floating Charges) (Scotland) Act 1961 (c. 46)
Credit-Sale Agreements (Scotland) Act 1961 (c. 56)
Trusts (Scotland) Act 1961 (c. 57)
Crofters (Scotland) Act 1961 (c. 58)

1962
Local Government (Financial Provisions etc) (Scotland) Act 1962 (c. 9)
Forth and Clyde Canal (Extinguishment of Rights of Navigation) Act 1962
    (c. 16)
Housing (Scotland) Act 1962 (c. 28)
Law Reform (Damages and Solatium) (Scotland) Act 1962 (c. 42)
Education (Scotland) Act 1962 (c. 47)
Licensing (Scotland) Act 1962 (c. 51)
Electricity (Borrowing Powers) (Scotland) Act 1962 (c. 7)

1963
Local Government (Financial Provisions) (Scotland) Act 1963 (c. 12)
Education (Scotland) Act 1963 (c. 21)
Sheriff Courts (Civil Jurisdiction and Procedure) (Scotland) Act 1963 (c. 22)
Forestry (Sale of Land) (Scotland) Act 1963 (c. 23)
Criminal Justice (Scotland) Act 1963 (c. 39)
Land Compensation (Scotland) Act 1963 (c. 51)

1964
Episcopal Church (Scotland) Act 1964 (c. 12)
Burgh Police (Amendment) (Scotland) Act 1964 (c. 33)
Succession (Scotland) Act 1964 (c. 41)
Tenancy of Shops (Scotland) Act 1964 (c. 50)
Local Government (Development and Finance) (Scotland) Act 1964 (c. 67)
Statute Law Reform (Scotland) Act 1964 (c. 80)
Spray Irrigation (Scotland) Act 1964 (c. 90)
Divorce (Scotland) Act 1964 (c. 91)

1965
Education (Scotland) Act 1965 (c. 7)
Rivers (Prevention of Pollution) (Scotland) Act 1965 (c. 13)
Teaching Council (Scotland) Act 1965 (c. 19)
Lost Property (Scotland) Act 1965 (c. 27)
Solicitors (Scotland) Act 1965 (c. 29)
Criminal Procedure (Scotland) Act 1965 (c. 39)
Housing (Amendment) (Scotland) Act 1965 (c. 40)
Local Government (Scotland) Act 1947 (Amendment) Act 1965 (c. 41)
Highlands and Islands Development (Scotland) Act 1965 (c. 46)
Registration of Births, Deaths and Marriages (Scotland) Act 1965 (c. 49)
Hire-Purchase (Scotland) Act 1965 (c. 67)

1966
Local Government (Pecuniary Interests) (Scotland) Act 1966 (c. 7)
Housing (Scotland) Act 1966 (c. 49)
Law Reform (Miscellaneous Provisions) (Scotland) Act 1966 (c. 19)
Local Government (Scotland) Act 1966 (c. 51)
Police (Scotland) Act 1966 (c. 52)
Universities (Scotland) Act 1966 (c. 13)

1967
Licensing (Certificates in Suspense) (Scotland) Act 1967 (c. 14)
Housing (Financial Provisions, etc.) (Scotland) Act 1967 (c. 20)
Remuneration of Teachers (Scotland) Act 1967 (c. 36)
Deer (Amendment) (Scotland) Act 1967 (c. 37)
Legal Aid (Scotland) Act 1967 (c. 43)
Police (Scotland) Act 1967 (c. 77)
Water (Scotland) Act 1967 (c. 78)
Countryside (Scotland) Act 1967 (c. 86)

1968
Teachers Superannuation (Scotland) Act 1968 (c. 12)
New Towns (Scotland) Act 1968 (c. 16)
Legitimation (Scotland) Act 1968 (c. 22)
Housing (Financial Provisions) (Scotland) Act 1968 (c. 31)
Sale of Venison (Scotland) Act 1968 (c. 38)
Sewerage (Scotland) Act 1968 (c. 47)

1968—*contd*
Social Work (Scotland) Act 1968 (c. 49)
Highlands and Islands Development (Scotland) Act 1968 (c. 51)
Law Reform (Miscellaneous Provisions) (Scotland) Act 1968 (c. 70)

1969
Electricity (Scotland) Act 1969 (c. 1)
Licensing (Scotland) Act 1969 (c. 13)
Agriculture (Spring Traps) (Scotland) Act 1969 (c. 26)
Town and Country Planning (Scotland) Act 1969 (c. 30)
Housing (Scotland) Act 1969 (c. 34)
Age of Majority (Scotland) Act 1969 (c. 39)
National Mod (Scotland) Act 1969 (c. 41)
Education (Scotland) Act 1969 (c. 49)

1970
Housing (Scotland) Act 1970 (c. 5)
Roads (Scotland) Act 1970 (c. 20)
Local Government (Footpaths and Open Spaces) (Scotland) Act 1970 (c. 28)
Conveyancing and Feudal Reform (Scotland) Act 1970 (c. 35)
Building (Scotland) Act 1970 (c. 38)

1971
Teaching Council (Scotland) Act 1971 (c. 2)
Hospital Endowments (Scotland) Act 1971 (c. 8)
Rent (Scotland) Act 1971 (c. 28)
Interest of Damages (Scotland) Act 1971 (c. 31)
Education (Scotland) Act 1971 (c. 42)
Redemption of Standard Securities (Scotland) Act 1971 (c. 45)
Sheriff Courts (Scotland) Act 1971 (c. 58)

1972
Social Work (Scotland) Act 1972 (c. 24)
Harbours, Piers and Ferries (Scotland) Act 1972 (c. 29)
Housing (Financial Provisions) (Scotland) Act 1972 (c. 46)
Chronically Sick and Disabled Persons (Scotland) Act 1972 (c. 51)
Town and Country Planning (Scotland) Act 1972 (c. 52)
National Health Service (Scotland) Act 1972 (c. 58)
Administration of Justice (Scotland) Act 1972 (c. 59)
Harbours Development (Scotland) Act 1972 (c. 64)
Companies (Floating Charges and Receivers) (Scotland) Act 1972 (c. 67)

1973
Law Reform (Diligence) (Scotland) Act 1973 (c. 22)
Succession (Scotland) Act 1973 (c. 25)
Prescription and Limitation (Scotland) Act 1973 (c. 52)
Land Compensation (Scotland) Act 1973 (c. 56)
Education (Scotland) Act 1973 (c. 59)
Local Government (Scotland) Act 1973 (c. 65)

1974
Lord High Commissioners (Church of Scotland) Act 1974 (c. 19)
Education (Mentally Handicapped Children) (Scotland) Act 1974 (c. 27)
Land Tenure Reform (Scotland) Act 1974 (c. 38)
Housing (Scotland) Act 1974 (c. 45)

1975
Offshore Petroleum Development (Scotland) Act 1975 (c. 8)
District Courts (Scotland) Act 1975 (c. 20)
Criminal Procedure (Scotland) Act 1975 (c. 21)
Housing Rents and Subsidies (Scotland) Act 1975 (c. 28)
Local Government (Scotland) Act 1975 (c. 30)

1976
Solicitors (Scotland) Act 1976 (c. 6)
Housing (Amendment) (Scotland) Act 1976 (c. 11)
Damages (Scotland) Act 1976 (c. 13)
Fatal Accidents and Sudden Deaths Inquiry (Scotland) Act 1976 (c. 14)
Education (Scotland) Act 1976 (c. 20)
Crofting Reform (Scotland) Act 1976 (c. 21)
Freshwater and Salmon Fisheries (Scotland) Act 1976 (c. 22)
Divorce (Scotland) Act 1976 (c. 39)
Electricity (Financial Provisions) (Scotland) Act 1976 (c. 61)
Valuation and Rating (Exempted Classes) (Scotland) Act 1976 (c. 64)
Retirement of Teachers (Scotland) Act 1976 (c. 65)
Licensing (Scotland) Act 1976 (c. 66)
Sexual Offences (Scotland) Act 1976 (c. 67)

1977
Town and Country Planning (Scotland) Act 1977 (c. 10)
Returning Officers (Scotland) Act 1977 (c. 14)
Marriage (Scotland) Act 1977 (c. 15)
New Towns (Scotland) Act 1977 (c. 16)
Presumption of Death (Scotland) Act 1977 (c. 27)
Control of Food Premises (Scotland) Act 1977 (c. 28)

1978
Local Government (Scotland) Act 1978 (c. 4)
Housing (Financial Provisions) (Scotland) Act 1978 (c. 14)
Theatres Trust (Scotland) Act 1978 (c. 24)
Adoption (Scotland) Act 1978 (c. 28)
National Health Service (Scotland) Act 1978 (c. 29)
Import of Live Fish (Scotland) Act 1978 (c. 35)
Local Government (Scotland) Act 1978 (c. 39)
Community Service by Offenders (Scotland) Act 1978 (c. 49)
Scotland Act 1978 (c. 51)

1979
Electricity (Scotland) Act 1979 (c. 11)
Administration of Justice (Emergency Provisions) (Scotland) Act 1979 (c. 19)
Confirmation to Small Estates (Scotland) Act 1979 (c. 22)
Land Registration (Scotland) Act 1979 (c. 33)

1980
Bail etc. (Scotland) Act 1980 (c. 4)
Slaughter of Animals (Scotland) Act 1980 (c. 13)
Highlands and Islands Air Services (Scotland) Act 1980 (c. 19)
Concessionary Travel for Handicapped Persons (Scotland) Act 1980 (c. 29)
Criminal Justice (Scotland) Act 1980 (c. 62)
Education (Scotland) Act 1980 (c. 44)
Water (Scotland) Act 1980 (c. 45)
Solicitors (Scotland) Act 1980 (c. 46)
Tenants' Rights, etc. (Scotland) Act 1980 (c. 52)
Law Reform (Miscellaneous Provisions) (Scotland) Act 1980 (c. 55)
Married Women's Policies of Assurance (Scotland) (Amendment) Act 1980 (c. 56)
Tenants' Rights, etc. (Scotland) Amendment Act 1980 (c. 61)

1981
Local Government (Miscellaneous Provisions) (Scotland) Act 1981 (c. 23)
Countryside (Scotland) Act 1981 (c. 44)
Education (Scotland) Act 1981 (c. 58)
Matrimonial Homes (Family Protection) (Scotland) Act 1981 (c. 59)
Housing (Amendment) (Scotland) Act 1981 (c. 72)

1982
Harbours (Scotland) Act 1982 (c. 17)
Deer (Amendment) (Scotland) Act 1982 (c. 19)
Local Government and Planning (Scotland) Act 1982 (c. 43)
Civic Government (Scotland) Act 1982 (c. 45)
Electricity (Financial Provisions) (Scotland) Act 1982 (c. 56)
Lands Valuation Amendment (Scotland) Act 1982 (c. 57)

1983
Divorce Jurisdiction, Court Fees and Legal Aid (Scotland) Act 1983 (c. 12)
Solvent Abuse (Scotland) Act 1983 (c. 33)
Mental Health (Amendment) (Scotland) Act 1983 (c. 39)
Agricultural Holdings (Amendment) (Scotland) Act 1983 (c. 46)

1984
Tourism (Overseas Promotion) (Scotland) Act 1984 (c. 4)
Education (Amendment) (Scotland) Act 1984 (c. 6)
Law Reform (Husband and Wife) (Scotland) Act 1984 (c. 15)
Tenants' Rights, etc. (Scotland) Amendment Act 1984 (c. 18)
Inshore Fisheries (Scotland) Act 1984 (c. 26)
Rating and Valuation (Amendment) (Scotland) Act 1984 (c. 31)

1984—*contd*
Mental Health (Scotland) Act 1984 (c. 36)
Prescription and Limitation (Scotland) Act 1984 (c. 45)
Roads (Scotland) Act 1984 (c. 54)
Foster Children (Scotland) Act 1984 (c. 56)
Rent (Scotland) Act 1984 (c. 58)

1985
Natural Heritage (Scotland) Act 1985 (c. 16)
Rating (Revaluation Rebates) (Scotland) Act 1985 (c. 33)
Family Law (Scotland) Act 1985 (c. 37)
Bankruptcy (Scotland) Act 1985 (c. 66)
Law Reform (Miscellaneous Provisions) (Scotland) Act 1985 (c. 73)

1986
Law Reform (Parent and Child) (Scotland) Act 1986 (c. 9)
Incest and Related Offences (Scotland) Act 1986 (c. 36)
Legal Aid (Scotland) Act 1986 (c. 47)
Housing (Scotland) Act 1986 (c. 65)

1987
Animals (Scotland) Act 1987 (c. 9)
Debtors (Scotland) Act 1987 (c. 18)
Register of Sasines (Scotland) Act 1987 (c. 23)
Housing (Scotland) Act 1987 (c. 26)
Prescription (Scotland) Act 1987 (c. 36)
Registered Establishments (Scotland) Act 1987 (c. 40)
Criminal Justice (Scotland) Act 1987 (c. 41)
Abolition of Domestic Rates etc. (Scotland) Act 1987 (c. 47)
Scottish Development Agency (Scotland) Act 1987 (c. 56)

1988
Civil Evidence (Scotland) Act 1988 (c. 32)
Electricity (Financial Provisions) (Scotland) Act 1988 (c. 37)
Solicitors (Scotland) Act 1988 (c. 42)
Housing (Scotland) Act 1988 (c. 43)
School Boards (Scotland) Act 1988 (c. 47)

1989
Transport (Scotland) Act 1989 (c. 23)
Self-Governing Schools etc. (Scotland) Act 1989 (c. 39)
Prisons (Scotland) Act 1989 (c. 45)

1990
Term and Quarter Days (Scotland) Act 1990 (c. 22)
Enterprise and New Towns (Scotland) Act 1990 (c. 35)
Law Reform (Miscellaneous Provisions) (Scotland) Act 1990 (c. 40)

1991
Crofter Forestry (Scotland) Act 1991 (c. 18)
Natural Heritage (Scotland) Act 1991 (c. 28)
Mental Health (Detention) (Scotland) Act 1991 (c. 47)
Age of Legal Capacity (Scotland) Act 1991 (c. 50)
Agricultural Holdings (Scotland) Act 1991 (c. 55)

1992
Licensing (Amendment) (Scotland) Act 1992 (c. 18)
Further and Higher Education (Scotland) Act 1992 (c. 37)

1993
Damages (Scotland) Act 1993 (c. 5)
Bankruptcy (Scotland) Act 1993 (c. 6)
Prisoners and Criminal Proceedings (Scotland) Act 1993 (c. 9)
Carrying of Knives etc. (Scotland) Act 1993 (c. 13)
Protection of Animals (Scotland) Act 1993 (c. 15)
Licensing (Amendment) (Scotland) Act 1993 (c. 20)
Crofters (Scotland) Act 1993 (c. 44)
Scottish Land Court Act 1993 (c. 45)

1994
State Hospitals (Scotland) Act 1994 (c. 16)
Inshore Fishing (Scotland) Act 1994 (c. 27)
Local Government etc. (Scotland) Act 1994 (c. 39)

1995
Civil Evidence (Family Mediation) (Scotland) Act 1995 (c. 6)
Requirements of Writing (Scotland) Act 1995 (c. 7)
Land Registers (Scotland) Act 1995 (c. 14)
Criminal Justice (Scotland) Act 1995 (c. 20)
Children (Scotland) Act 1995 (c. 36)
Criminal Law (Consolidation) (Scotland) Act 1995 (c. 39)
Criminal Procedure (Consequential Provisions) (Scotland) Act 1995 (c. 40)
Proceeds of Crime (Scotland) Act 1995 (c. 43)
Criminal Procedure (Scotland) Act 1995 (c. 46)

1996
Licensing (Amendment) (Scotland) Act 1996 (c. 36)
Education (Scotland) Act 1996 (c. 43)
Deer (Amendment) (Scotland) Act 1996 (c. 44)
Deer (Scotland) Act 1996 (c. 58)

1997
Local Government (Gaelic Names) (Scotland) Act 1997 (c. 6)
Town and Country Planning (Scotland) Act 1997 (c. 8)
Planning (Listed Buildings and Conservation Areas) (Scotland) Act 1997 (c. 9)
Planning (Hazardous Substances) (Scotland) Act 1997 (c. 10)

1997—*contd*
Planning (Consequential Provisions) (Scotland) Act 1997 (c. 11)
Transfer of Crofting Estates (Scotland) Act 1997 (c. 26)
Contract (Scotland) Act 1997 (c. 34)
Scottish Legal Services Ombudsman and Commissioner for Local Administra-
   tion in Scotland Act 1997 (c. 35)
Flood Prevention and Land Drainage (Scotland) Act 1997 (c. 36)
Crime and Punishment (Scotland) Act 1997 (c. 48)
Referendums (Scotland and Wales) Act 1997 (c. 61)

1998
Criminal Procedure (Intermediate Diets) (Scotland) Act 1998 (c. 10)
Registered Establishments (Scotland) Act 1998 (c. 25)
Scotland Act 1998 (c. 46)

1999
Scottish Enterprise Act 1999 (c. 5)
Mental Health (Amendment) (Scotland) Act 1999 (c. 32)

2003
Sunday Working (Scotland) Act 2003 (c. 18)

2004
Scottish Parliament (Constituencies) Act 2004 (c. 13)

SOURCE: Chronological Table of the Statutes [1235–2004] (London: TSO, 2005)

Notes to the Text

Prologue

1 Vincent, *Diaries of the 15th Earl of Derby*, 5/5/1883.
2 The *Scotsman* 17/1/1884.
3 *The Times* 17/1/1884.
4 3rd Hansard 287 c1664–65.
5 Ibid., c1668.
6 Ibid., c1669.
7 3rd Hansard 288 c810.
8 *The Times* 30/6/1885.
9 3rd Hansard 299 c95.
10 Ibid., c101.
11 *The Times* 13/7/1885.

6th Duke of Richmond

1 Blake, *Disraeli*, 516.
2 The Franchise Act 1884 and the Redistribution of Seats Act 1885 (the Third Reform Act) collectively increased the electorate to 56 per cent of the adult male population. Scotland also increased its number of constituencies from 60 to 72 – remaining at that level until 2005.
3 Johnson, *The Diary of Gathorne Hardy*, 573.
4 A rather contrived political compromise had seen education become the responsibility of the vice-president of the Scotch Education Committee of the Privy Council, who also happened to be the secretary for Scotland.
5 3rd Hansard 289 c1648–49. Richmond had also opposed the original creation of the Scotch Education Department as a result of the Education (Scotland) Act 1872. 'It means simply a room in Whitehall, with the word 'Scotland' painted on the door. It is a sham, and can be nothing but a sham.' (Mitchell, *Governing Scotland*, 16).
6 Goodwood MS 871.
7 Hanham, 'The Creation of the Scottish Office 1881–87', *Juridical Review* 10 (1965), 229.
8 Goodwood MS 871, 13/8/1885.
9 Dictionary of National Biography, *Duke of Richmond and Gordon*.
10 Ibid.
11 Queen Victoria, who held Richmond in high regard, proposed the revival of the dukedom of Gordon as a consolation prize for Richmond on ceasing to be Conservative leader in the Lords.
12 The *Scotsman* 14/8/1885.
13 Ibid. 17/8/1885.
14 Sir Francis made it clear he wanted the option of resigning at the end of the year.
15 'He seems to have the whole Scotch business entirely at his finger ends,' wrote Richmond to Sir Richard Cross on 25/9/1885 (Hanham, 236, MS 51267). Dunbar became the new department's lynchpin despite a severe speech defect.

16 Goodwood MS 871, 20/8/1885.
17 Ibid.
18 Hanham, 238. It actually says 'Secretary for Scotland's Office' and can still be made out above No. 6 Parliament Square.
19 Lothian Papers GD40/16/3, 24/8/1885.
20 Cross Papers MS 51267 f139.
21 Ibid. f144, 19/9/1885.
22 Ibid. f157, 25/11/1885.
23 Goodwood MS 871, 23/12/1885.
24 Hanham, 232.
25 Ibid., 221.
26 Salisbury told Richmond he would write to the Treasury on the principle that 'It would be a great pity to spoil the ship for a pennorth of tar.' (Hanham, 230).
27 CP MS 51267 f139.
28 Hanham, 233.

Sir George Otto Trevelyan, Baronet

1 3rd Hansard 302 c653.
2 Gladstone Papers MS 44335 f197.
3 Matthew, *Gladstone Diaries XI*, 508, GP MS 44548 f60.
4 GP MS 44335 f199.
5 Matthew, 511, GP MS 44335 f201.
6 Ibid., p519, GP MS 44335 f205.
7 Campbell-Bannerman Papers MS 41231 f4.
8 Rendell Papers NLW 20569D f66. Notes of a conversation with Gladstone dated 22/12/1897.
9 Anonymous, 'The Government and Scottish Affairs', *Blackwoods* (February 1894), 252–64.
10 Ibid.
11 DNB, *Sir George Otto Trevelyan*.
12 Brooks, *The Destruction of Lord Rosebery*, 4/4/1894. Sir Edward Hamilton considered Trevelyan 'a great wreck politically' (8/8/1894). South Aberdeen MP James Bryce was then chancellor of the Duchy of Lancaster but replaced A. J. Mundella at the Board of Trade in May 1894. A Glaswegian jurist and historian, Bryce had been a contender for the Scottish secretaryship in 1892.
13 RP NLW 20569D f59. Notes of a conversation with Gladstone on 1&4/2/1897.
14 Trevelyan had written to Rosebery earlier that month: 'It is worth considering whether a reference should be made to the Scottish Bills being sent to a Grand Committee containing all the Scotch members.' (Rosebery Papers MS 10145 f84).
15 4th Hansard 22 c1116–38.
16 The *Scotsman* 1/6/1894.
17 Althorp Papers MS 76967, 26/12/1892. Trevelyan also wrote to Principal Donaldson at St Andrews University on 27/10/1892: 'I am becoming very fond of my work – though the conditions under which it is carried on, with a scattered staff partly in Edinburgh and partly in London, make it somewhat difficult to keep the threads together.' (Donaldson Papers MS 7846).
18 Bryce Papers MSS Bryce 18–19 ff19–20, 21/9/1894.
19 *The Times* 15/9/1892.
20 4th Hansard 13 c1842–52.
21 There had been an earlier motion on home rule following the resolution on the Scottish Grand Committee. It was carried by ten votes in a full chamber, forcing Trevelyan to support a principle he had been arguing against the previous day.
22 DP MS 7845.
23 This Bill, unlike that of 1886, allowed for continuing Irish representation at Westminster.

24 DP MS 7982.
25 *The Times* 22/12/1894.
26 Balfour, *Lord Balfour of Burleigh*, 65–66.
27 Rosebery Papers MS 10130 f50.
28 Ibid. f54.
29 Kimberley Papers MS Eng c4474 f113.
30 RP MS 10130 f126. Letter to Rosebery marked 'Private and very confidential' dated 1/6/1895.
31 RP MS 10162 f148.
32 But Trevelyan was not wholly sympathetic to the crofters. '. . . they do not pay their private debts. Besides that they do not pay their municipal taxes, and still less any instalment of the money which they owe to our Treasury as the price of their farms.' (RP 10162 f95, 11/1894.)
33 Trevelyan, *Sir George Otto Trevelyan: A Memoir*, 136.

13th Earl of Dalhousie

1 Morley, *Life of Gladstone III*, 303fn.
2 Matthew, *Gladstone Diaries XI*, NLS 10023 f30, 30/9/1885.
3 Vincent, *The Diaries of Edward Henry Stanley, 15th Earl of Derby*, 15/2/1883.
4 Vincent, *The Later Derby Diaries*, 290.
5 Matthew, Althorp MSS K296.
6 Gladstone Papers MS 44496 f34.
7 The *Scotsman* 29/3/1886.
8 3rd Hansard 305 c1472.
9 Balfour Papers MSS 49838 f273.
10 The *Scotsman* and *The Times* 27/5/1886.
11 The *Scotsman* 22/7/1886.
12 *The Times* 28/11/1887.
13 McGonagall, *Collected Poems*, 'The Death of Lord and Lady Dalhousie'.

Arthur James Balfour

1 Zebel, *Balfour: A Political Biography*, 55.
2 3rd Hansard 308 c945.
3 Ibid., c948–56.
4 Balfour Papers MSS 49801, Dover House Letter book.
5 Gibson, *The Thistle and the Rose*, 27, SRO HH 1/3.
6 Dugdale, *Arthur James Balfour*, 87. Blanche Dugdale was a niece of Balfour, whose book was substantially revised by her friend Walter Elliot in the years before he became Scottish secretary.
7 Ibid., 88.
8 Ibid., 89–90.
9 Williams, *The Salisbury-Balfour Correspondence*, 163, BP MS 49688 f127.
10 3rd Hansard 310 c1688.
11 Gilmour Papers GD40/16/3–4. In a minute written on 31/1/1886 for the Duke of Richmond but never actually sent to the Home Office, His Grace had come to the same conclusion that law and order should be transferred to the secretary for Scotland.
12 Williams, 160, HH 3/29.
13 Lothian Papers GD40/16/3–4.
14 BP MSS 49801.
15 Ibid.
16 Williams, 161, HH 3/30.
17 Ibid., 164, BP MS 49688 f129. Cabinet leaks are not a new phenomenon: Lord Randolph Churchill passed this news to G. E. Buckle, the editor of *The Times*, who held back when Salisbury told him he was yet to receive the Queen's approval (Roberts, *Salisbury*, 403–04).

18 Ibid., 165, HH 3/37.
19 Egremont, *Balfour: A Life of Arthur James Balfour*, 79.
20 3rd Hansard 309 c218.
21 3rd Hansard 310 c1487.
22 Ridley & Percy, *The Letters of Arthur Balfour and Lady Elcho*, 30–31.
23 Egremont, 80.

9th Marquis of Lothian
1 Lothian's nephew, Philip Henry Kerr, the 11th marquis, was a Liberal and became British ambassador to the United States from 1939–40.
2 Williams, *The Salisbury-Balfour Correspondence*, 176, HH 4/13.
3 *Dundee Courier* 9/3/1887.
4 The *Scotsman* 9/3/1887.
5 Hanham, 'The Creation of the Scottish Office 1881–87', *Juridical Review* 10 (1965), 221.
6 Ibid., Cab 37/20/36 f1. Rosebery and Salisbury had tried to transfer law and order to the Scottish Office in 1884, but a Lords amendment to this effect was rejected by the Commons.
7 Lothian Papers GD40/16/12–13.
8 Thus far only the Duke of Richmond, and latterly Balfour, had sat in the Cabinet.
9 The *Scotsman*, 11/7/1888.
10 Lothian had himself become lord rector of Edinburgh University in 1887, continuing until 1890.
11 LP GD40/16/1–2.
12 Ibid.
13 3rd Hansard 325 c1183.
14 The new county councils were empowered to remove those suffering from diseases to purpose-built 'isolation' hospitals.
15 3rd Hansard 339 c20.
16 3rd Hansard 335 c72.
17 Ibid., c108.
18 LP GD40/16/4–5.
19 LP GD40/16/51.
20 LP GD40/16/11.
21 Ripon Papers MS 43636 ff116–17.
22 LP GD40/16/51.
23 LP GD40/16/24–25.
24 3rd Hansard 356 c1109.
25 The *Scotsman* 10/1/1890.
26 *The Times* 18/6/1892.
27 Mary Gladstone Papers MS 46229 f95.

6th Lord Balfour of Burleigh
1 Balfour, *Lord Balfour of Burleigh*, 74.
2 Balfour of Burleigh Papers NRAS 923 bundle 6, 29/6/1895.
3 *Vanity Fair* 14/8/1902.
4 Lord Balfour was later a director of The Eastern and Associated Telegraph Companies, which eventually became Cable & Wireless.
5 Scotland then sent only 16 peers to the Upper House, a relic from the 1707 Act of Union. 'General elections' were held at Holyrood Palace to coincide with elections to the House of Commons. Lord Balfour remained a representative peer until his death in 1921, and the system was scrapped under the Peerage Act in 1963.
6 The *Scotsman* 7/6/1921.
7 4th Hansard 96 c384.
8 Mitchell, *Governing Scotland*, 61.

9 *The Times* 17/4/1900.
10 Sir Henry was also a keen historian, producing two volumes, *A Century of Scottish History*, while at the SED in 1901.
11 Stodart-Walker, *Rectorial Addresses Delivered Before the University of Edinburgh 1859–1899*, 322–37.
12 Balfour Papers MS 49800 ff93–95, 18/5/1901.
13 Ibid., ff96–104.
14 Campbell-Bannerman Papers MS 41241 ff227–32, 20/5/1901.
15 NRAS 923 bundle 5, 29/9/1903.
16 The first Scottish secretary, the Duke of Richmond, chaired a special House of Lords Select Committee to scrutinise the Bill in 1896.
17 Balfour, 72–7.
18 Roberts, *Salisbury*, 252.
19 Cadogen Papers CAD/837. Letter from Salisbury to Cadogen dated 20/2/1896: 'Balfour of Burleigh declines to take the Irish Office . . .'
20 Roberts, 786.
21 Sandars Papers MSS Eng. hist. c733 f50, 12/11/1900. Balfour replied on 18/11/1900, f55.
22 Vincent, *The Crawford Papers*, 46.
23 BP MS 49800 ff109–10.
24 Fitzroy, *Memoirs I*, 142.
25 NRAS 923 bundle 6, 19/8/1903.
26 Gollin, *Balfour's Burden*, 132–33.
27 NRAS 923 bundle 6, 18/9/1903.
28 Ibid., bundle 5, 22/9/1903.
29 Ibid., 21/9/1903.

Andrew Graham Murray

1 The *Scotsman* 19/1/1904.
2 Ibid. 22/8/1942.
3 *Vanity Fair* 22/10/1896.
4 Sandars Papers MSS Eng. hist. c744 f121, 5/10/1903.
5 Ibid., ff121–24.
6 Craik Papers MS 7175 ff45–48, 5/11/1903.
7 Hansard 132 c864–882.
8 The *Scotsman* 29/3/1904.
9 Ibid. 31/1/1905.
10 DNB, *Andrew Graham Murray*.

1st Marquis of Linlithgow

1 Fitzroy, *Memoirs*, 235.
2 DNB, *Marquis of Linlithgow*.
3 *Vanity Fair* 19/5/1900.
4 Linlithgow's real ambition had been to become Viceroy of India. Poignantly, his son, the 2nd marquis, Victor Alexander John Hope, became the longest-serving Indian Viceroy from 1936–43.
5 The *Scotsman* 3/2/1905.
6 Hope Family Papers NRAS 888 bundle 1639, 30/1/1905. Linlithgow was also approached on 26/8/03: '. . . do you think you . . . could possibly allow you to become Scotch Secretary? As you know the work of the office in the Lords is light . . .'
7 Ibid., 3/2/1905.
8 Dalrymple Papers MS 25558 f180.
9 Sandars Papers MSS Eng. hist. c749 ff72–80, 12/3/1905.
10 HFP NRAS 888 bundle 1639, 30/1/1905.

11 Hansard 150 c847–49.
12 HFP NRAS 888 bundle 1638.

John Sinclair, 1st Lord Pentland

1 David, *Inside Asquith's Cabinet*, 79–80.
2 Agnes was the daughter of John Learmonth of Dean, a coach-builder and former lord provost of Edinburgh who built and presented the Dean Bridge to the city.
3 Sinclair planned an official life but only managed to edit a volume of early letters written by 'CB'. He later presented all Campbell-Bannerman's papers to the British Library.
4 Wilson, *A Life of Sir Henry Campbell-Bannerman*, 460.
5 Pentland, *Memoir of Lord Pentland*, 106.
6 Hazlehurst & Woodland, *A Liberal Chronicle*, 95. Sinclair had been born the year Sir Henry married.
7 Hansard 188 c175.
8 In 1912 Sinclair did attempt one minor reform: basing an assistant secretary in Edinburgh, but he was ticked off by the chancellor Lloyd George, who told him: 'So long as the seat of Government and consequently the Secretary for Scotland are in London, it will be necessary that the Secretary for Scotland should have at hand and consequently in London the services of a staff which watches Scottish interests in Parliament much more effectively than would be from Edinburgh.' (Levitt, *The Scottish Office*, 2, SRO, E828/4.)
9 A. J. Balfour thought some 'evils' still existed, but dropped the plans after complaints from the Crofters Commission and the Duke of Argyll.
10 Pentland, 87. Speech at the Royal Albert Hall 21/12/1905.
11 4th Hansard 173 c768.
12 4th Hansard 180 c986–90.
13 Rosebery Papers MS 10171 f155, 4/9/1907.
14 Wilson, 600.
15 Campbell-Bannerman Papers MS 52521 f501, 12/12/1907.
16 Ibid., ff214–15.
17 *The Times* 31/1/1908.
18 CBP MS 41230 f106.
19 Ibid., ff116–19.
20 Ibid.
21 Ibid., f105.
22 Ibid., ff130–37.
23 Ibid., ff151–54.
24 Ibid.
25 *The Times* 1/11/1909.
26 Hazlehurst & Woodland, 98. The opposition shared Asquith's view of Sinclair; Unionist whip William Bridgeman thought him a 'dismal failure', and his two land Bills 'childish measures'. A. J. Balfour believed he combined the 'greatest stupidity with the worst principles'. (Williams, *The Modernisation of Conservative Politics*, 35&41.)
27 Mitchell, *Governing Scotland*, 78.
28 Lady Marjorie was only daughter of John Campbell Gordon, 7th Earl and first Marquis of Aberdeen. She was, therefore, a niece of Lord Balfour of Burleigh.
29 Hazlehurst & Woodland, 94–95.
30 Ibid., 100.
31 *The Scotsman* 30/11/1907.
32 Ibid. 27/4/1909.
33 Wells, *The House of Lords*, 210.
34 The list of names included a reluctant Sir George Otto Trevelyan.
35 Pentland, 126.

36 Ibid., 127.
37 Bonham Carter, *Lantern Slides*, 29/1/1912.
38 Pentland, 128.
39 Ibid., 128.
40 The *Scotsman* 14/2/1912.
41 *The Times* 14/2/1912.
42 Pentland, 129.
43 By mid 1913, MPs were increasingly complaining that the Board was acting too slowly and needed more funds. Sinclair's successor, Thomas McKinnon Wood, announced a staffing increase and explained that its reticent behaviour was necessary to avoid early difficulties or criticisms.

Thomas McKinnon Wood

1 McKinnon Wood was similar, in many ways, to Ken Livingstone. Both made their name in London local government before being elected to the Westminster parliament, and both were London-born with Scottish family. Livingstone's father was from Dunoon.
2 Lloyd George Papers LG/C/9/5/4, 5/8/1913.
3 *The Times* 28/3/27.
4 DNB, *Thomas McKinnon Wood*.
5 The *Daily Telegraph* 28/3/1927. Thomas Power O'Connor sat for the Scotland Division of Liverpool until 1929, the only Irish Nationalist MP to hold a Commons seat outside Ireland (his constituency had a large Irish population).
6 5th Hansard 36 c885.
7 The *Scotsman* 10/2/1913.
8 Ramsden, *Real Old Tory Politics*, 16/2/1913. There was also a debate about 'disinterested management', whereby the state would become involved in the drinks trade as an alternative to prohibition, with decisions taken by local option.
9 The *Scotsman* 10/2/1913.
10 Ibid. 18/2/1913.
11 4th Hansard 54 c750–56.
12 Thomas McKinnon Wood Papers MS. Eng. hist. d312, 5/4/1927.
13 The *Scotsman* 18/2/1913.
14 Runciman Papers WR 75/14.
15 The *Scotsman* 23/10/1912.
16 The *Morning Post* 28/3/27.
17 The *Scotsman* 11/5/1912.
18 *The Times* 7/5/1912.
19 The *Scotsman* 17/7/1912.
20 The Young Scots Society was formed by pro-Boers in 1900. They supported Scottish home rule and 'real Scottish' MPs, as opposed to carpet-bagging Englishmen.
21 The *Scotsman* 28/4/1913.
22 Ibid. 1/6/1913.
23 3rd Hansard 62 c1473.
24 Ibid., c1546.
25 The *Scotsman* 16/5/1914.
26 Sir George admitted the Scottish secretary was overburdened, and suggested having under-secretaries for each Edinburgh board at the Scottish Office.
27 The feeling was not mutual. In Easter 1914, Asquith wrote in his diary: 'I am in for a rather dreary function tonight – a dinner here at the House of Scotch members given by McK. Wood.' (Jenkins, *Asquith*, 267.)
28 Jenkins, 325. The group included John Morley, Lloyd George and Herbert Samuel.
29 After the failure of the Battle of Neuve Chapelle, it was widely perceived that the quality of artillery shells for use by the British Army was inadequate.

30 TMWP MS. Eng. hist. d499 ff193–94.
31 Ibid., f195.
32 *The Times* 10/7/1916.
33 Wood and 25 other Liberal candidates stood with Irish 'coupons', or Irish Nationalist endorsement, in the 1918 general election. Many of them, including Wood, lost their deposits.
34 The *Daily Telegraph* 28/3/1927.

Harold John Tennant
1 *The Times* 10/7/1916.
2 Margot's half-sister Katherine later married Walter Elliot, Scottish secretary from 1936–38.
3 Margot Asquith's Diary MS Eng. d. 3206, 4/1908.
4 *Vanity Fair* 23/12/1909.
5 Margot had a wild theory that Jack's height was arrested by being allowed to walk several miles a day with the shooters on his father's estate. (Asquith, *The Autobiography of Margot Asquith I*, 12–13.)
6 The *Scotsman* 15/7/1916.
7 Edward Priaulx Tennant, 1st Baron Glenconner. He was Margot's brother and assistant private secretary to Sir George Otto Trevelyan as Scottish secretary between 1892–95.
8 Margot Asquith's Diary MS Eng. d.3215, 20/8/1916.

Robert Munro
1 Lloyd George Papers LG/F/1/7/1, 13/12/1916.
2 In his book, *No Gods and Precious Few Heroes*, Christopher Harvie calls Munro the 'the dim representative of a failing party'.
3 Alness, *Looking Back*, 299.
4 Lord Balfour of Burleigh had by then mellowed politically, having lost a son in the war.
5 Runciman Papers WR 88/16.
6 McLean, *The Legend of Red Clydeside*. 125.
7 Fry, *Patronage and Principle*, 139.
8 Pratt sat for the Cathcart Division of Glasgow from 1918 as a coalition Liberal. He was knighted on losing his seat and ministerial post in 1922. Sir John tried several times to re-enter parliament, latterly as a 'New Party' candidate in 1931.
9 Levitt, *The Scottish Office*, 245–48, PRO, CAB 24/107 CP[20]1437.
10 Ibid., 248–49, PRO, CAB 23/26 CC[21]60th Appendix IV.
11 McLean, 190.
12 Alness, 239.
13 LGP LG/1/7/23.
14 Alness, 290.
15 Ibid., 243–44.
16 Nicolson, *Lord of the Isles*, 178.
17 Ibid., 149.
18 Ibid., 151.
19 Ibid., 163.
20 Ibid., 175.
21 Ibid., 241. Novar zealously continued the previous government's land policy, hinting that he might divide every farm on the island except those immediately surrounding Stornoway.
22 The *Scotsman* 6/8/1919. The 1919 Supply debate was interrupted for two hours by a royal pageant on the Thames and not allowed to make up the time.
23 Levitt, 10, SRO HH1/887.
24 Even after leaving the Scottish Office, Munro continued to campaign for a raise in

status, saying in one speech that Scotland was being 'kept in a subsidiary position unbefitting her dignity'. (The *Scotsman* 13/3/1923.)

25 Alness, 282.

26 Munro supported an unconditional truce with the Irish leaders and was concerned about the effect of a delay upon Scottish public opinion. The civil servant Tom Jones described Munro's contributions to Cabinet discussions on Ireland as 'perfectly lucid' (Jones, *Whitehall Diary III*, 107).

27 5th Hansard 127 c2067–70. Sir Henry's Bill was counted out.

28 Reports Commissioners 5, XIII 1920. Most domestic policies were to be devolved to an executive committee appointed by each Grand Council. Back in 1918 Tom Jones noted in his diary that 'I do not see why Provincial Councils might not also be set up for England and Scotland.' (Jones, *III*, 11).

29 Asquith had persuaded Lowther to chair what became the first ever Speaker's Conference a few years earlier; it reported in January 1917 on electoral reform.

30 *The Times* 13/5/1920.

31 The *Scotsman* 10/4/1922. At the general election of December 1918 Munro was returned as a coalition Liberal for Roxburgh and Selkirk, his Wick Burghs seat having ceased to exist as a result of redistribution.

32 The *Scotsman* 13/5/1922.

33 Bonar Law Papers BL/97/3/32, 22/5/1919. 'It so happens that recently I have had an exceptional amount of domestic anxiety & expense,' wrote Munro to Bonar Law. 'At the moment my mother, who is 70, had the misfortune to break her leg, and she is critically ill.'

34 Munro appears to have been a fully paid-up member of the Lord Dunedin fan club, frequently suggesting him to head up various commissions. 'What about a man like Lord Dunedin? He was Lord Advocate as well as Secretary for Scotland – one of the most successful Secretaries of modern times. He is a man of exceptional ability and strength of character. He is intolerant of humbug . . .' (LGP LG1/7/34 2, 29/8/1919.)

35 LGP LG/1/7/44, 21/2/1920.

36 Ibid., LG/1/7/56, 25/3/1922.

37 Ibid., LG1/7/58, 1/9/1922.

38 Munro died on the same day, in a macabre twist of fate, as J. J. Robertson, joint under-secretary of state for Scotland from 1947–50.

39 Alness, 298–99.

40 The *Scotsman* 7/1/1920.

1st Viscount Novar

1 The great-grandfather of Margaret Thatcher's first Scottish secretary and also Sir John Gilmour's brother-in-law.

2 Vincent, *The Crawford Papers*, 455.

3 *The Times* of 11/10/22 also reported that the pensions minister, Ian Macpherson, would take over from Robert Munro at the Scottish Office.

4 Bonar Law Papers BL/109/1/26a. Memo dated 21/10/1922.

5 The London-born Charles Clinton was then a forestry commissioner, having been joint parliamentary secretary to the Board of Agriculture in 1918.

6 Vincent, 460–61.

7 They both hailed from the same part of Scotland. Novar's father took the additional surname of Munro on the death of his first cousin, Hugh Andrew Munro, in 1864, when he inherited the estates of Novar, Ross-shire, and Muirton, Moray.

8 The *Scotsman* 24/10/1922.

9 McKinstry, *Rosebery*, 516.

10 Cunneen, *King's Men*, 110.

11 Anstruther-Gray Papers NRAS 3363/445, 2/10/1918.

12 Liberal Imperialists had a habit of moving away from the centre, both to the right and

left. Most notably, Viscount Haldane became Ramsay MacDonald's lord chancellor in 1924. Novar's sister, Valentine, was briefly engaged to Haldane, but changed her mind and died insane in 1897.

13 Levitt, *The Scottish Office*, 253, PRO, CAB 26/5 HAC[23]7th:4.
14 Ibid., 150–51, PRO, CAB 24/161 CP[23]366.
15 Worthington Evans Papers MS Eng hist c.924 f85.
16 Ibid., f139.
17 Ibid., f141.
18 Ibid., letter dated 21/9/1923.
19 Hansard 34 c1454–58.
20 George Younger, Malcolm Rifkind and even Michael Forsyth were all pro-devolution to varying degrees during the 1970s.
21 Novar had two parliamentary secretaries for health: the Linlithgow MP, James Kidd, from 31/10/1922, and Walter Elliot from 15/1/1923.
22 Levitt, 13, SRO HH45/51.
23 Rosebery Papers MSS 10020 f205, 16/1/1925.
24 Vincent, 14/11/1923.
25 Cecil of Chelwood Papers Acc 51080 f108, c11/1923.
26 RP MSS 10020 f202, 9/11/1924.
27 Ibid., f203.

William Adamson

1 DNB, *William Adamson*.
2 Anonymous, *The Scottish Socialists*, 105.
3 Marquand, *Ramsay MacDonald*, 305. The *Scotsman* said: 'The Socialist Prime Minister has issued the list of his Cabinet with remarkable promptitude, and it must be admitted that he has made the most of the scanty material at his disposal.' (23/1/1924.)
4 Vincent, *The Crawford Diaries*, 494.
5 Macmillan, *A Man of Law's Tale*, 90. The prime minister also had to look outside his party for a lord chancellor, appointing the former Liberal MP Viscount Haldane.
6 Hansard 169 c1146.
7 Adamson's under-secretary for health was James Stewart, the MP for the St Rollox Division of Glasgow since 1922 and a hairdresser by profession. Known as the 'Barber MP', Stewart lost his seat in the 1924 general election.
8 Hansard 173 c869–70.
9 The *Scotsman* 25/8/1924.
10 The government had come under fire after suggesting that the Soviet Union should be granted diplomatic recognition.
11 Shinwell, *The Labour Story*, 111–12. Beatrice Webb wrote in her diary that 'The party is led by the respectable but dull-witted Adamson, elected chairman because he is a miner.' (Webb, *Diaries I*, 10/1/1919.)
12 Webb, 330.
13 Johnston, *Memories*, 101.
14 Johnston also recalls in his memoirs that the Treasury used to have a joke that so persistent were Scottish Office demands for more money that they ran to take in the cat's milk whenever they heard its ministers coming.
15 Hansard 229 c1030.
16 The *Scotsman* 19/7/1929. On 11/9/1929 Ramsay MacDonald told the House that if the Scottish Local Government Act worked for 12 months, then he would set up an inquiry into Scottish government to report the following year.
17 The *Scotsman* 28/12/1929, *Dunfermline Press* 28/12/1929.
18 The *Scotsman* 1/3/1930.
19 Ibid. 2/4/1931. On another occasion, an MP asked Adamson whether after he had given due consideration to the due consideration he had previously promised, he

might give due consideration to the advisability of giving an answer to the question. Adamson said he would also give that point his due consideration.

20 Pimlott, *Political Diary of Hugh Dalton*, 198–99.
21 Adamson had maintained during the campaign that the Labour Party had no responsibility for the election 'thrust upon' the country by the National Government. *Dunfermline Press* 10/10/1931.
22 Johnston, 101.
23 *The Times* 24/2/1936. The obituary was headed 'From Pitboy to Cabinet Minister'.
24 Anonymous, *The Scottish Socialists* 119.

Sir John Gilmour, Baronet

1 Carreras High-Class Cigarettes Notable MPs No 14.
2 Vincent, *Crawford*, 501.
3 Self, *The Neville Chamberlain Diary Letters*, 309.
4 Ibid., 322.
5 The *Scotsman* 13/1/1926.
6 Ibid. 6/3/1926.
7 Pottinger, *The Secretaries of State for Scotland*, 29.
8 Gilmour Papers GD383 20/9.
9 The *Scotsman* 8/6/1926.
10 Pottinger, 30.
11 The *Scotsman* 28/7/1926.
12 Hansard 204 c474.
13 Hansard 214 c265–66.
14 Levitt, 349–50, PRO, CAB 24/196 CP[28]201.
15 Hansard 223 c866.
16 Autograph Letters and Verse Add 49458 f77.
17 Hansard 224 c1465.
18 The *Scotsman* 6/2/1929.
19 One Labour councillor writing in *Forward* said it would uproot local government democracy in Scotland and establish in its place a 'semi-Fascist bureaucracy recruited mainly from the landlords and the profiteers'.
20 The *Student* 28/10/1927.
21 Hansard 206 c870–73.
22 The *Scotsman* 19/1/1929.
23 Ibid. 25/1/1929.
24 A paper prepared by the Scottish Unionist whip's office in July 1929 blamed misrepresentation of the Local Government Act for losing a considerable number of votes in several constituencies. The memo also criticised the lack of a 'definite and attractive future policy' which could be grasped by the Scottish electorate (GP GD383 29/30).
25 The *Scotsman* 4/6/1929.
26 Williams, *The Modernisation of Conservative Politics*, 229.
27 Jones, *Whitehall Diary*, 179.
28 *The Times* 1/4/1940.

Sir Archibald Sinclair

1 Hunter, *Winston and Archie*, letter dated c10/1931.
2 The National Government lasted until 1939 when it was replaced by the wartime coalition. Interestingly, Sinclair was distantly related to John Sinclair, later Lord Pentland, who was Scottish secretary from 1905 until 1912.
3 Thurso Papers THRS II 85/3.
4 Gilbert, *Winston Churchill III/2*, 1490.

5 Ball, *The Headlam Diaries*, 29/8/31. Lord Lothian was the former Scottish secretary's nephew.

6 In an earlier debate, Sir Archibald had identified two approaches to the question of Scottish administration, administrative efficiency and national sentiment. He favoured the former.

7 Hunter, 198. Churchill was then recovering from a car accident in the United States.

8 De Groot, *Liberal Crusader*, 88.

9 Self, *The Neville Chamberlain Diary Letters III*, 13/2/1932.

10 Pottinger, *The Secretaries of State for Scotland*, 50.

11 Hunter, 200.

12 THRS II 1/1 f67.

13 Ibid., f3.

14 Ibid., f36.

15 Ibid., f6.

16 Colville, *The Churchillians*, 141.

Sir Godfrey Collins

1 Ball, *The Headlam Diaries*, 28/9/32.

2 Ibid., 31/10/32. Sir Godfrey's predecessor, Sir Archibald Sinclair, also wrote on 29/9/1932 to wish him luck: 'This is a very happy office and I am very sorry to leave it – but I am thankful to know that you are to succeed me . . . With all good wishes for a term of office not happier than mine for that is impossible but as happy as and longer than my own.' (THRS II 1/1 f8).

3 Ibid., 24/11/32.

4 Hansard 272 c250–51.

5 Ibid., c294–98.

6 Chamberlain collected information for two returns, the second of which was published in 1935.

7 In 1989, Collins was taken over by Rupert Murdoch's News Corporation, which merged it with the US publisher Harper & Row. The firm now trades under the name of HarperCollins.

8 Scotland's Record Acc 7330 (55–56). Interview with Sir Charles Cunningham, 29/5/1980.

9 Hansard 287 c184.

10 SR Acc 7330 (55–56).

11 The *Scotsman* 16/2/35. At around this time, Edinburgh Castle was proposed as an official residence for the Scottish secretary. Nothing came of the idea, although Arthur Woodburn used it for official functions in the late 1940s.

12 The second Scottish commissioner was Sir Nigel Douglas-Hamilton. His nephew, Lord James Douglas-Hamilton, was a long-serving Scottish Office minister and is now a member of the Scottish parliament.

13 Levitt, 266–67, PRO, CAB 24/235 CP^{32}411. Memo dated 24/11/1932.

14 Hansard 298 c552.

15 Ibid., c564.

16 A sub-committee of the Cathcart Committee was, however, impressed with the Highlands and Islands Medical Service and thought it might provide valuable pointers for a future 'national' medical service.

17 *The Times* 5/4/1933.

18 Hansard 308 c1633.

19 This habit helps explain why no papers survive from Sir Godfrey's political career.

20 *The Times* 24/4/1934.

21 The *Scotsman* 8/12/1933.

22 Hansard 284 c177–78.

23 Home, *The Way the Wind Blows*, 59.

24 Mitchell, *Governing Scotland*, 204–05. Sir John continued: 'One would want to see one much younger given a chance – Clydesdale for instance, or Colville or Dunglass, all of whom seem to have some life in them.' It was a good call on Colville, who became Scottish secretary in 1938, and also on Dunglass – later the Earl of Home – who joined the Scottish Office as minister of state in 1951.

25 *The Times* 23/11/1935. Skelton was the first example of a candidate being elected posthumously. John Colville replaced him as under-secretary.

26 Self, *The Neville Chamberlain Diary Letters*, 211. The Earl of Dundee remembers his father telling him that Sir Godfrey was also quite senile just before his death.

27 The *Scotsman* 14/10/1936.

28 Ibid. 15/10/1936.

29 Hansard 316 c34.

Walter Elliot

1 *The Times* 14/1/1958. Violet Markham wrote: 'To him the past was not a page turned but part of the fabric which concerns the present.'

2 Elliot also described himself as a 'White Marxist', someone who argued against socialism on its own terms.

3 Pottinger, *The Secretaries of State for Scotland*, 64.

4 Self, *The Neville Chamberlain Diary Letters*, 31/10/1936.

5 The *Scotsman* 30/10/1936.

6 Elliot Papers Acc 12198, 11/4/1923.

7 Elliot won the Kelvingrove Division of Glasgow, which he held until 1945. He often campaigned with the slogan, 'Do not falter; vote for Walter'.

8 EP Acc 12198. Elliot soon got into the swing of things, writing to Baffy again on 23/12/1924: 'It's a quarter to nine o'clock at night and I'm alone in the Scottish Office where they must regard me as either a maniac or an imbecile since this is a nightly programme of mine.'

9 Jones, *Whitehall Diary I*, 304.

10 At the invitation of Sir John Boyd-Orr, Elliot conducted some research at the renowned Rowett Institute in Aberdeen, earning a PhD in 1923.

11 The *Saturday Review* 9/2/1929.

12 The *Glasgow Herald* 6/11/1926.

13 The *Aberdeen Press & Journal* 6/2/1928.

14 The *Yorkshire Evening Post* 5/1928.

15 Stanley Baldwin Papers vol 36 ff76–77. Letter dated 2/9/1928.

16 Harvie, *Travelling Scot*, 122.

17 Katherine Tennant was the half-sister of Margot Asquith and Harold John Tennant, the short-lived Scottish secretary during the latter half of 1916. She married Walter Elliot in 1934; his first wife, Helen Arabella Hamilton, had tragically died in a climbing accident on their honeymoon in 1919.

18 Ball, *The Headlam Diaries*, 28/9/1932.

19 A recent review of ministerial salaries perhaps softened the blow. The Scottish secretary's salary rose to £5,000.

20 EP Acc 12198/8, 3/11/1936. Timekeeping was not Elliot's strong point. Sir Ronald Johnson remembered Elliot's maxim being: 'To catch a train with half-an-hour to spare is more unsporting than shooting at a sitting pheasant.' (Scotland's Record Acc 7330).

21 Hansard 317 c141–42.

22 Levitt, *The Scottish Office*, 47.

23 Coote, *A Companion of Honour*, 189.

24 Levitt, 172, PRO, CAB 27/578 DA[34]11th.

25 *The Times* 27/11/1937.

26 Scotland's Record Acc 7330 (55–56). Interview with Sir Charles Cunningham, 29/5/1980.

27 Sir Archibald Sinclair and Lord Alness were also considered as possible chairmen. They later gave evidence favouring the retention of the board system.

28 Command 5563, 680.

29 The *Scotsman* 18/10/1937. Elliot must have agreed with the spirit of the report, writing to Baffy on 14/6/1937: 'I am arguing away here about the Agriculture Bill on which the English Ministry is bent on centralising everything in Whitehall which is a Bad Thing.' (Acc 12198/8.)

30 EP Acc 12198/8, 19/11/1937.

31 Finlay, *A Partnership for Good?*, 112. Elliot also wrote: 'Recently Scotland – largely, I think because of the unsatisfactory conditions mentioned in my Cabinet Memorandum – has become increasingly conscious of itself and of the need for a material and spiritual revival on a national scale.' (Mitchell, *Governing Scotland*, 120.)

32 EP Acc 12198/8, 29/12/1937.

33 Hansard 318 c2064–65.

34 The *Scotsman* 1/1/1937. Elliot said: 'Mr Walter Elliot, MP for Kelvingrove and Secretary of State for Scotland, wishes you all a happy and prosperous new year, and mony may ye see.' The audience applauded loudly.

35 The *Scotsman* 18/11/1937.

36 EP Acc 12198/8, 1/10/1937.

37 Ibid., 2/10/1937.

38 Hansard 328 c394–404.

39 EP Acc 12198/8, 13/1/1938.

40 Ibid, 21/2/1938 and 3/1938.

41 Since 1918, this seat elected three MPs by single-transferable-vote, with graduates of the four ancient Scottish universities forming the electorate. It was scrapped in 1948, and the three MPs disappeared at the 1950 general election.

42 The *Daily Herald* 21/9/1948.

David John Colville

1 Darling, *King's Cross to Waverley*, 42. Sir William's great-nephew, Alistair Darling, was Scottish secretary from 2003–6.

2 Pottinger, *The Secretaries of State for Scotland*, 75.

3 Scotland's Record Acc 7330 (55–56). Interview with Sir Charles Cunningham, 29/5/1980.

4 SR Acc 7330. Interview with Sir Ronald Johnson, 18/8/1979.

5 If dull public clerks like church organs then Colville stands guilty as charged. He kept one in his house at Braidwood, and gifted another to his local church.

6 Hansard 341 c259–66.

7 SR Acc 7330.

8 The *Scotsman* 27/1/1940.

9 Self, *The Neville Chamberlain Diary Letters*, 31/10/1936.

10 The *Scotsman* obtained one early in-house design which it dubbed the 'jam factory', ensuring an open competition to find an architect was eventually held.

11 Hansard 349 c2029. At around the same time John McEwen, later Sir John, became the new under-secretary at the Scottish Office. A former diplomat and Catholic convert, he had been PPS to Walter Elliot as Scottish secretary, and later chaired the Conservatives' 1922 Committee from 1944–45.

12 The wood reputedly came from a walnut tree planted at Balmerino Abbey in the 16th century.

13 Hansard 338 c2528.

14 Hansard 342 c1837–51; 342 c1858.

15 Ibid. c1858

Ernest Brown

1 The *Scotsman* 21/5/1940.
2 The former Leith MP, Tony Benn's father William Wedgwood Benn, had switched from the Liberals to the Labour Party, and instead fought North Aberdeen.
3 This was the first time since 1885 that Dover House had not been used as the Scottish Office. It was reoccupied by James Stuart in 1955.
4 Brown Papers BRO/1.
5 Dunnett, *Among Friends*, 188.
6 Darling, *So It Looks To Me*, 252.
7 Pottinger, *The Secretaries of State for Scotland*, 84.
8 Darling, *King's Cross to Waverley*, 42. Sir William added: 'His experience of the Scotchmen in his Constituency of Leith must have taught him much.'

Thomas Johnston

1 Hansard 374 c304–05.
2 Galbraith, *Without Quarter*, 238.
3 Darling, *King's Cross to Waverley*, 42.
4 The Primroses got off relatively lightly: '. . . the family to which Lord Rosebery belongs have only sprung up in comparatively recent times; and consequently they have not had many opportunities of perpetrating land robberies and of steeping themselves in deceit, cruelty and blood.' The 6th Earl of Rosebery later became a friend and used to quote this at Johnston to amuse himself. (Johnston, *Our Scots Noble Families*, 10.)
5 Beatrice Webb wrote that Johnston 'is the best of the Clyde lot and a good party man; but he is slight in mental makeup.' (Webb, *Diaries*, 138) The Tory MP Bob Boothby described him as 'among them but never quite of them'. (Boothby, *My Yesterday, Your Tomorrow*, 138.)
6 Walker, *Thomas Johnston*, 94. Johnston also suggested various relief schemes, one of which was a tourist road from Aberfoyle to the Trossachs.
7 It was such friendships that led to suspicion from other Clydesiders. After the 1931 election defeat, John Wheatley often attacked Johnston in the *Glasgow Eastern Standard*.
8 In his election address, Johnston boasted of several achievements during his time at the Scottish Office, including the Slum Clearance Act, an amendment to the Widows Pensions Act and his nutritional experiments with milk.
9 Johnston reputedly told a colleague that the best view of London was of Euston from the train. He always travelled by sleeper, buying a 'blood' at the station, a detective paperback which would see him off to sleep. (Scotland's War Acc 11307/177. Interview with Mary Knox, Johnston's daughter.)
10 'I also saw Tom Johnston,' wrote Churchill's private secretary Jock Colville, 'whom the PM thinks one of the best of the Labour Party. He is to be offered the Scottish Office.' (Colville, *The Fringes of Power*, 4/2/1941) Churchill later told *The Times* that Johnston was 'our good and faithful friend'.
11 Johnston, *Memories*, 148.
12 Gilbert, *Winston Churchill Companion III*, 187. Churchill also used Johnston to fend off accusations that he was anti-Scottish. 'I have taken very great pains, as you can see from recent appointments, to meet Scottish Nationalist sentiment,' he wrote to the East Edinburgh MP, Mr F. W. Pethick-Lawrence, 'but I get a little nettled sometimes by the very small clique who write indignant letters if ever the word England is mentioned. I do not believe that clique expresses at all the opinions of the Scottish people, who are too sure of themselves to be so petty.' (Gilbert, 226, 15/2/1941).
13 Haddow considered Johnston to be the greatest ever secretary of state for Scotland. When asked why, he reasoned: 'He could see through a brick wall!' (Letter to the *Scotsman* 12/9/1990) Another Scottish Office civil servant, Sir Horace Hamilton, later told Alastair Dunnett that Johnston ranked alongside Lloyd George in his ability to get straight to the heart of an issue.

14 Johnston Papers Dep 176 Box 26[4], 7/2/1941.
15 Beaverbrook Papers BBK, 1/3/1941.
16 This was despite an early injury which meant Johnston could not lift his right hand up to his face. His daughter remembers him always eating and writing with his left hand, and tying his bow tie with his left hand and teeth.
17 Colville, 8/5/1941.
18 Walker, 42.
19 Hansard 374 c1615.
20 The *Scotsman* 31/10/1941.
21 Campbell, 'The Committee of Ex-Secretaries of State for Scotland and Industrial Policy', *Scottish Industrial History*, 2 (1979), SRO DD 12/41.
22 Ibid., SRO DD 12/42. Letters dated 17 and 21/11/1941.
23 Reith, *Diaries*, 25/3/1943.
24 The *Scotsman* 9/6/1997. Article by Alastair Dunnett.
25 Darling, 65.
26 The *Scotsman* 6/8/1942.
27 Naomi Mitchison recorded this encounter with Johnston in her diary: 'After a bit T.J. came and looked at my Scots history books, signed my *History of the Working Classes* for me (I wondered if he would disown it!) and then talked about Scotland, rather inspiringly, I thought, about people coming back from Canada and America to find ancestors, about part of our job being to trace them. I said we mustn't make Scotland into an antique. And he said we would even do that to buy her future.' (Mitchison, *Among You Taking Notes*, 19/9/1944.)
28 Dunnett, *Among Friends*, 209.
29 Hansard 387 c184–93. One former Scottish secretary was once heard to describe opponents of the scheme as 'long-haired men and short-haired women living in Chelsea together and occasionally married'.
30 The *Scotsman* 20/10/1941.
31 Ibid. 28/10/1941.
32 Ibid. 13/3/1943.
33 Johnston, 165.
34 Darling, *So It Looks To Me*, 252.
35 Hansard 379 c1623–30.
36 Johnston moved its Second Reading on 14 February 1945: 'I do not claim that this Bill will bring the new Jerusalem to our Scottish towns, but it does four things . . .' (Hansard 408 c262).
37 The Convention was supposed to meet for the first time in 1939 but the meeting was cancelled due to the outbreak of war. It met instead in October 1942, and soon moved a resolution in Johnston's favour.
38 Muirhead Papers Acc 3721 Box 3. Letters dated 25/7 and 29/8/1942.
39 Reith, 25/3/1943.
40 Mitchison was a niece of Lord Haldane, the former Liberal MP and lord chancellor under Ramsay MacDonald. She was later elected to Argyll County Council, and served on the Highland Panel from 1947–1965, and also the Highlands and Islands Development Consultative Council from 1966.
41 Walker, 174.
42 Mitchison, 300. Mitchison was one of several writers commissioned by the social research organisation, Mass-Observation, to keep a diary to record social conditions in wartime Scotland. She also planned to write a book about Johnston and government by consent, but never did.
43 Levitt, *The Scottish Office*, 101–04, PRO, CAB 87/72 MGO 36.
44 Nicolson, *Diaries and Letters II*, 17/4/1945.
45 Hansard 396 c510.
46 Johnston, 169.

47 The *Scotsman* 7/4/1942.
48 At the Bill's Second Reading, Johnston said that if he were starting afresh, he would prefer an ad hoc system of education administration. 'But we are not starting afresh,' he told MPs, 'and it is a trite but a truthful observation that it is easier to scramble an egg than to unscramble it.' (Hansard 410 c1274)
49 Gibson, *Thistle and the Crown*, 111. Attlee rejected the idea, partly because Labour's showing in Scotland at the general election had been poorer than expected.
50 The *Glasgow Herald* 26/5/1945.
51 The *Scotsman* 26/5/1945.
52 Galbraith, 251–52.
53 Woodburn Papers Acc 7656 Box 3.
54 Johnston even waxed lyrical about devolution in a short film called the *Future of Scotland*, made by J. Arthur Rank in 1948.
55 *The Times* 6/9/1965.

6th Earl of Rosebery

 1 Despite the wartime coalition having broken up on 23/5/1945, Rosebery had continued to support Churchill and the Conservatives.
 2 The *Scotsman* 26/5/1945.
 3 Ibid. 28/5/1945. Peers, on the other hand, were delighted that one of their own was in the Cabinet, heaping praise upon Rosebery in the chamber. 'I can assure them that I shall do my utmost, fortified by these good wishes, to further what I can for Scotland' responded Rosebery. (Hansard 136 c371)
 4 McKinstry, *Rosebery*, 494–97.
 5 Beaverbrook Papers BBK/C/278, 23/1/1941.
 6 Darling, *King's Cross to Waverley*, 40.
 7 BBC Scotland documentary, *Secretary of State for Scotland*, c1966 (Scottish Screen Archive).
 8 In 1955 Rosebery also replaced Johnston as chairman of the Scottish Tourist Board.
 9 The *Scotsman* 14/6/1945.
10 Young, *Harry, Lord Rosebery*, 134.
11 Scotland's Record Acc 7330 (68). Interview with Lord Strathclyde, 10/7/1980.
12 The *Scotsman* 11/7/1945.
13 Despite supporting Churchill personally, Sinclair's Liberals fielded candidates against ten of his ministers.
14 The *Scotsman* 12/7/1945.
15 Young, 135.
16 House of Lords Archives HC/CL/CH/2/2/213.
17 Michael Noble's former private secretary, Archie Rennie, recalls this incident.

Joseph Westwood

 1 The *Scotsman* 3/8/1945.
 2 Dunnett, *Among Friends*, 188.
 3 Anonymous, *The Scottish Socialists*, 162.
 4 The *Scotsman* 1/10/1946.
 5 Ibid. 26/1/1946. Johnston had delivered the first such address in January 1945, and for a few years it became a fixture in the political life of Scotland. Westwood thought it 'should become a permanent part of the unwritten constitution for Scotland – a day when they could hear from the Secretary of State a brief review of the work of the past year, take with him a look at the present, and with him dip into the future.'
 6 The *Scotsman* 25/8/1945; Dunnett, *Among Friends*, 189.
 7 Ibid. 25/1/1947.
 8 Levitt, *The Scottish Office*, 61–62.
 9 The Highlands and Islands Medical Service. Westwood had also been a member of Sir Godfrey Collins' Cathcart Committee on Scottish Health Services.

10 Hansard 431 c1013.
11 Pottinger, *The Secretaries of State for Scotland*, 104–05.
12 Hansard 423 c2350.
13 Dalton, *High Tide and After*, 153.
14 The *Scotsman* 1/2/1947. Westwood also told a planning congress in Edinburgh that the planning of the 'Scotland of tomorrow' was in her own hands, without any interference from Whitehall. 'Certainly its planning will not be subject to those strange alien influences about which we hear so frequently,' he said. 'There will be no pattern drawn up in some dark office in Whitehall imposed willy-nilly on the Authorities of Scotland. Nor, may I say, do I intend to have one drawn up in St Andrew's House.' (The *Scotsman* 4/10/1947.)
15 Fry, *Patronage and Principle*, 195.
16 Levitt, 106, PRO, T 222/1048.
17 Ibid., 107, PRO, CAB 124/911.
18 Ibid., 109, PRO, CAB 124/911.
19 Ibid., 21, PRO, PREM 8/658.
20 The *Glasgow Herald* 1/7/1947.
21 Levitt, 110, PRO, CAB 124/911.
22 Harvie, *Forward!*, 67–68.
23 The *Daily Herald* 8/10/1947.
24 5th Hansard 450 c414–15.
25 5th Hansard 454 c428–29.

Arthur Woodburn

1 Brown, *Maxton*, 65.
2 The *Scotsman* 10/8/1947.
3 In his first speech as Scottish secretary, Woodburn also promised to 'try to pull the country through without party politics'. (The *Daily Mail* 11/10/1947).
4 Woodburn Papers Acc 7656/1/2. Letters dated 10/10 and 16/10/1947. Sir William Darling also led a campaign to give the Scottish secretary a 'Number 10' or official residence, preferably on the Royal Mile or near Princes Street. From January 1948 the lower banqueting hall of Edinburgh Castle was sanctioned for use by the secretary of state to entertain guests, but an official residence had to wait until 1970.
5 *Scottish Sunday Express* 10/1947.
6 Pearce, *Patrick Gordon Walker Political Diaries*, 2/8/1938.
7 House of Lords Archives HC/CL/CH/2/2/213.
8 Woodburn, *Some Recollections*, 147.
9 Levitt, *The Scottish Office*, 113, SRO, HH36/92.
10 Ibid., 115–16, SRO, HH1/1231.
11 Morrison argued that an inquiry would provide unwelcome scope for attacks on the government's programme of nationalisation. He also reminded Woodburn that he had no economic powers as Scottish secretary.
12 The *Scotsman* 1/12/1947.
13 Press cuttings in the Woodburn Papers Acc 7656/28/2.
14 The *Scotsman* 31/1/1948.
15 CAB 128/10.
16 5th Hansard 450 c409.
17 The *Scotsman* 29/4/1948.
18 Levitt, 'Britain, the Scottish Covenant Movement and Devolution', *Scottish Affairs* (1998), SRO, HH 1/1231c.
19 MacCormick went on to become lord rector of Glasgow University in 1950, and also became embroiled in the theft of the Stone of Destiny. The Scottish Convention gradually lost support, and in June 1951 he founded the Scottish Covenant Association to press for a Scottish parliament within the UK. MacCormick ended his political

career as a Liberal candidate at the 1959 general election, and died two years later.

20 MacCormick, *Flag in the Wind*, 126–27. Meetings of the Scottish Convention used to parade effigies of the 'Quisling' Woodburn.

21 The *Scotsman* 27/10/1947.

22 Woodburn, 153.

23 The austere chancellor did, however, announce plans to bring light industry to the Highlands, and create new community centres to stop depopulation.

24 In his unpublished memoirs, Woodburn says 'J. J.' was incapable of grasping the complexity of his housing brief due to failing health.

25 Woodburn, 157.

26 The *Scotsman* 26/4/1948.

27 Woodburn, 168.

28 The *Scotsman* 7/3/1948.

29 Levitt, 372–73.

30 The *Scotsman* 2/2/1949.

31 WP Acc 7656/16/1.

32 WP Acc 7656/1/1.

33 Hansard 469 c2097.

34 Ibid. c2107. Coincidentally, Woodburn's cousin was the actor James Woodburn, best known for his role in the Ealing Comedy, *Whisky Galore*. The SNP politician Winnie Ewing, née Woodburn, was also a relative of Arthur, and he sponsored her when she became an MP in 1967.

35 MacCormick, 132.

36 The *Bulletin* 17/11/1949.

37 Woodburn, 185.

38 WP Acc 7656/16/1.

39 Levitt, 123, SRO, HH41/454.

40 Woodburn, 187. Oddly, Woodburn maintains in his memoirs that he remained at the Scottish Office until 1951.

41 The *Scotsman* 1/3/1950.

42 Ibid. 9/3/1950.

Hector McNeil

1 Fisher, *Burgess and Maclean*, 58. Reputedly, this exchange took place at Burgess's farewell party at his London flat, a function also attended by fellow-communists, spy-hunters and male prostitutes. According to John Fisher, McNeil and Burgess got on well because both had close relationships with their mothers, both were intellectual snobs, and both liked occasional drinking sprees.

2 The *Scotsman* 1/3/1950. The *New Statesmen* described McNeil's appointment as 'an intelligent matching of the man to the moment'.

3 McNeil defended his relationship with Beaverbrook by arguing that as a Cabinet minister, he could act as a pacifier between the Labour government and the *Daily Express*. After McNeil's death, the press baron also helped pay McNeil's son's school fees.

4 Nicolson, *Diaries and Letters 1945–62*, 69.

5 Lord Maclennan, who looked upon McNeil as an uncle, remembers clearly his views on foreign affairs. (27/10/2005)

6 Williams, *Gaitskell Diaries*, 23/4/1948.

7 *The Times* 2/5/1950.

8 Hansard 472 c635.

9 Hansard 477 c218.

10 Levitt, 'Britain, the Scottish Covenant Movement and Devolution', *Scottish Affairs* (1998), SRO, HH 41/454c.

11 Ibid., 127.

12 Ibid., 128.

13 Herbison's relative (a cousin), Karen Whitefield, was elected a member of the Scottish parliament for Peggy's old seat in 1999.

14 McNeil had been offered 25 minutes on the NBC to talk about Scotland. 'It might have brought a few more light industries to the north, who knows,' wrote McNeil's wife Sheila to Lord Beaverbrook. (Beaverbrook Papers BBK/C/236. Letter dated 22/12/1950.)

15 The *Scotsman* 29/5/1950.

16 *The Times* 15/1/1951.

17 His friends' son, Robert Maclennan, was heavily influenced by McNeil and later became a Labour MP in 1966, holding Caithness and Sutherland despite his defection to the SDP in 1981.

18 Scotland's Record Acc 7330. Interview with Sir Ronald Johnson, 18/8/1979.

19 George John Gordon Bruce, 7th Lord Balfour of Burleigh. His father had been secretary for Scotland from 1895 to 1903.

20 McNeil said: 'However noble and dearly loved the right hon. Gentleman [Winston Churchill] may be – and he is – he will scarcely permit himself to be disentangled from the suspicion which reaches from Land's End to John O'Groats in relation to the Tory Party's housing programme, and today our suspicions have not been allayed.' (5th Hansard 480 c707–08)

21 Wheatley, *One Man's Judgement*, 115.

22 BP BBK/C/236.

23 Shawcross was quoted in the *Sunday Times*, 26 Feb 2006. The incident did no harm to Hamilton's career; he later became both a QC (taking silk before the very man who was to recommend against a prosecution, John Wheatley) and rector of Aberdeen University.

24 The *Sunday Times* 26/2/2006.

25 Rosie, *Curious Scotland*, 225–26. McNeil's successor, James Stuart, said in a Cabinet memo that 'nothing is to be gained by postponing the decision about the disposal of the Stone. On the contrary, we should avoid having any controversy about the Stone at or about the time of the Coronation.' Churchill even offered Tom Johnston a CH, arguing that it 'might even make them [the Scots] forget the Scone Stone'. (Letter to Johnston dated 2/5/1953, Copy in William Patrick Library, Kirkintilloch.)

26 BP BBK/C/236.

27 Pimlott, *Hugh Dalton: The Political Diary*, 9/2/1951.

28 BP BBK/C/236.

29 Ibid.

30 Levitt, *The Scottish Office*, 378–79, PRO, CAB 129/39 CP50'57.

31 5th Hansard 487 c338.

32 Levitt, 384, SRO, HH102/316.

33 As Scottish secretary, McNeil received a salary of £5,000, while as a back-bencher he got only £1,000.

34 BP BBK/C/236.

35 Woodburn Papers Acc 7656. Transcript dated 12/10/1955.

36 Brown, *In My Way*, 91.

James Stuart

1 Catterrall, *The Macmillan Diaries*, 97.

2 Ibid., 115.

3 Stuart, *Within the Fringe*, 161.

4 *Scottish Control of Scottish Affairs, Unionist Policy* (Glasgow 1949).

5 Home, *The Way the Wind Blows*, 103.

6 Hansard 494 c480.

7 Stuart, xiii.

8 The Conservative manifesto of 1951 also promised a minister for Welsh affairs, which was established and later upgraded to a minister of state in 1954.
9 Ibid., 161.
10 Kemp, *The Hollow Drum*, 107.
11 Stuart, 164.
12 Dickie, *The Uncommon Commoner*, 92.
13 Vickers, *Elizabeth the Queen Mother*, 47.
14 Stuart was also a contemporary of Macmillan at Eton.
15 Ball, *The Headlam Diaries*, 19/7/35.
16 Another standard tale of James Stuart as Scottish secretary was his wife telling him not to sound so bored during a placid speech at election time. 'Sorry darling,' he replied audibly, 'I just can't help it because I am so bored.'
17 SR Acc 7330. Interview with Lord Strathclyde, 10/07/1980.
18 Sir William Kerr Fraser, later permanent under-secretary at the Scottish Office, made this simile. (14/11/2005)
19 Levitt, *The Scottish Office*, 309.
20 Lord Sorn suffered from arthritis, and had to read committee papers through a glass screen while lying on his back. He died soon after his report was published.
21 Hansard 547 c1415.
22 Hansard 523 c375; Butskellism was the post-war consensual economic policy named after the Labour chancellor Hugh Gaitskell and the Conservative chancellor Rab Butler.
23 Levitt, 209.
24 SR Acc 7330(68).
25 Ibid.
26 SR Acc 7330(53). Interview with Sir Alec Douglas-Home, 8/7/1980.
27 SR Acc 7330(68).
28 Hansard 504 c770–71.
29 MacCormick, *The Flag in the Wind*, 139.
30 MacCormick v. Lord Advocate 1953 SC 396.
31 *The Times* 7/8/1954.
32 Macmillan, *Riding the Storm*, 97.
33 SR Acc 7330(68).
34 Stuart, 177.
35 SR Acc 7330(68).
36 Stuart, 167.

John Maclay

1 Boothby, *My Yesterday, Your Tomorrow*, 139–40. Boothby was a rather promiscuous bisexual who fathered one of Macmillan's daughters following an affair with Lady Dorothy. The Greenock MP Dick Mabon, who had ambitions to be Scottish secretary, used to quote Boothby approvingly.
2 See *The Choice for Liberals*, a speech Maclay made to the 21st meeting of the National Liberal Association of Scotland in Edinburgh on 22/2/1958.
3 *People's Journal* 17/1/1957.
4 Scotland's Record Acc 7330(54). Interview with Viscount Muirshiel, 17/11/1980.
5 Ibid.
6 A possible closure had been in the air since the previous November. 'Poor James Stuart is in trouble with the West Lothian shale oil industry,' wrote Macmillan in his diary. 'This employs 5000 men, but is hopelessly uneconomic. Of course it ought to be shut down; but there is the usual outcry about the men.' (Catterall, *The Macmillan Diaries*, 17/11/1955)
7 SR Acc 7330(54).
8 Lord Forbes was at time of writing still alive and well and living in Aberdeenshire,

easily the oldest surviving Scottish Office minister. He told me that he was the last minister of state mainly to be resident in Edinburgh.

9 Macmillan was criticised for awarding a life peerage to Browne so soon after he lost his seat.

10 In July 1957, Macpherson held a meeting with the directors of the *Dumfries and Galloway Standard* which resulted in its editor being sacked; it was said because he had written editorials critical of the government. The opposition leader Hugh Gaitskell got involved, and Emrys Hughes called an adjournment debate.

11 Hope was a grandson of the 1st Marquis of Linlithgow, who was briefly secretary for Scotland in 1905.

12 'I have always had a strong dislike of 5-year plans' wrote Maclay to James McGuiness on 21/11/1972. (Muirshiel Papers DC371.)

13 Lord Forbes remembered that many of Maclay's colleagues, himself included, thought the Scottish secretary would have been more successful had he been more forceful in Cabinet.

14 *The Times* 3/7/1957.

15 Archie Rennie, who became Maclay's private secretary in the spring of 1962, remembers him saying that he should not expect to be his PS for very long.

16 SR Acc 7330(54).

17 Ibid.

18 MP DC371. Both letters dated 15/7/1962.

19 Ibid. Letter dated 31/8/1968.

20 Ibid.

Michael Noble

1 Sir John was a relation of the Victorian engineer Isambard Kingdom Brunel, as was the wife of Gordon Campbell, Scottish secretary from 1970–74.

2 Interview with Archie Rennie, 7/11/2005.

3 Deedes, *Dear Bill*, 159–60.

4 *The Times* 9/11/1962. Macmillan apparently remarked: 'Very well, we shall retire, but we shall retire to the thunder of the guns.'

5 Bruno Pontecorvo was a Jewish-Italian atomic physicist who voluntarily moved to the USSR in 1950.

6 *The Times* 15/11/1962.

7 Tweedsmuir Papers Acc 11884/64. Thatcher and Tweedsmuir were two of only three female ministers in the Conservative government. The other was Mervyn Pike.

8 Tweedsmuir's son-in-law, Lord James Douglas-Hamilton, also became an under-secretary and minister of state at the Scottish Office, and from 1999 was a member of the Scottish parliament.

9 Noble's background, like Maclay's, was steeped in heavy industry. His grandfather, Sir Andrew Noble Bt, helped found the engineering and armaments firm Armstrong, Whitworth & Co., of which Noble's father was a director. His nephew, Ian Noble, also helped launch the Scottish merchant bank Noble Grossart in the late 1960s.

10 Hansard 663 c676.

11 Heath, *The Course of My Life*, 265.

12 Hansard 679 c698.

13 Hansard 685 c268.

14 Noble wrote in a memo dated 13/12/1963 that he favoured such a body if he 'could be persuaded that it could achieve what existing bodies could not do, and would not overlap'. (Muirshiel Papers DC371.)

15 Interview with Archie Rennie.

16 These proposals were largely the work of the civil servant George Pottinger.

17 Home became prime minister on 18 October 1963, and disclaimed his seat in the Lords five days later under the Peerage Act. Therefore, from 23 October until the

Kinross and West Perthshire by-election on 7 November, Sir Alec was prime minister without being a member of either house of parliament.

18 This was a great blow to Noble, who had come to rely heavily on Leburn, a classic 'safe pair of hands'.

19 Muirshiel Papers DC371.

20 Another former Scottish Office minister from the period, Niall Macpherson – now Lord Drumalbyn – also joined the Heath government as minister without portfolio.

21 Coutts, *Auld Acquaintance*, 64.

22 BBC Scotland documentary, *Secretary of State for Scotland*, c1966 (Scottish Screen Archive).

William Ross

1 Scotland's Record Acc 7339. Interview with Sir Ronald Johnson. Both Ross's former private secretary Peter Mackay, and the future permanent under-secretary (and former private secretary) Sir William Kerr Fraser, remember the atmosphere in 1964.

2 Ross, 'Approaching the Archangelic', *Scottish Government Yearbook 1978* (1978).

3 Ross was briefed by Sir Douglas, who feared that such competition would expose just how well the Scottish Office was doing in comparison with the rest of the UK.

4 On his appointment, Ross was summoned to Fielden House to meet the civil servant George Pottinger, who was then McNeil's private secretary. Pottinger was a renowned snob and had a low opinion of Ross. When he arrived and sent a message that 'Major Ross is waiting', Pottinger replied that 'Colonel Pottinger will see him in five minutes'. Ross was furious and never forgave Pottinger, who was still at the Scottish Office when he became Scottish secretary 13 years later. (Interview with Archie Rennie, 7/11/2005.)

5 Sir William Kerr Fraser made this comparison. He remembers watching the pair hold up a Bill on owners' rates in the mid 1950s. (11/4/2002)

6 Hansard 708 c1095.

7 Interview with Scottish TV (1985).

8 As home secretary, Callaghan led trade union-backed Cabinet opposition to Castle's Bill. (Castle, *Diaries 1964–70*, 767.)

9 Mabon's private secretary, Peter Mackay, remembers Ross phoning his office at about 8pm and demanding to know where Dick was. Mackay replied that he was 'out somewhere' and Ross growled: 'It is the duty of all Scottish ministers to be in parliament until after the 10 o'clock vote.' (11/4/2002)

10 Ewing, *Stop the World*, 8.

11 National Archives of Scotland HH41/1802. Note dated 4/8/1967.

12 Crossman, *Diaries of a Cabinet Minister III*, 895.

13 The *Scotsman* 1/1/1999.

14 Tam Dalyell, at that time Crossman's PPS, thought his boss was only pro-devolution because Ross was anti. When Crossman wanted to sit on the front-bench to listen to the Second Reading of the Social Work (Scotland) Bill in May 1968, Ross ordered him to be kept out of the chamber. 'You and Willie Ross,' Crossman thundered to Tam. 'You're just as bad as he is, really, though in a less uncouth, smoother way! – go around shouting about the Scottish Nationalists wanting separation, but what both of you and your friends actually want is to keep your Scottish business absolutely privy from English business. You and Willie Ross want a system which gives you the worst of both worlds, and that's why I'm in favour of a Scottish parliament.' (Dalyell, *Dick Crossman*, 224.)

15 The *Scotsman* 1/1/1999.

16 Former ministers and civil servants are divided over the issue of Ross's drinking habits. Harry Ewing remembers him enjoying a drink, certainly in the mid 1970s, while Peter Mackay, who was his private secretary in 1974/75, does not remember him ever touching a drop.

17 Castle, 532.

18 Peter Mackay, Ross's former private secretary, has this note.
19 Jim Sillars remembers a 'disastrous' *Daily Record* dinner where Mackintosh told Ross he was 'a stupid prick' after consuming vast quantities of alcohol. He later started dancing at a drunken Scots Night at the Labour Party conference. 'Look at him,' muttered Ross in disgust, 'just look at him.'
20 Interview with Jim Sillars, 3/2002.
21 Smith had been offered one of the Scots law officer posts, but was reluctant to become trapped in a Parliament House niche. Instead, Bruce Millan convinced him to become Ross's bag-carrier, a more traditional first step on the ministerial ladder.
22 This is richly ironic. Ross's daughter Fiona became a long-serving political correspondent for Scottish TV. Ross once told STV's political editor Colin Mackay that television was 'cheap, meretricious rubbish'. He did, however, get on well with individual reporters like Jim Naughtie from the *Scotsman*.
23 Interview with Sir William Kerr Fraser, 11/4/2002.
24 Sir William Kerr Fraser also remembers detailed sketches of the skyline from the Cabinet room window, while Peter Mackay recalls that junior members of staff used to save Ross's doodles as mementos.
25 Lord Thomson recalls that such rumours led to a great degree of tension between him and Ross, even though Thomson had no desire to move to the Scottish Office. (26/10/2005)
26 Hansard 866 c324. Dick Mabon quoted another member who said it was necessary in almost all circumstances to have beauty and the beast. 'Certainly she is the beauty,' he added, meaning MacDonald.
27 See following chapter on Gordon Campbell.
28 This was Peter Mackay, who remembers Number 10 phoning him to say that Ross was to become Scottish secretary for the second time and could he contact him. It turned out that the position had already been offered to another Willie Ross, the Ulster Unionist MP for Londonderry, who happened to stay at the same London hotel frequented by his Ayrshire namesake. He had said, 'for God's sake no, anything but that', and Mackay was eventually able to reach the other Willie Ross, who grumpily retorted: 'nobody told me'. There was much chaos at this time because the prime minister had miscalculated the number of ministers he could appoint, so the Scottish Office had to make do with only one under-secretary, Hugh Brown.
29 Interview with Alex Neil MSP, 31/5/2005.
30 Hansard 904 c1500.
31 The minority of five included Donald Dewar, the future secretary of state and Scottish first minister, and George Robertson, Labour's shadow Scottish secretary in the run up to the 1997 election.
32 Hansard 880 c371.
33 Alex Neil remembers the trade unionist John Pollock telling him of a nightcap he had once shared with Ross, when the Scottish secretary confessed that if he were starting out in politics again he would be a nationalist. He also lamented that he and Pollock were not leading the SNP, as they would do it so much better.
34 Donoughue, *Downing Street Diary*, 8/7/1974.
35 Crowther-Hunt, not to be confused with the Lord Crowther who chaired the royal commission, was then working on devolution with Ted Short at the Privy Council Office.
36 Donoughue, 8/7/1974.
37 Ibid., 17/1/1975.
38 Castle, *Diaries 1974–76*, 17/1/1975.
39 Donoughue, 10/9/1975.
40 Alex Neil, who had helped write the October 1974 manifesto, also left Labour to join the new party.

41 Hansard 903 c1056.
42 Ibid. c1064.
43 By 1 April 1976 Ross was telling colleagues: 'If things go wrong it would immediately lead to separation.' (Castle, 1/4/1976).
44 Donoughue, 6/11/1974.
45 Later Lord Hughes of Woodside and therefore not to be confused with the Lord Hughes who was minister of state. Robert Hughes resigned from the Scottish Office on 22 July 1975 over incomes policy and the sale of arms to South Africa.
46 Donoughue, 19/3/1975.
47 Ibid., 25/11/1975.
48 Wilson had recently learned of plans by Ross's old army chief, Lord Mountbatten, to lead a military coup against the Labour government.
49 The irony of this was widely noted at the time. Ross turned 65 the week he was sacked.
50 Interview with Lord Donoughue, 10/11/2005.
51 Lord Callaghan wrote to me on 18/4/2002: 'Dick Mabon attached himself to Jack Cunningham's team in 1976 which organised a campaign for me as PM & I believe worked hard. (I stayed a little aloof from the canvassing.) I am certain I did not discuss the name of Willie Ross's successor with him. That was not my practice. Perhaps Harry Ewing approached me at the time but I have no recollection of that – many people were anxious to talk to me as you can guess.'
52 The *Scotsman* 9/4/1976.
53 The *Sunday Times*, 20 March 1977.
54 Ross, 'Approaching the Archangelic', *Scottish Government Yearbook 1978* (1978).

Gordon Campbell

1 Willie Ross had agreed to the gift, and the trust to manage it. The Conservative MP Sir William Darling had led a campaign to give the Scottish secretary an official residence in the late 1940s.
2 Browne, *Long Sunset*, 68–69.
3 Tam Dalyell recalls that Campbell's disarming style in the Scottish Grand Committee made Labour attacks seem churlish. As Peggy Herbison put it to her colleagues, 'If you are offensive to Gordon Campbell, it'll simply rebound on us.'
4 On hearing about this, Willie Ross was furious. When I interviewed Lord Campbell in 2002, he still remembered his 'noisy and congratulatory' welcome at St Andrew's House. 'I think the reason was they wanted a change,' he said. 'Anyway I am afraid I have to say Willie Ross was very unpopular with the staff.'
5 Campbell had been at Wellington with Stodart, who was a few years older (and at the Scottish Office from 1963–64), and Peter Mackay remembers Stodart complaining that he would never have believed that his fag would turn on him in this way. Stodart actually retained his seat until retiring at the October 1974 election.
6 Letter from Sir Teddy Taylor to the author dated 13/4/2006.
7 When Sir Douglas retired in 1972, Campbell caused a political storm by appointing him chairman of the North of Scotland Hydro-Electric Board.
8 Sir Henry Hardman was a former head of the Ministry of Defence. His proposals became known as the 'Hardman dispersal'.
9 Interview with Peter Mackay, 11/4/2002.
10 Interview with Lord Gray of Coutin, 27/6/2005.
11 Hansard 833 c523.
12 Hansard 848 c436. Campbell did not make it known that his daughter Christina was at that time near death suffering from anorexia.
13 Interview with Lord Campbell of Croy, 26/4/2002. He was of course referring to today's Holyrood assembly. 'I wouldn't have liked to be in the Scottish parliament,' Lord Campbell told me with a smile, 'as they get continuous stick.'
14 The senior Scottish Office economist Gavin McCrone warned ministers that the

SNP's claims were impressive, the only mistake being that they wildly underestimated the amount of as yet undiscovered oil.

15 In 1971 Hurd had written an entertaining novel called *Scotch on the Rocks*, in which the Scottish secretary is assassinated by dissident nationalists.

16 *The Times* 23/11/1970.

17 Ibid. 3/8/1971.

18 Taylor had suggested to Heath that it would be helpful to have someone from Glasgow playing a part in the campaign.

19 Young, *Scotland*, 159.

20 Winnie Ewing, for example, had long been advertising her constituency surgeries under the banner: 'Come and have a noggin and a natter with Winnie.'

21 *The Times* 18/2/1974.

22 Campbell also said his disability had prevented him campaigning as energetically as Ewing, a claim the SNP matriarch dismissed rather bluntly.

23 Letter dated 7/3/1974. Peter Mackay kindly showed me this from his private papers.

24 The *Guardian* 30/4/2005.

25 Interview with Lord Campbell of Croy.

26 Harold Wilson coined the term Selsdon Man following a meeting of Heath's Shadow Cabinet at Selsdon Park Hotel which firmed up the party's free-market principles.

Bruce Millan

1 The *Scotsman* 9/4/1976.

2 Millan remembers being introduced to Roland Muirhead by Douglas Young during the 1951 contest. Muirhead asked him to support home rule and Millan replied that he had an open mind; Muirhead abstained. (17/6/2005)

3 Millan had been energetically anti-nationalist at the Glasgow Union.

4 Hugh Brown remembers all the junior ministers regularly going for an Italian meal together. Millan, however, rarely joined them.

5 The government's slim majority meant that all Scottish Office ministers were required to be in London all week. Lord Kirkhill, therefore, remained in Edinburgh for most of the time, even using Bute House as a domestic base.

6 Interview with Lord Ewing, 21/2/2002.

7 Smith had been Ross's PPS before going to the Department of Energy. It was said that Smith greeted guests to his birthday celebrations in Edinburgh by saying: 'Come in and have a "devolution special": not a lot of whisky, but plenty of water.' (Lang, *Blue Remembered Years*, 142.)

8 Morgan, *Callaghan*, 629. Memo dated 9/7/1976 (PU 199).

9 Lord Robertson had accused Millan of 'usurping the functions of the judiciary'. The Scottish secretary later invited another Scottish judge, Lord Hunter, to conduct an inquiry into the Meehan case. (Kennedy, *Thirty-Six Murders & Two Immoral Earnings*, 153.)

10 The removal of a sheriff needed a majority of both houses of parliament. Thompson was sheriff of South Strathclyde, Dumfries and Galloway.

11 *The Economist* 25/12/1976.

12 Interview with Kenneth MacKenzie, 24/11/2005.

13 Hansard 939 c69.

14 Benn, *Diaries 1977–80*, 6/7/1978. Benn considered Millan 'thoughtful and sensitive', and also voted against the Lib-Lab pact along with Peter Shore.

15 Ironically, Cunningham later defected to the pro-devolution SDP in 1982, having sat as an independent since 1981.

16 Millan later persuaded Shetland Islands Council to accept two amendments which provided for a commission to examine the government of Orkney and Shetland, and give the Scottish secretary power to over-ride the Assembly if it acted against the interests of islanders. Grimond recommended that the council accept Millan's offer.

17 Interview with Lord Donoughue, 10/11/2005.
18 *The Economist* 24/3/1979.
19 Ibid.
20 Willie Ross used the statement for his last Commons intervention. 'Is the Prime Minister aware that I wish him well,' he said, 'but I "hae ma doots"?' (Hansard 964 c1698)
21 Foot's winding up speech was a tour de force: 'What the right hon. Lady [Mrs Thatcher] has done today is to lead her troops into battle snugly concealed behind a Scottish nationalist shield, with the boy David holding her hand.'
22 Jenkins, *A Life at the Centre*, 333.
23 The Millan Committee was established by Sam Galbraith, the Scottish Office health minister, in February 1999.

George Younger

1 Many civil servants regarded Taylor's defeat as a stroke of good luck. He later said his first act as Scottish secretary would have been to abolish all arts subsidies in Scotland. Others believe Thatcher never really wanted to appoint Taylor and was secretly quite relieved. Lord Sanderson remembers Denis Thatcher – who was suspicious of Taylor – saying to him: 'Well, you've got your man' when Younger was appointed. (23/11/2005)
2 Thatcher's verdict was: '[George,] who for all his decency and common sense was very much of the paternalist school of Scottish Tory politician.' (Thatcher, *The Downing Street Years*, 620).
3 Younger was often heard to say 'I must go and have a word with Willie'. They had a similar military background and Whitelaw respected Younger for making way in 1963 for Sir Alec Douglas-Home.
4 Kenneth Younger was the Labour MP for Grimsby, a minister of state at the Home Office, and later director of the Royal Institute of International Affairs at Chatham House.
5 Roy, *Conversations in a Small Country*, 180.
6 Ibid., 179.
7 Younger's daughter, Joanna Davidson, remembers her father being particularly upset about losing this front-bench post. (24/1/2006)
8 When asked in 1992 if he had any regrets, Younger said: 'I had quite a role in the Sixties in persuading Mr Heath to go for a Scottish Assembly. I do regret that.' (Roy, 182–83.)
9 In 1975 Thatcher had written to Lady Tweedsmuir: 'We seem to have problems in Scotland and the difficulty from my point of view is to get agreement on how to reorganise and with whom.' (Tweedsmuir Papers Acc 11884, 283.)
10 When R. A. Butler (also Buchanan-Smith's cousin) met Thatcher in 1978, she asked him for advice. He took out a piece of chalk and wrote on the chest of his suit the word 'Scotland'. 'Mary died with the word "Calais" written on her heart,' he told her. 'You will die with the word "Scotland".' Butler thought Taylor a nasty piece of work and believed his cousin had been badly treated. (Pearce, *The Lost Leaders*, 6.)
11 Sir Teddy Taylor remembers Younger remaining aloof from the devolution issue during the 1970s. He recalled that 'George seemed to change his opinions a little depending on the stance of the Party leadership' and that on issues like devolution 'I gained the impression that he regarded them all as a bit irrelevant'. (Letter to the author 13/4/2006.)
12 www.margaretthatcher.org, 12/5/1979. During this speech, Thatcher also lamented the loss of Teddy Taylor in a way many thought was insensitive to Younger, who was sitting next to her on the podium.
13 Hansard 968 c1338.
14 Scotland's Record Acc 7330(79) Speech to the Royal Institute of Public Administration, 29/10/1982.

15 Noel Skelton, an under-secretary at the Scottish Office from 1931–35, coined the term in a 1923 *Spectator* essay.
16 Ironically, Hugh Brown's Housing Bill from the previous session had already made council house sales possible, although only in limited circumstances.
17 Sproat's name was mentioned as a possible Scottish secretary in 1983, but he lost his seat at that year's election.
18 Curiously, the Labour-dominated Strathclyde Regional Council remained quiet, its leader Dick Stewart having had a private meeting with Younger shortly after the election in 1979. The authority later tried to sue the secretary of state.
19 Stodart had been asked to focus on any overlaps and anomalies which existed in the two-tier structure of regions and districts.
20 www.margaretthatcher.org, 11/5/1984.
21 Interview with Godfrey Robson. 'Absolutely' was a word Younger used frequently as it could be construed both positively and negatively. (13/11/2005)
22 *The Times* 10/12/1982.
23 Clark, *Diaries – Into Politics*, 16/8/1982. Clark (a third generation Scot) also believed that the whole composition of Cabinet had become 'absurdly distorted' by PR considerations. 'And if there really have to be Secretaries of State for Wales and Scotland in the Cabinet then they should simply be selected by the Prime Minister.'
24 Younger's daughter, Joanna Davidson, remembers her father using this nickname in private.
25 The amendment was tabled by Robin Cook and carried by 203 votes to 80. Godfrey Robson remembers Younger overturning a refusal by Russell Fairgreave to grant funds to an Edinburgh organisation which ran a telephone helpline for gay people.
26 Both Sir William Kerr Fraser, Younger's permanent under-secretary, and Godfrey Robson, his private secretary, remember occasionally hitting what they called an 'invisible barrier' when talking to him.
27 Allan Stewart remembers it being said that Younger did lose his temper once, when his private secretary drove off in his official car, leaving him stranded.
28 Interview with Allan Stewart, 25/10/2005.
29 Campbell-Bannerman Papers Add 41231 f8. Letter dated 26/12/1894.
30 Thatcher snidely notes in her memoirs that if Younger and Ancram had warned her earlier, then she would have acted to delay the revaluation.
31 www.margaretthatcher.org, 10/5/1985. Absurdly, and as if unaware of the political impact of revaluation, Thatcher also challenged delegates to return Conservative support to its 1955 levels.
32 Baker, *The Turbulent Years*, 122.
33 Younger was later identified by Douglas Hurd and Geoffrey Howe as bearing most of the responsibility for the Pergau Dam scandal, in which Malaysia promised to buy £1 billion in arms from Britain in exchange for £200 million in aid for the controversial structure. Younger had agreed the ratio as defence secretary.

Malcolm Rifkind

1 Dalhousie was also 39. His appointment followed another ministerial Cabinet walk-out; Joseph Chamberlain and the secretary for Scotland, George Otto Trevelyan, stormed out as Gladstone unveiled his plans for Irish home rule.
2 Coincidentally, Rifkind would later serve in the same Cabinet as Leon Brittan, his cousin by descent from the same Lithuanian immigrant.
3 Kamm, *A Scottish Childhood*, 196.
4 Interview with Sir Malcolm Rifkind, 17/11/2005. Sir Malcolm wrote in his journal that 'The last few days have been the most difficult of my political career'.
5 Ibid.
6 Hansard 107 c200.
7 Hansard 110 c325.

8 Lord Glenarthur remembers meeting Lord Whitelaw in the House of Lords during the spring of 1987 as peers, including Lord Home, considered the Bill. 'Are you sure this bill is wise?' Whitelaw asked him, adding: 'I told them; they wouldn't listen to me.' (13/10/2005)

9 Alexander, *Donald Dewar*, 116.

10 They were reluctant for very different reasons. Stewart believed the election had gone badly because the party had not been right-wing enough in Scotland, while for Buchanan-Smith, serving as deputy to the man who had once been his junior would have been too humiliating.

11 Lord Gray and Allan Stewart had been sacked in September 1986 and replaced by Lord Glenarthur and Ian Lang.

12 Pagett was a former Scottish Office information officer who made it clear that he himself was not a member of any political party.

13 www.margaretthatcher.org, 13/5/1988.

14 *The Times* 23/5/1988.

15 'Instead of 50,000 demonstrating outside St Andrew's House,' Rifkind later reflected, 'there were half a dozen people who maintained a lonely vigil outside the old Royal High School. The rest of Scotland went on with its life.' (Alexander, *Donald Dewar*, 115.)

16 Interview with Sir Malcolm Rifkind.

17 Thatcher, *The Downing Street Years*, 620.

18 Blake, *Disraeli*, 481–82.

19 The sale of the two Scottish companies was recognised by the National Audit Office as being one of the most successful and well handled privatisations there had been, raising almost as much as all the English regional electricity companies put together.

20 Thatcher, 621.

21 Ibid.

22 Interview with Sir Malcolm Rifkind.

23 Wyatt, *The Journals of Woodrow Wyatt*, 171.

24 Lord Sanderson remembers Rifkind asking both him and Ian Lang in July if they thought he was being deliberately undermined. Independently, they both said yes. (23/11/2005)

25 Rifkind's analysis was this: 'The assumption was that when he was made party chairman that somehow the right of the party would be pleased but through inexperience he ended up alienating them as well. I was getting representations from impeccably right-wing people saying we can't work with this guy. What Michael did at central office was change the locks so people couldn't get in, place men were put in and it left such a bad taste and it was a silly thing to do, even people who would have been politically closer to him than me found him impossible to work with at that time.'

26 Forsyth also won back responsibility for education, much to the anxiety of the Scottish educational establishment. Rifkind assured them that no radical reforms would be forthcoming before the next general election, while Forsyth told teaching unions that he wanted a 'bloody revolution' in Scottish education.

27 Gavin McCrone remembers Sanderson telling him, 'we're all standing shoulder to shoulder against the opposition', meaning Forsyth. (16/12/2005)

28 Thatcher, 623.

29 Interview with Sir Malcolm Rifkind.

30 Thatcher, 852. Alan Clark thought Rifkind 'was a weasel' for saying the prime minister should resign.

Ian Lang

1 Interview with Lord Lang, 25/10/2005.

2 Lang, *Blue Remembered Years*, 15.

3 Henderson was the MP for Dunbartonshire East from February-October 1974, and for East and North-east Fife from 1979–87.

4 Lang and Henderson, *The Scottish Conservatives – A Past and a Future*, 10 & 19.

5 Lang did, however, regularly vote in favour of capital punishment.

6 Lang, 111. It was said that Margaret Thatcher, watching the announcement of Lang's promotion on television that evening, whisky glass in hand, complained that she had been 'told it couldn't be done'. That is, moving Rifkind from the Scottish Office.

7 Major, *The Autobiography*, 208.

8 Lang, 117.

9 The former Scottish Office minister, Alick Buchanan-Smith, had died from cancer on 29 August 1991. Polling suggested the Conservatives were going to lose the seat. They did, to the future Scottish Executive deputy first minister and Liberal Democrat, Nicol Stephen, although he lost the seat at the subsequent general election.

10 Macdonald, *Unionist Scotland 1800–1997*, 128.

11 Lang, 189.

12 One former private secretary believed the relationship was partly sustained by the Scottish secretary's reluctance to exploit his access to the prime minister.

13 Lang, 189.

14 In the event the choice of Devonport proved highly expensive. Completion was much delayed, and the National Audit Office was scathing in its criticism. So Lang was vindicated.

15 Lord Strathclyde was the third generation of his family to serve at the Scottish Office. His grandfather, Tom Galbraith, served under James Stuart in the 1950s, while his father, Tam Galbraith, was forced to resign in 1962 over the Vassall affair. Lang had briefly been a tenant of Tam's at his house in London.

16 The chancellor, Norman Lamont, was keen to privatise all of the UK's water authorities and was unconvinced by Lang's arguments against doing so. In the end, the Scottish Office produced eight plans of action, six of which meant retaining water in the public sector.

17 Lang himself used a private sector doctor.

18 The Marquis of Lothian in 1889, Sir John Gilmour in 1929, Gordon Campbell in 1973 and Ian Lang in 1995. All four reforms culminated in defeat for the Conservatives at each subsequent general election.

19 Lang, 152.

20 Ibid.

21 Stewart, *The Long March of the Market Men*, 92.

22 Ibid., 94–95.

23 Smith's death occurred during the Scottish Conservative conference at Inverness. An ashen-faced Lang had to face the television cameras with his reaction, and the gathering was suspended for the rest of the day. When Major arrived the following day, he and Lang discussed the party chairman's job; the Scottish secretary made it clear he did not covet it.

24 Lang, 164.

25 Lang became president of the Board of Trade, a title last held by Michael Noble, also his predecessor as Scottish secretary.

26 By 1997 Lord James Douglas-Hamilton had beaten this record by a year, having served as a Scottish Office minister since 1987.

27 Lang, 208.

28 The others were Tom Johnston's *Memories* and James Stuart's *Within the Fringe*. Robert Munro, later Lord Alness, did publish a book, but it was more a collection of speeches than a memoir.

Michael Forsyth

1 In March 2006 Lord Forsyth delivered the CPS Sir Keith Joseph memorial lecture. Lady Thatcher was in the audience, as was Sir Keith's widow.

2 The story goes that following a clash in the university debating chamber, Salmond decided to put political matters aside and invite Forsyth for a drink. He accepted and opted for a gin and tonic. Surprised, Salmond pointed out that Forsyth did not like gin, to which the young Conservative replied: 'No, but I am learning to.'

3 Forsyth and McLetchie, *The Scottish Conservative Party: A New Model for a New Dimension* (Edinburgh 1975). According to some, Forsyth did his best to destroy copies of this pamphlet more than a decade later, just as Tom Johnston had done with his *Our Scots Noble Families*. McLetchie became leader of the Scottish Conservatives in the Scottish parliament in 1999, resigning six years later.

4 Interview with Lord Forsyth, 7/12/2005.

5 Forsyth's devotion to Mrs. Thatcher sometimes reached comic extremes. Gyles Brandreth remembers him swooning over pictures of Baroness Thatcher in her robes, while one Scottish Office official recollects him bowing, as if in prayer, before a picture of her at the Department of Education.

6 Forsyth's predecessors at the Scottish Office, John Sinclair and Thomas McKinnon Wood, also began their careers in London local government.

7 Thatcher, *The Downing Street Years*, 623.

8 Clark, *The Last Diaries*, 7/6/1995.

9 Major consulted both Lang and Rifkind on Forsyth's appointment. They agreed with the prime minister that he had sufficiently mellowed to do the job well.

10 The *Sunday Times* 9/7/1995.

11 Brandreth, *Breaking the Code*, 347.

12 *The Times* 9/7/1995.

13 Lord James had become the 11th Earl of Selkirk following the death of his uncle, Nigel Douglas-Hamilton, on 24 November 1994. He had been Commissioner for Special Areas in Scotland from 1937–39.

14 Interestingly, Whitehall officials who worked with Forsyth at the Department of Employment and Home Office found him good-natured and could not understand why he had such a bad reputation at the Scottish Office.

15 Major, *The Autobiography*, 425–26.

16 This idea later floundered when it emerged that only a handful of government-owned crofting estates had shown any interest in Forsyth's offer to transfer ownership.

17 Brandreth, 390.

18 Private information.

19 Dick Stewart had been the first leader of Strathclyde Regional Council. John Smith, the late Labour leader, had given the first memorial lecture in 1994.

20 By 1997 the Scottish Grand Committee was meeting every two weeks in Scotland. Michael Portillo made an appearance, as did Michael Heseltine and Kenneth Clarke. Even the prime minister appeared at one meeting in Dumfries.

21 Interview with Lord Forsyth.

22 *The Times* 10/5/1996.

23 John McAllion, a Labour front-bench spokesman on Scotland, resigned as a result of this U-turn.

24 Interview with Lord Forsyth.

25 Hansard 280 c973.

26 Brandreth, 412.

27 Bennett, *Untold Stories*, 197.

28 *The Times* 11/2/1997.

29 The Labour candidate was Anne McGuire, later an under-secretary at the renamed Scotland Office.

30 *The Times* 1/5/1997.

31 Like Tony Blair inviting Margaret Thatcher to Downing Street soon after becoming prime minister in 1997, Jack McConnell invited Forsyth to Bute House soon after he became first minister in 2001. The former Scottish Enterprise minister Wendy

Alexander also dropped in to see him at work in London. Both Labour MSPs asked him the same thing: 'how on earth did you get officials to do what you wanted?'

Donald Dewar
1 The *Sunday Times Magazine* 18/4/1999.
2 Scottish TV documentary, *The Dewar Years*, 2001 (Scottish TV Archive).
3 Ibid. 'Crosland kept trying to persuade me that various trade unionists had brilliant intellects,' Dewar explained to Roy Hattersley, 'when we both knew that was rubbish.' (Alexander, *Donald Dewar*, 107.)
4 MacCormick, *The Scottish Debate*, 79.
5 Dewar had been a front-bench spokesman on Scotland since 1981. He joined the Shadow Cabinet in 1983.
6 Naughtie, *The Rivals*, 63.
7 The *Scotsman* also called for Dewar to swap places with the foreign secretary, Robin Cook.
8 Lord Sewel remembers Downing Street commenting that part of the revision was 'too tartan'.
9 Interview with Henry McLeish, 7/11/2005.
10 Rawnsley, *Servants of the People*, 240.
11 Hansard 304 c35.
12 Hansard 312 c803.
13 *Scotland on Sunday* 8/5/2005. Article by Brian Wilson.
14 Radice, *Diaries*, 421–22.
15 The *Financial Times* 7/5/1999.
16 Interview with Sam Galbraith, 5/11/2005.
17 The *Sunday Times Magazine* 18/4/1999.
18 Fiona Ross's father was Willie Ross, Scottish secretary from 1964–70 and 1974–76. Fiona Ross worked with Dewar at Radio Clyde in the 1970s and was political correspondent at Scottish TV throughout the 1980s and '90s.
19 Alexander, 46.
20 Ashdown, *The Ashdown Diaries I*, 495.
21 Macdonald replaced Brian Wilson, who had moved to the Department of Trade and Industry in July. Although now Lord Macdonald, he was a Scottish Office minister for several months without being a member of either house of parliament.
22 Officially, Tony Blair was – and is – leader of the Scottish Labour Party.
23 Canavan did stand as an independent and won, securing the largest majority of any MSP and winning in both his constituency and on the regional list.
24 *The Times* 28/4/1999. Scottish Questions was reduced to 30 minutes every month after the Scottish parliament began work in July 1999.
25 Sam Galbraith remembers Dewar telling him that he did not enjoy politics any more and was worried that he was now only liked by the establishment, and not by people like his constituents.
26 Speech by Donald Dewar 1/7/1999.
27 The *Sunday Times Magazine* 18/4/1999.

John Reid
1 Interview with Lord Sewel, 28/11/2005.
2 'I used to be a Communist,' admitted Reid during one interview. 'I used to believe in Santa Claus.'
3 The *Scotsman* 19/6/2003.
4 The *Observer* 3/10/1999.
5 According to *Private Eye*, when Reid was asked to take on the Health Department in June 2003, his reaction was 'Oh fuck, not health'.

Helen Liddell

1 Liddell, *Elite*, 201.
2 Healey, *The Time of My Life*, 460.
3 The *Scotsman* 25/8/1997.
4 It was said that Liddell was so attentive that she once followed Maxwell into the gents' toilets.
5 Interview with Helen Liddell (by email).
6 *Caledonia Magazine* 6/2002.
7 When I asked Liddell about the *Scotsman's* sustained campaign, she simply responded: 'Boys will be boys!'
8 Interview with Nick Comfort, 24/10/2005. Comfort's father was the late Alex Comfort, author of the bestselling sex manual, *The Joy of Sex*. He later left the Scotland Office to update his father's book.
9 Interview with Helen Liddell.
10 The *Scotsman* 13/6/2003.

Alistair Darling

1 The *Herald* 13/6/2003.
2 Ibid.
3 Private information.
4 Contemporaries in Aberdeen student politics included Lewis Robertson, who would become an MSP and Scottish transport minister when Darling was transport secretary at Westminster.
5 Darling did, during one early Scottish Questions session, refer to the Scottish parliament as the 'Scottish Assembly', but this was more a generational gaffe than a political one.
6 Formerly a Roman Catholic priest in Clapham, Cairns had previously been barred from standing for parliament under the House of Commons (Clergy Disqualification) Act 1801. Nevertheless, he was selected to fight his native Greenock in 2001, and the House of Commons (Removal of Clergy Disqualification) Act passed just days before the candidate deadline for the subsequent general election.
7 Clark had beaten Sir Malcolm Rifkind in Edinburgh Pentlands in 1997 and became advocate general for Scotland from May 1999. She stood down from the Commons at the 2005 general election but, as Baroness Clark of Calton, remained as advocate general. She resigned on 18 January 2006 and was replaced, after a long period in limbo, by the former solicitor-general for Scotland Neil Davidson.
8 Darling faced four Conservative shadows across the despatch box: Jacqui Lait, Peter Duncan, Eleanor Laing and David Mundell. A fifth, James Gray, lasted only two weeks as shadow Scottish secretary before reluctantly resigning on 19 May 2005. He had implied during a press interview that MSPs, although not necessarily the Scottish parliament, could be scrapped.

Douglas Alexander

1 Alexander's father, the Rev. Douglas Alexander, conducted the funeral of former Scottish secretary and Scotland's first First Minister, Donald Dewar, at Glasgow Cathedral in 2000.
2 *Daily Mail* 10/5/2006.
3 The *Guardian* 10/5/2006.
4 The *Scotsman* 20/5/2006.
5 Government Response to the Scottish Affairs Committee's report on 'The Sewel Convention: The Westminster Perspective', 20/07/2006.
6 Speech by Douglas Alexander, 26/07/2006.

Epilogue

1 *Donald Dewar: A Book of Tribute*, 13.
2 The *Scotsman* 8/2/1943.
3 The Scottish parliament's first meeting was on 12 May 1999, when MSPs took their oaths and elected a presiding officer and two deputy presiding officers.
4 Official Report 1/2 c25.
5 No former ministers interviewed, whether Labour or Conservative, considered lack of parliamentary time to be a problem.
6 For a period while Helen Liddell was Scottish secretary, the deputy prime minister John Prescott also occupied Dover House. He called Liddell his 'landlady'.
7 Interview with Helen Liddell (by email).

BIBLIOGRAPHY

Archives
Anstruther-Gray, William (National Archives of Scotland)
Autograph Letters and Verse (British Library)
Asquith, Margot (New Bodleian Library, Oxford)
Balfour, 1st Earl of (A. J. Balfour) (British Library)
Balfour of Burleigh, 6th Baron (National Archives of Scotland)
Beaverbrook, 1st Baron (Sir Max Aitken) (House of Lords Record Office)
Bonar Law, Andrew (House of Lords Record Office)
Brown, Ernest (House of Lords Record Office)
Bryce, James (New Bodleian Library, Oxford)
Cadogan, 5th Earl of (George Henry Cadogan) (House of Lords Record Office)
Campbell-Bannerman, Sir Henry (British Library)
Cecil of Chelwood, 1st Viscount (Edgar Algernon Robert Gascoyne-Cecil) (British Library)
Craik, Sir Henry (National Library of Scotland)
Cross, Lord (Sir Richard Cross) (British Library)
Dalrymple, Sir Charles (National Library of Scotland)
Donaldson, Sir James (St Andrews University Library)
Elliot, Walter (National Library of Scotland)
Gilmour, Sir John (National Archives of Scotland)
Gladstone, Mary (British Library)
Gladstone, William Ewart (British Library)
Johnston, Thomas (National Library of Scotland and Mitchell Library, Glasgow)
Kimberley, 1st Earl of (John Wodehouse) (New Bodleian Library, Oxford)
Linlithgow, 1st Marquis of (John Adrian Louis Hope) (National Archives of Scotland)
Lloyd George, 1st Earl (David Lloyd George) (House of Lords Record Office)
Lothian, 9th Marquis of (National Archives of Scotland)
Muirhead, Roland (National Library of Scotland)
Muirshiel, 1st Viscount (John Maclay) (Glasgow University Archive Services)
Pentland, 1st Baron (John Sinclair) (National Archives of Scotland)
Rendel, 1st Baron (Stuart Rendel) (National Library of Wales)
Richmond, 6th Duke of (West Sussex Records Office)
Ripon, 2nd Earl of (George Frederick Samuel Robinson) (British Library)

Ritchie, 1st Baron (C. T. Ritchie) (British Library)
Rosebery, 5th Earl of (National Library of Scotland)
Runciman, 1st Viscount (Walter Runciman) (Newcastle upon Tyne University, the Robinson Library)
Sandars, John Satterfield (New Bodleian Library, Oxford)
Scotland's Record (National Library of Scotland)
Scotland's War (National Library of Scotland)
Spencer, 5th Earl of (John Poyntz Spencer) (British Library)
Thurso, 1st Viscount (Sir Archibald Sinclair) (Churchill College, Cambridge)
Tweedsmuir, Lady (Priscilla Buchan) (National Library of Scotland)
Wood, Thomas McKinnon (New Bodleian Library, Oxford)
Woodburn, Arthur (National Library of Scotland)
Worthington-Evans, Sir Laming (New Bodleian Library, Oxford)

Published sources

Alexander, Wendy, ed., *Donald Dewar: Scotland's first First Minister* (Edinburgh 2005)
Anonymous, *The Scottish Socialists: A Gallery of Contemporary Portraits* (London 1931)
Anonymous, *Our Conservative and Unionist Statesmen I & II* (London *c.* 1899)
Ashdown, Paddy, *The Ashdown Diaries I & II* (London 2000, 2001)
Asquith, Margot, *The Autobiography of . . . I & II* (London 1936)
Attlee, C. R., *As It Happened* (London 1954)
Baker, Kenneth, *The Turbulent Years: My Life in Politics* (London 1993)
Balfour, Arthur James, *Chapters of Autobiography* (London 1930)
Balfour, Lady Frances, *A Memoir of Alexander Hugh Bruce, Lord Balfour of Burleigh KT, 6th Baron* (London 1924)
Ball, Stuart, ed., *Parliament and Politics in the age of Baldwin and MacDonald: The Headlam Diaries 1923–1935* (London 1992)
Benn, Tony, *Conflicts of Interest: Diaries 1977–80* (London 1990)
Bennett, Alan, *Untold Stories* (London 2005)
Blake, Robert, *The Conservative Party from Peel to Thatcher* (London 1985)
— *Disraeli* (London 1998)
Blow, Simon, *Broken Blood: The Rise and Fall of the Tennant Family* (London 1987)
Bonham Carter, Mark and Pottle, Mark, ed., *Lantern Slides: The Diaries and Letters of Violet Bonham Carter 1904–1914* (London 1996)
Boothby, Robert, *My Yesterday, Your Tomorrow* (London 1962)
Brandreth, Gyles, *Breaking the Code: Westminster Diaries* (London 1999)
Brooks, David, ed., *The Destruction of Lord Rosebery: From the Diary of Sir Edward Hamilton 1894–1895* (London 1986)
Brown, Gordon, *Maxton* (Edinburgh 1986)
Butler, David and Freeman, Jennie, *British Political Facts 1900–1968* (London 1969)
Butler, J. R. M., *Lord Lothian* (London 1960)
Campbell, John, *Margaret Thatcher Volume I: The Grocer's Daughter* (London 2000)
Campbell, R. H., 'The Committee of Ex-Secretaries of State for Scotland and Industrial Policy 1941–45', *Scottish Industrial History* 2 (1981), 3–11
Cannadine, David, *G.M. Trevelyan: A Life in History* (London 1992)

Carnegie, Andrew, *Autobiography of . . .* (London 1920)

Castle, Barbara, *The Castle Diaries 1964–70* (London 1984)

— *The Castle Diaries 1974–76* (London 1980)

Catterall, Peter, ed., *The Macmillan Diaries: The Cabinet Years 1950–1957* (London 2003)

Clark, Alan, *Diaries* (London 1993)

— *Diaries: Into Politics* (London 2000)

— *Diaries: The Last Diaries* (London 2002)

Clifford, Colin, *The Asquiths* (London 2002)

Cole, Margaret, ed., *Beatrice Webb: Diaries 1912–1924* (London 1952)

Colville, John, *The Fringes of Power: Downing Street Diaries* (London 2004)

— *The Churchillians* (London 1981)

Coote, Sir Colin, *A Companion of Honour – The Story of Walter Elliot* (London 1965)

Coutts, Ben, *Auld Acquaintance: Great Scots Characters I Have Known* (Edinburgh 1994)

Crathorne, Nancy, *Tennant's Stalk: The Story of the Tennants of the Glen* (London 1973)

Crewe, Marquess of, *Lord Rosebery I & II* (London 1931)

Cunneen, Christopher, *King's Men: Australia's Governors-General from Hopetoun to Isaacs* (Sydney 1983)

Curtis, Sarah, ed., *The Journals of Woodrow Wyatt I-III* (London 1998, 1999, 2000)

Dalton, Hugh, *Memoirs 1945–1960: High Tide and After* (London 1962)

Dalyell, Tam, *Dick Crossman: A Portrait* (London 1989)

Darling, Sir William, *King's Cross to Waverley* (London 1944)

— *So It Looks To Me* (London 1952)

Davenport-Hines, Richard, *The Macmillans* (London 1992)

David, Edward, ed., *Inside Asquith's Cabinet* (London 1977)

Davidson, Lorraine, *Lucky Jack: Scotland's First Minister* (Edinburgh 2005)

Deedes, Bill, *Dear Bill . . .* (London 2005)

De Groot, Gerard J., *Liberal Crusader: The Life of Sir Archibald Sinclair* (London 1993)

Devine, T. M. and R. J. Finlay, eds., *Scotland in the 20th Century* (Edinburgh 1996)

— *The Scottish Nation 1700–2000* (London 1999)

Dickie, John, *The Uncommon Commoner: A Study of Sir Alec Douglas-Home* (London 1964)

Donnachie, Ian, Harvie, Christopher and Wood, Ian S., eds., *Forward! Labour Politics in Scotland 1888–1988* (Edinburgh 1989)

Donoughue, Bernard, *Downing Street Diary* (London 2005)

Douglas-Home, Sir Alec, 'Scotland's Government: The Report of the Scottish Constitutional Committee' (Edinburgh 1970) (pamphlet)

— *The Way the Wind Blows* (London 1976)

Drucker, H. M. et al, ed., *Scottish Government Yearbook* (Edinburgh 1978–92)

Dugdale, Blanche E. C., *Arthur James Balfour* (London 1939)

Dunnett, Alastair, *Among Friends* (London 1984)

Egremont, Max, *Balfour: A Life of Arthur James Balfour* (London 1980)

Elliot, Major Walter, *Toryism and the Twentieth Century* (London 1927)

Ewing, Winnie, *Stop the World: The Autobiography of Winnie Ewing* (Edinburgh 2004)

422 THE SCOTTISH SECRETARIES

Finlay, Richard J., *A Partnership for Good? Scottish Politics and the Union Since 1880* (Edinburgh 1997)
Fisher, John, *Burgess and Maclean: A New Look at the Foreign Office Spies* (London 1977)
Fisher, Nigel, *Iain Macleod* (London 1973)
Fitzroy, Sir Almeric, *Memoirs I & II* (London 1925)
Forsyth, Michael and McLetchie, David, *The Scottish Conservative Party: A New Model for a New Dimension* (Edinburgh 1975) (pamphlet)
Fry, Michael, *Patronage and Principle* (Aberdeen 1987)
Galbraith, Russell, *Without Quarter: A Biography of Tom Johnston* (Edinburgh 1995)
George-Brown, Lord, *In My Way: Memoirs* (London 1971)
Gibson, John, *The Crown and the Thistle* (Edinburgh 1985)
Gilbert, Martin, ed., *Winston S. Churchill Companion III/2* (London 1972)
Glendinning, Miles, *The Architecture of Scottish Government* (Dundee 2004)
Goldman, Dr Lawrence, ed., *Oxford Dictionary of National Biography* (London 2004)
Gollin, Alfred, *Balfour's Burden* (London 1965)
Hanham, H. J., 'The Creation of the Scottish Office, 1881–1887', *Juridical Review* (1965), 205–44
Harris, Kenneth, *Attlee* (London 1982)
Harvie, Christopher, *No Gods and Precious Few Heroes* (London 1981)
— *Scotland & Nationalism* (London 1994)
— *Travelling Scot: Essays on the history, politics and future of the Scots* (Argyll 1999)
Hassan, Gerry, ed., *The Scottish Labour Party: History, Institutions and Ideas* (Edinburgh 2004)
Hazlehurst, Cameron and Woodland, Christine, *A Liberal Chronicle: Journals and Papers of J.A. Pease, 1908 to 1910* (London 1994)
—, Whitehead, Sally and Woodland, Christine, eds., *A Guide to the Papers of British Cabinet Ministers 1900–1964* (London 1996)
Healey, Denis, *The Time of My Life* (London 1990)
Heath, Edward, *The Course of My Life* (London 1998)
Henderson Scott, Paul, *A Twentieth Century Life* (Argyll 2002)
Horne, Alistair, *Macmillan I & II* (London 1988, 1989)
Hume, James, *Mandarin Grade 3* (Durham 1993)
Hunter, Ian, ed., *Winston and Archie: The Letters of Sir Archibald Sinclair and Winston S. Churchill 1915–1960* (London 2005)
Hurd, Douglas and Osmond, Andrew, *Scotch on the Rocks* (London 2001)
Hutchinson, Roger, *The Soapman: Lewis, Harris and Lord Leverhulme* (Edinburgh 2003)
Jefferys, Kevin, ed., *Labour and the Wartime Coalition: From the Diary of James Chuter Ede, 1941–1945* (London 1987)
Jenkins, Roy, *Asquith* (London 1986)
— *Baldwin* (London 1987)
— *A Life at the Centre* (London 1991)
— *Gladstone* (London 1995)
— *Churchill* (London 2001)
Johnson, Nancy E., ed., *The Diary of Gathorne Hardy 1866–1892* (Oxford 1981)

Johnston, Thomas, *The Financiers and the Nation* (London 1934)
— *Memories* (London 1952)
— *Our Scots Noble Families* (Argyll 1999)
Kamm, Antony and Lean, Anne, eds., *A Scottish Childhood* (Glasgow 1985)
Keating, Dr Michael and Midwinter, Dr Arthur, *The Government of Scotland* (Edinburgh 1983)
Keir, David, *The House of Collins* (London 1952)
Kellas, James G., *Modern Scotland* (London 1968)
— *The Scottish Political System* (Cambridge 1979)
Kemp, Arnold, *The Hollow Drum: Scotland Since the War* (Edinburgh 1993)
Kennedy, Ludovic, *Thirty-Six Murders & Two Immoral Earnings* (London 2002)
Knox, Dr William, ed., *Scottish Labour Leaders 1918–1939* (Edinburgh 1984)
Lamont, Norman, *In Office* (London 1999)
Lang, Ian, *Blue Remembered Years* (London 2002)
— and Henderson, Barry, 'The Scottish Conservatives – A Past and a Future' (Edinburgh 1975) (pamphlet)
Lawson, Nigel, *The View From No. 11* (London 1992)
Levitt, Ian, ed., *The Scottish Office: Depression and Reconstruction 1919–1959* (Edinburgh 1992)
Levitt, Ian, 'Britain, the Scottish Covenant Movement and Devolution, 1946–1950', *Scottish Affairs* 22 (1998), 33–57
Liddell, Helen, *Elite* (London 1990)
MacCormick, J. M., *The Flag in the Wind: The Story of the National Movement in Scotland* (London 1955)
MacCormick, Neil, ed., *The Scottish Debate: Essays on Scottish Nationalism* (Oxford 1970)
Macdonald, Catriona M. M., ed., *Unionist Scotland 1800–1997* (Edinburgh 1998)
Macdonald, Mary and Redpath, Adam, 'The Scottish Office 1954–79', *The Scottish Government Yearbook 1980* (1979), 101–34
McGonagall, William, *Collected Poems* (Edinburgh 1999)
McKinstry, Leo, *Rosebery: Statesman in Turmoil* (London 2005)
Maclay, John, *The Choice for Liberals* (National Liberal Association of Scotland 1958) (pamphlet)
McLean, Iain, *The Legend of Red Clydeside* (Edinburgh 1983)
McLeish, Henry, *Scotland First* (Edinburgh 2004)
McManus, Michael, *Jo Grimond: Towards the Sound of Gunfire* (Edinburgh 2001)
Macmillan, Harold, *Riding the Storm* (London 1971)
Macmillan, Lord, *A Man of Law's Tale* (London 1953)
Major, John, *The Autobiography* (London 1999)
Marquand, David, *Ramsay MacDonald* (London 1977)
Marr, Andrew, *The Battle for Scotland* (London 1995)
Matthew, H. C. G., ed., *The Gladstone Diaries XI and XIII* (Oxford 1990)
Middlemas, Keith, ed., *Thomas Jones: Whitehall Diary I–III* (London 1969, 1971)
Mileham, Patrick, ed., *'Clearly My Duty': Jack Gilmour's Letters from the Boer War* (East Linton 1996)

Milne, Sir David, *The Scottish Office* (London 1957)

Mitchell, James, *Governing Scotland: The Invention of Administrative Devolution* (London 2003)

Montague Brown, Anthony, *Long Sunset* (London 1995)

Morgan, Kenneth O., *Callaghan: A Life* (Oxford 1997)

Morley, John, *Life of Gladstone I–III* (London 1903)

Morris, David, *The Honour of Richmond: A History of the Lords, Earls and Dukes of Richmond* (York 2000)

Munro, Robert, *Looking Back: Fugitive Writings and Sayings* (London 1930)

Naughtie, James, *The Rivals* (London 2001)

Nicolson, Nigel, ed., *Harold Nicolson: Diaries and Letters 1939–1945, 1945–62* (London 1967, 1968)

Nicolson, Nigel, *Lord of the Isles* (London 1960)

Owen, David, *Time to Declare* (London 1991)

Parris, Matthew, *Great Parliamentary Scandals* (London 1995)

Pearce, Edward, *The Lost Leaders: The Best Prime Ministers We Never Had* (London 1997)

Pearce, Robert, ed., *Patrick Gordon Walker Political Diaries 1932–1971* (London 1991)

Pentland, Lady Marjorie, *The Right Honourable John Sinclair, Lord Pentland, G.C.S.I.: A Memoir* (London 1928)

Pimlott, Ben, *Harold Wilson* (London 1992)

— ed., *Hugh Dalton: The Political Diary, 1918–40, 1945–60* (London 1987)

Pottinger, George, *The Secretaries of State for Scotland 1926–1976* (Edinburgh 1979)

Radice, Giles, *Diaries 1980–2001* (London 2004)

Ramsden, John, ed., *Real Old Tory Politics: The Political Diaries of Robert Sanders, Lord Bayford 1910–1935* (London 1984)

Rawnsley, Andrew, *Servants of the People* (London 2000)

Riddell, Peter, *Honest Opportunism* (London 1993)

Ridley, J. and Percy, C., ed., *The Letters of Arthur Balfour and Lady Elcho, 1885–1917* (London 1992)

Roberts, Andrew, *Salisbury: Victorian Titan* (London 1999)

Rose, Richard, ed., *Ministers and Ministries: A Functional Analysis* (Oxford 1987)

Rosen, Greg, ed., *Dictionary of Labour Biography* (London 2001)

Rosie, George, *Curious Scotland* (London 2004)

Ross, William, 'Approaching the Archangelic?', *The Scottish Government Yearbook 1978* (1978), 1–20

Roy, Kenneth, *Conversations in a Small Country* (Ayr 1989)

Self, Robert, ed., *The Neville Chamberlain Diary Letters II–IV* (Aldershot 2000–2005)

Sheridan, Dorothy, ed., *Among You Taking Notes . . . The Wartime Diary of Naomi Mitchison 1939–1945* (Oxford 1986)

Shinwell, Emanuel, *The Labour Story* (London 1963)

Sillars, Jim, *Scotland: The Case for Optimism* (Edinburgh 1986)

Smith, W. C., *The Secretary for Scotland* (Edinburgh 1885)

Spicer, Matthew, *The Scotsman Guide to Scottish Politics* (Edinburgh 2004)

Stewart, Allan, with Conroy, Harry, *The Long March of the Market Men* (1996)

Stodart-Walker, Archibald, ed., *Rectorial Addresses Delivered Before the University of Edinburgh 1859–1899* (London 1900)

Stott, Gordon, *Lord Advocate's Diary 1961–1966* (Aberdeen 1991)

Stuart, Charles, ed., *The Reith Diaries* (London 1975)

Stuart, James, *Within the Fringe* (London 1967)

— *Scottish Control of Scottish Affairs, Unionist Policy* (Glasgow 1949) (pamphlet)

Stuart, Mark, *John Smith: A Life* (London 2005)

Taylor, Brian, *Scotland's Parliament: Triumph and Disaster* (Edinburgh 2002)

Thatcher, Margaret, *The Downing Street Years* (London 1993)

— *The Path to Power* (London 1995)

Thorpe, Andrew, *A History of the British Labour Party* (London 1997)

Thorpe, D. R., *Alec Douglas-Home* (London 1996)

— *Eden* (London 2003)

Toothill, J. N., *Committee of Inquiry into the Scottish Economy* (Paisley 1961)

Trevelyan, George Macaulay, *Sir George Otto Trevelyan: A Memoir* (London 1932)

Unsigned, 'The Government and Scottish Affairs' (*Blackwood's Edinburgh Magazine*, February 1894)

Various, *Donald Dewar: A Book of Tribute* (Norwich 2000)

Vickers, Hugo, *Elizabeth The Queen Mother* (London 2005)

Vincent, John, ed., *The Later Derby Diaries* (Bristol 1981)

— *The Crawford Papers: The Journals of David Lindsay* (Manchester 1984)

— *The Diaries of Edward Henry Stanley, 15th Earl of Derby* (Oxford 2003)

Walker, David, *St. Andrew's House: An Edinburgh Controversy 1912–1939* (1989)

Walker, Graham, *Thomas Johnston* (Manchester 1988)

Ward, Paul, *Unionism in the United Kingdom 1918–1974* (Basingstoke 2005)

Warner, Gerald, *The Scottish Tory Party: A History* (London 1988)

Wells, John, *The House of Lords* (London 1997)

Wheatley, Rt Hon. Lord, *One Man's Judgement* (London 1987)

Williams, Philip M, ed., *Diary of Hugh Gaitskell 1945–56* (London 1983)

— *The Modernisation of Conservative Politics: The Diaries and Letters of William Bridgeman, 1904–1935* (London 1988)

Williams, R. H., ed., *Salisbury–Balfour correspondence: letters exchanged between the third marquess of Salisbury and his nephew Arthur James Balfour, 1869–1892* (London 1988)

Wilson, Harold, *The Labour Government 1964–1970: A Personal Record* (London 1971)

Wilson, John, *A Life of Sir Henry Campbell-Bannerman* (London 1973)

Wolfe, J. N., ed., *Government and Nationalism in Scotland* (Edinburgh 1969)

Woodburn, Arthur, *An Outline of Finance* (London 1931)

— 'Some Recollections' (Unpublished)

Young, Douglas, *Scotland* (London 1971)

Young, Hugo, *One of Us* (London 1989)

Young, Kenneth, *Sir Alec Douglas-Home* (London 1970)

— *Harry, Lord Rosebery* (London 1974)

Zebel, Sydney H., *Balfour: A Political Biography* (London 1973)

INDEX